Morocco

Mediterranean Coast & the Rif
p220

Atlantic Coast
p153

Imperial Cities, Middle Atlas & the East
p281

Marrakesh & Central Morocco
p46

Southern Morocco & Western Sahara
p357

THIS EDITION WRITTEN AND RESEARCHED BY

Paul Clammer,
James Bainbridge, Paula Hardy, Helen Ranger

Contents

TEA SERVICE, MARRAKESH (P76)

COUSCOUS WITH TAJINE (P434)

Contents

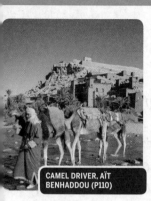

CAMEL DRIVER, AÏT BENHADDOU (P110)

Welcome to Morocco

Morocco is one of the most diverse countries in Africa, with high mountains, sweeping desert, rugged coastline, and the winding alleyways of ancient medina cities and souqs.

Mountains & Desert

From Saharan dunes to the peaks of the High Atlas, Morocco could have been tailor-made for travellers. Lyrical landscapes carpet this sublime slice of North Africa like the richly coloured and patterned rugs you'll lust after in local cooperatives. The mountains – the famous High Atlas but also the Rif and suntanned ranges leading to Saharan oases – offer simple, breathtaking pleasures: night skies glistening in the thin air, and views over a fluffy cloudbank from the Tizi n'Test pass. On lower ground, there are rugged coastlines, waterfalls, and caves in forested hills – and the mighty desert.

Traditional Life

The varied terrain may inform your dreams, but it shapes the very lives of Morocco's Berbers, Arabs and Saharawis. Despite en-croaching modernity, with motorways join-ing mosques and kasbahs as features of the landscape, Moroccan people remain closely connected to the environment. Nomadic southern 'Blue Men' brave the desert's burn-ing expanses in robes and turbans, mobile phones in hand. Traditional life continues – with tweaks – in the techniques of Berber carpet makers, in date cooperatives, in medina spice trading, and in the lifestyles in mountain hamlets and ports like Essaouira.

Moroccan Activities

Meeting the Moroccan people involves nothing more than sitting in a cafe and waiting for your mint tea to brew. The trick is to leave enough time to watch the world go by with the locals when there's so much else to fit in: hiking up North Africa's highest peak, learning to roll couscous, camel trekking, shopping in the souqs, getting lost in the medina, and sweating in the hammam. Between the activities, you can sleep in the famous riads, relax on panoramic terraces and grand squares, and mop up tajines flavoured with saffron and argan.

Ancient Medinas

Often exotic, sometimes overwhelming and always unexpected, these ancient centres are bursting with Maghrebi mystique and madness: the perfect complement to the serene countryside. When you hit the town and join the crowds, you follow a fine tra-dition of nomads and traders stretching back centuries. Unesco has bestowed World Heritage status on the Fez medina, the world's largest living medieval Islamic city, and on the carnivalesque street theatre of the Djemaa el-Fna in Marrakesh.

Why I Love Morocco

By Paul Clammer, Author

I first went to Morocco as a backpacking student in 1993. I didn't plan it – another trip had fallen through – but it was one of the happiest accidents of my life. I got wonderfully lost in the medina in Fez, got blisters climbing Jebel Toubkal and sunburn in the desert in Merzouga, and was hypnotised by the grand spectacle of Marrakesh's Djemaa el-Fna. Most importantly, I was inspired to come back, and over the past 20 years I've spent more time exploring this amazing land than any other country on the planet.

For more about our authors, see p520

Above: Fez medina (p284)

Morocco

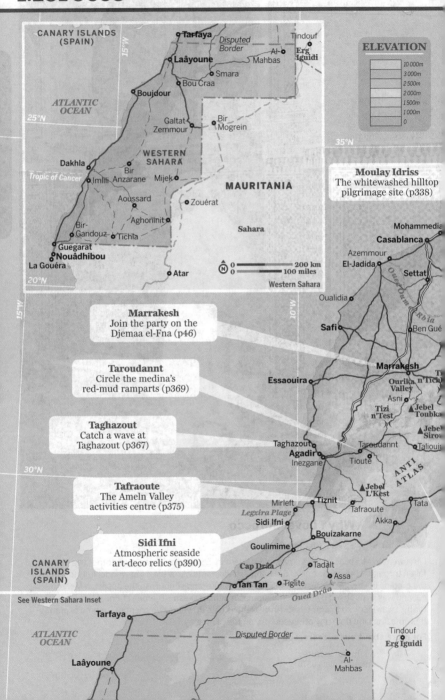

ELEVATION

10 000m
3 000m
2 500m
2 000m
1 500m
1 000m
0

Moulay Idriss
The whitewashed hilltop
pilgrimage site (p338)

Marrakesh
Join the party on the
Djemaa el-Fna (p46)

Taroudannt
Circle the medina's
red-mud ramparts (p369)

Taghazout
Catch a wave at
Taghazout (p367)

Tafraoute
The Ameln Valley
activities centre (p375)

Sidi Ifni
Atmospheric seaside
art-deco relics (p390)

CANARY ISLANDS
(SPAIN)

Tarfaya
Laâyoune
Tindouf
Al-Mahbas
Erg Iguidi
Smara
Bou Craa
Boujdour
Galtat Zemmour
Bir Mogrein

ATLANTIC OCEAN

Dakhla
Bir Anzarane
Imliti
Mijek
WESTERN SAHARA
MAURITANIA
Aoussard
Zouérat
AghonInit
Bir-Gandouz
Tichla
Guegarat
Nouâdhibou
La Gouéra
Atar

Sahara

Tropic of Cancer

25°N
20°N
15°W

0   200 km
0   100 miles

Western Sahara

Mohammedia
Casablanca
Azemmour
El-Jadida
Settat
Oualidia
Oued Oum Rbia
Safi
Ben Gué
Essaouira
Marrakesh
Ourika n'Tich Valley
Asni
Tizi n'Test
Jebel Toubka
Jebel Siro
Taghazout
Taroudannt
Talioui
Agadir
Inezgane
Tioute
ANTI ATLAS
Jebel L'Kest
Tata
Mirleft
Tiznit
Legzira Plage
Tafraoute
Sidi Ifni
Akka
Bouizakarne
Goulimime
Cap Drâa
Tadalt
Assa
Tan Tan
Tiglite
Oued Drâa

30°N

CANARY ISLANDS
(SPAIN)

See Western Sahara Inset

Tarfaya

ATLANTIC OCEAN

Disputed Border

Tindouf
Erg Iguidi

Laâyoune
Al-Mahbas

0 | 200 miles
0 | 400 km

Assilah
Murals colour the
seaside medina (p195)

Chefchaouen
A blue medina in the
Rif Mountains (p252)

Volubilis
Roman mosaics, arches
and olive presses (p335)

Fez
Explore the medina
and tanneries (p283)

Figuig
An oasis town with
mudbrick kasbahs (p355)

High Atlas
Sublime peaks and
Berber villages (p84)

Drâa Valley
Hop between kasbahs
and oases (p118)

Erg Chigaga
Saharan dune hikes
by moonlight (p125)

Anti Atlas
Trek in the granite
mountain range (p375)

Mediterranean Sea

SPAIN
Málaga
Cádiz
Algeciras • Gibraltar
Jebel Musa • Ceuta (Spain)
Tangier
Tetouan • Martil
Assilah • Larache
Chefchaouen • Al-Hoceima
Melilla (Spain)
Nador • Ras el-Mar
Mers el-Kebir
Oran • Mostaganem
Saïdia
Berkane • Ahfir
Tlemcen • Saida
Ketama • Targuist
Ouezzane
Souk el-Arba du Rharb
Moulay Bousselham
Kenitra
Sidi Kacem
Volubilis
Moulay Idriss • Fez
Salé
RABAT
Khémisset
Meknès • Sefrou
Ben Slimane
Jebel Tidiquin
Moulay Yacoub
Taza
Guercif
Taourirt
Oujda
Aïn-Benimathar
Jebel Tazzeka
Ifrane
Azrou
Missour
Tendrara
Ain Sefra
Khouribga
Oued-Zem
Khenifra
Midelt
Bouarfa
ALGERIA
Kasba-Tadla
Jebel Ayachi
Beni Mellal
Afourer
Imilchil
Figuig
Beni Ounif
Azilal
Bin el-Oudane
HIGH ATLAS
Demnate
Irhil M'Goun
Tinerhir
Béchar
Vallée des Roses
Aït Benhaddou
Boulmane du Dadès
Oued Ziz
Tafilalt
Erfoud
Skoura
Rissani
Merzouga
Erg Chebbi
Taghith
Ouarzazate
Tazenakht
Agdz
Taouzo
Grand Erg Occidental
Drâa Valley
Zagora
Tazzarine
Erg Chigaga
M'Hamid
Erg Er-Raoui
Timimoun
Tabelbala
Gourara
Hamada du Drâa
Tinfouchy
Adrar

Morocco's
Top 17

Djemaa el-Fna Street Theatre

1 Circuses can't compare to the mad-cap, Unesco-acclaimed *halqa* (street theatre) in Marrakesh's main square (p50). By day, 'La Place' draws crowds with astrologers, snake-charmers, acrobats and dentists with jars of pulled teeth. Around sunset, 100 restaurant stalls kick off the world's most raucous grilling competition. 'I teach Jamie Oliver everything he knows!' brags a chef. 'We're number one...literally!' jokes the cook at stall number one. After dinner, Djemaa music jam sessions get under way – audience participation is always encouraged, and spare change ensures encores.

Fez Medina

2 The Fez medina (p284) is the maze to end all mazes. The only way to experience it is to plunge in head first, and don't be afraid of getting lost – follow the flow of people to take you back to the main thoroughfare, or pay a local to show you the way. It's an adventure into a medieval world of hidden squares, enormous studded doors and colourful souqs (markets). Remember to look up and see intricate plasterwork, magnificent carved cedarwood and curly Arabic calligraphy, while at your feet are jewel-like mosaics.

Drâa Valley Kasbah Trail

3 Roads now allow speedy passage through the final stretches of ancient caravan routes from Mali to Marrakesh, but beyond the rocky gorges glimpsed through car windows lies the Drâa Valley of desert-traders' dreams. The palms and mud-brick castles of Tamegroute (p124), Zagora (p120), Timidarte (p120) and Agdz (p118) must once have seemed like mirages after two months in the Sahara. Fortifications that housed caravans are now open to guests, who wake to fresh dates, bread baked in rooftop ovens, and this realisation: speed is overrated.

The High Atlas

4 Hemmed in by the cracked and fissured summit of Aroudane (3359m), the valley of Zaouiat Ahansal (p88) is characterised by kilometres of cliffs, soaring buttresses and dramatic slot canyons. With the arrival of a paved road in 2013, this awesome natural canvas is just beginning to attract attention. For rafters and kayakers the valley is a green jewel where rafts whip between 2.5m-wide limestone walls; for climbers and trekkers the extreme topography and huge routes offer ridiculous views and a thrilling sense of wilderness.

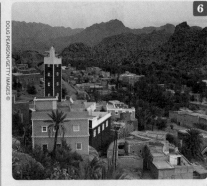

DOUG PEARSON/GETTY IMAGES ©

TIM E WHITE/GETTY IMAGES ©

Life in the Palmeraies

5 Thick with palms and networked by communal wells and *khettara* (irrigation channels), the *palmeraies* (palm groves) of Figuig (p355), Ziz Valley (p142), Tinejdad (p141), Tinerhir (p137) and Skoura (p128) are the historical lifeblood of the Moroccan south. Even today they continue to play a vital role in oasis life, with plots beneath the shaded canopy providing a surprising bounty of barley, tomatoes, mint, pomegranates, apricots, figs and almonds sustaining generation after generation.

Tafraoute

6 Tafraoute (p375) has a jumble of pink houses and market streets with extraordinary surroundings. The Ameln Valley is dotted with *palmeraies* and Berber villages, and the looming mountains stage a twice-daily, ochre-and-amber light show. With a relatively undeveloped tourist industry, despite the region's many charms, it's a wonderful base for activities including mountain biking and seeking out prehistoric rock carvings (p379). As if the granite cliffs and oases weren't scenic enough, a Belgian artist applied his paint brush to some local boulders (p379) – with surreal results.

Surfing

7 You can surf all along Morocco's Atlantic coast, but the best place to catch waves is Taghazout (p367). It's clear what floats the village's board as soon as you arrive: the usual cafes and *téléboutiques* are joined by surf shops, where locals and incomers wax boards and wax lyrical about the nearby beaches. On the same stretch of coast between Agadir and Essaouira, Tamraght (p367) and Sidi Kaouki (p218) are also set up for surfing; further south, Mirleft (p389) is Morocco's newest surf destination, with an annual longboard championship.

Beach at Taghazout (p367)

ASSILAH MOROCCO / ALAMY ©

SUSANNA WYATT / GETTY IMAGES ©

Assilah Medina Art

8 In a refreshing take on graffiti, large expanses of walls in Assilah medina (p195) are adorned with colourful murals. In July every year, local and foreign artists are invited to contribute to the Assilah Festival by painting the walls. Some murals, like those near the El-Khamra Tower or the lookout at the Koubba of Sidi Mansur, are huge. But you might round a bend in the medina and spot a small corner down an alleyway that has been brightly decorated.

Fès Festival of World Sacred Music

9 With intimate concerts in mosaic-studded riads, harmonic afternoons at the Batha Museum, mesmerising Sufi Nights in a Pasha's garden and grand performances in the magnificent crenellated Bab al Makina, this festival (p311) still charms and impresses after 20 years. A love of music that engenders harmony between civilisations and religions is the cornerstone here: it could be Mongolian fiddles or whirling dervishes, Sufi qawwali or Persian maqām, Irish laments or African drums. Qawwali singers, Faiz Ali Faiz ensemble

Anti Atlas Trekking

10 A granite range leading to the Sahara, the Anti Atlas remains unexplored compared with the High Atlas. The star attraction is the quartz massif of Jebel L'Kest (p383), the 'amethyst mountain', which you can walk to through the lush Ameln Valley. More farming villages and crumbling kasbahs are found around Jebel Aklim (p384), another of the excellent trekking possibilities in this area of blue skies and Berber shepherds. The landscape has enough variety, from palm-filled gorges to brooding, volcanic Jebel Siroua (p384), to justify multiple treks.

Moulay Idriss

11 Named for Morocco's most revered saint, this little town (p338) contains his mausoleum and is one of the most important pilgrimage spots in the country. It straddles two hills and whichever side of town you're on, the views across the green roofs and out to the rolling countryside beyond are arrestingly pretty, especially in the evening light. At the very top is Morocco's only cylindrical minaret, which is well worth the climb, while spread at its feet are olive groves that produce a fragrantly tasty oil.

Sidi Ifni

12 Shhh! Don't tell your friends, but this formerly Spanish seaside town (p390), a camel ride from the Sahara, is every bit as dilapidated, breezy and magical as well-trodden Essaouira. You can walk to the stone arches at Legzira Plage (p393), or just explore the blue-and-white backstreets of one of southern Morocco's most alluring hang-outs. The best time to appreciate the art-deco relics – more reminiscent of Cuba than Casa – is sunset, when the Atlantic winds bend the palms and fill the air with a cooling sea mist. Legzira Plage (p393)

Volubilis

13 Berber king Juba II, his wife the daughter of Antony and Cleopatra, was installed at Volubilis (p335) by the Romans. The town became a thriving farming community producing olive oil, wheat and wine for the Roman army. Stand on the basilica steps today, look out over the same fertile fields and survey his kingdom. This World Heritage site has few rules about where you can walk, little signage and lots of storks nesting on column-tops. It has some dazzling mosaics and a brand-new museum.

Camel Trekking in the Sahara

14 When you pictured dashing into the sunset on your trusty steed, you probably didn't imagine there'd be quite so much lurching involved. Don't worry: no one is exactly graceful clambering onto a saddled hump. But even if your dromedary leaves you knock-kneed, you'll instinctively find your way to the summit of the dunes at nightfall. Stars have never seemed clearer, and with good reason: at Erg Chigaga (p125), you're not only off the grid, but several days' camel trek from the nearest streetlights.

WALTER BIBIKOW/GETTY IMAGES ©

JULIAN LOVE/GETTY IMAGES ©

Chefchaouen Medina

15 Steep and cobbled, the Chefchaouen medina (p253) tumbles down the mountainside in a shower of red roofs, wrought-iron balconies and geraniums. The blue-washed lanes enchant, making the town a photographer's dream come true. With a grand red-hued kasbah lording it over the cafe-packed main square, you could be content for hours just people-watching over a mint tea. Alternatively, amble down the riverside walk, stroll to the Spanish mosque on the hill or even venture into the surrounding Talassemtane National Park to explore the Rif Mountains.

Taroudannt

16 With views of both the High Atlas and Anti Atlas, this Souss Valley trading centre (p369) is known as Little Marrakesh, offering a medina and souqs without the big-city hustlers. Day trippers from Agadir will certainly find it charming. The town's red-mud ramparts are unique, changing colour according to the time of day. Circle the 7.5km perimeter by foot, bike or horse-drawn calèche, then return to the medina through one of the gates. After the sunset glow fades from the walls, the town is a relaxing, everyday place with some good restaurants.

Casablanca's Architectural Heritage

17 If anyone tells you there's nothing to see in Casablanca except the Hassan II Mosque, they haven't looked up. Dating from the early 20th century, when Casa was the jewel of the French colonies, a wealth of Mauresque and art-deco buildings can be found in the downtown areas, with rounded corners, tumbling friezes of flowers and curved wrought-iron balconies. Some buildings have been cared for while others are shamefully neglected. The Casablanca walking tour (p164) showcases most of them.

Need to Know

For more information, see Survival Guide (p463)

Currency
Dirham (Dh)

Language
Moroccan Arabic (Darija)
Berber
French

Money
ATMs widely available. Major credit cards widely accepted in main tourist centres.

Visas
Not required for most nationalities for stays of up to 90 days. Passports must be valid for six months beyond date of entry.

Mobile Phones
GSM phones work on roaming. For unlocked phones, local prepaid mobile SIM cards are a cheaper option (about Dh20).

Time
GMT/UTC

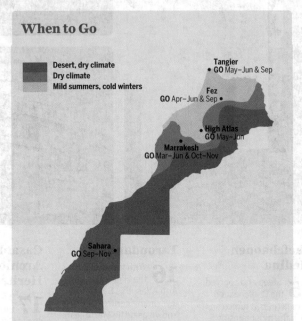

When to Go

- Desert, dry climate
- Dry climate
- Mild summers, cold winters

Tangier
GO May–Jun & Sep

Fez
GO Apr–Jun & Sep

High Atlas
GO May–Jun

Marrakesh
GO Mar–Jun & Oct–Nov

Sahara
GO Sep–Nov

High Season
(Nov–Mar)

➡ Spring and autumn are the most popular times to visit.

➡ Accommodation prices are highest.

➡ Marrakesh and the south are popular at Christmas and New Year, but the north of the country can be chilly.

Shoulder
(Apr & Oct)

➡ Spring sandstorms in the Sahara and persistent rain in the north.

➡ Popular elsewhere.

➡ Accommodation prices and demand jump around Easter.

Low Season
(May–Sep)

➡ Discounts in accommodation and souqs (markets).

➡ Domestic tourism keeps prices high on the coast.

➡ Ramadan will fall between late May and late July during the lifetime of this guidebook.

Useful Websites

The View from Fez (http://riadzany.blogspot.com) News and opinions.

Visit Morocco (www.visitmorocco.com) Moroccan National Tourist Office website.

Maroc Mama (http://marocmama.com) Food and travel blog from Marrakesh.

Al-Bab (www.al-bab.com/maroc) Handy links.

Lonely Planet (www.lonelyplanet.com/morocco) Info, bookings and forums.

Important Numbers

Dial the local four-digit area code even if you are dialling from the same town or code area.

Ambulance	☑15
Fire	☑15
Police (city)	☑19
Police (countryside)	☑177

Exchange Rates

Australia	A$1	Dh7.24
Canada	C$1	Dh7.37
Europe	€1	Dh11.22
Japan	¥100	Dh7.95
Mauritania	UM100	Dh2.84
New Zealand	NZ$1	Dh6.80
UK	UK£1	Dh13.62
USA	US$1	Dh8.22

For currency exchange rates see www.xe.com.

Daily Costs
Budget:
Less than Dh350

➡ Basic double (shared bathroom): from Dh50

➡ Soup or sandwich: Dh4–30

➡ Four-hour local bus trip: Dh60

Midrange:
Dh550–1000

➡ Admission to sights: Dh10–50

➡ Hotel room: Dh400–800

➡ Dinner main: Dh70–150

Midrange:
More than Dh1400

➡ Hire car: Dh300

➡ Day tour: Dh300

➡ Double in a city riad: from Dh1000

Opening Hours

Morocco keeps the Western working week, but some businesses may close early or completely on the Muslim prayer day or Friday. Opening hours may vary

Banks 8.30am to 6.30pm Monday to Friday

Restaurants noon to 3pm and 7pm to 10pm (cafes generally open earlier and close later)

Shops 9am to 12.30pm and 2.30pm to 8pm Monday to Saturday

Arriving in Morocco

Mohammed V International Airport (Casablanca; p171) Trains to Casa Voyageurs station (Dh40, 35 minutes) run hourly from 6am to 10pm, and again at midnight. A taxi to central Casablanca (45 minutes) is Dh300 to Dh350.

Tanger Med ferry terminal (p237) Shuttle buses to central Tangier (Dh25, 45 minutes) run hourly.

Menara Airport (Marrakesh; p81) Bus to central Marrakesh (Dh30) every 20 minutes. A taxi to central Marrakesh costs Dh70/100 day/night. Private hotel transfers in the city are Dh170 to Dh200.

Getting Around

Transport in Morocco is reasonably priced, and mostly quick and efficient.

Train Reasonably priced, with good coverage and frequent departures between the major cities, but no lines in the south or along the Mediterranean coast.

Car Useful for travelling at your own pace, or for visiting regions with minimal public transport. Cars can be hired in every town or city. Drive on the right, but beware erratic local drivers.

Bus Cheaper and slower than trains, ranging from modern coaches to rickety local affairs. Useful for destinations not serviced by trains.

Taxi Mercedes 'grands taxis' run set routes between nearby towns and cities. Cheap but cramped.

For much more on **getting around**, see p485

If You Like...

Medinas

If you pause for a moment in the medina, stepping out of the stream of shoppers, you can watch Morocco's very essence flash by. These ancient, crowded quarters – with winding lanes, dead ends, riad hotels, piles of spices, traders, tea drinkers, and a sensory assault around every corner – offer a strong dose of Morocco's famous Maghrebi mystique.

Fez The planet's largest living Islamic medieval city and its biggest car-free urban environment, with donkeys trekking to tanneries in the leather district. (p284)

Marrakesh Exuberant Marrakshis course between souqs (markets), palaces and the Djemaa el-Fna within the medina's 19km of ramparts. (p47)

Tangier Hop off the ferry for a fitting introduction to North Africa in this gem of a medina, contained by the walls of a 15th-century Portuguese fortress. (p222)

Chefchaouen Medinas aren't always like diving from the top board; smaller, stylish examples include this Andalucian-blue one. (p253)

Craft & Culture

Whether you want to catch some Gnaoua (bluesy music developed by freed slaves), see the Maghreb's hottest contemporary art or forever transform your mantel with quality craftwork, Morocco will inundate you with options.

Taroudannt Pick up Chleuh silver jewellery, influenced by Saharan tribes and Jewish silversmiths, in the souqs. (p369)

Fès Festival of World Sacred Music In June, Morocco's premier music festival features international names and intimate concerts by tariqas (Sufi orders). (p311)

Marrakesh Shop beyond the souqs, alongside design fanatics in Quartier Industriel Sidi Ghanem, and collectors in the hip art galleries of Guèliz. (p47)

Carpets Compared with the cities, towns like Ouarzazate and Tafraoute have cooperatives, ensembles and shops that are low-pressure spots to bag a tasselled souvenir. (p116)

Tangier The American Legation Museum contains the 'Moroccan Mona Lisa' and a wing devoted to Paul Bowles, William Burroughs and the Beat writers' associates in Tangier. (p224)

Off the Beaten Track

Morocco's small towns and picturesque villages are ideal for unwinding and meeting the locals over mint tea.

Afella-Ighir The road to these oasis villages is little visited; in Tiwadou, stay in an auberge with a local museum. (p379)

Agdz Watch other travellers hurry along the Drâa Valley from your relaxing vantage point amid the palmeraie (palm grove) and mudbrick kasbahs of Agdz. (p118)

Imilchil The Middle Atlas village is famous for its marriage moussem (festival), but the journey there is stunning year-round. (p140)

Midelt Between the Middle and High Atlas, visit the surrounding villages and kasbahs, enjoy the mountain views and leave with a carpet. (p344)

Tarfaya Clean up in a tented pool hall near a shipwrecked ferry, and watch the Saharawi world go by. (p397)

Around Essaouira Leave the crowds in the medina and follow the surf trail south to Sidi Kaouki and Taghazout. (p218) (p367)

Food Adventures

Morocco offers culinary adventures from couscous rolling to eating camel tajine.

Fez On a culinary course or walking tour, pack your *tanjia* (slow-cooked stew) at the butcher's, then leave it to cook in the hammam's woodfired oven. (p300)

Desert food Learn Saharawi recipes or the secrets of elaborate traditional couscous at M'Hamid's Saharan retreats. (p87)

Marrakesh Buy ingredients at the souq, learn to cook like a *dadas* (chef) and feast on the results in the comfort of a riad. (p64)

Seafood Buy your dinner fresh off the boat in Al-Hoceima port, or try Atlantic catches at Essaouira's fish souq and outdoor fish grills. (p261) (p208)

Taliouine Tour saffron and argan producers and learn how to make a saffron-tinted tajine. (p374)

Demnate Try local almonds, olive oil and wildflower honey, and choose between 40 restaurants in this Berber foodie hub near Marrakesh. (p84)

Architecture

Morocco's buildings, whether reinvented as a boutique medina retreat or crumbling into a hillside, reflect the country's long history as a cultural melting pot.

Ali ben Youssef Medersa Inside this splendid 14th-century theological seminary in Marrakesh are five-colour *zellij* (tilework) walls and stucco archways. (p51)

Art deco The Atlantic Coast has some wonderful art-deco architecture, mostly in Casablanca, where it influenced the local Mauresque style, and in white-and-blue Sidi Ifni. (p164) (p390)

(Above) Decorating pottery, Fez (p283)
(Below) Prayer time, Marrakesh medina (p58)

Kairaouine Mosque and University One of Africa's largest mosques and the world's oldest universities, this 1150-year-old complex in Fez has a green pyramidal roof. (p285)

Essaouira The town's name means 'well designed', and it still suits the whitewashed medina behind 18th-century seafront ramparts. (p208)

Rissani On a 21km loop, you can see a *zawiya* (shrine), a ruined Saharan trading post, multiple *ksour* and a museum about life in the fortified strongholds. (p145)

Berber Culture

Morocco's proud indigenous people are a memorable part of many travellers' journeys here. Their Amazigh colour and character are a big part of special spots such as Marrakesh and the Atlas.

Regional costumes Women display their local allegiances; from black shawls and colourful dresses around Tata to Riffian hats and candy-striped skirts in Tangier. (p381) (p222)

Demnate Just 1½ hours from Marrakesh, immersion in indigenous culture and cuisine awaits, with Morocco's best olive oil and a Berber Romeo and Juliet. (p84)

Imilchil marriage moussem Berbers look for marriage material in the Middle Atlas village. (p140)

Maison Tiskiwin Understand how the Berbers tie into the rest of North Africa in Marrakesh's museum of trans-Saharan culture. (p55)

Al-Hoceima The seaside town is the unofficial capital of Morocco's northern Berbers. (p261)

Beaches

Its coastline stretching from the Mediterranean to the Sahara, Morocco packs in beaches for every taste between its coves, cliffs, boardwalks and ports. Some are fit for family fun, others wait for development to happen, and many are untrodden apart from the odd surfer and migratory bird.

Marabout's Beach With its eponymous saint's tomb and savage rocks, this is the most dramatic of Mirleft's half-dozen Atlantic beaches. (p389)

Agadir The city is a concrete grid, but its long, curving beach, clean and well lit at night, will have families scrambling for buckets and spades. (p359)

Yellich Facing a small Mediterranean island you can walk to; visit Yellich and Cala Iris' other beaches before the fishing village becomes a resort. (p266)

Tangier Escape the city on a day trip to Plage Robinson, at the northwestern extremity of Africa's Atlantic Coast, or Ksar es-Seghir on the Strait of Gibraltar. (p238) (p239)

Deserts

Morocco's Saharan expanses are some of Africa's safest and most evocative places to experience the great desert. Not only can you see curvy dunes and harsher *hammada* (stony desert), you can also meet blue-robed Berbers and try the nomadic lifestyle.

Erg Chebbi This classic Saharan sandscape, its dunes rising to 160m, can be explored by camel, 4WD or sandboard, followed by a night in a Berber tent. (p148)

Figuig It's worth trekking east to Morocco's oasis par excellence, with *palmeraies, ksour* and views of Algeria. (p355)

Erg Chigaga Enlist a 'Blue Man' in M'Hamid, where dunes nuzzle against the guesthouses, to find this 40km stretch of sand mountains reaching 300m. (p125)

Drâa Valley Timbuktu-bound caravans once passed through this desolate valley; now you can board a 'ship of the desert' (read: camel) to palm-shaded oases. (p118)

Mountains

With Berber villages nestling beneath snowy peaks, the High Atlas is one of the world's most awe-inspiring mountain ranges. Whether you want to climb, trek, experience rural life or just escape the rat race far below, Morocco's other mountains are also worth exploring.

Jebel Toubkal Trek to the top of North Africa for thin air and views across the High Atlas. (p103)

Ameln Valley Stay in a traditional village house among *palmeraies* and the gold-pink Anti Atlas. (p380)

Middle Atlas Around towns like Azrou and Midelt, the mellower northern Atlas range is ideal for day hikes though hills and forests. (p342) (p344)

Jebel el-Kelaâ There's more to the Rif than kif crops – as you'll see from this peak, walkable in a day from the idyllic mountain town of Chefchaouen. (p257)

Eastern Atlas Barren, Martian-red mountains overlook the Ziz Gorges and the wedding-festival village of Imilchil. (p142) (p140)

Month by Month

January

Moroccan winter: the north is wet and snow makes many mountains impassable for trekkers and even motorists. Marrakesh and the south receive the most tourists, especially around New Year.

⁂ Moussem of Sidi ben Aïssa

One of Morocco's largest *moussems* (festivals) takes place at the Sufi saint's mausoleum, outside the Meknès medina walls. Public displays of glass-eating, snake bites and ritual body piercing are no longer allowed, but *fantasias* (musket-firing cavalry charges), fairs and the usual singing and dancing are.

🏃 Marrakesh Marathon

The year-round Djemaa el-Fna carnival acquires a sporty dimension with this annual road race, when 5000 marathoners cross the finish line on the grand square. The route follows the city ramparts and alleys of palms, orange and olive trees. (p66)

February

Winter continues: the weather is generally poor, although drier, balmier spots such as Marrakesh and Agadir are bearable. Outside overlanders and city-breakers, few visitors are spotted.

March

The country wakes up with the beginning of spring, when the mountains thaw and the wildflowers and almond and cherry trees blossom. Winds begin to disturb the desert and the Souss Valley, continuing through April.

⁂ Almond Blossom Festival

A very pretty festival held in the Anti Atlas in spring, when the Tafraoute area is awash with blossoms. Traditionally about celebrating the harvest in Morocco's almond capital, the festival is now also about local folklore, with singing, dancing, theatre and storytelling. (p377)

🏃 Marathon des Sables

Starting and finishing in Morocco's movie town, Ouarzazate, the Saharan ultramarathon is as epic as films made in 'Ouallywood'. The gruelling six-day challenge, held in March or April, crosses 243km of desert. Water is provided. (p113)

April

Springtime continues: the country is lush and green and temperatures are now reliably hot nationwide. Tourist numbers are high, particularly around Easter, when prices jump.

✨ Festival of Sufi Culture

Fez' cultural festival hosts events including films and lectures, and concerts with Sufi musicians from around the world. The setting is the Andalucian-style garden of the Batha Museum, which is housed in a 19th-century summer palace. (p302)

🏃 Riffian Trekking

Between the wet northern winter and fierce summer, spring is perfect for trekking trails in the Rif Mountains. The best scenery is found in Talassemtane National Park (p266), including the God's Bridge rock formation and, closer to the Mediterranean, Al-Hoceima National Park (p265).

May

Prices drop in hotels and souqs (markets) as the tourist season ends, although the heaviest summer heat is yet to come; the average temperature in Marrakesh is about 28°C. Ideal for mountain trekking.

✨ Rural Festivals

During the Festival du Desert, Er-Rachidia hosts performers from across the Sahara, including local Gnaoua band Les Pigeons du Sable. Down the Dadès Valley, garlands come out for Kelaâ M'Gouna's festival to celebrate the rose harvest. (p142)

June

Summer is hotting up, although High Atlas peaks

are still snowy. Northern Morocco and the coast are good places to be. During the Fès Festival of World Sacred Music, there is major demand for local accommodation.

✨ Gnaoua & World Music Festival

This passionate celebration is held in Essaouira on the third weekend of June, with concerts featuring international, national and local performers, and art exhibitions. It offers a great chance to hear some bluesy Gnaoua music, developed here by freed slaves. (p211)

✨ Cherry Festival

Sleepy Sefrou awakes for Morocco's longest-running town festival, held in mid-June. Folk music, artists' displays, parades, *fantasias* and sports events celebrate the cherry harvest – culminating in the picturesque crowning of the Cherry Queen. (p324)

✨ Fès Festival of World Sacred Music

Organise tickets well in advance for Fez' successful world-music festival, which has hosted the likes of Ravi Shankar and Youssou N'Dour. Equally impressive are the concerts by Moroccan *tariqas* (Sufi orders); fringe events include exhibitions, films and talks. (p311)

July

Snow melts from the mountains, the High Atlas is scorching and Ramadan adds intensity to the temperatures, hovering

around 30°C. The beaches are breezy, but busy with domestic and European tourists in the north.

✨ Festival of Popular Arts

Unesco praised this street-theatre festival, a typically colourful Marrakshi event, as a 'masterpiece of cultural patrimony'. Djemaa el-Fna is even more anarchic than usual during the opening-night parade, featuring 500-plus performers. (p66)

✨ Assilah Festival

Assilah confirms its arty leanings with this cultural jamboree, which attracts some 200,000 spectators to three weeks of public art demonstrations, workshops, concerts and exhibitions. A concurrent three-day horse festival features a *fantasia*. (p197)

August

This month is a scorcher with an average of 40°C in Marrakesh, and it can easily exceed that in the interior. Head to southern Atlantic beaches to avoid the crowds.

✨ Moussems

During Morocco's largest *moussem,* picturesque whitewashed Moulay Idriss fills with *fantasias,* markets and music. Five pilgrimages to this *moussem* are said to equal one to Mecca. *Moussems* also take place in Setti Fatma, southeast of Marrakesh, and Ouarzazate. (p338)

September

With autumn, Morocco is once again prime territory for foreign travellers. Accommodation prices go up, but everyone's in high spirits after Ramadan. Beaches empty of local holidaymakers and even the desert is pleasant, with dates and gentle breezes.

TANJAzz

Attracting an ever-growing roster of international as well as local musicians, Tangier's annual jazz festival is a great way to take in the cosmopolitan side of Morocco's music scene. (p228)

Marriage Moussem

At this famous three-day marriage festival in the Middle Atlas village of Imilchil (p140), local Berbers search for a partner. Everyone looks their best, sporting woollen cloaks, white *jellabas* (flowing garments) and elaborate jewellery.

Religious Moussems

Hamdouchi Moussem (p84) is a dance-off between religious fraternities outside Demnate's two *zawiyas* (shrines); Fez' Moussem of Moulay Idriss sees a musical, rosewater-showered procession through the medina; thousands of pilgrims head east to the *moussem* at Sidi Yahia Ben Younes (p352), which includes a *fantasia*. (p302)

October

Another popular month to visit, although, north of the Middle Atlas, rain is beginning to set in. Eid al-Adha interrupts transport and life in general for a few days in late October/early November.

Rallye Toulouse Saint-Louis

In late September to early October, this event in Tarfaya remembers the colonial French airmail service that stopped here, and its most famous pilot, the writer Antoine de Saint-Exupéry. Planes pass through here en route from Toulouse in France to Saint Louis in Senegal. (p398)

November

This is a busy time in Marrakesh and further south, with more people heading to the desert or trekking nearby. Birdwatchers stake out wetlands, and Mauritania-bound overlanders roll through.

Harvests

Around the Immouzzer des Ida Outanane waterfalls in the High Atlas foothills, villagers climb into the trees to shake out olives from the branches. In Taliouine, a festival celebrates the saffron harvest, and you can see locals picking the flowers.

December

The country is busy at the end of the month with Christmas holidaymakers. Snow closes High Atlas passes, but the white blanket is good news for skiers.

Marrakesh International Film Festival

The Marrakesh event lives up to its name, with stars from Hollywood to Bollywood jetting in to walk the red carpet. The week culminates in wildly eclectic awards shows – recent honourees include Ben Kingsley and Harvey Keitel. (p66)

Itineraries

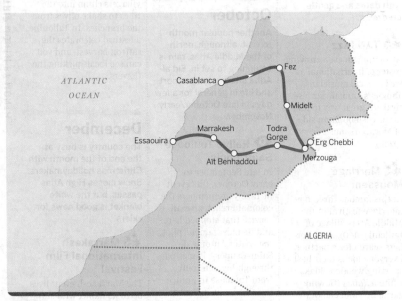

ATLANTIC
OCEAN

Fez

Casablanca

Midelt

Marrakesh

Todra
Gorge

Essaouira

Erg Chebbi

Aït Benhaddou

Merzouga

ALGERIA

Essential Morocco

Touch down in **Casablanca**, the commercial capital, and start with a tour of the stupendous Hassan II Mosque. Head by train to the easternmost imperial city of **Fez**, venerable heart of Moroccan religious and cultural life, with its ancient yet thriving medina.

Next, head south over the Middle Atlas via **Midelt**, for your first startling taste of Moroccan kasbah architecture, and to shop for the region's distinctive Berber carpets. Continue all the way to **Merzouga**, Morocco's gateway to the Sahara. Saddle up your camel and sleep under the stars amid Morocco's largest sand sea, the perfectly sculpted **Erg Chebbi**.

Shadowing the High Atlas as you head west brings you to the sharp cleft of the **Todra Gorge** for a day's hiking amid the canyons and *palmeraies* (palm groves). From here, head past Ouarzazate to **Aït Benhaddou**, with its fairytale-like 11th-century kasbah.

En route to the Atlantic, check into a luxurious riad in **Marrakesh**, where you can spend as many sunsets as possible on the theatrical Djemaa el-Fna, and then don't stop until you reach **Essaouira**, with its artsy seaside medina and fishing port.

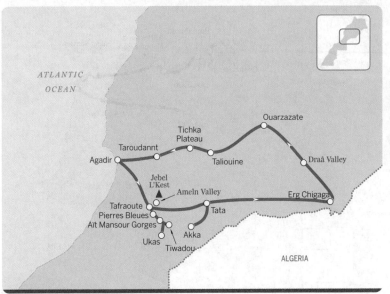

 Circling the South

This itinerary takes you deep into the south for wild mountain and desert landscapes, far from clicking cameras, with plenty of activities to stimulate the mind and body.

Agadir is a handy entry point, but adventurers will want to leave quickly. Head to tiny but vibey **Tafraoute**, surrounded by beautiful Anti Atlas scenery such as the **Ameln Valley**, with its lush *palmeraies* and pink-hued houses. Spend a few days trekking through the valley and up **Jebel L'Kest**, bike past rock formations and engravings to the surreal **Pierres Bleue**s (Painted Rocks), and continue south through the **Aït Mansour Gorges**. At the far end of the gorges, where the beautiful scenery belies the ancient slave routes that passed this way, stay in the Afella-Ighir oasis. Use **Tiwadou** as a base for more trekking or discovering the rock carvings at **Ukas**.

By now you've developed a taste for Morocco's secluded southern corners. Once back in Tafraoute, wind east through the Anti Atlas and descend to the equally silent and epic Sahara. The last stop before Jebel Bani and a whole lot of *hammada* (stony desert), **Tata** makes a convenient base for exploring the oases, kasbahs, *agadirs* (fortified granaries) and magnificent rock engravings in spots such as **Akka**. A dusty journey to the east, the yellow-gold dunes of **Erg Chigaga** are more remote and less visited than Merzouga. In nearby M'Hamid, find yourself a camel to lead you north into the kasbah-littered **Drâa Valley**.

At the top of valley, head back towards the mountains. Commandeer a bike (mountain or motor), horse, mule or dromedary in film favourite **Ouarzazate**, where the stony desert landscape has been a celluloid stand-in for Tibet, Rome, Somalia and Egypt. Return to the coast via **Taliouine**, where you can buy the world's most expensive spice in Africa's saffron capital. Pause here or in **Taroudannt** for a trekking reprise in a mountainous area such as the **Tichka Plateau**. With its red walls and backdrop of snow-capped peaks, Taroudannt has hassle-free echoes of Marrakesh. Its souqs and squares are pleasant places to relax, and it's handy for Agadir's Al-Massira Airport.

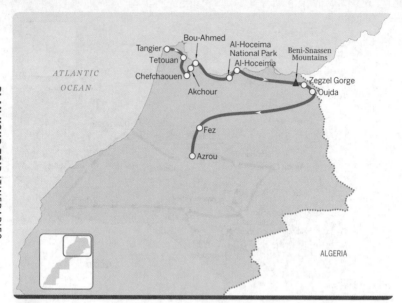

ALGERIA

The Med & the Mountains

In the north the Mediterranean littoral and the Rif Mountains have seen huge investment from the government, and there are plans to push tourism in the area. But if you get in now, you'll be ahead of the pack.

Start in **Tangier**, ideally arriving by ferry across the Strait of Gibraltar to feel the thrill of crossing from Europe to Africa. In the mid-20th century, characters from gunrunners to Beatnik literati mixed in this legendary port city. After a few days taking in the history, nightlife and restaurants, skip inland to **Tetouan**, the old capital of Spanish Morocco, with its charming blend of Arab medina and Andalucian architecture. The Spanish left a lighter imprint on nearby **Chefchaouen**, nestled in the Rif Mountains, with its gorgeous blue-painted medina. It's tempting to spend a string of sunsets listening to the minarets chorus each other's call to prayer, but this is a good trekking spot. You can head deep into the mountains on a five-day trek via riverside **Akchour** to **Bou-Ahmed**, a fishing village in the Oued Bouchia valley.

Continue east along the coast to the proud, modern seaside resort **Al-Hoceima**, gateway to the dry canyons and limestone cliffs of **Al-Hoceima National Park**. Walk to the park along the coast, or book a memorable tour including hiking or mountain biking and a homestay with a Berber family. En route to the Algerian border, there's more fine scenery in the **Beni-Snassen Mountains**, which you can enjoy in a swimming pool with mountain views, or a 300-year-old rural lodge. With its gorges, caves, mesa and Barbary sheep, this verdant area is far removed from classic images of Morocco. In the **Zegzel Gorge**, pluck a cumquat and see why the Romans remarked on this small citrus fruit.

From here, head to **Oujda** to refresh yourself with some city comforts, before taking the train to that grandest of imperial cities, **Fez**. Dive into the medina and relax in a riad, but if you find yourself missing the countryside, you can make an easy day (or several-day) trip into the cedar-clad Middle Atlas around the Berber market town of **Azrou**.

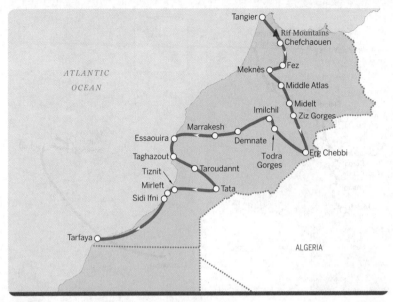

6 WEEKS Highlights & Hidden Gems

Climb off a ferry in famously decadent **Tangier**, with its Europe-facing medina, and head into the **Rif Mountains**. European influence continues in **Chefchaouen**, with its bright blue, Andalucian-tinted medina. Further south, the imperial cities **Fez** and **Meknès** are more quintessentially Moroccan in their ancient medinas.

After a few days of labyrinthine lanes and dye pits, you'll be ready for more mountains. Wind through the **Middle Atlas** to the Berber village of **Midelt**, then on through the Martian landscape of the **Ziz Gorges**. It's now just a few dusty hours to **Erg Chebbi**, the achingly beautiful expanse of rolling dunes, which you can explore on a camel or sandboard.

Brush off the Sahara and return to the High Atlas at **Todra Gorge**. Hike between the enclosing rock walls, then jump in a market-bound truck through tiny villages and deeper into the mountains. **Imilchil**, surrounded by red rock and turquoise lakes, is the site of a wedding *moussem* (festival) in September.

Descend through the Middle Atlas and turn southwest, pausing to refuel in Berber foodie and cultural hub **Demnate**. The next stop is **Marrakesh**, with its famous riad hotels, medina shopping and Djemaa el-Fna. Hit the Wild West coast at hippie-turned-boutique hang-out **Essaouira**, then head south to vibrant **Taghazout**, Morocco's premier surf spot. Then take the N10 to **Taroudannt**, the Souss Valley's prettiest market town with its mud-walled medina and kasbah.

Travel barren mountains and empty roads to **Tata**, a Saharan gateway where blue-robed guides can show you the desert. The road back to the Atlantic passes oases, *palmeraies,* kasbahs, *agadirs* and rock carvings. Near the coast, detour north to the **Tiznit** jewellery souq, particularly if it's a Thursday (market day).

Arcing west and south, you come to **Mirleft**, with its pink-and-blue arches, and **Sidi Ifni**, a jumble of wind-whipped art-deco relics surrounded by coastal walks. End your journey on the edge of the Western Sahara in sandy, gloriously isolated **Tarfaya**.

Atlantic Adventure

3 WEEKS

Morocco's Atlantic seaboard takes you from the clamour of the north to the quieter coastline of the south.

Take the ferry from Spain to **Tangier**, at once a quintessentially Moroccan mosaic and a decadent outpost of Europe. Catch the train south, first to artsy **Assilah**, with its whitewashed charms, and then to \Rabat, with its colonial architecture and palm-lined boulevards. Follow suburbanites to the sleepy 'Cité Portugaise', **El-Jadida**, then take the spectacular ocean road to **Oualidia**, the St Tropez lookalike with a perfect crescent lagoon.

Further south, the hippies once gravitated to **Essaouira**, and its white-walled ramparts, bohemian beat and renovated riads still make travellers linger. When you've eaten your fill at the outdoor fish grills, follow Jimi Hendrix and today's surfers to the peaceful beaches at **Diabat** and **Sidi Kaouki**.

Past more surf spots, **Agadir** is a family-friendly seaside resort, but the beaches and boutique accommodation of **Mirleft** are more appealing, as is art-deco **Sidi Ifni**.

Empire & Atlas

10 DAYS

This trip begins in two cities once ruled by enlightened dynasties. Throw back a shot of Maghrebi exoticism in **Fez**, where modern Morocco and its rich past crowd for space in the extraordinary medina. Next, catch your breath in nearby **Meknès**, bypassed by many travellers despite its echoes of Sultan Moulay Ismail's glory days.

A detour north takes you to **Volubilis**, Morocco's best-preserved ancient city, and testament to the Roman Empire's astonishing breadth. Nearby **Moulay Idriss**, with the mausoleum of the founder of Morocco's first imperial dynasty, is another wonderful antidote to urban clamour.

Unless you're a completist and want to visit all four Moroccan imperial cities, skip Rabat and head into the Middle Atlas. We've suggested a few stops in our Moroccan Odyssey itinerary; another is the Berber town of **Sefrou**, its medina pierced by the Oued Aggaï, 30km south of Fez. Take the cross-country route via Beni Mellal, skirting the edge of the **High Atlas** to the icon of contemporary Morocco: **Marrakesh**. The city's souqs, street performers and imperial architecture form an intoxicating mix.

Plan Your Trip
Morocco Outdoors

Morocco may be well known as one of Africa's top trekking destinations, but the country's diverse terrain means there are many other outdoor activities on offer. Birdwatching enthusiasts, cyclists, climbers and horse riders will all find options to challenge and excite. Another bonus: whether you're skiing, surfing or camel trekking, between activities you can enjoy the Moroccan culture and hospitality.

Birdwatching

Morocco is a birdwatcher's paradise. A startling array of species inhabits the country's diverse ecosystems and environments, especially the coastal wetlands.

Around 460 species have been recorded in the country, many of them migrants passing through in spring and autumn, when Morocco becomes a way station between sub-Saharan Africa and breeding grounds in Scandinavia, Greenland and northern Russia. Other birds fly to Morocco to avoid the harsh northern European winters. The lagoon at Merja Zerga National Park (p191) near Larache is the best site in the country for migratory birds.

A pleasant time for birdwatching is March through May, when the weather is comfortable and a wide variety of species is usually present. The winter is also a particularly active time in the wetlands and lagoons.

Guides & Tours

In addition to local birdwatching guides, the following UK-based companies offer Moroccan tours:

Top Activity Spots

Mountains

Hoist yourself up here for rock climbing from bouldering to mountaineering; downhill skiing and ski trekking; wildlife spotting, including apes, sheep and leopards, all of the Barbary variety; trekking; mountain biking; and white-water rafting.

Desert

Hotfoot it to the Sahara to take part in camel treks, moonlight dune hikes and sandboarding, and to watch wildlife – including desert warblers and the bat-eared fennec foxes – and sleep in a Berber tent.

Coast

Hit the beach for surfing, windsurfing, kitesurfing, kayaking and canoeing; and for marine mammals and bird life such as the endangered bald ibis.

Birdfinders (www.birdfinders.co.uk)

Naturetrek (www.naturetrek.co.uk)

Wild Insights (www.wildinsights.co.uk)

Camel Treks

Exploring the Sahara by camel – whether on an overnight excursion or a longer desert safari – is one of Morocco's signature activities and most rewarding wilderness experiences.

Morocco's most evocative stretches of Saharan sand are Erg Chebbi, near Merzouga, and Erg Chigaga, near M'Hamid and Zagora, and past the more accessible Tinfou Dunes.

Only consider doing your camel trek in autumn (September and October) or winter (November to early March). Outside these months, the desert experiences gruelling extremes of heat, as well as sandstorms in the spring.

Prices start at around Dh300 per person per day, but vary depending on the number of people, the length of the trek and your negotiating skills.

The agency organises the bivouac (temporary camp), which may be a permanent camp for shorter trips, and may offer Berber music and *mechoui* (barbecued lamb).

Organising a Camel Trek

Travellers with lots of time can organise a guide and provisions in situ. This benefits the local community and counters the trend towards young guides leaving home to look for work in more popular tourist centres.

M'Hamid is probably the most hassle-free of the main desert gateways, although the choice is wider at Zagora and Merzouga. Try to get recommendations from other travellers.

It's quicker and easier, involving less negotiations and waiting, to organise a trip in advance – either through an international tour operator or a company based in Ouarzazate or Marrakesh.

Horse Riding

Southern Morocco is popular for horse riding, from beaches such as Diabat to hills, mountains, valleys, gorges and the desert.

Specialist travel companies offer guided horse-riding tours:

Club Farah (www.clubfarah.com) Meknès-based Swiss-Moroccan company running trips throughout Morocco, from the imperial cities to the southern Atlantic coast.

Unicorn Trails (www.unicorntrails.com) UK-based operator offering four expeditions in the High Atlas, Sahara and Essaouira area.

Mountain Biking

Ordinary cycling is possible in Morocco, but mountain biking opens up the options considerably.

For the very fit, the vast networks of *pistes* (dirt tracks) and footpaths in the High Atlas offer the most rewarding biking. The Anti Atlas, the Jebel Saghro plateau and the Drâa Valley also offer excellent trails.

Travel agencies, hotels and shops hire out mountain bikes, for example in Tafraoute, but the quality isn't really high enough for an extended trip. Adventure-tour companies cater to serious cyclists.

The following operators offer mountain-bike tours in Morocco:

Saddle Skedaddle (www.skedaddle.co.uk)

Biking Morocco (www.mountain-biking-morocco.com)

Freeride Morocco (www.freeridemorocco.com)

Rock Climbing

There is a growing climbing scene in Morocco, with some sublime routes. Anyone contemplating climbing should have plenty of experience and be prepared to bring all their own equipment.

The Anti Atlas and High Atlas offer everything from bouldering to very demanding mountaineering routes that shouldn't be attempted unless you have a great deal of experience.

The Dadès and Todra Gorges are prime climbing territory.

Des Clark's guidebook *Mountaineering in the Moroccan High Atlas* (published by Cicerone), subtitled 'Walks, climbs and scrambles over 3000m', is destined to become a classic. It covers some 50 routes and 30 peaks in handy pocket-sized, plastic-covered form, with plenty of maps, photos and practical information.

The following are useful for information and hooking up with other climbers:

Nicolò Berzi (nicolobe@tiscalinet.it) Italian climbing guide organising trips to Todra Gorge.

PlanetMountain.com (www.planetmountain.com/english/rock/morocco) Has a section on Morocco.

Royal Moroccan Ski & Mountaineering Federation (www.frmsm.ma) Has a list of routes.

Skiing

Skiing is viable from November to April, although Morocco's ski stations are somewhat ramshackle.

Downhill Skiing & Snowboarding

Popular resort Oukaïmeden, about 70km south of Marrakesh, has North Africa's highest ski lift, and equipment for hire. There are other spots dotted around the Middle Atlas, most notably Mischliffen, near Fez, although some seasons the snow is thin on the ground. There's ad hoc equipment hire, but no ski-lift.

Ski Trekking

Ski randonné is increasingly popular, especially from late December to February, when the Aït Bougomez Valley has prime routes.

Surfing, Windsurfing & Kitesurfing

With thousands of kilometres of coastline, the Moroccan Atlantic is a fine, if under-

rated, destination for surfing, windsurfing and kitesurfing. Lessons, equipment hire and surf holidays are available.

Northern & Central Morocco

North of Rabat, Mehdiya Plage has strong currents but reliable year-round breaks. Moving south, Plage des Nations and Temara Plage, both within 20km of Rabat, are also good for surfing. Sidi Bouzid and the beaches around El-Jadida also attract surfers.

Oualidia is known for surfing, windsurfing and kitesurfing. En route to Safi, the Lalla Fatna area has some of Morocco's best breaks: one of the world's longest tubular right-handers has drawn some of the biggest names in surfing.

Southern Morocco

Essaouira has been singled out by some surfers, although the 'Windy City of Africa' is a better windsurfing and kitesurfing destination year-round. Nearby Sidi Kaouki is an up-and-coming destination for all three sports.

Near Agadir, the Taghazout area has some of Morocco's best surfing beaches and numerous businesses catering to surfers.

Other destinations to consider in southern Morocco are Agadir, Aglou Plage, Mirleft, and Sidi Ifni.

White-Water Rafting & Kayaking

Although white-water rafting and kayaking are underdeveloped in Morocco, the rivers in the High Atlas near Bin el-Ouidane have stunning scenery.

Water by Nature (www.waterbynature.com) The specialist UK- and USA-based adventure company offers rafting and kayaking trips, including family rafting trips, and caters to all levels of experience.

Plan Your Trip

Trekking in Morocco

Morocco is blessed with some of the world's most beautiful mountains, and is a year-round trekking destination. In summer, head to Jebel Toubkal (North Africa's highest peak). In winter, when snow makes the High Atlas impossible to trek, there's Jebel Saghro to explore, while the Rif Mountains are ideal for the seasons in between.

Trekking Regions

High Atlas

Tackle North Africa's highest peak, Jebel Toubkal, and meet the Berbers on the longer Toubkal Circuit.

Escape the crowds and be inspired by the remote M'Goun Massif's spectacular valleys and beautiful villages.

Jebel Saghro

Head southeast to some of Morocco's most rugged and stunning scenery, perfect for winter walking.

Rif Mountains

Take a gentler path through little-visited cedar forests in the Talassemtane National Park, near Chefchaouen.

Anti Atlas

Visit a few of the Ameln Valley's 26 villages, en route to an ascent of the 'amethyst mountain', Jebel L'Kest.

Enjoy serious trekking and stark beauty among the remote villages and tremendous gorges beneath volcanic Jebel Siroua.

Getting Started

Where to Trek

These are some of the best trekking spots in the country.

Toubkal Summit & Circuit

An ascent of Jebel Toubkal (p103), north Africa's highest peak (4167m), is Morocco's most iconic trek. The two-day hike starts at Imlil near Marrakesh; those wanting more can hire mules to make a Toubkal Circuit trek of up to 10 days.

M'Goun Traverse

Despite the sometime fearsome reputation of the M'Goun Traverse, this four-day trek (p93) is suitable for most levels of fitness. The landscape is both varied and spectacular, from dry gorges to lush valleys, but be prepared to get your feet wet sometimes hopping or wading across shallow rivers.

Rif Mountains

Morocco's lowest mountain range is ideal for springtime trekking (p266), when the Rif's oak forests are greenest and slopes are carpeted with wildflowers. Trek through the Talassemtane National Park, past Berber villages to arrive at the audacious natural rock formation of God's Bridge.

Jebel Saghro

This trek (p132) of five to six days threads a path between the High Atlas and the Dadès Valley. The traverse of Jebel Saghro is arid but starkly beautiful, and is a prime winter trek when other mountain trails are closed due to snow.

Anti Atlas

The Anti Atlas (p382) is where Morocco's ripple of mountains finally peters out into the Sahara. In these much over-looked mountains hardcore trekkers can take a week to tackle the volcanic peak of Jebel Siroua, or hike for five days through the villages of the Ameln Valley to Jebel L'Kest.

Maps

Morocco is covered by a 1:100,000 and also a 1:50,000 topographical map series.

Some of the 1:50,000 series are unavailable to the public; travellers exploring wide areas are advised to stick to the 1:100,000 series.

Although marked in Cyrillic script, 1:100,000 maps of Morocco made by the Soviet military are as topographically accurate as any available.

The best place in Morocco to buy maps is Direction de la Cartographie (p185) in Rabat, which lists the maps it sells online.

Maps and photocopies are also available at other bookshops around Morocco, as well as at stalls around the Djemaa el-Fna (p50) in Marrakesh and, as a last resort, on the approaches to the Atlas trekking routes.

The Foyle Reading Room of the **Royal Geographical Society** (www.rgs.org; cnr Exhibition Rd & Kensington Gore, Kensington, London, UK; admission per day £10) has one of the world's largest private collections of maps, and you can view its catalogue online.

Websites including **Amazon** (www.amazon.com) sell maps such as West Col Productions maps of the Toubkal and M'Goun Massifs.

Books

The booklet *Morocco: Mountain and Desert Tourism* (2005), published by Office National Marocain du Tourisme (ONMT), the Moroccan tourist office, has a good introduction to trekking in Morocco, plus lists of car-hire companies, *bureaux des guides* (guide offices), tourist offices, *gîtes d'étape* (trekkers' hostels), huts, *refuges* (huts), campsites, souq (market) days and other information.

You should be able to pick it up in ONMT offices overseas and in Marrakesh and other major cities, or at Imlil's *bureau des guides*.

Edisud/Belvisi publishes *Gravures Rupestres du Haut Atlas,* which looks at the rock art of Plateau du Yagour, northeast of Setti Fatma, and *Randonnées Pédestres Dans le Massif du Mgoun.* These are available online, and sporadically at tourist offices, in bookshops in Rabat and Marrakesh, from the Club Alpin Français (CAF) and in the CAF's Oukaïmeden *refuge.*

The Mountains Look on Marrakech is Hamish Brown's atmospheric account of a 96-day trek across the mountains.

Clubs, Information & Tours

Club Alpin Français (CAF; http://cafmaroc 2011.ffcam.fr; Casablanca) Operates *refuges* in the Toubkal area. Its website is a good source of information.

La Fédération Royale Marocaine de Ski et Montagne (Royal Moroccan Ski & Mountaineering Federation, FRMSM; www.frmsm.ma; Casablanca) Has basic information on its website.

Clothing & Equipment

Clothing

All year round you will need to pack strong, well-broken-in walking boots. You will also need a waterproof and windproof outer layer. It's amazing how quickly the weather can change, so you'll also need a sunhat, sunglasses and high-factor sunscreen.

In the summer (June to August) light, baggy cotton trousers and long-sleeved shirts are musts, and because the nights can still get cold even at lowish altitudes, you should also bring along a fleece or jumper.

When trekking during winter (November to March) always pack walk clothing, including a woollen hat and gloves for High Atlas trekking. You should be prepared for very cold weather wherever you trek in the country.

Trekking Areas

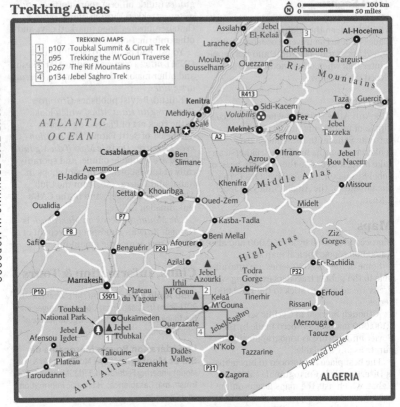

TREKKING MAPS
1 p107 Toubkal Summit & Circuit Trek
2 p95 Trekking the M'Goun Traverse
3 p267 The Rif Mountains
4 p134 Jebel Saghro Trek

Tents

The key decision, when planning a route, is whether or not to sleep in a tent. A good tent opens up endless trekking possibilities and will get you away from the crowds.

You can hire tents from tour operators and guides, and at trailheads.

If you would rather not carry a tent, in most regions you can stay in the villages.

Sleeping Bags

Whether you are camping or staying in houses, a four-season sleeping bag is essential for the High Atlas and Jebel Saghro from September to early April, when temperatures as low as -10°C are not unknown.

In lower ranges, even in high summer, a bag comfortable at 0°C is recommended. A thick sleeping mat or thin foam mattress is a good idea since the ground is extremely rocky. Guides can usually supply these.

Stoves

Many *gîtes* have cooking facilities, but you may want to bring a stove if you are camping. Multifuel stoves that burn anything from aviation fuel to diesel are ideal.

Methylated spirits is hard to get hold of, but kerosene is available. Pierce-type butane gas canisters are also available, but are not recommended for environmental reasons.

Your guide will be able to advise you on this.

Other Equipment

Bring a basic medical kit as well as water-purification tablets or iodine drops or a mechanical purifier. All water should be treated unless you take it directly from the source.

To go above 3000m between November and May, as well as having experience in winter mountaineering, you will need essentials including crampons, ice axes and snow shovels. Again, this equipment is available for hire.

If you are combining trekking with visits to urban areas, consider storing extra luggage before your trek rather than lugging around unwanted gear. Most hotels will let you leave luggage, sometimes for a small fee. Train stations in larger cities have secure left-luggage facilities.

Guides

However much trekking and map-reading experience you have, we strongly recommend that you hire a qualified guide – if for no other reason than to be your translator (how is your Tashelhit?), chaperone (*faux guides* – unofficial guides – won't come near you if you are with a guide), deal-getter and vocal guidebook.

A good guide will also enhance your cultural experience. They will know local people, which will undoubtedly result in invitations for tea and food, and richer experiences of Berber life.

If something goes wrong, a local guide will be the quickest route to getting help. Every year foreigners die in the Moroccan mountains. Whatever the cause – a freak storm, an unlucky slip, a rock slide – the presence of a guide would invariably have increased their chances of survival. So however confident you feel, we recommend that you never walk into the mountains unguided.

Choosing a Guide

A flash-looking, English-speaking *faux guide* from Marrakesh is no substitute for a gnarled, old, local mountain guide who knows the area like the back of his hand.

Official guides carry photo-identity cards. Guides should be authorised by the Fédération Royale Marocaine de Ski et Montagne or l'Association Nationale des Guides et Accompagnateurs en Montagne du Maroc. They should be credited as *guides de montagne* (mountain guides), which requires study for at least six months at the Centre de Formation aux Métiers de Montagne, a school for mountain guides at Tabant in the Aït Bougomez valley.

Accompagnateurs (escorts) will have had only one week's training, and will not be insured to lead mountain trips; *guides de tourisme* (tourist guides) are not qualified to lead treks.

Official mountain guides, who can always show an identity card as proof of their status, have been trained in mountain

---

INTERNATIONAL SPECIALIST TRAVEL MAP & BOOKSHOPS

Australia

Melbourne Map Centre (www.melbmap.com.au; Malvern East, Victoria) Australia's largest map shop stocks half-a-dozen Morocco maps.

France

Au Vieux Campeur (www.au-vieux-campeur.fr)

UK

Stanfords (www.stanfords.co.uk; London & Bristol) It sells maps including Editorial Piolet's 1:40,000 map of the Jebel Toubkal area; and West Col's series of 1:160,000 maps of the Atlas, based on the Soviet military survey maps.

The Map Shop (www.themapshop.co.uk; Upton upon Severn, Worcestershire)

USA

East View Map Link (http://store.maplink.com) Has a list of other map shops in the United States and elsewhere.

Omnimap (www.omnimap.com; Burlington, North Carolina) Sells an excellent range of maps, including the West Col and Soviet military survey maps, some available digitally.

Rand McNally (http://store.randmcnally.com)

craft, including first aid. In times of uncertain weather or in an emergency, they will be infinitely more efficient than a cheaper guide lacking proper training. If a guide is reluctant to show a photo card, it probably means he/she either doesn't have one or it has expired (they should be renewed every three years).

Some *guides de montagne* have additional training in rock climbing, canyoning and mountaineering. All guides speak French, and some also speak English, Spanish or German. Several young Moroccan female guides, who have succeeded in breaking into the previously all-male world of mountain guiding, are in high demand.

Hiring a Guide

There are more than 400 accredited mountain guides in Morocco, and many can be found through the *bureaux des guides* in Imlil, Setti Fatma, Chefchaouen, and Maroc Profond in Tabant (Aït Bougomez Valley).

At the time of writing, the minimum rate for official guides was Dh300 per day (per group, not per person). This rate can vary according to season and location. The rates do not include food and accommodation expenses.

Guides generally get free accommodation in *refuges* and *gîtes,* but you may be asked to cover their meals. If you walk a linear route, you'll also be expected to pay for their return journey.

Negotiate all fees before departure and count on giving at least a 10% tip at the end, unless you have been unhappy with the service.

If your guide (rather than a tour operator) is organising your trip, be sure to go through all aspects of the trek ahead of time. Discuss where each day will start and end; whether tents will be shared (most guides have a tent and/or sleeping bag); how many mules will be hired; who will be cooking (if there are enough of you, the guide may insist on hiring a cook, usually for about Dh100 a day); food preferences, water provision, and the division of food and equipment among the group.

Mules

Mules (and the odd donkey) are widely used in Morocco for transporting goods through the mountains, and you can easily hire one to carry your gear.

If you are relying on heavy local supplies, or are in a large group, hiring a mule makes especially good sense. As a rough guide, mules can carry up to 120kg – or up to four sets of gear. If the route is very steep or demanding, the muleteer may insist upon carrying less. He will have the wellbeing of his meal ticket in mind, although Moroccans are generally unsentimental about their pack animals.

Some trekking routes are not suitable for mules, although detours (for the mule) are often possible. If high passes are covered in snow, porters may have to be used instead of mules (one porter can carry up to 18kg).

There is usually a standard charge for a mule and muleteer of about Dh100 per day. As with guides, if you trek a linear route, you'll also be expected to pay for the muleteer's return journey.

TREKKING GUIDEBOOKS

➡ *Great Atlas Traverse* by Michael Peyron. The two-volume work by the Morocco-based British writer is the definitive text for the great traverse. Less useful for the casual trekker.

➡ *The Atlas Mountains: A Walking and Trekking Guide* by Karl Smith. Published by the walking specialist Cicerone, this has route descriptions and information on subjects such as ski-touring, although it gets mixed reviews.

➡ *Mountaineering in the Moroccan High Atlas* by Des Clark. Also published by Cicerone, this guide covers some 50 routes and 30 peaks in handy pocket-sized, plastic-covered form, with plenty of maps, photos and practical information.

➡ *Trekking in the Moroccan Atlas* by Richard Knight. Has 43 maps and information ranging from green hiking tips to language advice, although it also has both fans and detractors. Likely to be the most useful book for inexperienced trekkers, but it's also the bulkiest.

On the Trek

Accommodation

If you would rather not carry a tent, you can often stay in *refuges* and in villages at either *gîtes d'étape* (basic homestays or hostels) or *chez l'habitant* (in someone's home). Especially in more remote areas, village rooms may not even have a mattress on the floor, although in places such as Imlil they often come with the luxury of a bed.

The bulk of trekking accommodation options in the High and Middle Atlas are *gîtes*. In the Rif and Anti Atlas, *gîtes* are uncommon, and accommodation is more often in local homes or in tents.

Gîtes d'Étape

Gîtes provide basic accommodation, often offering little more than a foam mattress in an empty room, or on a roof terrace or balcony. They have basic bathrooms and toilets, although the better ones have hot showers. Given notice, the proprietor can rustle up a tajine.

At the time of writing, the standard rate was Dh50 per person per night, although the price can vary according to season and location. Meals are extra (usually Dh30 to Dh50 per person), as are hot showers (usually Dh10 to Dh15 per shower).

The more upscale, privately owned *gîtes* typically charge up to Dh200 per person for half-board, while rooms at one luxury kasbah in Imlil cost up to Dh2780.

Refuges

CAF operates *refuges* in Imlil, Oukaïmeden, Tazaghart, Tacheddirt and on Toubkal. Officially, bookings should be made in advance through the Oukaïmeden *refuge*. However, in practice you can usually find out if space is available at the other *refuges* in the Toubkal region by asking in Oukaïmeden or Imlil. *Refuges* are often packed in July and August.

CAF members and HI members get the cheapest price for a bed. Members of affiliated and recognised alpine organisations (eg the UK's Alpine Club) and children aged under 16 years are also eligible for discounts.

Food

The choice of dry rations is limited in rural Morocco. You cannot be sure of finding much beyond powdered milk, a range of dried fruit and sachets of soup, biscuits, some tinned fish and dates. Supermarkets in larger towns and cities are a much better option, and if you take a mule, you will be able to plan a more varied diet.

Bread, eggs, vegetables and some basic supplies (eg tea and tinned tuna) may be available in some mountain villages, but you cannot count on it. Meals can also be arranged in some villages (Dh30 to Dh50 per person is standard), especially at *gîtes* and *refuges,* although they usually need to be ordered in advance. Again, do not rely on local suppliers as your only source of food unless you have made previous arrangements.

Change money in the nearest major town and ensure that you have plenty of small notes. If you do get stuck, euro notes may be accepted.

Responsible Trekking

Morocco is being developed as a walking destination, but many regions remain remote – and susceptible to the cultural and environmental impact of tourism. Many travellers return home warmed and heartened by Berber hospitality, but as visitor numbers increase so too does the pressure on locals. In response, travellers should adopt an appropriate code of behaviour.

Cross-Cultural Considerations

Dress

The way you dress is important, especially among remote mountain people, who remain conservative. In villages, wear buttoned shirts or T-shirts and not sleeveless vests, which villagers use as underwear. Above all, trousers should be worn rather than shorts. This applies equally to men and women.

The importance of dress in the villages cannot be overemphasised (as many a frustrated and embarrassed trekking tour leader will affirm). However much you might disagree with this conservatism,

WORDS TO TREK BY

Even just a few words in a foreign language can make a big difference to your experience. The following words may be helpful on these treks. (A) indicates Arabic, (B) indicates Berber; other useful Arabic and Berber words can be found in the Glossary (p502).

adfel (B) – snow

adrar (B) – mountain (plural *idraren*)

afella (B) – summit

agdal (B) – pasture (also *aougdal*)

aghbalu (B) – water spring

ain (A) – water spring

aman (B) – water

anzar (B) – rain

argaz (B) – man

asserdoun (B) – mule

assif (B) – watercourse, river

azaghar (B) – plane/plateau (also *izwghar*)

azib (B) – seasonal shelter for shepherds

brhel (A) – mule

hâba (B) – ravine

iferd (B) – lake

ifri (B) – cave

jebel (A) – mountain or hill

kerkour (B) – cairn

taddart (B) – house

talat (B) – dried-up ravine/watercourse

tamada (B) – lake

tigm (B) – house

tizi (B) – mountain pass

respecting local traditions will bring great rewards, not least by way of contact, hospitality and assistance.

Hospitality

Invitations for tea and offers of food are common in the mountains. By taking a guide, who may have friends in many villages, you'll open yourself up to even more offers of genuine hospitality.

While these offers are unconditional, it is worth bearing in mind that the mountain economy is one of basic subsistence farming. No one has large supplies, and in outlying villages there may be no surplus food. Offering your hosts some Chinese gunpowder tea and some sugar (preferably in cones) is a very welcome gesture. Dried fruits are also appreciated, as is a taste of any imported food you may have.

For this reason, it is important to be generous when buying provisions for yourself and guides.

Medicine

In remote areas, people along the way will often ask for medicine, from disinfectant and bandages to painkillers or cream for dry skin (which many children have). Always make sure the guide explains what to do with what you offer – how often to take it and so on.

Environmental Considerations

Rubbish

Carry out all your rubbish; never bury it or burn it (Western-style packaging never burns well). Your guide may be happy to bag up all your rubbish and hurl it over a cliff, but that approach is unsustainable, especially given that more and more people are now trekking in Morocco. So if you have carried it in, then you should carry it out.

Minimise the waste you'll carry out by taking minimal packaging, and by repackaging provisions into reusable containers when appropriate. If you want to make a gesture, consider carrying out some of the rubbish left by others.

Don't rely on bought water in plastic bottles, as disposal of these bottles is creating a major problem in Morocco. Instead purify locally sourced water.

Human Waste Disposal

Contamination of water sources by human faeces can lead to the transmission of hepatitis, typhoid and intestinal parasites. This is a particular problem in more populated trekking areas.

Where there is a toilet, it is a good idea to use it; where there is none, bury your waste. Dig a small hole 15cm (6in) deep and at least 100m from any watercourse – an important point to remember, given how many trekking routes follow rivers and streams. Consider carrying a lightweight trowel: in the arid Atlas Mountains, digging without one can be difficult. In snow, dig down to the soil; otherwise, your waste will be exposed when the snow melts.

Use toilet paper sparingly, burn it when possible or bury it with the waste. Cover the waste with soil and a rock.

Washing

Don't use detergents or toothpaste in or near watercourses, even if they are biodegradable. For personal washing use biodegradable soap and wash at least 50m away from any watercourse. Disperse the waste water widely to allow the soil to filter it fully before it makes its way back to the watercourse. Use a scourer, sand or snow to wash cooking utensils rather than detergent. Again, make sure you're at least 50m from any watercourse.

Erosion

Hillsides and mountain slopes, especially at high altitudes, are prone to erosion. Stick to existing tracks and avoid short cuts that bypass a switchback. If you blaze

a new trail straight down a slope, it will turn into a watercourse with the next heavy rainfall, eventually causing soil loss and deep scarring.

Low-Impact Cooking

Don't depend on open fires for cooking. As you will see, cutting wood for fires has caused widespread deforestation in Morocco. Ideally, cook on a lightweight multifuel or kerosene stove and avoid those powered by disposable butane gas canisters.

If you do make a fire, ensure that it is fully extinguished after use by spreading the embers and dousing them with water. A fire is only truly safe to leave when you can comfortably place your hand in it.

Camping

Vegetation at high altitude is highly sensitive. When camping, minimise your impact on the environment by not removing or disturbing the vegetation around your campsite. In order to avoid aggravating the persistent and serious problem of overgrazing in many of the regions, sufficient fodder (barley) for all baggage mules and donkeys should be brought in. Enquire about this before setting off.

Plan Your Trip

Travel with Children

Morocco has plenty to capture a child's imagination. The souqs of Marrakesh and Fez are an endlessly fascinating sensory explosion, and nights around a campfire or camel rides on the beach are equally memorable – but factor in some time by the hotel pool at the end of a hot day.

Best Regions for Kids

Marrakesh
All generations can retire to pool, park, horse-drawn calèche or camel back. The Djemaa el-Fna is Morocco's carnival capital.

Coast
The Atlantic Coast offers plenty of beaches and water and wind sports. Agadir's long, sandy beach is popular; mix it with somewhere more colourful like Essaouira, with its fun-to-explore ramparts and medina.

Drâa Valley
Tour Ouarzazate's film studios and kasbah, then head down the valley for dunes and dromedary rides.

Rabat
With souqs, ruins and gardens, this is a relatively mellow slice of urban Morocco. Attractions include a zoo, amusement park and pony rides.

Middle Atlas
For mountain scenery, waterfalls, forest walks and less hair-raising passes than in the High Atlas. Easily visited from spots like Azrou and Fez.

Morocco for Kids

Morocco is ideal for parents who once travelled to intrepid destinations, and don't necessarily fancy a Western poolside now they have knee-high travelling companions. Compared with Asia, Morocco is easily accessible from Europe and North America; Marrakesh is less than four hours from London. And when you touch down, you'll find that children open numerous doors, getting you closer to the heart of this family-oriented country.

Meeting the Locals

Moroccans love children so much that you may even want to bring a backpack to carry smaller kids, in case they grow tired of the kissing, hugging, gifts and general adulation. Locals have grown up in large families, and children break the ice and encourage contact with Moroccans, who are generally very friendly, helpful and protective towards families.

As you travel the countryside, women may pick up their own child and wave from their doorway. Such moments emphasise your children's great benefit: having yet to acquire any stereotypes about Africa and the Middle East, their enduring impression of Morocco is likely to be its people's warmth and friendliness.

Of course, this certainly doesn't mean parents receive special treatment from the salesmen in the country's souqs. However, even the grizzliest shopkeepers generally welcome Western women and children, as it gives their store the image of having a broad, family-friendly appeal. Letting your kids run amok in carpet shops can also be an excellent bargaining technique!

Adapting to Morocco

Morocco will be an unfamiliar environment to many, and children will probably take a day or so to adapt, but it has plenty of familiar and fun aspects that kids can relate to. Hectic first impressions will be countered by exciting finds like the snakes charmers on the Djemaa el-Fna. In the countryside, simple things like beehives and plants endlessly fascinate children. Dedicated play facilities in parks and public gardens are very rare.

Taking Your Time

A key to successful family travel in Morocco is to factor in lots of time: to acclimatise at the beginning, and to just relax and muck about at the end. Trying to cram everything in, as you might if you were by yourself, will lead to tired, cranky kids. Distances are deceptive due to factors such as bad roads, and you need to build in contingency plans in case children get ill. However, having to slow your pace to that of your kids – for example, having to stay put in the hottest hours between noon and 4pm – is another way children draw you closer to the Moroccan landscape, people and pace of life.

Eating Out

Tajines contain many familiar elements, such as potatoes and carrots. Although you may want to encourage your child to try Moroccan food, you may struggle if they don't like potatoes or bread, in which case Western foods, such as pasta, pizza and fries, are available. High chairs are not always available in restaurants, although staff are almost universally accommodating with children.

Be careful about choosing restaurants; steer clear of salads and stick to piping-hot tajines, couscous, omelettes and soups such as *harira* (lentil soup). Markets sell delicious fruit and veggies, but be sure to wash or peel them.

To avoid stomach upsets, stick to purified or bottled water. Milk is widely available – UHT, pasteurised and powdered – but you should bring any special foods you require.

Children's Highlights

Animal Encounters

➡ Travelling by road to a High Atlas trailhead such as Imlil (p101), then taking a day walk in the mountains with a guide and mule.

➡ Camel or horse rides along the beaches around Essaouira (p208) or in the Sahara, with accessible dunes in the Drâa Valley (p118) and Merzouga (p147).

➡ Calèche (horse-drawn carriage) rides around the ramparts of places like Marrakesh (p47) and Taroudannt (p369).

Splashing Around

➡ Wind and water sports around Essaouira, or the beach at Agadir (p359) for young children.

➡ Oualidia lagoon (p204), with safe, calm waters and a wide, sandy beach.

➡ Ceuta's creative Parque Marítimo del Mediterráneo, its pools surrounded by restaurants and cafes.

Fun & Games

➡ Jardin Majorelle (p60) and Djemaa el-Fna (p50), Marrakesh; on the latter, children enjoy amusements such as the 'fishing for a bottle' game.

➡ Atlas Film Corporation Studios (p112), Ouarzazate, featuring sets and props from famous films made hereabouts.

Planning

If you look hard enough, you can buy just about anything you need for young children in Morocco. Before leaving home, think about what you can take with you to Morocco's various environments; wet-weather gear is vital in the mountains in case the weather turns bad.

Lonely Planet's *Travel with Children* has more information and tips.

Accommodation

Some hotels are more family-friendly than others, so check your children will be well catered for before booking.

Like the airlines, many hotels will not charge children under two years of age. For those between two and 12 years sharing a room with their parents, it's often 50% off the adult rate. If you want reasonable toilet and bathroom facilities, you'll need to stay in midrange hotels.

Transport

Northern Morocco has a great rail infrastructure, and travel by train may be the easiest, most enjoyable option: children can stretch their legs, and fold-out tables are useful for drawing and games. Travellers and children are eligible for reductions and discount cards.

Grands taxis and buses can be a real squeeze with young children, who count not as passengers in their own right but as wriggling luggage, and have to sit on your lap. The safety record of buses and shared taxis is poor, and many roads are potholed.

Hiring a vehicle – a taxi in Marrakesh or a 4WD to the mountains – is well worth the extra expense. It's worth bringing a child seat – it will allow children to see out of the window and hire-car companies normally don't have them. Seats generally cost more in Morocco than they do in Europe.

Health & Hygiene

Alcohol gel (hand sanitiser) is essential, as children tend to touch everything. Disposable nappies are a practical solution when travelling despite the environmental drawbacks; international brands are readily available. All travellers with children should know how to treat minor ailments and when to seek medical treatment.

Make sure the children are up to date with routine vaccinations, and discuss possible travel vaccines well before departure, as some are not suitable for children aged under a year.

Upset stomachs are always a risk for children when travelling, so take particular care with diet. If your child is vomiting or experiencing diarrhoea, lost fluid and salts must be replaced. It may be helpful to take rehydration powders for reconstituting with sterile water; ask your doctor. Be aware that at roadside stops and cheaper hotels, squat-style toilets are more common than Western-style toilets.

In Morocco's often-searing heat, sunburn, heat exhaustion and dehydration should all be guarded against, even on cloudy days. Bring high-factor sunscreen with you, and avoid travelling in the interior during midsummer, when temperatures rise to 40°C plus.

Encourage children to avoid dogs and other mammals because of the risk of rabies and other diseases – although there isn't likely to be a risk on camel rides in the desert, or with donkeys and mules working in places like Fez medina.

Regions at a Glance

Marrakesh & Central Morocco

Adventure
Architecture
Food

Adventure

With its dunes, mountains, souqs and kasbahs, Central Morocco is an adventure. But before you leave Marrakesh, dive into the Djemaa el-Fna. The square's peculiar magic – like a circus meeting a giant barbecuing competition – soon sweeps travellers into a jubilant party mood.

Architecture

Marrakesh has more riads than any other city, kasbahs dot the Drâa Valley, and *ksour* (fortified strongholds) line the Rissani road. White window frames and blue doors distinguish stone, mud and thatch villages from their High Atlas settings.

Food

Fantastic street food, lavish riad dining, local organic ingredients – and that's just in Marrakesh. Slow Food is even taking off, from Saharan date syrup to honey from medicinal herbs. Try some local wines, particularly the crisp rosé and gris varieties.

p46

Atlantic Coast

Beaches
Architecture
Birdwatching

Beaches

This stretch encompasses the aptly named Paradise Beach, a carriage ride from Assilah, and Sidi Kaouki, a top surfing and windsurfing spot. In between, Temara Plage and Haouzia beach are near Rabat and Casablanca, and chic Oualidia has a sand-fringed lagoon.

Architecture

Gems include Essaouira and El-Jadida, fortified seaside towns with wavelashed ramparts. Hispano-Moorish Larache recalls its two spells under Spanish rule and murals decorate nearby Assilah's medina. Mauresque beauties are found in Casablanca (which also has the world's third-largest mosque) and Rabat.

Birdwatching

Beaches and coastal wetlands offer excellent birdwatching, particularly around Moulay Bousselham: Merja Zerga (Blue Lagoon) attracts thousands of birds. Lac de Sidi Bourhaba is one of the last places to see large numbers of marbled ducks.

p153

Mediterranean Coast & the Rif

Beaches
National Parks
Trekking

Beaches

The Mediterranean coast ripples east from beaches near Tangier. Top beaches include Oued Laou, Cala Iris, Al-Hoceima and Saïdia, all unruffled in comparison with Europe's Mediterranean beaches.

National Parks

Two stunning national parks offer the best of the region's coastline and mountains. Talassemtane National Park encompasses green mountains, tiny villages, an eco-museum and the God's Bridge rock formation; and the Al-Hoceima National Park's great mesas, dry canyons and thuya forests lead to limestone sea cliffs.

Trekking

Trekking through the Rif Mountains in Talassemtane National Park is superb, and largely undiscovered compared with High Atlas routes. From Chefchaouen, multiday trails lead through forests of cedar, cork oak and fir.

p220

Imperial Cities, Middle Atlas & the East

Souqs
History
Food

Souqs

Fez medina includes the Henna Souq (actually best for blue pottery) and the Carpenters' Souq, with thrones built for weddings. Meknès has souqs devoted to textiles, jewellery, carpets and embroidery, and Middle Atlas souqs are piled with Berber carpets.

History

Fez medina is the world's largest living medieval Islamic city, and the Fès Festival of World Sacred Music showcases Sufi music. Elsewhere, memories of Meknès' past glories remain; Volubilis was a Roman outpost; Moulay Idriss is dedicated to its 8th-century namesake; and an 11th-century minaret overlooks oasis town Figuig.

Food

Fez' dishes include wild thistle/artichoke stew, and the medina has a snail stand. The Middle Atlas has homegrown delights, such as the red goodies at Sefrou's Cherry Festival.

p281

Southern Morocco & Western Sahara

Coastal Hideaways
Oases
Activities

Coastal Hideaways

Remote seaside escapes offer empty beaches and dilapidated charm. Mirleft is a favourite hang-out with its cafes and boutique accommodation; art-deco Sidi Ifni is as perfectly faded as a sepia photo; and Tarfaya's colonial Spanish relics peel between the eddying sands.

Oases

Beneath ochre cliffs, palms worthy of *Lawrence of Arabia* nestle in the Aït Mansour Gorges and Ameln Valley. Palms also line the winding road through Paradise Valley, and refresh Saharan travellers around Tata and Tighmert.

Activities

Taghazout is Morocco's premier surf spot, the sun-and-sand fun continues year-round in Agadir, and Mirleft and Sidi Ifni offer wind and water sports. Inland, the Anti Atlas is a mountain-biking and trekking playground, and Tata is an emerging destination for desert excursions.

p357

On the Road

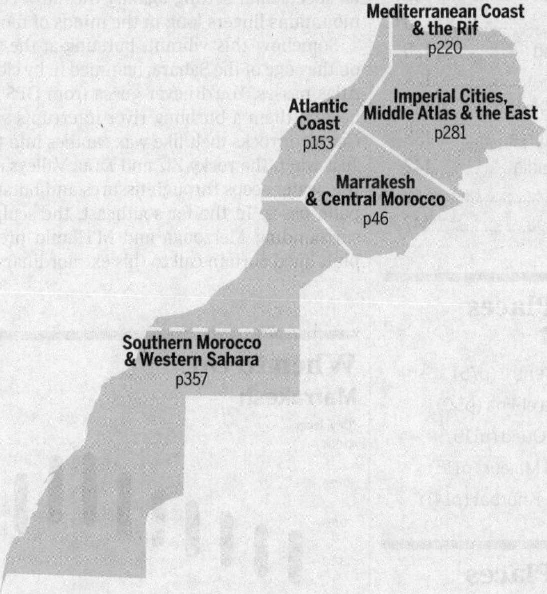

Mediterranean Coast
& the Rif
p220

Atlantic
Coast
p153

Imperial Cities,
Middle Atlas & the East
p281

Marrakesh
& Central Morocco
p46

Southern Morocco
& Western Sahara
p357

Marrakesh & Central Morocco

مراكش وسط المغرب

Best Places to Eat

➡ Amal Centre (p75)
➡ Djemaa el-Fna (p50)
➡ Bab el-Oued (p119)
➡ Accord Majeur (p116)
➡ Ksar el-Khorbat (p141)

Best Places to Stay

➡ Dar al Assad (p69)
➡ Tizouit (p85)
➡ Dar Ahansal (p89)
➡ Jardins de Skoura (p130)
➡ La Dune Blanche (p124)

Why Go?

The central region of Morocco is the most exciting and diverse destination in the entire country. The biggest drawcard is the pink city of Marrakesh. Founded almost 1000 years ago, it is one of the great cities of the Maghreb and its spectacular setting against the snow-capped High Atlas mountains lingers long in the minds of most travellers.

Somehow this vibrant, bursting-at-the-seams city exists on the edge of the Sahara, hemmed in by cloud-busting High Atlas passes. You'd never guess from GPS coordinates that beyond them a burbling river interrupts stony-faced Todra Gorge, or rocks melt like wax candles into the Dadès Gorge. Just when the rocky Ziz and Drâa Valleys seem utterly barren, water seeps through fissures and bursts into exuberant palm oases. In the far southeast, the sculpted sand dunes surrounding Merzouga and M'Hamid provide the perfect pink-hued curtain call to this extraordinary region.

When to Go
Marrakesh

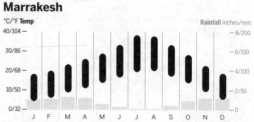

Mar–Apr Mountains thaw, desert blooms. Skip Easter holidays when prices jump.

May–Jun Ideal High Atlas hiking: hot, not scorching. Accommodation and souq bargains.

Oct–Nov Prime desert time: gentle breezes, dates galore.

MARRAKESH

مراكش

POP 1,070,800

From the moment you arrive in Marrakesh, you'll get the distinct feeling you've left something behind – a toothbrush or socks, maybe? But no, what you'll be missing in Marrakesh is predictability and all sense of direction. Never mind: you're better off without them here. Start at action-packed Djemaa el-Fna and head north into Marrakesh's maze of souqs, where Berber tribes once traded slaves, gold, ivory and leather, and where modern tourists scour people-packed alleys for carpet bargains and *babouches* (leather slippers). Look carefully, and you'll also spot a number of creative new boutiques and galleries. They signify the evolving face of the medina as a new generation of craftspeople and artists try to connect the city's hankering for modernity with its traditional craft heritage.

Beyond the souqs, the medina is an ideal place to explore private palaces and riad mansions, many of which now provide the city's most atmospheric accommodation. But it's worth leaving the old city occasionally for dinner, drinks and art galleries in the ville nouvelle (new town), mountain bike rides in the *palmeraie* (palm oasis) or horse-riding and weekend retreats in the Agafay Desert and Ouirgane.

History

Many desert caravans passed through this outpost before Almoravid Berber leader Youssef ben Tachfine and his savvy wife Zeinab recognised its strategic potential, and built ramparts around the encampment in AD 1062. The Almoravids established the city's *khettara* (underground irrigation system) and signature pink mudbrick architecture. But when Almohad warriors stormed the city, they left only the plumbing and the Koubba Ba'adiyn intact. Almohad Yacoub el-Mansour remodelled Marrakesh with a fortified kasbah, glorious gardens, *qissariat* (covered markets), a rebuilt Koutoubia and a triumphal gate (Bab Agnaou). But the Almohads soon lost their showpiece to the Merenids, who turned royal attention to Meknès and Fez.

Life improved again in the 16th century, when the Saadians made Marrakesh the crux of lucrative sugar-trade routes, established a trading centre for Christians and a protected *mellah* (Jewish quarter) in 1558. Ahmed al-Mansour ed-Dahbi (the Victorious and Golden) paved the Badi Palace with gold and took opulence to the grave in the gilded Saadian Tombs.

Alawite leader Moulay Ismail preferred Meknès to Marrakesh, and moved his headquarters there – though not before looting the Badi Palace. Marrakesh entered its Wild West period, with big guns vying for control. Those who prevailed built extravagant riads, though much of the population lived hand to mouth in crowded *funduqs* (rooming houses). In 1912 the French protectorate granted Pasha Glaoui the run of southern Morocco, while French and Spanish colonists built themselves a ville nouvelle.

Without a clear role post-Independence, Marrakesh resumed its fall-back career as a caravanserai – and became the nation's breakaway success. Roving hippies built the city's mystique in the 1960s and '70s, and visits by the Rolling Stones, Beatles and Led Zeppelin gave the city star power. In the 1990s private medina mansions were converted into B&Bs, just in time for low-cost airlines to deliver weekenders to brass-studded riad doors.

Marrakesh was amid a major tourism boom in 2008 when the global financial crisis started to wreak havoc on European markets, which account for over 80% of the city's visitors. Hot on the heels of this fiscal collapse, an Islamist militant disguised as a guitar-carrying hippie walked into Café Argana on the Djemaa el-Fna and planted two bombs that killed 17 people in April 2011.

Confidence in the Red City plummeted: tourists cancelled bookings and investment tumbled. But while economic growth hit the skids, dropping from 4.9% in 2011 to 2.9% in 2012, Morocco's circumspect handling of Arab Spring tensions saw a gradual return to growth in 2013. What's more, the city's dynamic entrepreneurs are determined to put Marrakesh back on track with audacious plans for Africa's largest contemporary art museum scheduled for completion in 2016.

👁 Sights

👁 Medina

Most monuments are inside the medina ramparts (a 19km circuit). If you wander off course exploring souqs and palaces, ask someone to point you towards Djemaa el-Fna (preferably a shopkeeper – kids sometimes mislead tourists) or head towards the Koutoubia minaret, the tallest in town.

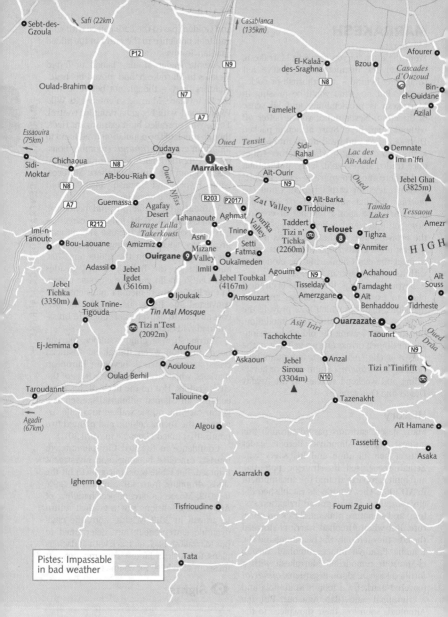

Marrakesh & Central Morocco Highlights

1 Contrast the outrageous antics of **Djemaa el-Fna** (p50) street performers with the serenity and social graces hidden behind the austere pink walls of authentic **Marrakshi riads** (p67)

2 Walk through Morocco's Shangri-la, the stunning and secluded **Aït Bougomez Valley** (p90)

3 Follow desert caravan routes from kasbah to kasbah through the **Drâa Valley** (p118)

4 Stargaze in the rolling dunes at **Erg Chigaga** (p125)

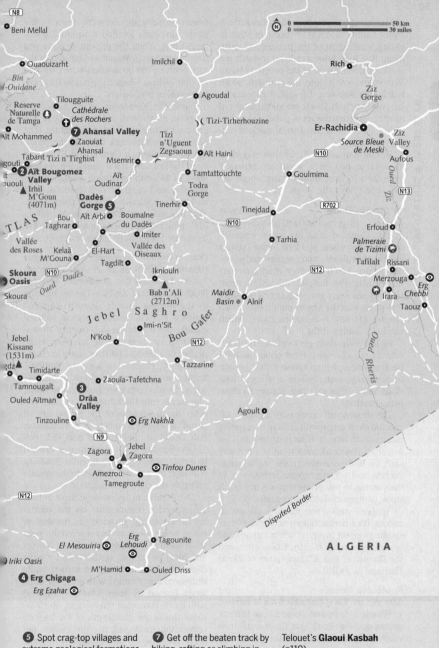

Beni Mellal

N8

Ouaouizarht

Bin
el-Ouidane

Reserve
Naturelle
de Tamga

Tilougguite

Cathédrale
des Rochers

Aït Mohammed

7 **Ahansal Valley**

Zaouiat
Ahansal

gouti

Tabant Tizi n'Tirghist

Tizi
n'Uguent
Zegsaoun

2 **Aït Bougomez
Valley**

Msemrir

Aït
Oudinar

Irhil
M'Goun
(4071m)

**Dadès
Gorge** 5

Bou
Taghrar

Aït Arbi

Boumalne
du Dadès

ATLAS

Vallée
des Roses

Kelaâ
M'Gouna

El-Hart

Imiter

Tagdilt

Ikniouln

Vallée
des
Oiseaux

**Skoura
Oasis**

N10

Oued   Dadès

Skoura

Jebel   Saghro

Bab n'Ali
(2712m)

Imi-n'Sit

Jebel
Kissane
(1531m)

N'Kob

Bou Gafer

N12

Imilchil

Agoudal

Tizi-Tirherhouzine

Aït Haini

Tamtattouchte

Todra
Gorge

Tinerhir

Tinejdad

N10

Tarhia

Maïdir
Basin

Alnif

Tazzarine

Timidarte

Zaouïa-Tafetchna

Tamnougalt

3 **Drâa
Valley**

Ouled Aïtman

Tinzouline

N9

Zagora

Jebel
Zagora

Amezrou

Tamegroute

N12

Erg Nakhla

Tinfou Dunes

Agoult

Rich

Ziz
Gorge

Er-Rachidia

Source Bleue
de Meski

Ziz
Valley

Aufous

N10

Goulmima

Oued   Ziz

N13

R702

Erfoud

Palmeraie
de Tizimi

Tafilalt

Rissani

Merzouga

Irara

Erg
Chebbi

Taouz

Oued   Rheris

N12

El Mesouiria

Erg
Lehoudi

Tagounite

Iriki Oasis

4 **Erg Chigaga**

Erg Ezahar

M'Hamid

Ouled Driss

Disputed Border

ALGERIA

N   0   50 km
0   30 miles

5 Spot crag-top villages and
extreme geological formations
in the **Dadès Gorge** (p135)

6 Stroll amid swaying palm
trees in the Unesco-protected
oasis of **Skoura** (p128)

7 Get off the beaten track by
hiking, rafting or climbing in
the **Ahansal Valley** (p88)

8 Witness troubled history
and impeccable artistry at

Telouet's **Glaoui Kasbah**
(p110)

9 Join weekending
Marrakshis for lunch, lounging
and fun in **Ouirgane's**
countryside retreats (p83)

Marrakesh's main souqs, mosques and *za-wiyas* (saints' shrines) are north of Djemaa el-Fna, while most of the palaces are south along Rue Riad Zitoun el-Jedid towards the *mellah*. Turning west at the covered Mellah Market and south along the ramparts, you'll reach Bab Agnaou, triumphal gateway to the royal kasbah. Inside are gilded tombs of Saadian princes, the royal palace (closed to visitors), and 16 acres of royal gardens dating from AD 1166.

During Ramadan, official sites may close an hour or two early; souqs are generally open 9am to 7pm, though many shops are closed on Friday afternoon.

★ **Djemaa El-Fna** SQUARE
(Map p56; ⊙approx 9am-1am, later during Ramadan) Think of it as live-action channel-surfing: everywhere you look in the Djemaa el-Fna, Marrakesh's main square and open-air theatre, you'll discover drama already in progress. The hoopla and *halqa* (street theatre) has been non-stop here ever since this plaza was the site of public executions around AD 1050 – hence its name, which means 'assembly of the dead'.

By 10am, the daily performance is underway. Snake charmers blast oboes to calm hissing cobras; henna tattoo artists beckon to passersby; water-sellers in fringed hats clang brass cups together, hoping to drive people to drink.

The show doesn't peak until shadows fall and 100 chefs arrive with grills in tow, cueing musicians to tune up their instruments. This is a show you don't want to miss – but stay alert to horse-drawn-carriage traffic, pick-pockets and rogue gropers. Arrive early in the evening to nab prime seats on makeshift stools (women and elders get preference).

Applause and a few dirhams ensure an encore. It's a bargain show, and critically acclaimed too: for bringing urban legends and oral history to life nightly, Unesco declared the Djemaa el-Fna a 'Masterpiece of World Heritage' in 2001.

Koutoubia Mosque MOSQUE
(Map p52; cnr Rue el-Koutoubia & Ave Mohammed V; ⊙mosque & minaret closed to non-Muslims, gardens open 8am-8pm) Five times a day, one voice rises above the Djemaa din in the *adhan* (call to prayer): that's the muezzin calling the faithful from atop the Koutoubia Mosque minaret. Excavations confirm a longstanding Marrakshi legend: the original mosque built by Almoravid architects

wasn't properly aligned with Mecca, so the pious Almohads levelled it to build a realigned one. When the present mosque was finished by Sultan Yacoub el-Mansour in the 12th century, 100 booksellers were clustered around its base – hence the name, from *kutubiyyin*, or booksellers.

While the Koutoubia serves a spiritual purpose, its minaret is also a point of reference for international architecture. The 12th-century 70m-high tower is the prototype for Seville's La Giralda and Rabat's Le Tour Hassan, and it's a monumental cheat sheet of Moorish ornament: scalloped keystone arches, jagged *merlons* (crenellations), and mathematically pleasing proportions. The minaret was sheathed in Marrakshi pink plaster, but experts opted to preserve its exposed stone in its 1990s restoration.

Douiria Derb el Hammam MUSEUM
(Map p56; ☏0524 38 57 21; www.douiria.com; Fontaine Mouassine, Derb el Hammam; admission Dh30; ⊙10am-6pm Sat-Thu) House hunting in the medina Patrick Menac'h stumbled across a historic treasure of great cultural significance beside the 16th-century Mouassine mosque. Beneath the layers of white plaster of a modest 1st-floor *douiria* (guest apartment) emerged a jewel of domestic Saadian architecture and decor, circa 1560, when the Saadians were busy transforming Marrakesh into their Imperial capital. The other major projects of the period are all grand in scale – the mosques at Mouassine, Bab Doukkala, Ben-Youssef and Sidi Bel-Abbes. But this bijou *douiria* was created by a *chorfa* (noble) family after the Saadians relocated the Mouassine Jews to the *mellah* and gave the city a new dynamic.

The Douiria in its restored form is thus an important commentary on the courtly art of hospitality. Imagine the mindset of travel-weary guests as they entered the main salon with its symphony of colours; flowers and birds in saffron, verdigris and apricot climb the walls in a vertical garden, while bedrooms are trimmed with sculpted Kufic script framed by azure blue and finished with a fine Pompeian red skirting. You'll assume this is the handiwork of the 24-man restoration team, but no, the colour and decor are uniquely and amazingly original, their vibrancy preserved for four centuries beneath thick layers of plaster.

Part of the Douiria's ongoing restoration will be undertaken in public view (groups will be limited to 25 people at a time) as part of the museum's efforts to showcase modern restoration techniques. A sequence of fascinating photographs details each step of the journey, which is momentous enough to appear as part of the curriculum of the École d'Architecture de Marrakech introducing students to the concept of patrimony. Beyond that the space will be utilised for exceptional temporary exhibitions focusing on the very best examples of Islamic art and craftsmanship. And with patrons like Xavier Salmon from the Louvre, they promise to be as exquisite as the apartment itself.

Mouassine Fountain   FOUNTAIN
(Map p56; Rue Sidi el-Yamani) The medina had 80 fountains at the start of the 20th century, and each neighbourhood had its own for cooking, public baths, orchards and gardens. The Mouassine Fountain, near Rue el-Mouassine, is a prime example, with carved wood details and continued use as a neighbourhood wool-drying area and gossip source.

Funduqs   HISTORICAL BUILDINGS
(⊙ 9am-7pm) Since medieval times, these creative courtyard complexes featured ground-floor stables and workshops and rented rooms for desert traders and merchants upstairs – and from this flux of artisans and adventurers emerged the inventive culture of modern-day Marrakesh. Only 140 *funduqs* remain in the medina, many of them now converted into artisan complexes, and although you'll find them in various states of disrepair, many retain fine original woodcarving, romantic balconies and even some stuccowork.

You'll find notable examples near Pl Bab Fteuh, along Rue Amesfah (Dar Bellarj is a converted *funduq*) and a cluster at the junction (Map p56) of Rue el-Mouassine and Rue Dar el-Bacha, including one featured in the film *Hideous Kinky*.

Dar Bellarj   GALLERY
(Map p56; ☑ 0524 44 45 55; www.darbellarj.org; 9-7 Toualate Zaouiate Lahdar; ⊙ 9.30am-12.30pm & 2-5.30pm Mon-Sat) **FREE** Flights of fancy come with the territory at Dar Bellarj, a stork hospital (*bellarj* is Arabic for stork) turned into Marrakesh's premier arts centre. Each year the nonprofit Dar Bellarj Foundation adopts a program theme, ranging from film to women's textiles and storytelling. Calligraphy demonstrations, art openings, craft exhibits and arts workshops are regular draws, and admission is usually free (there's a charge for some events).

During Ramadan, the foundation also hosts a series of evening music concerts in the central courtyard.

★ Ali ben Youssef Medersa   MEDERSA
(Map p56; ☑ 0524 44 18 93; Pl ben Youssef; adult/child Dh50/30, with Musée de Marrakesh Dh60; ⊙ 9am-6pm winter, to 7pm summer) 'You who enter my door, may your highest hopes be exceeded' reads the inscription over the entryway to the *medersa* (theological college), and after almost six centuries, the blessing still works its charms on visitors. Founded in the 14th century under the Merenids, this Quranic learning centre was once the largest in North Africa, and remains among the most splendid.

Sight lines are lifted in the entry with carved Atlas cedar cupolas and *mashrabiyya* (wooden-lattice screen) balconies. The courtyard is a mind-boggling profusion of Hispano-Moresque ornament: five-colour *zellij* (mosaic) walls; stucco archways; cedar windows with weather-worn carved vines; and a curved mihrab (eastern-facing niche indicating the direction of Mecca) of prized, milky-white Italian Carrara marble.

The *medersa* is affiliated with nearby Ali ben Youssef Mosque (Map p56; ⊙ closed to non-Muslims), and once 900 students in 132 dorms arranged around the courtyard studied religious and legal texts here. Despite upgrades with its 19th-century renovation, the Ali ben Youssef Medersa gradually lost students to its collegiate rival, the Medera Bou Inania in Fez, but the *medersa* still exudes magnificent, studious calm.

Musée de Marrakech   MUSEUM
(Map p56; ☑ 0524 44 18 93; www.museedemarrakech.ma; Pl ben Youssef; admission Dh50, with Ali ben Youssef Medersa Dh60; ⊙ 9am-6.30pm) Maybe the rumours are true of a curse on the Mnebhi Palace, now home to Musée de Marrakesh. Its low walls and inner courtyard left no place to hide for Mehdi Mnebhi, defence minister during Sultan Moulay Abdelaziz' troubled 1894–1908 reign. While Minister Mnebhi was away receiving a medal from Queen Victoria, England conspired with France and Spain to colonise North Africa. In Mnebhi's absence, autocrat Pasha Glaoui filched his palace – but after independence, it was seized by the state and became Marrakesh's first girls' school in 1965.

The palace's fortunes turned around in 1997 with restoration by the Omar Benjelloun Foundation. Now displayed within are

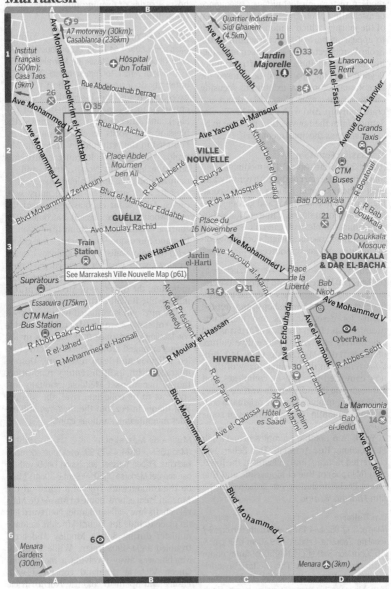

See Marrakesh Ville Nouvelle Map (p61)

traditional arts, including Rabati embroidery, inlaid daggers and Fassi pottery.

Koubba Ba'adiyn   HISTORIC BUILDING
(Map p56) The Almohads destroyed everything else their Almoravid predecessors built in

Marrakesh, but overlooked this small, graceful 12th-century *koubba* (shrine) across from Ali ben Youssef Mosque, which was probably used for ablutions. This architectural relic reveals what Hispano-Moresque architecture owes to the Almoravids: keyhole arches,

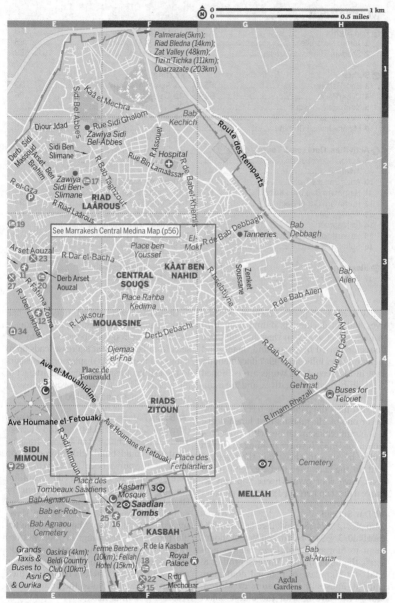

Palmeraie(5km);
Riad Bledna (14km);
Zat Valley (48km);
Tizi n'Tichka (111km);
Ouarzazate (203km)

See Marrakesh Central Medina Map (p56)

ribbed vaulting, interlaced arabesques and domed cupolas on crenellated bases.

★ **Maison de la Photographie** GALLERY
(Map p56; ☎0524 38 57 21; www.maison-dela photographie.com; 46 Souq el-Fassi; adult/child Dh40/free; ☺9.30am-7pm) When Parisian Patrick Menac'h and Marrakshi Hamid Mergani realised they were both collecting vintage Moroccan photography, they decided to open a gallery to show their collections in their original context. Together they

Marrakesh

'repatriated' 4500 photos, 2000 glass negatives and 80 documents dating from 1870 to 1950; select works on view here fill three floors, organised by region and theme, and include a rare, full-colour 1957 documentary shot in Morocco. Most works are editioned prints from original negatives, and are available for sale.

Don't miss the panoramic terrace for coffee or one of Marrakesh's best lunch deals: a fragrant chicken tajine with preserved lemon for Dh35. If you're heading to Ourika Valley, be sure to check out their second venture, the Ecomusée Berbere (p98). If you don't have your own wheels, you can arrange a day trip here for Dh150 per person.

★ **Dar Si Said**　　　　　　　　　　MUSEUM
(Map p56; ☏0524 38 95 64; Derb Si Said; adult/child Dh10/3; ⊙9am-4.45pm Wed-Mon) A monument to Moroccan *mâalems* (master artisans), the home of Bou Ahmed's brother Si Said is a showcase of regional craftsmanship. It houses the Museum of Moroccan Arts, starting with the oldest object in Marrakesh: an AD 1002–1007 chest that belonged to a chamberlain of Spain's Umayyad Caliphate. Arrows direct visitors past antique yet fashion-forward Marrakshi man-bags; 20th-century High Atlas carpets; and doors carved with talismans, warding off the evil eye.

Upstairs, flower-painted musicians' balconies flank the spectacular painted domed wedding-reception chamber credited to artisans from Fez. The rear staircase leads up to a musical instruments display, or downstairs to the exit via the most delightful artefact of all: a Ferris wheel for babies, with pint-sized palanquins on a hand-cranked axis.

★ **Bahia Palace**　　　　　　　　　MUSEUM
(Map p56; ☏0524 38 95 64; Rue Riad Zitoun el-Jedid; admission Dh10; ⊙9am-4.30pm) Imagine what you could build with Morocco's top artisans at your service for 14 years, and here you have it: *La Bahia* (the Beautiful) has floor-to-ceiling decoration begun by Grand Vizier Si Moussa in the 1860s and embellished from 1894 to 1900 by slave-turned-vizier Abu 'Bou' Ahmed. But the Bahia proved too beguiling: in 1908 warlord Pasha Glaoui claimed the palace as a suitable venue to entertain French guests, who were so impressed that they booted out their host in 1911, and installed the protectorate's *résident-généraux* here.

Though only a portion of the palace's 8 hectares and 150 rooms is open to the public, you can see the unfurnished, opulently ornamented harem that once housed Bou Ahmed's four wives and 24 concubines. The quarters of his favourite, Lalla Zineb, are the most spectacular, with original woven-silk panels, stained-glass windows, intricate marquetry and ceilings painted with rose bouquets.

Maison Tiskiwin
MUSEUM

(Map p56; ☑ 0524 38 91 92; www.tiskiwin.com; 8 Rue de la Bahia; adult/child Dh20/10; ◷ 9.30am-12.30pm & 2.30-6pm) Travel to Timbuktu and back again via Dutch anthropologist Bert Flint's art collection, displayed at Maison Tiskiwin. Each room represents a caravan stop along the Sahara-to-Marrakesh route, with indigenous crafts from Tuareg camel saddles to High Atlas carpets. The accompanying text is often more eccentric than explanatory (an example: 'By modifying his pristine nakedness Man seeks to reveal his image of himself') but Tiskiwin's well-travelled artefacts offer tantalising glimpses of Marrakesh's trading-post past.

★ Saadian Tombs
HISTORIC SITE

(Map p52; Rue de la Kasbah; admission Dh10; ◷ 9am-4.45pm) Anyone who says you can't take it with you hasn't seen the Saadian Tombs, near the Kasbah Mosque. Saadian Sultan Ahmed al-Mansour ed-Dahbi spared no expense on his tomb, importing Italian Carrara marble and gilding honeycomb *muqarnas* (decorative plasterwork) with pure gold to make the Chamber of the 12 Pillars a suitably glorious mausoleum.

Al-Mansour played favourites even in death, keeping alpha-male princes handy in the Chamber of the Three Niches, and relegating to garden plots some 170 chancellors and wives – though some trusted Jewish advisors earned pride of place, literally closer to the king's heart than his wives or sons. All tombs are overshadowed by his mother's mausoleum in the courtyard, carved with poetic, weathered blessings and vigilantly guarded by stray cats.

Al-Mansour died in splendour in 1603, but a few decades later, Alawite Sultan Moulay Ismail walled up the Saadian Tombs to keep his predecessors out of sight and mind. Accessible only through a small passage in the Kasbah Mosque, the tombs were neglected by all except the storks until aerial photography exposed them in 1917.

Mellah
NEIGHBOURHOOD

(Map p56) In the narrow *derbs* (alleys) of the city's historic Jewish quarter are the tallest mudbrick buildings in Marrakesh. Most of the Jewish families moved away in the 1960s, but the *mellah* remains notable for tall mudbrick homes along single-file streets and cross-alley gossip through

MARRAKESH & CENTRAL MOROCCO MARRAKESH

MARRAKESH MUSEUM FOR PHOTOGRAPHY & VISUAL ARTS (MMP+)

In two years the world's largest Museum for Photography and Visual Arts (www.mmpva.org; Badi Palace) will open in Marrakesh. British architect David Chipperfield has been commissioned to complete the build, which will open near the Menara Gardens in 2016. Until then, a section of the Badi Palace has been restored as a gallery space and the dynamic Kamal Laftimi (the entrepreneur behind Terrasse des Epices and Le Jardin) has been put in charge of creating the site's cafe-bookstore.

The museum is part of an ambitious plan to fashion Marrakesh into a North African cultural hub, building on the success of its Biennale and International Film Festival, much as Venice did in the early 20th century. Interestingly, the two cities share a lot in common. Both are historic trading depots benefiting from centuries of cross-cultural influence; both inhabit a strange mid-ground between medieval city and modern metropolis; and both retain a dynamic artistic and artisanal community.

It is the latter that the 6000-sq-metre museum is focused on promoting through a permanent collection of lens-based contemporary art and revolving exhibitions related to architecture, design, fashion and culture. Even the museum's new location is significant. Sited beside the 12th-century Menara Gardens, the architecturally distinct sandstone cube aims to form a temporal link between the historical output of the medina and 21st-century art practices, with the emphasis firmly on Moroccan and North African talent.

With a theatre, bookshop and extensive educational facilities, David Knaus, the museum's director, hopes the space will be transformative rather than static, attracting students, scholars, designers and artists from around the world. 'With a rich program of exhibitions, education and cultural exchange, the museum will be the first such institution on the African continent', he proudly points out.

Marrakesh Central Medina

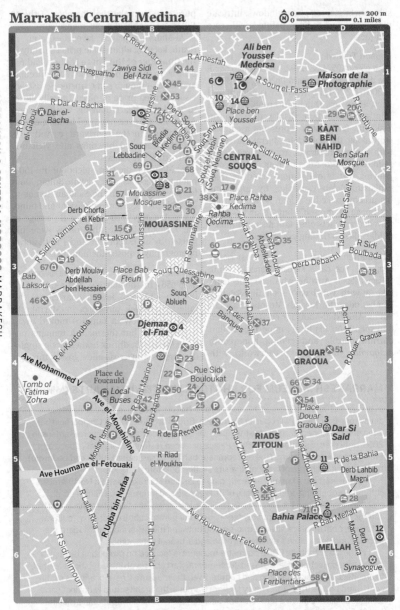

wrought-iron balconies. Local guides may usher you into the local synagogue, and the **miaâra** (Map p52), or Jewish cemetery, where the gatekeeper admits visitors paying respects to whitewashed tombs topped with rocks for remembrance (Dh10 tip expected).

To see the living legacy of *mellah* artisans and spice traders, check out the Place des Ferblantiers, the Grand Bijouterie and the Mellah Market (p74).

Marrakesh Central Medina

Badi Palace HISTORIC SITE

(Map p52; palace/palace plus Koutoubia minbar Dh10/20; ◉9am-4.45pm) As 16th-century Sultan Ahmed el-Mansour was paving the Badi Palace with gold, turquoise and crystal, his court jester wisecracked, 'It'll make a beautiful ruin'. That jester was no fool: 75 years later the place was looted. Today it's hard to guess the glories of *el-Badi* (the Incomparable) from the vast courtyard, although its four sunken gardens and reflecting pools give a hint of its former majesty and make for instant atmosphere during the Festival of Popular Arts in July.

Check out the view of Marrakesh from atop the pisé (rammed-earth) ramparts, and the temporary exhibits of the new Marrakesh Museum for Photography & Visual Arts (p55) housed in the **Khaysuran Pavilion** on the south side of the courtyard.

El-Badi's other key attraction is the Koutoubia *minbar* (prayer pulpit), its cedarwood steps intricately inlaid with marquetry, and gold and silver calligraphy by 12th-century Cordoban artisans.

To reach the entrance, head through Pl des Ferblantiers and turn right along the ramparts.

Marrakesh Medina

HALF-DAY TOUR OF THE MEDINA

To discover the medina's hidden treasures begin this leisurely stroll at **Dar Si Said ❶**, the home of tastemaker Si Said, a model of restrained 19th-century elegance. Then head north up Rue Riad Zitoun el-Jedid and emerge into the **Djemaa el-Fna ❷**, from where you can see the iconic **Koutoubia minaret ❸**. You'll need to dodge scooters and snake charmers as you cross the plaza to Pl Bab Fteuh in the northwest corner. On your right is the Bab Fteuh Funduq where jewellery and trays are hammered out in crammed studios.

Follow Rue el-Mouassine north past the Mouassine mosque and duck down a small *derb* (alley) beside the monumental **Mouassine Fountain ❹** to marvel at the 16th-century splendour of the **Douiria Derb el Hammam ❺**, once the guest pad of choice for visiting Saadian aristocrats. Emerge dazzled into the sun and continue north.

At the next arched junction with Rue Dar el-Bacha you'll spot grand courtyard **funduqs ❻** (medieval merchant inns). Some date back to the 16th century and most are populated by artisan workshops. Lunch a few steps further north in the brilliant green garden of **Le Jardin ❼**.

Refuelled, turn right out of Le Jardin and right again after the small arch onto Rue Amesfah, which takes you past more *funduqs* and the Ben Youssef Mosque, before you see signs for the **Ali ben Youssef Medersa ❽**. Once the most splendid Quranic school in North Africa, it's decorated with Hispano-Moresque wonders wrought in high-lustre *zellij* (mosaic) and intricate stucco. Finish the tour amid vintage photographs of the medina and a spectacular sunset view from the rooftop of **Maison de la Photographie ❾**.

Funduqs
These medieval caravanserai once provided lodging and stabling for desert traders visiting the souqs. Of the 140 remaining in the medina, many have now been converted into artisan workshops.

PAULA HARDY ©

Douiria Derb el Hammam
The central room of the *douiria* is covered with stucco in brightly coloured *testir*, geometric tracery radiating from a central star called 'the cobwebs of the Prophet'.

PAULA HARDY ©

Koutoubia minaret
This 12th-century, 70m-high tower is the architectural prototype for Seville's La Giralda, and it's a monumental cheat sheet of Moorish ornamentation: scalloped keystone arches, jagged *merlons* and mathematically pleasing proportions.

PAULA HARDY ©

Le Jardin
This popular medina hang-out is a true urban oasis. The lush green colour scheme echoes the soothing canopy of palms and banana trees that shade the 17th-century riad courtyard, which comes complete with trilling songbirds.

Ali ben Youssef Medersa
In its heyday, 900 students lived in the medersa's 132 dorms – and shared one bathroom. Upstairs, a 3-sq-metre room shows how students lived, with a sleeping mat, writing implements and Quran bookstand.

PAULA HARDY ©

Maison de la Photographie
This riad gallery displays fascinating works from 1870 to 1960, including a 1907 Djemaa el-Fna vista, a 1920 photo of Ali ben Youssef Medersa with students, and a rare 1957 documentary shot in Morocco.

Mouassine Fountain
Built in the mid-16th century by Abdallah el Ghalib, the Mouassine Fountain is one of 80 original medina fountains. Its installation was a pious act, providing water for people and animals.

LONELY PLANET/GETTY IMAGES ©

Djemaa el-Fna
PT Barnum was bluffing when he called his circus 'the greatest show on earth'; that title has belonged to the Djemaa el-Fna ever since this plaza was used for public executions in about 1050.

SCOTT E BARBOUR/GETTY IMAGES ©

Dar Si Said
Si Said's artisans outdid themselves in the upstairs wedding chamber, covering the walls, musicians' balconies and ceiling with a truly joyous profusion of floral ornament.

PAULA HARDY ©

☉ Ville Nouvelle

If the medina starts to wear down your nerves and shoe leather, escape to Guéliz for art galleries around Rue Yougoslavie, fixed-price boutiques along Rue de la Liberté, and perennially fashion-forward Jardin Majorelle.

Count on a 30-minute walk from downtown ville nouvelle to Djemaa el-Fna. Since the blocks are long and boring until you enter the medina, you might take a bus or taxi.

★ **Jardin Majorelle**   HISTORIC PARK
(Map p52; ☎ 0524 31 30 47; www.jardinmajorelle. com; cnr Aves Yacoub el-Mansour & Moulay Abdullah; garden Dh50, museum Dh25; ☉ 8am-6pm summer, 8am-5.30pm winter) Other guests bring flowers, but Yves Saint Laurent gifted the Jardin Majorelle to Marrakesh, the city that adopted him in 1964. Saint Laurent and his partner Pierre Bergé bought the electric-blue villa and its garden to preserve the vision of its original owner, landscape painter Jacques Majorelle, and keep it open to the public. Thanks to Marrakshi ethnobotanist Abderrazak Benchaâbane, the garden Majorelle began cultivating in 1924 is now a psychedelic desert mirage of 300 plant species from five continents.

Majorelle's art-deco studio houses a Berber Art Museum, showcasing the rich panorama of Morocco's indigenous inhabitants in displays of some 600 artefacts, including wood, leather and metalwork, carpets and textiles, musical instruments and a display of traditional dress that makes *Star Wars* costumery look staid and unimaginative. Best of all is the mirrored, midnight black, octagonal chamber displaying a sumptuous collection of chiselled, filigreed and enamelled jewels that reflect into infinity beneath a starry desert sky.

Exit into the boutique with its handsome coffee-table books and pricey souvenirs: Majorelle blue slippers, perfume, and pillows embroidered with YSL. The cafe offers drinks at high-fashion prices but you can't argue with the view.

CyberPark   GARDEN
(Map p52; Ave Mohammed V; ☉ 9am-7pm; 🖥️) Stop and smell the roses while checking email at this 8-hectare royal garden, dating from the 18th century but now offering free wi-fi. Wait for free outdoor kiosks or pay to use the air-conditioned cybercafe (Dh10 per hour).

Menara Gardens   GARDEN
(Map p52; Ave de la Menara, Hivernage; garden free, picnic pavilion Dh20; ☉ 9am-5pm) Local lore tells of a sultan who seduced guests over dinner, then lovingly chucked them in the Menara's reflecting pools to drown. Nowadays dunking seems the furthest thing from the minds of couples canoodling amid these royal olive groves, or families picnicking in the stately

---

TOP FIVE ART GALLERIES

While the tourist market still trades in harem girls, men with muskets and other Orientalist clichés, these Guéliz galleries offer original talent.

Galerie Rê (Map p61; ☎ 0524 43 22 58; www.galeriere.com; Résidence Al Andalous III, cnr Rues de la Mosquée & Ibn Toumert; ☉ 10am-1pm & 3-8pm Mon-Sat) A showcase for next-generation Moroccan art stars. Don't miss gallery opening soirées – always packed, always fabulous.

Galerie Noir sur Blanc (Map p61; ☎ 0524 42 24 16; www.galerienoirsurblanc.com; 1st fl, 48 Rue Yougoslavie; ☉ 3-7pm Mon, 10am-1pm & 3-7pm Tue-Sat) Major Moroccan and international talent covers the walls while friendly, well-informed staff provide useful insights.

Matisse Art Gallery (Map p61; ☎ 0524 44 83 26; www.matisseartgallery.com; 43 Passage Ghandouri; ☉ 9.30am-noon & 3-7.30pm Mon-Sat) Nationally recognised gallery showcasing the work of Biennale contenders and vintage Orientalists such as Jacques Majorelle.

David Bloch Gallery (Map p61; ☎ 0524 45 75 95; www.davidblochgallery.com; 8 bis Rue des Vieux Marrakchis; ☉ 10.30am-1.30pm & 3.30-7.30pm Tue-Sat, 3.30-7.30pm Mon) Artists from both sides of the Mediterranean strike fine lines between traditional calligraphy and urban graffiti.

Gallery 127 (Map p61; ☎ 0524 43 26 67; www.galerienathalielocatelli.com; 2nd fl, 127 Ave Mohammed V; ☉ 3-7pm Tue-Sat) A scuffed entry, dimly lit stairway and exposed brick walls set the scene for new and vintage works by international photographers at reasonable prices.

Marrakesh Ville Nouvelle

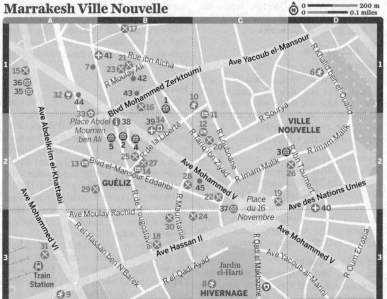

Marrakesh Ville Nouvelle

19th-century pavilion. On clear days, come for dromedary rides and photo ops against the Atlas Mountain backdrop.

🏃 Activities

Cycling

Rent bikes from budget hotels around Djemaa el-Fna and at hotels along Ave Abdelkrim el-Khattabi in the ville nouvelle for Dh70 to Dh120 per day. To escape city traffic, head 5km northwest to the Palmeraie, where you'll spot celebrity villas amid the palms.

Marrakech Roues CYCLING

(Map p56; ☑ 0663 06 18 92; www.marrakech-roues. com; Imm Roux, 3 Rue Bani Marine; per hr/half day/ full day Dh50/80/120) Well-located bike rental geared towards those who want to rent a bike for a day to explore the medina. It also arranges 90-minute dromedary rides in the *palmeraie* (Dh250), including transport.

Action Sport Loisirs CYCLING

(Map p52; ☑ 0661 24 01 45; www.marrakechbike action.com; Apt 4, 2nd fl, Ave Yacoub el-Mansour, Guéliz; half day Dh280-350, full day Dh750) Organises circuits of the Palmeraie and Marrakesh gardens and longer excursions to the Ourika Valley and the Lalla Takerkoust lake replete with barbecue lunch. *Palmeraie* tours leave from the Tikida Garden Resort in the Palmeraie.

Horse Riding

Les Cavaliers de L'Atlas HORSE RIDING

(☑ 0672 84 55 79; www.lescavaliersdelatlas.com; Rte de Casablanca; half-day ride Dh350-565, full day Dh1000-1350) Run by passionate horsewoman Sophie Chauvat, this is a professional stables with a mix of Arab, Anglo-Arab and Berber horses and Welsh and Shetland ponies. With riad-style accommodation available (Dh1010 to Dh1690), options include fully packaged horse-riding holidays, lessons for children and beginners, and half-/full- and multi-day horse treks in the Atlas.

All equipment is provided, including hard hats, half chaps and body protectors for children. The centre is located five minutes north of Marrakesh on the Rte de Casablanca (N9) and is clearly signposted on the road.

WORTH A TRIP

GREAT ESCAPES: THE AGAFAY DESERT

If you don't have time to traverse mountain passes, you can take an overnight trip to the Agafay Desert, a rough, dry, moon-like expanse 40km southwest of Marrakesh down the Rte d'Amizmiz. This is a favourite playground for weekending Marrakshis who come for a spot of horse-riding, dune-gazing and canoeing on Lalla Takerkoust, a manmade reservoir on the edge of the Agafay. In spring, the desert is covered with wheat and wildflowers, but in summer and autumn it really does look like the desert. Here's our pick of the region's country retreats and camps:

★ Scarabeo (☑ 0661 44 41 58; www.scarabeo-camp.com; standard/ste/child tent incl half board Dh2020/2580/1240) This nomadic eco-camp moves its 12 elegant bivouacs according to season, but there are always views of the desert and High Atlas. During the day spend your time trekking, camel riding, paragliding or flying kites, and by night dozens of lamps light your way to open-air film projections and unforgettable stargazing.

La Pause (☑ 0661 30 64 94; www.lapause-marrakech.com; N 31°26.57, W 008°10.31, Douar Lmih Laroussiéne; per person incl full board Dh1685; ⊠) Skip off the grid to this desert getaway for days spent playing turf-free golf or Frisbee or hanging out in hammocks by the pool. Kids can ride off into the sunset on mountain bikes, Arabian stallions or dromedaries and return to candlelight feasts.

Jnane Tihihit (☑ 0668 46 55 45; www.riad-t.com/jnane-tihihit; Douar Makhfamane; d Dh500-850; P⊠) 🍃 Relax in whitewashed pisé (rammed-earth) bungalows amid pomegranate trees. Foodies can tend saffron gardens and learn to make couscous (meals Dh80 to Dh160), while kids can go riding or head out to the lakefront beach or lounge by the chemical-free pool.

Dar Zitoune (☑ 0662 40 83 80; www.dar-zitoune.com; Douar Zii; s incl breakfast Dh480-530, d Dh660-810; P⊠⊠) Escape the urban hustle at this stone-walled country house, with a pool in the garden. Your host Anouar organises eco-excursions from canoeing and dromedary riding to trekking on the Kik Plateau.

Public Hammams

For authentic Moroccan spa experiences at bargain prices, head to your local neighbourhood hammam, where entry costs about Dh10, *gommage* (scrub) Dh15 to Dh30 and massage Dh50 to Dh100. All public hammams are single sex and have three main rooms: one cool, one hot, one very hot.

Bring your community hammam kit: towel, flip-flops, plastic mat and a change of knickers or boxer shorts (you'll be expected to wear yours).

Hammam Dar el-Bacha   HAMMAM

(Map p52; 20 Rue Fatima Zohra; admission Dh10; ⊙men 7am-1pm, women 1-9pm) The city's largest traditional hammam, with star-shaped vents in the vast domed ceiling. It's the public hammam of choice for women, who get prime afternoon/evening hours here.

Hammam Bab Doukkala   HAMMAM

(Map p52; Rue Bab Doukkala; admission Dh10; ⊙women noon-7pm, men from 8pm) A historic hammam in the southeast corner of Bab Doukkala Mosque, dating from the 17th century. It has heated *tadelakt* (polished plaster) floors in good repair and a mellow atmosphere during men's hours.

Private Hammams

A private hammam might sound decadent, but it's one of the best deals in Marrakesh, although like everything you need to choose carefully – some hammams are so oversubscribed they can feel anything but relaxed.

Le Bain Bleu   HAMMAM

(Map p56; ☎0524 42 69 99; www.lebainbleu.com; 32 Derb Chorfa Lakbir; ⊙by appointment 10am-9pm) This riad spa-hammam delivers top-notch style and value in a secret location. Follow signs for Dar Cherifa off Rue el-Mouassine onto Derb Chorfa, where this double riad features secluded patios, sleek subterranean steam rooms and professional services (massages Dh350 per hour, hammam/*gommage* Dh150, couples hammam/massage Dh600 per person, manicure or pedicure Dh280).

Sultana Spa   HAMMAM

(Map p52; ☎0524 38 80 08; www.lasultanamarrakech.com; Rue de la Kasbah) An opulent, all-marble spa near the Saadian Tombs offering services from hammam (Dh200, cinnamon *gommage* Dh350) to three-hour-plus 'absolute pleasure' treatments for couples: hammam/*gommage,* mineral-enriched tub soak, mani/pedi, sauna and Jacuzzi (Dh3500).

Les Secrets de Marrakesh   HAMMAM

(Map p61; ☎0524 43 48 48; www.lessecretsdemarrakech.com; 62 Rue de la Liberté; ⊙10am-8pm Mon-Sat) Upscale treatments in an art-deco villa, with hammam, *gommage* and massage (Dh480) in a sleek graphite-*tadelakt* hammam, argan-oil and Atlas cedar body wraps (Dh350 to Dh500) and rose-petal massages (Dh220 for 30 minutes).

Swimming

Medina riads are restricted to plunge pools, since leakage from larger pools endangers mudbrick foundations. The following are some attractive day-use pool options in or near Marrakesh.

★Beldi Country Club   SWIMMING, TENNIS

(☎0524 38 39 50; http://beldicountryclub.com; Km6 Rte de Barrage 'Cherifa'; adult/child incl lounger & lunch Dh370/250) Located just 6km south of the city centre, the Beldi feels a million miles away from the dust and chaos of the medina. Lie back and smell the 15,000 roses at Dominique Leymarie's eco-chic paradise with its two pools, spa, hammam, tennis courts and much else besides.

Le Jardins de la Medina   SWIMMING, SPA

(Map p52; ☎0524 38 18 51; http://lesjardinsdelamedina.com; Derb Chtouka 21; lunch & pool pass Dh350) This 19th-century palace-cum-boutique hotel is the most beautiful place in the medina for a light lunch and afternoon lounging poolside. The huge riad garden is planted with old palms, orange and olive trees, and jacarandas, which burst into dramatic blue bloom in early summer.

Ferme Berbère   SWIMMING, HAMMAM

(☎0524 38 56 85; www.lafermeberbere.net; 9km Rte d'Ourika; incl lunch & hammam per person from Dh400) Getaway packages to this family-friendly rustic retreat in an olive grove include hammam, *gommage,* massage, lunch and access to a small pool. Families get the best deal: hammam and *gommage* for two adults, donkey rides for two kids, lunch and pool access costs Dh730. You'll find it 9km south on Rte d'Ourika.

La Mamounia   SWIMMING

(Map p52; ☎0524 38 86 00; www.mamounia.com; Ave Bab Jedid; day pass Dh500) A Mamounia day pass provides access to Mamounia's ozone-treated pool, historic gardens, fitness centre, three swanky bars and *zellij*-paved spa (basic treatment hammam/*gommage*/orange honey scrub Dh900).

MARRAKESH FOR CHILDREN

The mutual admiration between kids and Marrakesh is obvious. Kids will gaze in wonderment at fairy-tale souq scenes: snake charmers serenading cobras, herbalists trading concoctions straight out of Harry Potter and cupboard-sized shops packed with spangled Cinderella-style slippers.

That said, for families with toddlers and babies, the city can be overwhelming and logistically challenging. Strollers are impractical in the medina, baby-changing facilities scarce and restaurants can make few dietary concessions. But with a greater degree of planning and a careful selection of accommodation it is still possible to enjoy a memorable Moroccan holiday with younger children.

The majority of museums have reduced rates for under-12s, but Marrakesh museums are a poor substitute for the live theatre of the souqs and the Djemaa el-Fna. Try to plan your time in each carefully for the best experience: early mornings (before noon) are quieter in the souqs, allowing for easy strolling, less hassle and a better view of craftspeople at work. Early evening (from 6pm to 8pm) are best for Djemaa storytellers and offer chance encounters with Moroccan families also doing the rounds and taking carriage rides around the ramparts.

Key to a successful trip is child-friendly accommodation. Fair warning: riad plunge pools and steep stairs aren't exactly child-proof, and sound reverberates through riad courtyards. Most riad owners and staff, however, dote on babies and will provide cots and high chairs, and cater special meals on request. To find the most child-friendly venues, look for the ⛵ symbol throughout this chapter. The following are our top 10 sights and activities for children.

Arterre (Map p52; ☑ 0524 43 10 71; www.arterremarrakech.com; 44 Lot Akioud, Semlalia) Family-friendly art centre, just north of Guéliz, offering workshops and short courses in ceramics, drawing and painting.

Beldi Country Club (p63) A 15-hectare country retreat designed with families in mind, including two children's pools and activities ranging from bread-making and pottery workshops to tennis, cycling and cinema.

Riad Bledna
SWIMMING

(☑ 0661 18 20 90; www.riadbledna.com; 2km Route de Ouarzazate; incl lunch & transfer per person Dh250) ⚓ The top-value, eco-friendliest option: day rates cover lounging by an oxygen-filtered pool, tasty homemade lunches and transfers to/from the Djemaa el-Fna at this family-friendly, 4-acre organic garden retreat in a quiet Marrakesh suburb east of the city centre.

🍴 Courses

Many riads in the medina organise sessions with their cook. Cafe Clock (p73) is also a one-stop shop for a fascinating range of courses from belly dancing to calligraphy to language classes.

★ Ateliers d'Ailleurs
CRAFT, COOKING

(☑ 0672 81 20 46; www.ateliersdailleurs.com) Engaging a select network of professional craftspeople with robust businesses in pottery, *tadelakt*, *zellij*, brassware, woodwork, basketry and jewelry, these ateliers (studios) offer a unique insight into traditional craft techniques, with student interpreters from Marrakesh University on hand to help with the translation of concepts, as well as any language barriers. The three- to five-hour sessions (Dh550 to Dh750), where you'll work alongside craftspeople utilising traditional materials, ensure enough time to practise several techniques and to realise your own objects.

For more serious amateurs or design professionals longer courses are tailormade to specific requirements (from Dh3200 for three days), and for those who don't want to get their hands dirty it is possible to take a guided circuit of three workshops.

Also popular are the studio's cookery courses (Dh750): relaxed, in-depth interactions held in Marrakshi homes with expert home cooks.

Souk Cuisine
COOKING

(Map p56; ☑ 0673 80 49 55; www.soukcuisine.com; Zniquat Rahba, 5 Derb Tahtah, Medina; per day incl meal & wine Dh520) Learn to cook as the *dadas* (chefs) do: shop in the souq for ingredients with English-speaking Dutch hostess

Calèche rides When kids' legs and parents' backs start to give out, do what Marrakshi parents do: hire a horse carriage in the Djemaa el-Fna and take a grand tour.

Dromedary rides Calèche circuits of the Palmeraie usually stop at Café le Palmier d'Or, which has a small playground and dromedaries in the parking lot. With some gentle bargaining, Dh100 should cover a 15- to 30-minute guided ride.

Horse-riding & mountain biking For professional lessons and horse treks in the *palmeraie* and Atlas mountains look no further than the stables at Les Cavaliers de L'Atlas (p62); mountain bikers should contact Action Sports Loisirs (p62).

Jardin Harti (Map p61; Rue Ouadi el-Makhazine; ⊙8am-6pm) As well as soccer fields and two life-sized dinosaurs, this Guéliz park offers a playground and an outdoor amphitheatre where free shows are held.

Kawkab Jeux (Map p52; ☑0524 43 89 29; www.kawkab-jeux.com; 1 Rue Imam Chafaï) Activity centre where you can let Junior loose on arts-and-crafts projects, a mini-train, playground slides, video games, a foosball table and a snack bar for around Dh100 to Dh200.

Le Kech (Opera Plaza Hotel; Map p61; ☑0524 35 15 18; Ave Hassan II; admission noon-7pm/7pm-midnight Dh30/45; ⊙noon-midnight) Marrakesh's only tenpin bowling alley offers six bowling lanes alongside pool tables and table football.

Oasiria (☑0524 38 04 38; www.oasiria.com; Km 4, Rte d'Amizmiz; adult/child 0.8-1.5m/child under 1.5m Dh150/90/free; ⊙10am-6pm) All-day family fun whizzing down kamikaze and cobra slides and playing in wave pools and pirate lagoons. There are also massages, Jacuzzi and restaurants, and an on-site infirmary to ensure everyone stays safe.

Terres d'Amanar (☑0524 43 81 03; www.terresdamanar.com; Douar Akli, Tahanaoute) For active kids not easily impressed by pools: learn to master zip-lines, river-rafting, BMX cycling and donkey polo. Overnight accommodation is available. It's located 36km south of Marrakesh, outside the village of Tahanaoute. Overnight accommodation is available.

Gemma van de Burgt, work alongside two Moroccan *dadas*, then enjoy the four-course lunch you helped cook. Courses are two-person minimum, 12 participants maximum; vegetarian courses possible.

Institut Français LANGUAGE
(☑0524 44 69 30; http://if-maroc.org/marrakech/; 60 Rte de Targa, Guéliz; ⊙9am-12.30pm & 3-7pm Mon-Sat) Offers private classes in Arabic and French (adult/under 26 years Dh380/150 per hour), plus courses in Moroccan dialect (Dh1800) and French (from Dh900). Also hosts worthwhile concerts, films and dance performances.

Centre for Language & Culture LANGUAGE
(Map p61; ☑0524 44 76 91; www.clcmorocco.org; Rue Sourya, Guéliz) American and Moroccan teachers with years of experience offer summer language courses with homestay hookups. Lessons are immersive and the school applies the Communicative Language Learning (CLL) technique in its Arabic language classes, the only school in Morocco to do so.

Study Arabic in Marrakech LANGUAGE
(www.studyarabicmarrakech.com) Private teachers here cover the basics of polite Arabic conversation in five lessons.

☞ Tours

Guided tours of the medina will help you cover specific landmarks in an hour or two. Just don't expect sweet souq deals: guides get commissions on whatever you buy. Hotels, riads and travel agencies can arrange guides, or you can book official guides directly via the tourist office for Dh250/400 for a half/full day.

Many travel agencies have offices in Guéliz and arrange multi-city, mountain and desert tours. Other specialist desert tour operators can be found in Ouarzazate, Zagora and M'Hamid. For a good, safe time had by all, request licenced, insured guides and specify English-speaking guides as needed.

★**Inside Morocco Travel** TOURS
(Map p61; ☑0524 43 00 20; www.insidemorocco travel.com; 4th fl, 29 Rue de Yougoslavie, Guéliz;

⊙9am-noon & 3-7pm Mon-Sat) Get to know Morocco inside-out on bespoke adventures designed for you by ecotourism expert Mohamed Nour and his multilingual team – sunset tea for two in the Sahara, hikes off-the-beaten track in the Zat and Ouirgane Valleys, home cooking in pristine Berber mountain villages and crafts workshops with inspiring women's cooperatives.

Morocco Adventure & Rafting RAFTING
(☑0614 97 23 16; www.rafting.ma; Rue Beni Marine, Guéliz) This local company has been leading rafting expeditions in the Atlas for over 12 years with a team of local and international guides all with a minimum of five years guiding experience. Excursions range from half-day trips to Ourika to a highlight, week-long excursion in the Ahansal valley. In addition, it runs a seasonal kayak school for beginners at Bin el-Ouidane and kayak clinics for the more experienced. Groups are limited to 12 to 16 people.

Morocco Exchange CULTURAL
(www.moroccoexchange.org) Morocco Exchange (MoEx) is part of Crossing Borders Education, and is a nonprofit organisation offering short-term student exchange and travel programs with a focus on cross-cultural education through visiting cities and rural villages. The program aims to be different by encouraging participants to engage in discussions and share ideas with young English-speaking Moroccans. Previous custom-made programs have explored Morocco's medical system, the use of the French language, and women's rights.

Tawada Trekking HIKING, CULTURAL
(☑0618 24 44 31; www.tawadatrekking.com) Trekking tours and cultural immersion experiences are the speciality of Hafida H'doubane, one of the first Moroccan women to be licenced as a mountain guide.

Desir du Maroc CULTURAL
(☑0661 16 35 85; www.desirdumaroc.com) Marrakshi Abdelhay Sadouk has 30 years' experience introducing visitors to Moroccan culture, leading history and culture tours around Marrakesh's lesser-known sites and further afield to the coast, desert and mountains. Yoga and tai-chi workshops also available.

★ Festivals & Events

Marrakesh Marathon SPORT
(www.marathon-marrakech.com; half-marathon fee €30, full €50; ⊙Jan) Run like there's a carpet salesman after you from the Djemaa to the Palmeraie and back for this annual marathon.

Marrakech Biennale CULTURAL, ART
(www.marrakechbiennale.org; ⊙Feb) Promoting debate and dialogue through artistic exchange, this major trilingual (Arabic, French and English) festival invites local and international artists to create literary, artistic, architectural and digital works throughout the city. Held every second year (in even years).

MadJazz MUSIC
(www.madjazz-festival.com; ⊙Mar) Marrakesh invents new sounds nightly with Gnaoua castanets, jazz riffs and Jimi Hendrix guitar licks.

Festival of Popular Arts STREET CARNIVAL
(www.marrakechfestival.com; ⊙Jul) The only thing hotter than Marrakesh in July is this free-form folk fest. Berber musicians, dancers and street performers from around the country pour into Marrakesh to thrill the masses.

TEDx Marrakesh CULTURAL
(www.tedxmarrakesh.net; day/weekend Dh700/800; ⊙Sep) Like any self-respecting cultural capital, Marrakesh has it own TEDx talkfest, where Marrakshi movers and shakers take on challenging themes such as 'Driving Forces' and 'Dare to Question'.

Marrakesh International Film Festival FILM
(http://en.festivalmarrakech.info; ⊙Dec) Stars from Hollywood to Bollywood strut the Berber red carpet at this week-long festival, culminating in wildly unpredictable awards shows.

🛏 Sleeping

Marrakesh has it all: you can sleep anywhere from the funkiest fleapit to palaces straight out of some Orientalist Hollywood fantasy. Take your pick: authentic riads hidden in the heart of the medina; budget-friendly inns right off the Djemaa; ville nouvelle hotels, ranging from budget to business class; or Palmeraie villas, with pools amid swaying palms. Luxury resorts from the likes of Amanjena, Taj Hotels and Bulgari are closing ranks around Marrakesh, offering suburb-sized rooms at stratospheric rates – but for personal attention and Marrakshi style, they can't compete with medina riads and Palmeraie villa guesthouses.

Wherever you go, know that the rates for Marrakesh accommodation are more expensive than anywhere else in Morocco.

R&R WITH B&B: MARRAKESH RIADS

Paris has its cathedrals, New York its skyscrapers, but riads are what set Marrakesh apart. These spectacular mudbrick courtyard mansions are oases of calm in the bustling medina: push through the brass-studded ancient door and you'll find yourself listening to songbirds, ice clinking in drinks and your own thoughts – suddenly, Marrakesh's balance of extremes makes perfect sense.

Over the past decade, hundreds of these historic family homes have been sold and reinvented as guesthouses, mainly by Europeans. The best are not just marvels of the Marrakshi tradition of craftsmanship – which guesthouses helped revive – but unforgettable experiences of Marrakshi hospitality, complete with insights into the local culture and shifting social mores. 'Riad' is now a synonym for guesthouse, and the ones recommended here have been selected not on looks alone, but for convenient locations, gracious staff, home-cooked meals and prime opportunities for relaxation and cultural immersion. Staying in a riad isn't just about sleeping in posh digs; it's about gaining an understanding of Marrakesh behind those studded doors.

Specialist agencies dealing specifically in riads are as follows:

Marrakech Riads (www.marrakech-riads.com)

Marrakech Medina (www.marrakech-medina.com)

Hip Marrakech (www.hipmarrakech.com)

Marrakech & Beyond (www.marrakechandbeyond.com)

Low season is mid-June to August, mid-January to mid-March and mid-November to mid-December. Book a month ahead and expect high-season rates during major European holidays. The cheapest hotels line the sinuous Rue Sidi Bouloukat just south of the Djemaa between Rue Bab Agnaou and Riad Zitoun el Kedim.

🏛 Medina

⭐ **Equity Point Hostel** HOSTEL €
(Riad Amazigh; Map p56; ☎0524 44 07 93; www.equity-point.com; 80 Derb el-Hammam, Mouassine; dm per person Dh100-180, d Dh620; 🖥📶) Award-winning international hostel chain Equity Point spotted a yawning gap in the market and set up one of their 'FUNtastic' hostels in the heart of Mouassine. Here you get all the perks of historic-riad living – a private courtyard pool, *zellij*-tastic *bhous* (nooks) and ornate decorative effects from brass lanterns to carved cedar doors – plus a convivial hostel crowd. Dorm rooms sleep six to eight and each has its own bathroom. The hostel has a bar, a restaurant and no curfew restrictions.

Le Gallia HOTEL €
(Map p56; ☎0524 44 59 13; www.ilove-marrakesh.com/hotelgallia; 30 Rue de la Recette; s/d/tr Dh350/550/780; 🖥) Madcap Djemaa el-Fna is around the corner, but the Gallia maintains the calm and grace of another era with 19 comfortable,

air-con/heated rooms with gleaming brass lamps and marble sinks. Get tanned over rooftop breakfasts (Dh45), and chat in stuccoed salons around bougainvillea-bedecked courtyards. Run by the French Galland family since 1929, the Gallia is often packed with repeat visitors; book ahead by fax.

Hotel du Trésor RIAD €
(Map p56; ☎0524 37 51 13; www.hotel-du-tresor.com; 77 Derb Sidi Bouloukat; incl breakfast s Dh400-470, d Dh410-580; 🖥📶🏊) Not since the Rolling Stones tumbled down these *derbs* has Marrakesh seen such rock-and-roll style. Fourteen rooms flank a cool whitewashed courtyard with chequered tiles, a towering orange tree and mod Panton chairs perfect for posing by the large plunge pool. Behind painted doors are walls of vintage mirrors reclaimed from the Mamounia, crystal chandeliers over a red-velvet-padded bed, and in the terrace Blue Suite, a soaking tub and gold-mosaic fireplace.

Hôtel Cecil INN €
(Map p56; ☎0524 44 22 03; http://djemaaelfna hotelcecil.com; Rue Sidi Bouloukat; incl breakfast r without bathroom Dh220, s/d/tr with bathroom Dh250/300/400; 🖥📶) Cecil's twin courtyards in hot Marrakshi pink with a green-and-white *zellij* trim offer chic, modern digs minutes from Djemaa el-Fna. Rooms with and without en suites are allocated their own courtyard. En-suite rooms boast a slightly higher

level of comfort and decoration with carved cedar wood beds, *tadelakt* showers and reversible air-con/heaters. For those sharing bathrooms there are toilets and showers on each floor, while breakfast is on the shared roof terrace beneath a Berber tent.

Hôtel Atlas INN €

(Map p56; ☑0524 39 10 51; www.hotel-atlas-marrakech.com; 50 Rue Sidi Bouloukat; s/d/tr without bathroom Dh90/170/250, d/tr with bathroom Dh350/450; ※ ☎) Tucked in an unassuming niche along Rue Sidi Bouloukat is this surprisingly quiet and peaceful inn. Its 32 rooms (12 en suite) encompass two shaded courtyards, one with a mosaic fountain, the other with potted palms and trailing creepers. Top-quality coverlets, small bedside rugs, stained-glass lunettes, a comfortable TV salon and jewel-coloured lanterns lift an otherwise standard budget hotel above the norm.

Hôtel Sherazade INN €

(Map p56; ☑0524 42 93 05; www.hotelsherazade.com; 3 Derb Djemaa; s/d without bathroom Dh180/230, s Dh220-480, d Dh270-550, ste Dh690; ※ ☎) Conversation comes easily in this inn off Riad Zitoun el-Kedim, run by a Moroccan-German family, with 23 rooms (18 with air-con), sunny terraces and a mellow-yellow courtyard with a trickling fountain. Terrace rooms are bargains, but you'll want earplugs to sleep through the muezzin's call and the breakfast rush (Dh50 extra). Light sleepers should ask for rooms in the ivy-covered rear courtyard.

Hotel Essaouira INN €

(Map p56; ☑0524 44 38 05; www.jnanemogador.com/hotelessaouira-marrakech.htm; 3 Derb Sidi Bouloukat; s/d without bathroom Dh70/100, r with bathroom Dh380-480, mattress on roof Dh40) No frills, just the cheapest hotel in the medina with 28 rooms and breakfast (Dh25 to Dh40) views of the Koutoubia.

★ Riad Le J RIAD €€

(Map p56; ☑0524 39 17 87; www.riadlej.com; 67 Derb el-Hammam; r Dh850-1450; ※ ☎) What do you get if you cross Italian furniture designers with Marrakshi craftsmanship? The wonderfully furnished Riad Le J. Whichever room you choose from the range of four spicy options – Mint, Saffron, Pepper and Cinnamon – you can lie back and gaze at antique painted ceilings, silk kaftans, vintage Mamounia mirrors and enviable, embroidered *babouches*. Delicious dinners of cardamom-spiced *tanjia* (slow-cooked stew) are served at a communal table on the balcony.

Riad Wo RIAD €€

(Map p56; ☑0665 36 79 36; www.riadw.com; Derb Boutouil 41, Kennaria; r Dh1000-1350, ste Dh1460; ※ ☎ ☎) Minimalist Mallorcan chic makes Riad Wo a medina haven. Artful Elsa Bauza oversaw every aspect of her riad's renovation, retaining its handsome central courtyard, installing a generous L-shaped pool in the patio and a sleek *tadelakt* fireplace in the salon, stripping rooms down to their elegant essentials, and designing upholstery, linens and sculptural raffia lampshades to create a finish that deserves a spread in *Architectural Digest*.

Dar Attajmil RIAD €€

(Map p56; ☑0524 42 69 66; www.darattajmil.com; 23 Rue Laksour; d incl breakfast Dh1000-1230; ※ ☎) This riad is rosy and relaxed, and you will be too after a few days within these Marrakshi pink *tadelakt* walls near the heart of the souqs. Lucrezia and her attentive staff offer a warm welcome and an even warmer rooftop hammam, plus Moroccan-Italian dinners, cooking classes, *tadelakt* workshops, music concerts, Arabic calligraphy lessons and Essaouira escapes.

Dar Zaman RIAD €€

(Map p52; ☑0524 37 66 12; www.darzaman.com; 29 Derb Bouelilou, Sidi Ben Slimane; r Dh730-1065; ※ ☎) What Dar Zaman may lack in size it makes up for in heart, with extraordinary personal attention from Peter, Hassan and Karima. Other guests obviously think the same, as dinner dates quickly transform into social events offering opportunities to trade tips on overnight excursions, cookery courses and hammams – certainly, no one seems keen to retire to their snug, stylish rooms. Highly recommended for solo and female travellers.

Riad Magellan HOSTEL €€

(Map p56; ☑0661 08 20 42; www.riadmagellan.com; 62 Derb el-Hammam; r Dh780-1350; ※) The long and winding *derb* leads to your door at this hip hideaway behind the Mouassine Fountain. The English-speaking French owner Philippe has anticipated every world explorer's needs: *tadelakt* hot tub on the terrace, multilingual library stocked with Tintin adventures in the fireplace salon, and deep-tissue massages to soothe away economy-airfare kinks. Antique globes, steamer trunks and rocking chairs add retro flair to sleek *tadelakt* guest rooms strewn with rose petals.

Maison Mnabha
RIAD €€

(Map p52; ☑0524 38 13 25; www.maisonmnabha. com; 32-33 Derb Mnabha, Kasbah; d incl breakfast Dh840-1290, tr Dh1750; ❋☀@) Treasure-hunters will seek out this 17th-century kasbah mansion for adventure and authenticity. Rose petals and candles mark the way to chandelier-lit salons and roof terraces, where fellow travellers chat over seasonal cocktails and creative canapés. Brothers Peter and Lawrence and manager Aziz offer valuable antiques advice and cultural insights (Peter holds a PhD in kasbah history), and arrange restorative massages and eco-adventures.

Marhbabikoum
RIAD €€

(Map p56; ☑0524 37 52 04; www.marhbabikoum. com; 43 Derb Lahbib Magni; s Dh730-900, d Dh840-1010; ❋☀@) The name means welcome, and you'll feel it when you step through the door. Khalil and Véronique run a mellow, family-style riad, so you're automatically invited for tea, chats, card games and Moroccan jam sessions. If you can tear yourself away, mountain excursions can be arranged.

Riad Hanane
RIAD €€

(Map p56; ☑0524 37 77 37; www.dar-hanane.com; 9 Derb Lalla Azzouna, Kâat ben Nahid; d incl breakfast Dh1120-1570; ❋☀) Lounging comes naturally at this chic retreat. Sunny guest rooms have architect-designed details – skylights, bold niches, domed bathrooms – and mod cons: iPod docks, safes, hairdryers, les Sens de Marrakech toiletries, free coffee and mineral water. Guests are drawn to the panoramic terrace, honour bar and English- and French-speaking concierge, who arranges car hire, guides and dinners. If it's full, the owners have three other riads in the medina, which you can book through www.pureriads.com.

Riad Tizwa
RIAD €€

(Map p56; www.riadtizwa.com; 26 Derb Gueraba, Dar el-Bacha; r incl breakfast Dh680-1060; ❋☀) Adding to their places in Fez and Sidi Ifni, the Bee brothers have now converted this large, six-room riad near Dar el-Bacha. Opting to keep the original fabric of the building, each room wears a warm patina of age and some unique decorative touches in stucco and antique tile. Other standout features are an airport pick-up, ample ecofriendly bath products and a breakfast fit for a king served at any time of day.

Riad Helen
RIAD €€

(Map p52; ☑0524 37 86 11; www.riadhelen.com; 138 Derb Arset Aouzal; r Dh560-700; ❋☀) This quaint *dar* (small house) steps from Dar el-Bacha is home to Maxime and Mario and offers five of the best-value riad rooms in town. Unlike other riads, Helen has a 1950s vibe with its grey-green balconies and ceilings, pink pillared courtyard, tall French doors and shuttered windows. Light streams into 1st-floor rooms furnished with comfortable, dream-inducing beds dressed in thick cotton coverlets.

★ Dar Al Assad
RIAD €€€

(Map p56; ☑0524 42 70 65; daralasad@yahoo. fr; Derb el Hajra 29; s/d Dh1100/1300; ❋☀) For over 10 years gorgeous Dar al Assad was the home of fabric designer and interior decorator Daniel Bainvel, but now you have the privilege of booking one of its five royally appointed suites decked out in museum-quality furniture, luxurious textiles, rare Rabati embroidery and artworks commissioned from internationally recognised artists. Sink into statement beds in brass and carved cedar, curl up with a book in salons crammed with busts and baroque chairs, and wash the souqs off beneath rain showers in bathrooms equal in size to many other riad rooms.

Dar Housnia
RIAD €€€

(Map p56; ☑0524 37 66 97; www.dar-housnia.com; Derb Lalla Azzouna 2, Kâat Benahid; r Dh1570-1740, 4-person douiria Dh3480; ❋☀☀) Tradition and modernity blend seamlessly in Eveline Donnez' quietly stylish *dar*, where a thoughtful approach to luxury puts the well-being of guests ahead of glitzy frippery. No comfort is overlooked from the individually hand-crafted tassels on each curtain to enormous, buffed *tadelakt* bathrooms, which are heated in winter. Winding staircases and clever design divide public and private spaces, keeping the art-hung salon snug, the self-contained *douiria* (guest apartment) private and the terrace pool secluded.

Tchaikana
RIAD €€€

(Map p56; ☑0524 38 51 50; www.tchaikana.com; 25 Derb el Ferrane, Azbest; d incl breakfast Dh1000-1800; ❋☀) With a Tuareg tent-post bed in one room and a boat suspended from the ceiling in another, Tchaikana has the adventurous spirit of a true Marrakesh caravanserai. Travellers plot souq forays over lavish breakfasts hosted by English-speaking Belgian owner Jean-Francois, and return at happy hour to plan Sahara eco-adventures. Navigating the winding *derb* is a challenge, but staff can walk you at night.

Riyad el Cadi

RIAD €€€

(Map p56; ✆0524 37 86 55; www.riyadelcadi.com; 87 Derb Moulay Abdelkader; s Dh1235, d Dh1560-2020, ste from Dh2800; ✳@⩎) A medina within the medina, this labyrinth of five riads offers unexpected delights at every turn: lovers' balconies, secret alcoves, a Marrakshi red hammam and glimpses of an outstanding collection of rare Berber textiles. A staff of 15 keeps occupants happy in 12 pristine rooms and suites, ranging from the mod black-and-white double Aleppo to the elegant two-bedroom Douiria junior suite.

Riad Al Massarah

RIAD €€€

(Map p52; ✆0524 38 32 06; www.riadalmassarah.com; 26 Derb Jedid; d incl breakfast Dh1000-2000; ✳@⩎) 🌿 The ultimate feel-good getaway: British-French owners Michel and Michael redesigned this ancient riad to maximise comfort and sunlight, and minimise electrical and water waste, putting the well-being of guests and the planet first. Each guest room is distinct, with original art, handmade textiles, and *tadelakt* fireplaces. The riad's local engagement and energy-saving efforts have earnt it Green-Key certification. Children under 12 years old are not accepted.

Riad L'Orangeraie

RIAD €€€

(Map p56; ✆0661 23 87 89; www.riadorangeraie.com; 61 Rue Sidi el-Yamani; d incl breakfast Dh1450-1900; @⩎) 🌿 Smooth and suave, with perfectly buffed *tadelakt* walls, massaging showers (the best in town), sprawling rooms, and a generous chlorine-free pool. This place has all the right moves, with five employees looking after seven rooms, a car and driver on call, excellent breakfasts, soothing hammam treatments, a babysitting service and a pioneering recycling program.

🛏 Ville Nouvelle

Hotels in Guéliz are handier if you're passing through town quickly or are seeking disabled-accessible accommodation.

Hôtel Toulousain

INN €

(Map p61; ✆0524 43 00 33; http://hoteltoulousain.com; 44 Rue Tariq ibn Ziyad; incl breakfast s Dh150-180, d Dh200-280; ⩎) An easygoing budget hotel run by a kindly Moroccan-American family in a prime Guéliz location, with restaurants, boutiques, laundry, local travel agency and a literary cafe right at your doorstep. Book ahead for spacious, cheerful 1st-floor guest rooms with classic blue *beldi*

(country-style) tiles. When upstairs rooms get stuffy, guests hang out on patios under banana trees.

Hôtel du Pacha

HOTEL €

(Map p61; ✆0524 43 13 27; www.hotelpacha.net; 33 Rue de la Liberté; s/d Dh320/400; ✳⩎) Novels beg to be set in this faded colonial hotel, with tall French windows to catch breezes and neighbourhood gossip. Ground-floor rooms come with marble sinks and dark woodwork, while those upstairs have art-deco tiles and turquoise bath tubs. The shadowy stuccoed entry, hidden courtyard and salon club chairs add *noir*-novel intrigue.

Villa Marguerite

GUESTHOUSE €€

(Map p61; ✆0672 41 82 64; www.ilove-marrakech.com/villamarguerite; 62 Blvd Mansour Eddahabi; d Dh670-1010, ste Dh1235-1680; ✳⩎) This classic colonial villa is located steps from fashionable Rue de la Liberté in the heart of Guéliz. Hidden behind high walls is a flower-draped patio with a small pool and a spacious house with seven rooms. Apart from the stuccoed lobby and lounge (complete with piano), rooms are contemporary in style with terrazzo floors, large queen-sized beds and polished-concrete bathrooms, many of which have baths.

Breakfast is rather disappointing, but with one of the best Moroccan bakeries, al-Jawda (Map p61; ✆0525 433897; www.al-jawda.com; 11 Rue de la Liberté; ◷8am-7.30pm), just around the corner, eating out is easy.

Le Printemps

HOTEL €€

(Map p61; ✆0524 43 96 04; www.hotelleprintemps.com; 19 Ave el-Mansour Eddahbi; d Dh600-800, ste Dh1500; P✳✳⩎) The wood-fired poolside pizza restaurant was so successful, Le Printemps invested upwards creating 110 luxurious new rooms with scalloped balconies overlooking central Guéliz. Plump, divan beds with Mediflex mattresses and soft suede throws sit amid acres of space beside en-suite bathrooms clad in shiny marble. Still, it's the locally popular restaurant and poolside pizza that makes this place a real winner.

🛏 Palmeraie & Outskirts

When the medina seems a bit much, villas in the Palmeraie let you chill out in a palm oasis. Once your blood pressure dips and you begin to miss the madness of Marrakesh, it's only a 30-minute drive back to the heart of the action. A taxi into town is the easiest

ETHICS & AESTHETICS: FELLAH HOTEL

Part Berber farm, part modern-art installation, part spa resort and community outreach program, the Fellah Hotel (☑0525 06 50 00; www.fellah-hotel.com; Km 13 Rte de l'Ourika, Tassoultante; d from Dh1900; P❄🛜❄) 🗲, southeast of Marrakesh, defies easy definitions and that's exactly how they like it. The visionaries behind the concept hope that the hotel, with its chocolate-coloured adobe-style villas framed picturesquely by High Atlas peaks, will become a meeting place between resident artists, travellers and the local community of Akara, who are engaged through activities and classes at the Dar al Ma'mûm Foundation (www.dam-arts.org).

The latter, housed in the comprehensive library in villa 7, collaborates with Unesco through the Aschberg program, which defends mobility for young artists, who are regularly hosted in one- to three-month residencies and contribute to the Fellah's dynamic cycle of poetry readings and musical jam sessions. No wonder guests wandering the cactus-flanked gardens or floating in the heated pool exude an air of quiet contentment that can't be wholly attributed to the Wat Po Massage Centre or a round with personal trainer, Freddie, in the sunken boxing ring.

Even nonguests can feel the love by booking in for lunch or Sunday Brunch (Dh250), when daydreaming by the pool never felt so worthwhile.

way, but is rather costly (Dh150 to DH250) since you often have to pay for the driver's round-trip to fetch you.

Riad Bledna
MAISON D'HÔTE €€
(☑0661 18 20 90; www.riadbledna.com; Km 19 Rte de Ouarzazate; d incl breakfast Dh680; P🛏) 🗲 Welcome home to the garden villa of the Moroccan-British Nour family, who pamper visitors like favourite house guests, urging them to relax by the filtered pool, enjoy more quail and apricot tajine, and sip more fresh-squeezed juice (made with organic fruit from their 4-acre gardens). Daily transit to/from the medina are included in the rates, and your hosts can arrange airport pick-ups, babysitting, desert trips, mountain eco-excursions and hands-on Moroccan craft workshops.

You'll find it 19km east of Marrakesh, signposted off the Rte de Ouarzazate. From the turn-off it's a further 2.5km to the house.

Casa Taos
MAISON D'HÔTE €€€
(☑0661 20 04 14; www.casataos.net; Km 8 Rte de Souihla; incl breakfast d Dh1595-2035, ste Dh1815-2585; P❄🛜❄) As if taking its cue from the blue pool and rosy apricots in the orchard, Casa Taos comes in an uplifting palette of colours, blending indoor and outdoor space seamlessly thanks to award-winning architect Abderrahim Charaï. Rooms sport natural finishes in *tadelakt*, terracotta, cedar and *talaouh* (a mix of clay, lime and straw) and overlook 3 hectares of biodynamic garden that mirror their symphony of colours

in minty and sage greens, vibrant lemon, pomegranate red and dusky pink.

Lunch and pool formulas are also possible with advanced booking (Dh300 to Dh450). The house is located in Souihla, 9km northwest of Marrakesh.

Jnane Tamsna
RESORT €€€
(☑0524 32 94 23; www.jnanetamsna.com; Douar Abiad, Palmeraie; d incl breakfast from Dh2800-3300, ste from Dh4000; ❄@🛜) 🗲 Sustainability meets style at Meryanne Loum-Martin's oasis of water-conserving plants, filtered pools, all-organic cuisine, fair-trade design gallery (www.inspired-by-marrakech.com) and cultural excursions organised by her English ethnobotanist husband, Gary Martin, founder of the Global Diversity Foundation (www.global-diversity.org). Book ahead for excursions, cooking classes, yoga retreats and literary salons with Booker Prize winners.

You'll find the palm-fringed property 15 to 20 minutes northwest of Marrakesh in the village of Douar Abiad off the Circuit de la Palmeraie. Transfers from the medina cost Dh200.

🍴 Eating

Slow-roasted lamb cooked in a hammam, roasted-eggplant caviar, hearty white bean soup...Marrakesh's traditional specialities are mouth-watering. That said, Marrakshis don't eat out often and there isn't much of a local dining scene in the medina, and with Dh65 to Dh80 for a scrawny chicken tajine on the Djemaa and set-price menus at riad restaurants starting at Dh300-plus, you can see why. In many cases, meals prepared by riad *dadas* may be your best medina eating experience.

Cheap eateries, such as **Chez Chegrouni** (Map p56; Djemaa el-Fna; mains Dh25-70; ⊘ 8am-11pm; ⊘) and **Cafe du Grand Balcon** (Map p56; Djemaa el-Fna; mains Dh30-50; ⊘ 8am-11pm), cluster around the southern end of the square and serve standard fare of brochettes and tajine (Dh30 to Dh45) with overpriced drinks and views of the spectacle.

A better bet for food are restaurants off the square such as **El Bahja** (Map p56; ⊘ 0524 44 13 51; 24 Rue Bani Marine; meals Dh60-70; ⊘ noon-11pm) and **Oscar Progrès** (Map p56; 20 Rue Bani Marine; mains Dh30-40; ⊘ noon-11pm) on Rue Bani Marine, cafes along Rue Bab Agnaou and a cluster of small restaurants such as **Bakchich** (Map p56; Rue des Banques; ⊘ 9.30am-10.30pm) on Rue des Banques. There are also several popular fast-food stalls along Rue Riad Zitoun el-Jedid.

In the middle-class ville nouvelle, it's another story. Good-value French, Moroccan and increasingly international fare can be found in abundance alongside high-end concept restaurants and buzzy cafes and bars.

✕ Medina

★ Henna Cafe   CAFE, MOROCCAN €
(Map p52; www.hennacafemarrakech.com; 93 Arset Aouzal; salads & snacks Dh30-80; ⊘ 11am-8pm; ☎) Tea, coffee, salad, henna tattoo, Darija class...they're all on the menu at the funky Henna Cafe, where a local *nquasha* (henna artist) draws intricate scorpions and climbing creepers on hands and feet while volunteers staff language lessons and serve up tasty *kefta* (spiced meatball) sandwiches on the rooftop terrace. A hundred percent of all profits go to local residents in need, while foreign volunteers can return the kindness by teaching French, Spanish and English classes alongside CV-writing skills.

Prices for henna tattoos start at Dh50 for a small design and range up to Dh500. Only organic, brown henna is used at the cafe and the catalogue of designs has been donated by top henna artists from around the world.

Mechoui Alley   MOROCCAN €
(Map p56; east side, Souq Ablueh; 250g lamb with bread Dh30-50; ⊘ 11am-2pm) Just before noon, the vendors at this row of stalls start carving up steaming sides of *mechoui* (slow-roasted lamb). Point to the best-looking cut of meat, and ask for a *nuss* (half) or *rubb* (quarter) kilo. The cook will hack off falling-from-the-bone lamb and hand it to you with fresh-baked bread, cumin, salt and olives in a takeaway baggie, or serve it to you on paper in a nearby stall.

Souk Kafé   MOROCCAN €
(Map p56; ⊘ 0662 61 02 29; 11 Derb Souk Jedid, near Rue Riad El-Arous; mains Dh65-80; ⊘ 9am-9pm) Pull up a hand-hewn stool under terrace sun umbrellas and stay awhile: this is authentic local food worth savouring. The Moroccan *mezze* of six savoury, cooked vegetable dishes qualifies as lunch for two, and the vegetarian Berber couscous is surprisingly hearty – but wait until you get a whiff of the aromatic Marrakshi *tanjia*, beef that flakes apart after slow-cooking in a hammam across the street.

Earth Café   FUSION, VEGETARIAN €
(Map p56; ⊘ 0661 28 94 02; 2 Derb Zouak; mains Dh60-80; ⊘ 11am-11pm; ⊘) Now for something completely different: a vegetarian spring roll stuffed with organic spinach, pumpkin, blue cheese and grated carrot with a sesame dressing, right in the heart of the souqs off Rue Riad Zitoun el-Kedim. The Earth Café's sunshine-yellow courtyard is small, but its veggie culinary ambitions are great – the warm beet salad with goat cheese may make believers out of carnivores and the freshly squeezed fruit and veg smoothies give souq-weary shoppers a much-needed boost.

Haj Mustapha   MOROCCAN €
(Map p56; east side, Souq Ablueh; tanjia with bread & olives Dh35-50; ⊘ 6-10pm) As dusk approaches, several stalls set out paper-sealed crockpots of *tanjia*. This 'bachelor's stew' makes for messy eating, but Haj Mustapha offers the cleanest seating inside a scuffed stall. Use bread to scoop up *tanjia,* sprinkle with cumin and salt, and chase with olives.

Café des Épices   CAFE, SANDWICHES €
(Map p56; ⊘ 0254 39 17 70; Pl Rahba Kedima; breakfast Dh25, sandwich or salad Dh25-50; ⊘ 8am-9pm) Watch the magic happen as you sip freshly squeezed OJ while overlooking the Rahba Kedima potion dealers. Salads and sandwiches are fresh and made to order – try the tangy chicken spiked with herbs, nutmeg and olives – and service is surprisingly efficient, given the steep stairs.

Un Dejeuner á Marrakesh
MEDITERRANEAN, SANDWICHES €

(Map p56; ☑0524 37 83 87; 2-4 Rue Kennaria, cnr Rue Riad Zitoun el-Jedid; mains from Dh60; ☺9am-5pm; 🖋) Come early or forfeit to ravenous vegetarians just-baked quiche of the day with asparagus. Omnivores pig out on decadent *croque monsieur* (grilled sandwich) made with turkey slices and served with a tangy side salad. Ground-floor booths are comfy and quick; the tented terrace has pillows, Koutoubia views and leisurely service.

Restaurant Place Ferblantiers
MOROCCAN €

(Map p56; west entrance Pl des Ferblantiers; tajines Dh45-65; ☺lunch) Plop down on a plastic chair in the courtyard, and have whatever's bubbling away and well-caramelised on the burner. The meat and produce are fresh from the Mellah Market across the street, and the chef whips up dishes in front of you.

★ Cafe Clock
CAFE €€

(Map p52; ☑0655 21 01 72; www.cafeclock.com; 224 Derb Chtouka, Kasbah; mains Dh40-100; ☺9am-11pm) The Marrakesh sibling of the phenomenally successful Cafe Clock in Fez is housed appropriately in an old school with a light-filled courtyard and unimpeded sunset views over the Kasbah. Star chef Tariq Hadine has also relocated to work his magic on the seasonal Marrakshi menu of fresh sandwiches and salads and, of course, the signature camel burger.

But beyond Clock's yummy menu, it's the revamped classrooms and cross-cultural vibe that'll keep you returning. Join Beyaz for belly dancing in a private room or watch Abdelali's pen dance across the page in the calligraphy class before signing up for a 101 session on Marrakshi culture and cookery classes (Dh600). On Sundays there are sunset concerts (adult/student Dh20/10), and best of all, Djemaa storytellers have agreed to perform here accompanied by English and French translators.

★ Le Jardin
RIAD, FUSION €€

(Map p56; ☑0524 37 82 95; www.lejardin.ma; 32 Rue El Jeld, Sidi Abdelaziz; meals Dh80-180; 🖋) The aptly named 'Garden' is the latest inspired idea from entrepreneur Kamal Laftimi, who transformed this 17th-century riad into a tranquil, green-hued oasis in the heart of the medina. Its cosmopolitan clientele sits beneath an overarching canopy of banana trees, sipping mint tea in green glasses seranaded by songbirds as tiny tortoises inch across the emerald-green floor tiles. Come for espresso in the morning, burgers at lunch, tea in the afternoon and well-executed tajines at dinner.

Kui-Zin
MOROCCAN, MEDITERRANEAN €€

(Map p56; www.kui-zin.com; 12 Rue Amesfah; meals Dh80-120; ☺11am-10pm Tue-Sun) Just like its clever name suggests, Kui-Zin combines top-quality cuisine with attractive surroundings ('zin' means beautiful in Arabic). As you're munching on complimentary olives and fresh-baked bread, choose from Moroccan favourites such as lamb tajine with apricots and almonds or international fare such as chicken and mango salad, vegetable lasagna and even lemon meringue pie. Chef Kenza takes real pride in the preparation while Hassan serves everything with a heartfelt smile.

Kasbah Café
MOROCCAN €€

(Map p52; ☑0524 38 26 25; http://kasbahcafemarrakech.com; 47 Boutouil, Kasbah; meals Dh100-200, pizza Dh85; ☺8am-10pm; 🖋) Say hello to your neighbours, the beak-clacking storks perched atop the Saadian Tombs, and then tuck into the sizzling brochette skewers dangling on the stand beside a healthy plate of salad and chips. The Kasbah Café wins top marks for stylish presentation of

---

DJEMAA EL-FNA DINNER THEATRE

Arrive just before sunset to watch chefs set up shop right in the heart of the action in the Djemaa el-Fna. Djemaa stalls have a better turnover of ingredients than most fancy restaurants, where you can't typically check the meat and cooking oil before you sit down to dinner. Despite alarmist warnings, your stomach should be fine if you clean your hands before eating, use your bread instead of rinsed utensils and stick to your own bottled water.

Pull up a bench and enjoy the show: the action continues in 'La Place' until after midnight. Storytellers recite ancient tales near dentists' booths displaying jars of teeth, not far from a performance involving clowns and worryingly amateur boxers. Some of the Djemaa's evening entertainments haven't changed much in a millennium, including astrologers, potion sellers and cross-dressing belly dancers.

SELF-CATERING

For a solid selection of fresh produce, dried fruits and nuts, try **Marché Municipale ibn Toumert** (Map p61; Rue ibn Toumert), off Ave Mohammed V. Souqs are also filled with food stalls selling olives, dates and sweets, and carts loaded with fruit and vegetables; the **Bab Doukkala food souq** offers the best value and a nice local vibe, as does the **Mellah Market** (Map p56; Ave Houmane el-Fetouaki; ⊙8am-1pm & 3-7pm), which serves the south side of the city.

For staples such as cheese, cereal and alcohol (often difficult to find elsewhere), plus speciality items, a few supermarkets in the ville nouvelle are useful. ACIMA Supermarket has branches in **Guéliz** (Map p61; ☑0525 43 04 53; cnr Aves Mohammed V & Mohammed Abdelkrim el-Khattabi, Guéliz; ⊙9am-10pm) and **Jardin Marjorelle** (Ave Yacoub el-Mansour, Jardin Majorelle; ⊙9am-10pm). Or you can try **Aswak Assalam** (Map p52; Ave du 11 Janvier, Bab Doukkala; ⊙9am-10pm) or **Carrefour** (Al-Mazar Mall, Rte d'Ourika, Aguedal; ⊙9am-11pm).

well-executed Moroccan standards, as well as Medi-Moroccan pizza and a range of fresh juices, milkshakes and non-alcoholic beer. For sunset views over the *mellah* arrive around 6.30pm to 7pm.

PepeNero ITALIAN, MOROCCAN €€€
(Map p56; ☑0524 38 90 67; www.pepenero-marrakech.com; 12 Derb Cherkaoui, Douar Graoua; meals Dh350; ⊙12.30-2.30pm & 7.30-10.30pm Tue-Sun; ☎) Never mind the exquisitely twirled cone of linguine topped by ruby-red cherry tomatoes on your plate, PepeNero's jewel-like interiors with their rose-filled fountains and citrus-scented courtyards almost steal the show. Housed in part of Riyad al Moussika, Thami el Glaoui's one-time pleasure palace, this Italian-Moroccan restaurant is one of the finest in the medina. Choose from either a Moroccan or Italian menu, the latter offering slivers of salmon carpaccio, succulent fillet of beef and fresh house-made pastas. Reservations required.

La Maison Arabe MOROCCAN €€€
(Map p52; ☑0524 38 70 10; www.lamaisonarabe.com; 1 Derb Assehbi; menus from Dh330; ⊙7.30pm-midnight; ☎☑) La Maison Arabe was serving Moroccan fine dining decades before other riads, and viva la *diffa* (feast) difference: here the focus is on the food and company, get-cozy booth seating, excellent classical Andalucian musicians instead of cheesy belly dancers, and the humble Marrakshi *tanjia* elevated to a main attraction. Even the scaled-down Dh330 menu qualifies as a feast, so make an evening of it – and tomorrow you can take classes here to learn how it's done.

Le Tobsil MOROCCAN €€€
(Map p56; ☑0524 44 40 52; 22 Derb Abdellah ben Hessaien; 5-course menu incl wine Dh600; ⊙7.30-11pm Wed-Mon) In this intimate riad near Bab Laksour, 50 guests max indulge in button-popping, five-course Moroccan menus with aperitifs and wine pairings, as musicians strum quietly in the courtyard. No excess glitz or belly dancers distract from noble attempts to finish 11 salads, *pastilla* (rich savoury-sweet pie), tajines (yes, that's plural) and couscous, capped with mint tea, fresh fruit and Moroccan pastries. Booking required.

Zourouni SUSHI €€€
(Map p56; ☑0666 74 67 28; 14 Derb Jdid, Riad Zitoun el-Kedim; 3-course menu Dh250; ⊙7-11pm Sat, Sun & Tue-Thu) What started out as a hobby for long-time resident Yumiko, who would prepare traditional sushi for homesick Japanese tourists, has now become one of the hottest restaurants in town with a wait list at least two weeks long. And no wonder: housed in her beautiful riad home, a maximum of 50 diners sit on purple velvet sofas waiting to be served plates of homemade *nigiri*, miso soup and two kinds of fish sushi. No alcohol is served out of respect for Yumiko's neighbours.

Ville Nouvelle

At lunchtime local office workers head to the string of restaurants along **Rue ibn Aicha** for barbecued meats, well caramelised tajines and offal (Dh35 to Dh70).

Kaowa VEGETARIAN, CAFE €
(Map p52; ☑0524 33 00 72; 34 Rue Yves Saint Laurent; snacks Dh40-80; ⊙9am-6pm; ☎☑) Breezy Kaowa brings a touch of California cool to the Majorelle gardens with a multicoloured juice bar stacked with zesty coloured watermelon, blood oranges, lemons and pomegranates. Down detox smoothies on the decked terrace or join the cool crowd

munching vegetarian wraps and *briouat* (filo pastry parcels) inside.

Samak al-Bahriya
SEAFOOD, MOROCCAN €

(Map p61; 75 Ave Moulay Rachid, cnr Rue Mauritanie; seafood with chips Dh30-80; ⊙10am-midnight) The best option along this stretch of side-walk stalls, al-Bahriya serves fresh fish and perfectly tender fried calamari with gener-ous chunks of lemon, plus salt, cumin and hot sauce.

Café du Livre
CAFE €

(Map p61; ☎ 0524 43 21 49; www.cafedulivre.com; 44 Rue Tariq ibn Ziyad; dishes Dh55-90; ⊙9.30am-9pm Mon-Sat; 🖥🍴) A bookish beauty, with walls of used books in English and French to browse, board games, cushy seating, quiz nights and poetry readings, plus free wi-fi and tasty salads.

Café 16
PATISSERIE €

(Map p61; ☎ 0524 33 96 70; 18 Pl du 16 Novembre; desserts Dh20-50; ⊙9am-midnight) The blonde-wood decor and the prices may seem Euro-pean, but the welcome is Marrakshi and so are intriguing ice-cream flavours like mint tea and *kaab el-gazelle* (almond cookie). Light lunches and salads are available, if only to justify homemade, gold-leafed chocolate-coffee cream cake and raspberry-mousse cake afterwards.

★ Amal Centre
MOROCCAN €€

(Map p61; ☎ 0524 44 68 96; www.facebook.com/amalnonprofit; cnr Rues Allal ben Ahmad & Ibn Sina; meals Dh60-80; ⊙noon-3.30pm) Given the lack of an 'eating out' culture, often even the best restaurants in Marrakesh are a poor reflec-tion of the food served in a Moroccan home. The Amal Centre hopes to change that by using their friendly restaurant as a means of supporting and training disadvantaged Mo-roccan women (providing literacy courses, management training, accounting skills and hospitality services), in exchange for one home-cooked meal a day. The bonus for you is a truly tasty array of dishes including unu-sual salads composed of lentils, cauliflower and leeks, fish tajine, spiced *tanjia* and tra-ditional Friday couscous.

Prices are also locally focused so the res-taurant's clientele is a happy mix of local families, expats and in-the-know tourists. Crèche facilities are provided and there's an in-demand takeaway window. If you're inter-ested in finding out more about the centre or supporting its work, check out http://hope-amal.org.

La Cuisine de Mona
LEBANESE €€

(Map p52; ☎0618 13 79 59; http://lacuisinedemona. com; 5 Residence Mamoune, 115B; meals Dh70-120; ⊙10am-10.30pm Mon-Sat; 🍴) Tiny and tasty, Mona's serves delicious, vegetarian-friendly food on painted plates in a colourful, mod-ern venue. If you can, grab one of the three tables outside and wait for a parade of mezze including citrus-glazed chicken wings, clas-sic baba ganoush, chicken livers, hummus and mercifully fresh vegetables with a minty yoghurt dip. There are even a few bottles of Lebanese wine on the menu, or fruit cocktails for non-drinkers.

If arriving in a taxi, ask the driver to drop you off at Pizzeria Niagara around the corner.

Mamma Mia
ITALIAN €€

(Map p61; ☎0524 43 44 54; www.mammamia-mar rakech.com; 18 Rue de la Liberté; meals Dh50-170; ⊙noon-11pm) This new, family-friendly Italian trattoria packs in punters with good-value pizzas and generous bowls of pasta alongside more unusual specialities such as osso bucco, escalope and a good selection of charcuterie.

TOP FIVE SWEET TREATS

Amandine (Map p61; ☎0524 44 96 12; www.amandinemarrakech.com; 177 Rue Mohamed El Beqal ; ⊙6am-11pm) Out-standing Viennoiserie and now multi-coloured macaroons.

Pâtisserie al-Jawda (Map p61; www. al-jawda.com; 11 Rue de la Liberté; ⊙8am-7.30pm; 🍴) Sweet and savoury delica-cies featuring figs, orange flower water and desert honey.

Venezia Ice (Map p61; www.venezia -ice.com; train station, Ave Mohammed VI; ⊙9am-10pm) Rich ice creams and tangy sorbets made by a Casablanca-based company and scooped to order.

Patisserie des Princes (Map p56; ☎0524 44 30 33; 32 Rue Bab Agnaou; ⊙9am-9pm) The city's most famous pa-tisserie, with enough *pain au chocolat* and petits fours to keep Djemaa el-Fna dentists in business.

Panna (Map p52; ☎0524 43 65 65; www. pannagustoitaliano.com; cnr Rue du Capi-taine Arrigui; cone Dh20; ⊙7.30am-10pm) A master gelato artisan from Italy, proprietory recipes and top ingredients make Panna the best place for ice cream in Morocco.

Exposed brickwork, red-and-white-checked tablecloths and vintage 1950s posters make for a warm and laid-back atmosphere. Families should come early before the smoking crowd gets comfortable at 9pm.

Catanzaro
ITALIAN €€

(Map p61; ☑ 0524 43 37 31; 42 Rue Tariq ibn Ziyad; pizzas Dh60-80, meals Dh100-150; ⊙ noon-2.30pm & 7.15-11pm Mon-Sat) Where are we, exactly? The thin-crust, wood-fired pizza says Italy, the wooden balcony and powerful air-con suggest the Alps, but the spicy condiments and spicier clientele are definitely mid-town Marrakesh. Grilled meat dishes are juicy and generous, but the Neapolitan pizza with capers, local olives and Atlantic anchovies steals the show.

Chez Mado
SEAFOOD €€

(Map p61; ☑ 0524 42 14 94; 22 Rue Moulay Ali; menu du jour Dh100-120, meals Dh250-350; ⊙ noon-3pm & 7.30-11.30pm Tue-Sun) With the fragrance of Oualidia's salty shallows still fresh on them, Chez Mado's oysters are the prettiest and plumpest in Marrakesh. Shellfish and seafood are delivered daily here, and under chef Alex Chaussetier's direction they are transformed into the lightest lunches: elegant sole meunière, grilled prawns and mayonnaise, John Dory with chorizo and a seafood platter to blow your mind.

★ Al-Fassia
MOROCCAN €€€

(Map p61; ☑ 0524 43 40 60; http://alfassia.com; 55 Blvd Mohammed Zerktouni, Guéliz; meals Dh180-250; ⊙ noon-2.30pm & 7.30-11pm Wed-Sun) Glassy-eyed diners valiantly grip morsels of bread, scraping the last savoury caramelised onion from what was once a Berber pumpkin and lamb tajine. The *mezze* of nine starters alone is a proper feast, but there's no resisting the classic mains perfected over a decade by the Marrakshi sisters who own the place. Book ahead for the Guéliz location, which is cosier and more convenient. Their Agdal restaurant (Al Fassia Aguedal; ☑ 0524 38 38 39; www.alfassia-aguedal.com; MH 9 Bis, Rte de l'Ourika, Zone Touristique de l'Aguedal), just south of the Kasbah quarter, offers rooms (Dh1680 to Dh2020) and views over the Agdal gardens.

L'Annexe
FRENCH €€€

(Map p61; ☑ 0524 43 40 10; www.lannexemarrakech.com; 14 Rue Moulay Ali; meals Dh200-250; ⊙ noon-3.30pm & 7.30-11:30pm Mon-Sat; ☎) French lunches in a mirrored cafe-bistro setting, handy to all the ville nouvelle boutique action. After the umpteenth tajine, L'Annexe offers a welcome switch to light, clean flavours: Provençale fish soup, *duck confit* (duck slowly cooked in its own fat) atop salad, and a mean crème brûlée.

Azar
MIDDLE EASTERN €€€

(Map p61; ☑ 0524 43 09 20; www.azarmarrakech.com; cnr Ave Hassan II & Rue de Yougoslavie; meals Dh180-250; ⊙ noon-3pm & 7pm-midnight; ☎) Imagine a Beirut lounge teleported to Marrakesh via Mars, and here you have it. With space-captain chairs and star-patterned stucco walls, the decor is out of this world – and the Lebanese-inspired fare isn't far behind. Authenticity sticklers will appreciate the shish *taouk* (plump marinated chicken cubes), and though they may want more lemon in the hummus, shared *mezze* with Dh50 glasses of wine keep vegetarians happy and bills in this stratosphere.

Le Studio
FRENCH €€€

(Map p61; ☑ 0524 43 37 00; www.restaurant-le studiomarrakech.com; 85 Ave Moulay Rachid; meals Dh200-250; ☎) Upmarket winebar-cum-restaurant Le Studio serves impeccable French food and a sophisticated wine list. Drinkers sip smooth glasses of Domaine de Sahari and nibble on spiced olives perched at high tables, while diners sit beneath the open, retractable roof mopping up plates of fricasseed langoustine and beef fillet dusted with truffle shavings. Suave hosts Steeve and Didier circle the room lapping up compliments.

Grand Café de la Poste
MEDITERRANEAN €€€

(Map p61; ☑ 0524 43 30 38; Blvd Mohamed Eddahbi, cnr Rue Imam Malik; meals Dh180-300; ⊙ 8am-1am) Restored to its flapper-era, potted-palm glory, this landmark bistro delivers swanky comfort and a seared beef tartare to write home about just behind the main post office. Prices run high for dinner, and service can be agonisingly slow – but during the 6pm to 8pm happy hour, a parade of appetisers is offered with drinks, and the wine list is the best in town.

🍷 Drinking & Nightlife

As with elsewhere in Morocco, traditional bars in Marrakesh are mostly frequented by men. Trendy lounge bars are more accommodating for women, as are restaurant-bars that turn into party places later at night, such as Grand Café de la Poste.

Nightlife begins around midnight. Most of the hottest clubs are in the Hivernage, or in the fast-expanding city suburb along Blvd Mohammed VI known as Zone Aguedal. Admissions range from Dh150 to Dh350 including the first drink, but midweek those who arrive early and dress smartly may get in free (especially women). Taxis back from out-of-town clubs like Pacha are expensive – taxi drivers know they've got you stranded.

★ **Riad Yima**   TEAHOUSE, GALLERY
(Map p56; ☑0524 39 19 87; www.riadyima.com; 52 Derb Aarjane, Rahba Kedima; ⊙9am-6pm Mon-Sat; ⏣) Marrakesh is full of riads, palaces and restaurants designed to fulfill every *Arabian Nights* fantasy, but after a while all the candlelit lanterns, arches and belly dancers can feel a bit false. At least that's what Hassan Hajjaj, acclaimed Marrakshi artist and photographer, thought when he created his kitsch-crammed tea room and gallery. Here all your preconceived notions of Morocco are revamped with a tongue-in-cheek sense of humour, accompanied with a traditional glass of mint tea, of course.

Djellabar   BAR, RESTAURANT
(Map p52; ☑0524 42 12 42; 2 Rue Abou Hanifa, Hivernage; cocktails Dh100; ⊙7pm-2am) If you've been to a branch of Buddha Bar, you'll be familiar with the playful pop-art, fusion menu and fashion-forward crowd at Claude Challe's newest venture. Challe's Maroc n'Roll style works a treat in this converted stucco-tastic 1940s wedding hall with an eye-popping *zellij*-backed bar, snakeskin loungers and a collection of portraits sporting fez-wearing icons from Marilyn Monroe to Nelson Mandela.

Check out its Facebook page for impromptu private sales and events. Reservations required.

Dar Cherifa   CAFE
(Map p56; ☑0524 42 64 63; 8 Derb Chorfa Lakbir; tea & coffee Dh20-25; ⊙noon-7pm) Revive souqsore eyes at this serene late-15th-century Saadian riad near Rue el-Mouassine, where tea and saffron coffee are served with contemporary art and literature downstairs, or terrace views upstairs.

Churchill Bar   HOTEL BAR
(Map p52; ☑0524 38 86 00; www.mamounia.com; La Mamounia, Ave Bab Jedid; ⊙6pm-1am; ⏣) The bar named for the Mamounia regular and sometime head of state retains its speakeasy appeal, with padded fuchsia leather walls, wood panelling and splashy leopard print. Call ahead to book, dress to impress strict doormen, and go retro with 20-year-old Scotch or flapper-favourite Mamoune Lady: gin, lemon and orange-flower water. At about €20 per cocktail, let heads of state buy the first round.

Comptoir   BAR, RESTAURANT
(Map p52; ☑0524 43 77 02; www.comptoirdarna. com; Ave Echouhada, Hivernage; menus Dh400-700; ⊙4pm-2am) Never mind the restaurant downstairs; the flash lounge upstairs is the place for visiting fashion designers and married Casa playboys to mingle over cocktails. There's no avoiding the belly dancers, who descend en masse every other hour.

Sky Bar 23   HOTEL BAR
(Map p61; www.renaissance-hotel-marrakech.com; Renaissance Hotel, Mohammed V; ⊙11am-1am; ⏣) The rooftop bar of the Renaissance Hotel is the best ville nouvelle option for a drink with a view. Canoodling couples sneak up to the shadowy corners of the top deck for great drinks and a view of city lights framing the giant, retro, red neon 'Bar' sign that bathes the hotel terrace in a rosy glow.

Kosybar   BAR
(Map p56; ☑0524 38 03 24; http://kozibar.tripod. com; 47 Pl des Ferblantiers; ⊙noon-1am) The Marrakesh-meets-Kyoto interiors are full of plush, private nooks, but keep heading upstairs to low-slung canvas sofas and Dh40 to Dh60 wine by the glass on the rooftop terrace. At the aptly named Kosybar you can enjoy drinks with a side of samba as storks give you the once-over from nearby nests. Skip the cardboard-tasting sushi and stick with bar snacks.

Piano Bar   HOTEL BAR
(Map p56; ☑0524 38 88 00; www.lesjardinsdela koutoubia.com; Les Jardins de la Koutoubia, 26 Rue el-Koutoubia; ⊙5pm-1am) Step from the red Berber carpet into the classiest gin joint in Marrakesh, with powerful long drinks (Dh70 to Dh90) delivered to leather club chairs as jazz classics soar to carved cedar ceilings. A second plush seating area behind the reflecting pool makes a serene escape for nonsmokers and jazz-avoiders, and the terrace restaurant serves a decent Indian curry quite late.

Café Arabe   BAR, CAFE
(Map p56; ☑0524 42 97 28; www.cafearabe.com; 184 Rue Mouassine; ⊙10am-midnight) Gloat over

souq purchases with cocktails on the roof or alongside the Zen-*zellij* courtyard fountain. Wine prices here are down to earth for such a stylish place, and you can order half bottles of better Moroccan wines such as the peppery red Siroua S. The food is bland but the company isn't – artists and designers flock here – so grab a bite and join the conversation.

555 Famous Club CLUB
(⏺0678 64 39 40; www.beachclub555.com; Blvd Mohammed VI, Zone Aguedal; admission Dh100-300; ⊙11.30pm-4am) After its success in Tangier, 555 opened a Marrakesh branch of its famous club at the end of 2012. True to form the club has impressive stats: a 1600-sq-metre club room, top security (with metal detectors at the entrance), floor-to-ceiling screens, psychedelic light shows, oxygen on tap and LED table buzzers for when drinks need to be replenished. More importantly the DJ booth is the width of the whole club, providing a suitable platform for some of Morocco's hottest house talent.

Theatro CLUB
(Map p52; ⏺0524 44 88 11; www.theatromarrakech.com; Hôtel es Saadi, Rue Ibrahim el Mazini, Hivernage; admission Dh200; ⊙11.30pm-5am) The most convenient club in Marrakesh is the old-time favourite Theatro, actually located as its name suggests in an old theatre. Themed nights, bizarre floor shows with acrobats and jugglers and a lively mix of house, R&B and Middle Eastern pop keep the punters coming. A recent collaboration saw Wednesday nights dedicated to aspiring Marrakshi DJs, dancers and performers.

Pacha CLUB
(⏺0661 10 28 87; www.pachamarrakech.com; Blvd Mohammed VI, Zone Aguedal; admission Dh150-200; ⊙8pm-1am Mon-Thu, 8pm-2am Fri & Sat) Pacha Ibiza was the prototype for this clubbing complex, which is now Africa's biggest, with DJs mashing up international and Maghrebi hits for weekend influxes of Casa hipsters. Ladies arrive en masse Thursdays to drink gratis at Rose Bar.

☆ Entertainment

For a good selection of French and sometimes Moroccan films, check out the program at the Institut Français (p65), where films are usually in French or subtitled in French. The plushest cinema in town, Le Colisée (Map p61; ⏺0524 44 88 93; Blvd Mohammed Zerktouni; orchestra/balcony Dh25/35; ⊙3pm, 5pm, 7pm & 9.30pm) sometimes shows films in the original language and subtitled in French.

For Sunday night music concerts, check out the website of Cafe Clock (p73).

🛍 Shopping

🏠 Medina

Souq means 'market', but when locals refer to 'the souqs' they mean the maze of market streets north of the Djemaa el-Fna and southwest of the Musée de Marrakesh. The main thoroughfare from the Djemaa el-Fna, **Souq Semmarine** (Leather Souq), sells a hotchpotch of local crafts. Prices are at their most expensive here given the high price of real estate on the main drag, and products often come from specialist souqs just a few streets away. It is always better to buy products direct in dedicated souqs, especially in the case of *babouches*, carpets and leatherwork, which can be found in smaller *qissariat* (covered markets) between **Souqs Smata** and **el-Kebir** (literally, 'the big souq for leatherwork').

Souk Cherifa MARKET
(Map p56; Derb Souq Kchachbia; ⊙10am-7pm) Short-circuit souq fatigue and head straight for this mini-market where younger, edgier designers congregate. Pick-up Berber-style knitted beanies from **Ipanema** (⏺0676 04 67 67), personalised straw hats and bags from **Original Marrakech** (www.paniermarocain.com), Parisian-style purses from **Lalla** (www.lalla.fr), contemporary embroidered linens from **La Maison Bahira** (www.maison-bahira.com) and the latest crushed-velvet boots from couturier **Art/C** (http://art-c-fashion.com).

Maktoub FASHION, ACCESSORIES
(Map p56; ⏺0524 37 55 70; 128 Fontaine Mouassine; ⊙10am-7pm) Maktoub by Max & Jan is the medina's first concept store selling a range of sexy, slouchy streetwear in a multitude of colours. But where the fashion is understated, ethnic-chic accessories are big, bold and bright with jewelry from Joykech and Virginia W and super-cool clutches from Maella One of a Kind.

Pop-Up Shop FASHION
(Map p56; www.norya-ayron.com; Le Jardin, 32 Rue El Jeld, Sidi Abdelaziz; ⊙11.30am-5pm & 7-10pm Wed-Mon, 11.30am-4pm Tue) Located in Le Jar-

din (p73), Norya Nemiche's Pop-up Shop counts Erykah Badu and Maggie Gyllenhaal among its fans thanks to her contemporary take on traditional kaftans and abayas in fabulous silk prints. Velvety soft suede and leather bags, kitsch clutches and a select range of jewellery and perfume from Hérit-age Berbère mean you can buy your complete Marrakesh wardrobe here.

Cooperative Artisanale des Femmes de Marrakesh
ARTS & CRAFTS

(Map p56; ☑0524 37 83 08; 67 Souq Kchachbia; ⏱10am-1pm & 3.30-7pm Sat-Thu) A showcase for Marrakesh's women *mâalems* (master artisans), the cooperative is eye-opening and a total bargain. Original, handcrafted designs include handbags made from water-bottle caps wrapped in wool, hand-knitted *kissa* (hammam gloves), and black-and-white kaftans edged with red silk embroidery. Ask cooperative director Souad Boudeiry about getting tunics and dresses tailor-made.

Art Ouarzazate
FASHION, ACCESSORIES

(Map p56; ☑0648 58 48 33; 15 Zinkat Rahba; ⏱9am-8pm) Tried-and-tested techniques in weaving, leatherwork and embroidery are transformed into high-fashion dandy jackets, sari-grafted coats and wire-rimmed 'papillon' dresses by dynamic duo Samad and Malek. Beyond the clothes racks their creative tentacles extend to bags, *babouches* and punk-rock homewares, such as pouffes and cushions in shredded midnight-blue suede with lime-green lining.

Naturom
BEAUTY

(Map p56; ☑0673 46 02 09; www.naturom.fr; 213 Rue Riad Zitoun el-Jedid; ⏱9.30am-8pm Sat-Thu, 9.30am-noon Fri) There are lots of good things about Naturom, not least its 100% organic certification and the use of pure essences and essential oils (argan, avocado and wheat germ), which ensure that all of its beauty products are completely hypoallergenic. And with its own medicinal and herbal garden, there's full traceability of all its raw materials. Trained in cosmetology in London, Rachid Jaafari also hosts fascinating workshops at an atelier on the Rte de Ourika (Km 17), where you can learn to put together your own signature perfumes. Check the website for details.

Al Nour
ARTS & CRAFTS

(Map p56; ☑0524 39 03 23; www.alnour-textiles. com; Rue Laksour 57; ⏱9am-2pm & 3-7pm Sat-Wed) A smart cooperative run by local disabled women where you can find household linens minutely embroidered along the edges. You can also get fabulous hand-stitched Marrakesh-mod tunics, dresses and shirts for men, women and kids, and there's no extra charge for alterations. Purchases pay for salaries, training programs and a childcare centre.

Michi
ARTS & CRAFTS

(Map p56; ☑0661 86 44 07; http://michi-morocco. com; 21 Souq Kchachbia; ⏱10am-7pm Mon-Thu & Sat) When an intrepid Japanese traveller met a hip Marrakshi designer, they discovered a shared love for craft, reclaimed materials and *wabi-sabi* (organic forms). Hicham and Michiko now have a family and this highly original boutique, featuring *babouches* made from flour sacks, mirrors made of Libya oil drums, and hammam tote bags made with recycled feed bags.

L'Art du Bain Savonnerie Artisanale
BEAUTY

(Map p56; ☑0668 44 59 42; http://savonnerielart dubain.com; Souq Lebbadine; ⏱10am-7pm Mon-Sat) Do your skin and the planet a favour with biodegradable, pure plant-oil soaps made in Marrakesh with fragrant blends of local herbs, flowers and spices, including prickly-pear cactus extract and donkey's milk. A recent partnership with artist Martine Goron has added some beautiful and truly unique scented necklaces to the mix. It's near Souq Sebbaghine.

Kif-Kif
ARTS & CRAFTS

(Map p56; ☑0661 08 20 41; www.kifkifbystef.com; 8 Rue Laksour; ⏱9am-9pm) 🌿 A hip boutique near Bab Ksour that engages the city's most inventive artisans to come up with clever gifts: handbags woven from recycled T-shirts, rings with interchangeable felt baubles and adorable children's nightgowns embroidered with 'good night' in Arabic. Ten percent of the price on all kids' items goes to a local non-profit children's organisation.

Assouss Cooperative d'Argane
ACCESSORIES, FOOD & DRINK

(Map p56; ☑0524 38 01 25; 94 Rue Mouassine; ⏱9am-1pm & 3-7pm Sat-Thu, 9am-noon Fri) 🌿 For pampering and foodie finds, this is the Marrakesh retail outlet of a women's argan cooperative outside Essaouira. The all-women staff will ply you with free samples of *amlou* (argan-nut butter) and proudly explain how their ultra-emollient cosmetic oil and gourmet dipping oils are made. You'll find it near Mouassine Fountain.

Jamade ARTS & CRAFTS
(Map p56; ☎0524 42 90 42; 1 Pl Douar Graoua, cnr Rue Riad Zitoun el-Jedid; ☺10am-noon & 3-7.30pm) Standout collection of locally designed items at fixed prices. Recent scores include graphite ceramic olive-oil cruets, breezy ice-blue linen tunics, citrus seed-bead necklaces with a clever antique-coin closure, and hip, hand-sewn coasters from Tigmi women's cooperative.

Creations Pneumatiques ARTS & CRAFTS
(Map p56; ☎066 09 17 46; 110 Rue Riad Zitoun el-Kedim; ☺10am-7pm) 🍃 To buy crafts directly from Marrakesh's recycling artisans, head over to Riad Zitoun el-Kedim and check out lanterns, bowls and belts cleverly fashioned from tin cans and tyres. There are several to choose from, but this place has a good selection of Michelin mirrors, inner-tube jewellery boxes, and man-bags with street cred (look for the framed Bob Marley poster).

🏠 Ville Nouvelle

Upscale fixed-price boutiques worth checking out for gifts, fashion and household linens line Rue de la Liberté and intersecting Rue Vieux Marrakshis. Another hot spot centres around the Majorelle gardens. To give your home a complete Marrakshi makeover, though, take a cab to the design outlets of Sidi Ghanem.

⭐ **33 Rue Majorelle** CONCEPT STORE
(Map p52; ☎0524 31 41 95; www.33ruemajorelle. com; 33 Rue Yves Saint Laurent; ☺9.30am-7pm) The quiet calm of this elegant concept shop is the antithesis of the souq's visual overload, but don't be fooled: 33 Rue Majorelle

---

QUARTIER INDUSTRIAL SIDI GHANEM

Modern Moroccan design fanatics hire taxis in the morning or late afternoon to scour the local designer factory outlets in this warehouse district, 4km outside Marrakesh on the Rte de Safi. Most of the original designs you'll see in Sidi Ghanem are made for export, with prices to match.

Negotiate a set rate of Dh150 to Dh250 for the round-trip ride from the medina, and score a map of the quarter at an open showroom. Hours are erratic, but many storefronts open 9am to 6pm Monday to Friday and 9am to noon Saturday.

---

represents over 60 designers, mostly from Morocco, and co-owner Yehia Abdelnour dedicates much of his time to sourcing local *mâalems* who make the majority of what's on view. The final edit, though ample in variety, is artfully displayed in a trio of rooms over three floors. Recent finds include super-cool clutches made in vintage upholstery from the Harakat sisters; silk harem pants from couturier Maroc n'Roll and plaited, pop-art charm bracelets from Zinab Chahine.

Atika SHOES
(Map p61; ☎0524 43 95 76; 34 Rue de la Liberté; ☺8.30am-12.30pm & 3.30-8pm Mon-Sat) With more colours than a candy store, Atika loafers are a Marrakesh must-have. Some customers have been known to buy their favourite shoe in 10 different colours but at Dh650 to Dh700 a pair, a quarter of the price of designer TOD's lookalikes, who can blame them?

L'Atelier du Vin WINE
(Map p52; ☎0524 45 71 12; www.atelierduvin.ma; 87 Rue Mohamed el-Beqal; ☺9.30am-1pm & 3.30-8pm Tue-Thu & Sat, 2.30-8pm Mon, 9.30am-12.30pm & 3.30-8pm Fri) Volubilis and Meknès are key growing regions for Moroccan reds, but due to heat stability issues in transit, coastal gris, rosé and crisp whites from nearby Essaouira are safer bets. For Moroccan wines at realistic prices, head to this dedicated wine shop; check the store's Facebook page for wine-tasting events.

Ensemble Artisanal ARTS & CRAFTS
(Map p52; Ave Mohammed V; ☺9.30am-12.30pm & 3-7pm Mon-Sat) To get a jump-start on the souqs, come to this government-sponsored showcase, across from Cyber Park, to glimpse master artisans at work and see the range of crafts and prices Marrakesh has to offer. The set prices are higher than in the souqs, but it's hassle-free shopping and the producer gets paid directly.

ℹ Information

EMERGENCY

Ambulance (☎150)

Brigade Touristique (Map p56; ☎0524 38 46 01; Rue Sidi Mimoun; ☺24hr)

Police (Map p56; ☎19; Rue Ouadi el-Makhazine)

Polyclinique du Sud (Map p61; ☎0524 44 79 99; cnr Rues de Yougoslavie & Ibn Aicha; ☺24hr) Private hospital for serious cases and emergency dental care.

INTERNET ACCESS

Many hotels, riads and cafes offer free internet access or wi-fi. Cybercafes ringing the Djemaa el-Fna charge Dh8 to Dh12 per hour; just follow signs reading 'c@fe'. Most open by 10am and close around 10pm.

Cyber Café in CyberPark (Map p52; www. arsatmoulayabdeslam.ma; Ave Mohammed V; per hr Dh10; ☺9am-6pm) Surprise: 15 termi-nals with fast connections amid the olive trees in the CyberPark, near the entry across from Ensemble Artisanal.

MONEY

Most banks change cash or travellers cheques and there's no shortage of ATMs. On Sundays, ATMs on Rue Bab Agnaou (near Djemaa el-Fna) and in Rahba Kedima often run out of funds; try ATMs on Rue Fatima Zohra near Bab Ksour, or in the ville nouvelle. Private *bureaux de change* (exchange bureaus) offer official exchange rates but may charge commission. Hotel Ali, on Djemaa el-Fna, nearly always offers fractionally better rates than anywhere else.

Voyages Schwartz (Map p61; ☑0524 43 74 69; 22 Rue Moulay Ali; ☺8.30am-noon & 2.30-6.30pm Mon-Fri, 8.30am-noon Sat) Represents American Express.

PHARMACIES

A list of pharmacies operating night hours (known as Pharmacie de Garde) is posted on or beside the door of all chemists. For public holidays, the list will include pharmacies that are open during the day. For an online list and loca-tion map, refer to www.syndicat-pharmaciens -marrakech.com.

Pharmacie Centrale (Map p61; ☑0524 43 01 58; 166 Blvd Mohammed V; ☺9am-7pm) The go-to place for excellent advice, personal care and a reliable stock of medication.

Pharmacie de l'Unité (Map p61; ☑0524 43 59 82; Ave des Nations Unies; ☺8.30am-11pm) Open late for all your imported drug, homeo-pathic remedy and aromatherapy needs; off Pl de la Liberté.

POST & TELEPHONE

Public card phones are widely available, espe-cially near Rue de Bab Agnaou in the medina and Ave Mohammed V in Guéliz, and cards can be bought from news vendors and *téléboutiques* (private phone offices).

DHL (Map p61; ☑0524 43 76 47; www.dhl-ma. com; 113 Ave Abdelkrim el-Khattabi; ☺8.30am-12.30pm & 2.30-6.30pm Mon-Fri, 8.30am-12.30pm Sat) International courier service; insurance subject to surcharge.

FedEx (Map p61; ☑0524 44 82 57; 113 Ave Abdelkrim el-Khattabi; ☺8.15am-12.15pm & 2.30-6.30pm Mon-Fri, 8.15am-12.30pm Sat) International courier service.

Main Post Office (Map p61; ☑0524 43 19 63; Place du 16 Novembre; ☺8am-4pm Mon-Fri, 8.30am-noon Sat) Poste restante is at window 3 and the parcel office is around the corner on Ave Hassan II. The section for stamps and foreign exchange stays open until 8pm Monday to Friday and to 6pm on Saturday.

Post Office (Map p56; Rue de Bab Agnaou; ☺8am-noon & 3-6pm Mon-Fri) A convenient branch office in the medina.

TOILETS

When nature calls in the medina, brave the toilets in cafes ringing the Djemaa or make an OJ pit stop at the Café des Épices. Along Ave Mohammed V in Guéliz there are dozens of spiffy cafes where you can nip to the loo.

TOURIST INFORMATION

Office National Marocain du Tourisme (ONMT; Map p61; ☑0524 43 61 79; Pl Abdel Moumen ben Ali) Offers boosterish pamphlets and numbers of licenced guides.

USEFUL WEBSITES

For more tips on events, restaurant openings and shopping head to:

Pocket Marrakech (www.pocketmarrakech. com) Monthly *What's On?* guide to the Red City. Also stocked in most hotels and bars.

Best Restaurants Maroc (www.bestrestau rantsmaroc.com) A good resource for higher-end restaurants.

Marrakech Train Tickets (www.marrakech traintickets.com) The only advance reservation ticketing service, although reservations include a Dh75 fee.

❶ Getting There & Away

AIR

Menara Airport (RAK; ☑0524 44 79 10; http:// marrakech.airport-authority.com; ☺informa-tion desk 8am-6pm) is located 6km southwest of town and continues to expand due to the grow-ing number of international and charter flights serving Marrakesh. In the arrivals hall you'll find currency exchange, an information desk and phone providers where you can equip yourself with a Moroccan SIM card.

Royal Air Maroc (RAM; Map p61; ☑0524 43 62 05, call centre 0890 00 08 00; www. royalairmaroc.com; 197 Ave Mohammed V; ☺8.30am-12.20pm & 2.30-7pm) has several flights daily to and from Casablanca (round trip from Dh525, 40 minutes), where you can pick up domestic and international connec-tions. Reconfirm your flight with its 24-hour call centre, and leave extra time for connections in Casablanca. Flights from New York connect to Marrakesh via Casablanca.

BUS

CTM bus station (Map p52; ☎0524 43 44 02; www.ctm.ma; Rue Abou Bakr Seddiq; ☺6am-10pm), southwest of the train station (about 15 minutes on foot), is CTM's main bus station, from where most services arrive and depart. Get tickets for early-morning departures the day before (especially for Essaouira), as morning buses fill quickly on holidays and weekends. There's not much at the station in the way of facilities, beyond a smoky 24-hour cafe with stuttering wi-fi.

Some CTM buses also stop outside the city walls near **Bab Doukkala** (Map p52), a 15-minute walk northeast of Pl du 16 Novembre or a 20-minute walk from Djemaa el-Fna. A number of local transport companies offer services from Bab Doukkala to Fez (from Dh130, 8½ hours, six daily) and Meknès (from Dh120, six hours, three daily). Each day there's at least one local **bus to Telouet** (Map p52; Dh50, four hours) that leaves at 1pm from Bab Gehmat in the medina's southeast wall.

Supratours (Map p52; ☎ 0524 43 55 25; www.oncf.ma; Ave Hassan II) is located west of the train station, in the old station building. To popular destinations like Essaouira and Agadir, Supratours offers a regular and more expensive 'comfort plus' service on slightly smaller, nicer buses.

Supratours also offers connecting buses to trains. The Supratours bus station has a room where you can check baggage (per day Dh10, open 6am to 10pm).

The parking lot in front of the Supratours office is the arrival and departure point for most international buses, including CTM buses to/from Paris (from Dh1780, 48 hours, Tuesday and Friday) and Madrid (from Dh1350, 36 hours, daily Monday to Saturday).

CAR

Local car-rental companies often offer more competitive deals than international operators, with quoted rates starting at around Dh350 per day with air-con and unlimited mileage. For 4WD rentals, count on Dh950 to Dh1300 per day with minimal insurance; the top end of the range reflects the largest vehicles, which can carry up to seven people. You should be able to negotiate a 10% to 20% discount in the low season (late October to mid-December and mid-January to the end of February).

A car with a driver starts at an additional Dh150 per day within Marrakesh and Dh200 per day for excursions outside Marrakesh.

International agencies Avis, Hertz, Europcar and Budget all have desks at the airport; otherwise check out these local agencies:

KAT (Map p61; ☎ 0524 43 35 81; www.katcar-marrakech.com; 68 Blvd Mohammed Zerktouni; ☺8am-9pm) Friendly, English-speaking local agency.

BUSES FROM MARRAKESH

CTM Services

DESTINATION	PRICE (DH)	DURATION (HR)	FREQUENCY (DAILY)
Agadir	105	3½	9
Casablanca	85	3½	5
Er-Rachidia	160	10	1
Essaouira	70	3	3
Fez	165	9	3
Laâyoune	325	15½	5
Ouarzazate	85	4	5
Tan Tan	200	10	7
Tiznit	130	5½	8
Zagora	120	7½	1

Supratours Services

DESTINATION	PRICE (DH)	DURATION (HR)	FREQUENCY (DAILY)
Agadir	100/150 regular/comfort plus	3½	7
Dakhla	450	25	1
Essaouira	70/100 regular/comfort plus	3	5
Laâyoune	320	15-17	3
Tan Tan	180	10½	3

La Plaza Car (Map p61; ☏ 0524 42 18 01; www.laplazacar.com; Immeuble 141, 23 Rue Mohammed el-Beqal; ⊘ 8.30am-noon & 2.30-6.30pm Mon-Sat)

Lhasnaoui Rent (Map p52; ☏ 0524 31 24 15; www.lhasnaouirent.com; cnr Blvd Allal el-Fassi & Ave Yacoub el-Mansour, 15 Immeuble el-Omairi; ⊘ 9am-5pm Mon-Sat)

TAXI

Departing from outside Bab er-Rob near the royal palace are **grands taxis** (Map p52) to destinations in the High Atlas, including Asni (Dh30), Ouirgane (Dh40) and Setti Fatma (Dh40). Those serving destinations further afield gather on a dirt lot near **Bab Doukkala** (Map p52), including grands taxis bound for Agadir (Dh150), Azilal (Dh75), Beni Mellal (Dh110), Demnate (Dh70), Essaouira (Dh130), Ouarzazate (Dh120) and Taroudannt (Dh110). Prices can fluctuate by Dh10 to Dh20 depending on demand.

TRAIN

Marrakesh's **train station** (Gare; ☏ 0524 44 65 69, information only 0890 20 30 40; www.oncf.ma; cnr Ave Hassan II & Blvd Mohammed VI), next door to the Supratours station, is big, clean and convenient, with ATMs, cafes and fast-food outlets. From the train station you can take a taxi or city buses 3, 8 or 10 (Dh3) into the centre.

Casablanca 1st/2nd class Dh140/90, three hours, nine daily

Fez Dh295/195, seven hours, eight daily

Meknès Dh265/174, 6½ hours, eight daily

Rabat Dh120/185, four hours, 10 daily

Safi Dh62 (2nd class), three hours, one daily

Tangier Dh310/205, 9½ hours, five daily

The last Tangier train travels overnight. Tickets cost Dh350 each for a sleeping-car compartment; book at least two days in advance.

❶ Getting Around

TO/FROM THE AIRPORT

A petit taxi (local taxi) to Marrakesh from the airport (6km) should be no more than Dh100 by night, but you may have difficulty convincing the driver of this. Airport transfers to the Palmeraie or arranged through hotels or riad guesthouses in the medina or ville nouvelle cost Dh170 to Dh250. Alternatively, airport bus 19 runs every 20 minutes from outside the airport carpark to near the Djemaa el-Fna (Dh30), and local bus 11 runs irregularly to Djemaa el-Fna (Dh3.50).

BUS

Local buses (Map p56; all fares Dh3.50) leave for the ville nouvelle at seemingly random intervals from Pl de Foucauld near the Djemaa el-Fna.

Key bus lines include the following:

No 1 medina–Guéliz (along Ave Mohammed V)

Nos 3 & 10 medina–train station

Nos 11 & 18 medina–Menara Gardens

Nos 4 & 12 Jardin Majorelle–medina

CALÈCHES

These are the horse-drawn green carriages you'll see at Pl de Foucauld next to the Djemaa el-Fna. They're a pleasant way to get around, if you avoid the rush hours (8am, noon and 5.30pm to 7.30pm). One-way trips on set medina routes down Rue Debachi officially cost Dh20 per person; otherwise, state-fixed rates of Dh120 per hour apply (rates are posted inside the carriage). Expect a tour of the ramparts to take 1½ hours, and allow three hours for the Palmeraie.

CAR & MOTORCYCLE

If you're feeling brave and/or foolhardy, you might join the fray on a scooter or motorcycle. Rentals are available from Action Sports Loisirs (p62).

If you do rent a car or motorcycle, there are public parking lots near the Koutoubia Mosque and just south of Pl de Foucauld on Ave el-Mouahidine; expect to pay Dh20/40 during the day/24 hours. If you find street parking, a guardian will expect a Dh10 tip for keeping an eye on your car; look for the guy in the blue coat, and pay your tip afterwards.

TAXI

The creamy-beige petits taxis around town charge Dh8 to Dh20 per journey, with a Dh10 surcharge at night. They're all supposed to use their meters, but you may need to insist, especially coming from the airport – but if the meter is mysteriously broken, just know that no trip within town should cost more than Dh20 by day, or Dh30 at night. If your party numbers more than three you must take a grand taxi (long-distance tax), which requires negotiation.

AROUND MARRAKESH

Ouirgane

When Marrakesh is sweating it out 60km to the northeast and tourists and daytrippers are swamping Ourika, Marrakshis sneak off to mellow Ouirgane for High Atlas breezes, peaceful hikes through unspoilt villages and romantic country retreats. For those crossing the Tizi n"Test to or from Taroudannt, Ouirgane makes an excellent stopover.

🛏 Sleeping

⭐ **L'Oliveraie de Marigha** BOUTIQUE HOTEL €€€
(☏ 0524 48 42 81; www.oliveraie-de-marigha.com; Km 59 R203, Douar Marigha; d/ste Dh900/1300; 🗟 ⊠) Weekend escapees come all the way

from Casa to lunch in this olive grove on woodfired pizza and float in the pool admiring High Atlas views. Chic bungalows in subtle earth tones sit amidst the trees, equipped with walnut furniture, double-glazed French doors and shiny, marble bathrooms. Children are also made welcome with a separate pool, playroom and mini-golf.

Chez Momo   INN €€€
(✆0524 48 57 04; www.aubergemomo.com; Km 61 R203, Ouirgane; d/ste with half board Dh890/1100; P✳🔊🏊) Country living comes with Marrakesh style at Chez Momo. Garden bungalows have *tadelakt* baths, pine-beam ceilings, kilim-upholstered armchairs, and panoramic patios that overlook the wildflower garden and pool; suites have fireplaces and extra beds for kids (Dh360 half board). The inn is also a weekend dining destination, the restaurant offers Berber couscous (Dh120 to Dh180) and a Saturday night barbecue.

Domaine Malika   MAISON D'HÔTE €€€
(✆0661 49 35 41; www.domaine-malika.com; Rte d'Amizmiz, Douar Marigha; d Dh1450, ste Dh1700-2000; P✳🔊🏊) The perfect antidote to inward-facing medina riads, this modern villa is all about the great outdoors. Floor-to-ceiling patio doors overlook a keyhole-shaped pool shaded by drooping pepper trees, while 1st-floor rooms enjoy views of High Atlas peaks from double aspect windows and private terraces. The decor, likewise, is modern with a slight vintage vibe and a zesty colour palette. With only seven rooms, service and food is impeccable.

THE HIGH ATLAS

Welcome to North Africa's highest mountain range, known by local Berbers as 'Idraren Draren' (Mountains of Mountains), and a trekker's paradise from spring through to autumn. The High Atlas runs diagonally across Morocco for almost 1000km, encircling Marrakesh to the south and east from the Atlantic Coast just north of Agadir to Khenifra in the northeast. Its saw-toothed Jurassic peaks act as a weather barrier between the mild, Mediterranean climate to the north and the encroaching Sahara to the south.

In its highest reaches, snow falls regularly from September to May, allowing for winter sports in Oukaïmeden, while year-round rivers flow northwards towards Marrakesh creating a network of fertile valleys – the Zat, Ourika, Mizane and Ouirgane. Happiest of all are the secluded valleys of the central High Atlas, which include Zaouiat Ahansal, Aït Bougomez, Aït Bououli and Aït Blel.

In the High Atlas the main language is the Berber dialect of Tashelhit, with some pockets of Tamazight.

Central High Atlas

The road less travelled lies to the east of Marrakesh in the central High Atlas, accessible through the regional hub of Demnate. Here a chalky mass of muscular mountains, weather-worn canyons and sculpted gorges (providing the best climbing in the country) hide fertile valleys, many inaccessible to vehicles until a few years ago. Several peaks in the area exceed 4000m including Irhil M'Goun, which at 4071m is the highest point.

Demnate   دمنات

POP 23,400
The once-grand Glaoui kasbah and mudbrick ramparts have been left to crumble, yet Demnate's fascinating interfaith heritage has survived. At the heart of town is a mellah (Jewish quarter), with an entry about 150m on the right after the town's main gate. Hundreds of Jewish families from Morocco, France, Israel, Canada and the United States arrive each July for the Jewish moussem (festival), a week-long mystical event said to offer miracle cures. Demnate also has two *zawiyas* (Islamic religious shrines), making the annual Hamdouchi Moussem in September twice as raucous. Pilgrims visiting each *zawiya* dance to a different rhythm in an all-day music festival in the town centre before going their separate ways in three-hour parades to the *zawiyas*. Sometimes the *moussem* peaks in blood purification, with dancers cutting themselves on the scalp in dramatic acts of ritual cleansing.

The 100-year-old olive groves dotting hillsides around Demnate produce Morocco's best olive oil, with trace mineral salts, a golden colour and subtle woodsy flavours that compare favourably to Tuscan oils. Almonds are another renowned local product, and the flowering of the local orchards makes March a lovely time to visit. Meals at Café-Restaurant Al Jazeera and Kasbah Timdaf are prime opportunities to sample Demnati olive oil and almonds.

🛏 Sleeping & Eating

Kasbah Timdaf   MAISON D'HÔTE €€€

(☑0523 50 71 78; www.kasbah-timdaf.com; GPS coordinates N 31°46,50 W 007°01; s B&B/half board Dh605/790, d B&B/half board Dh770/1140, extra adult/child Dh275/165; P) 🕭 A cosy eco-castle 15 minutes from Demnate on the road to Azilal, with artful rooms warmed by vintage woodburning stoves and snazzy *tadelakt* bathrooms. It may seem palatial, but this stone and mudbrick kasbah is a working farm surrounded by almond and olive groves, providing inspired Mediterranean-Berber meals (Dh110 to Dh185) on a vine-draped terrace with expansive views.

Owners Jacqueline and Yannick can organise cycling, trekking and fishing trips around Demnate. Transfers from Marrakesh cost Dh500.

Café-Restaurant Al Jazeera   BERBER €€

(☑0524 45 82 39; near Gare Routiére, Demnate; 3-course menus from Dh130; ☺8am-8pm) Call ahead to reserve a table for savoury seasonal salads that are a prelude to Demnate's signature fine-grain couscous, decadently laced with local olive oil and sprinkled with toasted Demnati almonds. Then enjoy a refreshing dip in the courtyard pool (open in summer) and an excellent espresso in the garden.

Snak Itrane   MOROCCAN €

(quarter/whole chicken with chips or bread Dh20/65) Some 300m after the city gate on the left, this sidewalk restaurant serves a mean rotisserie chicken.

🛍 Shopping

The weekly **Sunday souq** 10 minutes south of town is an opportunity to taste-test local olives, olive oils and almonds, and browse Demnate's local woodwork and yellow-glazed pottery painted in henna. On other days, you can hunt down the **potteries** 2km outside town in the village of Boughlou; turn right at the mosque and head 4km off-road.

Honey that's considered rare elsewhere abounds in the hills around Demnate. You'll notice a sign with a bee on it at the hanout (grocer) on your right on the main road east out of town towards Imi n'Ifri: approach the counter and ask the grocer to let you sample local honey (Dh100 per 500g). The mountain herb and wildflower honey is a standout with a peppery, thyme flavour while the *zriga* (a local blue wildflower) honey tastes fruity, almost like guava.

ⓘ Getting There & Away

Grands taxis to Marrakesh (Dh50) and Azilal (Dh35) leave from the main gate in Demnate.

Buses leave for Marrakesh (Dh35, two hours) from 6am to 9pm and to Azilal (Dh25, one hour) from 7am to noon from the bus station (take the road to the right before the town gate and turn left at the roundabout). To reach nearby Imi n'Ifri, you'll need to take a taxi (Dh35 for the whole taxi).

Imi n'Ifri

Just 6km east of Demnate along the R307 is Imi n'Ifri ('Grotto's Mouth' in Berber), a natural travertine bridge that formed over a gorge 1.8 million years ago. You can walk down into the **gorge** and through this toothy maw by yourself – the paths are clearly marked by the bridge and post office and comprise 300 steps down – but you might want to pay a small tip (Dh20) to a local guide to help you over some tricky boulders and explain local lore.

The two sides of the bridge are said to represent two local lovers whose families kept them apart, so this Romeo and Juliet held hands and turned to stone. On the south side of the gorge is a **spring** with water rich in natural mineral salts, where brides come for pre-wedding rites; in summer you may hear women singing and playing drums and tambourines at Berber bachelorette parties. On the other side of the gorge is a freshwater spring said to cure acne, which explains the number of teens hanging out here. Pass under the bridge, and suddenly you're in a *Lord of the Rings* setting, with flocks of crows swooping down from dramatic stalactites overhead.

🛏 Sleeping & Eating

★Tizouit   MAISON D'HÔTE €€

(☑0658 34 61 48; www.tizouit.ma; Aït Oumghar; r Dh600-660, tr Dh825; P🛜❄) 🕭 Stepped into the hillside overlooking Demnate and shaded by flourishing gardens filled with banana, pomegranate and olive trees, Tizouit is a labour of love and it shows. Henri and Nadja, who has family ties with the nearby village of Aït Oumghar, have brought their considerable talents in construction and agronomy to bear on this superb ecolodge with its eight individual cottage rooms (each with its own private terrace), natural biological pond and luxurious native planting scheme.

A relaxed, Euro-ethnic vibe – combining raffia rugs, Moroccan antiques and textiles and squashy European sofas – characterises the living areas and rooms where floor-to-ceiling patio doors overlook sun-kissed views of Demnate's ancient olive groves. Activities are naturally laid-back: long, leisurely walks along ancient irrigation channels to Imi n'Ifri's awesome grotto, or treks in dinosaur footprints at Aït Blel. And keep an eye out for future yoga retreats.

Kasbah Illy BERBER €€

(☎0523 50 89 53; set lunch menu Dh130) This splashy kasbah-hotel, 5km from Demnate on the road to Imi n'Ifri, offers lunch by a dolphin-tiled pool overlooking the valley. Reserve ahead.

Aït Blel

Follow the road that forks to the left at Imi n'Ifri into the breathtaking Aït Blel Valley, which connects to Aït Bougomez Valley via Aït Bououli Valley. In spring, Aït Blel is like an animated Impressionist painting, with the breeze rippling golden wheat fields dotted with red poppies.

The road here is fairly new, so the entire valley seems untouched by time. Mountains are striped gold, orange and purple, with green crops sprouting from stone-walled terraces. Follow the road 6km from Imi n'Ifri to the village of louaridene and you're in prehistoric territory. Signs point you towards what geologists claim are dinosaur footprints dating from the mid-Jurassic period, about 170 million years ago. Quadruped and carnivorous dinosaurs once roamed this area, and local kids do a mean impersonation of a T-rex.

Cascades d'Ouzoud شالا لد ت أزوض

Northeast of Demnate, just 167km from Marrakesh and a world away from the city heat are the Cascades d'Ouzoud, one of the most popular day trips from Marrakesh for tourists and Moroccans alike. The Oued Ouzoud drops 110m into the canyon of Oued el-Abid in three-tiered waterfalls, and the view only gets better as you descend into the cool of the canyon, past the late-afternoon rainbow mists to the pools at its base. The falls are most dramatic from March to June when there's more water, but young Moroccans often camp here in summer on terraces facing the falls. To reach the falls, walk past the signs for Riad Cascades d'Ouzoud towards the precipice, where converging paths wind down towards the falls.

But, be prepared: you won't have this natural idyll to yourself. The cascades are so universally beloved that during summer weekends the cafe-lined paths that lead down to the falls are filled with local families and tourists browsing souvenir stalls and taking pictures.

◉ Sights & Activities

Locals might lead you into the gorge for a few dirham, but you can follow well-trodden paths to viewing points and down into the gorge. Along the way, Barbary apes clamour for attention – though a signpost advises not to feed them.

At the bottom, you can hike further along the riverbed to more peaceful pools where you can swim, or cross the river to another path for extended hikes. To see the picturesque Berber village of Tanaghmelt, follow

---

AÏT BLEL TO AÏT BOUGOMEZ

From Aït Blel the only way is up, east over the Tizi-n-Oubadou pass (2173m) towards Aït Bououli (p93), Aït Bougomez (p90) and beyond. It's a spectacular drive through mountain oak forests set against striking, vertically striped sedimentary rock formations formed during the Triassic period some 230 million years ago. You'll need a 4WD and dry weather (thunderstorms and flash floods often wipe out bridges) between April and November.

The road sometimes narrows to one lane, but it's paved or graded the entire way. The cliff-edge villages and centuries-old way of life you'll encounter make it worth the additional two hours it takes to reach Aït Bougomez, instead of going the faster route via Aït Mohammed. Gas up before you go: the biggest town is Khemis Aït Blel, with a Tuesday souq and stalls selling sundries and occasionally petrol.

Near the pass, Gîte Tizi-n-Oubadou (☎0661 44 36 02) offers wraparound views over meticulously trimmed terraces with carob and almond groves. If you call as you leave Demnate in the morning, it may be able to provide lunch (Dh60 to Dh80).

the path by the lower pools past a farmhouse and up the slopes for about 1.5km. For longer treks, follow the course of the river to the Gramaa Nakrouine caves (two hours) and the Gorges of Oued el-Abid (another two hours).

🛏 Sleeping & Eating

Most cafes flanking the falls offer meals comprising of salad, tajine, chicken and chips for Dh60 to Dh80, and several offer rudimentary campsites for Dh15 – but until serious steps are taken to keep garbage and outhouses in check, the environmental cost of these establishments is too high to recommend them to nature lovers. You can help keep the falls beautiful by packing out trash and using the portable toilets.

★ **Camping Zebra** CAMPGROUND, GUESTHOUSE €
(☑0666 32 85 76; www.campingzebra.com; GPS coordinates N 32°00,351 W 006°42,177; 2-person pitch without/with electricity Dh75/95; r without/ with bathroom Dh200/400; P🛜) After four years overlanding in their B&W-striped 4WD (which gave the camp its name), Renata and Paul landed in Ouzoud and decided to create their own dream campground. The result is this welcoming mixed site with 25 tent pitches (20 of them are equipped for mobile homes), five garden rooms and a mini kasbah with four en suites. The decor is as cheerful as your hosts, with brightly painted rooms, up-cycled coke-bottle chandeliers and a communal *khaima* (tent) decked out in multicoloured Moroccan textiles.

In addition, there's a hammam, two washing machines and kitchen facilities, and if you want to arrange activities, Paul and Renata can put you in touch with guides from Ouzoud.

Riad Cascades d'Ouzoud MAISON D'HÔTE €€
(☑0662 14 38 04; www.ouzoud.com; s incl breakfast Dh570, d Dh710-810, tr Dh950, ste Dh1050; ✳) This stylish mudbrick guesthouse located just 30m from the top of the cascades offers the best accommodation in Ouzoud, along with a range of activities in the surrounding area. Solar-heated showers, ceilings painted with Berber talismans, and family-style welcomes from local staff make you feel part of the scenery. Souq visits and kayaking need to be booked in advance, as do lunches (Dh130 for a three-course menu) if you're not staying the night.

ℹ Getting There & Away

From Marrakesh, it's easiest to get transport direct to Azilal, from where grands taxis run when full to Ouzoud (per person/taxi Dh25/300 return). Head back to Azilal before 4pm, when taxis become scarce and drive hard bargains.

Azilal أزيلال

POP 27,700
This regional centre is mainly of interest to travellers as a handy transport hub between Demnate, the Cascades d'Ouzoud and the Zaouiat Ahansal and Aït Bougomez Valleys. This is also the last place you'll be able to stock up on cash and log on to the internet. There's a **Thursday souq**, and the town's **Complexe Artisanal** (⊙Mon-Sat) is on the right across from the town hall.

🛏 Sleeping & Eating

Hôtel Souss HOTEL €
(☑0672 32 84 95; Ave Hassan II; s/d with shared bathroom Dh40/80) This laid-back hotel offers a friendly welcome and basic pink rooms with shared showers and thick blankets. You'll find it on the corner on your right-hand side just after Hotel France. The entrance is through the cafe around the corner just off the main drag, Avenue Hassan II.

Ibnou Ziad Restaurant MOROCCAN €
(Ave Hassan II; meals Dh40) A good pit stop for lunches of rotisserie chicken and chips, though football fans might be delayed by matches shown on TV here.

ℹ Information

You'll find a number of banks along Ave Hassan II, including Attijariwafa, next to the police station.
Cyber Espace Bleu (Ave Hassan II; per hr Dh8; ⊙9am-12.30pm & 4-10pm Mon-Sat) One of the last internet outposts before heading into Aït Bougomez is next to Hôtel Assounfou.

ℹ Getting There & Away

Buses run between Azilal and Marrakesh (Dh60, 3½ hours, three daily) and Azilal and Demnate (Dh20, 1½ hours, three daily). Arrivals in Azilal will drop you on Avenue Hassan II, while departures leave from the bus station behind the main mosque. Plenty of grands taxis run from Marrakesh to Azilal (Dh90) and, less frequently, from Azilal to Demnate (Dh35). In the afternoon, when full, local minibuses depart from Azilal to Zaouiat Ahansal (Dh50, 3½ to four hours) and Tabant (Dh40, three hours), the main town in Aït Bougomez.

WORTH A TRIP

KAYAKING AT BIN EL-OUIDANE

From Azilal it's possible to take a detour to the huge dam of Bin el-Ouidane. The dam provides the majority of the electricity in the region, but more importantly it's the location for the increasingly popular 10-day kayak school of Morocco Adventure & Rafting (p66). Held once a year between April and May, the school spends two days on the lake running through the basics (no previous experience is assumed) before launching off into the Ahansal river gorge. What follows are seven spectacular days of running rapids through 8ft-wide gorges, river camping and turtle-spotting before returning in a loop to the lake.

Aside from being awesome fun, it's a wonderful way to visit the dramatic Cathédrale des Rochers and the Ahansal Valley and affords a dramatically different perspective of the sheer rock gorges from the valley floor. Groups are limited to 12 people and are accompanied by two guides, a safety kayaker and a photographer. Sleeping bags are also available for hire if you don't want to carry your own. Exclusive trips can also be organised for a minimum of six people.

A shorter, three-day rafting excursion down the Ahansal is also possible as is canyoning, although a good level of fitness is required for the latter.

Zaouiat Ahansal زأحنصال

Fantastically remote and fiercely independent, Zaouiat Ahansal was founded in the 13th century by travelling Islamic scholar Sidi Said Ahansal, who, according to local legend, was instructed to establish a religious school wherever his cat leapt off his mule. Happily for Sidi Ahansal that location sits astride a prominent crossroads between the Central High Atlas and the plains of Marrakesh and is blessed with fresh water and abundant grazing frequented by the powerful Aït Abdi and Aït Atta nomads.

As a result, the region prospered materially and intellectually. Libraries, religious schools, saints' houses and highly decorative *ighirmin* (collective granaries) testify to this wealthy cultural heritage. Even today a significant number of pilgrims continue to visit the region during the Islamic month of *sha-waal* bearing gifts of clothing and food for Saint Sidi Said Ahansal and his descendants.

Arriving in Zaouiat Ahansal, cross the bridge towards the mudbrick *douar* (village) atop a steep hill; this structure once housed the entire 300-person community. You can stay here or in the nearby villages of Amezrai or Agoudim (tell the bus driver which village you need). The village of Taghia is a further two-hour trek upstream and is located at the base of a stunning limestone cirque. You'll need to hire a mule to reach it (Dh120 including muleteer).

Sights & Activities

With the tarmac road from Azilal only arriving in 2013, Zaouiat Ahansal is only now making a name for itself among serious climbers and adventurous trekkers. To explore the region's dramatic scenery and sights, it is advisable to hire a local, licenced mountain guide (Dh300 to Dh400 per day). It is worth noting these guides are not climbing guides and are only certified in trekking, hiking and multiday camping excursions.

For those serious about climbing, the majority of Zaouiat Ahansal's routes run from 200m to 800m in length, although a handful of single-pitch moderate routes are being established. Part-time resident, the North Face athlete and international climbing guide Kristoffer Erickson can be hired to help you scale the region's technical rock face (€350 per day). In the winter months, Erickson also guides single or multiday backcountry ski tours in the surrounding peaks. You can contact him through Atlas Cultural Adventures.

Atlas Cultural Adventures ROCK CLIMBING, CULTURAL
(http://atlasculturaladventures.com) If you are looking for a hands-on cultural experience, ACA organises service programs for artists, university and high-school students, and independent travellers. These programs are in partnership with the non-profit Atlas Cultural Foundation (ACF; p90) and a portion of all program costs is donated to ACF.

Historic Walking Tours WALKING TOUR

Zaouiat Ahansal is blessed with an abundance of historical and natural sites: old saints' houses, places of pilgrimage and hand-tended community gardens. To enable easy exploration, a map of self-guided walking tours will be available at local guesthouses for a small donation from summer 2014. For a more in-depth tour an ACF staff member can be hired for a half-day (Dh250) and multiday tours of the region and their community projects.

Tagoujimt n'Tsouiannt TREKKING

At 853m (2800ft) high, Tagoujimt n'Tsouiannt is the highest, scalable cliff face, accessible also by trek via the aptly named Tire-Bouchon (Corkscrew) Pass, as hikers must 'corkscrew' themselves through a tight and winding series of stone and wood stacks to reach the top. Other worthwhile local treks include a circumnavigation of Oujdad, the muscular rock formation that defines the valley, and a short walk upstream to 'The Source', an impressive waterfall that marks the start of the Ahansal River.

🛏 Sleeping

Advance reservations are recommended for the months of March through to June, and for September and October.

Gîte Ahmed El Hansali GÎTE D'ÉTAPE €

(📱 0678 53 88 82; amahdar.ahmed@gmail.com; Agoudim; per person incl half board Dh120) Bunk at Sidi Ahmed Amahdar's *gîte* for hot showers, clean shared bathrooms and a clamorous welcome from the women who manage the place. Lunch is an extra Dh50.

Gîte Tawajdat GÎTE D'ÉTAPE €

(📱 0523 45 92 90; gitesaid@yahoo.fr; Taghia; per person incl full board Dh120) Basic accommodation is provided at the home of guide Said Massaoudi and his son Mohammad. It consists of mattresses on wooden pallets accompanied by simple, but tasty meals. Lunch is an extra Dh50.

⭐ Dar Ahansal GUESTHOUSE €€

(📱 0678 96 25 84; www.darahansal.net; Amezrai; s/d incl half board Dh380/560, child incl half board Dh145; P) As you round the final corner to Amezrai, Youssef Oulcadi's impressive rock-hewn *dar* rises organically out of the tough mountain landscape, its terraces built around Aleppo pines and landscaped with blushing roses and oleanders. Inside, rooms are beautifully finished with terracotta floors, *zellij* bathrooms and raffia-framed beds covered with thick blankets.

The large, cosy dining room and vast terrace overlook Amezrai's pisé granary (recently restored by the Atlas Cultural Foundation), as do the camping facilities, which are provided with a shared shower unit, traditional hammam and washing facilities.

ℹ Information

Youssef Oulcadi, a licensed Moroccan mountain guide and native of the region, can hook you up with guides through Dar Ahansal or online via www.randomaroc.net.

Climbers and trekkers are advised to bring a medical kit as the small clinic in Agoudim has poor facilities. In the case of emergencies, there is a new government ambulance that runs between Agoudim and the Azilal hospital.

ℹ Getting There & Away

Zaouiat Ahansal is 84km southeast of Azilal. From Azilal through Aït Mohammed follow the old route for Aït Bougomez for 25km. When you reach the junction below the snowy sail of Azourki, take the left-hand road heading northeast across the Tizi n'Tselli-n-Imanain (2763m) to the market town of Assemsouk. Beyond Assemsouk the road climbs again to Tizi n'Illissi (2606m) and then snakes down the Illissi valley to Zaouiat Ahansal.

Minivans ply the route between Zaouiat Ahansal and Azilal (Dh50, 3½ to four hours, two daily), leaving Zaouiat Ahansal in the morning and returning from Azilal in the afternoon. Grands taxis only originate in Azilal and cost Dh600 (for six people), although you may have a job convincing them to go beyond Aït Mohammed.

ℹ RESPONSIBLE TOURISM

The locals of Zaouiat Ahansal take immense pride in the natural beauty and traditional culture of their region and are making a collective effort to influence foreigners visiting this region to do so in an environmentally sustainable and respectful manner with the following suggestions:

➡ Pack out all rubbish and empty containers.

➡ Bring a water-treatment system rather than purchasing bottled water.

➡ Dress conservatively around locals and avoid wearing shorts or tank tops.

➡ Avoid drinking alcohol in front of or with locals.

THE ATLAS CULTURAL FOUNDATION

The Atlas Cultural Foundation (ACF; www.atlasculturalfoundation.org) is a registered US non-profit organisation with the mission of helping under-served Moroccans, especially women and children, improve their quality of life through locally determined development projects focusing on cultural preservation, community and environmental health, and education. In partnership with the local Moroccan Association Amezray SMNID, they are responsible for the restoration of three historic saints' houses and the extraordinary communal granaries, which now form some of the major sights in the valley.

Another core component of ACF's work is its international service learning and volunteer programs, which are run through Atlas Cultural Adventures (p88). Participants assist in ACF's ongoing community development projects, work side by side with locals, and experience rural Moroccan village life. Programs are focused on community leader capacity building, historic preservation, design and construction of small community projects, public health workshops and sustainable farming. Programs are open to students or independent travellers and are from three days to five weeks in length.

For more information, contact the ACF president Cloe Medina Erickson (medina morocco@gmail.com).

Cathédrale des Rochers & Reserve Naturelle de Tamga

Continuing north off-road along the main road from Zaouiat Ahansal leads to La Cathédrale des Rochers, the 'rock cathedral', and the Reserve Naturelle de Tamga, a vast national reserve with eight separate parks. Bird-watchers will have a field day (or several) observing 107 species of birds, including rare and endangered species. A botanical garden 3km from the sign marking the park's entry highlights the park's diverse flora, including medicinal herbs said to cure rheumatism.

Overnight stays, camping and meals (Dh50) are available at Gîte le Cathédrale (☑ 0523 44 20 23; dm with/without breakfast Dh50/30, half/full board Dh150/200), 2km after the sign for the *cathédrale*.

Aït Bougomez Valley

وادي عيت بو غومز

Though some roads are still accessible only by mule or 4WD, paved roads have given unprecedented entry to Morocco's 'happy valley' with its mudbrick towers, reddish *ighremt* (stone-reinforced houses) and rich, cultivated terraces. Scattered throughout the valley, 25 *douars* (villages) blend mimetically with their spectacular backdrops. Cliff sides are dotted with tiny plots of wheat and barley inside stone-walled terraces. High in the hills, you'll spot villagers collecting wild mountain plants to make herbal remedies and natural dyes for carpets, and in the broad alluvial valley acres of apple, almond and apricot orchards are lovingly tended beside carob, quince, pomegranate and cherry trees.

The Y-shaped valley centres around the *zawiya* of Sidi Moussa, which sits on a cone-shaped hill with the villages of Imelgas and Ikhf-n-Ighir to the northeast, Tabant to the east and Tikniouine and Agouti to the southwest. Tabant, with its weekly Sunday souq, school and official mountain-guide training centre, is the heart of the valley and the main transport hub.

⊙ Sights & Activities

Although there are plenty of mountainous hikes in the region – with summit-baggers heading straight for Irhil M'Goun (4068m) – ambling between villages along the valley floor is enormously rewarding. Along the way, drop in at some of the valley's 40 local associations and cooperatives and find out more about how these mountain communities are evolving their own unique brand of sustainable tourism and providing much needed education to future generations. One such example is the non-profit école vivante (www.ecolevivante.com), a free primary school that is part of a global educational youth project.

At the very upper (northeastern) end of the valley at Ifrane a track heads east to Zaouiat Oulmzi. From here you can trek down to the seasonal Lac Izoughar, a favoured watering hole for the nomadic Aït Atta tribe.

★ **Sidi Moussa**   MONUMENT, VIEWPOINT

For a spectacular sunset, take the road west out of Tabant, and you'll find the trailhead leading up to the Unesco-heritage *zawiya* of local *marabout* (saint) Sidi Moussa. It's a straightforward 20-minute uphill hike (15 minutes downhill), and you won't need a guide. The round structure served as a collective granary and has been restored through a community effort, with fitted-stone walls and weather-beaten wooden doors making a worthy photo backdrop.

★ **Cooperative**
Tikniouine   CULTURAL BUILDING

(☑0678 52 08 80; Tikniouine; ⊗9am-4pm Mon-Thu & Sat) 🖉 Some 5km east along the main road from Agouti is the village of Tikniouine, a key stop for gourmet treats and cultural immersion. The cooperative was formed in 2005 by plucky young women who secured EU funding to start cultivating organic walnuts, collecting mountain wildflower honey, and making their own mild, aged cow's-milk cheese, which tastes like a cross between gouda and emmental. At the cooperative's centre, which now employs 17 women full-time, you can sample and purchase the products. It is signposted off the main road 50m down a rutted track.

If you're trekking and don't have room to carry jars of syrupy mountain honey, you can buy the honey and nut oils at www.apanart.fr.

Souq   MARKET

(Tabant; ⊗8am-2pm Sun) The valley's main market takes place on Sunday and offers a great insight into valley life. Traders and shoppers start arriving in Tabant on Saturday evening, 'parking' their donkeys at the top of town. Expect an unedited experience of busy butchers' stalls and veg vendors, alongside traders selling everything from used clothes to teapots and tajines and even the kitchen sink (literally).

Petroglyphs   PETROGLYPH

Exiting the northern end of the valley 5km northeast of Ifrane towards Azilal you'll crest the dramatic Tizi n'Tirghist pass (2626m). Around this area are petroglyphs some geologists estimate are 4000 years old; ask a local guide to point out the enigmatic symbols, which local lore links to ancient rain-making ceremonies.

Association Ighrem Atelier
du Sculpture   ARTS & CULTURAL CENTRE

(☑0673 75 31 63; www.theanou.com; Agouti; ⊗8am-6pm) In Agouti at this centre, 500m from Flilou, on the left, visitors can watch artisans carve free-form spoons and bowls from fragrant walnut, juniper and boxwood salvaged from fallen trees. With proceeds from sales, the association is reforesting the valley with fast-growing boxwood and planting vetiver to harvest for weaving baskets.

LOCAL KNOWLEDGE

ARTISANS ONLINE

Inhabitants in Aït Bougomez are a surprisingly resourceful bunch. Take, for example, the launch of Anou (www.theanou.com), a new artisan-managed online platform that enables illiterate artisans to sell their work independently.

Unlike Etsy or eBay the resource isn't open to anyone, but rather is limited to locally recognised artisans peer-verified by Anou's leadership team, the benchmark being the quality of the products produced and the motivation of the artisans to expand and develop their product line.

Anou then assists artisans in creating a profile page with a biography of each member, photographs of their studio and tools, and GPS coordinates of their workshops. Each piece created is subsequently approved by Anou's administration team before being posted to the site, ensuring that every product you see is exactly the item that will be shipped to you. When products sell, artisans pop the purchased item in the post and, voila, in two to three weeks your new handcrafted carpet/bag/sculpture will arrive on your doorstep.

It's a great resource for travellers, as Anou's primary buyers so far are conscientious tourists keen to ensure that they are buying direct from artisans. At the time of writing there were 200 artisans on the site and 35 cooperatives and associations now extending well beyond Aït Bougomez across the whole country.

🛏 Sleeping & Eating

The valley is dotted with a network of *gîtes d'étape* (hostels or homestays). Many of them are located within a 30-minute walk west of Tabant in the villages of Imelgas and Ikhf-n-Ighir. Closer to the M'Goun trailhead is Agouti, which is the favoured base for trekkers.

Most establishments offer half-board lodging, although basic cafes and restaurants can also be found in Tabant.

Flilou
GÎTE D'ÉTAPE €

(☑0524 34 37 98; tamsilt@menara.ma; Agouti; dm/d incl half board Dh130/180, d with bathroom incl half board Dh460; [P]) The first *gîte* on your left offers clean dorm rooms, doubles with hand-painted beds around the rear courtyard, savoury meals and clean, updated bathrooms. Climb the ladder to the roof terrace, where Berber tents beckon and mirrored wedding blankets reflect sunsets. Hot showers cost an additional Dh10.

Chez ben Ali
GÎTE D'ÉTAPE €

(☑0523 45 87 26; Agouti; s/d/tr/q with shared bathroom Dh90/160/230/290; @) A large pinkish retreat with welcome amenities at the northeast end of Agouti. Cheerfully painted rooms share clean bathrooms, washing machine, terrace, three kitchens for guest use, and a computer with a slow internet connection. Ask for rooms with garden views; if you're sensitive to hard beds, opt for softer foam mattresses on the floor. Breakfast is Dh20 and lunch or dinner Dh60, plus drinks.

Gîte Intimou
GÎTE D'ÉTAPE €

(☑0670 71 47 12; Ikhf-n-Ighir; per person incl half board Dh250) So new you can almost smell the yellow and pink paint job drying, Intimou has five sunny doubles and triples and one large dorm room. All of them share the gleaming black-and-white-tiled washing facilities, which include two showers and two toilets. You'll find it on the hillside on your left as you head north, opposite the sign for the Association Ikhf-n-Ighir.

Gîte Timit-La Maison Imazighne
HOMESTAY €

(☑0641 53 34 80; www.highatlashome.com; Timit; dm/d incl breakfast Dh70/200) This historic Berber home is a breath of fresh mountain air with family-friendly dorms and brightly painted doubles. Your host family lives in the rear courtyard, and can arrange birdwatching excursions, treks and botanical hikes. Meals are served family-style on cushions in the living room, under a painted ceiling.

★ Touda Ecolodge
GUESTHOUSE €€

(☑0662 14 42 85; www.touda.fr; Zaouiat Oulmzi; adult/child incl full board Dh395/195) 🍴 Quite literally off-the-beaten track, Touda is located down a rutted *piste* in the village of Zaouiat Oulmzi, 5km east of Ifrane and the Tizi n'Tirghist pass and 4km west of the seasonal Lac D'Izoughar. Here you'll be overwhelmed by magnanimous Berber hospitality, plentiful home-cooked meals, impromptu fireside music sessions and stunning treks in the foothills of Jebel Azourki (3677m).

Dar Si Hamou
RIAD €€

(☑0667 64 48 62; www.nuancesmarocaines.com; Tabant; per person b&b/half board Dh200/250) Set around a pretty garden courtyard with undisturbed views over emerald-green fields to snow-capped M'Goun beyond, Dar Si Hamou is Tabant's first 'stylin' guesthouse. Pristine white linens on cosy duvets offset minimal Berber-chic decor of saffron stencils, ochre-and-red-striped woollen cushions and painted chests, while hungry trekkers keep warm around the free-standing fireplace in the salon.

Ecolodge Dar Itrane
INN €€€

(☑0610 08 69 30; www.origins-lodge.com; Imelghas; per person incl half board Dh350-500) 🍴 Located in Imelghas village (an easy 30-minute walk west of Tabant) is this rural-hip ecolodge. Eighteen whitewashed guest rooms are kitted out with handmade Berber-style furnishings, plus en-suite bathrooms in *tadelakt* with solar-powered hot showers. Pack lunches (Dh50), guides (Dh300 per day) and donkeys (Dh120 per day) are all available, as are a whole host of excursions and activities.

Café des Amis
CAFE €

(meals Dh20-30) Across from the Tabant post office, 50m down the main street, this cafe whips up piping-hot tajines in 30 minutes from garden-fresh vegetables for just Dh20.

❶ Getting There & Away

Access to Aït Bougomez is from Azilal south along the R301. At Aït Mohammed the road forks southeast (accessing the valley from the north over Tizi n'Tirghist and off-piste through ancient juniper and oak forests to Aghbalou) and southwest, from where a paved road leads all the way to Agouti.

Minibuses occasionally run from Azilal to Tabant (Dh40, three hours) in the morning when full, from near the mosque. You might share a grand taxi (Dh35 per person) or ride in trucks headed to Azilal on Thursday for its market.

Aït Bououli Valley

Heading southwest from Aït Mohammed you'll pass through hills marking geologic time in red-, purple- and white-striped mineral deposits. Five kilometres before you reach Agouti, adventurers equipped with a 4WD and steely nerves can detour south through a steep red-clay gorge to the Aït Bououli Valley, which until a couple of years ago was inaccessible even by mule for months at a time.

◎ Sights

Sebt Aït Bououli   VILLAGE

In the remote outpost of Sebt Aït Bououli, 14km off the main road, trekkers stock up on food for their M'Goun traverse at the Saturday souq.

Some 2.5km beyond Sebt Aït Bououli, you'll have to squint to make out a picturesque trio of villages built right into a two-toned purple and ochre bluff. On green terraces are gambolling lambs that are the valley's claim to fame: Bououli means 'those who keep sheep'.

🛍 Shopping

★ **Cooperative Feminin de Tissage Aït Bououli**   ARTS & CRAFTS

(✆ 0671 41 91 06; ⊗ 8am-5pm) Immediately below Aït Bououli's trio of mimetic villages is a stone-walled community association with a sign pointing visitors towards the Aït Bououli women's carpet-weaving cooperative. This 40-member cooperative takes every aspect of carpet-making into its own hands, tending and shearing sheep, carding and spinning fluffy lambswool into yarn; and collecting plants to dye yarn fascinating tertiary hues. The members also take turns minding the shop, so you'll be buying carpets from the woman who made it, her sister or her neighbour.

If you find the door closed, just call Fatima, the dynamic director, and she'll come down from the village to open the co-op's small storeroom.

Trekking the M'Goun Traverse
جبل المكون

While crowds flock to Jebel Toubkal, nature lovers head to the M'Goun Massif, where pristine, prehistoric landscapes make for rewarding challenges for trekkers.

If you're going in spring, dress warmly and be prepared to get your boots wet: walking river gorges is one of the great pleasures of M'Goun. The M'Goun Traverse outlined here follows one river up to its mountain source, crosses the mountain range, and then follows another river down into its valley.

The M'Goun Massif has some of Morocco's highest peaks and toughest trekking. But this walk will suit all grades of trekkers, including families.

ARRIVAL DAY

To stretch your legs and camp overnight, you could stroll down the valley to Agerssif to a riverside camping spot near the bridge. Alternatively, there is accommodation around Tabant and right near the trailhead in Agouti.

DAY 1: AGOUTI TO ROUGOULT

DURATION SIX TO SEVEN HOURS / DISTANCE 17KM / ASCENT & DESCENT 326M

After a leisurely 1½-hour walk south along the road from Agouti, a *piste* road forks to the left. Continue on this road, or take a steeper, shorter path that zigzags down into the valley, rejoining the tarmac road at the village of Agerssif (1469m), which you should reach less than three hours from Agouti. Agerssif sits at the confluence of the Lakhdar and Bougomez Rivers, and there's a good resting/camping spot by the bridge.

THE TREK AT A GLANCE
....

Duration four days

Distance 57km

Standard medium

Start Agouti

Finish Aït Alla

Highest Point Tizi n'Rougoult (2860m)

Accommodation camping and *gîtes*

Public Transport yes

Summary This walk, which traverses the northeastern slopes of the M'Goun massif and then drops down into the Tessaout river valley, will suit most trekkers, even younger ones. There is one long day of walking, but this varied trek crosses stunning mountain landscapes, and travels through river gorges and remote valleys.

BEFORE YOU GO: M'GOUN TRAVERSE TREKKING CHECKLIST

Maps & Books The 1:100,000 survey sheets *Azilal, Zawyat Ahannsal, Qalat M'Gouna* and *Skoura* cover all of the major trekking areas. West Col Productions' 1:100,000 *Mgoun Massif* is occasionally available in Morocco, and often stocked by Stanfords (www.stanfords.co.uk) and Omnimap (www.omnimap.com). Although devoid of contours, this map is a good trail reference. The German-produced *Kultur Trekking im Zentralen Hohen Atlas* shows the trek from Aït Bougomez to Kelaâ M'Gouna, and usefully marks and grades *gîtes* throughout the range.

Guide Since Morocco's main mountain-guide school is in Tabant, there are many licenced local guides with M'Goun expertise. Guides with High Atlas training from the Imlil, Marrakesh and Dadès also have the know-how to lead M'Goun trips.

Food Basic food supplies are available in Tabant and sometimes in Abachkou.

Water Purifying locally sourced water is the most responsible option.

Fuel For gas canisters, a supermarket in Marrakesh is the best bet. Petrol, diesel and kerosene can be bought in Azilal.

Gear When walking in spring or after heavy rain, a stick or trekking pole will help you vault over streams. When water is high, you may want plastic or waterproof sandals to wade through rocky riverbeds.

Tent There is no *gîte* in Rougoult, but there is excellent camping beside the river. Your guide should be able to arrange tents. If you don't have a tent and don't want to sleep under the stars, you'll need to spend the night in Sebt Aït Bououli, making the second-day walk longer.

Mule Guides can sort out local muleteers and mules.

The Lakhdar Valley narrows as the road climbs its south side. A half-hour upstream is the picturesque village of Taghoulit (1519m), surrounded by juniper trees, and with a simple gîte (per person Dh50). The road scales the gorge, then enters the broad, fertile upper valley, until it reaches Sebt Aït Bououli, where you'll find Gîte Hassan Benkoum (per person Dh100) – but we advise continuing to Rougoult for a head start on day two. Several valleys meet at Sebt Aït Bououli, and looking up past the village of Abachkou you'll notice Jebel Rat (3781m).

A graded *piste* road heads left to the south, through a valley of wheat and barley fields. The village of Tazouggart, on the opposite side of the valley, marks a more-than-halfway point between Sebt Aït Bououli and Rougoult (1850m). In Rougoult you'll find a Tifra River campsite and possible homestays (per person Dh30) – ask around to see who has space.

DAY 2: ROUGOULT TO AMEZRI
DURATION SIX TO SEVEN HOURS / DISTANCE 14KM / DESCENT 600M / ASCENT 970M

For two hours, the morning walk follows the Tifra along a stony path criss-crossing the river. As the well-trodden mule path climbs, the landscape becomes more barren, occasionally leading above rocky gorges – but the path always follows the course of the river south.

The source of the Tifra River is no more than a trickle at the best of times, as you'll discover just below the pass of Tizi n'Rougoult (2860m). From the broad saddle beneath the pass, a path leads left (east) to a ridge that climbs to over 3500m. The well-worn Rougoult pass is straight ahead, and the summit of Irhil M'Goun (4068m) – only 100m lower than Jebel Toubkal – due east. In the near distance across the Tessaout River, exposed mountain slopes reveal great gashes of rust, green and grey rock.

From the Rougoult pass, the mule path is clearly marked, winding gradually downhill for two hours before reaching the village of Tasgaïwalt (2521m). Curious village children may keep you company on the easy 40-minute walk along the track, keeping the river to your left, to the village of Amezri (2250m). The Gîte d'Étape Agnid Mohamed (per person Dh100) has large sleeping rooms, some overlooking the valley, with a rudimentary shower and toilets, and convenient camping (Dh20).

Trekking the M'Goun Traverse

Trekking the M'Goun Traverse

START

M'Goun Traverse Trek

END

Jebel Tamadout

Tighremt n'Aït Ahmed (2230m)

Taouigalt

Ihihit Igoudamene

Jebel Asselda (2984m)

Tabant

Tizi n'Aït Imi (2905m)

Tinoughine

Assif Ahouli

Assif Ayt Oullimt

Jebel Aklim (3432m)

Arous

Tizi n'Tanout (3074m)

3519m

3266m

3996m

3993m

Irhil M'Goun (4068m)

Tighouzzirine

Assif n'Arous

Tizi Asderent n'Aït Bou Oully (3066m)

Assif Ikt Oucan

Taghra

Taïsnant

Taghzout

Agouti

Imi n'Talat

Irhil n'Tikkis (3207m)

Tizi n'Oumsoud (2969m)

Tizi n'Oumassin (3640m)

Irhil n'Nig Oumassine (3883m)

Jebel Tajouija (3391m)

1989m

Agerssif (1469m)

Taghoulit

Jebel Tifaïniwine (3449m)

Tizi n'Aït Taziyt

Jebel Tarkeddid

Jebel Tazoukt n'Ouguerd (3381m)

Jebel Tadaghast (2891m)

Jebel Tafenfent (2513m)

Jebel Tifaïniwine (3449m)

Ifri n'Aït Kherfalla

Idrmaman

Sebt Aït Bououli (1858m)

Tizi n'Tizit

Tizi n'Roogoult (2860m)

Tizi n'Oulawn (2767m)

Tarbat n'Aït Moussa

Abachkou

Tazzougart

Rougoult (1850m)

Assif n'Tizit

Jebel Wagraraz (3272m)

Tizi n'Roogoult (2860m)

Amezri (2250m)

Tasgaïwalt (2521m)

Jebel Alimmane (2586m)

Tagassalt

Tarbat n'Tirsal

Tizi n'Tighist (2399m)

Tazgagalt

Assif Aït Mallal

Tignousti (3819m)

Tizi n'Wani (3017m)

Imi-n-Ikkis

Jebel Azegza (2663m)

Jebel Rat (3781m)

Tizi n'Tibouzene

Aghoulid n'Ichbbakne

2809m

Ichbbakene

Tala n'Izri

Jebel Amerziaz (2522m)

Jebel Aguendra (3060m)

Tissili

2864m

Oued Tessaout

Imi n'Larba

Jebel Timlilt (2862m)

Jebel Waguerset (2882m)

Tizi n'Wawat

Ifoujou

Fakhour

Aït Ali n'Ito (1833m)

Aït Alla

N

5 miles

10 km

DAY 3: AMEZRI TO AÏT ALI N'ITO
DURATION SIX HOURS / DISTANCE 18KM / DESCENT 427M / ASCENT 150M

Your path follows the Tessaout River, shelving gently from 2250m to 1833m. The valley is flanked by impressive cliffs, particularly the sheer Ichbbakene escarpment, which rises 600m above the river.

The river has few fish, but it does irrigate exceptionally lovely terraces cultivated by Aafan Berbers. In spring, the area is covered with wildflowers and blooming fruit and nut trees. Here the Tessaout flows west, fed by streams of melted mountain snow.

Where the path crosses the river, you can often hop across on stones. In spring, you may have to wade, as at the village of Imi-n-Ikkis, 5km from Amezri. The village has a shop (no sign) that sometimes stocks water, soft drinks, tinned food and plastic shoes to ford rivers.

Downstream 1½ hours, the path passes beneath the larger village of Ichbbakene, backed by a sheer escarpment. The path becomes a *piste*, and keeping the river on your left for another 2½ hours, the *piste* squeezes between the stone and mud houses of Aït Hamza. Another hour leads to the village of Aït Ali n'Ito, where you'll find great views at the Gîte d'Étape Assounfou (⌂ 0668 96 82 63; half board per person Dh200) plus electricity, hot showers (Dh10) and even a hammam.

DAY 4: AÏT ALI N'ITO TO AÏT ALLA
DURATION 2½ TO THREE HOURS / DISTANCE 8KM / DESCENT 150M

A dirt road leads alongside the river with gentle climbs to the lovely village of Fakhour, where the houses scale the hillside. Fakhour is noted for its *agadir* (fortified granary), which can be visited (a Dh10 tip for the guardian is customary).

Less than an hour beyond Fakhour, the village of Ifoulou sits on a bend of the river and road, drawing villagers from miles around for its Monday souq. From here, a tarmac road leads to the main Demnate–Skoura road by the bridge over the Tessaout River, below the village of Aït Alla. Here it's possible to find transport.

Western High Atlas

South of Marrakesh, Morocco's highest peak, Jebel Toubkal (4167m), sits at the centre of Toubkal National Park. Since these peaks are just 2½ hours from Marrakesh, Jebel Toubkal is the most frequently visited High Atlas

region and has long been a key route south. It is most easily accessible via the Ourika and Mizane Valleys. The heavily touristed Ourika Valley deposits you at the trekking base of Setti Fatma, while the Mizane Valley leads you to the more atmospheric village of Imlil. The ski resort of Oukaïmeden sits between the two.

Zat Valley

When Marrakesh is sweating it out 50km to the northwest, breezes are rippling through barley and swaying poplar trees along this charmed river valley.

To reach Zat Valley from Marrakesh, take the N9 towards Ouarzazate until it crosses the Oued Zat at Aït Ourir, then turn off south and head towards the transport town of Tighdouine at the near end of the valley. Tighdouine offers tasty roadside tajines before you enter Zat's land of make-believe: gardens built right into cliff faces, stone houses with bright-blue doors, white-framed windows with families leaning out to say hello. This is all best appreciated on foot or mule.

Three- to five-day walking tours are organised by Inside Morocco Tours (p65). They wend their way up the rich valley (most of Marrakesh's potatoes, turnips, olives, figs and tomatoes come from here) to the village of Talatassat, where you can visit the local potteries before continuing on up to the red sandstone Yaggour Plateau, the location of an important concentration of prehistoric rock engravings. Nearby Tizi N'Rhellis leads to the neighbouring Ourika Valley.

⊙ Sights & Activities

★ Isafarne Honey Collective   FOOD & DRINK
(⌂ 0677 78 75 48; Ighalen; ⊙ 9am-1pm & 2.30-6pm Thu-Tue) On the left about 13km after the turn-off from the Ouarzazate road (about 2km before Tighdouine), you'll spot an eye-catching pink building with the sign of a bee on your left. This initiative involves 120 Zat locals in the production of a truly exceptional dark, spicy honey from wild Berber medicinal plants that thrive in the Zat Valley. The president of the collective, Mr Ahmed Zaki, will gladly treat you to a taste of the collective's honey (Dh250 per kilogram) with local bread.

Mr Zaki can also help you identify the complex flavours you're tasting, which, depending on the time of year, may include verbena, wild sage, lavender, carob flower, wild mint, walnut and mountain thyme. There are also cheaper pots of orange-blossom honey (Dh80) on sale, harvested from the myriad orchards in the valley.

Ourika Valley وادة اوريكة

Temperatures are cooler in the shadow of snowcapped High Atlas peaks, and this blooming valley 45 minutes by car south of Marrakesh is the city's escape hatch from the soaring summer heat. The valley is especially mood-altering from February to April, when almond and cherry orchards bloom manically and wildflowers run riot.

Sadly Ourika's beauty and easy accessibility have lead to significant development, which now threatens to mar its mountain-valley vibe. At Oulmes makeshift cafes and BBQ joints line the riverside strung together by flimsy rope bridges that allow day-trippers to cross the river (it seems that everyone has forgotten the flash floods of 1995), while at the end of the valley sits the summer resort and well-worn trekking base of Setti Fatma.

For High Atlas scenery with fewer tourist coaches and moped-mounted salesmen, you may prefer the Mizane or Zat Valleys.

❶ Getting There & Away

Grands taxis to Setti Fatma leave frequently from Bab er-Rob in Marrakesh (Dh35) and you may also find less-frequent minibuses to Ourika Valley destinations (Dh15 to Dh25). Most grands taxis will drop you anywhere along the Route d'Ourika, but return taxis and minibuses are easiest to find in Setti Fatma, Tnine and Aghbalou. Transport returns when full.

AGHMAT أغمات

Drivers speeding past Aghmat (aka Rhmat, Ghmat or Jemaa Rhmat) 31km from Marrakesh are missing a key turning point in Moroccan history. This town was an Idrissid dynastic capital from AD 828 to 1058, and an important stop on the camel caravans from sub-Saharan Africa through Sijilmassa (the ruins of which now lie near Rissani).

When the Almoravids conquered the city in 1058, one of Aghmat's leading citizens was killed in the fray, leaving his brilliant, wealthy widow Zeinab en-Nafzawiyyat free to marry Almoravid leader Abu Bakr. When Abu Bakr was recalled to the Sahara to settle disputes, he divorced Zeinab so that she could remarry his cousin, Youssef ben Tachfine. With Zein-

ab's financing and counsel, Youssef ben Tachfine proved unstoppable, founding a new capital at Marrakesh and expanding the Almoravid empire to the doorstep of Barcelona.

Once Almoravids moved to Marrakesh, Aghmat became a place of exile for political dissidents, including Andalucian poet-king Al-Mutamid ibn Abbad. Arts continue to prevail in Aghmat: in April the town hosts Awaln'art (www.awalnart.com), an international festival of street artists.

◉ Sights & Activities

Visitors can glimpse Aghmat's former glories just behind the town's main market-place, where Aghmat's Friday souq is held.

Archaeological Site HISTORIC SITE
(http://aghmatarchaeology.org) Excavations about 200m to the left off the main road began in 2010, co-financed by the state, revealing ancient urban foundations, including a hammam, mosque, marketplace and irrigation. Work at the site has so far unearthed over 7000 artefacts and there are hopes for a future museum.

Mausoleum HISTORIC SITE
Al-Mutamid's tomb is marked with a domed Almoravid-style mausoleum. It's signed right off the main road after the commune building, inside a garden enclosure 200m along on the left. The dissident's tomb was the site of a 1950 protest against French occupation that was violently suppressed by Pasha Glaoui – an inciting incident in Morocco's independence movement.

TNINE

Beyond the turn-off for Aghmat and 33km from Marrakesh along Rte d'Ourika is the town of Tnine (aka Tnin l'Ourika), where you may run into donkey traffic at the Monday souq.

◉ Sights & Activities

★ Nectarôme GARDENS
(☑ 0524 48 21 49; www.nectarome.com; Km 34 Rte de l'Ourika, Tnine; garden visits Dh15; ⊙ 9am-7pm Sep-Jul) Just after the bridge in Tnine, signs off the main road point down a dirt track towards the organic botanical gardens of a Franco-Moroccan natural bath-product company that combines Berber herbal remedies with modern aromatherapy. The garden certainly smells great, and a footbath and foot massage with organic essential oils (Dh250) is just the thing after a trek.

If you're in Tnine for the Monday souq, the gardens are also a good place to stop for lunch (Dh60 to Dh80).

Safranerie GARDENS
(☑0522 48 44 76; www.safran-ourika.com; Km 34 Rte de l'Ourika, Tnine; garden tours adult/under 16yr Dh20/free; ☉7am-5.30pm) Almost anything thrives in Ourika's rich soil, including saffron (*Crocus sativus*), organically grown here from bulbs that are cultivated near Talouine. Saffron is a high-maintenance plant, with flowers harvested before dawn for maximum potency. You can watch the harvest take place during the first three weeks of November, although you'll need to get here between 4am and 5am. At other times of the year, guided tours are given by staff who reiterate key points on explanatory placards.

Tours end with a complimentary mint tea and a soft-sell of Safranerie saffron (Dh13 per gram) and estate-grown herbal tisanes (Dh20 to Dh40).

Ecomusée Berbere MUSEUM
(☑0524 38 57 21; www.museeberbere.com; Douar Tafza, Km 37 Rte de l'Ourika, Tafza; adult/under 16yr Dh20/free; ☉9.30am-7pm)🖉 Four kilometres after Tnine a discreet sign points up a dirt path into the Berber village of Tafza: here, the three-storey mudbrick *ksar* (fort) that once housed the local *caid* (chief) is now a museum. Enthusiastic guided visits cover every detail of household life, from symbols carved in door frames to silver dowry jewellery. Call ahead to reserve meals on the terrace (Dh60) or arrange to visit Tafza pottery workshops.

🛏 Sleeping & Eating

Kasbah Bab Ourika ECOLODGE €€€
(☑0668 74 95 47; http://kasbahbabourika.com; Tnine Ourika; d Dh1695-2825; 🅿🖼)🖉 Occupying an outstanding location in the Ourika Valley, this rammed-earth kasbah puts Richard Branson's bombastic Kasbah Tamadot in the shade. Understated luxuries include uninterrupted views of snowy Atlas peaks, top-quality meals any time anywhere, superbly finished interiors, sleep-inducing orthopaedic mattresses and underfloor heating powered by solar panels. The kasbah's dedication to sustainability is serious (water is recycled, electricity is produced by a biodigester and solar panels provide heat and hot water), and everything contrives to highlight the beauty of the surrounding environment.

ⓘ Information

From December to March, flash floods can make hiking dangerous and render parts of Ourika Valley inaccessible – in 1995, winter floods nearly wiped out the village of Oulmes.

Centre d'Informations Touristique Ourika
(☑0668 46 55 45; ☉8.30am-7pm Mon-Sat, 8.30am-1pm Sun) Just outside Tnine, this local NGO-operated information office provides maps of valley vista points and updates on trekking conditions.

AGHBALOU

A red stone mosque and minaret are the signature landmarks of Aghbalou, the Ourika Valley's largest village, located some 47km southwest of Marrakesh. Most buses make a stop here, and from here to Oulmes the river is lined with cafes and restaurants.

🛏 Sleeping & Eating

Cafes dot the riverbanks serving kebabs and salad (Dh50) or tajines big enough for two (Dh60), with carpets spread out under shady trees in good weather.

Auberge le Maquis HOTEL €€
(☑0524 48 45 31; www.le-maquis.com; Km 45 Rte de l'Ourika; half board s Dh320-440, d Dh480-680; 🖼) A warm welcome awaits at this eight-room, family-style getaway and launching pad/finish line for bikers and trekkers. The local management makes meals (Dh80 to Dh150) feel like dinners among friends, and there's a play-yard where kids cut loose. The *auberge* also arranges plenty of treks and excursions including to the Yaggour plateau petroglyphs (from where you can descend to the Zat Valley) and mule treks for little ones.

Ourika Garden HOTEL €€
(☑0524 48 44 41; www.ourika-garden.com; Km 49.5 Rte de l'Ourika; outside Aghbalou; s Dh600, d Dh660-880; 🏵🛜🖼) A gardener's dream, with flagstone paths through aromatic herbs leading over footbridges to a stone-walled lodge. Guest rooms have fireplaces, seating nooks, hewn-wood furnishings and en-suite bathrooms with variable hot water (shower early). Breakfasts on the terrace feature High Atlas views, local honey and olive oil, and there's wi-fi by the patio bar.

SETTI FATMA ستي فتما

A little village that's seen a whole lot of tourist action in the past decade, Setti Fatma is a scenic stop for lunch by the river and for hikes to seven waterfalls. The village is neatly nestled in a canyon beneath the High Atlas mountains at the southern end of the Ourika Valley road, 24km south of the Oukaïmeden turn-off at Aghbalou. Waterfall hikes range from an easy 20-minute stroll to arduous stream hikes; ignore the faux guides and follow the paths, or find a licenced guide to lead the way on foot or mule at the *bureau des guides*.

Prime times to visit are in early March when the cherry and almond trees are in bloom, or in August for the four-day moussem, with its fair and market at the *koubba* of Setti Fatma. During the summer the place is clogged with visitors from Marrakesh; our advice is to head instead to the splendidly untrammelled neighbouring valleys of Zat and Ouirgane.

🏃 Activities

Served by frequent buses and grands taxis, Setti Fatma is the most accessible High Atlas trekking base, although trailheads for many of the more impressive hikes lie on the other side of Tizi n'Tacheddirt pass (3230m) in Imlil. One popular hike has been to traverse the pass via the villages of Tadrart, Timichi, Tacheddirt and Ouaneskra, but now a paved road covers two-thirds of the route forcing trekkers to make a steeper two-day ascent to avoid walking along the road.

Other possible treks from Setti Fatma head east to Tourcht, north to Imi-n-Taddert, to Anammer and Tiz n'Oucheg in the Aït Oucheg Valley, and from the Yaggour Plateau into the Zat Valley (p96), the latter being the most impressive trek on offer. The bureau des guides (p99) can hook you up with licenced guides.

🛏️ Sleeping & Eating

From Oulmes to Setti Fatma, both sides of the river are lined with cafe-restaurants offering tajines priced to move. Two of the better choices in Setti Fatma proper are Café-Restaurant Imlil (near the parking at the end of town), and Café-Restaurant Azrrabzou (opposite the river) over a plank bridge in a patch of almond trees. Both offer set meals with salad, tajine/kebabs and bottled water for Dh50 to Dh60.

⭐ **Au Bord du l'Eau**　　　GUESTHOUSE €
(📞 0661 22 97 55; www.obordelo.com; d Dh250, ste Dh450-525; 🛜) This jaunty little guesthouse is tucked down a steep pebble staircase below the busy streets of Setti Fatma. As a result, it

is wonderfully secluded, with just the sound of the rushing river to disturb dreams of summit ascents. With Martine and Poulou's easygoing hosting and shared conversations around central fireplaces, you'll feel right at home. Rooms are kitted out with cute quilts, Berber rugs and personal knick-knacks. Bring a torch for night-time navigation.

Hôtel Asgaour　　　CAFE, GUESTHOUSE €
(📞 0524 48 52 94; tr without/with bathroom Dh150/200) Basic but clean rooms with lumpy pillows and hot showers upstairs, plus a restaurant downstairs serving well-caramelised tajines (Dh50 to Dh60).

ℹ️ Information

Bureau des Guides (📞 0524 42 61 13) Located 200m beyond the Hôtel Asgaour.

Pharmacy Asgaour (🕐 10am-8pm) A good selection of first aid, medicine and women's products.

Oukaïmeden　　　اوكيمدين

Best known as Morocco's ski resort, Oukaïmeden (elevation 2650m, 75km from Marrakesh) is also a High Atlas trekking destination, with outer-space landscapes, ancient petroglyphs and alpine wildflowers in spring; Club Alpin Français (CAF) can point you towards trailheads.

In snow season, skiers will find seven ski runs from nursery to black, six tows and the highest ski lift in Africa (3243m). Gear, passes and lessons are available in town at prices that will delight skiers used to European and American rates. Peak season has historically been late January to March, but in recent years snow has been scarce by March.

When snow is low on the slopes, skiers can cross-country ski.

🛏 Sleeping & Eating

CAF Refuge
HOSTEL €

(☏ 0524 31 90 36; https://tinyurl.com/lzvgx2k; dm CAF or HI members/nonmembers Dh80/130; 🛜) Offers heated dormitories, a bar-restaurant (breakfast/meal Dh25/110), a well-equipped kitchen, a library and wi-fi, but you'll need your own sleeping bag. Bathrooms are on the 1st floor, but the nicest bunk beds are in pine-ceilinged rooms upstairs. Kids under 16 are eligible for discounts (dorm bed members/nonmembers Dh42/65). They can arrange group pick-ups from Marrakesh (Dh400 by grand taxi or Dh700 to Dh900 for nine to 12 by minibus or 4WD).

Hôtel Chez Juju
HOTEL €€€

(☏ 0524 31 90 05; www.hotelchezjuju.com; d incl half board Dh1100-1580; 🛜) Reliable restaurant with a bar (whiskey and wine Dh60 to Dh120), plus simple alpine-style rooms with en-suite bathrooms. Nicer renovated doubles have mountain views, pine panelling, cotton quilts and flowered drapes; grimmer rooms out the back have frayed carpet and bathrooms curtained off in the corner.

Le Courchevel
FRENCH €€

(☏ 0524 31 90 95; www.lecourchevelouka.com; meals Dh80-200) With a long sun terrace and a cosy fireside bar, this is a good place for lunch and aprés-ski.

❶ Getting There & Away

If you're not travelling by rental car, your best bet is transport through CAF. Otherwise, you can charter a grand taxi from Marrakesh's Bab er-Rob (Dh400 to Dh600).

Toubkal National Park

For pure mountain air that cuts through the heat and leaves you giddy, don't miss the highest mountain in North Africa: snow-capped Jebel Toubkal (4167m), situated in the heart of the Toubkal National Park. Mountain trails criss-crossing Jebel Toubkal start from Imlil, which is located at the end of the Mizane Valley. On the way to Imlil, you could make a pit stop 47km south of Marrakesh at Asni for roadside tajines and the Saturday souq.

❶ Getting There & Away

Frequent local buses (Dh18, 1½ hours) and grands taxis (Dh20, one hour) leave south of Bab er-Rob in Marrakesh for Asni. Local minibuses and occasional taxis travel the final 17km between Asni and Imlil (Dh10, one hour). Expect a car journey from Marrakesh to Imlil to take at least 2½ hours.

BERBER BOTANY IN THE HIGH ATLAS

Despite icy winters and scalding summers, the High Atlas Mountains are extremely fertile. Overgrazing, agriculture and wood collection for fuel has impacted the High Atlas; much of its indigenous vegetation has disappeared. But through painstaking reforestation and resourceful mountainside terrace farming using *targa* (channel) irrigation, the hills are alive with a diversity of flora.

Here's what you'll spot on High Atlas walks:

Valleys Riots of flowers erupt in spring, when valley almond, cherry and apricot orchards bloom. In summer, you'll enjoy the shade of carob, quince, pomegranate, apple and fig trees. Resourceful farmers manage to eke multiple crops from terrace plots: barley October through to May, and potatoes, carrots, turnips, onions, lentils and beans from spring through to autumn. Walnuts are a major crop in higher villages, with harvest in late September.

Subalpine zone (2400m to 3200m) Thickets of gnarled Spanish juniper (*Juniperus thurifer*) are blasted into extraordinary shapes by the wind, and exposed roots cling like fingers to the rock. Aleppo pine is being planted to prevent erosion, and replace fragrant Atlas cedar used for woodworking.

High elevations The easiest to spot are 'hedgehog plants', spiny, domed bushes that briefly burst into flower in spring. Even when you don't spot plants on the trail, you'll get a whiff of lavender, rosemary and wild thyme underfoot, perfuming your boots as you walk.

Imlil إمليل

A favourite hitching post for mountain trekkers, Imlil (elevation 1740m) is just a five-hour hike from the base of Jebel Toubkal, and in spring you won't want to miss waking up in these flowering High Atlas foothills.

🏃 Activities

Imlil is the main trekking base for Jebel Toubkal and the whole town caters to trekkers and their needs. Ascents to the summit leave daily from here, although the traffic in high season may rub the edge off that lone-mountain-ranger fantasy. To escape the well-worn path consider trekking southwest over Tizi n'Mzik (2489m) to the wonderful Cascades d'Irhoulidene near Azib Tamsoult and either ascending the Toubkal summit from the west (covered on Day 6 and 7 of the Toubkal Circuit trek), or heading east down the unspoilt Azzadan Valley.

For those really short on time you can easily walk to the village of Aroumd and back in a couple of hours. Follow the mule track along the western edge of the Mizane river.

Bike Adventures in Morocco MOUNTAIN BIKING
(📱0666 23 82 00; www.bikeadventuresinmorocco. com; Imlil) Run by mountain guide and biking expert Lahcen Jellah, this well-equipped outfit offers a range of itineraries crisscrossing the Atlas. Routes range from an easy four-day Toubkal circuit to an epic 10-day Atlas traverse from Imlil to M'Goun.

Imlil Mountain Bike MOUNTAIN BIKING
(📱0661 82 02 65; www.imlil-mountain-bike.com; Imlil; ⊙9am-7pm) Located on your left as you pass Hôtel Etoile de Toubkal is this new bike outlet offering 16 good mountain bikes (Dh200 to Dh400 per day). Prices include helmet, gloves and pump. A guide will cost a further Dh500 per day.

Mountain Travel Morocco TREKKING
(📱0524 48 57 84; www.mountain-travel-morocco. com; Imlil; ⊙9am-6pm Mon-Sat) Established by four of Imlil's most experienced trekking guides, MTM is Imlil's first fully registered, private guiding outfit offering treks to suit all levels. Guides are trained in first aid and are experienced in dealing with altitude sickness. To ensure you can undertake the trek you want when you want, book in advance.

🛏 Sleeping

Imlil is full of *gîtes d'étape* and small hotels, but during high season (April and October) it's essential to book ahead; some places close between November and February. Additional options are available in nearby Aroumd, but the village has minimal facilities by comparison.

★Riad Atlas Toubkal GUESTHOUSE €
(📱0524 48 57 82; www.riadatlastoubkal.com; Imlil; d Dh250-400, ste Dh600; P❄🔊) This brand new guesthouse tucked behind the clinic is already in hot demand. No wonder: eight spacious rooms with large picture windows catch mountain breezes and boast views as fine as those at the pricey Kasbah. Iman graciously staffs a reception desk where piles of board games and books keep idle hours filled. Guest showers for sweaty trekkers, panoramic views from the restaurant and parking (Dh20 per night) complete the excellent service.

Imlil Lodge GUESTHOUSE €
(📱0671 15 76 36; www.toubkalguide.com; Tamatert; d Dh300-380, 6-person dm Dh550; ❄🔊) Run by Jamal Imrehane, one of the founders of Mountain Travel Morocco, this friendly stone-faced guesthouse looks out over Imlil and the Mizane Valley from Tamatert. Arranged around an internal courtyard, four riad-style rooms come with fancy stucco ceilings, brass lanterns and stripey Asni blankets. There's also a dormitory that sleeps six on three sturdy bunk beds. Needless to say, with one of the most experienced guides as your host, all your trekking needs are covered here.

Dar Ouassaggou RIAD €
(📱0667 49 13 52; www.guesthouseouassaggou. com; Douar Aït Soukka; d incl breakfast Dh320-400; ❄@) A walnut orchard shades the valley path east of Imlil to this eight-room guesthouse, where visitors are received like long-lost relatives by Houssein, an English-speaking mountain guide. The cosy, comfortable bedrooms here have en-suite bathrooms, one with a *tadelakt* tub. The sunny terrace is ideal after a morning trek, and internet and washing machines are available (Dh10).

Dar Adrar RIAD €
(📱0668 76 01 65; www.daradrar.com; Achayn; incl breakfast s/d without bathroom Dh130/200, r Dh300-370) Sitting in a shaded grove in the village of Achayn, a steep, five- to 10-minute

walk uphill from the Atlas Trek Shop in Imlil, Dar Adrar has simple, comfortable rooms, a flower-filled yard and an in-house hammam (Dh50). The owner, mountain guide Mohamed Aztat, is a co-founder of Mountain Travel Morocco and also owns the trek shop in Imlil.

CAF Refuge
HOSTEL €

(☏0524 48 56 12; https://tinyurl.com/n5mxdhs; dm CAF & HI members/nonmembers Dh60/80, camping incl shower per person/tent Dh25/15) A climbers' hostel offers dorm-style bunks, camping, cooking facilities, hot showers, picnics (Dh50), hot meals (Dh80) and baggage storage (Dh10 per day).

★ Douar Samra
RIAD €€

(☏0524 37 86 05; www.douar-samra.com; Tamatert; per person incl half board Dh450-660; ☏) At the east end of the valley in Tamatert, a trail zigzags among low-slung houses made of pisé; the triple-decker one is Douar Samra. Take the hewn stone steps to the candlelit, wood-beamed guest rooms. Donkeys deliver your luggage, but there's wi-fi in the organic garden and aperitifs with terrace sunsets.

Riad Dar Imlil
MAISON D'HÔTE €€€

(☏0524 48 49 17; www.darimlil.com; d Dh1300-1600; ❄☏) Marrakesh style heads for the mountains in this 20-room stone guesthouse. Bedrooms are comfortable and climate-controlled with hewn wood furnishings, wrought-iron windows and modern en-suite bathrooms with complimentary babouches and warm woollen jellabas (flowing garments). Cheaper rooms facing the courtyard are quieter but darker; there's in-room wi-fi, and dining on the terrace or by the salon fireplace.

Kasbah du Toubkal
KASBAH €€€

(☏0524 48 56 11; www.kasbahdutoubkal.com; dm incl breakfast Dh1460-1800, d Dh1800-2800, ste Dh3800-4950; ☏) ✔ This converted historic kasbah (1800m) lords it over Imlil with views of snowy peaks and verdant valleys. The 11 bedrooms range from quaintly cute to kasbah cool, and 'Berber salons' allow families and groups to bunk communally. At guests' disposal are a traditional hammam, mountain guides, board games, wi-fi and tasty meals (Dh165 to Dh300). Two nights minimum; a 5% community tariff has helped build three boarding schools and supply two ambulances.

✗ Eating

Hôtel Etoile de Toubkal
PIZZERIA, MOROCCAN €

(☏0524 48 56 18; meals Dh70-120) Tiled tables in the garden at this downtown hotel offer a tranquil dining retreat. Aside from the standard selection of tajines, you can also order Imlil's only pizza (Dh45 to Dh60).

Patisserie La Maison des Association
PATISSERIE €

(☉10am-7pm) Follow your nose to this tiny pastry shop opposite Imlil Mountain Bike for melt-in-your-mouth, almond-flavoured biscuits and honey sweets baked daily by Berber village girls at this local association. Supported by the Kasbah du Toubkal, the association helps local villagers learn and perfect new skills.

❶ Information

Bureau Des Guides (☏0524 48 56 26; bureau.guides@yahoo.fr; ☉8am-7pm) This information bureau is open daily during the season. If you arrive without having made arrangements, head here and let them know your requirements and they'll hook you up with a guide for a fixed-price rate (Dh300/400 per half/full day). Guides speak a range of languages, including French, English and Spanish.

Aroumd

For Berber hospitality above the trekker fray, head 3km up to the hilltop village of Aroumd (aka Armed), at 1960m. You could take the drivable piste from Imlil, but the walking path passes a burbling stream, stone houses and shady orchards.

🛏 Sleeping & Eating

Les Roches Armed/Chez Lahcen
RIAD €

(☏0667 64 49 15; dm Dh60, d per person incl half board Dh180) Atop Aroumd, guests enjoy 360-degree mountain views, admire courtyard gardens and chat by the living-room fireplace before retreating to private rooms with tataoui (woven palm) ceilings or clean dorms. Five shared bathrooms come with hot showers, and hearty High Atlas cooking comes served on Berber crockery.

Dar Warawt/Chez Omar Jellah
RIAD €

(☏0667 41 46 23; omarjellah@yahoo.co.uk; per person Dh50) Ideal for families trekking together, this guesthouse is a fully equipped apartment downstairs from the family home of English-speaking guide Omar Jellah. Through arched doorways are a salon, stucco-edged bedrooms and an enviable kitchen. You can cook here, or arrange meals (Dh100).

Camping-Auberge Atlas Toubkal/ Chez Omar le Rouge CAMPGROUND, INN €
(⏱ 0524 48 57 50; www.trekkingatlasmorocco.com; half board per person Dh50, camping per person Dh20; ⓟ) Hillside campsite with parking (Dh10), or basic rooms with communal facilities, including hot showers (Dh10) and meals (breakfast/tajine Dh20/50).

Jebel Toubkal Ascent تساق جبل توبقال

North Africa's tallest peak, **Jebel Toubkal** (4167m), doesn't require climbing experience. In summer, anyone in good physical condition can reach the summit. In early October runners of the **Toubkal Marathon** (www.toubkaltrail.com) scamper 42km up and down Jebel Toubkal. For extreme ultramarathoners, the organisers tacked a 106km High Atlas trail onto the marathon, calling it the **Toubkal Trail**.

Although the 3313m ascent from Imlil isn't technically difficult, challenges include Toubkal's fast-changing climate, steep slopes of volcanic scree and altitude sickness. Hikers should factor in sufficient time to ascend slowly and steadily; for a more leisurely ascent, camp en route at Sidi Chamharouch. An ascent of Toubkal can be combined with satellite peaks, and very fit trekkers ascend **Ouanoukrim** (4088m) as well.

THE TREK AT A GLANCE

Duration two days

Distance 22km

Standard medium to hard

Start/Finish Imlil village

Highest Point Jebel Toubkal (4167m)

Accommodation camping and mountain *refuges*

Public Transport Yes

Summary The most popular walk in the High Atlas, with magnificent views. The route is straightforward, but the trek up the scree slope is hard, and trekkers can be struck with altitude sickness. The trek is best in summer and autumn, but check conditions before departure – there can be snow even in June.

DAY 1: IMLIL TO TOUBKAL REFUGE
DURATION FIVE TO SIX HOURS / DISTANCE 10KM / ASCENT 1467M

Ideally leave **Imlil** early morning – it's uphill all the way, with little shade past Aroumd. Follow the dirt track leading to **Aroumd** (Armed) past the **Kasbah du Toubkal**. Beyond the kasbah, the path zigzags steeply upwards to rejoin the road at Aroumd, where towering slopes begin to close around you.

Past Aroumd, cross the stony valley floor and follow the well-defined mule trail uphill towards a very large rock above the eastern side of the Assif Reraya, which leads to the hamlet and *marabout* of **Sidi Chamharouch** (2310m). Beyond the *marabout* to the left of the track are cascades, pools and a prime picnic spot in the shady overhang of the rocks.

After crossing the river by the bridge at Sidi Chamharouch, the rocky path veers away from the river for 2km and zigzags above the valley floor. It then levels off, before rejoining the course of the river. The **Toubkal Refuge** is visible for an hour before you reach it, immediately below the western flank of Jebel Toubkal.

DAY 2: THE ASCENT
DURATION NINE HOURS / DISTANCE 12KM / ASCENT & DESCENT 960M

Set off as early as possible to avoid climbing in the sun – there is no shade, only rocks – and be sure to dress warmly and pack extra water and snacks. If you've trekked here directly from Imlil you may not be acclimatised, so walk at a steady, slow pace to avoid altitude sickness. If you experience severe headache or vomiting, descend immediately. However tempting, do not lie down to sleep on the slope.

Two cwms (valleys formed by glacial activity) run down the western flank of Toubkal, divided by the west-northwest ridge, which leads down from the summit. The southern cwm is the more usual route, and starts immediately below the *refuge* to the left, where you cross the river and head eastwards up the scree slope.

Start to climb the well-defined path to the left of the slope, cross the field of boulders, then follow the path that zigzags up to **Tizi n'Toubkal** (3940m), straight ahead on the skyline. From there the path turns left (northeast) and follows the ridge to the summit (4167m). Allow up to four hours to reach the top, depending on your fitness and weather conditions.

BEFORE YOU GO: JEBEL TOUBKAL ASCENT CHECKLIST

Maps The same maps are recommended as for the Toubkal Circuit (p106).

Water Purifying locally sourced water is a responsible alternative to bottled water, but don't count on finding available water sources between June and October.

Guide Although the route is marked, a guide (p102) is recommended for the ascent, especially for inexperienced mountaineers and in variable conditions from October to June.

Food Meals and snacks are available at Toubkal Refuge and Refuge Mouflon, but you can also find lunch supplies in Imlil and a wide selection of portable snacks in Marrakesh supermarkets.

Mule For this two-day trek with limited gear requirements, most experienced trekkers won't require a mule. If you want one, guides can organise mules and muleteers for you.

Gear Bring a sleeping bag. You won't need a tent, unless you'd rather camp than stay at *refuges* – just ask your guide to arrange tents in advance.

Stick to the same route coming down, bearing left when the *refuge* comes into view. The descent to the *refuge* should only take 2½ hours, after which you can return to Aroumd or Imlil. If you are planning on spending a second night at the *refuge,* you could come down the longer route via the Ihibi sud, or south circuit. It's a straightforward four-hour walk down to the *refuge* for well-earned congratulations and celebratory chocolate.

Toubkal Circuit جولة جبل توبقال

Beyond the majestic peaks and fabulous views of Jebel Toubkal, this circuit offers fascinating glimpses into Berber life in remote High Atlas villages. You will need camping gear for this route, though with short detours you could use basic village accommodation and mountain *refuges*.

Since this trek is fairly strenuous, you might want an extra rest day. The ascent of Jebel Toubkal takes place on the sixth day, allowing five days of acclimatisation to altitude. Most of the route is above 2000m, with several passes over 3000m.

Late April to late June is ideal: alpine flowers bloom April to May, and by June daytime temperatures often drop below freezing November to May, and snow covers higher peaks and passes. Only lower-valley walking is possible during this season, unless you're prepared to bring ropes and crampons.

Midsummer guarantees long daylight hours and snow-free passes (though not always a snow-free Toubkal), but in the lower valleys temperatures can be extremely hot and water nonexistent. July and August are the busiest months in the High Atlas, but

trekking is best done early morning and later in the afternoon.

Flash flooding can occur in summer after thunderstorms – something to bear in mind when deciding where to camp. Rivers have maximum flow in autumn (November) and late spring (April or May).

DAY 1: IMLIL TO TACHEDDIRT
DURATION 3½ TO 4½ HOURS / DISTANCE 9.5KM / ASCENT 560M

Much of day one's relatively gentle route follows the road linking Imlil (1740m) to the village of Ouaneskra, 2km west of Tacheddirt (2300m). The road climbs gently eastwards zigzagging up to Aït Souka.

After an hour, just past a stream known as Talat n'Aït Souka, you can either take the road north directly to the pass at Tizi n'Tamatert (2279m), or follow a fairly well defined but rocky path east, skirting Tamatert village. The rocky path continues eastwards for 15 minutes, passing through a small pine grove and crossing the road, before climbing steeply northeast to reach Tizi n'Tamatert. The walk up takes 30 to 45 minutes.

At the pass is Bivi Thé, a weather-beaten shack selling pricey soft drinks. To the northeast are great views of Tizi n'Eddi (2960m), the pass leading to Oukaïmeden, and Tizi n'Tacheddirt (3130m).

The path and tarmac meet at Tizi n'Tamatert, where it's an easy 45-minute walk to Ouaneskra. Along this stretch you'll be treated to views across the valley to neat Berber houses and lush terraces in Talate n'Chaoute, Tamguist and Ouaneskra.

Shortly before Ouaneskra, the path divides. The mule track to the right traverses the southern side of the valley to an ideal camping place near the track, close to the Irhzer n'Likemt stream and the starting place for tomorrow's climb.

The longer route via Ouaneskra and Tacheddirt takes the northern side of the valley after crossing Tizi n'Tamatert. There are three *gîtes* in Ouaneskra and a pleasant little restaurant – but tomorrow's walk is long, so it's best to have lunch and carry on. The village of Tacheddirt is 2km further along the tarmac road. In Tacheddirt, 50 people can sleep at Tigmi n Tacheddirt (📞0662 10 51 69; www.highatlaslodges.com; per person incl half board & shared/private bathroom Dh180/200). From Tacheddirt, the hiking track loops south, up to the campsite near Irhzer n'Likemt.

DAY 2: TACHEDDIRT TO AZIB LIKEMT
DURATION FIVE TO SIX HOURS / DISTANCE 9KM / ASCENT 1200M / DESCENT 900M

Leave Tacheddirt early to make the two- to three-hour walk up to Tizi Likemt (3550m), winding around the head of the valley on a more gentle ascent instead of heading straight down and across the Assif n'Imenane and up past the campsite. Though the walk is mostly shaded by mountain shadows in the morning, it's a hard climb, especially a very steep scree slope towards the top.

Close to the campsite, a well-defined rocky path heads up the centre of the gully on the east side of the riverbed (though it

THE TREK AT A GLANCE

Duration seven to 10 days

Distance 60.2km

Standard medium to hard

Start/Finish Imlil village

Highest Point Jebel Toubkal (4167m)

Accommodation camping, village *gîtes* and mountain *refuges*

Public Transport yes

Summary Easily accessible from Marrakesh, this circuit around (and up) Jebel Toubkal passes through landscapes ranging from lush, cultivated valleys and Berber villages to forbidding peaks and bleak passes. This is a demanding trek, with long, gruelling climbs over rocky terrain. A guide is highly recommended, fitness essential.

crosses over twice). It climbs for about 50 minutes before bearing left (southeast) up to the col (pass). Atop Tizi Likemt are views of verdant valleys and jagged peaks, including Oukaïmeden and Jebel Toubkal on clear days.

The rocky path leading down the other side (southeast) passes a semipermanent water source on the left after 30 minutes, and irrigated pastures above Azib Likemt after another hour. An *azib* is a summer settlement, and Azib Likemt (2650m) is occupied from May through October by local people growing crops on irrigated terraces.

You may be offered shelter or a place to pitch your tent in Azib Likemt. Otherwise, walk through terraces down to the Assif Tifni, cross the river, turn right and walk upstream to a group of large boulders, where you'll find a flat campsite close to the river.

DAY 3: AZIB LIKEMT TO AMSOUZERT
DURATION SIX TO 6½ HOURS / DISTANCE 15.2KM / ASCENT 470M / DESCENT 1380M

This direct route south to Amsouzert is less demanding, but offers some good ridge walking. From Azib Likemt, the well-worn trail leads behind the campsite south, up the mountainside and into the tremendous gorge formed by Assif n'Tinzer. Above the river's eastern bank, the trail snakes above the Tombe Asmine waterfall before descending close to the river. Follow the river for about two hours past stunning cliffs and through wide pastures, until an obvious track leads up the valley to Tizi n'Ououraïne (3120m; also known as Tizi n'Ouaraï) and brilliant views of the eastern face of Toubkal, Dôme d'Ifni (3876m) and the rest of the jagged Toubkal massif.

Continue over the col, where the trail traverses the head of the valley to a spur and trail crossroads. Heading southwest, a trail leads down the ridge to Tagadirt (after 50m there's a fantastic viewpoint south to Jebel Siroua), but turn left (southeast) and follow the mule track south. Traverse the head of another valley and along the side of a spur to reach the ridge after 90 minutes; Lac d'Ifni is visible to the west. After a further 15 minutes, just before two pointed outcrops, the path forks. Turn right and continue descending slowly southwards to a large cairn. Descend southwest, then west down the end of the spur to Amsouzert (1797m) in 30 minutes.

Amsouzert is a prosperous village spread on both sides of the river. If you're planning a rest day, this is an excellent place to take

BEFORE YOU GO: TOUBKAL CIRCUIT CHECKLIST

Maps The 1:50,000 sheet map *Jebel Toubkal* covers the whole Toubkal Circuit and is sometimes available through the *bureau des guides* (p102) in Imlil. Four-sheet, 1:100,000 topographical *Toubkal Massif Walking Map* also covers the circuit, produced by the Division de la Cartographie (Moroccan Survey) and obtainable from its office in Rabat, in London at Stanfords (p94) or in Marrakesh on the Djemaa el-Fna at Hotel Ali (Dh150). Government-produced 1:100,000 *Cartes des Randonnées dans le Massif du Toubkal* marks trekking routes but includes less topographical detail.

Guide Engage licenced guides at Imlil's *bureau des guides* (p102). Allow at least a day to hire a guide and make trekking arrangements – though if you have specific needs or are travelling in high season, it may take more time.

Mule Mountain guides can organise mules and muleteers for you. Trekkers should be aware that mules have problems crossing Tizi n'Ouanoums, west of Lac d'Ifni, and from November to June, some areas may be impassable. If mules have to take lengthy detours, you may need to carry one day's kit and food. Talk this through with your guide and muleteer.

Food Basic food supplies are available in Imlil, and trail mixes, packaged soups and other light, portable food is stocked by Marrakesh supermarkets.

Water Purifying locally sourced water is a responsible alternative to bottled water, but don't count on finding available water sources – pack plenty of water.

Gear A stick or trekking pole is useful. Petrol, diesel and kerosene can be bought in Marrakesh or Asni.

Tent Your guide can arrange tents. The circuit outlined here requires some camping, but you could add detours to seek out lodging, or possibly do without tents in summer.

it. Next to the school is an outdoor tearoom shaded by an enormous walnut tree where you may be able to **camp** (per tent Dh20). Otherwise, you can stay at **Gîte Himmi Omar** (dm Dh50, tajine Dh30).

In Amsouzert are small shops, a couple of cafes west of the river and early morning transport to the N10 highway connecting Marrakesh and Ouarzazate. About 3km south of Amsouzert is another village called Imlil (not to be confused with the Imlil trailhead on the northern side of the range), which hosts a wildly popular **Wednesday souq**.

DAY 4: AMSOUZERT TO AZIB IMI N'OUASSIF

DURATION 5½ TO SIX HOURS / DISTANCE 10.5KM / ASCENT 1100M

Between November and June, mules won't make it much beyond Lac d'Ifni, the largest lake in the High Atlas, so you'll have to carry your kit to Azib Imi n'Ouassif over **Tizi n'Ouanoums** (3600m) to Toubkal Refuge.

From Amsouzert follow the level, well-used 4WD track that continues northwest towards Lac d'Ifni above the north side of the river. The path takes you through the villages of **Ibrouane**, **Takatert** and **Tisgouane** before reaching **Aït Igrane**, where

there are a couple of cafes and **Gîte Belaïde** (dm Dh50). There is also a shady **campsite** (Dh30) on a flat, stony site just beyond the Café Toubkal, with a cold shower and toilet.

Follow the 4WD track along the riverbed northwest out of Aït Igrane, picking up the narrow rocky mule path where the 4WD track crosses the river then turns sharp left. The mule path leads around the north side of **Lac d'Ifni** (2295m), across sharp, rocky, barren, inhospitable terrain. The climb is steep at first, but it descends to the northeastern corner of Lac d'Ifni, an inviting expanse of green water (safe for swimming). The walk to the lake should take three hours. Before you reach the shore, you will pass a **shack** marked 'café'. There's no coffee here, but if it's attended you may be able to buy water, soft drinks and, with any luck, a tajine.

On the small beach on the northern shore are shady (if occasionally fly-filled) **stone shelters**. If it's rainy, camping nearer the next pass is treacherous, and you're better off finding a campsite above the lake.

Every October, villagers from the surrounding area gather at Lac d'Ifni for a three-day *moussem* in honour of a local *marabout,* whose tomb, **Sidi n'Ifni,** sits high above the southeastern corner of the lake. A track leads from the northeast shore up to the tomb.

From the northwestern side of the lake, the track crosses the wide, dry part of Lac d'Ifni before the long trudge towards Tizi n'Ouanoums. The path climbs through a rocky gorge, keeping to the south side of the river. About 3.5km from the lake, you'll reach **Azib Imi n'Ouassif** (2841m), situated at a crossing of dramatic gorges. Beyond this point the path climbs steeply to Tizi n'Ouanoums, with winds near the summit and small, frigid waterfalls. You'll find flat, rocky areas for pitching tents and shelters in surrounding cliffs long used by local shepherds.

DAY 5: AZIB IMI N'OUASSIF TO TOUBKAL REFUGE

DURATION FOUR HOURS / DISTANCE 4KM / ASCENT 759M / DESCENT 393M

The path to Tizi n'Ouanoums is immediately northwest of the campsite. It's a steep, de-

manding climb, but the views are spectacular from the top over **Assif n'Moursaïne**, hemmed in by jagged ridges of **Adrar bou Ouzzal** and **Ouimeksane**. The path crosses the river several times after leaving the camp, reaching a stone shelter and water source after an hour and the col another hour further. Even in midsummer it's cold and blustery at the top.

Coming down the other side, there's treacherous loose rock and snow until July. From here you can see Jebel Toubkal and, to the west, the path to **Tizi n'Melloul** (3875m). After the descent, the track levels out and heads due north to Toubkal Refuge (3207m), about two hours from Tizi n'Ouanoums.

CAF's **Toubkal Refuge** (☎ 0661 69 54 63; www.refugedutoubkal.com; dm CAF members/HI members/nonmembers Dh60/80/130), sometimes labelled Neltner on maps, suffers from overcrowding, damp and a lack of facilities. The newer **Refuge Mouflon** (☎ 0661 21 33 45; www.refugetoubkal.com; dm Dh140, half board

Toubkal Summit & Circuit Trek

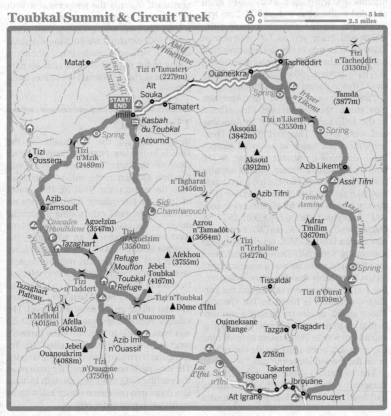

per person Dh319) provides more facilities, a better-stocked shop and good meals (Dh90) in the chilly lounge. You can also camp downstream from the *refuge* or 20 minutes south of the *refuge* on flat pasture (Dh20).

Assuming you reach the *refuge* before lunch, there are trekking options to occupy the afternoon – including the three- or four-hour descent directly north back to the starting point, Imlil, if you don't want to climb Jebel Toubkal. You could ascend the second-highest mountain in the region, Jebel Ouanoukrim (4088m, five to six hours return). The best option is to rest all afternoon to prepare for the climb up Jebel Toubkal the following morning.

DAY 6: TOUBKAL REFUGE TO AZIB TAMSOULT

DURATION FIVE HOURS / DISTANCE 8KM / ASCENT 493M / DESCENT 1300M

From the Toubkal Refuge pick up the mule track that heads northwest then gently climbs north across the slope for about 15 minutes. You will come to a fork near a small rounded wall, used as a sheepfold. Turn left, westwards, up the zigzagging mule path, which will bring you to Tizi n'Aguelzim (3560m) after two hours. It's a slower trail but less treacherous than the southern route at Tizi n'Taddert, which is often abruptly closed due to dangerous conditions.

Panoramic views await at Tizi n'Aguelzim pass: east to the Toubkal summit, northeast to the Imlil valley, northwest to Azzadene and west to the Tazaghart plateau. From here, the track twists in some 92 hairpin bends downhill for almost an hour. At the bottom, it crosses a stream. Twenty minutes further on, at a fork, take the left-hand track, and take another left 15 minutes later. Here the track leads uphill for 10 minutes to cosy CAF Tazaghart Refuge (☎ 0667 85 27 54, Oukaïmeden 0524 31 90 36; dm CAF/HI members/ nonmembers Dh60/80/130), which sits beside a stunning waterfall. There are mattresses for 22 people, gaslights and a basic kitchen. You'll probably find the place closed unless you've made a reservation, and the *gardien* (attendant) is based in Tizi Oussem. Phone ahead, or else try passing a message to him via muleteers or shepherds, who may run all the way to Tizi Oussem to fetch him. Campers can pitch tents beside the *refuge*, or on flat ground above the falls.

Tizi n'Melloul (3875m), southeast of Tazaghart *refuge*, offers a harder route to and from the Toubkal Refuge, but provides access to Afella (4045m) southeast of the pass and to the jagged ridge leading north to Biginoussen.

The route down to Azib Tamsoult (2400m) passes the impressive Cascades d'Irhoulidene, where vegetation and tree coverage increases. A five-minute walk from the falls brings you to a pleasant wooded area for camping. To reach the village, walk north for 10 to 15 minutes.

DAY 7: AZIB TAMSOULT TO IMLIL

DURATION FOUR TO FIVE HOURS / DISTANCE 7KM / ASCENT 89M / DESCENT 749M

If you have made good time and you have the legs, you could continue down to Imlil at the end of day six. From the vegetable patches of Azib Tamsoult, with the Assif n'Ouarzane down to the left, a mule track traversing the forested valley is visible to the north. Head towards it past the village and over the stream, and stay on it, avoiding left forks into the valley.

Climbing slightly and heading steadily northeast, towards the juniper forest with Tizi Oussem due west, you arrive at Tizi n'Mzik (2489m), where a sheep shed might serve as shelter. Imlil is a 90-minute descent along a well-worn mule track; there's a spring to the right of the trail after 40 minutes. Comfortable beds and hot tajines await in Imlil.

Tizi n'Test

Blasted through the mountains by the French in the late 1920s, the awe-inspiring road over the Tizi n'Test pass (2092m) was the first modern route linking Marrakesh with the Souss plain. Vital for the control of trade its hair-raising hairpin bends offer one of the most exhilarating panoramic drives in the country. As if the single-lane road weren't enough of an adventure, the weather is subject to sudden changes. Heavy clouds and mist often cut visibility to near zero and you might find your way blocked by snow in winter.

Heading south from Marrakesh, you'll see Tin Mal village on the right of the road. The village's Almohad-era mosque (tip Dh10-20) was built in 1156 in honour of the dynasty's strict spiritual leader, Mohammed ibn Tumart, and it remains an architectural wonder. The mosque is no longer used for prayers, so the guardian will usher you through its massive doors into the serene prayer hall with its intricately carved cedar ceilings.

Beyond Tin Mal, as you approach the pass, you may suddenly break through fog into clear blue sky, and catch breathtaking airplane-window views over cloudbanks. On the south side of the pass, the van ominously embedded into the hillside is your cue for a pit stop at Cafe Dar Issouga (☎0670 10 65 21; tajine Dh60-90). The balcony offers stunning valley views of green terraces and cypress forests cascading down the hillside all the way to Taroudannt.

THE SOUTHERN OASES

Break through the granite curtain of the High Atlas over the Tizi n'Tichka pass and you'll find yourself descending from forested slopes into the flat, stony landscape of Morocco's pre-Sahara. Cypress, juniper and apple blossom quickly give way to thorny acacias and palm trees that flash in sudden bursts of green against a backdrop of mudbrick kasbahs and secretive *ksours* (fortified villages). Snaking through the great *hammada* (stony desert) down to the sandy fringes of the Sahara proper are the southern oases – the Drâa, Dadès and Ziz – long green river valleys thick with date palms that once served the caravan routes to Timbuktu, Niger and Sudan.

The hub of the region is the administrative centre of Ouarzazate, from where you can embark on excursions south through the Drâa to M'Hamid and the impressive Erg Chigaga dunefield, or east via Skoura along the Dadès Valley to Merzourga and the smaller dunefield of Erg Chebbi.

Tizi n'Tichka

Higher than Tizi n'Test to the west but an easier drive along the N9, the Tizi n'Tichka pass (2260m) connects Marrakesh with the southern oases. It was built to bypass the old caravan route to the Drâa, which meandered through the Ounilla Valley and was controlled throughout the nineteenth century by the powerful Glaoui clan.

If you have a date with the desert, you can make it over Tizi n'Tichka from Marrakesh within three hours. As you pass Aït Ourir, the road ascends and takes a turn for the scenic amid oak trees and walnut groves. Past the village of Taddert, the road gets steeper and the landscape is stripped of colour, except for hardy wildflowers and kids along the road selling geodes dyed shocking red. In winter, check with the Gendarmerie of the Col du Tichka (☎0524 89 06 15) that the pass is open.

Once over the pass, you can choose one of two routes to Ouarzazate: the quicker journey is to continue along the N9, while the more scenic route takes you via the splendid Glaoui Kasbah in Telouet and the lush green Ounilla Valley all the way to Aït Benhaddou. You'll find the turn-off to Telouet on the south side of the road some 20km after the pass. While the road is pockmarked and bumpy, it is possible to navigate all 36km to Aït Benhaddou with a 2WD. The worst section of road is the 11km stretch between Telouet and Anmiter.

🛏 Sleeping & Eating

⭐ I Rocha   MAISON D'HÔTE €€
(☎0667 73 70 02; www.irocha.com; Douar Tisselday; d per person incl half board Dh460; ✦) This cliffside stone guesthouse, on the N9 road from Marrakesh to Ouarzazate, lifts travel-worn spirits above the green river valley. Ten sunny, cream-coloured rooms have easy-going Berber charm, with wood-beamed ceilings, plush local carpets and *beldi*-tiled bathrooms. Owners Ahmed and Katherine make terrific French-Moroccan dishes with herbs fresh from the terrace garden.

Dar Isselday   GUESTHOUSE €€
(☎0666 17 48 81; www.dar-isselday.com; Douar Tisselday; s/d Dh340/500) Prepared with love, Najat's traditional lunches are served on Dar Isselday's panoramic terrace beneath the shade of a pink peppercorn tree. Inside, six comfortable rooms sport *tadelakt* bathrooms, and brothers Kamal and Lahcen are on hand to lead interesting walks through the family orchards and to nearby quartz mines. You'll find the house just down the hill from I Rocha on the N9 Marrakesh–Ouarzazate road.

Telouet   تلوات

Telouet occupied a privileged position as the birthplace of French collaborator and autocrat Pasha Glaoui, until he was ousted in 1953 by the Moroccan independence movement. Legend has it that when the imposing doors of Telouet's Glaoui kasbah were thrown open at last, locals who had mysteriously disappeared from their villages years before stumbled dazed onto Telouet streets, after years locked in the pasha's basement.

Telouet also once had a thriving Jewish community, entrusted by the Glaoui with managing the all-important salt trade. Salt mines are still active in the area; prized pink salt found along the nearby Oued Mellah (Salt River) was once accepted as currency.

Near the Glaoui Kasbah is what remains of an ancient slave village. But Morocco's government remains ambivalent about the Glaoui clan's home town, and with little outside investment and a highway bypassing the town entirely, Telouet seems arrested in time half a century ago.

Narrow river-valley oases beyond Telouet are lined with crumbling Glaoui kasbahs, gorges riddled with caves, and ancient fortified villages such as Anmiter (11km east of Telouet), which has two well-preserved red kasbahs and a historic mellah.

◉ Sights & Activities

★ **Glaoui Kasbah**   HISTORIC SITE
(admission Dh20) The once-glorious stronghold has been left to crumble, and the best indication of Telouet's former position as the centre of a trans-Saharan trading empire is the 2nd-floor reception rooms. No less than 300 artisans worked on salons faceted with stucco, *zellij* and painted cedar ceilings that make Marrakesh's royal Bahia Palace seem like a freshman artisan effort. After independence, Pasha Glaoui was ousted from the Bahia Palace and died shortly thereafter of cancer in exile in Telouet.

**Baraka Community
Partnerships**   VOLUNTEERING
(www.barakacommunity.com) In cooperation with the Tighza Village Association, UK NGO Baraka Partnerships offers volunteer vacations in the remote, rural village of Tighza (16km east of Telouet). Current long-term projects involve the replacement of 2km of irrigation channels and larger groups can assist with tree planting. The work is funded through donations (Dh350 and upwards depending on the project), which can be made locally or through the website.

⌖ Sleeping & Eating

Restaurants around Telouet's central square serve simple Dh40 tajines and Dh30 Berber omelettes (with tomato, olives and herbs).

Dar Aissa   GÎTE D'ÉTAPE €
(☑0670 22 22 47; www.maisondhotesdaraissa telouet.com; Telouet; per person incl breakfast/half board Dh120/200; @) In downtown Tel-

ouet, this simple guesthouse offers clean, mattress-on-floor accommodation in pink and yellow rooms with modern shared bathrooms.

★ **Riad Kasbah Oliver**   GUESTHOUSE €€
(☑0524 89 18 28; www.homestaysmorocco.net; Tighza; per person adult/child 6-12yr Dh300/100) Owned by Tighza native Mohamed El Qasemy and his British wife, Carolyn, Riad Kasbah Oliver is a labour of love. Built by hand in stone and earth by local village craftspeople, the result is simple, sustainable accommodation. Doors were fashioned in Telouet and furniture up-cycled, and hot showers are solar-powered. Walking tours, salt-mine visits, souq trips and tea with local villagers are just some of the activities that can be arranged.

You'll find the turn-off to Tighza 11km east of Telouet, from where it is a 5km drive on *piste* to the village.

Le Lion d'Or Atlas   MOROCCAN €
(☑0524 88 85 07; meals Dh120) Take a seat on the terrace overlooking the valley and order a tajine with Telouet's speciality figs. You'll find the restaurant on your left 500m from the kasbah.

ⓘ Getting There & Away

From the N9 Marrakesh–Ouarzazate Rd, the turn-off to Telouet is signed 20km beyond the pass. There's a daily bus from Bab Gehmat in Marrakesh (Dh50), which returns to Marrakesh at 7am. Grands taxis are Dh70 per seat, but you might get stuck renting out all six seats. There are no buses from Ouarzazate, only taxis.

Aït Benhaddou   آيت بنحدو

Like certain Botoxed stars, this Unesco-protected kasbah seems suspiciously frozen in time: with Hollywood touch-ups, it still resembles its days in the 11th century as an Almoravid caravanserai. Movie buffs may recognise this red mudbrick kasbah 32km from Ouarzazate from *Lawrence of Arabia*, *Jesus of Nazareth* (for which much of Aït Benhaddou was rebuilt), *Jewel of the Nile* (note the Egyptian towers) and *Gladiator*.

If you're headed to the desert, Aït Benhaddou is a worthy detour for a tasty lunch and kasbah stroll. From the Hôtel la Kasbah, head down past the souvenir stalls to the kasbah across the parched Oued Ounilla riverbed. But where are all the people? The few remaining residents make a few dirham providing access through their family homes to the **kasbah** (customary tip Dh10). Climb the kasbah to a ruined **agadir** (fortified granary) with magnificent views of the surrounding *palmeraie* and unforgiving *hammada*.

A less retouched kasbah can be found 6km north along the tarmac from Aït Benhaddou: the **Tamdaght kasbah** (tip to caretaker Dh10), a crumbling Glaoui fortification topped by storks' nests.

🛏 Sleeping

Auberge Ayouze
B&B €

(🕿 0524 88 37 57; www.auberge-ayouze.com; GPS coordinates N 31°04,066 W 007°08,526; s/d/q Dh180/260/370; P@☎) Located in the village of Asfalou, 3km north of Aït Benhaddou, Zoé and Abderrahmane's B&B is a haven from the tourist throngs. The simple, rustic style and practical, good-value rooms make this a great place for families and single travellers. Plan to stay a while so you can enjoy mountain hikes, river walks and treks to Aït Benhaddou and Tamdaght. Advance reservations are recommended.

Auberge Baghdad Cafe
GUESTHOUSE €€

(🕿 0524 88 25 06; www.auberge-baghdad-cafe.com; d incl breakfast/half board Dh430/610; P❄☎☎) The friendly Baghdad Cafe is well known for its good food – a few, simple homecooked dishes done to a high standard – but it also has jaunty rooms decked out with rattan-framed beds, rag rugs and bright, modernist bed linens. It's probably the best-value accommodation in town. You'll find it on your left on the main drag past Riad Makhtoub.

Etoile Filante d'Or
GUESTHOUSE €€

(🕿 0524 89 03 22; www.etoilefilantedor.com; d incl breakfast/half board Dh440/605; ❄@☎) Moonlit desert nights on the Etoile's roof terrace lure guests out of 19 spacious rooms for movie-script-inspiring kasbah views. Guest rooms feature traditional touches (*tataoui* ceilings, Berber blankets). The guesthouse also has wi-fi and à la carte lunches (meals Dh60 to Dh90). Trust Moroccan-French hosts Hind and Aurélien to organise dromedary rides, picnics and bike tours.

★ Kasbah Ellouze
KASBAH €€€

(🕿 0524 89 04 59; www.kasbahellouze.com; Tamdaght; incl half board s Dh765, d Dh965, ste Dh1400; ❄@☎☎) Located 6km north of Aït Benhaddou in the village of Tamdaght, this

THE OUNILLA VALLEY

Travellers equipped with a sturdy 2WD or 4WD, mountain bikes or good walking shoes can follow the ancient desert caravan routes from Telouet to Aït Benhaddou through the splendid **Ounilla Valley**. Although the first 12km is bumpy and slow going, the remaining 25km to Tamdaght is on good graded *piste*. The fascinating route follows the course of the Oued Mellah passing through **Anmiter** (whose red-tower kasbah gives a glimpse of what Aït Benhaddou may have looked like in its original state), Assaka, Tizgui and other picturesque villages dotting the **Gorge Assaka**. Exiting the Ounilla Valley to the south, you'll spot **limestone threshing terraces** notched into an east-facing hillside. In harvest season, you'll see villagers threshing grain on these stone platforms, just as they've done for centuries.

pisé guesthouse blends in with the adjacent kasbah. The best rooms have orchard views (*luz* means almonds), especially stylish doubles by the heated pool. Guests gather in the kitchen to learn to make local bread, for aperitifs and wi-fi in the jazz salon, and for watercolour-painting excursions into the Ounilla and Drâa Valleys.

🍴 Eating

Chez Brahim
MOROCCAN €

(🕿 0671 81 63 12; meals Dh70; ☺10am-9pm) Sure, there are other tajines in town, but only Brahim's improve international relations: the chef/owner has a letter from Hilary Rodham Clinton thanking him for a meal in her First Lady days. The set menu includes salads, tajine and dessert in a pisé-walled salon with Kasbah views.

Auberge Cafe-Restaurant Bilal
MOROCCAN €

(🕿 0668 24 83 70; ☺10am-9pm) For lunch or tea with a view, pull up a patio chair and gaze at Aït Benhaddou across the way. À la carte options include omelettes (Dh35), couscous (Dh50) and kebabs (Dh60).

ℹ Getting There & Away

To get here from Ouarzazate take the main road towards Marrakesh to the signposted turn-off

(22km); Aït Benhaddou is another 9km down a bitumen road. Cycling from Ouarzazate takes three hours.

Grands taxis run from outside Ouarzazate bus station when full (Dh15 per person) and from the turn-off (Dh90 one-way or Dh250 return). Minibuses run from Tamdaght to Ouarzazate in the morning when full.

Ouarzazate ورزازت

POP 270,300

Strategically located Ouarzazate (war-zazat) has gotten by largely on its wits instead of its looks. For centuries, people from the Atlas, Drâa and Dadès Valleys converged to do business at Ouarzazate's sprawling Taourirt Kasbah, and a modern garrison town was established here in the 1920s to oversee France's colonial interests. The movie business gradually took off in Ouarzazate after the French protectorate left in the 1950s, and 'Ouallywood' movie studios have built quite a resumé providing convincingly exotic backdrops for movies supposedly set in Tibet, ancient Rome, Somalia and Egypt.

Since King Mohammed VI started visiting here and fixing up the roads, Ouarzazate has been developing quickly with vast new residential areas marked out to the south of town along with new condo-hotel complexes, a spacious pedestrian plaza and well-stocked supermarkets. With scores of agencies offering bikes, motorbikes and camels, this is an ideal launching pad for mountains, desert and gorges. But from November to March, be prepared for the icy winds that can come whipping down from the High Atlas.

◉ Sights

Ouarzazate is more of a staging post in most travel itineraries. If you're here for a day or two, it's worth hiring a taxi and taking a day trip to the nearby **Fint Oasis** or the **Barrage El Mansour Eddahbi**, a popular fishing and birding spot.

★ Taourirt Kasbah KASBAH
(Ave Mohammed V; admission Dh20; ⊙8am-6.30pm) Unlike other Glaoui kasbahs, this one escaped ruin by moonlighting as a Hollywood backdrop (*Sheltering Sky, Gladiator, Prince of Persia*) and attracting the attention of Unesco, which has carefully restored small sections of the inner sanctum. Follow the maze of stairwells to the top floor, where you'll find a prayer room through keyhole archways, traces of stucco and an original

tataoui ceiling. Wander through the village inside the kasbah walls, and you might also find deals on local crafts in backstreet shops.

Atlas Film Corporation Studios NOTABLE BUILDING
(☑0524 88 22 23, 0524 88 22 12; www.studiosatlas.com; adult/child Dh50/35; ⊙8.15am-5.15pm Oct-Feb, to 6.45pm Mar-Sep) The first 'Ouallywood' studio, established in 1983, displays sets and props from movies filmed here, including *Jewel of the Nile, Kingdom of Heaven* and *Kundun*. Who knows, you may even get discovered by a talent scout – though as locals point out, the Dh40 to Dh100 day rates for extras aren't exactly Screen Actors Guild pay. Guided tours run every 20 to 40 minutes and take you through some of the stages, sets and workshops incorporated in the 150-hectare site.

The studio is 5km west of town on the Marrakesh road and easily accessible on the yellow STUDID bus. Buy tickets at Hotel Oscars next door.

Musée de Cinema MUSEUM
(☑0524 89 03 46; Ave Mohammed V; adult/student Dh30/15; ⊙8am-6pm) This small, dusty cinema museum is housed in a former studio and exhibits a collection of old sets, props and cinematic equipment. Located opposite the Taourirt Kasbah, it is a convenient alternative if you can't get to the larger studios out of town.

✦ Activities

Though many agencies and hotels still offer them, quad bikes cause considerable damage to the fragile desert ecosystem and are not recommended. On motorbikes and bicycles, riders are advised to stay on well-marked trails to minimise displacement of native species.

Photo Emotion TOUR
(☑0642 98 89 47; www.rosafrei.com; ⊙10am-4pm Mon-Fri) Swiss photographer and Ouarzazate resident Rosa Frei offers custom-made photography workshops and tours between September and June. Workshops (starting at Dh3150 per person for one day) focus on technique, composition, visual awareness and lighting, while tours range down the Drâa and Dadès Valleys to desert and kasbah retreats. Shorter trips are possible to the film studios, Fint Oasis and the El Mansour Eddahabi dam. Teaching is in English or German.

Saïd Mountain Bike
CYCLING

(☎0662 86 93 24; www.saidmountainbike.com; Ave Moulay Rachid) In addition to 43 rental mountain bikes (Dh250 per day), this local tour company offers guided trekking tours (Dh3800 per person per week with mules and dromedaries) and desert expeditions on mountain bike (Dh1520 to Dh1800).

Wilderness Wheels
ADVENTURE SPORTS

(☎0524 88 81 28; www.wildernesswheels.com; 61 Hay al-Qods; 3-day, 2-night excursions from Dh8470) Professionally guided motorbike tours are organised by this British-run company. Prices include overnight stays, complete riding gear and a support car for up to 20 bikes. Sell-out tours include a girls-only Desert Camp and the classic five-day Desert Tour.

☞ Tours

Désert et Montagne
TOUR

(☎0524 85 49 49; www.desert-montagne.ma; Dar Daïf, Douar Talmasla) Morocco's first female mountain guide and her company organise trips to meet Berber families in the mountains, walking and 4WD trips in the desert and High Atlas, and longer trips following caravan routes. The agency operates out of Dar Daïf in Douar Talmasla. To reach it, continue south on the N9 and cross the Oued Ouarzazate, after which it is signposted to the left.

Desert Majesty
TOUR

(☎0524 89 07 65; www.desertmajesty.com; 18 Pl al-Mouahidine) A highly recommended local agency offering trips to the High Atlas and the desert. Airport pick-ups, multilingual guides originating in Erfoud, Merzouga, M'Hamid and Taouz and reassuringly safe drivers are offered at competitive prices. Booking queries are handled by Felicity who is fluent in English, German, French and Darija.

Ksour Voyages
TOUR

(☎0524 88 28 40; www.ksour-voyages.com; 11 Place du 3 Mars) Books flights and organises trips from mountain hikes to 4WD desert excursions with English-speaking drivers; also rents mountain bikes.

Ouarzazate Unlimited
TOURS

(☎0524 89 06 41; www.ouarzazate-unlimited.com; 6 Rue Du Marché) A reader-recommended provider delivering well-organised camel treks, 4WD desert tours and multi-city itineraries.

Select accommodation includes midrange to top-end riads, kasbahs and camps.

★★ Festivals & Events

The *moussem* of Sidi Daoud is held in Ouarzazate each August.

Marathon des Sables
SPORTS

(www.marathondessables.co.uk) This gruelling six-day, 250km desert ultramarathon is held in March/April. The course changes each year, and is revealed when runners converge in Ouarzazate.

☐ Sleeping

With the rapid growth of the city, Ouarzazate's hotel scene is slowly evolving to offer a better selection of mid-priced B&Bs and *maisons d'hôtes*, alongside larger, tour-group-friendly hotels such as the Ibis and Kenzi Azghor, which cluster near the Taourirt Kasbah and along the Rte de Zagora.

Camping-Bivouac
La Palmeraie
CAMPGROUND €

(Douar Tajda; campsite for 2 people incl car/caravan Dh70/75, berber tent/d incl breakfast Dh250/270; ⓟ⑤) Sleep in one of five cosy Berber tents or pitch your own beneath palms and fruit trees in the Ouarzazate *palmeraie*. There's also room for 15 camping cars (electricity is Dh20), and meals are laid on in the shocking pink salon with its gauzy, tent-like roof. Canoeing excursions (Dh250 per person) and half-day trips to the Fint Oasis (Dh550 per person) are also possible.

Hotel Amlal
HOTEL €

(☎0524 88 40 30; www.hotelamlal.com; 24-25 Rue du Marché; s/d/tr/q Dh200/250/300/400; ⓟ✳) With its peppermint-coloured staircase, zigzagging tilework and cool terrazzo floors, Hotel Amlal is a cheerful budget option. Twenty-eight air-conditioned rooms feature simple wrought-iron furnishings, narrow but comfortable beds and snug, tiled bathrooms. Bring ear-plugs as the mosque is located next door.

★ Dar Bergui
GUESTHOUSE €€

(☎0524 88 77 74; www.darbergui.com; Sidi Hussain Ben Nacer; s/d incl breakfast Dh500/660; ✳⑤✉) This sleek pisé villa with crenellated turrets is the home of Jean-Michel and Martine and is located within walking distance of the Place al-Mouahidine. The six villa bedrooms arranged around the courtyard swimming pool are simply and tastefully furnished

Ouarzazate

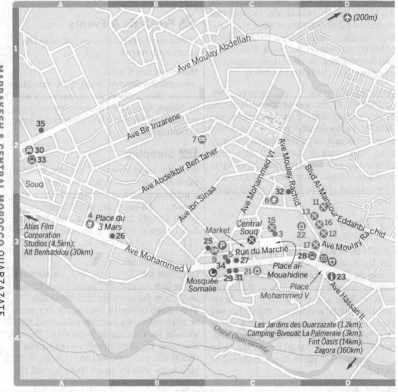

and offer good value for money, especially considering the bountiful breakfast of pancakes, homemade yoghurt, fruit and cake. Non-guests can also book for one of Souad's delicious dinners (Dh165).

Le Petit Riad
MAISON D'HÔTE €€
(☏0524 88 59 50; http://petitriad.com; Blvd Moulay Abdellah, Hay el Wahda; r incl breakfast Dh700-780; ❄️ 🛜 ☒) For those craving light after the shady seclusion of Drâa Valley kasbahs, book a room at the family home of mountain guide Fatima Agoujil. The modern villa has six large rooms with large picture windows overlooking the flowering gardens and the Atlas mountains. The decor is flamboyant (family artworks, plush quilts, dozens of scatter cushions) and the home-cooked meals are authentic.

Les Jardins de Ouarzazate
HOTEL €€
(☏0524 85 42 00; http://hotel-les-jardins-de -ouarzazate.com; Rte de Zagora, Tabounte; s/d incl half board Dh300/500; 🅿️ ❄️ 🛜 ☒) True to its name this hotel hides a large blooming garden inside the rather formidable exterior. Bungalow-style rooms sit along meandering pathways that cut through rose bushes and oleanders. Inside they're capacious with queen-sized beds topped with grand painted headboards. It's popular with groups.

Dar Chamaa
BOUTIQUE HOTEL €€€
(☏0524 85 49 54; www.darchamaa.com; Tajdar; s/d incl half board Dh570/875; 🅿️ ❄️ 🛜 ☒) At the fringe of Ouarzazate's palm oasis, this stylish hotel offers Moroccan-minimalist guest rooms around a central courtyard photography gallery. Rooms are architect-designed to the last detail, from fossilised stone sinks to *tadelakt* niches serving as wardrobes. Ask for rooms with balconies overlooking the pool in the palm-shaded garden. You'll find it on the south side of Oued Ouarzazate signed left off the Zagora road; Dar Chamaa is about 3km along the *piste* on the left.

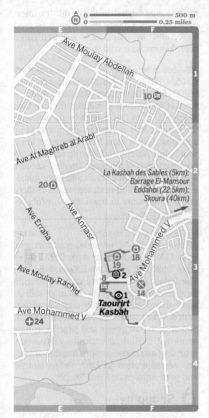

Dar Kamar   MAISON D'HÔTE €€€

(☎ 0524 88 87 33; www.darkamar.com; 45 Kasbah Taourirt; incl breakfast s Dh1020-1275, d Dh1200-1500, ste Dh2400-3000; ⊗ closed Jul; ❄ ☏) Once a stern 17th-century Glaoui courthouse, this cosy pisé guesthouse has a sense of humour: upturned tajines serve as sinks and sewing-machine tables are repurposed as desks. Local iron-workers went wild decorating en-suite bathrooms, though showers are poorly ventilated – a fine excuse to use the in-house hammam and massage room. Ask for upstairs doubles – as nice as suites, only smaller and at half the price.

✖ Eating

Ouarzazate has a nascent dining scene with a few good restaurants worth venturing out of your hotel to visit. For quick eats the cafes that line Place al-Mouahidine are a good bet. Fresh cheese, meat and vegetables can be found at the daily central souq.

Aux Delices   PATISSERIE €

(☎ 0524 88 28 29; Ave Moulay Rachid; ⊗ 6am-midnight) Legendary for its *chnek* (custard cinnamon-raisin twirl), this patisserie also rivals the best in Marrakesh.

Patisserie des Habouss PATISSERIE, CAFE €

(Pl al-Mouahidine; ⊙6am-10pm) On a balmy evening, all strolls lead here for French éclairs (Dh7), Moroccan pastries and ice cream in summer. In the mornings, trekkers and locals line up for fresh baguettes (Dh10), croissants (Dh2.50) and coffee.

Pizzeria Veneziano ITALIAN €

(📞0524 88 76 76; Ave Moulay Rachid; pizzas Dh39-43; ⊙noon-9.30pm) Friendly, central and reasonably priced, Veneziano serves thin-crust pizzas with local toppings like desert herbs, anchovies and goat cheese, plus real Italian espresso.

Restaurant 3 Thés MOROCCAN €

(📞0524 88 63 63; Ave Moulay Rachid; mains Dh25-55; ⊙8am-10pm) The wrought-iron sidewalk seating and get-cosy interiors say Paris cafe, but the menu says tasty vegetarian tajines, cheeseburgers and meaty tajines with figs, prunes and almonds.

Chez Nabil MOROCCAN €

(📞0524 88 45 45; Ave Moulay Rachid; mains Dh45-75; ⊙10am-midnight) With its blue-and-white-checked tablecloths and fast, friendly service, Chez Nabil is a local favourite. Choose between quick and easy burgers, chicken skewers and merguez sausages and traditional favourites of liver tajine and couscous.

Douyria MOROCCAN €€

(📞0524 88 42 62; www.restaurant-ouarzazate.net; 72 Ave Mohammed V; meals Dh140-200; ⊙8am-11pm) Romantic candlelit dinners served in cushion-lined nooks on a terrace overlooking the Taourirt Kasbah. Dare to dine on roasted goat basted in argan oil, try unexpectedly tasty rabbit tajine with preserved lemon and olives, or stick to well-marinated beef skewers with wild thyme.

★**Accord Majeur** FRENCH, ITALIAN €€€

(📞0524 88 24 73; Ave Moulay Rachid; meals Dh200-250; ⊙11am-10pm Mon-Sat) After a week of desert dining, you may find yourself sleepwalking to this French bistro opposite the Berbère Palace. Here in cosy nooks lit by a mellow, yellow glow from dozens of brass wall lamps Aurélie and Charlie serve an impressive menu of foie gras, smoked salmon, beef carpaccio, duck confit and even homemade liquorice-and-mint ice cream. If there are any film stars in town, they'll probably be dining here, too.

Le Relais Saint Exupéry FUSION €€€

(📞0524 88 77 79; www.relais-ouarzazate.com; 13 Blvd Moulay Abdellah; set menu Dh270, dinner mains Dh80-150; ⊙11.30am-2.30pm & 6-10pm) The Relais serves creative dishes featuring local ingredients such as Talouine saffron and Saharan salt. Try flaky *pastilla* of fish, or dromedary meat in a Mali-inspired sauce of garlic, cumin, ginger and paprika. It may seem odd to find adventurous gastronomy near the Ouarzazate airport, but this airport was an inspiration to *Little Prince* author and pilot Antoine de Saint-Exupéry.

 Shopping

Coopérative de Tissage ARTS & CRAFTS

(Weaving Cooperative; 📞0662 61 05 83; Ave Mohammed V) Opposite the kasbah, glimpse female artisans at work on *hanbels* (woven carpets) and embroidered straw mats, and

---

WORTH A TRIP

LA KASBAH DES SABLES

Putting Ouarzazate's film credentials to good use, there is little about La Kasbah des Sables (📞0524 88 54 28; www.lakasbahdessables.com; 195 Hay Aït Kdif; meals Dh200-320; ⊙noon-2pm & 7-11pm) that won't leave you slack-jawed. The 5km journey west of Ouarzazate to the old neighbourhood of Al Kdif is a suitable adventure to whet your appetite for the Arabian Nights spectacle within.

Housed behind the walls of an old Glaoui kasbah, this 900-sq-metre restaurant is the creation of Brigitte Babolat, who conceived an extraordinary medley of art-filled lounges and nooks arranged around patios hung with grand cut-brass chandeliers dangling like oversized Christmas baubles. The centerpiece is an enormous shallow pool backed by a wall of jewel-coloured lights and surrounded by romantic, candlelit tables where diners are served a mix of Moroccan and French dishes such as barbot and saffron or chicken with Atlas morels. Afterwards recline in cushion-lined cubbyholes filled with objets d'art crafted in Ouarzazate and Marrakesh. In the morning you'll have to shake yourself and wonder if you didn't dream the whole experience.

take one home at posted fixed prices of Dh550 to Dh1100 per sq metre.

Horizon Artisanat
ARTS & CRAFTS

(📞0524 88 69 38; 181 Ave Annasr; ⏱9am-7pm) Henna-painted pottery, hand-painted tea glasses, and silver filigree rings are sold at reasonable fixed prices, supporting Horizon's programs to provide vocational training for adults with disabilities and integrate disabled children and adults into the community. The association supports some 2500 people, including 53 permanent staff members.

Ensemble Artisanal
ARTS & CRAFTS

(Ave Mohammed V; ⏱9am-12.30pm & 1.30-6pm) State-run showrooms feature local stone carvings, inlaid daggers and embroidered linens.

Supermarché
SUPERMARKET

(Ave Mohammed V) Carries all the desert essentials: water, toothpaste, lip balm, packaged soups, cookies, film, vodka and argan anti-cellulite lotion.

Supermarket
SUPERMARKET

(Ave Moulay Rachid) This large supermarket has imported European foods.

ℹ Information

Banks with ATMs line the northern end of Ave Mohammed V, as do internet cafes offering one hour online for Dh10. Most hotels and guesthouses also offer free wi-fi.

EMERGENCY

Police (📞19; Ave Mohammed V)

LAUNDRY

Lavanderie (Rue du Marché; ⏱9am-noon & 2-8pm) Modern appliances (per load wash/dry Dh30/18) and wash-and-fold services (per item wash/dry/press Dh4/2/3).

MEDICAL SERVICES

Pharmacies line Ave Mohammed V and post a list of night pharmacies in their windows after hours.

Hôpital Bougafer (📞0524 88 24 44; Ave Mohammed V) Public hospital east of the tourist office.

POST & TELEPHONE

There are numerous *téléboutiques* in the centre.

Main Post Office (Ave Mohammed V; ⏱8.30am-4.30pm Mon-Fri) Postal services and a direct-dial international phone.

TOURIST INFORMATION

Délégation Régionale du Tourisme (ONMT; 📞0524 88 24 85; Ave Mohammed V; ⏱8.30am-4.30pm) Stocks a few brochures and offers limited advice. Hotels will be able to provide more information.

ℹ Getting There & Away

AIR

North of town 2km is **Taourirt airport** (📞0524 88 23 83). **Royal Air Maroc** (RAM; 📞0524 88 51 02; 1 Ave Mohammed V) has daily, direct flights to Casablanca, plus charter flights from Belgium, France and Germany. Flights arriving in Ouarzazate from Casa land inconveniently at 11.35pm when night fares apply to taxi services.

During the annual Haj pilgrimage and popular events such as the Marathon des Sables there are extra flights.

BUS

Supratours operates buses from Marrakesh (Dh80, 4½ hours, three daily) and one daily service to Zagora (Dh50, 2½ hours), Er-Rachidia (Dh80, 5½ hours) and Merzouga (Dh180, eight hours). **Supratours Al Hizam** (📞0661 08 26 56; Ave Moulay Abdellah; ⏱7.30am-11pm) sells tickets, and the bus stops outside.

CTM (📞0524 88 24 27; Ave Mohammed V; ⏱7am-10pm) buses also serve Marrakesh (Dh85, five daily), Agadir (Dh145, 7½ hours, one daily), Er-Rachidia (Dh95, one daily), Zagora (Dh50, two daily) and M'Hamid (Dh75, five hours, one daily). During local holidays and busy periods, book your tickets at least a day in advance.

The main, local **bus station** (Gare Routière; Mahta) is 1km northwest of the town centre off Ave Moulay Abdellah. Several buses a day leave from here to Marrakesh (Dh65, four to five hours), Boumalne du Dadès (Dh30), Taroudannt (Dh75, five hours), Tazenakht (Dh25, three hours), Foum Zguid (Dh40, four hours), Tata (Dh80, five hours) and M'Hamid (Dh70, seven hours) via Zagora (Dh45, four hours).

CAR

For desert detours you might want to rent a car (from Dh350 per day). Car hire with a driver runs Dh900 (car) to Dh1250 (4WD). There are dozens of agencies in town and international outfits such as **Avis** (📞0524 88 80 00; www.avis. com; cnr Ave Mohammed V & Place du 3 Mars), **Hertz** (📞0524 88 20 84; www.hertz.com; 33 Ave Mohammed V), **Budget** (📞0524 88 42 02; www.budget.com; 28 Ave Mohammed V) and **National** (📞0524 88 20 35; www.nationalcar. com; Place du 3 Mars). All have booths at the airport, although they are more expensive than local operators. Other operators:

Desert Evasion (⌖0524 88 86 82; www.desert-evasion.net; Imm El Ghifari, Ave Mohammed V) Payment due upon receipt of keys.

ESON Maroc (⌖0524 89 05 62; www.eson-maroc.com; Ave Mohammed VI) Reliable and much cheaper than the international agencies; also has 4WDs.

Ilana Car (⌖0524 88 41 42; www.ilana-car.com) New cars and professional service located behind Accord Majeure.

TAXI

Taxis leave from outside the main bus station to Agdz (Dh40), Boumalne du Dadès (Dh30), Marrakesh (Dh90 to Dh110), Skoura (Dh15), Tinerhir (Dh60) and Zagora (Dh80).

ⓘ Getting Around

Petits taxis run up and down Ave Mohammed V for flat rates of Dh5 per person (based on three people sharing). The yellow STUDID bus (Dh5) runs half-hourly services up and down Ave Mohammed V. Taxis to/from the airport cost Dh50 during the day and Dh75 at night.

DRÂA VALLEY   وادة درعة

From Ouarzazate the N9 plunges southeast into the Drâa Valley, formed by a narrow ribbon of water from the High Atlas that occasionally emerges triumphantly in lush oases particularly between Agdz and Zagora, a stretch of about 95km. The drive from Agdz to Zagora takes three to four hours, though the more scenic Circuits Touristiques route (p120) follows the *piste* through the oasis. Beyond that, a road takes you 96km further south to M'Hamid, a town 40km short of the Algerian border that marks the end of the road and the start of the desert proper.

If you don't want to retrace your steps back to Ouarzazate along the N9, it's possible to continue west of M'Hamid through the desert to Foum Zguid from where you can pick up the N10 north via Tazenakht. For those with more time, it's possible to complete an enormous circuit east on the N12 from Tansikht (29km southeast of Agdz) to the Erg Chebbi dunefield near Merzouga and return to Ouarzazate via the Todra and Dadès Gorges.

Agdz   اكدز

POP 9400

Travellers who zoom from Ouarzazate to Zagora are missing out on Agdz (ag-daz), a classic caravanserai oasis with ancient mudbrick kasbahs, a still-pristine *palmeraie* and a secret desert prison.

As you approach Agdz, you'll see tajine-shaped Jebel Kissane on the horizon, and spot mountain bikers heading off from Agdz to 1660m Tizi n'Tinififft, some 20km away. The mountains glisten with what looks like snow, but that's a mirage: it's sunlight bouncing off deposits of reflective mica. Agdz craft traditions include carving, pottery and basket-weaving, and you might spot a few prime examples outside shops downtown or at the Thursday souq (October and November).

That said, none of the key attractions of Agdz are apparent from the main road. The historic centre of Agdz is east of the N9 about 1.5km along a dusty *piste,* so the old town has been largely bypassed by mass-tourism development schemes. For that very reason, an unusual number of authentic mudbrick kasbahs have been preserved. Overnight visitors might also take a morning stroll through the vast Agdz palmeraie, just to the north of the village.

◉ Sights

Caïd's Kasbah   KASBAH
(adult/child Dh40/20) The 170-year-old kasbah that once belonged to the *caïd* (leader) of Agdz is now owned by his descendants. Stop at Casbah Caïd Ali's reception next door for admission to the mudbrick structure, and explore a maze of rooms spread over three storeys. The play of light and shade in the ancient kasbah could obsess photographers for hours – but best of all are rooftop views over the neighbouring oasis.

Glaoui Kasbah   KASBAH
(customary tip Dh20) Long-time residents of Agdz reported their shock at discovering that the walled Glaoui kasbah in Agdz (marked 307 on the gate, located on the south side of the *piste* near Rose du Sable guesthouse) was used as a secret desert detention centre. Hassan II's purges to suppress political dissidents led to the establishment of such secret detention centres, details of which emerged after 2004 through Morocco's Equity and Reconciliation Commission.

In the meantime, if you see the next-door neighbour who keeps an eye on the place, you can ask him to let you in the door to look around (Dh20 tip customary).

🛏 Sleeping

Casbah Caïd Ali KASBAH €

(☑0524 84 36 40; www.casbah-caidali.net; Rue
Hassan II; d with/without breakfast Dh220/190,
mattress on roof Dh35, tent Dh20; ▣) Descendants of the local *caïd* welcome guests to
their partially restored kasbah, in courtyard
guest rooms. Rooms are so-so, but the camping is good beneath the palms.

Dar Laurli GUESTHOUSE €€

(☑0524 84 39 34; www.laurli-location-sud-maroc.
com; s/d incl breakfast Dh500/620; ▣❋❂▤)
Tucked away in the centre of Agdz is Dar
Laurli, the bijou, four-room guesthouse of
Patrick and Agnès. Small, cosy rooms with
platform beds, colourful flatweave desert
carpets, romantic uplighting and gauzy
mosquito nets overlook the gardens and
an emerald-green pool. The atmosphere is
soporific, but stir yourself for excellent bike
rides through the *palmeraie* and hikes up
Jebel Kissane.

Kasbah Azul KASBAH €€€

(☑0524 84 39 31; www.kasbahazul; Agdz; d incl
breakfast Dh880, q & ste Dh1375; ▣❋❂▤) Hiding in a garden at the eastern end of the
historic centre like an arty recluse, this kasbah has seven rooms with en-suite *tadelakt*
bathrooms in contrasting hues: acid green
and plum, terracotta and powder blue. The
owner contributed her own collaged lamps
and paintings to the striking decor – and
this artist's retreat has a keyhole pool and
copious breakfasts.

✕ Eating

At the entry to town on the left, there's a gas
station with a convenience store and cafe,
the **Kasbah Total** (◷8am-9pm), where you
can fuel up on good espresso and packaged
snacks galore. Cafes ring Pl Marché Vert in
downtown Agdz, including **Sables d'Or**,
which serves rotisserie chicken with chips
for Dh35.

ℹ Getting There & Away

Buses from Ouarzazate (Dh35, one hour) and
Zagora (Dh35, two hours) stop in the Grand
Place; the CTM office is in the northeast corner
of the square. You can also pick up grands taxis
here for Ouarzazate (Dh40), Zagora (Dh40)
and N'Kob (Dh25). The back country road
(N12) to Rissani meets the N9 29km east of
Agdz.

Tamnougalt

Perched on a hill 6km from Agdz is a star
attraction of the Drâa Valley: Tamnougalt,
a 16th-century fortified village that's among
the oldest mudbrick *ksour* still standing.

◉ Sights

★**Tamnougalt Ksar** KSAR

(admission Dh 10, compulsory guide Dh50) The
maze of rooms at Tamnougalt *ksar* (fortified
stronghold) leads through a sizeable *mellah*,
dips underground with strategically placed
skylights and candle nooks, and emerges
into sunny courtyard stables lined with
horseshoe arches. See if you can distinguish
between the Arab, Andalucian and Berber
Jewish motifs that blend so seamlessly here –
or at least recognise scenes shot here from
Oscar-winning movies *Babel* and *The English Patient*.

🛏 Sleeping & Eating

★**Bab el-Oued** MAISON D'HÔTE €€

(☑0524 88 53 95; www.babeloued-maroc.com;
d Dh825-935, tr Dh1155, ste Dh935; ▣❋▤) ✑
Shaded by date palms in a walled organic
garden, these ecofriendly bungalows fairly
beam with local pride thanks to wooden
doors carved in town, carpets from nearby
Tazenakht, palm-beamed ceilings and glossy
tadelakt bathrooms. By keeping the pool
small and the toilets low-flow, the French-
and English-speaking owners conserve
enough water to grow 60 types of plants, including herbs and vegetables for Moroccan-
Mediterranean meals.

Nonguests can call ahead for delicious
organic lunches (Dh165), and nap in hammocks by goldfish ponds afterwards. It's
6km south of Agdz.

Chez Yacob KASBAH €€

(☑0524 84 33 94; www.lavalleedudraa.com; half
board per person Dh300; ❋) Next door to Tamnougalt's ancient *mellah* are eight snug
rooms with en-suite bathrooms ringing a
soaring courtyard, capped by a scenic terrace overlooking the *palmeraie*. Set menus
are Dh90, and bountiful enough to count as
lunch and dinner. It's 2km from Rte de Zagora down an unpaved lane.

ℹ Getting There & Away

Turn left off the main road 4km past Agdz, then
2km east up a *piste*.

Circuits Touristiques

Those with a 4WD shouldn't miss the slower, scenic *piste* that runs from Tamnougalt to just north of Zagora, parallel to highway N9. The dirt road winds along the north side of the valley through palm oases, villages, patchwork fields and river vistas all the way to Zagora. For shorter 4WD excursions along the scenic north side of the Drâa, follow signposts for 'circuits touristiques' off N9 (near the Afriquia petrol station) just before Ouled Aïtman that lead past Kasbah Said Arabi and the Tinzouline kasbah. At Tansikht, about 29km before Zagora, look out for the old watchtower guarding the *palmeraie,* signposted 'Oasis Du Drâa'.

Timidarte

If you want to (all together now) rock the kasbahs, turn west off N9 to check out prime specimens in Timidarte village. The finest example dates from the 17th century; it was recently converted by Timidarte's tourism association into an authentic kasbah guesthouse, Kasbah Timidarte.

🛏 Sleeping & Eating

Kasbah Timidarte   KASBAH €
(☎0668 68 00 47; www.kasbahtimidarte.com; d incl half board without/with bathroom Dh200/300) For a night, you can live much as kasbah inhabitants have for centuries: in seven mudbrick rooms arranged around a central light well, with palm-frond mats and mattresses on floors. Instead of TV, there's socialising under the stars on the roof terrace, next to a Berber bread oven. Some improvements have been made since the 17th century – there's electric light for reading and a couple of rooms have en-suite bathrooms.

Association members have taken to the task of cooking for guests with gusto, and home-style Berber meals are a point of pride. It's 1km east of Rte de Zagora, 15km south of Agdz.

Zagora   زاكورة
POP 35,100

The original, iconic 'Tombouctou, 52 jours' (Timbuktu, 52 days) sign featuring a nomad with a smirking camel may have been swept away in an inexplicable government beautification scheme, but Zagora's fame as a desert outpost remains indelible. The Saadians launched their expedition to conquer Timbuktu here in 1591, and desert caravans passing through Zagora gave this isolated spot cosmopolitan character. These days Zagora remains a trading post and meeting place, hosting a regional souq on Wednesdays and Sundays and putting on a variety of lively festivals.

⊙ Sights

★ **Musée des Arts et Traditions de la Valleé du Drâa**   MUSEUM
(☎0661 34 83 88; Kasbah de Tissergat; admission Dh20; ⊙8.30am-7pm) Eight kilometres north of town, below a spectacular viewing point over the *palmeraie,* follow 'Musée' signs to a triple-storey mudbrick home that houses this fascinating desert-culture museum. In the tea salon, you'll find key equipment for desert entertaining c 1930: a vintage

---

THE IDEAL DATE

For prime date selection, head to Tinzouline, about 56km south of Agdz during the September to November date season. You're getting close when you spot vendors with dates overflowing from palm-frond baskets along the Zagora road. You may run into traffic for the Monday souq, where you'll be elbow to elbow with local grandmothers vying for the best local-speciality boufeggou dates. This is a date to remember: nicely caramelised outside by the desert sun, and tender and savoury-sweet inside.

If you're not visiting the valley in autumn, you still have a standing dessert date in Timidarte, where local dates become Slow Food sensations at Timarine Tijara (☎0661 91 32 25; ⊙by appointment), 18km south of Agdz. Head past historic mudbrick kasbahs, through the garden of a traditional family home, and into a spotless white-tiled kitchen with a single industrial cauldron bubbling merrily away and dozens of jars of Timarine Tijara's signature date jam and *tahalout* (date syrup). 'Try drizzling some on warm goat cheese – it brings out the nutty, fruity flavours in our dates', advises owner and date gourmet innovator Abderrahim Ouagarane.

ham radio, a gramophone and tea glasses believed to shatter on contact with poison. Artefacts are tagged with insightful explanations of their origins and purpose in French and English – very helpful for explaining otherwise mysterious tattooing implements, the intriguing birthing room and markedly different wedding garments from five local tribes.

Amezrou
NEIGHBOURHOOD

Zagora's desert-crossroads culture can be glimpsed in the adjacent village (south of downtown Zagora, across the Oued Drâa), where artisans in the historic mellah work good-luck charms from African, Berber, Jewish and Muslim traditions into their designs. In the 1930s, Amezrou had some 400 Jewish households, but almost all had left town by the 1960s.

Ask an elderly resident to point you towards the tiny synagogue. The family opposite will let you into the prayer room (Dh20 tip customary).

Jebel Zagora
MOUNTAIN

This spectacular mountain rises over the Oued Drâa – worth climbing for the views, provided you have stamina, water and sunblock and set off in the early morning. The round trip to Jebel Zagora takes about three hours on foot, or 45 minutes by car along the *piste* to the right beyond Camping de la Montagne. Halfway up are the faint ruins of an 11th-century Almoravid fortress, but the military installation at the summit is off-limits.

🏃 Activities

Nearly every tourist in Zagora is heading for the Sahara and many plan their trips here. That said, the desert gateway of M'Hamid is still a three-hour drive further south with the undulating dunes of Erg Chigaga an additional (and expensive) 56km off-road southwest from M'Hamid. When planning trips with local operators make sure you know where your trip is headed. The closest dunes to Zagora are Erg Nakhla (12km northeast of town), Tinfou (25km south beside the N9), El Messouira and Erg Lihoudi (both approximately 90km south near M'Hamid).

For dromedary rides all-inclusive prices range between Dh350 and Dh500 depending on the campsite and the size of the group.

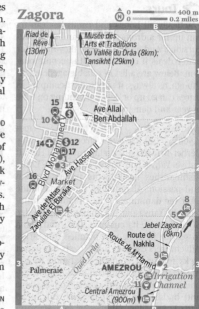

Zagora

🏃 Activities, Courses & Tours
1 Caravane Desert et Montagne	A2
2 Caravane du Sud	B3
3 Caravane Hamada Drâa	A2

🛏 Sleeping
4 Auberge Restaurant Chez Ali	A2
5 Camping Oasis Palmier	B2
6 Hotel la Fibule du Draa	B3
7 La Petite Kasbah	B3
8 Riad Dar Sofian	B2
9 Villa Zagora	B3

🍴 Eating
10 Souq	A2

🍷 Drinking & Nightlife
11 African Bar	B3

ℹ Information
12 Banque Populaire	A2
13 BMCE	A1
14 Pharmacy Zagora	A2

🚍 Transport
15 Bus Station	A1
16 CTM Bus Station	A2
Grands Taxis	(see 15)
17 Supratours	A2

☞ Tours

Practically all hotels and campsites can fix you up for a dromedary ride and desert excursions. And, in some cases, they may offer better deals if combined with accommodation. Below are a list of reliable agencies, although, as always, it pays to cost-compare as prices can go up or down depending on time of year and demand.

Wild Morocco   TOUR
(☑ 0655 77 81 73; www.wildmorocco.com) This Berber-British partnership run by M'Hamid native Yahya and corporate-escapee Emily distinguishes itself by its professionalism and passion. Abandoning the nomadic life after the damming of the Drâa made it unfeasible, Yahya put his immense knowledge of the desert, its customs, flora and fauna to service in these well-planned itineraries. Adventurers can join three- to six-day desert treks following nomadic migration routes, musicians find guitars conjured from neighbours for impromptu desert jam sessions and budding anthropologists break bread with Drâa Valley families or join Harratin inhabitants in M'Hamid's old *ksar* for tea and local gossip.

Larger excursions combining Altas mountain trekking, the gorges and desert tours are also possible, as are desert trips to Erg Chebbi.

Caravane Hamada Drâa   DESERT SAFARI
(☑ 0524 84 69 30; www.hamadadraaa.com; Blvd Mohammed V) English-speaking guides; treks to nomadic camps by licenced guide and native nomad Youssef M'hidi.

Caravane Desert et Montagne   DESERT SAFARI
(☑ 0524 84 68 98; www.caravanedesertetmontagne .com; 112 Blvd Mohammed V) Partners with local nomads to create adventures off the beaten track for individuals and small groups.

Caravane du Sud   DESERT SAFARI
(☑ 0524 84 75 69; www.caravanedusud.com; Amezrou) Three- to 14-day camel treks, 4WD circuits and a three-day round-trip to Erg Chigaga for Dh1900. It also offers cheaper departures from M'Hamid. You'll find it on the roundabout in Amezrou.

Discovering South Morocco   DESERT SAFARI
(☑ 0524 84 61 15; www.zagora-desert.info) Run by highly regarded English- and French-speaking, Zagora-born Mohamad Sirirou.

✿ Festivals

Moussem of Sufi Moulay Abdelkader Jilali   RELIGIOUS
This *moussem*, which takes place at the same time as Moulid an-Nabi, is the biggest shindig in the Drâa. Members of the Sufi Jilala brotherhood make a pilgrimage to Zagora to pay their respects, and you may hear their hypnotic music of praise and celebration with the *bendir* (handheld drum).

⌂ Sleeping

Many of the better accommodation options are located in the *palmeraie* in the atmospheric hamlet of Amezrou.

★ **Auberge Restaurant Chez Ali**   INN €
(☑ 0524 84 62 58; http://chezali.net; Ave de l'Atlas Zaouiate El Baraka; d incl breakfast without bathroom Dh70, with bathroom Dh200-300; ❀ ❄) The peacocks stalking the pool can't be bothered, but otherwise the welcome here is enthusiastic. Sky-lit upstairs rooms have simple pine furnishings, bathrooms and air-con, and 'traditional' rooms have mattresses on carpets and shared bathrooms. Enjoy fantastic Berber meals (Dh80) and overnight trips run by English-speaking guides Mohamed and Yusuf.

La Petite Kasbah   MAISON D'HÔTE €
(☑ 0524 84 80 43; www.hotelzagora.com; Amezrou; per person b&b/half board Dh150/250) Expect a warm welcome and a fresh glass of mint tea when you arrive at La Petite Kasbah. Originally the family home of Brahim Badri, the mini kasbah now has five rooms around a flower-filled courtyard, a cushion-strewn tea salon and a terrace overlooking the Amezrou *palmeraie*. Good mountain bikes are available to hire (Dh100 per day) as are well-priced camel rides (Dh100 per person) and longer excursions to Erg Nakhla and Erg Lihoudi.

Camping Oasis Palmier   CAMPGROUND €
(☑ 0613 98 52 31; pixameharee@hotmail.com; Rte de Nakhla; camping per person Dh20, per tent Dh20-30, per car Dh15, campervans Dh20; 🅿 🛜) Located almost next door to Dar Sofian, this campsite has a mixture of palm-shaded pitches and Berber tents. It also has a cafe, free wi-fi, hot showers (Dh15) and electric hook-ups (Dh20), and it'll even deliver fresh bread to your door.

Riad de Rêve
GUESTHOUSE €€

(☑0677 19 13 37; 353 Hay Moulay Rachid; s/d/ste incl half board Dh370/560/1100; ✳🖥) Escape the typical tourist accommodation and spend a night at Abdesalem's intimate riad home, where he'll whip up tasty traditional dishes and a variety of home-baked breads. With a nomadic background and years of experience working in Switzerland, your host is a master of hospitality and a knowledgeable guide to local history and folklore and the surrounding desert.

Hotel la Fibule du Draa
HOTEL €€

(☑0524 84 73 18; s/d/tr incl breakfast Dh560/680/780; P🖥🌊) Unexpected calm at the Amezrou crossroads, with a palm-shaded pool, garden bar, in-house hammam (from Dh100) and on-site massages (from Dh330). The 24 basic rooms have pisé walls, en-suite bathrooms, fridges and climate control of varying reliability. Choose garden-view rooms as the pool area can be noisy. It's 50m to the right off the Rte de M'Hamid in Amezrou.

★ Riad Dar Sofian
MAISON D'HÔTE €€€

(☑0524 84 73 19; www.riaddarsofian.com; Rte de Nakhla, Amezrou; s/d/tr incl breakfast Dh680/880/1100, tent Dh220; P✳🖥🌊) Setting new standards in Zagora, Dar Sofian is a stunning desert oasis. The fabulous pisé edifice was constructed by a team from Skoura, while Fassi craftspeople executed the acres of tilework inside. The decor is a successful take on contemporary Moroccan with a mix of modern beds and bathrooms, antique furnishings and traditional detailing. Massages, cooking courses and excursions can all be arranged but guests seem reluctant to leave the palm-fringed pool.

If you can't spend the night, it's certainly worth booking lunch here to sample Zagora's speciality cabbage couscous and enjoy a dip in the pool.

Villa Zagora
MAISON D'HÔTE €€€

(☑0524 84 60 93; www.mavillaausahara.com; Rte de Nakhla, Amezrou; d incl half board without/with bathroom Dh1010/1200, ste Dh1520; ✳🌊) Light, breezy and naturally charming, this converted country home makes desert living look easy. French doors reveal plush Moroccan carpets, soaring ceilings and an eclectic art collection, including Zagora-inspired abstracts. Staff fuss over you like Moroccan relations you never knew you had, and marathon meals feature oasis-fresh ingredients.

Pool water is wisely reused on aromatic herb gardens; forget dromedaries and read your days away on the verandah.

🍴 Eating & Drinking

Hotels provide Dh100 to Dh150 set meals to guests and nonguests by prior reservation. Auberge Restaurant Chez Ali is a standout for quality and freshness, and you can join off-duty desert guides at **La Rose des Sables** (☑0524 84 72 74; Ave Allal Ben Abdallah; meals Dh40-60). Cafes and *laterie* (juice shops) cluster around the intersection of Boulevard Mohammed V and Ave Allal Ben Abdallah and serve a good selection of staples like roast chicken, tajine and pizza for Dh20 to Dh30. Lateria Younes and Lateria Ayoub both serve fruit smoothies (Dh7).

Picnic ingredients can be found at the daily **souq** (Blvd Mohammed V; ⏱9am-7pm), the supermarket at the northern end of town (no alcohol) and a bakery on Mohammed V. For a stiff drink, head to La Fibule du Draa's garden bar, or the **African bar** (☑0524 84 83 88; www.riadlamane.com; Amezrou) at Riad Lamane.

ℹ Information

Most hotels offer wi-fi and there are several internet cafes along Blvd Mohammed V and Ave Allal Ben Abdallah (Dh10 per hour).

Banque Populaire (Blvd Mohammed V) Stock up on cash at one of the last ATMs you'll find before you hit the Sahara.

BMCE (Blvd Mohammed V) ATM.

Pharmacy Zagora (☑0524 84 71 95; Blvd Mohammed V; ⏱8.30am-1pm & 3-8pm Mon-Fri, 8.30am-1pm Sat)

ℹ Getting There & Away

AIR

Zagora has a small airport, southwest of town off the N12, that caters to private charter flights only. Both **Heliconia** (www.heliconia-aero.com) helicopter services and **Alfa Air** (www.alfaair. aero) light aircraft fly into the airport.

BUS

The **CTM bus station** (☑0524 84 73 27) is at the southwestern end of Mohammed V, while the local **bus station** (Blvd Mohammed V) is beside the mosque, where grands taxis also depart. **Supratours** (☑0524 84 76 88; Blvd Mohamed V) is near the Banque Populaire and offers a daily 6am bus to Marrakesh (Dh125, eight hours) and Ouarzazate (Dh50, 2½ hours). There are also three daily CTM buses to Ouarzazate (Dh50, four hours), one of which continues to Marrakesh (Dh120, 9½ hours).

Other companies, which are based at the local bus station, have at least one run a day to Marrakesh (Dh110) and Ouarzazate (Dh45, three hours). There are buses to Rissani (Dh90, six hours) via N'Kob (Dh20, two hours) and Tazzarine (Dh30, 2½ hours) three times a week. A bus passes through Zagora to M'Hamid (Dh20, two hours) in the morning. More frequent minibuses run to M'Hamid (Dh25) throughout the day when full.

TAXI

Grands taxis can be found in the centre of town beside the new mosque. They are more regular early in the morning. Destinations include Tamegroute (Dh8, 20 minutes), Agdz (Dh35, 1½ hours), Ouarzazate (Dh80, three hours), M'Hamid (Dh25, 1½ hours) and N'Kob (Dh60, 1½ hours).

Tamegroute   تامكروت

Stressed out? You've come to the right place: Tamegroute's Zawiya Nassiriyya is said to cure anxiety and high blood pressure, thanks to the post-mortem calming influence of Sidi Mohammed ben Nassir – founder of the influential and learned Nassiri brotherhood who were famed for their ability in settling Drâa Valley disputes in the 17th century. The *zawiya* is still a place of pilgrimage for the sick and a working Quranic school. Bibliophiles should plan desert trips around visits to the *zawiya's* library of ancient illuminated texts or try to coincide with the annual moussem between the 12th and 22nd of November.

Besides miracle cures, Tamegroute is known for its labyrinth of *ksour,* which you can explore with a local guide or by yourself to test your internal compass. Tamegroute also has a Saturday souq.

> ### QUICK GETAWAY: TINFOU DUNES
>
> M'Hamid's grand Erg Chigaga or the great inland sea of dunes in Merzouga can make this small patch of two to three dunes seem like a kiddie sand box by comparison. Around 8km south of Tamegroute, you'll spot them marooned by the road on your left. On busy days it can feel like a playground here, but it's still fun to climb and run down the big dunes.

◉ Sights

★ Zawiya Nassiriyya   MEDERSA

(suggested donation Dh20; ⊘ morning & late afternoon Sat-Thu) While non-Muslims can't visit Sidi ben Nassir's green-roofed mausoleum, anyone can visit the library inside the adjacent *medersa* for Quranic scholars. Among the 4000 books on these glassed-in shelves are ancient medical, mathematics, algebra and law texts, in addition to splendid 13th-century Qurans written on gazelle hide. You'll find it through an arch in the northwest corner of the main square.

★ Cooperative des Potiers   GALLERY

(⊘8am-6pm Mon-Fri) Oxidised copper yields the distinctive 'Tamegroute green' glaze used on the local pottery, which originated when the Nassiri brotherhood invited craftsmen from Fez to settle in the village. Two families remain, turning out irridescent rustic bowls, stamped tiles and elegant platters. Heading south, you'll find it on your left as you leave the village.

🛏 Sleeping & Eating

Auberge-Restaurant-Camping-Jnane Dar Diafa   GUESTHOUSE €

(☑0524 84 06 22; www.jnanedar.ch; s/d from Dh280/340, with shared bathroom Dh170/200) In this breezy garden-gazebo restaurant, enjoy leisurely lunches made with vegetables grown on the premises. Scuffed but winsome pisé-walled guest rooms overlook the garden, some featuring air-con, mosquito nets over beds and star-patterned walls. Prices include breakfast.

Tamegroute to M'Hamid

From Tamgroute the road south narrows to a single lane highway (being widened at the time of research) and takes you through a dauntingly bleak landscape of sun-scorched rubble, until the road ascends up and over Tizi Beni Selmane pass. Midway, the village of Tagounite has petrol and several cafes. It's also a jumping-off point for the El Mesouira and Erg Lihoudi dunes, which lie southwest of Tagounite.

★ La Dune Blanche   DESERT CAMP €€

(☑0667 96 64 64; www.bivouac-laduneblanche -zagora.com; GPS coordinates N 29°56'05.53, W 005°41'28.13; per person incl half/full board Dh400/480) La Dune Blanche offers a great alternative to staying in M'Hamid and gets you into the desert fast. Surrounded by dunes, 22km south of Tagounite, accommodation is in beautiful pisé cottages dressed with fabric inside to mimic the feel of a tent. Each 'tent' has a different colour and is furnished with comfortable beds dressed in natural woollen blankets, carpets and cut-metal lanterns, which cast swirling patterns on the walls. From here any number of excursions are possible.

Given the location, it is necessary to book in advance. Salah will meet you at the petrol station at Tagounite with a 4WD to take you the remainder of the way.

M'Hamid المحاميد

POP 3000

Once it was a lonesome oasis, but these days M'Hamid is a wallflower no more. Border tensions between Algeria (which lies just 40km south), Morocco and the Polisario had isolated this caravan stop until the 1990s, when accords allowed M'Hamid to start hosting visitors again. From here, it doesn't take long to reach the dunes – some nuzzle right up against guesthouses on the west side of town – but to be enveloped by large dunes, you'll have to head out across the *reg* (hard-packed rocky desert) by dromedary or 4WD.

◉ Sights

M'Hamid itself encompasses two towns and five different ethnic groups: the Harratine, Berber, Chorfa, Beni M'Hamid and the fabled nomadic 'Blue Men'. M'Hamid Jdid, the prematurely aged 'new' town, has a mosque, roadside cafe-restaurants, small budget hotels and a Monday souq (on your right opposite the water tower as you enter town). There's a frontier-town feel here, with tough guys in *shesh* (turban) and sunglasses hanging around dusty cafes, swapping stories.

The old kasbah sits in the *palmeraie*, 3km away across the Oued Drâa. Another worthwhile stop is the Ksar Ouled Driss, 5km before M'Hamid, which includes a small ethnographic museum (admission Dh20; ⊙hours vary) displaying traditional household objects in a lovely mudbrick courtyard.

★ **Erg Chigaga** SAND DUNE
The soft sculpted peaks of Erg Chigaga are located several days' trek or two hours' drive from M'Hamid. It is the largest sand sea in Morocco, snaking along the horizon for

40km and bordered to the north and south by mountain ridges. This sea of golden crescents, which peak at 300m, hides small, semi-permanent camps in its troughs. As a result the desert experience here is quiet and enveloping, offering spectacular night skies illuminated by the enormous arc of the Milky Way.

Erg Ezahar SAND DUNE
This tall 'screaming' dune set amid a sea of smaller dunes wails eerily when the wind kicks up. Located 65km southwest of M'Hamid it takes three days to reach it by camel, passing an old marabout shrine and the flat plain of Bousnaïna where artefacts from a long disappeared village are sometimes turned up. There are no fixed camps here.

Erg Esmar SAND DUNE
Located close to Erg Ezahar this collection of smaller dunes rising to just 80m are well off the main radar with no permanent camps. With its mixture of red and white dunes, it is particularly photogenic at sunset.

Erg Lihoudi SAND DUNE
The most easily accessible dunes to M'Hamid are the 100m-high Erg Lihoudi (Dunes of the Jews), located 8km northeast of M'Hamid. Characterised by their white river sand due to their proximity to the Drâa, they are frequented by a higher number of day trippers and some of the semipermanent camps are in need of attention.

El Mesouiria SAND DUNE
Located just 8km northwest of M'Hamid, El Mesouiria is another possibility for an easy overnight camel trek. Dunes range between 60m and 80m in height and are characterised by their white sand and a smattering of tamarisk trees.

🏃 Activities

Many overnight camel treks (from Dh350 per person) from M'Hamid head to Erg Lihoudi or the smaller dunes of El Mesouiria, 8km from M'Hamid. You can arrive there by *piste* off the main road 18km before M'Hamid, but a guide is advisable.

The star attraction, though, is the misnamed Erg Chigaga, not a single dune (*erg*) but an awesome stretch of golden sand sea some 56km southwest of M'Hamid. The best way to reach them is in classic movie style: by camel, which takes five days or a week (from Dh500 to Dh600 per day) round trip.

ⓘ BOOKING ERG CHIGAGA EXCURSIONS: TOP TIPS

Book ahead Given the considerable logistics of desert travel (and the fact that top guides are often booked in advance through Marrakesh agencies), it's always best to book ahead. It also gives you time to nail down the details of your camp and itinerary.

First time? Keep it short As any Sufi mystic will attest, being alone with your thoughts in the desert can be an illuminating, uplifting experience – but those not accustomed to such profound isolation may get bored quickly.

Camel riding or camel trekking Be aware that not all camels are for riding. In fact, most dromedaries are used for transporting luggage and food. If you want to ride your camel you need to specify that at the outset and it may cost more if additional animals are needed.

Before you commit to a longer trip, get names The guide (and the guide's language ability) can make or break your experience. Ask for the name of the guide with whom you'll be travelling, do an internet search for reviews, and solicit feedback on Lonely Planet's Thorn Tree (www.lonelyplanet.com/thorntree).

To reach the area in a few hours, you'll need a 4WD, which costs Dh1000 to Dh1300 per day with insurance, plus another Dh350 to Dh500 for the camp.

Other nearby desert destinations include Erg Ezahar and the Iriki oasis mirage. And if you get the hang of camel-riding, you might consider an epic 12-day camel trip to Foum Zguid.

☞ Tours

Treks on foot, by camel or 4WD to Erg Chigaga can be arranged in Marrakesh, Zagora or M'Hamid. Sales ploys come with the territory, so don't be reeled in by *faux guide* scare tactics. Prices are fairly standard: around Dh350 per person per day for an overnight camel trek and Dh500 to Dh600 per day for a camel trek to Erg Chigaga. Also bear in mind that many desert tour operators only accept payment in cash.

Bivouac Sous Les Étoiles　DESERT SAFARI
(☎0644 77 74 05; www.bivouacsouslesetoiles.org) Expert and friendly 4WD excursions and camel treks led by the personable Hassan and a team of M'Hamid locals.

Caravan de Rêves　DESERT SAFARI
(☎0670 02 00 33; www.caravane-de-reve.com) A small operation of French, German and English-speaking Saharawi (indigenous people of Western Sahara) offering camel treks, walking tours, sand-boarding and 4WD excursions, including a well-priced overnight Erg Chigaga trip including 4WD, three meals and accommodation for Dh1000.

Sahara Services　DESERT SAFARI
(☎0661 77 67 66; www.saharaservices.info) All-inclusive desert trips via camel and 4WD, including overnights to an encampment of walled Berber tents in Erg Chigaga. A large outfit, it uses many of the other guides in town and thus prices are on the high side.

Zbar Travel　DESERT SAFARI
(☎0668 51 72 80; www.zbartravel.com) Offers overnights at an Erg Chigaga encampment, sleep-outs under the stars, sand-boarding and dromedary treks.

🛏 Sleeping & Eating

Most hotels can also arrange excursions and overnight camps in the desert.

Auberge la Palmeraie　INN €
(☎0668 72 98 51; www.sable-voyage.com; per person b&b/half board Dh150/200) Located across the Oued Drâa in the shade of the palm grove is the Laghrissi brothers' budget-friendly camp. Mixing traditional goat hair Berber tents and modest pisé rooms with mattress beds on flat-weave carpets, it provides simple accommodation. Showers and toilets are basic, with the latter of the squat variety. The brothers are both experienced guides and offer well-priced excursions.

Turn left at the mosque as you enter M'Hamid and you'll find it just past Hamada du Drâa.

Dar Sidi Bounou　GUESTHOUSE €
(☎0524 84 63 30; www.darsidibounou.com; per person incl half board Berber tent/r Dh340/450; ⓅⓈ) A desert dream: dunes in the backyard, sand hammams, Saharawi music jam

sessions and *mechoui* (whole roast lamb) feasts on starry terraces. Retreat to Berber tents and mudbrick huts that sleep six to eight, sleep on the roof, or curl up between crisp cotton sheets in the main house. Instead of the usual sandy pool, Dar Sidi Bounou offers desert immersion experiences such as landscape-painting, cooking or belly dancing classes.

It's 4km beyond Ouled Driss.

Le Drom'Blanc INN €€
(☏0524 84 68 52; www.ledromblanc.com; GPS coordinates N 29°49.054, W 005°40.681; per person incl breakfast bivouac/s/d Dh190/430/585; ⓟ❋ⓢ) Well off the beaten track down a seemingly endless bumpy *piste*, Le Drom'Blanc is an excellent place for families and groups. Guest rooms are available in the air-conditioned riad or in small cottages dotted around the garden. Your hostess, Maguy, is an excellent cook, and if you book ahead, she'll prepare her famous spice-infused lamb baked in a traditional clay oven in the garden.

★**Erg Chigaga Luxury Desert Camp** DESERT CAMP €€€
(www.desertcampmorocco.com; per person all-inclusive main/private/wild camp Dh2530/2980/3150) Set in the shadow of Erg Chigaga's highest dune is Morocco's most luxurious tented camp. Co-owned by M'Hamid native, Mohammed Boulfrifi (aka Bobo) and British expat Nick Garsten, the 13 sumptuous caidal tents (25 sq metres each) are furnished with wall-to-wall carpets, handcrafted beds, snug duvets, percale cotton sheets and solar-powered lighting. Camel-rides, guided walks, chill-out zones furnished with hammocks, board games and magical evenings filled with Gnaoua ballads played with goatskin drums – the experience here is second to none.

For those seeking more privacy, the camp also operates two private camps (each with only two tents) and offers the option of wild camping on treks of three days or more.

Jnan Lilou MAISON D'HÔTE €€€
(☏0671 51 74 77; www.jnanlilou.com; Ksar Bounou; s/d incl half board Dh935/1430; ⓟ❋ⓢ▤) When siroccos blow through town, retreat to air-conditioned candy-coloured rooms featuring en-suite *tadelakt* bathrooms with shiny brass sinks. Lunch and evening menus mix French and Moroccan cuisine, with fireside dining in winter and lunches under the

poolside pergola in summer. The three-night, full-board packages including camel rides and an overnight excursion to Erg Chigaga are good value (Dh2360 to Dh3100).

❶ Getting There & Away

A daily CTM bus leaves M'Hamid for Zagora (Dh30, 1½ hours), Ouarzazate (Dh75, five hours) and Marrakesh (Dh130, 10 hours). Local buses and taxis leave for Zagora (Dh25) throughout the day. Buses and taxis all depart from the main square in M'Hamid.

West of Erg Chigaga

Exiting Erg Chigaga by 4WD, head north to Ouarzazate or Marrakesh via Foum Zguid. En route through the *sahel* and *reg*, you'll pass the Iriki 'oasis' under an imposing plateau on your right. From here, you'll spot thirsty birds and gazelles drinking from a vast lake. But look again: 'Lake Iriki is actually a salt pan shimmering in the heat haze, with deceptive silhouettes of poisonous calotropis bushes.

Travel another 30km or so and you'll hit the N12 tarmac road. From here the road heads south to Tata and north to Foum Zguid. Foum Zguid is a strategic military base, so you may be asked to show your passport here. Downtown is a crossroads with all the necessities: water, petrol, a public phone, restaurants and coffee. As you head north out of town, past the guardhouse, a road east leads to the town's two hotels. The road north is rough, ruined by trucks serving the nearby titanium mines, but the scenery is spectacularly barren.

Eighty-five kilometres north of Foum Zguid is Tazenakht, a handy stop for a quick bite, coffee, petrol and, yes, carpets. The distinctive local carpets (a mix of flat-weave and thick pile) with their extraordinary zigzagging patterns and bold colour schemes of red, orange and blue, are hung all around town. You can skip the middlemen and browse fixed-price pieces inside the government-run Agence de L'Artisanat (⏰7am-7pm), within a walled compound on your right as you enter the town from the south.

More carpets await discovery 26km north in the village of Anzal at Jemaite Tifawin Carpet Cooperative (Association of Light; ☏0642 59 29 80; ⏰carpet showroom 9am-noon & 2-6pm Mon-Thu, studio open house 9am-5pm Sun). If you phone a week in advance, they'll happily organise a studio visit and show you how to create natural dyes and spin raw wool into yarn. Approaching from the south, turn left at the sign for Khouzama in the centre of Anzal.

🍴 Sleeping & Eating

You'll find Foum Zguid's two hotels signposted east at the police checkpoint at the northern entrance to the town.

Maison d'Hôtes Hiba   MAISON D'HÔTE €€
(☑0615 72 72 82; www.maisondhoteshiba.com; GPS coordinates N° 30°07.549, W°006°52.411, Foum Zguid; per person incl half board Dh220-250; ☀🍴) A rock-studded guesthouse and restaurant serving restorative meals of tajine, salad and fruit (Dh80) on the scenic terrace or in the air-conditioned salon. Comfy grotto-style rooms have en-suite bathrooms making this a welcome overnight stop after roughing it in the desert.

Bab Rimal   HOTEL €€
(☑0524 39 41 95; www.babrimal.com; GPS coordinates N 30°07.722, W 006°52.062, Foum Zguid; s/d/ste incl half board Dh530/780/1460; ⓟ☀🛜🍴) A complex of faux-pisé cottages centred around a large, flower-fringed pool. Standard rooms come with platform beds, *zellij* floor tiles and Tazenakht carpets. More luxurious suites are housed in mini villas with double-aspect windows and their own garden terraces. It's a popular lunch stop for tour groups, who relish a few hours in the pool on the long drive south or north.

Restaurant Chigaga   MOROCCAN €
(Foum Zguid; sandwiches Dh20-35, mains Dh35-60; ⏰7am-9pm) A popular restaurant on the east side of Foum Zguid's main town square with outdoor seating, barbecued brochettes and monster sandwiches.

Bab Sahara   MOROCCAN €
(☑0524 84 10 70; Tazenakht; mains Dh60-80; ⏰8am-11pm; 🛜) This Peace Corps–certified hotel on Tazenakht's main drag is a popular pitstop for pizza, brochette and bubbling tajines. It also does a mean *nous-nous* (half-half) coffee that would almost past muster in an Italian bar.

❶ Getting There & Away

Sitting at the crossroads between Ouarzazate and Agadir, Tazenakht is something of a transport hub, although without your own 4WD transport onward travel to Foum Zguid and Erg Chigaga is impossible from here. If you're driving

yourself, fuel up in Tazenakht as the two gas stations further south don't have a reliable supply of petrol. And for those contemplating the westward drive east along the R108, don't attempt it in a 2WD vehicle as the road is particularly bad.

DADÈS VALLEY & THE GORGES سهول داداس والمضايق

Nomad crossings, rose valleys and two-tone kasbahs: even on paper, the Dadès Valley stretches the imagination. From the daunting High Atlas to the north to the rugged Jebel Saghro range south, the valley is dotted with oases and mudbrick palaces that give the region its fairy-tale nickname – Valley of a Thousand Kasbahs. Some of the best views are only glimpsed on foot, on hidden livestock tracks between the Dadès and Todra Gorges and nomad routes across the Saghro.

Paved roads from Tinerhir to Imilchil and the intersection of the N8 between Beni Mellal and Khenifra, and from Er-Rachidia north up the N13 to Meknès, allow travellers to connect easily with Middle Atlas itineraries.

Skoura سكورة
POP 2800

By the time caravans laden with gold and spice reached Skoura, the camels must've been gasping. After a two-month journey across the Sahara, blue-robed Tuareg desert traders offloaded cargo from caravans in Skoura, where Middle Atlas mountaineers packed it onto mules headed to Fez. Ouarzazate is now the region's commercial centre 39km west, but Skoura's historic mudbrick castles remain, and desert traders throng Monday and Thursday souqs brimming with intensely flavourful desert produce. When market days are done and palm-tree shadows stretch across the road, no one seems in a hurry to leave.

◉ Sights & Activities

Navigating the network of dirt tracks in Skoura's vast *palmeraie* is challenging, so invest in a guide (Dh50 per hour). Most hotels offer their own excursions.

★**Palmeraie**   PALM GROVES
Skoura's defining features remain its mudbrick kasbahs and vast Unesco-protected

palm groves, earning the moniker 'Oasis of 1000 Palms'. Under this green canopy, a 15-mile patchwork of carefully tended garden plots are watered by an ingenious, centuries-old *khettara* system of locks, levers and canals. More than 100 bird species flourish here. Stay overnight in a pisé guesthouse and explore the *palmeraie* on foot or bicycle.

Kasbah Amridil   KASBAH

(unguided/guided visit Dh10/50) Morocco's most coveted kasbah is this 17th-century wonder, which appears on Morocco's 50-dirham note. Signposted just a few hundred metres from the main road, this living museum shows that traditional kasbah life hasn't changed much over the centuries, with hand-carved door locks, an olive-oil press, still-functioning bread ovens, and goats bleating in the courtyard.

🛏 Sleeping & Eating

Skoura is a wonderfully peaceful place to overnight with the best accommodation hidden in the *palmeraie*. Most places here tend towards the higher end of the budget, but they're absolutely worth it. Given that this is a small oasis, there are no real restaurants, so hotels offer full board, or half board with some light lunch options. If you're just passing through, you may be able to book lunch (depending on numbers), but you'll need to reserve ahead.

Note that there is no ATM in Skoura, and since most local guesthouses don't accept credit cards, you'll need to stop for cash in Ouarzazate.

Chez Slimani   MAISON D'HÔTE €

(☑ 0524 85 23 59; www.chezslimani.com; Douar Magramane; r incl half board Dh120-160) With the local mayor for host, this Skoura homestay offers a pleasant insight into *palmeraie* life: a garden filled with pomegranate trees, dates drying in the yard and a few sheep and goats for neighbours. Rooms are simple and light-filled with shared bathrooms, while homemade breakfasts and dinner are served communally on the shady garden terrace.

It's signed off the N10 west of the village. Follow orange painted rocks 1.5km along a *piste* road.

Kasbah Aït Abou   KASBAH €

(☑ 0524 85 22 34; www.kasbahaitabou.com; Palmeraie de Skoura; per person incl breakfast/half board Dh180/250; ℗) Sleep like a dignitary in this 1825 kasbah built by the local *caïd*, with a 25m mudbrick tower that's an engineering marvel. Ground-floor rooms are big, plain and naturally cool, with wonky en-suite bathrooms, or you may opt for newer rooms around the vegetable garden. Thanks to a unique partnership with the UCPA youth club, horse rides through the *palmeraie* (per hour/day Dh150/400) can also be arranged.

Follow red arrows from the main road.

EVERY PALM TREE DESERVES A HAND

Walking the Skoura Oasis, feet naturally fall into rhythm with the bossa-nova sway of stately palms. But they're not here for looks: palms have work to do in the oasis, providing dates, shade and fronds to be woven into roofing material, floor coverings and fencing.

Palms are plentiful in this 'Oasis of 1000 Palms', but not one of them can be taken for granted. One concern is Bayoud disease, a fungus that passes from palm to palm. Unesco is taking steps to protect palm oases from Aït Benhaddou to Figuig, declaring the oases a biosphere reserve, and the Moroccan government is planting palms believed to be Bayoud-resistant.

But Skoura's majestic palms face another danger, reports the director of the **Skoura Cultural Centre's** (☑ 0524 85 23 92) palm-preservation initiative. 'The biggest threat to our palms isn't actually Bayoud: it's poverty,' he says. 'When crops fail, to support their families, some people illegally sell palms to decorate big-city resorts.'

To address this problem, the centre recently opened an **oasis arts showcase** (⊙ 8.30am-noon, 3.30-5pm) on the N10 on the eastern edge of town. Here Skoura residents sell items made with palm fronds, sustainably harvested without harming the trees. For travellers who've admired Morocco's majestic palm groves, these sun hats, breadbaskets, mats and frond-framed lanterns make meaningful mementos – and purchases support the centre's palm-preservation efforts.

★ **Dar Lorkam** MAISON D'HÔTE €€
(✆0524 85 22 40; www.dar-lorkam.com; GPS coordinates N 31°05.57, W 06°35.03; d/ste incl half board Dh800/1000; ⊗closed Jan & Jul; P✿🖥🛜✍)
With a garden full of roses and views of Jebel M'Goun from the vine-draped terraces there's hardly any reason to venture beyond the snug confines of Dar Lorkam. Six cosy rooms with understated decorative details sit beneath shady olive trees overlooking a small, child-friendly pool. Mornings slip by with walks in the *palmeraie* and visits to the souq while evenings are best spent in the royal purple hammam.

Follow green triangle markers from the main road.

Sawadi MAISON D'HÔTE €€
(✆0524 85 23 41; www.sawadi.ma; Douar Tajanate; s/d/ste incl breakfast Dh660/780/930; P✿🛜✍)
🌿 An oasis within an oasis, 9 acres of walled organic gardens make a bucolic setting for pisé bungalows – and they also yield sumptuous evening meals. Unwind after visits to local artisans or kasbah architecture tours with a steamy hammam, or chilled white wine by the salt-filtered, chlorine-free pool. Follow white triangle markers from the road into the north end of the oasis.

★ **Jardins de Skoura** MAISON D'HÔTE €€€
(✆0524 85 23 24; www.lesjardinsdeskoura. com; Palmeraie de Skoura; r/ste incl breakfast Dh880/1320; ⊗closed during Ramadan; ✿✍)
🌿 Low-key, high-romance Skoura style: this garden guesthouse offers intimate rooms with nooks carved from pisé walls, custom-designed rugs and attractive artworks. Lunch on light salads and fresh-baked pizza amid the magical blooming garden, then nap beside the small pool beneath your courtesy palm-woven sunhat. You might struggle to raise yourself for donkey rides in the *palmeraie*, aperitifs on the rooftop and French-Moroccan dinners (Dh200), but they're worth it.

Follow orange triangle markers from the main road.

Kasbah Aït ben Moro KASBAH €€€
(✆0524 85 21 16; www.aitbenmoro.com; s/d incl half board Dh670/780-1000; P✿🖥🛜✍) An 18th-century kasbah given a stylish makeover that remains true to its desert roots with original palm-beam ceilings, moody low-lit passageways and water-conserving cactus gardens. The three tower rooms are the sweetest deals, with shared bathrooms and

oasis views; ask for the one with a fireplace. It's located on the N10, 2km west of Skoura.

ⓘ Getting There & Away

There are regular but infrequent buses from Ouarzazate (Dh10, 45 minutes) and Tinerhir (Dh40, two hours) to the centre of Skoura, which lies just off the N10 at the eastern end of the oasis. Tickets can be bought at Restaurant La Kasbah, which is located on the main road in Skoura. Grands taxis from Ouarzazate (Dh15) and Kelaâ M'Gouna (Dh15) stop just after the crossroads.

Kelaâ M'Gouna قلعة مكونة

Although it takes its name from the nearby M'Goun mountain, the small town of Kelaâ M'Gouna is famous for roses and daggers. Some 50km from Skoura, pink roses start peeking through dense roadside hedgerows, and you can't miss the bottles of local rosewater for sale in town. During the May rose harvest you'll see rose garlands everywhere, especially during the town's signature rose festival (⊗1st weekend May). At Wednesday souqs, you can load up on dried edible roses.

To stop and smell the roses with a nature walk, call the bureau des guides (✆0662 13 21 92, 0661 79 61 01) or book official guides through local hotels (Dh300 per day). At Kelaâ's downtown crossroads are some handy facilities: an ATM, pharmacies and internet cafes.

🛏 Sleeping & Eating

Kasbah Iswan MAISON D'HÔTE €€
(✆0658 96 28 89; www.kasbahiswan.com; per person incl half board Dh350) Spend a few days in comfortable Kasbah Iswan and you'll start to feel as at home as the storks that nest on the turrets. Nights are dark and peaceful, filled with friendly conversation and delicious plates of coucous and fried sardines conjured up by Azzedine, while days are spent reading in the flower-filled courtyard or wandering through rose gardens along the M'Goun River.

The kasbah is located 7km north of Kelaâ M'Gouna in the village of Tazroute. A taxi costs Dh10.

Kasbah Itran KASBAH €€
(✆0524 83 71 03; www.kasbahitran.com; d incl half board without bathroom Dh400, with bathroom Dh550-600; 🛜✿) A maze of terraces, fire-

places and simple rooms that are in need of some maintenance. Most come with en-suite bathrooms (three with air-con), stiff beds and views over the M'Goun River. Trekking excursions are available. It's 2km northwest of Kelaâ M'Gouna; minivans from town run past en route to the village of Torbis (Dh5).

🛍 Shopping

Unité de Distillation de Rose   SOUVENIRS
(☑0661 34 81 77; ⊙8am-5.30pm) Located 500m before you reach downtown on your right, this rosewater distillery purchases buds direct from farmers in the valley. The adjoining showroom offers a full range of perfume, creams and bath products, including uncoloured, untreated rosewater used locally as aftershave.

**Cooperative Artisan
du Poignards Azlag**   ARTS & CRAFTS
(⊙9am-6pm) At this set-price showroom on the main road at the eastern edge of town, ceremonial daggers range from Dh250 to Dh1200. On the wall is a collection of local styles, ranging from Tuareg (leather-handled, straight blade) to Aït Aitta (inlaid hilt, curved blade). It's sometimes closed for lunch.

❶ Getting There & Away

Buses run between Ouarzazate and Tinerhir via Kelaâ, but are often full. You can catch buses and grands taxis from the centre of Kelaâ, where they pull up beside the road. Taxis serve Ouarzazate (Dh30), Skoura (Dh15), Boumalne du Dadès (Dh7) and Tinerhir (Dh30).

Boumalne du Dadès

بوملنه داده

POP 11,200

Head 24km northeast of Kelaâ M'Gouna until you reach a fork: the main road continues over the river to the hillside town of Boumalne du Dadès, while the left-hand road leads into stunning Dadès Gorge. The town is at its liveliest during the Wednesday and Sunday souq.

◎ Sights & Activities

A few kilometres to the east of town, where the *piste* leads south into the seemingly lifeless *hammada* to the village of Tagdilt, you'll find a surprisingly rich variety of bird life in the aptly named Vallée des

Oiseaux (Valley of the Birds). Horned lark, wheat-ears, sand grouse, buzzards and eagle owls are among some of the species you may spot here along with a healthy reptile population and small herds of Edmi gazelle and Addax antelope. Organise trips with knowledgeable, local guide Hamou Aït Lhou at the *bureau des guides*, which also rents out mountain bikes (Dh120 per day) and organises treks further afield to Jebel Saghro.

Bureau des Guides   TREKKING, CYCLING
(☑0667 59 32 92; hamou57@voila.fr; Ave Mohammed V) Located on the main road near the junction for the Dadès Valley.

🛏 Sleeping

Hôtel Almanader   HOTEL €€
(☑0524 83 01 72; www.hotelmanader.com; Ave Mohammed V; s/d incl half board Dh200/400) High above the river valley, Almanader makes a splash with colourful murals and 12 tidy, quirky rooms with candy-coloured stucco ceilings; four have air-conditioning. Easy-going staff are quick with hellos, espresso and homestyle Berber cooking (meals Dh70 to Dh100).

Xaluca Dadès   HOTEL €€€
(☑0535 57 84 50; www.xaluca.com; s/d incl break-fast Dh850/1120; ℙ❋@🛜🐾) A sub-Saharan makeover transformed this 1970s convention centre into a destination hotel. The 106 guest rooms have balconies with Tuareg chairs, plush beds with thick duvets and mud-cloth bedspreads. Expect all the mod cons, plus hammam (Dh100), bar, billiards, panoramic terrace swimming pool, Jacuzzi and noisy gym. It's signposted at the top of the hill on Ave Mohammed V.

🍴 Eating

Restaurant Oussikis   MOROCCAN €
(Place de Souk; dishes Dh50-90) Inside the souq plaza on your left, you'll spot chef Fadil Faska in his spotless open kitchen transforming fresh, local ingredients into savoury tajines, flaky *pastilla,* or quick, satisfying salads (Dh10) and roast chicken (Dh30).

Hôtel-Restaurant Adrar   MOROCCAN €
(☑0524 83 07 65; Ave Mohammed V; meals Dh35-70) Handy to the bus station yet clean, with popular, filling meals of salads and brochettes or the local speciality: *gallia* (game hen) tajine.

ⓘ Information

On Ave Mohammed V there's a Banque Popu-laire, four pharmacies and internet access.

ⓘ Getting There & Away

BUS

Supratours offers a daily service to Ouarzazate (Dh40, two hours), Tinerhir (Dh25, 45 minutes), Marrakesh (Dh115, six hours) and Merzouga (Dh150, six hours). The ticket office is near Banque Populaire and buses stop near the covered market.

Other, cheaper, private buses also leave daily to Ouarzazate (Dh30), Tinerhir (Dh10) and Marrakesh (Dh100), and multiple times daily to Er-Rachidia (Dh40).

TAXI, TRUCK & MINIBUS

You may have to wait awhile for a grand taxi or minibus to fill up; fares are Dh40 to Ouarzazate, Dh20 to Tinerhir and Dh10 to Aït Oudinar (inside the Dadès Gorge).

Trekking Jebel Saghro

Few tourists venture into the starkly beauti-ful Jebel Saghro (aka Jebel Sarhro or Djebel Sahro) as most of the flat-topped mesas, volcanic pinnacles and deep gorges dotted with palm groves are only accessible on foot. This arid, isolated territory is home turf to the seminomadic Aït Atta, legendary warri-ors famous for their 1933 stand against the French here, on Jebel Bou Gafer.

THE TREK AT A GLANCE

Duration five to six days

Distance 56km

Standard medium

Start Tagdilt

Finish Kelaâ M'Gouna

Highest Point Tizi n'Ouarg (approxi-mately 2300m)

Accommodation camping and gîtes/homestay

Public Transport yes

Summary A great alternative to the classic Saghro traverse, showcasing the staggering and varied beauty of the range. Given demanding climbs and long days of walking, you might add another night to the route.

Jebel Saghro is accessed from three trek-king hubs: Kelaâ M'Gouna and Boumalne du Dadès on the north side of the range, and the southern village of N'Kob. The most scenic routes head through the heart of the range, between Igli and Bab n'Ali.

This circuit has one big advantage over the classic Saghro north–south traverse: it begins and ends on the north side of the mountains, so you can easily resume jour-neys to Dadès gorges, Merzouga and the dunes.

When to Go

While many High Atlas trails are impassable between November and February, Saghro is a prime winter trekking destination. Winter temperatures can dip below freezing, and snow may fall as low as 1400m, but even when it does snow, it is usually possible to trek. In autumn and spring, night-time tem-peratures rarely fall below zero. When sum-mer temperatures get scorching hot (above 40°C), water sources disappear, and even scorpions hunker under rocks for shade.

ⓘ Getting There & Away

Minibuses run from Boumalne du Dadès to Ikniouln (Dh25), at the northern edge of the range, departing around noon and returning to Boumalne early the next morning. There may be extra buses on Wednesdays, when Ikniouln has its weekly souq.

Day 1: Tagdilt to the Assif Ouarg Valley

DURATION FOUR HOURS / DISTANCE 17KM / ASCENT 200M

Tagdilt is an uninspiring village but a useful trailhead, with three gîtes and a daily cami-onette (pick-up truck) from Boumalne. For 2½ hours, you could follow the piste used by vans crossing the mountain to N'Kob, or veer onto the track that occasionally strays to the side, rejoining the piste further up the slope.

At Imi n'Ouarg, the third village above Tagdilt, the path leaves the road (which con-tinues to mines at Tiouit). The path turns right (southwest) beside the village school, marked by a Moroccan flag.

The path follows the right-hand side of the winding Assif Ouarg valley, beneath the summit of Jebel Kouaouch (2592m). After an hour (about 3km), there's a farm above terraced fields where you can arrange a

BEFORE YOU GO: JEBEL SAGHRO CHECKLIST

Maps The 1:100,000 *Boumalne* and *Tazzarine* maps cover the region, but a more detailed trekking map with history and information on the back is 1:100,000 *Randonnée culturelle dans le Djebel Sarhro* by Mohamed Aït Hamza and Herbert Popp, published in Germany, written in French and available in Morocco, including at hotels in Boumalne and N'Kob (Dh150).

Guide Several foreign tour operators (including Explore, Exodus and Walks Worldwide) run good-value trips here, but many of them subcontract to local guides. You can find a licenced local guide directly through a *bureau des guides* in any of the three Saghro trekking centres: Kelaâ M'Gouna, Boumalne and N'Kob. Expect to pay Dh300 a day for a guide and Dh100 for a mule.

Water Dehydration is common any time of the year, so pack extra water.

Food Stock up in Ouarzazate or Boumalne de Dadès. The three Saghro departure towns all have tea, tinned fish, biscuits and bread, and you may find eggs, dates, almonds, bread and tinned sardines in some villages.

Mule Given the amount of water you must carry, mules are a worthwhile investment. Your guide can organise mules and muleteers.

Gear Bring a sleeping bag. You won't need a tent, unless you'd rather camp than stay at *refuges*.

---

homestay ([phone]0661 08 23 21; per person Dh30-50). The host's sons can be hired as muleteers and hot meals may be available.

Day 2: Assif Ouarg Valley to Igli

DURATION SIX TO SEVEN HOURS / DISTANCE 19KM / ASCENT 620M / DESCENT 860M

The most memorable walk on this trek is also the most difficult, starting with a 35-minute climb towards the head of the valley. The path leads left (south) and Jebel Kouaouch is the highest of a row of peaks straight ahead. The path zigzags over a stream, up towards Kouaouch and a lone juniper tree – a good place for a breather. Depending on fitness and weather, it could take another hour to reach the pass. As you climb, there are good views back towards Tagdilt, and once over the ridge, the High Atlas and Jebel Saghro come into view.

The path drops steeply down ahead, but our track veers right (southwest) across the valley's shoulder and over another ridge, with views south to the palms and kasbahs of N'Kob. Igli is due south over a series of slopes, with the famous Tête de Chameau (Camel's Head) cliffs appearing as you walk down towards the settlement. Three low buildings form a gîte (per person Dh30) with a toilet and wood-fired hot showers (Dh10). There's no electricity or sleeping mats here, but the friendly *gardien* runs a shop selling trekkers' necessities, including mule shoes,

and if you bring flour, he'll have it baked into bread.

For breathtaking mountain sunsets, you've come to the right place. You might add a round trip to Bab n'Ali, one of the most spectacular rock formations in the Saghro, returning to Igli for another night or continuing to the Irhazzoun n'Imlas gîte (per person Dh30).

Day 3: Igli to Tajalajt

DURATION SEVEN TO 7½ HOURS / DISTANCE 24KM / ASCENT 350M / DESCENT 400M

Looming on the right-hand side as you walk is the peak of Jebel Amlal, sacred to the Aït Atta and the site of August pilgrimages. The morning's walk is gentler than the previous day's, leading through wide, rocky valleys. After 1½ hours, beneath the village of Taouginte, the path curves around an Aït Atta cemetery, where graves are marked with piles of stone. The path then leads below the Needles of Saghro, a long, dramatic cliff that slopes down after another 1½ hours to the Amguis River. Several valleys meet at a beautiful camping spot, amid palms and oleander. Half an hour southwards down the valley is Irhazzoun n'Imlas, a village above well-tended fields with a riverside lunch spot.

At Irhazzoun n'Imlas the path joins a *piste* that runs left to N'Kob and right towards the Dadès. Take the right (northwest)

Jebel Saghro Trek

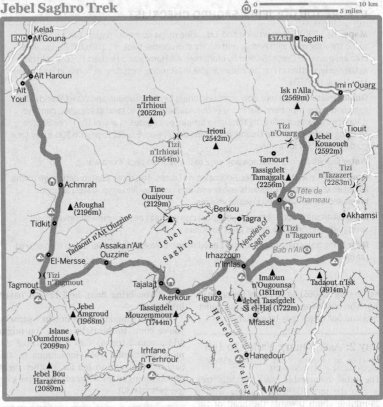

track towards a sheer cliff on the left, with the rocky path leading beneath it and up to a broadening valley. The *piste* loops around the north side of Jebel Tassigdelt Si el-Haj (1722m) and then south again towards Tiguiza, where there is a basic gîte (☎ 0671 72 80 06; per person Dh30). Before Tiguiza, another *piste* leads right (west) to Akerkour village, into a narrowing valley dotted with palms, and up an incline to Tajalajt, where you can arrange a homestay (per person Dh30) and maybe obtain basic meals.

Day 4: Tajalajt to Achmrah

DURATION EIGHT TO 8½ HOURS / DISTANCE 26KM / ASCENT 200M / DESCENT 300M

Take the valley *piste* from Tajalajt, above splendid terraced palm and almond groves. Less than 1½ hours brings you to Assaka n'Aït Ouzzine (1584m), its ruined kasbah teetering above the beautiful valley. Next,

the *piste* leads out of the valley into a rocky, windy steppe.

After 1½ hours from Assaka spent wedged between 2000m ridges, you'll arrive at Tagmout (also called Amgroud after one of the mountains overlooking the village) and a well-kept gîte (per person Dh30, breakfast Dh25) with electricity, mattresses, blankets and possibly lunch (Dh25 to Dh30).

From Tagmout the *piste* leads northwest to Kelaâ M'Gouna and south to N'Kob, with transport headed to N'Kob's Sunday souq. The trek heads due north, climbing over an hour to Tizi n'Tagmout (1754m) for stunning views to the M'Goun Massif. Another hour leads to El-Mersse, where shade and a year-round spring facilitate camping.

The track continues due north, mostly in gentle descent, but with occasional climbs. Less than 1½ hours after El-Mersse, there's a riverside campsite at Tidkit under shade trees and it may be possible to sleep *chez l'habitant* here or in Achmrah, another hour down the track. However, the Berbers on this side of Jebel Saghro are seminomadic and may be absent April to May. If the houses are empty, the animal shelters will be too – a less glamorous but practical place to sleep.

Day 5: Achmrah to Kelaâ M'Gouna

DURATION FOUR HOURS / DISTANCE 14KM / ASCENT 150M / DESCENT 450M

The best parts of this morning walk are the beginning and end. The track north of Achmrah makes a short climb, suddenly revealing M'Goun and Siroua vistas. Less than half an hour later, it crosses a *piste* that leads to an anthracite mine and should not be followed. Instead continue north, occasionally northwest, on a well-worn track that leads down a gully towards the Dadès Valley. As you get closer, you will see the villages of Aït Youl on your left, Aït Haroun on the right, and a valley studded with old kasbahs. Head for Aït Haroun, where there is a bridge over the Dadès River. The Boumalne–Kelaâ M'Gouna road is nearby, but long after you return to the modern world, Saghro's seminomadic spirit stays with you.

Dadès Gorge

مخنف ا مفيق ا دادس

As the local saying goes, the wind has a son who lives in Boumalne, which is why he rips down this valley to visit him in winter. Sitting in the rain shadow of the Central Atlas, the Dadès Gorge presents a dramatic landscape: ancient rust-red and mauve mountains stripped back to zigzagging layers of strata and knobbly rock formations reminiscent of Utah. A rush of springtime water puddles in the valley where irrigation channels siphon it off to fields of wheat and orchards of fig, almond and olive trees. A series of crumbling kasbahs and *ksour* line the valley in the Berber villages of Aït Youl, Aït Arbi, Aït Oudinar, Aït Ouffi and Aït Toukhsine.

Nomads still live in the surrounding mountains with their herds (you can see some of their troglodyte caves from the Berbere de la Montagne campground) and use the valley as a seasonal livestock between their High Atlas summer pastures and their winter home in Jebel Saghro. In spring and autumn, if you're lucky, you'll see them on the move with laden camels and mules.

The R704 road is sealed all the way to Msemrir (63km north of Boumalne de Dadès), but you'll need a 4WD beyond that – especially for the *piste* that leads southeast into Todra Gorge. If you're up for a challenge, you could travel north from Msemrir over the High Atlas to Imilchil. Lots of transport heads up the valley on Saturday for the Msemrir market. There's also a market in Aït Oudinar on Sunday.

◉ Sights & Activities

The most dramatic gorge scenery commences 26km up the gorge where the road crosses the river and starts to climb through an extraordinary series of hairpin bends (see www.dangerousroads.org). When the road flattens out again, you might take that as your cue to turn around: you've covered the best gorge scenery you can see without 4WD or good hiking shoes.

There's a good trekking trail heading northwest, beginning just across the river, 28km from Boumalne du Dadès. The energetic could cover the distance from Dadès and Todra Gorges on foot (a two- to three-day walk). Most hotels in the gorge and Boumalne du Dadès can arrange hiking guides (Dh200 to Dh300 per day) and 4WD trips to the Todra Gorge (Dh1400 per day).

Aït Youl
KASBAH

Those art-deco tourism posters you'll see all over Morocco showing a red-and-white kasbah in a rocky oasis aren't exaggerating: just 6.5km into the gorge the old Glaoui kasbah of Aït Youl is set against a lush backdrop of almond and fig trees. A couple of kilometres past Aït Youl, the road crosses an *oued;* this river valley offers a sneaky back way to Kelaâ M'Gouna on foot.

Gorge de Miguirne
GORGE

Cresting over a small pass, 14km from Boumalne, is the hidden Gorge de Miguirne (Sidi Boubar Gorge), which joins the Dadès Gorge from the south. It offers a pleasant half-day hike amid its springs and rock pools. The owner of Restaurant Meguirne, 14km from Boumalne, can provide guides.

Tamlalt Valley
VALLEY

Eighteen kilometres from Boumalne brings you to extraordinary red rock formations that look like wax, melting right into the green carpet of the *palmeraie* below Aït

GORGE YOURSELF: DADÈS TO TODRA

The 42km *piste* drive from Dadès Gorge to Tamtattouchte in the Todra Gorge is a tough five-hour journey through twisting hills and the boulder-strewn valley of Tizgui n'Ouadda. The crossing is prone to flash floods, so seek up-to-date advice on the state of the *piste* before setting off. The route starts with a bone-rattling ascent at Tilmi, 15km north of Msemrir and then crests the 2639m-high **Tizi n'Uguent Zegsaoun** before descending through a long valley to emerge just north of Tamtattouchte.

The trip should only be attempted by 4WD during the summer months (May to September), and a local guide is recommended. In May, many nomadic Berbers with homes in Aït Haini head to this valley to pitch tents and graze large herds of sheep. If you stop, you may be invited into tents to sip tea and swap stories.

Arbi. They're known locally as *Les Doigts de Singes* (or 'Monkey's Fingers') given their bizarre wind-worn shapes. A little further on is the more colourfully named 'Valley of Human Bodies', where famished travellers are said to have died of hunger and been turned to stone.

Association Gorge du Dadès ARTS & CRAFTS (☑0677 90 96 70, 0666 39 69 49; 24km Aït Oudinar; ☺2-5pm Mon-Sat) Tufted carpets are made at this weaving cooperative, but soft kilim blankets made with undyed, extra-fluffy lambswool are signature pieces. The women are introducing non-chemical dyes made from local walnuts shells (brown), onion skins (yellow) and poppies (black). Items are sold at fixed prices and the weaver is paid directly.

From the roadside sign, follow arrows to the western bank to find the converted stable currently housing the cooperative.

🛏 Sleeping

Most accommodation listed here is within 28km of Boumalne du Dadès, and the kilometre markings refer to the distance from Boumalne. Most will let you sleep in the salon or on the terrace (even in summer you may need a sleeping bag) for around Dh30, or camp by the river for Dh15 to Dh30.

In Msemrir the best place to sleep is the run-down but friendly **Hotel Agdal** (☑0671 53 20 52; Msemrir; s/d Dh40/80; ℗), which offers simple en-suite rooms opposite the market.

Chez L'Habitant Amazigh MAISON D'HÔTE € (☑0670 71 45 51; zaid.azul@hotmail.fr; Km 20, Aït Arbi; incl breakfast s Dh180, d Dh200-300; 🛜) Spend a night at the Tair family home and you may find yourself invited to a local wedding, dressing up in Berber finery or taking

impromptu walks through valley orchards learning the names of local herbs and flowers. Pink pisé rooms and exuberantly decorated salons can't compete with first-class terrace views over the river and valley rock formations.

Auberge des Gorges du Dadès INN € (☑0524 83 02 21; www.aubergeaitoudinar.com; Km 24, Aït Oudinar; camping per person/tent/car Dh20/30/10, s/d per person incl half board Dh250/200; ℗❄) Bubbly with personality and overlooking the river, the Auberge has 30 rooms that cover the waterfront with Moroccan motifs: pisé Amazigh designs and fossil sinks in one wing, ornate stucco and *beldi* tile in another. Some have balconies and all have basic en-suite bathrooms and tiled floors. Bring socks or slippers.

Le Berbère de la Montagne CAMPGROUND, GUESTHOUSE € (☑0524 83 02 28; www.berbere-montagne.com; Km 34; per person incl half board Dh250-300, camping per person/car/tent/caravan Dh15/12/15/30; ℗🛜) With tent pitches overlooking the river and the hotel within a few metres of the narrowest point of the gorge, this friendly place offers peaceful accommodation far from the madding crowds. It's also perfectly located for hikes into the Petit Gorge and up into the hills to visit nomad encampments and secret caves hung with stalactites. The eight pleasant rooms come with *tataoui* ceilings, terracotta tiled floors and pine beds heaped with warm blankets.

Laundry facilities/electricity are an additional Dh30/20, and guides will cost Dh200 per day.

Chez Pierre INN €€ (☑0524 83 02 67; www.chezpierre.org; Km 27, Aït Ouffi; s/d/q incl breakfast Dh465/605/880; 🛜❄) Eight light-filled rooms and one apartment are notched right into the gorge wall, with tasteful, minimalist decor, flowering terraces and poolside sun decks. A rosy gorge sunset is the prelude to spectacular five-course dinners (Dh220) featuring inventive appetisers, delicately cooked duck in red-wine jus and impeccable *tarte tatin* served beside the snug wood-burning stove.

Brothers Ismael and Lahcen Sibiri run the inn with great pride and passion and offer guided day trips in English, French and Spanish.

Maison 4 Saisons   MAISON D'HÔTE €€
(☑ 0524 83 17 55; www.chambresdhotesdades.com; Km 24, Aït Oudinar; s/d incl half board Dh330/500) Book early for one of the four 'seasonal' rooms at Youssef Azrarag's welcoming new guesthouse where Berber hospitality, vintage French furniture and bright local decor blend seamlessly. All the rooms overlook the lovely patio garden where numerous varieties of mountain mint and verveine perfume the air. After High Atlas treks, walkers collapse on Moroccan cushions in the large open-plan kitchen, where you're free to lend a hand cooking.

★Kasbah de Mimi   MAISON D'HÔTE €€€
(☑ 0524 83 05 05, 0671 52 38 55; http://kasbah-mimi.webliberte.net; Km 12, Aït Ibrine; per adult/child incl half board Dh500/335; 🌐🕸) Save yourself the trouble of cultivating friends with fabulous country houses, and book a weekend at one of four rooms in Kasbah de Mimi. At this painstakingly restored cliffside getaway, everything is in excellent taste: Berber *baraka* (blessings) painted on living-room walls, pâté hors d'oeuvres, water-conserving rose gardens tumbling to the valley floor and a grand piano in the fully stocked library. The 500m cliffhanger of a driveway is harrowing, but village kids will cheer your arrival.

✗ Eating

The best dining in the valley is at Chez Pierre. Other than that there are a few casual eateries along the valley. To snap that iconic image of the road snaking up the valley, stop for coffee or a snack at Cafe Timzzillite (☑ 0524 83 05 33; Km 29; ☺ 6am-7pm).

Le Jardin de Source   MOROCCAN €
(☑ 0600 68 51 29; Km 11, Aït Ibrirne; mains Dh55-60; ☺ 10am-6pm) Quick lunches at this garden restaurant near the mouth of the gorge include flavourful vegetarian options, omelettes (Dh30) and marinated turkey kebabs.

Restaurant Isabelle   MOROCCAN €
(Km 15; menu Dh70; ☺ 9am-9.30pm) Hearty omelettes or tajines with salad and drink are served on the terrace with a side of wonder at the melting rocks across the valley.

❶ Getting There & Away

Grands taxis and minibuses run up the gorge from Boumalne and charge Dh10 per person to the cluster of hotels in Aït Oudinar and Aït Ouffi and Dh30 to Msemrir (1½ to two hours). To return, flag down a passing vehicle. Hiring a taxi for a half-day trip into the gorge costs around Dh200. Minibuses run up to Msemrir regularly; the last one back to Boumalne leaves around 4pm.

Tinerhir   تنرهير

POP 36.000

Charm falls a distant third to dust and hustle in Tinerhir (aka Tinghir), a busy mining-town transit hub recently benefiting from a rash of expansion and construction thanks to an administrative upgrade to independent provincial capital. If you need a break after the 51km drive from Boumalne du Dadès, head to the eastern edge of town, where a palm oasis unfolds like a green umbrella. Under the canopy, you'll discover crumbling kasbahs, the abandoned 19th-century Medersa Ikelane (look for the whitewashed mudbrick cupola) and to the north of town, the ruins of Ksar Asfalou, where Muslim and Jewish students once studied under the same roof. An enormous souq is held 2.5km west of the centre on Monday, and there's a Saturday livestock souq in town.

Bicycles and oasis guides are available at Hôtel Tomboctou.

🛏 Sleeping

Hôtel de l'Avenir   HOTEL €
(☑ 0672 52 13 89; 27 Rue Zaid Ouhmed; terrace/r Dh30/150) Cheap, clean rooms, hot showers and a nice roof terrace on the main market square. Ask for a room away from the square or bring earplugs.

Kasbah Petit Nomade   KASBAH €
(☑ 0668 49 58 38; http://kasbah-petitnomade. com; GPS coordinates N 31°31.683, W 005°33.386, Douar Ichmarine; per person incl half board Dh300) Cecile and Lahcen's restored kasbah is a find amid Tinerhir's bleak hotel scene. Three simple rooms decked out in bold reds and mauve sit around an internal courtyard while terrace tables look out over a dense

thicket of *palmeraie*. Tours of Tinerhir's historic Jewish quarter and mosque help you look beyond the unattractive town centre, while hiking, climbing or cycling excursions in the gorge can easily be arranged.

You'll find the kasbah 2km north of Tinerhir at the start of the gorge in the village of Ichmarine.

Hôtel Tomboctou
KASBAH €€

(📞 0524 83 51 91; www.hoteltomboctou.com; 126 Ave Bir Anzarane; s/d/tr incl breakfast Dh470/550/730; ❄ 🖥) Quirky, cosy rooms with en-suite bathrooms in a renovated kasbah built in 1944 for the local *caïd*. For more space, upgrade to the converted kitchen guest room with high, palm-beam ceilings. Traditional kasbah windows are porthole-sized, but sunshine surrounds the courtyard pool and bar. Oasis walking tours and bicycle trips are organised onsite.

Hôtel Saghro
HOTEL €€

(📞 0524 83 41 81; http://bougafer-saghro.com; s/d incl breakfast Dh560/720; 🅿 ❄ 📶 🖥) This large chain hotel situated on a hill north of the centre offers the best views over the *palmeraie* from its panoramic terrace. It is much favoured by tour groups, offers large balconied rooms and rather unremarkable food (menu Dh150). Still, nonguests can use the pool for Dh50 and the terrace is pleasant for sundowners.

✗ Eating

Grill restaurants line Ave Mohammed V and Ave Hassan II, including Café des Amis (Ave Hassan II), Café Central (Ave Hassan II) and Restaurant Essaada (Ave Hassan II). The roof terrace restaurant of the Hôtel l'Oasis (📞 0524 83 36 70; Ave Mohammed V; meals Dh80-100) is a convenient place to eat opposite Pl Principale (bonus: clean toilets).

Chez Michelle Supermarket SUPERMARKET €

(📞 0524 83 46 68; Ave Mohammed V; ⏱ 9am-9pm Sat-Thu) Excellent range of trekking provisions and snacks, and the only place that sells alcohol.

ℹ Information

Banks with ATMs flank Ave Mohammed V, including BMCE and Crédit du Maroc. There's a Banque Populaire opposite Pl Principale.

Tichka Internet (Rue Zaid Ouhmed; per hr Dh6; ⏱ 7am-9.30pm) Next to Hôtel de l'Avenir.

ℹ Getting There & Away

BUS

Buses leave from Pl Principale, off Ave Mohammed V. Supratours stops in Tinerhir en route to Boumalne du Dadès (Dh25, 75 minutes), Ouarzazate (Dh50, three hours), Marrakesh (Dh125, 7½ hours) and, heading in the other direction, Er-Rachidia (Dh30, three hours), Erfoud (Dh55, 3½ hours) and Merzouga (Dh80, 4½ hours). You'll find the ticket office to the right of the bus lot in front of the mosque.

On other lines, there's frequent bus service from Tinerhir to Marrakesh (Dh120) via Ouarzazate (Dh40), and to Erfoud (Dh40), Meknès (Dh110) and Boumalne du Dadès (Dh15).

TAXI & MINIVAN

Grands taxis to Ouarzazate (Dh60), Alnif (Dh25) and Er-Rachidia (Dh45 to Dh70) also leave from Pl Principale, where you'll also find minivans or pick-up trucks into Todra Gorge (Dh7) and beyond to Tamtattouchte (Dh15). An 8am minivan runs to Tamtattouchte (Dh15), Aït Haini (Dh20) and Imilchil (Dh40).

Todra Gorge

مخنف ا مفيق ا تودرغة

Being stuck between a rock and a hard place is a sublime experience in the Todra Gorge, where a 300m-deep fault splits the orange limestone into a deep ravine at some points just wide enough for a crystal-clear river and single-file trekkers to squeeze through. The road from Tinerhir passes green *palmeraies* and Berber villages until, 15km along,

---

TODRA LOOP HIKE

For a vigorous morning hike, try a three-hour loop from north of the gorge to Tizgui, south of the gorge. A 30-minute walk beyond the main gorge is the Petite Gorge, where you'll find a trailhead near Auberge le Festival. Take the track leading uphill to the left (southwest) – regular donkey and mule traffic keeps this path well defined. Head to the pass, and from there, ascend southeast to the next pass. This would be a good place to stray from the main route to look over the rim of the gorge – but be careful, as the winds are powerful up here. From the second pass, descend to the Berber village of Tizgui, where you can stroll through the *palmeraies* back to the gorge.

high walls of pink and grey rock close in around the road. The approach is thrilling, as though the doors of heaven were about to close before you.

The best time to visit is in the morning, when the sunshine briefly illuminates the gorge in a golden moment of welcome. Souvenir vendors and tour buses clog the centre in afternoons, until it suddenly turns dark and bitterly cold. Through the gorge and 18km up the road is the Berber village of Tamtattouchte, with Imilchil some 95km beyond.

🏃 Activities

Besides day hikes in and around the gorge, Todra's vertical rock faces offer sublime rock-climbing routes (French grade 5 to 8), some of them bolted. Many of the routes are over 25m long, although there is some spectacular multi-pitch climbing where routes run over 300m. Pillar du Couchant, near the entrance to the gorge, offers classic long climbs; the Petite Gorge is better for novice climbers, with good short routes. Few of the routes are mapped, although many hotels keep logbooks detailing current information on local routes. Otherwise, internationally certified guides and reliable equipment can be hired from Aventures Verticales.

From the centre of the gorge, you can walk back to Tinerhir through *palmeraies* in three or four hours. With a 4WD or a couple of days walking, you can cover the rough *piste* west of Todra to Dadès Gorge (p136).

There are no banks in the gorge and limited connectivity and phone coverage, so carry enough cash.

Aventures Verticales   ROCK CLIMBING
(☏0524 89 57 27; www.escalade-au-maroc.com; Km 14, Tizgui; 1hr/half-/full day per person for 4 Dh60/160/250) Finally, Todra has a professional climbing outfit with four internationally certified guides offering climbing, alpinism and trekking excursions for all levels. The small shop in Tizgui also stocks top gear for hire and sale, including Rock Pillar climbing shoes, Petzl helmets, Beal ropes and powder sacks, as well as tents and sleeping bags.

The Moroccan-Portuguese venture hopes to develop a serious climbing scene in the gorge, including establishing a school for climbing guides and developing a series of *via ferrata* routes (permanent, bolted routes linked by a safety cable modelled on

those in the Italian Alps), which will facilitate more DIY climbing.

Assettif Aventure   HORSE RIDING
(☏0618 53 07 90; www.assettif.org; Km 14, Tizgui; per hr/day Dh150/500) Arranges treks and horse riding. Advance booking is recommended for overnight horse treks with guide and food (Dh800).

🛏 Sleeping & Eating

Most of the accommodation listed following is within 20km of Tinerhir, and the kilometre markings refer to the distance from Tinerhir.

Camping le Soleil   CAMPGROUND €
(☏0524 89 51 11; www.hotelcampinglesoleil.com; Km 8; campsite per person Dh18, plus per tent/car/campervan/electricity Dh18/18/28/25, d incl half board Dh220-250; 🅿🕸🛜🍴) The first site you reach is among the best, with a good restaurant, clean hot showers, shady sites and a washing machine (per load Dh29). Basic rooms with en-suite bathrooms are also available.

Hôtel Restaurant la Vallée   HOTEL €
(☏0524 89 51 26; Km 15.5; d without bathroom incl breakfast Dh120, d with bathroom incl breakfast/half board Dh150/300; 🍴) Overlooking

Todra Gorge Walk

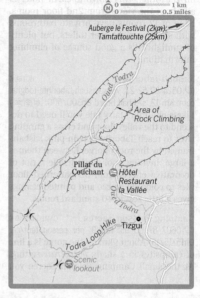

Auberge le Festival (2km);
Tamtattouchte (25km)

Oued Todra

Area of Rock Climbing

Pillar du Couchant
Hôtel Restaurant la Vallée

Oued Todra

Todra Loop Hike

Tizgui

Scenic lookout

the river on one side and facing the gorge on the other, this down-to-earth hotel is all about the views from 2nd-floor rooms. Nine of 12 rooms have private bathrooms with showers right over toilets, but plenty of sunlight. It's a good source of climbing information.

Kasbah Taborihte HOTEL €
(☑ 0524 89 52 23; www.kasbah-taborihte-todgha. com; Km 12; s/d half board Dh300/500; ❋ ☎ ☲) Like a children's fairy tale you'll need to descend to the valley floor and cross a gurgling river to reach Taborihte's twin pink kasbahs framed by the rocky gorge. Between them is a large, inviting pool while inside a riot of decorative effects from 3D-patterned floor tiles to coloured stucco and painted ceilings gives a little zest to 40 standard rooms.

Camping Poisson Sacrée CAMPGROUND €
(☑ 0607 87 05 95; Km 9; per person/tent/car Dh15/15/15) About 9km up the gorge is a line of campsites in a shady *palmeraie* setting. At the small Camping Poisson Sacrée you can camp or dine (Dh70) in the garden beside a 'sacred' pool filled with the namesake freshwater fish, which miraculously survive in saltwater.

Auberge Baddou INN, CAMPGROUND €
(☑ 0672 52 13 89; www.aubergebaddou.com; Km 36, Tamtattouchte; d without/with bathroom incl half board Dh200/250, camping per person/caravan Dh30/100; ❋ ☲) Head to Tamtattouchte for Berber tents or bungalows with candy-coloured walls and a dominant Flintstones aesthetic.

Auberge Les Amis INN, CAMPGROUND €
(☑ 0670 23 43 74; www.amistamt.com; Km 34, Tamtattouchte; s incl half board Dh400, d incl half board Dh460-600, camping per person/car/tent/caravan Dh20/10/10/70) This kasbah-style guesthouse goes the extra mile with generous home cooking, vast bathrooms (most en suite), local rugs and jugs repurposed as sink basins. There's camping out back with electrical hook-ups (included) and laundry (Dh15 per load).

IMILCHIL: MOROCCO'S MEET MARKET

Just another striking Middle Atlas Berber village most of the year, Imilchil is flooded with visitors during its three-day September **marriage moussem**. At this huge festival, local Berbers scope the scene for marriage material. Women strut their stuff in striped woollen cloaks and elaborate jewellery, and boys preen in flowing white jellabas.

The festival usually runs Friday to Sunday in the third or fourth week of September; dates are posted at tourist offices throughout the country. Organised tours to the event are available from cities throughout Morocco, and newly paved roads from Rich and Aït Haini to Imilchil have brought busloads of tourists to see romance blossom. With hustlers, *faux guides* and souvenir stalls eyeing the tourists, onlookers are beginning to outnumber the young lovers – but there's no denying the voyeuristic fascination of the event.

Accommodation
During the festival, the area is covered in tented accommodation. Otherwise, there is basic hotel accommodation at the following:

Chez Bassou (☑ 0523 44 24 02; www.chezbassou.com; s/d incl half board Dh260/400) Forty rooms, some with en-suite bathrooms.

Hotel Izlane (☑ 0661 22 48 82; www.hotelizlane.com; s/d incl half board Dh195/360) Fifteen rooms, four with en-suite bathrooms.

Getting There & Away
To get to Imilchil from Marrakesh, head northeast by bus or grand taxi to Kasba Tadla, and onward by grand taxi to El-Ksiba. At El-Ksiba there is a daily bus to Aghbala. The turn-off for Imilchil is near Tizi n'Isly, about 10km before Aghbala. From the turn-off, 61km of paved road leads south to Imilchil. You may also find local grands taxis or trucks Imilchil-bound for **Friday and Sunday souqs**.

It's possible to reach Imilchil (a breathtaking 160km by 4WD or souq-bound lorry) from Boumalne du Dadès or more easily along a paved road from Tinerhir. Grands taxis leave Imilchil for Tinerhir (Dh40, 2½ to three hours) daily.

★ **Auberge Le Festival** INN €€
(☑ 0661 26 72 51; www.auberge-lefestival.com; Km 22; main house with half board s/d Dh350/500, cave s/d Dh700/1000; [P] [❋]) [✦] Get back to nature in romantically lit cave rooms dug right into the hillside and finished in moulded *tadelakt*, or rock-walled, solar-powered lodge rooms surveying the Petit Gorge. After self-guided treks and climbs (Dh250 per hour) arranged by the multilingual owner, relax in the hillside hot tub or help harvest vegetables in the organic garden for dinner.

Dar Ayour GUESTHOUSE €€
(☑ 0524 89 52 71; www.darayour.com; Km 13; s/d incl half board Dh350/600; [P] [❋]) Riads have arrived in Todra with this warm, artsy five-storey guesthouse that's all Middle Atlas rugs, winking mirrorwork pillows and colourful Berber-inspired abstract paintings. All 14 rooms have en-suite bathrooms, and eight have balconies with matchless valley views. There's even garage parking for an additional Dh15 per night.

❶ Getting There & Away

The road from Aït Haini north to Imilchil and the intersection of the N8 Beni Mellal–Fez road was paved in 2011, opening up the route to normal vehicles. Grands taxis run up the gorge from Tinerhir to Imilchil (Dh40, 2½ hours) and there's usually one transit minivan heading up the gorge every day, with more on Wednesday for Aït Haini's Thursday market and on Friday for Imilchil's Saturday market. Hotels can usually advise on when the next public transport is scheduled.

Tinejdad

POP 7500

Back when caravans arrived loaded with gold, five Berber and Saharan tribes crossed paths at this hitching post (Tinejdad means 'nomad' in Tamazight), quenching their thirsts at the Sources de Lalla Mimouna natural springs, sleeping peacefully in well-fortified *ksour* in the Ferkla oasis and conducting business at 1000-year-old Ksar Asir, a medieval commercial centre that housed an Almoravid mosque and a sizeable Jewish community. Water, shelter, business and *baraka*: what more could a nomad need?

◉ Sights

Tinejdad's crossroads culture remains remarkably intact just off the N10. The Lalla

Mimouna springs are signposted on the left (north) 3km before town, and the green line of the Ferkla oasis begins on the southwest edge of town, where you'll spot towering Ksar Asir.

To see what treasures you can find from desert traders, hit the Sunday and Wednesday souqs on the west side of town.

★ **Musée de Oasis** MUSEUM
(www.elkhorbat.com/en.museum.htm; GPS coordinates N 31°29.693, W 005°05.206; admission Dh20; ⊙ 9am-7pm) Inside restored Ksar el-Khorbat is this award-winning museum that traces tribal migrations through 22 rooms of carefully curated artefacts of seminomadic life: saddles worn shiny; contracts inscribed on wooden tablets in Arabic and Hebrew; Tinejdad jars for water and preserved butter; heavy silver jewellery; and to protect it all from would-be thieves, inlaid muskets and handcuffs.

Interesting multilingual explanations in French, English and Spanish illuminate tribal and family affiliations and explain the vexing architectural differences between a *ksour* and a *kasbah*. Useful indeed when you wander around the labyrinthine alley of the *ksar* in which the museum is housed and which is still home to some 80 families.

Musée Sources Lalla Mimoun MUSEUM
(☑ 0535 78 67 98; admission Dh50; ⊙ 8am-6pm; [P]) This rambling private museum encompasses the fizzing, magnesium-rich springs of Lalla Mimouna and is the passion project of Tinejdad native Zaïd Abbou. Artefacts collected over 30 years – including agricultural implements, textiles, pottery, construction tools, calligraphy tablets and painted prayer books – offer an insight into desert life and are housed in an unfolding series of spaces that encompass an internal garden dotted with words of wisdom from *The Little Prince*.

🛏 Sleeping & Eating

Gîte-Restaurant el-Khorbat KSAR €€
(☑ 0535 88 03 55; www.elkhorbat.com; Ksar el-Khorbat; s/d incl breakfast Dh475/550; [❋][🛜][🏊]) [✦] Seasonal meals of garden-grown pumpkin soup and beef tajines with dates (Dh80 to Dh100) are served in the walled garden of the *ksar*, a regular stop for 19th-century Aït Merghad nomads. The *ksar* is still inhabited, and you too can spend the night in this living museum. Ten rooms are big enough to house a small, seminomadic tribe of your

own, with en-suite bathrooms, air-con and Tinejdad clay pots as lampshades. Excellent maps of the *palmeraie* enable self-guided bike rides.

🛍 Shopping

Galerie d'Art Chez Zaid ARTS & CRAFTS
(☑ 0661 35 16 74; ⊙ 9am-1pm & 3.30-6pm) Snoop around this converted home of a local calligrapher and you might find Tinejdad-made crockery in the courtyard, sand-worn bracelets in the salon, and wonderful, well-patched nickel silver teapots in the kitchen. Located in downtown Tinejdad, 200m after the Shell station on the right.

ℹ Information

There's an Attijariwafa ATM on the left side of the street across from the Tinejdad commune.

ℹ Getting There & Away

Grands taxis run from the main market in the centre of town to Goulmima (Dh10, 45 minutes), Er-Rachidia (Dh20 to Dh30, 1½ hours) and Tinerhir (Dh20, one hour).

Goulmima غولميما

POP 16,600

Located midway between Tinejdad and Er-Rachidia, Goulmima was once an ancient hub of Berber culture but is now little more than a stopover on journeys east to the desert. In fact, most travellers skip this featureless stretch of the N10 altogether and head direct to Erfoud along the more scenic R702 from Tinejdad.

If you are stopping over here, the main attraction is the labyrinthine Ksar Aït Goulmima, a walled village on the southeast end of Goulmima's oasis that's home to several hundred. A guide can lead you through the *palmeraie* and *ksar* to the 500-year-old mosque and historic Jewish mellah. To get there, head through downtown and turn right at the Er-Rachidia roundabout; the *ksar* is signed straight on. A pre-Islamic necropolis can be found northeast of town (signposted from N10), and there are also three souqs a week on Tuesday, Thursday and Saturday.

ATMs and internet cafes line the main street and grands taxis run to Er-Rachidia (Dh20) and Tinerhir via Tinejdad (Dh10) when full.

ZIZ VALLEY & THE TAFILALT وادة زيز و تافلالت

Snaking down through the dramatic Ziz Gorges from Rich, the Oued Ziz brings to life the last southern valley of the Ziz and the Tafilalt oases before puttering out in the rose gold dunes of Merzouga. Starting just south of the Middle Atlas town of Rich and about 30km north of Er-Rachidia, the tremendous Ziz Gorges provide a rocky passage south through the Tunnel du Légionnaire (built by the French in 1928). To the south, the valley widens presenting a spectacular sight: a dense canopy of palms wedged between ancient striated cliffs, which date back to the Jurassic period. It's worth taking some time here to explore the rich, untouristed *palmeraie*.

South of Erfoud the tough Tafilalt – once the main caravan terminus for the lucrative Salt Road and the original homeland of Morocco's ruling Alawite dynasty – was one of the last areas to succumb to French control under the protectorate, with tribes putting up sporadic resistance until 1932. Two years later Morocco was officially considered 'pacified', but just to be on the safe side, Erfoud was built as a garrison town. Today the provincial capital is located in Er-Rachidia, a convenient pitstop for those travelling north along the N13 to Midelt and Meknès.

Er-Rachidia الراشيدية

POP 76,800

Established as a military garrison for the French Foreign Legion, Er-Rachidia is still home to a sizeable military population stationed here to keep an eye on the nearby border with Algeria. Much like Ouarzazate, it is an expanding modern town staking out ever larger residential suburbs thanks to a significant injection of development funds.

Garrison towns aren't generally known for their hospitality or culture, but Er-Rachidia is trying to change that. Every May, its enormous theatre hosts performers from throughout the Sahara at the Festival du Desert (www.festivaldudesert.ma). The market days are Sunday, Tuesday and Thursday.

🛏 Sleeping

Despite its regional importance, Er-Rachidia has a limited number of decent hotels, so you may want to push on towards camping options at Meski and along the road south to Aufous.

Hôtel Errachidia HOTEL €

(☎0535 57 04 53; 31 Rue Ibn Battuta; s/d/tr incl breakfast Dh250/320/410; ❄) Don't be fooled by the setting behind the bus station (handy for early or late arrivals): inside are 26 comfortable, quiet rooms (half with air-con) with en-suite bathrooms, plus a cafe downstairs.

Hotel le Riad HOTEL €€€

(☎0535 79 10 06; www.hotelleriad.com; Rte de Goulmima, Er-Rachidia; s/d incl breakfast Dh700/900; P❄@⊛❄) Er-Rachidia's best business-class hotel has 30 sprawling guest suites with marble bath tubs, a huge pool, a spa and conference facilities. It's rather expensive for what it is, especially the Dh100 breakfast. You'll find it on your right along the N10 as you drive into town from Goulmima.

✗ Eating

Restaurant Imilchil MOROCCAN €

(☎0535 57 21 23; Ave Moulay Ali Cherif; set meal Dh70) Good tajines served on a big terrace, and sports matches on a giant flat screen.

Cafe-Restaurant Merzouga MOROCCAN €

(Ave Moulay Ali Cherif; mains Dh15-60; ⊙7am-9.30pm) A large, popular cafe with double-fronted French windows and a '50s vibe near the main bus station and market. Serves a good selection of local favourites, including rotisserie chicken, brochettes and omelettes.

ℹ Information

Banque Populaire and Attijariwafa ATMs are on Ave Mohammed V, as is the post office.

ℹ Getting There & Away

At the time of writing there were no domestic or international flights to Er-Rachidia's Moulay Ali Cherif airport.

BUS

Buses operate from the central **bus station** (Rue M'Daghra). **CTM** (☎0535 57 20 24) has one service daily to Marrakesh (Dh160, 10½ hours) and Meknès (Dh120, six hours) and an overnight service to Fez (Dh130, 7½ hours).

Private buses run to Ouarzazate (Dh70, six hours, three daily), Marrakesh (Dh140, 11 hours, three daily), Fez (Dh90 to Dh100, five daily) and Rissani (Dh20, two hours, nine daily) via Erfoud (Dh15).

TAXI

Grands taxis depart from three blocks northeast of the main bus station. Destinations include Erfoud (Dh25, one hour), Meknès (Dh120, five hours), Fez (Dh120, five hours), Tinerhir (Dh50, 1½ hours), Rissani (Dh25, 1½ hours) and Merzouga via Rissani (Dh30, 1½ hours).

Around Er-Rachidia

Driving south to Erfoud you pass the origins of the Oued Ziz at Meski, 17km south of Er-Rachidia. From here the road crests a desert plateau to a striking viewpoint over the Ziz *palmeraie* before descending to the town of Aufous, 40km south of Er-Rachidia and midway to Erfoud. Formidable *ksour* line the route, peeking above the palm tops, and Aufous has some stunning pisé buildings and an impressive kasbah ruins as well as useful services such as petrol, coffee and phones.

◉ Sights

Source Bleue de Meski SPRING

The origins of the Oued Ziz can be found in Meski, where warm, natural springs bubble to the surface beneath the picturesque ruins of the Ksar Meski. The French Foreign Legion extended the main pool and added steps forming a pleasant swimming pool much used by weekending locals. Beside it is a well-shaded campsite, and if you walk downstream and cross over the river, you can hike up to the deserted *ksar* for fabulous sunset views.

The spring is signposted about 1km west of the main road.

Cooperative Al Ouaha CULTURAL CENTRE

(⊙10am-4pm daily Oct-Nov, Tue, Thu & Sun Dec-Sep) ✎ Seven kinds of date are grown in the Aufous oasis, and you can sample them all here. In the October-to-November season, the women of this cooperative in Aufous will walk you through a date tasting (Dh20), and in the off-season on Tuesday, Thursday and Sunday, they'll offer you tastes (Dh20) of nutty *tahalout* (date syrup) and natural energy bars made with dates. The cooperative is signed on the main road past the village mosque on the left, next to the village commune.

🛏 Sleeping & Eating

Camping Tissirt CAMPGROUND €
(📞 0661 35 82 19; http://campingtissirtziz.free.
fr; GPS coordinates N 31°78.535, W 004°23.118;
per person/car/tent/caravan Dh15/15/15/30, per
person incl half board Dh150) At the edge of
the *palmeraie* 12km before Aufous is this
palm-shaded camp with two appealing pisé
bungalows and meals of local *kalia* (spiced,
minced mutton; Dh40 to Dh80). Showers
(Dh10) and electricity (Dh15) are extra.

Maison Vallée de Ziz MAISON D'HÔTE €€
(📞 0661 53 31 93; www.gite-detape.com; GPS coordinates N 31°45.835, W 004°12.220; s/d incl half
board Dh350/600; ❋ 🛜) Ignore the rather featureless facade of this small roadside hotel
and walk through to the terrace for gorgeous
valley views above the swaying palms. Steps
down into the *palmeraie* allow for frequent
morning and evening walks, after which you
can collapse in enormous king-sized beds
beneath cut-steel lanterns and oil paintings
inspired by desert dreams. Mohammed and
Said are desert guides, so excursions further
afield are easily arranged.

ℹ Getting there & Away

Public buses travel from Er-Rachidia to a terminal above the Source Bleue spring from 7am to
9pm (Dh3.50). Any bus or grand taxi to Erfoud or
Aufous can drop you at the turn-off. When leaving, flag down a grand taxi from the main road.

Erfoud ارفود

POP 24,000

Now that the tarmac road connects Rissani
with Merzouga, Erfoud has been left high
and dry, although plans are afoot to surface
the well-maintained *piste* from Erfoud to
Merzouga. For now, savvy travellers heading south from Fez and Meknès brake here
for wood-fired *madfouna* (Berber calzone),
fossils and a look at ancient **Ksar M'Aadid**
(5km north of Erfoud).

In October Erfoud has an increasingly
popular date festival, with dancing and
music. The souq at the southern end of
town sells local dates and fresh produce.

⊙ Sights

Erfoud lies in the heart of Morocco's fossil beds, and the Paleozoic strata south
of the highway between Erfoud and Alnif
are a prime hunting ground for diggers.
Kilometres of shallow trenches have been
hand-dug by Berber miners in their search
for trilobite fossils. Few of them are found
in perfect condition so diggers take broken
trilobites to 'prep' labs like Brahim Tahiri's
facility in Erfoud where they are restored.

The best place for an introduction to
Morocco's fossils is at Tahiri's **Museum of
Fossils & Minerals** (📞 0535 57 68 74; www.
tahirimuseum.com; Rte de Rissani; ⊘8am-7pm),
the only private fossil museum in Morocco,
where scientifically important specimens
are exhibited beside their lesser cousins for
sale in the boutique. Brahim's efforts at raising awareness of Morocco's rich geological
heritage have even been recognised internationally with the naming of his very own
trilobite, *Asteropyge tahiri*. You'll find the
museum 6km along the Rissani road.

Trilobite replicas can be made from plaster, plastic or auto-body putty, and can be
hard to distinguish from real fossils.

🛏 Sleeping

Hotel Cannes HOTEL €€
(📞 0535 57 86 95; www.hotelrestaurantcannes.
com; 85 Ave Hassan II; s/d/tr Dh160/210/270)
Cheap, clean, central rooms sporting a
range of '70s colour schemes from apricot
hallways to aubergine rooms and turquoise
bath suites. Breakfast is an additional Dh25,
and the cafe does decent meals. It's within
walking distance of the market, CTM and
Supratours ticket offices on Ave Mohammed
V and the bus stop at Pl des FAR.

Kasbah Tizimi HOTEL €€
(📞 0535 57 61 79; www.kasbahtizimi.com; Rte de
Jorf; s/d/ste Dh650/820/1500; 🅿❋🛜☗) If it's
good enough for Kate Winslet, Kasbah Tizimi's laid-back vibe, flowering courtyards and
tasteful riad-style rooms are good enough
for us. Pad across *zellij*-and-terracotta floors,
lounge on funky wrought-iron beds or sun
yourself beneath thatched parasols around
the pool. The poolside family room is spacious and has a prime position.

Kasbah Xaluca Maadid RESORT €€€
(📞 0535 57 84 50; www.xaluca.com; s/d
Dh845/1120, ste Dh1620-2220; 🅿❋🛜☗) A
flashy pool-party scene straight out of music
videos, only with more kids. Junior suites
come with fossilised marble bedsteads and
mineral lamps; suites are frilly, with chintz
dust ruffles on four-poster beds. Desert travellers appreciate the spa, but kids head for
the pool and minigolf course. It's 5km before
Erfoud on the right.

Eating

Cafes and restaurants line Ave Mohammed V and cluster around Pl des FAR.

★Pizzeria-Restaurant
des Dunes
BERBER, ITALIAN €

(☎0535 57 67 93; www.restaurantdesdunes.com; Ave Moulay Ismail; pizza Dh40, set menu Dh80-100; ☺9am-10pm) You'll find authentic wood-fired pizza here, including a pizza margherita with local anchovies, olives and oregano. If you can wait 15 minutes longer, order the stellar *madfouna*, a dough pocket stuffed with minced onions and herb-spiked lamb, baked until it's puffy and golden.

Hotel-Restaurant
Benhama
CAFE, SANDWICHES €

(☎0661 82 64 57; Ave Moulay Ismail; sandwiches Dh20-25; ☺8am-9pm) Roast chicken or cheese sandwiches, hamburgers, fruit smoothies and espresso served at spiffy sidewalk tables on the main road or inside the glam, air-conditioned lobby-restaurant.

🛍 Shopping

Manar Marbre
SOUVENIRS

(☎0535 57 81 26; www.manarmarble.com; Rte de Jorf; ☺8am-6pm) Watch fossilised marble being cut into prehistoric sinks at this showroom selling some portable items, including prehistoric bookends and trilobite earrings.

ℹ Information

Banks, internet cafes, the post office and a small supermarket are all located along Ave Moulay Ismail.

ℹ Getting There & Away

BUS
CTM (☎0535 57 68 86; Ave Mohammed V) runs overnight bus services to Meknès (Dh125, 7½ hours) and Fez (Dh140, 8½ hours) via Er-Rachidia (Dh30, 1¼ hours), and an early-morning service to Rissani (Dh15, 20 minutes).

Supratours and other buses leave from Pl des FAR to Tinerhir (Dh90, 3½ hours, twice daily), Ouarzazate (Dh125, 6½ hours, three daily), Marrakesh (Dh165, 11 hours), Meknès (Dh130, eight hours) and Fez (Dh130, nine hours, three daily).

TAXI
Grands taxis and taxi minivans depart Pl des FAR and opposite the post office for Merzouga (Dh30, one hour), Rissani (Dh8, 20 minutes), Er-

Rachidia (Dh25, one hour) and Tinerhir (Dh60, five hours).

Rissani
الريصاني

POP 20,500

Rissani is where the Oued Ziz quietly ebbs away, but between the 14th and 18th centuries it was the location of the famed desert capitol, Sijilmassa, where fortunes in gold and slaves were traded via caravans crossing the *sahel*. Rissani was so strategic that the Filali (ancestors of the ruling Alawite dynasty) staged their epic battle here to supplant the Saadians.

Today, Rissani is a dusty shadow of its former self. Barely a quarter of the population lives in the 17th-century *ksar*, while the modern town constitutes a single street and one square. Still, echoes of the past can be heard in the price haggling over birds, sheep and desert jewellery on Sunday, Tuesday and Thursday souqs.

👁 Sights & Activities

The ruins of Sijilmassa and the Circuit Touristique are both signed off the N13 to the west of the town centre. More mudbrick *ksour* flank the road to Merzouga, including Dar el-Beidha and Ksar Haroun; look for signposts on your left as you're leaving town.

Sijilmassa
HISTORIC SITE

Just before you reach Rissani are the ruins of Sijilmassa, the capital of the first virtually independent Islamic principality in the south. Its foundation is lost in myth, but by the end of the 8th century it was a staging post for trans-Saharan trade. Caravans of up to 20,000 camels departed Sijilmassa for the remote desert salt mines of Taodeni and Tagahaza (in modern-day Mali), then continued to Niger and Ghana, where a pound of Saharan salt was traded for an ounce of African gold.

By the 12th century, Sudanese gold that had been refined in Sijilmassa had made it to Europe, where it was minted into European coins. The identical quality between European and Moroccan coins attests to the importance of trade between these regions. But as Berbers say, where there's gold, there's trouble. Internal feuding led to the collapse of the city in the 14th century, and although it was rebuilt by Alawite Sultan Moulay Ismail in the 18th century, it was finally destroyed by Aït Atta nomadic

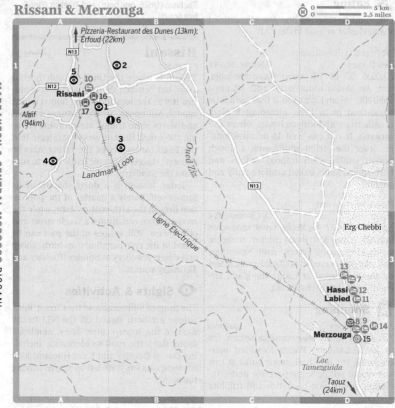

Rissani & Merzouga

warriors in 1818. Sijilmassa has remained a ruin ever since, with only two decorated gateways and other partially standing structures.

Ksar El Fida KSAR
(suggested donation Dh10; ⊙8am-7pm) This enormous, restored Alawite kasbah (1854–72) served as the palace of the local caïd right up until 1965, after which it housed a museum of archaeology. Now only the septuagenarian owner remains and is happy to give you a short guided tour in French and Arabic.

Circuit Touristique TOUR
Dune-bound visitors may be tempted to zoom through Rissani, but photographers, history buffs and architecture aficionados could spend a few days exploring decrepit ksour and artfully crumbling kasbahs on this 21km 'Landmark Loop' circuit. It's best tackled in a clockwise direction from the

regal ruins of Kasbah Abbar – a favourite palace in exile for sidelined members of the Alawite dynasty – past half a dozen crumbling ksour to the still-inhabited Ksar Tin-heras situated on a rise offering spectacular views over the Tafilalt.

Also of note en route are the Zawiya Moulay Ali Ash-Sherif (⊙8am-6pm) FREE, the shrine built to honour the Alawite dynasty's founder, and the royal Ksar Oulad Abdelhalim, a glorious 19th-century ruin with huge ramparts once called the 'Alhambra of the Tafilalt'.

The circuit is signed 1.5km west of Rissani along the N13.

🛏 Sleeping & Eating

With the dunes barely 35km further south, few people choose to spend the night in Rissani, instead visiting on a day trip either from Erfoud or Merzouga. Centrally located hotels, such as Hôtel Sijilmassa (🖂 fax 0535

Rissani & Merzouga

⊙ Sights
1	Ksar Abbar	A1
2	Ksar El Fida	B1
3	Ksar Oulad Abdelhalim	B2
4	Ksar Tinheras	A2
5	Sijilmassa	A1
6	Zawiya Moulay Ali Ash-Sharif	B2

🛏 Sleeping
7	Auberge Camping Sahara	D3
8	Chez Julia	D4
9	Chez Youssef	D4
10	Hôtel Sijilmassa	A1
11	Kasbah Kanz Erremal	D3
12	Kasbah Mohayut	D3
13	Maison Merzouga	D3
14	Riad Ali Totmarroc	D4

ⓘ Information
	Bank	(see 16)
15	Cyber Shop Les Amis	D4

ⓘ Transport
16	CTM	A1
	Grands Taxis	(see 8)
	Grands Taxis	(see 10)
17	Local Bus Station	A1
	Supratours	(see 8)

57 50 42; Pl al-Massira al-Khadra; s Dh80, d Dh140-160; ❄) near the grand taxi lot, are cramped and grubby and are better suited to male travellers.

Eating options here are limited to a few cafes along the main road and around the souq.

ⓘ Information

There's a post and phone office at the northern end of the medina, and two banks with ATMs on Pl al-Massira (the last place to withdraw cash before hitting the desert).

ⓘ Getting There & Away

CTM (Pl al-Massira) has an office in the centre of town next to Hotel Filalia, and runs one bus a day at 8pm to Meknès/Fez (Dh140/150, eight to nine hours) via Erfoud (Dh15, 20 minutes) and Er-Rachidia (Dh30, 1½ hours).

Supratours runs an evening service to Meknès (Dh135) and Fez (Dh135) via Er-Rachidia (Dh50), a morning service to Marrakesh (Dh220, 12 hours) and an early morning and evening service to Merzouga (Dh25, 30 minutes).

Local buses leave from the central bus station 400m north of the square on the road to Erfoud. There are services to Fez (Dh130, 13 hours) via Meknès (Dh100, nine hours) and to Marrakesh (Dh180, 10 hours). Buses run occasionally to Tinerhir (Dh35, six hours); check at the station for departures. There are six buses a day to Er-Rachidia (Dh20, three hours) via Erfoud.

Grands taxis run frequently from opposite the Hôtel Sijilmassa to Erfoud (Dh8), Er-Rachidia (Dh30), Tinerhir (Dh70), Merzouga (Dh13) and occasionally Taouz (Dh25).

You can also reach Merzouga by *camionette* (minivan; Dh10); they leave hourly from outside Chez M'Barek on Rue Moulay Ali Cherif.

Merzouga

When a wealthy family refused hospitality to a poor woman and her son, God was offended, and buried them under the mounds of sand called Erg Chebbi. So goes the legend of the dunes rising majestically above the twin villages of Merzouga and Hassi Labied, which for many travellers fulfil Morocco's promise as a dream desert destination.

But Erg Chebbi's beauty coupled with Merzouga's accessibility has its price. Paved roads across the Middle Atlas from Midelt and east from Ouarzazate mean that desert tourism is booming. In high season, coaches and convoys of 4WDs churn up huge dust clouds as they race across the *hammada* in time for sunset camel rides, and purists lament the encroachment of hotels flanking the western fringes of the dunes – although there's no denying the spectacular dune views from rooms and terraces.

To best experience Erg Chebbi's ethereal beauty, plan carefully and come out of season. The end of November, and January and February are the quietest times and some of the best weatherwise.

⊙ Sights & Activities

Most hotels offer excursions into the dunes, ranging from Dh100 to Dh250 for two-hour sunrise or sunset camel treks. Overnight trips usually include a bed in a Berber tent, dinner and breakfast, and range from Dh300 to Dh650 per person. Outings in a 4WD are more expensive: up to Dh1200 per day for a car taking up to five passengers. Invasive quads (dune buggies), which level dunes and disturb residents and wildlife, are not recommended.

If you show up in town unaccompanied by a guide or a dromedary, you can anticipate repeated offers of both. Try to keep it in

CAMEL QUERIES

With over 70 camps in the Erg Chebbi dunes, picking your place is key. Before you agree to a dromedary trek, ask the guide the following questions.

How big is your camp, and how many people are headed there tonight? Overnight treks often congregate in the same spot, so if you have a romantic notion of being alone in the dunes under the stars, find an outfit with a separate camp.

How far is it to the campsite? Not everyone is cut out for dromedary-riding – it makes some seasick and others chafe. For long treks, bring motion-sickness pills and corn-starch or talcum powder.

Does the trek guide speak English, or another language I know? This is important in the unlikely case of emergency in the desert, and to avoid awkward hand-gesture explanations when you need to use the bathroom.

Are the camels well rested? Don't take it personally. Cranky, overtired camels are notorious for sudden shifts, dead stops and throat-rattling spitting.

perspective, since getting by in the desert is notoriously tough. If you feel pressured, step away from the interaction.

★ **Erg Chebbi**   SAND DUNES

Shape-shifting over 28km from north to south and reaching heights of 160m, Erg Chebbi may be modest compared with the great sand seas of Algeria, Libya and Namibia, but it is extraordinarily scenic. The rose gold dunes rise dramatically above a pancake-flat, black *hammada* and glow stunning shades of orange, pink and purple as the afternoon sun descends.

Lac Tamezguida   BIRD-WATCHING

At the southern end of Erg Chebbi, between November and May, you'll find the seasonal lake of Tamezguida (also known as Lac de Merzouga or Dayet Sriji). This is perhaps the best area in Morocco for spotting many desert birds, including Egyptian nightjars, desert warblers, fulvous babblers and blue-cheeked bee-eaters. Sometimes, in good years, the lake even attracts flocks of flamingos and other waterbirds.

🛏 Sleeping & Eating

Many hotels are reached by *pistes* that run 1km or more east off the N13 tarmac road. Since they're strung out over 5km between the village of Hassi Labied to the north and Merzouga to the south, book in advance and find out the exact location of your hotel. At most places you can sleep on a terrace mattress or in a Berber tent for Dh30 to Dh50 per person. Bring warm clothing for overnight trips in desert bivouacs as it can get very cold.

🛏 Hassi Labied

Auberge Camping Sahara   INN, CAMPGROUND €

(☎0535 57 70 39; www.aubergesahara.com; GPS coordinates N 31°08.100, W 004°01.122; d per person incl half board Dh200-300, terrace camping per person/caravan Dh50/70; 🅿❋❉) Twenty basic, spotless rooms with en-suite bathrooms in a friendly Tuareg-run place with a pool, backing right onto the dunes at the southernmost end of the village. Four rooms feature dune views and air-con.

★ **Corner of Repose**   INN €€

(☎0641 99 48 28; www.corner-repose.com; GPS coordinates N 31°11.766, W 004°01.803; tent per person incl half board Dh225, s/d incl half board Dh450/550; 🅿❋) In the shade of a grove of tamarisk trees at the foot of Merzouga's highest dune, this pint-sized auberge packs a better desert punch than many of Merzouga's grand castle kasbahs. Low-key and friendly, its simple, understated rammed-earth-and-straw rooms ring a desert garden of mint and cactus. That's because the operators know the real views are outside, where the dune colours slide through the Pantone chart as the sun descends.

If you want to get out in them, camel rides cost Dh225 per person and overnight camping trips cost Dh550 per person, including dinner and breakfast.

Kasbah Kanz Erremal   HOTEL €€

(☎0535 57 84 82; www.kanzerremal.com; GPS coordinates N 31°07.765, W 004°00.769; d/ste incl half board Dh630/890; 🅿❋❉❉) Eschewing the rustic vibe of many other Merzouga hotels, Kanz Erremal favours understated stylish decor. Cushioned banquettes line the airy, central courtyard while rooms with desert views are swathed in cool, white linens, gauzy curtains and bluish-silver coverlets. Best of all is the wide terrace that peters out in the sand and a sleek infinity pool with dreamy dune views.

Kasbah Mohayut INN €€
(📞0666 03 91 85; www.mohayut.com; d/ste per person half board Dh350/450; 🏊) Find your niche in 24 sculpted-*tadelakt* guest rooms, in the shade by a small pool, or on the roof overlooking the dunes. Canopied beds, Berber rugs and *tataoui* ceilings add charm, although the finish is a bit rough in places; angle for a room with a fireplace.

Maison Merzouga MAISON D'HÔTE €€
(📞0535 57 72 99; www.merzouga-guesthouse. com; GPS coordinates N 31°07.869, W 004° 01.034; per person incl half board Dh350-500; 🏊🏊) This 16-room local family-run guesthouse focuses on Berber hospitality and not just desert-themed decor. Lounge poolside and enjoy the in-house hammam, or join local holiday celebrations, bake bread in the kitchen and explore the *palmeraie*. The best room is the cheapest tower room, with dune views.

🛏 Merzouga

Chez Julia GUESTHOUSE €
(📞0535 57 31 82; www.chez-julia.com; s/d/ tr Dh200/400/600; 🏊) Pure charm in the heart of Merzouga, behind the mosque: seven simply furnished rooms (with three shared bathrooms) in sun-washed colours with straw-textured pisé walls, antique mantelpieces, and white-tiled shared bathrooms, plus a furnished family apartment (Dh400 to Dh800). Ask about birdwatching tours, Saharan music concerts and fossil hunting.

Chez Youssef MAISON D'HÔTE €
(📞0535 57 89 04; www.chezyoussef.com; Merzouga village; s/d incl half board Dh255/510; 🏊🏊) Youssef's simple pisé home offers four rooms arranged around a tiny courtyard shaded by a single palm. The oasis-inspired decor is sparing, but beds are firm, linens are spotlessly clean and food home cooked. Your host can also help arrange good-value camel treks and 4WD excursions (Dh400 to Dh500 per person).

Riad Ali Totmarroc MAISON D'HÔTE €€
(📞0670 62 41 36; www.totmarroc.com; GPS coordinates N 31°05.799, W 004°00.302; s/d incl half board Dh400/600; 🅿🏊🏊) A mod kasbah provides instant relief from the white-hot desert with 11 guest rooms in Majorelle blue and lemon arranged around a courtyard pool. Overnight dromedary trips are led by an experienced, local official tour leader, and are inclusive of standard or luxury bivouac accommodation (per person Dh450/900), the latter boasting en-suite chemical toilets. It's conveniently located 600m from the centre of Merzouga where the bus terminates.

⭐ **Ali & Sara's Desert Palace** CAMPGROUND €€€
(📞0668 95 01 44; thedesertpalace@hotmail.com; price per person incl full board Dh850) 🏊 Make friends with Angel, Romeo and Casanova – no they aren't local lads trying it on, but your trusty dromedaries – as you head out from Merzouga for a trip of a lifetime. Husband-and-wife team, Ali and Sara, have spent four years crafting a personalised experience that gets rave reviews. Coming from a nomadic family of 11 brothers, Ali's knowledge of the desert is second to none, while Sara's know-how makes for a luxurious and organised camp, first-class cooking and beautifully decorated tents.

To keep things small, intimate and hassle-free, the camp (8km east of Merzouga) accommodates only 12 people and the rates are fully inclusive, including non-alcoholic drinks. Reserve in advance.

ℹ Information

Merzouga has *téléboutiques*, a post office, supply kiosks, a mechanic, a couple of carpet shops and **Cyber Shop Les Amis** (internet per hr Dh5; ⊗9am-10pm).

ℹ Getting There & Away

The N13 runs from Rissani to Merzouga, and the *piste* from Erfoud will probably be sealed in the next few years. That said, most of the hotels are some distance from the road on *pistes* marked with signs. If you're driving a standard rental car, don't head off-road as you'll likely get stuck in the sand. Minibuses will pick up or drop off in Hassi Labied – your hotel can make arrangements. Minivans run from Merzouga between 7.30am and 9.30am in the high season.

THE END OF THE ROAD... OR NOT

Instead of turning back at Taouz, you could take the *piste* by 4WD about one hour/30km southwest towards the 2km stretch of dunes at Ouzina, a seldom-visited desert destination known only to Sahara savants. Here you'll find Kasbah Ouzina (☑0668 98 65 00; per person incl half board Dh270), a small, tidy auberge with mercifully sand-free beds. At Ouzina the *piste* turns west towards the Drâa Valley, heading 45km to Mharje village, where you can turn north onto a well-graded *piste* to Alnif, where it intersects with the tarmac road to Zagora. Otherwise, you could follow a bumpy *piste* from Taouz west towards the Drâa Valley south of Zagora. Either way, the Taouz–Zagora journey takes at least seven hours, equipped with plenty of water, petrol, food, a spare tyre, a mobile phone and a Sahara-savvy guide.

Grands taxis leave from Merzouga centre, opposite Dakar Restaurant, heading north to Rissani (Dh13), and minibuses head south to Taouz (Dh15).

Supratours offers a daily 8am service from Merzouga to Marrakesh (Dh250, 12½ hours) and a 7pm bus to Fez (Dh180, 10½ hours).

Taouz   تاوز

Come to Taouz to spot mineral formations and possibly dinosaur bones where the desert swallows the road. Between Merzouga and Taouz is the village of Khamlia, whose inhabitants are believed to be descended from escaped slaves. This frontier town is home to notable Gnaoua musicians, including Les Pigeons du Sable (Sand Pigeons). Their music is available on CD in Europe, and they occasionally perform locally and at Er-Rachidia's Festival du Desert (p142). Ask at their house (marked by a banner) for details.

A house beyond Taouz village, Casa Taouz, offers tea and occasionally food. If you have a 4WD, several places to stay in the desert are signposted from the road with GPS locations.

RISSANI TO ZAGORA

Rather than retracing the N10 back to Marrakesh via Tinerhir and Ouarzazate, adventurous desert travellers opt for the N12, which traces the southern foothills of Jebel Saghro via Alnif, Tazzarine and N'Kob. The road sees little traffic and few tourists and provides an interesting link through prime fossil-hunting territory to the Drâa Valley, where it emerges at Tansikht 63km north of Zagora and 98km south of Ouarzazate.

Kasbah-studded N'Kob is the most atmospheric place to stay in the area, and provides a good base for Jebel Saghro treks and exploration.

Alnif   النيف

Much of Morocco's Anti-Atlas Mountains are built of Paleozoic rocks, dating back to between 245 and 570 million years. When these rocks were deposited, a shallow sea covered the region. Trilobites scuttled along the seafloor, and huge schools of *Orthoceras,* squid-like nautiloids with cone-shaped shells, swam above. When they died, their shells were preserved in the limy mud of the Maidir basin located between Erfoud and Alnif, awaiting resurrection as the polished curios, coffee tables and ornamental sinks that now cram Alnif's roadside shops.

Today more than 50,000 Moroccans earn their livelihoods in the fossil and mineral specimen mining and export business. It's hard, labour-intensive work where men hand-work the fossil-rich seams and old mining spoil heaps with chisels, picks and hoes. Prices depend on rarity, condition and the quality of the workmanship in the preparation, and can range from tens of dirhams to tens of thousands of dirhams for museum-quality specimens. Ihmadi Trilobites Centre (☑0666 22 15 93; trilobites@caramail.com; Alnif; ☺9am-5pm), on the main road, sells genuine fossils at fixed prices. The geologist owner also leads short trips to local fossil sites (Dh180 for the afternoon).

🛏 Sleeping & Eating

Few travellers spend the night in Alnif

Kasbah Meteorites   KASBAH €€
(☑0535 88 22 82; www.kasbahmeteorites.com; Alnif; per person half board Dh300; ❄ 🛜 ☀) A pleasant pitstop 13km west of Alnif. Comfortable

rooms with air-con and an oversized pool. Popular with tour groups.

La Gazelle du Sud MOROCCAN €
(☎0670 23 39 42; meals Dh35-60; ⊙8am-7pm) A popular lunch stop, serving large meals of tajine, brochettes, and chicken and chips.

Hotel Restaurant Bougafer CAFE €
(☎0535 78 38 09; Alnif; meals Dh30-60; ⊙8am-10pm) Tajine, brochettes and rotisserie chicken and chips. Generous portions. Popular for lunch.

Tazzarine تزارين

The small desert town and oasis of Tazzarine is located in the heart of the Aït Atta tribal area, midway between Alnif and N'Kob. Despite many years of drought, the palm groves and henna fields are pretty. Although there is little to stop for in the small straggly town, a few kilometres southwest you'll find the prehistoric site of **Aït Ouazik** with its wonderful petroglyphs clearly depicting images of elephants, giraffes, buffalos and antelopes. They date from about 5000 BC when the area had a savannah-like character.

Also south of Tazzarine is the small but picturesque dune field of **Foum Tizza**, an area of sandy *sahel* contrasting with blue-black rocks. The dunes are rarely visited and offer travellers a chance to appreciate the *désert profond* on a small scale.

French travel specialist **Voyaguers du Monde** (www.voyageursdumonde.fr) offer a luxurious camping experience at **Camp Nomades** (☎0524 43 48 08; www.camps-nomades.com; Tazzarine; tent Dh1650-3900; ⊙closed Jan & May-Sep). For those on a budget **Camping Serdrar** (☎0667 23 80 22; camping.serdrar@yahoo.com; GPS coordinates N 30°43.318, W 005°28.547, Tazzarine; Berber tent per person half board Dh190, tent/campervan incl shower Dh60/60, electricity Dh20) is a family-run palm farm set in a wonderful location 11km south of Tazzarine and 6km off the main road in the shadow of Jebel Rhart. Sleep in Berber tents or camp beneath the palms and get Youssef to guide you to the fossil fields.

N'Kob نيكو ب

One of Morocco's best-kept secrets is the Berber oasis of N'Kob, where 45 **mudbrick ksour** make you stop and stare. On the main square at the eastern edge of town, you might also spot a member of the local Aït Atta warrior tribe striding into the N'Kob post office wearing a scimitar.

Opposite the post office is **Aït Atta Chassures**, a cobbler banging out traditional walking sandals with leather, rope and used tyre treads – more comfortable than they sound and quite stylish (Dh80 to DH120). Wander 500m down the side street with signs for Kasbah Baha Baha and through a doorway bedecked with dented pots to find N'Kob's teapot mender, whose services are in demand during the **Sunday souq**.

For trekkers, N'Kob provides a gateway for treks across Jebel Saghro (three days) and is particularly well-located for shorter treks to the spectacular rock pinnacles of **Bab n'Ali**. Also possible is a spectacular off-road drive up over **Tizi n'Tazazert** (2283m) and through the swirling rock formations of the **Taggourt Plateau** before dropping down to Iknjouln and the Dadès Valley. There's a **bureau des guides** (☎0667 48 75 09) on the main road where you can arrange local hikes to explore N'Kob's kasbahs, rock formations and palm oasis.

Sleeping

Auberge-Camping Ouadjou CAMPGROUND €
(☎0524 83 93 14; www.ouadjou.com; N'Kob; tent without/with half board Dh50/150, r incl half board Dh250; P≋) Welcome comforts for desert-dazed travellers: dark courtyard rooms with hot showers in en-suite bathrooms, or Berber tents in the garden. Guests can use the pool free, as can visitors ordering lunch (Dh90 to Dh120). It's 1km west of N'Kob.

Kasbah Baha Baha KASBAH €€
(☎0524 83 97 63; www.kasbahabaha.com; N'Kob; Berber tents s/d/tr Dh200/300/390, d without/with bathroom Dh370/500; P❄📶≋) A gorgeously restored kasbah with a vast Berber botany garden, wood-fired bread oven, gourmet poolside meals (breakfast/dinner Dh40/120), on-site ethnographic museum (Dh30) and 360-degree oasis views. Guests are greeted like neighbours, and are even invited to local marriages hosted at the kasbah in summer.

Kasbah Imdoukal KASBAH €€
(☎0524 83 97 98; www.kasbah-imdoukal.com; N'Kob; d/tr/ste Dh700/900/1000; ❄≋) Berber pride meets minimalist chic: chip-carved beds, Amazigh friezes atop *tadelakt* walls, oasis mule treks with poolside lounging after, and dinners of *madfouna* (local pizza; Dh120

to Dh190) by the restaurant fireplace with private concerts. Most rooms have air-con.

★ Kasbah Hôtel Aït Omar
HOTEL €€€

(☎ 0524 83 99 81; www.hotel-aitomar.de; N'Kob; s/d incl breakfast Dh560/1000; P❄🔊🛋) Rebuilt to pisé perfection, Aït Omar's crenellated rooftop and descending terraces offer unparalleled views over N'Kob's forest of kasbahs. Zigzagging staircases reveal private patios with potted citrus trees, a domed, marble hammam and 11 individually decorated rooms linked by turquoise accents in *zellij* tiles, luxe sofa fabrics and mosaic mirrors. No detail has been left to chance: even the bathroom plumbing and fittings have been imported from Germany.

Ksar Jenna
MAISON D'HÔTE €€€

(☎ 0524 83 97 90; www.ksarjenna.com; d incl half board Dh700; ❄🔊🛋) Holding its own with Marrakesh riads, Ksar Jenna offers light-filled rooms in pastel blue, lemon yellow and the palest mauve decorated artfully with carved furniture, Tazenakht carpets and designer-fabulous *zellij* and *tadelakt* bathrooms. Dinner is served under the painted dining-room ceiling, breakfasts amid the luxuriant flowering garden, and aperitifs or espresso in the patio bar (it's a Moroccan-Italian venture). It's 2km west of N'Kob.

❶ Getting There & Away

Local buses ply the road between Rissani and Zagora (six hours), via Alnif, Tazzarine and N'Kob. More reliable though are grands taxis between Rissani and Alnif (Dh25), Alnif and Tazzarine (Dh25), Alnif and Tinerhir (Dh25) and Tazzarine and Ouarzazate (Dh70).

CTM runs a 6.30am bus from Tazzarine to Marrakesh (Dh125, 7½ hours) via N'Kob (Dh15, 30 minutes) and Ouarzazate (Dh55, three hours).

Atlantic Coast

شاطىء الأطلنطي

Best Places to Eat

➡ Outdoor fish grills (p214)

➡ Restaurant du Port de Pêche (p166)

➡ Le Petit Beur – Dar Tajine (p182)

Best Places to Stay

➡ Dar el-Manar (p202)

➡ La Sultana (p204)

➡ Riad Oudaya (p181)

Why Go?

The Atlantic coast is one of Morocco's most prosperous regions. The French called it 'Maroc utile' (useful Morocco), and it's home to both the nation's capital Rabat and the economic hub of Casablanca. These cities' Mauresque architecture, excellent restaurants, stylish cafes and liberal attitudes are a far cry from traditional Morocco.

It's more than just these great modern cities though. Miles of glorious sands, peppered with small fishing villages, historic ports and fortified towns, weave along the blustery coastline. Outside the towns, farmland rolls gently down to the sea and wetland reserves showcase rich birdlife.

The region is bookended by Assilah and Essaouira, fishing ports both, with whitewashed medinas. There's art and plenty of seafood, and a history written across the landscape – from the times of the Phoenicians and Romans, to the Portuguese, Spanish and French – begging to be explored.

When to Go
Casablanca

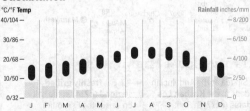

May–Jun Rabat's world-music Mawazine fest in May, Essaouira's Gnaoua Festival in June.

Sep Hit the beaches after the Moroccan tourists leave, while the weather's still good.

Dec–Mar Huge flocks of bird species descend on wetlands and lagoons.

SPAIN

0 — 100 km
0 — 60 miles

ATLANTIC
OCEAN

Tangier
Tangier-Boukhalef Airport ✈
Had Gharbia
Assilah ⑥ Dchar Ghanem
Souq Tnine de Sidi el-Yamani
Larache ⑧ Lixus
Moulay Bousselham
Ksar el-Kebir
⑤ Merdja Bargha
Merdja Zerga
Souk el-Arba du Rhurb
Lac de Sidi Bourhaba A1
Sidi-Kacem
Mehdiya Plage
Plage des Nations ⑦ Kenitra
Jardins Exotiques
Salé
Volubilis
Rabat-Salé Airport
Rabat ①
Temara Plage ⑦ Aïn el-Aouda
Meknès
Mohammedia Sidi-Yahya N6
A2 Khemisset
Casablanca ③ ⑨
Ben Slimane
Sidi Bettache Merchouch
Rommani
Azemmour
Mohammed V International Airport
Oued Mellah
Azrou (25km)
El-Jadida ⑦
Sidi Bouzid
Moulay Abdallah
Oued-Zem
N1
Ez-Zhiliga
Aïn-Leuh
S-Smaïl
Settat
Boulâouane
Khouribga
Oualidia ②
A7
N9
Oued-Zem
Khenifra
Khemis
S-Bennour
Skhour Rehamna
Mechra Benâbbou
El Borouj
Boujad
Cap Beddouza
Lalla Fatna
Sidi Bouzid
Safi
Youssoufia
Fkih-Ban-Salah
Kásba-Tadla
El-Ksiba
Bouguedra
Benguérir
Beni-Mellal
Souira Kedima
R204
N7
A7
Bin-el-Ouidane
Sidi-Bou-Othmane
Azilal
Essaouira ④
Oued Tensif
HIGH ATLAS
Diabat
Île de Mogador
Sidi Kaouki (15km)
R207
Chichaoua
N8
Marrakech
Ménara Airport
Demnate

Atlantic Coast Highlights

① Sip tea at the Andalucian Gardens in the **Kasbah Les Oudaias** (p177) in Rabat

② Swim in the warm waters of the **Oualidia lagoon** (p204), before gorging on local oysters for lunch

③ Take the shiny new tram to Casablanca's smart pavement **cafes** (p168)

④ Eat **freshly grilled seafood** (p214) in the salty breeze of the Essaouira harbour

⑤ Birdwatch on the lagoon at **Moulay Bousselham** (p191)

⑥ Gaze at the murals in Assilah's **medina** (p195)

⑦ Marvel at the water cistern in El-Jadida's **Cité Portugaise** (p200)

⑧ Imagine yourself as a Roman at the ancient site of **Lixus** (p194)

⑨ Look up in Casablanca at the glorious **Mauresque buildings** (p164)

Casablanca (Dar el-Baïda)

الدار البيضاء

POP 4 MILLION

Many travellers stay in Casablanca just long enough to change planes or catch a train, but the sprawling metropolis deserves more time. It may not be as exotic as other Moroccan cities, but it is the country's economic capital, and it represents Morocco on the move: Casablanca is where the money is being made, where the industry is, where art galleries show the best contemporary art and where fashion designers have a window on the world. The old pirate lair is looking towards the future, showing off its wealth and achievements.

The first French resident-general, Louis Hubert Gonzalve Lyautey hired French architect Henri Prost to redesign Casablanca in the early 20th century as the economic centre of the new protectorate and, indeed, as the jewel of the French colonies. His wide boulevards and modern urban planning still survive, and mark the city as more European than Moroccan. However, Lyautey underestimated the success of his own plans and the city grew far beyond his elaborate schemes. By the end of WWII, Casablanca had a population of 700,000 and was surrounded by heaving shanty towns.

Casablancais are cosmopolitan, and are more open to Western ways than other places in Morocco. This is reflected in their dress, and in the way men and women hang out together in restaurants, bars, beaches and hip clubs. But Europe is not the only inspiration. More and more young Casablancais are realising that they come from a country with a fascinating history.

Casablanca is full of contradictions. It is home to wide boulevards, well-kept public parks, fountains and striking colonial architecture, but is also fringed by large shanty towns and simmering social problems.

The bleak facades of the suburbs stand in sharp contrast to the Mauresque, art deco and modernist gems of the city centre, and to Casablanca's exceptional landmark, the enormous and incredibly ornate Hassan II Mosque.

The medina – the oldest part of town – is tiny and sits in the north of the city close to the port. To the south of the medina is Pl des Nations Unies, a large traffic junction that marks the heart of the city. The city's main streets branch out from here: Ave des Forces Armées Royales (Ave des FAR), Ave Moulay Hassan I, Blvd Mohammed V and Blvd Houphouët Boigny.

Ave Hassan II leads to Pl Mohammed V, easily recognised by its grand art deco administrative buildings. Quartiers Gauthier and Maarif, west and southwest of the Parc de la Ligue Arabe, are where most of the action is, with shops, bars and restaurants.

To the southeast is the Quartier Habous (also known as the nouvelle medina) and to the west is Aïn Diab, the beachfront suburb home to upmarket hotels and nightclubs.

Development in Casablanca today is so exciting that you'd think the ghosts of General Lyautey and Henri Prost were working on a new plan for the city, though this time with Moroccan pride rather than French colonial might. The new tramway has eased some of the pressures of Casablanca's interminable traffic, and improved the city centre environment enormously. Along the coastal road in Anfa, huge new projects are being built. The new environmentally friendly, award-winning 200,000-sq-metre Morocco Mall, the biggest 'destination mall' in North Africa, houses shops and offices as well as a large aquarium and a 400-seater IMAX theatre. On the coast east of the Hassan II Mosque the Casablanca Marina remains a few years from being completed, along with the under-refurbishment Casa Port train station. Casablanca today is showing a confident face to the rest of Morocco – and the world.

History

The Phoenicians established a small trading post in the now-upmarket suburb of Anfa from the 6th century BC onwards. In the 7th century AD, Anfa became a regional capital under the Barghawata, a confederation of Berber tribes. The Almohads destroyed it in 1188, and 70 years later, the Merenids took over.

In the early 15th century, the port became a safe haven for pirates and racketeers. Anfa pirates became such a serious threat later in the century that the Portuguese sent 50 ships and 10,000 men to subdue them. They left Anfa in a state of ruins. The local tribes, however, continued to terrorise the trade routes, provoking a second attack by the Portuguese in 1515. Sixty years later the Portuguese arrived to stay, erecting fortifications and renaming the port Casa Branca (White House).

The Portuguese abandoned the colony in 1755 after a devastating earthquake destroyed Lisbon and severely damaged the walls of Casa Branca. Sultan Sidi Mohammed ben Abdullah subsequently resettled and fortified the town, but it never regained its former importance. By 1830 it had only around 600 inhabitants.

By the mid-1800s Europe was booming and turned to Morocco for increased supplies of grain and wool. The fertile plains around Casablanca were soon supplying European markets, and agents and traders flocked back to the city. Spanish merchants renamed the city Casablanca and by the beginning of the 20th century the French had secured permission to build an artificial harbour.

Increased trade brought prosperity to the region, but the activities and influence of the Europeans also caused resentment. Violence erupted in 1907 when Europeans desecrated a Muslim cemetery. The pro-colonialist French jumped at the chance to send troops to quell the dispute; a French warship and a company of marines soon arrived and bombarded the town. By 1912 it was part of the new French protectorate.

Sights

Casablanca is Morocco's commercial hub and locals are far more interested in big international business than in tourism. Tourists are relatively few in town and it's very much a workaday place with remarkably few traditional tourist attractions. Apart from the grand Hassan II Mosque, the city's main appeal is in strolling around its neighbourhoods: the wonderful Mauresque architecture of the city centre, the peaceful Parc de la Ligue Arabe, the gentrified market district of the Quartier Habous and the beachfront views of the Corniche. Join the Casablancais in enjoying the cosmopolitan pleasures of their city, go out for dinner, visit an art gallery, shop till you drop in the Morocco Mall in Anfa, try out the funky nightlife or go roller skating outside the Hassan II Mosque.

Downtown Casa

It is often said that Casablanca has no sights apart from the Hassan II Mosque, but the French-built city centre is packed with grand colonial buildings, some of which are being restored. The best way to take it all in is by strolling in the area around the Marché Central (p166), or by doing the walking tour (p164). The Marché Central quarter is slowly being revived, driven on by the removal of traffic from Blvd Mohammed V to make way for Casablanca's new trams.

Place Mohammed V   NEIGHBOURHOOD
(Map p160) This is where the architect Henri Prost really went to town. The grand square is surrounded by public buildings whose designs were later copied in buildings throughout Morocco, including the law courts, the splendid *wilaya* (old police headquarters, now the governor's office), the Bank al-Maghrib, the post office and the Ministry of Defence building. Many grand boulevards lined with wonderful architecture go off this

---

CASABLANCA IN...

One Day

As no visit to Casablanca is complete without marvelling at the seaside mosque, hop in a taxi first thing to the **Hassan II Mosque** and take in a tour. Then head to **Sqala Restaurant** in the ramparts for lunch in the garden. Browse the artisan shops in the **Quartier Habous** for Moroccan souvenirs, stopping for tea and cakes. Treat yourself to stunning views over the ocean by dining at one of the **cliff-top restaurants** by el-Hank lighthouse before joining the city's pretty young things in the bars and clubs along **Blvd de la Corniche**.

Two Days

With another day to enjoy the city, start with breakfast at **Patisserie Bennis Habous** in the beautiful Zevaco building. Work it off by following our **walking tour** (p164), taking in the best of Casa's Mauresque heritage. After lunch, take the tram out to **Aïn Diab** to check out the trendy boutiques or take in an IMAX movie at **Morocco Mall** before a hammam and massage at **Gauthier Bain Turc**. **Restaurant du Port de Pêche** is just the place for local fish before a nightcap at **Blue Parrot**.

DON'T MISS

HASSAN II MOSQUE

Built by the late King Hassan II to commemorate his 60th birthday, this enormous mosque (Map p158; guided tours adult/child/student Dh120/30/60; ⊗ tours 9am, 10am, 11am & 2pm Sat-Thu, 9am, 10am & 2pm Fri) was funded by public subscription. It was completed in 1993 and provides Casablanca with an important landmark. A new Islamic media centre and library (⊗ 8am-6pm Mon-Fri) FREE can be found in the grounds.

Designed by French architect Michel Pinseau the mosque rises above the ocean on a rocky outcrop reclaimed from the sea, echoing the verse from the Quran that states that God's throne was built upon the water. The 210m-high minaret, the tallest minaret in the world, is topped by a spectacular laser beam that shines towards Mecca. It is the world's third-largest mosque, accommodating 25,000 worshippers inside, and a further 80,000 in the courtyards and squares around it. Believers can enjoy praying on a centrally heated floor, seeing the Atlantic washing the rocks underneath the glass floor in the basement and feel the sunlight through the retractable roof.

Above all, the vast size and elaborate decoration of the prayer hall is most striking. Large enough to house Paris' Notre Dame or Rome's St Peter's, it is blanketed in astonishing woodcarving, *zellij* (tilework) and stucco moulding. A team of over 6000 master craftspeople was assembled to work on the mosque, delicately carving intricate patterns and designs in cedar from the Middle Atlas, marble from Agadir and granite from Tafraoute.

To see the interior visitors must be 'decently and respectfully dressed' and, once inside, will be asked to remove their shoes. Hour-long tours are conducted in French, English, German and Spanish, and take in the prayer hall, the ablutions rooms and the hammam.

---

square. To the south is the Parc de la Ligue Arabe, designed in 1918 with a majestic palm-tree-lined promenade.

Villa des Arts   GALLERY
(Map p163; ☑ 0522 29 50 87; www.fondationona. ma; 30 Blvd Brahim Roudani; ⊗ 10am-7pm Tue-Sat) FREE Located in a converted art deco building with a pleasant garden near the Parc de la Ligue Arabe, this gorgeous 1930s gallery holds exhibitions of contemporary Moroccan and international art.

◉ Ancienne Médina

Casablanca's small and dilapidated medina gives an idea of just how petite the city was before the French embarked on their massive expansion program. Most of the buildings date from the 19th century, so it lacks the medieval character of other medinas. Plans are afoot to restore many buildings.

Enter the medina from the northeast corner of the Pl des Nations Unies near the restored clock tower (Map p160), and note the dilapidated Excelsior Hotel opposite it. Narrow lanes to the east are piled high with cheap shoes, high-sheen underwear and household goods. The rest of the medina remains largely residential. The old city's main

Friday mosque is the Jemaa ash-Chleuh along Rue Jemaa ash-Chleuh Arsalane.

On the north side of the medina, facing the port, you'll see the last remains of Casablanca's 18th-century fortifications. Known as the sqala, the bastion offers panoramic views over the sea.

◉ Maarif

Southwest of the Parc de la Ligue Arabe is the city's business centre and the place to head for international designer brands.

Jewish Museum   MUSEUM
(☑ 0522 99 49 40; www.casajewishmuseum.com; 81 Rue Chasseur Jules Gros, Quartier Oasis; admission Dh25; ⊗ 10am-5pm Mon-Fri, 11am-5pm Sun) South of Maarif in the suburb of Oasis is this museum housed in a beautiful villa surrounded by lush gardens. It's the only Jewish museum in the Islamic world. It relates the history of the once-thriving Jewish community (two thirds of whom live in Casablanca) and its influence on modern Moroccan society, with more than 1500 historical artefacts including documents, traditional clothing, ceremonial items and a vast collection of photographs. Oasis is a 15-minute taxi ride (Dh30) from the city centre.

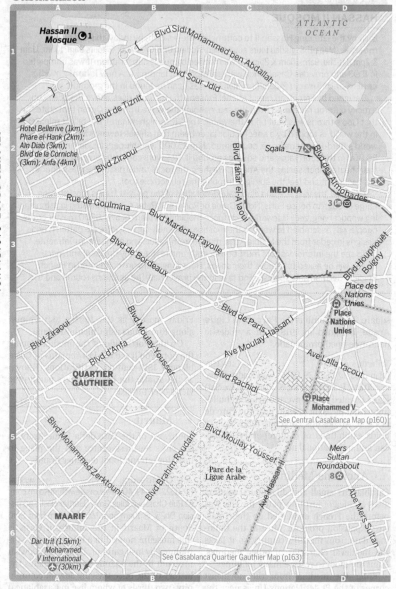

ATLANTIC COAST CASABLANCA

Hassan II Mosque 1

ATLANTIC OCEAN

Blvd Sidi Mohammed ben Abdallah

Blvd Sour Jdid

Blvd de Tiznit

Hotel Bellerive (1km);
Phare el-Hank (2km);
Aïn Diab (3km);
Blvd de la Corniche
(3km); Anfa (4km)

Blvd Ziraoui

Rue de Goulmina

Blvd Maréchal Fayolle

Blvd de Bordeaux

Blvd Tahar el-Alaoui

MEDINA

6

Sqala 7

Blvd des Almohades

5

3

Blvd Houphouët Boigny

Place des Nations Unies

Place Nations Unies

Blvd de Paris

Ave Moulay Hassan I

Ave Lalla Yacout

Blvd Ziraoui

Blvd d'Anfa

Blvd Moulay Youssef

QUARTIER GAUTHIER

Blvd Rachidi

Place Mohammed V

See Central Casablanca Map (p160)

Blvd Mohammed Zerktouni

Blvd Brahim Roudani

Blvd Moulay Youssef

Parc de la Ligue Arabe

Ave Hassan II

Mers Sultan Roundabout

8

Abe Mers Sultan

MAARIF

Dar Itrit (1.5km);
Mohammed
V International (30km)

See Casablanca Quartier Gauthier Map (p163)

Quartier Habous (Nouvelle Medina)

The Quartier Habous, or nouvelle medina, is Morocco-lite – an idealised, almost Disney version of a traditional medina, with neat rows of streets and shop stalls. Built by the French in the 1930s, it was a unique experiment: a medina built to Western standards to accommodate the first rural exodus in the 1920s. As such, it blends Moroccan architecture with French ideals, epitomised by a

Casablanca

● Top Sights
  1 Hassan II Mosque A1

● Activities, Courses & Tours
  2 Hammam Ziani................................E5

● Sleeping
  3 Youth Hostel.............................D3

● Eating
  4 Ostréa......................................E2
  5 Restaurant du Port de Pêche.............D2
  6 Rick's Cafe C2
  7 Sqala Restaurant D2

● Drinking & Nightlife
  Blue Parrot.............................(see 6)
  Sqala Café Maure ....(see 7)

● Entertainment
  8 Cinéma Lynx..........................D5

and has a decent selection of bazaars, craft shops, bakeries and cafes.

The **Royal Palace** (closed to the public) is to the north of the district, while to the south is the old **Mahakma du Pasha** (courts & reception hall; ⏰8am-noon & 2-6pm Mon-Sat) **FREE**, which has more than 60 rooms decorated with sculpted wooden ceilings, stucco-work, wrought-iron railings and earthenware floors. It's not always open to visitors.

The Quartier Habous is located about 1km southeast of town. Take bus 81 from Blvd de Paris, across from the main post office.

● Aïn Diab & Anfa

These affluent suburbs on the Atlantic beachfront, west of the centre, are home to the happening **Blvd de la Corniche**. Lined with beach clubs, upmarket hotels, restaurants, bars and clubs, it is the city's entertainment hub and *the* place for young, chic professionals to see and be seen.

However, in between the busy beach clubs along the promenade, the view is spoiled by abandoned pleasure grounds and concrete swimming pools filled with construction rubbish. Nevertheless, the beach remains extremely popular. The easiest way to find space on the sand is to visit one of the beach clubs. Two of the better ones, **Miami Plage** (☎0522 79 71 33; per day Dh80-150) and **Tahiti** (per day Dh80-150) have beach umbrellas, a pool, restaurant and bar.

mosque and a strip of grassy lawn, reminiscent of European village churches.

However sanitised it may feel, if you have some last-minute souvenir shopping to do, Habous is more peaceful than most souqs

Central Casablanca

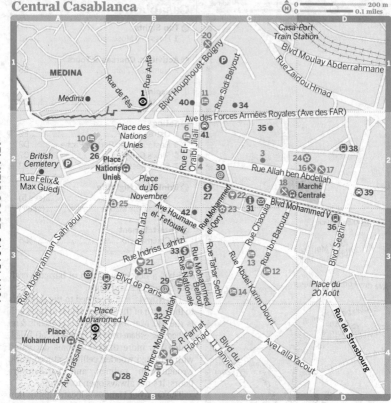

The Casablanca tramway goes to Aïn Diab, which is the furthest stop on the line. The ride takes around 30 minutes from Pl Mohammed V. A taxi from the centre costs around Dh30 (Dh70 at night).

The new Dubai-esque Morocco Mall (p170) in Anfa is some 4km west of the city centre. It sports a large aquarium and three floors of shops plus a food court with international cuisines, an IMAX cinema and – for evening entertainment – a 250m-long dancing fountain and light show.

🏃 Activities

Hammam Ziani   HAMMAM
(Map p158; ☎ 0522 31 96 95; 59 Rue Abou Rakrak; admission Dh45; ⏰ 7am-10pm) Sparkling clean and decidedly modern, this is an upmarket hammam offering the traditional steam room and *gommage* (scrub) for Dh50, and massage, as well as a jacuzzi and gym. It's off Rue Verdin. As is the case when visiting any

public hammam, it may be better to leave your valuables at your hotel.

Gauthier Bain Turc   HAMMAM
(Map p163; ☎ 0661 14 59 26; 25 Rue Jean Jaures; Mon-Fri Dh50, Sat & Sun Dh60; ⏰ 7am-10pm) You'll find a steam room, jacuzzi and gym at this ultra-modern hammam, where a scrub costs Dh15 and a 30-minute massage Dh100.

Spa 5 Mondes   HAMMAM
(☎ 0522 99 66 08; www.cinqmondes.com/spa-cinq -mondes.html; 18 Rue Ibrahim En-Nakhai, Maarif; ⏰ 10am-8pm) For a traditional hammam, a Japanese bath, a Balinese massage or an ay-urvedic treatment, head for this trendy spa.

🎓 Courses

Casablanca has a multitude of language schools, almost all of which have French classes.

Central Casablanca

Institut Français   LANGUAGE
(Map p163; ☎ 0522 77 98 70; www.ambafrance-ma.
org; 121-123 Blvd Mohammed Zerktouni; ◷ 9am-
2.30pm Tue-Sat) Only runs semester-long
French-language courses. Also offers a good
library, films, lectures, exhibitions and other
events.

École Assimil-Formation   LANGUAGE
(Map p160; ☎ 0522 31 25 67; 71 Rue Allah ben Abdellah) Offers private tuition in Arabic.

☞ Tours

Olive Branch Tours   TOUR
(Map p160; ☎ 0522 22 03 54; www.olivebranch-
tours.com; 35 Rue el-Oraïbi Jilali) This outfit offers a Grand Tour of Casablanca, which
takes in the main squares in the city centre,
the medina and Quartier Habous, as well as
a stroll along the Corniche.

★ Festivals

L'Boulevard Festival of Casablanca   MUSIC
(www.boulevard.ma; ◷ Jun) Three-day urban-
music festival that features hip hop, electro,

rock, metal and fusion music, with bands
from Morocco, France, the USA and the UK.

Jazzablanca   JAZZ
(http://jazzablanca.com; ◷ Apr) A five-day jazz
festival.

🛏 Sleeping

Most of Casablanca's hotels are in the centre of town with the exception of the youth
hostel, which is in the medina, and the
upmarket hotels along the Blvd de la Corniche. Hotels fill up fast during the summer months, particularly in August, so it's a
good idea to make reservations in advance.

Casablanca's budget hotels are pretty basic. The medina hotels are invariably grotty
and overpriced and don't offer good value
compared with their ville-nouvelle counterparts. Casablanca has a good selection of
midrange accommodation scattered around
the city centre. You'll also find some nice alternatives with ocean views and easy access
to the beach along Blvd de la Corniche. Casablanca has a glut of top-end hotels, with all
the major international chains represented

in town. Most are along Ave des FAR, with a few others along Blvd de la Corniche.

★ Hôtel Guynemer
HOTEL €

(Map p160; ☑0522 27 57 64; http://guynemerhotel.net; 2 Rue Mohammed Belloul; s/d Dh350/480; ❋🛜) The family-run Guynemer, in a gorgeous Mauresque building, is always reliable. The 29 well-appointed rooms are tastefully decked out in cheerful colours. Flat-screen TVs, wi-fi access and firm, comfortable beds make rooms a steal at these rates and the service is good, but note that some bathrooms are quite tiny. There's an airport pick-up service (Dh400) and city tours. The hotel also rents out two contemporary, fully equipped flats on the same street, which are ideal for longer stays and for families.

Hôtel Astrid
HOTEL €

(Map p160; ☑0522 27 78 03; hotelastrid@hotmail.com; 12 Rue 6 Novembre; s/d Dh315/368; 🛜) Tucked away on a quiet street south of the centre, Astrid offers the most elusive element of Casa's budget hotels – a good night's sleep. There's little traffic noise and the spacious, well-kept rooms are all en suite, with TV, telephone and frilly decor. There's a friendly cafe downstairs and wi-fi in the lobby.

Hôtel de Paris
HOTEL €

(Map p160; ☑ 0522 27 42 75; fax 0522 29 80 69; cnr Rues Ech-Cherif Amziane & Prince Moulay Abdallah; s/d/tr Dh350/450/550; 🛜) This small hotel has spacious rooms that are clean and relatively quiet. Rooms are decorated with dark wood and equipped with good mattresses, satellite TV and decent bathrooms. There's a swish cafe downstairs on the pleasant pedestrian street (great for breakfasts), and the hotel is in a good central location.

Youth Hostel
HOSTEL €

(Map p158; ☑ 0522 22 05 51; lesauberges@menara.ma; 6 Pl Ahmed el-Bidaoui; s/d/tr Dh80/150/190, tr with bathroom Dh200; ☺8-10am & noon-midnight; ☻) Clustered around a bright central lounge area, the rooms here are basic but well kept and quiet, with high ceilings and a lingering smell of damp in winter. The staff are friendly and the hostel is on a leafy square. There are good hot showers. No IYHF or YHA cards are required.

Hôtel Maamoura
HOTEL €

(Map p160; ☑ 0522 45 29 67; www.hotelmaamoura.com; 59 Rue Ibn Batouta; s/d/ste Dh440/580/900; ❋🛜☻) A favourite with readers, this modern hotel offers excellent value for money.

The spotless and spacious rooms may lack period detail, but they are very quiet for this central location, tastefully decorated in muted colours and have neat bathrooms. The staff are friendly and helpful.

Hôtel du Palais
HOTEL €

(Map p160; ☑ 0522 27 61 91; 68 Rue Farhat Hachad; s/d without bathroom Dh90/130, d/tr with bathroom Dh140/240) At the lower end of the price range, this basic hotel is a fair choice for those stretching their budgets, offering clean, spacious rooms with large windows. It's fairly spartan and can be noisy. A hot shower costs Dh10.

Hotel de Foucauld
HOTEL €

(Map p160; ☑ 0522 22 26 66; 52 Rue el-Oraïbi Jilali; s/d without bathroom Dh100/150, s/d/tr with bathroom Dh150/180/220) Rooms in this simple hotel in the centre of town don't live up to the decoration in reception, but they're much bigger than average and have a certain faded charm. Some rooms have en-suite bathrooms. Streetside rooms can be noisy.

Hôtel Mon Rêve
HOTEL €

(Map p160; ☑ 0522 41 14 39; 7 Rue Chaouia; s/d/tr Dh180/250/300, without bathroom Dh110/150/200) This old-style hotel has been a favourite with budget travellers for years. It is conveniently located near the Central Market but can be quite noisy, and the rooms painted in blue are spartan but clean. Choose a higher room to avoid the noise. Note that Rue Chaouia is sometimes referred to by its old name, Rue Colbert.

East-West Hotel
HOTEL €€

(Map p163; ☑ 0522 20 02 10; www.eastwest-hotel.com; 10 Ave Hassan Souktani, cnr Rue Washington, Quartier Gauthier; s/d incl breakfast Dh450/600; 🛜) Readers recommend this bright and cheerful three-star hotel. All rooms have clean bathrooms with modern fittings, free internet and a safe, and the hotel boasts a good restaurant and an Irish pub. Located in the residential but upcoming Quartier Gauthier, this choice is very quiet.

Hotel Ibis Casa Voyageurs
HOTEL €€

(☑ 0522 40 19 84; www.ibishotel.com; Pl de la Gare; r Dh1100; ❋🛜) Conveniently located both next door to Casa Voyageurs train station and on the new tram line, the Ibis is a strong midrange accommodation choice. As part of a chain, it's reliable if unsurprising, with modern comfy rooms, a decent breakfast and good service.

Casablanca Quartier Gauthier

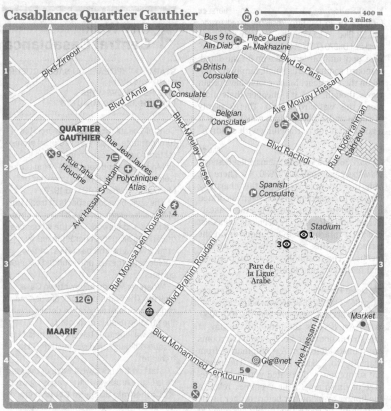

Casablanca Quartier Gauthier

Hôtel Transatlantique   HOTEL €€

(Map p160; ☏0522 29 45 51; www.transatcasa. com; 79 Rue Chaouia; s/d/tr Dh800/960/1100; ❄🞈) Set in one of Casa's architectural gems, the decor at this 1922 hotel is all a bit over the top. Popular with tour groups, it has a snack bar, a shady outdoor seating area and comfortable, but fairly plain, bedrooms. Avoid the 1st floor, as it gets the brunt of noise from the popular and very rowdy piano bar and nightclub. There are several newly decorated suites. Staff are keen to tell you that Édith Piaf was a resident and Telly Savalas of *Kojak* fame sucked his lollipop here.

Hôtel Bellerive

HOTEL €€

(☑ 0522 79 75 04; http://bellerive.terredumaroc. net; 38 Blvd de La Corniche, Aïn Diab; s/d/tr incl breakfast Dh570/720/950; ❋ 🛋) The lovely terrace, pool and garden make up for the dated, standard rooms at this small, family-run hotel on the Corniche. Many rooms have ocean views though, and it's cheaper than most along this waterfront strip. There's plenty of space and a playground, which makes it a good bet if you're travelling with children.

Dar Itrit

B&B €€

(☑ 0522 36 02 58; www.daritrit.ma; 9 Rue Restinga; s/d without bathroom Dh870/980; 🛜) There are only three double rooms in this charming B&B set in a residential area, each decorated in a different Moroccan style – Marrakesh, Berber and Mogador. A delicious breakfast is served in a bright living room or on the terrace, in this slightly out-of-the-centre location. The hospitality is warm, but note that bathrooms are shared.

★ Doge Hotel

HOTEL €€€

(Map p163; ☑ 0522 26 97 46; www.hotelledoge.com; 9 Rue du Docteur Veyre; s/d from Dh2300/3050; ❋🛜) Art deco is the order of the day at this stylish boutique hotel – even the rooms are named after Jazz Age luminaries from Man Ray to F Scott Fitzgerald. The rooms are sumptuously decorated with a high degree of finishing. In the evenings, relax in the library or piano bar before dinner in the restaurant, or sooth the travel days away at the splendid spa.

Hôtel Hyatt Regency

HOTEL €€€

(Map p160; ☑ 0522 43 12 34; www.casablanca.hyatt. com; Pl des Nations Unies; r Dh2200; 🅿 ❋ 🛜 🛋) The best and the most central of all the five-star hotels, the Hyatt is a favourite meeting place for Casablancais for a meal in one of the many restaurants, or a drink at the bar. The spacious rooms are equipped with modern amenities and decorated in an elegant contemporary style, and have magnificent views of Casablanca, the old medina, the ocean and the Hassan II Mosque. The hotel also has a gym, spa and nightclub.

Hôtel les Saisons

HOTEL €€€

(Map p160; ☑ 0522 49 09 01; www.hotellessais onsmaroc.ma; 19 Rue el-Oraïbi Jilali; s/d Dh1100/ 1400; ❋🛜) This small hotel offers extremely comfortable, well-appointed and quiet rooms with all the usual facilities: a safe, minibar, satellite TV and direct-dial phone. It's a more personal place than the larger

---

🚶 City Walk
Central Casablanca

START CATHÉDRALE DU SACRÉ COEUR, BLVD RACHIDI
END PL 16 NOVEMBRE
LENGTH 3KM, 50 MINUTES

Central Casablanca has a rich architectural heritage. The style of colonial architecture found here in abundance is known as Mauresque and came into being during General Lyautey's term as governor of Morocco between 1912 and 1924.

The style blended aspects of traditional Moroccan design such as Islamic arches, columns and tilework with the influences of Parisian art deco, characterised by ornate wrought-iron balconies, carved facades and friezes, and rounded exterior corners.

Wherever you go in downtown Casa, look up! The humblest block of apartments can sport ornate decorative details, even if the building itself is neglected.

This walking tour takes in the best Mauresque buildings, and some other Casa treasures.

Start on the northwest edge of the Parc de la Ligue Arabe, with the imposing white ❶ **Cathédrale du Sacré Coeur**, a graceful cathedral designed by Paul Tornon and built in 1930. This is a good example of the style, with some neo-Gothic influence.

From here, walk two blocks east to Pl Mohammed V, which is the grand centrepiece of the French building scheme. The vast square, beloved by Casablancais who congregate here in the evenings and on weekends, is surrounded by impressive administrative buildings, most designed by Robert Marrast and Henri Prost. The 1930 ❷ **wilaya** (old police headquarters, now governor's office) dominates the square's south side and is topped by a modernist clock tower.

The nearby ❸ **palais de justice** (law courts) dates from 1925. The huge main door and entrance were inspired by the Persian *iwan*, a vaulted hall that opens into the central court of the *medersa* (theological college) of a mosque.

Stroll across the grand square and admire the 1918 ❹ **main post office** (p170), fronted by arches and stone columns and

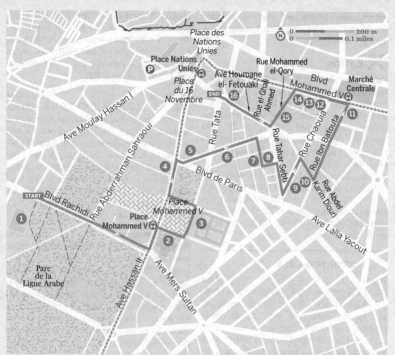

decorated with bold mosaics. More in the style of traditional Moroccan architecture is the **5 Banque al-Maghrib**, on Blvd de Paris. Fronted with decorative stonework, it was the last building constructed on the square.

From here, walk east on Rue Indriss Lahrizi, where impressive facades line both sides of the street, the best being **6 La Princière Salon de Thé**, with its huge stone crown on the roofline. Turn right into Rue Mohammed Belloul to see **7 Hôtel Guynemer** (p162) with its restored art deco panelling, and almost opposite, the **8 Hotel Oued Dahab**. Then walk a block east and turn right down Rue Tahar Sebti, which is lined with colonial buildings that are now apartments and offices.

Turn left into Rue Chaouia and look for **9 Hôtel Transatlantique** (p163), which dates from 1922 and has been beautifully restored. Just around the corner, another restored gem, the **10 Hotel Volubilis**, has a great facade.

Turn left up Rue Ibn Batouta and continue to the corner of Blvd Mohammed V. On your right is the derelict shell of the **11 Hôtel Lincoln**, a Mauresque masterpiece built in 1916. Sadly its owner cannot afford to carry

out restoration work, but the authorities won't allow such an important building to be torn down.

Turn left into Blvd Mohammed V and look out for an array of wonderful facades along the street's south side. The **12 Central Market post office** (p170), with its delicate motifs, and the **13 Le Matin/Maroc Soir** building, with its classic style, are two of the most impressive. There are plans to restore this entire area.

At the end of this block, on the corner of Rue Mohammed el-Qory, is **14 Petit Poucet** (p169) bar and pavement cafe, once frequented by Antoine de Saint-Exupéry, Édith Piaf and Albert Camus. It's worth looking inside at the original bar counter. Turn left here into Rue Mohammed el-Qory to find the **15 Cinéma Rialto** (p170). Continue south to the junction with Ave Houmane el-Fetouaki and turn right to reach **16 Pl 16 Novembre**, home to art deco buildings.

For information on Casablanca's architectural heritage, see *Casablanca: Colonial Myths and Architectural Ventures* by Jean-Louis Cohen and Monique Eleb, and *Casablanca – Portrait d'une Ville* by JM Zurfluh.

international hotels and offers good value for money and an excellent location. The staff speak English.

Eating

Casablanca has a great selection of restaurants, and you can eat anything from excellent tajine to French pâté and Thai dumplings. However, as elsewhere along the ocean, fresh fish and seafood are the local speciality and it's worth checking out the restaurants at the port or on the way to Aïn Diab for a culinary treat.

Rue Chaouia, located opposite the Marché Central, is the best place for a quick eat, with a line of rotisseries, stalls and restaurants serving roast chicken, brochettes and sandwiches (Dh20 to Dh30). It's open until about 2am.

✕ Downtown Casa

Ifrane　　　　　　　　　　　　CAFE €
(Map p160; cnr Rues Tata & Mouftakar; mains Dh40-65; ☺10am-10pm) Almost always crowded and spilling customers onto the streetside seating, this friendly cafe serves a choice of grills and brochettes at bargain prices. It's a relaxed place with a mixed clientele and offers hassle-free eating for women.

Patisserie Bennis Habous　　　PATISSERIE €
(☑0522 30 30 25; 2 Rue Fkih el-Gabbas; pastries from Dh10; ☺9am-8pm) One of the city's most famous and traditional patisseries, this place in the Quartier Habous is Casa's best spot for traditional Moroccan treats, including some of the best *cornes de gazelle* (gazelle horns; sweet almond pastries) in town, as well as made-to-order *pastillas*.

Marché Central　　　　　　　　MARKET €
(Map p160; meals from Dh40; ☺9am-6pm) The Marché Central is a great place to go for lunch – busy tables from half a dozen restaurants thrum with diners and waiters, serving up huge platters of fish, grilled vegetables, bread, salads and seafood soup. Cheap, filling and perfect for people-watching.

**★Restaurant du
Port de Pêche**　　　　　　　　SEAFOOD €€
(Map p158; ☑0522 31 85 61; Le Port de Pêche; mains Dh150; ☺lunch & dinner) This authentic and rustic seafood restaurant in the middle of the fishing harbour is packed to the gills at lunch and dinner as happy diners tuck into fish freshly whipped from the sea and

cooked to perfection. The fish and tangy paella are some of the best in town. The decor is very 1970s with paper tablecloths. Service is professional and swift. Book ahead as this place is very popular with Casablancais from all walks of life.

La Bodéga　　　　　　　　　　TAPAS €€
(Map p160; ☑0522 54 18 42; 129 Rue Allah ben Abdellah; mains Dh120; ☺Mon-Sat noon-4pm & 7pm-1am, 7pm-1am Sun) Hip, happening and loved by a mixed-aged group of Casablanca's finest, La Bodéga is essentially a tapas bar with good (meaty) mains, where the music (everything from salsa to Arabic pop) is loud and the *rioja* (Spanish wine) flows freely. It's a fun place with a lively atmosphere and a packed dance floor after 10pm.

Sqala Restaurant　　　　　　MOROCCAN €€
(Map p158; ☑0522 26 09 60; Blvd des Almohades; mains Dh90-160; ☺lunch & dinner Tue-Sun, daily summer) Nestled in the ochre walls of the *sqala*, an 18th-century fortified bastion north of the centre, this lovely restaurant is a tranquil escape from the city. The cafe has a rustic interior and a delightful garden surrounded by flower-draped trellises. No alcohol is served, but there's a good selection of teas and fresh juices. It's a lovely spot for a Moroccan breakfast or a selection of salads for lunch. Tajines are a speciality and the menu features plenty of fish, as well as a selection of meat brochettes.

Taverne du Dauphin　　　　　　FRENCH €€
(Map p160; ☑0522 22 12 00; 115 Blvd Houphouët Boigny; mains Dh70-90; set menu Dh110; ☺noon-11pm Mon-Sat) A Casablanca institution, this traditional Provençal restaurant and bar has been serving up *fruits de mer* (seafood) since it opened in 1958. On first glance it's a humble, family-run place, but one taste of the succulent grilled fish, fried calamari and *crevettes royales* (king prawns) will leave you smitten. Alcohol is served.

Ostréa　　　　　　　　　　　　SEAFOOD €€
(Map p158; ☑0522 44 13 90; Le Port de Pêche; mains Dh150; ☺lunch & dinner) Across the road from Restaurant du Port de Pêche inside the port is this more upmarket seafood restaurant specialising in Oualidia oysters, fresh lobster and other shellfish. Wash it all down with a glass of wine or beer.

Restaurant al-Mounia　　　　MOROCCAN €€
(Map p160; ☑0522 22 26 69; 95 Rue Prince Moulay Abdallah; mains Dh150; ☺dinner) Eat the best

Moroccan food in Casablanca's centre at this delightful traditional restaurant where you can choose to sit in the Moroccan salon elegantly decorated with *zellij* (tilework) and sculpted wood, or under the pepper tree in the cool, leafy garden. There's a selection of salads worthy of any vegetarian restaurant and an array of exotic delicacies such as pigeon *pastilla* (rich, savoury pie) and sweet tomato tajine.

Chez Flavio   ITALIAN €€
(Map p163; ☑0522 29 45 29; 3 Blvd Mohamed Abdou; pizzas Dh80, mains Dh120; ⊙lunch & dinner) One of the most popular Italian restaurants, Chez Flavio makes for a welcome break from tajine if you've been in Morocco for some time. These are definitely some of the best pizzas in town.

★ Le Rouget de l'Isle   FRENCH €€€
(Map p163; ☑0522 29 47 40; 16 Rue Rouget de l'Isle, off Blvd Moulay Hassan I; mains Dh200; ⊙lunch Mon-Fri, dinner Mon-Sat) One of Casa's top eateries, Le Rouget is set in a glorious 1930s villa and has a wonderful garden redolent with night-blooming jasmine. Sleek, stylish and charming, it's renowned for its simple but delicious and light French food. The owner's contemporary artworks grace the walls. The impeccable food is reasonably priced; book in advance.

Rick's Cafe   MEDITERRANEAN €€€
(Map p158; ☑0522 27 42 07; www.rickscafe.ma; 248 Blvd Sour Jdid; mains Dh160; ⊙lunch & dinner) Cashing in on the Hollywood classic *Casablanca*, the bar, lounge and restaurant is run by a former American diplomat. It's not remotely authentic, but great fun nevertheless. The menu features excellent French and Moroccan specialities, concentrating on fresh fish. At lunchtime, the Obama family's chilli con carne is on offer. The pianist, Issam, will play 'As Time Goes By', and there's a Sunday jam session and the inevitable souvenir T-shirts. You can watch the film again and again on the 1st floor.

La Brasserie la Bavaroise   FRENCH €€€
(Map p160; ☑0522 31 17 60; 129 Rue Allah ben Abdellah; mains Dh150-200; ⊙dinner) Locals and expats like to hang out in this upmarket brasserie behind the Marché Central, partly for the French cuisine, partly to see and be seen. It offers a good selection of fish as well as French classics such as veal, steak and pheasant cooked to perfection. Meat is grilled on a wood fire. It has a pleasant atmosphere and a friendly welcome. Every month the menu features specialities from a different region of France. The same owners also run La Bodéga next door.

La Maison du Gourmet   FRENCH, MOROCCAN €€€
(Map p163; ☑0522 48 48 46; Rue Taha Houcine, Maarif; meals Dh400-500; ⊙lunch Mon-Fri, dinner Mon-Sat) This upmarket gourmet restaurant serves an inventive menu of the finest of French and Moroccan cuisine; it's run by a couple, he French, she Moroccan, both trained by Paul Bocuse. Specialities include a heavenly *pastilla* with confit of duck and foie gras. The elegant surroundings, excellent service and exceptional food make this the perfect address for a special occasion. Book ahead.

✖ Aïn Diab & Anfa

The best of this neighbourhood's restaurants are clustered together on a cliff top overlooking the crashing Atlantic waves near el-Hank Lighthouse.

CASABLANCA FOR CHILDREN

Casablanca is a big, grimy city and your best bet when travelling with children is to retreat from the noise and traffic of the city centre. The beaches and beach clubs in **Aïn Diab** are the places to go. Along with swimming pools, slides and playgrounds, they have various sports courts and countless facilities. Staying at a hotel along the Blvd de la Corniche means you'll probably have your own swimming pool and won't have too far to walk for entertainment.

Continuing west from Aïn Diab, the upmarket suburb of **Anfa** is home to the enormous **Morocco Mall**, which has a giant aquarium and an IMAX theatre in addition to its shops.

Back in town, Casa's biggest open space is the **Parc de la Ligue Arabe** (Map p163). It's a good place for games and walks, and has a choice of small cafes and the **Yasmina amusement park** (Map p163; admission Dh150; ⊙10am-7pm), with plenty of small-scale rides and fun-fair atmosphere.

THE SHANTY TOWNS

In May 2003, 13 suicide bombers blew themselves up at public places in Casablanca, killing themselves and 32 other people. They belonged to Salafia Jihadia, a radical Islamic group whose founding members trained in Afghanistan. The bombers were all young Moroccan men living in Casablanca's worst slums, less than half an hour from the city centre.

In 2007, 24 Islamists were arrested for plotting another wave of bombings after their leader blew himself up at an internet cafe. Many came from the same slums.

Most Casablancais openly condemn the killings, and claim their city is the most tolerant in the country. But a quarter – perhaps even a third – of the city's population lives in shanty towns, where living conditions are harsh: makeshift houses are made of cardboard and plastic, with no running water, sewage system or electricity, no schools, no work and no hope. Many youngsters feel they have nothing to lose.

After the bombings, many charities were set up to improve the conditions, and the government has become more aware of the problems. The Housing Ministry has announced plans to abolish all slums in Casablanca, and several slums have been destroyed, but new shanties seem to spring up faster than the authorities can knock them down. Tens of thousands of houses are under construction, but slum residents complain that the new housing is too expensive and too small for extended families. There has been a serious improvement, but many feel it's not enough, and unless the government addresses the underlying problems there will be no improvement in conditions. It is hoped this will happen before anger and frustration boil over into support for violent alternatives.

Frédéric Cassel Haute Patisserie PATISSERIE €€
(8 Blvd Moulay Rachid, Anfa; pastries from Dh12; ⊙9am-10pm) Be seen at the latest trendy cafe in upmarket Anfa serving mouth-watering breakfasts and light meals, along with ice cream and cakes that display mind-boggling artistry.

Hediard PATISSERIE €€
(☑0522 79 72 32; Résidence Jardin d'Anfa, Blvd Lido Route Côterie, Aïn Diab; meals & sandwiches Dh50-90; ⊙9am-10pm) Very slick, and popular with the young and beautiful, this cafe in Aïn Diab serves a range of sumptuous cakes as well as light meals and deli-style sandwiches.

La Fibule MOROCCAN, MEDITERRANEAN €€€
(☑0522 36 06 41; Blvd de la Corniche, Phare el-Hank; meals Dh300-500; ⊙lunch & dinner) The subtle lighting, warm colours and elegant decor give La Fibule an inviting atmosphere. The food here is a mixture of well-prepared Moroccan and Lebanese, served at low tables overlooking the ocean through large windows.

La Mer SEAFOOD €€€
(☑0522 36 33 15; Blvd de la Corniche, Phare el-Hank; meals Dh400; ⊙lunch & dinner) This seafood restaurant is a refined place with white linen and bone china. The menu and service is very French, bordering on stuffy, but the food is divine.

A Ma Bretagne SEAFOOD, FRENCH €€€
(☑0522 36 21 12; Sidi Abderrahman, Blvd de la Corniche; meals Dh500; ⊙dinner) Locally promoted as the best restaurant in Africa, this self-consciously cool establishment is all modern lines and superb food. Although seafood tops the bill here, you can opt for some other French delicacies, cooked by the *maître cuisinier* (master chef) André Halbert. It's 5km out of town.

🍷 Drinking & Nightlife

Although there are plenty of classic French-style drinking dens in the centre of town, they are pretty much a male preserve and are usually intimidating for women. Casablanca's bars can be pretty rough around the edges, and they generally attract a male-only clientele (plus prostitutes). In general, the bars in the larger hotels are more refined places to drink, especially for women.

The beachfront suburb of Aïn Diab is the place for late-night drinking and dancing in Casa. However, hanging out with Casablanca's beautiful people for a night on the town doesn't come cheap. Expect to pay at least Dh150 to get in and as much again for drinks. Heavy-set bouncers guard the doors and practise tough crowd control – if you don't look the part, you won't get in. Many of these clubs cater for well-heeled Middle Easterners (a Saudi prince has a palace on the Corniche), with Egyptian or Lebanese performers.

Men are always expected to pay for drinks, and women shouldn't expect hassle-free drinking – but some of the more female-friendly venues are listed here.

Café Alba   CAFE
(Map p160; ☑0522 22 71 54; 59-61 Rue Indriss Lahrizi) High ceilings, swish, modern furniture, subtle lighting and a hint of elegant colonial times mark this cafe out from the more traditional smoky joints around town. It's hassle-free downtime for women and a great place for watching Casa's up-and-coming.

Sqala Café Maure   CAFE
(Map p158; Blvd des Almohades; ⊙noon-3pm & 7-11pm Mon, 8am-11pm Tue-Sun) Another exception to the men-only rule, this lovely cafe is set behind the *sqala* in the medina wall. The flower-filled garden is quiet all afternoon and makes a great place for coffee or delicious juices.

Blue Parrot   BAR
(Map p158; 248 Blvd Sour Jdid; ⊙6.30am-11.30pm) Upstairs at Rick's Cafe, this Caribbean-style bar is partially open-air with wonderful views over the port. It's a great place for a drink (and comfortable for women) and also serves a simple menu of barbecued fish and grills (mains Dh75 to Dh160).

Petit Poucet   BAR
(Map p160; cnr Blvd Mohammed V & Rue Mohammed el-Qory) A die-hard relic of 1920s France, this strictly male-only bar was where Saint-Exupéry, the French author and aviator, used to spend time between mail flights across the Sahara. Today, the bar is low-key but is an authentic slice of long-ago Casa life. Look out for the old-time advertising signs.

Le Trica   BAR
(Map p163; ☑0522 22 07 06; 5 Rue el-Moutanabi, Quartier Gauthier; ⊙closed lunch Sat & Sun) This bar-lounge, set over two levels with brick walls and 1960s furniture, is the place to feel the beat of the new Morocco. The atmosphere is hot and trendy at night, stirred by the techno beat and the flow of beer and *mojitos* (rum cocktails), but things are a lot calmer at lunch.

Balcon 33   CLUB
(33 Blvd de la Corniche) A Fellini-esque, cabaret-style bar-cum-restaurant.

Le Carré Rouge   CLUB
(Hotel Villa Blanca, Blvd de la Corniche; ⊙11.30pm-4am) An ultramodern pop sensation.

VIP Club   CLUB
(Rue des Dunes) Gay-friendly.

Le Village   CLUB
(11 Blvd de la Corniche) Also has a slightly gay-friendly atmosphere.

Armstrong Legend   CLUB
(41 Blvd de la Corniche) Incredibly packed and one of the few places with funky live music.

Hôtel Transatlantique   CLUB
(Map p160; www.transatcasa.com; 79 Rue Chaouia) The seedy nightclub here is good for late-night *couleur locale* as the belly dancers and singers provoke the mostly male locals into throwing money at them.

Sky 28   CLUB
(Kenzi Tower Hotel, Twin Centre, Maarif) Serves cocktails to the sounds of more middle-of-the-road live music.

☆ Entertainment

Theatre

Complex Culturel Sidi Belyout   THEATRE
(Map p160; 28 Rue Léon L'Africain; ⊙performances 9pm) This 200-seat theatre hosts plays (usually in Arabic) and the occasional music recital or dance performance.

Les Abattoirs de Casablanca   PERFORMING ARTS
(☑0537 73 26 50; www.abattoirs-casablanca.net; Quartier Hay Mohammadi) The old city abattoirs built in 1922 have been transformed into an impressive cultural centre dubbed the Culture Factory. Near Casa Voyageurs railway station, the centre hosts exhibitions and performances, plays, concerts and workshops in anything from mask-making to rollerblading, including some for children.

Cinemas

Most English-language films are dubbed in French, unless it specifically mentions '*version originale*'.

Megarama   CINEMA
(☑0522 79 88 88; www.megarama.info; Blvd de la Corniche; afternoon/evening shows Dh40/50) The plushest cinema in town, this huge complex

in Aïn Diab has four comfortable theatres that are usually packed.

Cinéma Lynx
CINEMA

(Map p158; ☎0522 22 02 29; 150 Ave Mers Sultan; screen/balcony/club Dh30/40/50) A good option if you don't want to trek out to Aïn Diab, this spacious and comfortable cinema has an excellent sound system.

Cinéma Rialto
CINEMA

(Map p160; ☎0522 26 26 32; Rue Mohammed el-Qory; screen/balcony/club Dh30/40/50) Classic, cavernous, single-screen, art-deco cinema.

IMAX Theatre
CINEMA

(Morocco Mall, Rte Azemmour, Anfa) This cinema at Morocco Mall offers the country's glitziest movie-going experience.

🔒 Shopping

Although not an artisan centre, Casablanca has a good choice of traditional crafts from around Morocco. The most pleasant place to shop is Quartier Habous, south of the centre. Merchants here are pretty laid-back, but the quality of crafts can vary and hard bargaining is the order of the day. There are craft shops of varying quality along Blvd Houphouët Boigny that aim to attract the tourist dirham.

Exposition Nationale d'Artisanat
ARTS & CRAFTS

(Map p160; ☎0522 26 70 64; 3 Ave Hassan II; ☺8.30am-12.30pm & 2.30-8pm) If you'd rather avoid haggling altogether, head here where you'll find three floors of fixed-price crafts.

Morocco Mall
MALL

(www.moroccomall.net; Anfa; ☺10am-9pm Sun-Thu, 10am-10pm Fri & Sat) Morocco's fanciest shopping destination, this new mall in Aïn Diab has stores galore, from recognised international brands to a dedicated 'souq' area with traditional Moroccan crafts. Take a shopping break to gawp at the two-storey-high aquarium, and fill up in the multi-national food court.

Twin Center
CLOTHING

(Map p163; cnr Blvd Mohammed Zerktouni & Al-Massira al-Khadra) Twin Center marks the high end of the chic shopping area and contains a shopping mall, luxury hotel and office space. Smaller boutiques on the side streets and around the covered Maarif market are more atmospheric and good for bargains.

ℹ Information

EMERGENCY
Fire/Ambulance (☎15; ☺24hr)
Police (☎19; ☺24hr)
Service d'Aide Médicale Urgente (SAMU; ☎0522 25 25 25; ☺24hr) Private ambulance service.

INTERNET ACCESS
EuroNet (Map p160; ☎0522 26 59 21; 51 Rue Tata; per hr Dh10; ☺8.30am-11pm) Internet.
G@.net (Map p160; ☎0522 22 95 23; 29 Rue Abdelkader al-Moftaker; per hr Dh8; ☺9am-midnight) Very clean and modern, with fast connection.
Gig@net (Map p163; ☎0522 48 48 10; 140 Blvd Mohammed Zerktouni; per hr Dh10; ☺24hr) Internet.
LGnet (Map p160; ☎0522 27 46 13; 81 Blvd Mohammed V; per hr Dh8; ☺9am-midnight) Internet.

MEDICAL SERVICES
Polyclinique Atlas (Map p163; ☎0522 27 40 39; 27 Rue Mohammed ben Ali, Quartier Gauthier; ☺24hr) Off Rue Jean Jaures.
SOS Médecins (☎0522 25 30 49, 0522 44 44 44; house call Dh400; ☺24hr) Private doctors who make house calls.

MONEY
There are banks – most with ATMs and foreign-exchange offices – on almost every street corner in the centre of Casablanca.
BMCE (Map p160; Hôtel Hyatt Regency, Pl des Nations Unies; ☺9am-9pm) Good for after-hours and weekend services.
Crédit du Maroc (Map p160; ☎0522 47 72 55; 48 Blvd Mohammed V; ☺8.30am-6.30pm Mon-Fri) Separate *bureau de change* that is very central; American Express (Amex) travellers cheques cashed for free.
Voyages Schwartz (Map p160; ☎0522 37 63 30; Rue Prince Moulay Abdallah; ☺9am-6pm Mon-Sat) Amex representative; does not cash or sell travellers cheques.
Wafa Cash (Map p160; ☎0522 20 80 80; 15 Rue Indriss Lahrizi; ☺8am-8pm Mon-Sat) Open longer hours; has an ATM and cashes travellers cheques.

POST
Central Market Post Office (Map p160; cnr Blvd Mohammed V & Rue Chaouia; ☺8.30am-4.30pm Mon-Fri)
FedEx (☎0522 54 12 12; 313 Blvd Mohammed V; ☺8.30am-4.30pm Mon-Fri)
Main Post Office (Map p160; cnr Blvd de Paris & Ave Hassan II; ☺8.30am-4.30pm Mon-Fri)

Medina Post Office (Map p158; Pl Ahmed el-Bidaoui; ⊗ 8.30am-4.30pm Mon-Fri) Near the youth hostel.

TOURIST INFORMATION

Although the staff are polite, tourist offices in Casablanca are of very little practical use. Try **Visit Casablanca** (www.visitcasablanca.ma) for information before you travel or ask the receptionist at your hotel for help.

Syndicat d'Initiative (Map p160; 0522 22 15 24; 98 Blvd Mohammed V; ⊗ 8.30am-6.30pm Mon-Fri) Tourist information.

ⓘ Getting There & Away

AIR

Casablanca's **Mohammed V International Airport** (0522 53 90 40; www.onda.ma) is 30km southeast of the city on the Marrakesh road. Regular flights leave here for most countries in western Europe, as well as to West Africa, Algeria, Tunisia, Egypt, the Middle East and North America.

Internally, the vast majority of Royal Air Maroc's (RAM) flights go via Casablanca, so you can get to any destination in Morocco directly from the city.

BUS

The modern **CTM bus station** (Map p160; 0522 54 10 10; www.ctm.ma; 23 Rue Léon L'Africain) is close to Ave des FAR. It's a pretty efficient place with a cafe. There are daily CTM bus departures.

CTM also operates international buses to Belgium, France, Germany, Italy and Spain from Casablanca.

The modern Gare Routière Ouled Ziane, located 4km southeast of the centre, is the bus station for almost all non-CTM services. The main reason to trek out here is for destinations not covered by CTM. A taxi to the bus station will cost about Dh20; alternatively take bus No 10 or 36 from Blvd Mohammed V near the market.

Also on Rte Ouled Ziane, but more than 1km closer to town, is the SAT bus station. SAT runs national and international buses of a similar standard to CTM, though to fewer destinations. Fares are slightly cheaper.

CAR

Casablanca is well endowed with car-rental agencies, many with offices around Ave des FAR, Blvd Mohammed V and at the airport.

Casablanca has parking meters (Dh2 per hour, two hours maximum), operating from 8am to noon and 2pm to 7pm daily, except on Sunday and public holidays. If you don't pay, you may be fined or have your wheels clamped. There is a guarded car park next to the British cemetery

 STREET NAMES

Casablanca's French street names are slowly being replaced with Moroccan names. Be very specific when asking for directions, as many people, including taxi drivers (and some local street directories) have yet to make the transition. You'll often see several different names for one street.

(per day/night Dh20) and another just off Rue Tata (Dh5 per hour). Anywhere else a guard will ask for a tip for watching your car; it is common practice to pay Dh5.

Avis Airport (0522 53 90 72; Mohammed V International Airport); City (Map p160; 0522 31 24 24; 19 Ave des FAR)

Budget Airport (0522 33 91 57; Mohammed V International Airport); City (Map p160; 0522 31 31 24; Tours des Habous, Ave des FAR)

National Airport (0522 53 97 16; Mohammed V International Airport); City (Map p160; 0522 27 71 41; 12 Rue el-Oraïbi Jilali)

President Car (Map p160; 0661 21 03 94, 0522 26 07 90; presidentcar@menara.ma; 27 Rue el-Ghali Ahmed) A reliable local agency that has a well-maintained fleet of cars, very competitive rates, and comes much recommended by the local expat community. The Bouayad brothers will do their utmost to help, and can deliver a car to the airport or Marrakesh if requested. It's off Blvd Mohammed V.

TAXI

Shared grands taxis to Rabat (Dh30) and to Fez (Dh120) leave from Blvd Mohammed V opposite the old Hôtel Lincoln. However, the train is more convenient and comfortable.

TRAIN

If your destination is on a train line, it's generally the best way to travel. Casablanca has five train stations, but only two of interest to travellers.

All long-distance trains as well as trains to Mohammed V International Airport depart from Casa Voyageurs train station, 4km east of the city centre. Catch bus 30 (Dh4), which runs along Blvd Mohammed V, or hop in a taxi and pay about Dh15 to get there.

The Casa Port train station is a few hundred metres northeast of Pl des Nations Unies. Although more convenient, trains from here only run to Rabat (Dh35, one hour, every 30 minutes) and Kenitra (Dh48, 1½ hours, every 30 minutes). Casa Port was under extensive reconstruction at the time of research.

DAY BUSES FROM CASABLANCA

DESTINATION	COST (DH)	DURATION (HR)	DAILY FREQUENCY
Agadir	190	6½	9
Chefchaouen	120	7	1
El-Jadida	40	2	6
Essaouira	130	6	3 with CTM; hourly with private companies
Fez	85	4	8
Laâyoune	435	20	4
Marrakesh	85	3½	15
Meknès	80	3½	7
Ouezzane	90	4	1
Tangier	130	5½	5 with CTM; regularly with private companies
Taza	140	7	5
Tetouan	145	6	6

Destinations from Casa Voyageurs include the following:

Azemmour Dh31, one hour, seven daily
El-Jadida Dh35, 1½ hours, eight daily
Fez Dh110, 3½ to 4½ hours, 16 daily
Marrakesh Dh90, three hours, nine daily
Meknès Dh90, 3½ hours, 18 daily
Nador Dh185, 11 hours, five daily
Oujda Dh205, 10 hours, three daily
Tangier Dh125, five hours, eight daily

🛈 Getting Around

TO/FROM THE AIRPORT

The easiest way to get from Mohammed V International Airport to Casablanca is by train (2nd class Dh40, 35 minutes). The trains are comfortable and reliable, and leave every hour from 6am to 10pm and at midnight. You can also continue to Rabat (Dh75) or Kenitra (Dh88), though you'll have a change of train at Casa Voyageurs or Aïn Sebaa. The trains leave from below the ground floor of the airport Terminal 1 building.

From Casa Voyageurs train station to the airport, the first train leaves at 4.40am and then every hour from 6.07am to 10.07pm. Additional trains go from Casa Port, with a change at Aïn Sebaa.

A grand taxi between the airport and the city centre costs Dh300, though you may be asked for Dh350 at unsocial hours. Some taxi drivers receive commissions if they bring clients to particular hotels.

BUS

The local bus system has been revamped, but you're more likely to find the new tramway or petits taxis more useful. Buses cost Dh4 and stop at designated bus stops.

Bus 2 Blvd Mohammed V to Casa Voyageurs train station.
Bus 4 Along Blvd de Paris and down Ave Lalla Yacout to the nouvelle medina.
Bus 9 From Blvd d'Anfa to Aïn Diab and the beaches.
Bus 10 From Pl de la Concorde, along Blvd Mohammed V to Gare Routière Ouled Ziane.
Bus 11 From Ave des FAR to Gare Routière.
Bus 15 Northbound from Pl Oued al-Makhazine to the Hassan II Mosque.

TAXI

Casa's red petits taxis are excellent value and can generally get you to your destination far faster than any bus. You can hail one anywhere, or there's a petit-taxi stand on Ave des FAR. The minimum fare is Dh7, but expect to pay Dh15 in or near the city centre. Most drivers use the meter without question, but if they refuse to, just get out of the cab (note that taxi drivers at Casa Voyageurs never put their meters on, and demand extortionate prices, even for locals). Prices rise by 50% after 8pm. Have plenty of small coins to hand, and check your change.

TRAM

The long-awaited **Casa Tramway** (www.casa tramway.ma) is finally in operation, and makes for an easy and efficient way of getting across the city. The most useful section of line for travellers is from Casa Voyageurs train station to Pl Mohammed V, via the Marché Central and Pl des Nations Unies. Trams also go to the beach at Aïn Diab (about 30 minutes from central Casablanca). Trams run every 15 minutes, with the first and last departures from the termini at 5.30am and 10.30pm. Fares are Dh7, bought from easy-to-use ticket machines on the platforms (multiple journey tickets are also available).

Rabat الرباط

POP 2.5 MILLION

While Rabat, Morocco's political and administrative capital since independence in 1956, has not established itself as a tourist destination, visitors who do go find a gem of a city. The colonial architecture is stunning, the palm-lined boulevards are well kept and relatively free of traffic, and the atmosphere is as cosmopolitan as its economic big brother down the coast. All in all, life here is pleasant and civilised. Casablancais say that, with all the bureaucrats, Rabat is dull, and they have a point. Yet the city is more laid-back, pleasant and more provincial than Casablanca, and far less grimy and frantic.

The quiet medina has an authentic feel to it, some good shops and fascinating architecture. You'll be blissfully ignored on the streets and souqs, so it's easy to discover the city's monuments and hidden corners at your own pace. The picturesque kasbah, with its narrow alleys, art galleries and magnificent ocean views, is also worth exploring.

Rabat has a long and rich history, and plenty of monuments to show for it from the Phoenician, Roman, Almohad and Merenid times. The power shifted at times between Rabat and Salé, the whitewashed town across the Bou Regreg river where time appears to have stood still.

Rabat is also a good place to eat; there are plenty of wonderful restaurants around town. The nightlife is not what it is in Casablanca, but an early afternoon stroll along the main avenues of the happening suburb of Agdal, where local hipsters flaunt their skinny jeans, is entertaining enough. And if city life gets you down, you can escape to the beaches further north.

History

The fertile plains inland from Rabat drew settlers to the area as far back as the 8th century BC. Both the Phoenicians and the Romans set up trading posts in the estuary of the Bou Regreg river in Sala, today's Chellah. The Roman settlement, Sala Colonia, lasted long after the empire's fall and eventually became the seat of an independent Berber kingdom. The Zenata Berbers built a *ribat,* a fortress-monastery after which the city takes its name, on the present site of Rabat's kasbah. As the new town of Salé (created in the 10th century) began to prosper on the north bank of the river, the city of Chellah fell into decline.

The arrival of the Almohads in the 12th century saw the *ribat* rebuilt as a kasbah, a strategic jumping-off point for campaigns in Spain, where the dynasty successfully brought Andalucia back under Muslim rule. Under Yacoub el-Mansour (the Victorious), Rabat enjoyed a brief heyday as an imperial capital, Ribat al-Fatah (Victory Fortress). El-Mansour had extensive walls built, added the enormous Bab Oudaia to the kasbah and began work on the Hassan Mosque, intended to be the greatest mosque in all of the Islamic West, if not in all of the Islamic world.

RABAT IN...

One Day

Start with a delicious breakfast at the **Pâtisserie Majestic** on Ave Mohammed V. A stroll through the medina will bring you to a superb lunch at **Riad Oudaya**. Cross Blvd Tariq al-Marsa and enter the **Kasbah les Oudaias** through the spectacular gate, Bab Oudaia. Climb to the top for magnificent views, then head to **Galérie d'Art Nouiga**. Stop for tea at **Café Maure** overlooking the Bou Regreg river. Take a taxi to the **Archaeology Museum** to see the famous Volubilis bronzes. By this time, you'll have earned a beer on the terrace at the **Hôtel Balima**, before dinner at the swish **Le Grand Comptoir**.

Two Days

Take the tram to **Salé** for a Moroccan-style breakfast at a cafe on **Pl Bab Khebaz**. Head into the medina to view the beautiful **Grande Mosquée** and **zawiyas** (shrines). Wander down to the river and be rowed across to Rabat, have fish for lunch at **Borj Eddar** overlooking the ocean, then take a taxi to **Le Tour Hassan** and the **Mausoleum of Mohammed V**. Another short taxi ride gets you to the **Chellah**, perfect for an afternoon stroll. For dinner, **L'Entrecôte** in trendy Agdal hits the spot, before dancing the night away at **Amnesia**.

Rabat

Enlargement

Rue Jerrada

Beach

Rue Bazzo

Andaluchan Gardens

Blvd Tariq al-Marsa

1
11
9
5
6
2
10
23
1

ATLANTIC OCEAN

Light House

Beach

See Enlargement

12
18
13

Cemetery

See Salé Map (p188)

Beach

25

Blvd Tariq al-Marsa

15
3
14
7
21
16

MEDINA

Ave Mohammed V

Ave Abdelkrim al-Khattabi

Blvd Mokhtar Gazouit

Ave Abdelkrim Gazouit

Line 1

OCEAN

Place al-Mellah

R Abdelmoumen

Place Mellia

Jardins Triangle de Vue

Ave Hassan II

R Mansour-ad-Dahbi

VILLE NOUVELLE

R al-Nmar

Oued Bou Regreg

Lines 1 & 2 Blvd Arrabah

7
8
31
34

Blvd Ab'l Rad'qa

Rue Idriss el-Azhar

SALÉ

Ave de Fès

SALÉ MEDINA

Rue Bab Sebta

MELLAH

Place Hassan II

Train Station

Ave Mohammed V

Line 1 Ave Hassan II

Line 2

Hypermarché Marjane (50m); Magic Park (250m); Salé (1.25m); Salé (12km)

0   1 km
0   0.5 miles

N

100 m

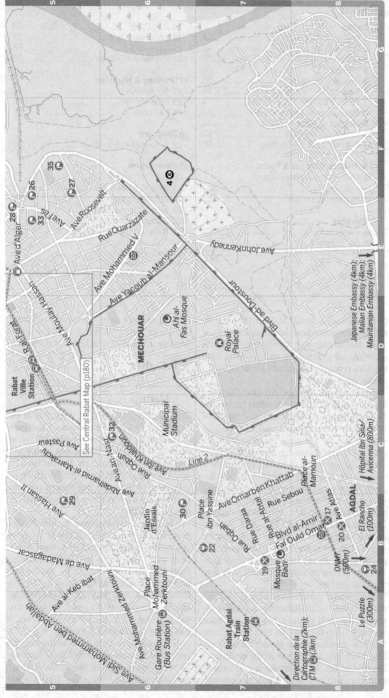

See Central Rabat Map (p180)

Rabat Ville Station

Ave Moulay Hassan

R. d'Égypte

Ave d'Alger

Ave Fès

Ave Roosevelt

Rue Ouarzazate

Ave Mohammed V

Ave Yacoub al-Mansour

MECHOUAR

Ahl al-Fas Mosque

Royal Palace

Blvd ad-Doustour

Ave John Kennedy

Japanese Embassy (4km); Malian Embassy (4km); Mauritanian Embassy (4km)

Hôpital Ibn Sina/ Avicenna (800m)

Municipal Stadium

Ave Pasteur

Ave Abdelhamid el-Marrakchi

Rue Oqbah

Ave Ibn Khaldoun

Line 2

Ave an-Nasr

Ave Hassan II

Ave de Madagascar

Jardin d'Essais

Place ibn Yassine

Ave Omar ben Khattab

Rue Daraa

Place al-Mamoun

Rue Sebou

Rue al-Abtal

Rue Oqbah

Mosque Badr

Blvd al-Amir Fal Ould Omar

AGDAL

El Rancho (100m)

Ave Atlas

ONMT (500m)

Le Puzzle (300m)

Place Mohammed Zerktouni

Ave Mohammed ben Abdallah

Ave al-Keb ibat

Ave Mohammed Zerktouni

Gare Routière (Bus Station)

Rabat Agdal Train Station

Direction de la Cartographie (2km); CTM (3km)

Rabat

El-Mansour's death in 1199 brought an end to these grandiose schemes, leaving the great Hassan Mosque incomplete. The city soon lost all significance and it wasn't until the 17th century that Rabat's fortunes began to change.

As Muslim refugees arrived from Christian Spain, so did a band of Christian renegades, Moorish pirates, freebooters and multinational adventurers. Rabat and Salé became safe havens for corsairs – merciless pirates whom English chroniclers called the Sallee Rovers. At one point they even created their own pirate state, the Republic of Bou Regreg. These corsairs roved as far as the coast of North America seeking Spanish gold, and to Cornwall in southern England to capture Christian slave labour. The first Alawite sultans attempted to curtail their looting sprees, but no sultan ever really exercised control over them. Corsairs continued attacking European shipping until well into the 19th century.

Meanwhile, Sultan Mohammed ben Abdallah briefly made Rabat his capital at the end of the 18th century, but the city soon fell back into obscurity. In 1912 France strategically abandoned the hornet's nest of political intrigue and unrest in the traditional capitals of Fez and Marrakesh and instead shifted power to coastal Rabat, where supply and defence were more easily achieved. Since then, the city has remained the seat of government and official home of the king.

◎ Sights

◎ Medina

Rabat's walled medina, all there was of the city when the French arrived in the early 20th century, is a rich mixture of spices, carpets, crafts, cheap shoes and bootlegged DVDs. Built on an orderly grid in the 17th century, it may lack the more intriguing atmosphere of the older medinas of the interior, but it's a great place to roam, with no aggressive selling.

The main market street is Rue Souika, lined with food and spice shops at the western end, then textiles and silverware as you head east. The **Souq as-Sebbat** (Jewellery Souq; Map p180) specialises in gaudy gold and begins roughly at Rue Bab Chellah. The **Grande Mosquée** (Map p180; off Rue Bab Chellah), a 14th-century Merenid original that has been rebuilt in the intervening years, is just down this road to the right.

If you continue past the Rue des Consuls (so called because diplomats lived here until 1912), you'll come to the *mellah* (Jewish quarter) with an interesting **flea market** going down to Bab el-Bahr and the river. Turning north along Rue des Consuls is one of the more interesting areas of the medina, with craft shops and some of the grand diplomatic residences. After the **carpet souq** (Map p174) the street ends in an open area lined with craft shops, which was once the setting for the slave auctions in the days of the Sallee Rovers. From here you can make your way up the hill to the kasbah.

East of the Centre

Le Tour Hassan   HISTORIC SITE

(Hassan Tower; Map p174) Towering above Oued Bou Regreg, and surrounded by well-tended gardens, is Rabat's most famous landmark. The Almohads' most ambitious project would have been the second-largest mosque of its time, after Samarra in Iraq, but Sultan Yacoub el-Mansour died before it was finished. He intended a 60m-tall minaret, but the tower was abandoned at 44m. The mosque was destroyed by an earthquake in 1755, and today only a forest of shattered pillars testifies to the grandiosity of El-Mansour's plans. The tower is built to the same design as the Giralda in Seville, and the Koutoubia in Marrakesh.

Mausoleum of Mohammed V   LANDMARK

(Map p174; ☺ sunrise-sunset) **FREE** Near the Hassan Tower stands this marble mausoleum, built in traditional Moroccan style. The present king's father (the late Hassan II) and grandfather have been laid to rest here. The decoration, despite the patterned *zellij* and carved plaster, gives off an air of tranquillity. Visitors to the mausoleum must be respectfully dressed, and can look down into the tomb from a gallery.

Chellah   HISTORIC SITE

(Map p174; cnr Ave Yacoub al-Mansour & Blvd Moussa ibn Nassair; admission Dh20; ☺9am-5.30pm) Abandoned, crumbling and overgrown, the old Roman city of **Sala Colonia** and the Merenid necropolis of Chellah is one of Rabat's most evocative sights. The Phoenicians were the first to settle on the grassy slopes above the river, but the town grew when the Romans took control in about AD 40. The city was abandoned in 1154 in favour

---

DON'T MISS

KASBAH LES OUDAIAS

The **kasbah** (Map p174; Rue Jamaa) occupies the oldest part of the city, the site of the original *ribat* (fortress-monastery), and commands magnificent views over the river and ocean from its cliff-top perch. Predominately residential, with tranquil alleys and whitewashed houses mostly built by Muslim refugees from Spain, this is a picturesque place to wander. Many foreigners are buying up the houses here, and it's easy to see the appeal. Some 'guides' offer their services but there is no need.

The 12th-century Almohad **Bab Oudaia** (Map p174), the most dramatic kasbah gate, is elaborately decorated with a series of carved arches. Inside the gateway, the main street, Rue Jamaa, runs straight through the kasbah. About 200m ahead on the left is the **Mosque el-Atiqa** (Map p174), the oldest mosque in Rabat, built in the 12th century and restored in the 18th century. You'll also find a number of low-key tourist shops and a couple of art galleries, such as the **Galérie d'Art Nouiga** (Map p174; Rue Jamaa), along this street.

At the end of the street is the **Plateforme du Sémaphore** (Signal Platform; Map p174; Rue Jamaa), with sweeping views over the estuary and across to Salé. The elevated position provided an excellent defence against seagoing attackers negotiating the sandbanks below.

Returning from the Plateforme, turn left down Rue Bazzo, a narrow winding street that leads down to the popular Café Maure (p184) and a side entrance to the formal **Andalucian Gardens** (Map p174; ☺ sunrise-sunset). The gardens, laid out by the French during the colonial period, occupy the palace grounds and make a wonderful shady retreat.

The palace itself is a grand 17th-century affair built by Moulay Ismail. The building now houses the **Musée des Oudaias** (Map p174; ☑ 0537 73 15 37; admission Dh20), the national jewellery museum containing a fascinating collection of prehistoric, Roman and Islamic jewellery found in the different regions of Morocco.

of Salé, but in the 14th century the Merenid sultan Abou al-Hassan Ali built a necropolis on top of the Roman site and surrounded it with the towers and defensive wall that stand today.

Overgrown by fruit trees and wildflowers, it is an atmospheric place to roam around. From the main gate, a path heads down through fragrant fig, olive and orange trees to a **viewing platform** that overlooks the ruins of the Roman city. Making out the structures takes a bit of imagination, but the mystery is part of the magic of this place. A path leads through the ruins of the triple-arched entrance known as the **Arc de Triomphe**, past the **Jupiter Temple** (to the left) and to the **forum** (at the end of the main road), while another goes to the octagonal **Pool of the Nymph**, part of the Roman system of water distribution.

Far easier to discern are the remains of the **Islamic complex**, with its elegant minaret now topped by a stork's nest. An incredible colony of storks has taken over the ruins, lording over the site from their tree-top nests. If you come in spring, the clacking bills of mating pairs is a wonderful soundtrack to a visit.

Near the ruined minaret is the **tomb of Abou al-Hassan Ali** and his wife, complete with ornate *zellij* ornamentation. A small *medersa* is nearby, where the remains of pillars, students' cells and scalloped pools – as well as the blocked-off mihrab (prayer niche) – are still discernible. On leaving the mosque, the path passes the **tombs** of several saints on the far right. To the left, the murky waters of a walled pool (marked '*bassin aux anguilles*') still attract women who believe that feeding boiled eggs to the eels here brings fertility and easy childbirth.

⊙ Central Rabat

Archaeology Museum   MUSEUM
(Map p180; ☑ 0537 70 19 19; 23 Rue al-Brihi Parent; admission Dh10; ⊙9am-4.30pm Wed-Mon) The interesting Archaeology Museum (even if the labels are only in Arabic and French) gives a good account of Morocco's history. Prehistoric finds include a beautiful neolithic rock carving of a man surrounded by concentric circles. The highlight of the collection is the **Salle des Bronzes**, which displays ceramics, statuary and artefacts from the Roman settlements at Volubilis, Lixus and Chellah. Look out for the beautiful head of Juba II and don't miss the tiny

acrobats – all found at Volubilis. The fate of the artefacts here is uncertain as a new ethnographical museum is planned, as well as a museum at Volubilis itself.

Moroccan Museum of Money   MUSEUM
(Map p180; www.bkam.ma; cnr Ave Mohammed V & Rue al-Qahira; admission Dh20; ⊙9am-5.30pm Tue-Fri, 9am-noon & 3-6pm Sat, 9am-1pm Sun) Housed in the historic Mauresque building of the Bank al-Maghrib, this quirky museum and art gallery is an unexpectedly interesting tour of Moroccan history through its coinage, from the Roman period to today – we especially liked the gloriously colourful notes that introduced the dirham in 1961. Also enjoy the galleries of French Orientalist art (including Marjorelle, of the famed gardens in Marrakesh), and the large collection of Moroccan abstract, naive and figurative painting.

Museum of Contemporary Art   MUSEUM, GALLERY
(Map p180; Ave Moulay Hassan) Still under construction at the time of research, this will be the first public gallery of contemporary art in Morocco.

🏃 Activities

Oudayas Surf Club   WATER SPORTS
(Map p174; ☑ 0537 26 06 83; www.surfmaroc.info/oscr; Plage des Oudaias; 90min surfboard/bodyboard lesson Dh150) One of Morocco's original surf clubs, it offers lessons and board hire, and has a swish clubhouse/cafe facing the waves. King Mohammed VI was a founding member.

Club Nautique de la Plage de Rabat   WATER SPORTS
(Map p174; ☑ 0537 26 16 09; www.cnprabat.com; Plage des Oudaias) Below the kasbah, this club offers lessons and equipment hire for surfing, bodyboarding, windsurfing and sea-kayaking.

🍃 Courses

Rabat has many language schools offering year-long courses, but the following offers short-term classes.

Center for Cross-Cultural Learning   LANGUAGE
(CCCL; Map p180; ☑ 0537 20 23 65; www.cccl.ma; Ave Hassan II, Bab el-Had) Intensive short courses in Modern Standard Arabic, Darija and Tamazight.

✨ Festivals & Events

Rabat hosts a number of festivals and events each year.

Festival Mawazine   MUSIC

(www.festivalmawazine.ma; ⊙ May) This festival draws the biggest names from the international pop music scene, as well as some major Arabic music stars. Rihanna's headline act in 2013 drew 150,000 people – claimed to be the biggest music concert in Moroccan history.

Festival International de Rabat   MUSIC, FILM

(www.rabatfilmfestival.org; ⊙ Jun-Jul) The biggest drawcard, attracting hoards of music lovers and film buffs to the capital for two weeks in late June and early July.

🛏 Sleeping

Most of Rabat's better accommodation is in the new city between Ave Mohammed V and Ave Abderrahman, while the old medina has a host of low-budget dives and a couple of upmarket riads (townhouses set around an internal garden). Rabat caters mainly for business travellers and has a disproportionate number of top-end hotels.

The medina and kasbah are full of budget hotels that are pretty basic and many lack any kind of creature comforts, including showers. However, there are some good options, too. Rabat has a limited choice of midrange accommodation, most of it located on or just off Ave Mohammed V. The city offers all the usual top international chain hotels, but for something with a little more local flavour the medina options offer ultrachic style and service.

🛏 Ville Nouvelle

Hôtel Splendid   HOTEL €

(Map p180; ☑ 0537 72 32 83; 8 Rue Ghazza; s/d without bathroom Dh125/160, with bathroom Dh190/250; ☎) In a 1930s building with enough original features left to give some character, the Splendid has spacious, bright rooms with high ceilings, big windows and simple wooden furniture set around a pleasant courtyard (with wi-fi). Bathrooms are modern and rooms without bathrooms have a hot-water washbasin.

Hôtel Majestic   HOTEL €

(Map p180; ☑ 0537 72 29 97; www.hotelmajestic.ma; 121 Ave Hassan II; s/d Dh260/320) Another decent option, though not as palatial as it

sounds. Readers recommend this modern place with smallish rooms and sleek new furniture and fittings – if not a lot of character. Despite the double glazing the rooms can be noisy, so it's best to forgo the medina view for a room at the back.

Hotel Central   HOTEL €

(Map p180; ☑ 0537 70 73 56; 2 Rue Al-Basra; s/d Dh170/250, without bathroom Dh120/200) Opposite the imposing Balima and right in the heart of town, the Hotel Central has a good-value range of simple rooms. It's a little past its best, but remains a friendly place handy to everything in town. Rooms with shared bathrooms have their own sinks. Hot showers are Dh10.

★ Le Piétri Urban Hotel   HOTEL €€

(Map p180; ☑ 0537 70 78 20; www.lepietri.com; 4 Rue Tobrouk; s/d Dh720/790; ❄ ⌘) ∥ This good-value boutique hotel in a quiet street in a central, but more residential, part of town is modern and chic. The 36 spacious bright rooms with wooden floors are comfortable, well equipped and decorated in warm colours in a contemporary style. Fifth-floor rooms have huge balconies. The hotel has an excellent restaurant, Les Sessions du Piétri, with live jazz several times a week.

Hôtel Royal   HOTEL €€

(Map p180; ☑ 0537 72 11 71; www.mtds.com/royal-hotel; 1 Rue Ammane; s/d Dh528/748) In a very central location, the Royal has tastefully renovated rooms that are very comfortable, with polished wooden furniture, new mattresses and sparkling clean bathrooms. The rooms on the 4th floor have the best views over the park and city, are quieter and come with a large terrace. An adequate breakfast is served in the downstairs restaurant.

Hôtel Balima   HOTEL €€

(Map p180; ☑ 0537 70 77 55; www.hotel-balima.net; Ave Mohammed V; s/d incl breakfast Dh563/746; ❄ ⌘) The grand dame of Rabat hotels is showing its age a bit, but still offers newly decorated and comfortable en-suite rooms, all immaculately kept and with great views over the city. The hotel has a decent restaurant and nightclub. The glorious shady terrace facing Ave Mohammed V is still the place to meet in Rabat.

Hôtel Bélère   HOTEL €€

(Map p180; ☑ 0537 20 33 02, 0537 20 33 01; www.belere-hotels.com; 33 Ave Moulay Youssef; s/d from Dh650/980; ☯ ❄ ⌘) This four-star hotel is a

Central Rabat

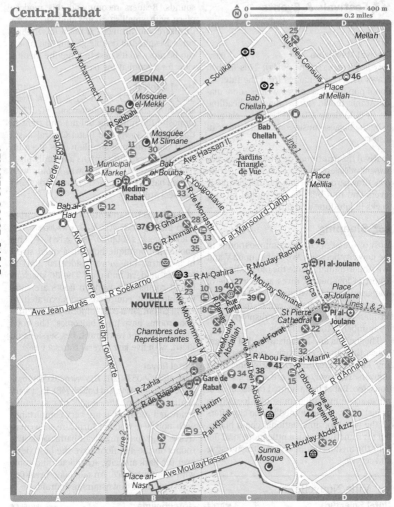

step up from the other options in this price range and offers small but extremely comfortable nonsmoking rooms with tasteful (albeit very 1970s) modern decor, now back in fashion. It has a bar and restaurant and it's handy to the train station.

🛏 Medina & Kasbah

Hôtel Dorhmi
HOTEL €
(Map p180; ☑0537 72 38 98; 313 Ave Mohammed V; s/d/tr Dh140/220/300) Immaculately kept, very friendly and keenly priced, this family-run hotel is the best of the medina cheapies.

The simple rooms are bright and tidy and surround a central courtyard on the 1st floor above the Banque Populaire. Despite being in the hub of things, the Dorhmi (also spelt Doghmi) offers quiet rooms. Hot showers are Dh10.

Hôtel Darna
HOTEL €
(Map p174; ☑0537 73 47 05; www.hoteldarna.ma; Blvd el-Alou; s/d Dh300/500; ☎) The Darna offers a tidy selection of comfortable and modern, if unexciting, rooms. It's a good choice well located close to the kasbah and medina.

Central Rabat

Hôtel al-Maghrib al-Jadid
HOTEL €

(Map p180; ☑0537 73 22 07; 2 Rue Sebbahi; s/d Dh80/120) Although the rooms at this hotel are fairly small and spartan, they are pristinely clean, with shuttered windows that let in lots of light. You'll either love or hate the shocking-pink walls but it's all part of the rather quirky character of this place. Hot showers are Dh10.

Dar Al Batoul
RIAD €€

(Map p174; ☑0537 72 72 50, 0661 40 11 81; www.riadbatoul.com; 7 Derb Jirari; d/ste Dh870/1400; ☜) This grand 18th-century merchant's house tucked down a *derb* (alley) off the main street has been transformed into a sumptuous hotel with just eight rooms in traditional Moroccan style. Centred on a graceful columned courtyard, each room is different, with stunning combinations of fabrics, stained glass and intricate hand-painted tilework.

★ Riad Oudaya
RIAD €€€

(Map p180; ☑0537 70 23 92; www.riadrabat.com; 46 Rue Sidi Fateh; s/d/ste Dh1100/1300/1650) Tucked away down an alleyway in the medina (it's near the mosque with the octagonal minaret), this brightly painted guesthouse is a gem. The rooms around a spectacular courtyard are tastefully decorated with a blend of Moroccan style and Western comfort. Subtle lighting, open fireplaces, balconies and the gentle gurgling of the fountain in the tiled courtyard below complete the romantic appeal. Meals here are sublime but need to be ordered in advance.

Dar El Kebira
RIAD €€€

(Map p174; ☑0537 72 49 06; www.darelkebira.com; Rue Ferrane Znaki, Impasse Belghazi; r Dh1350-1600, ste Dh1850; ☜) A plush and expansive riad, Dar El Kebira has a selection of large and well-appointed rooms with plenty of traditionally decorated ones that stay just the right side of Moroccan-riad-bling.

RABAT FOR CHILDREN

Hassle-free shopping in the souqs and the impressive **kasbah** make Rabat a pleasant place to visit with children. The Chellah (p177) offers a wide open space. However, there are few specific attractions in the city for younger visitors. The best bet is to head out of town to the beach, or the Jardins Exotiques (p189).

The 52-hectare **Jardin Zoologique de Rabat** (Zoological Gardens; www.rabatzoo. ma) northwest of Temara was being upgraded at the time of research. Long a neglected place with concrete pens for the animals, the recently refurbished zoo is divided into five ecosystems, including the Atlas Mountains (featuring captive-bred Atlas Lions).

The **Poney Club de Rabat** (☑ 0537 66 63 63; 45min private lesson Dh150), to the west of town, offers riding lessons and events for children and has English-speaking staff.

Across the river in Salé is the **Magic Park** (☑ 0535 88 59 90; Rte N6; admission Dh10; ⊙ 12.30-11pm Mon-Fri, 4.30-11pm Sat & Sun) with rides and cafes, providing just about enough entertainment to while away an afternoon.

There's a restaurant (book in advance), a terrace looking over the medina for breakast or sunset drinks, and an in-house hammam to soothe your travel cares away.

✗ Eating

Rabat has a wonderful choice of restaurants from cheap and cheerful holes-in-the-wall to upmarket gourmet pads feeding the city's legions of politicians and diplomats.

The best place for quick, cheap food in Rabat is on Ave Mohammed V just inside the medina gate. Here you'll find a slew of small joints dishing out tajines, brochettes, salads and chips for cheap and cheaper. You'll know the best ones by the queue of locals waiting patiently to be served.

Another good spot is around Rue Tanta in the ville nouvelle, where you'll find fast-food joints serving everything from burgers and brochettes to pizza and panini.

✗ Ville Nouvelle

La Rive MOROCCAN €
(Map p180; ☑ 0537 73 00 01; www.larive.com; Pl Moulay Hassan; mains from Dh40) Modern and airy, this is one of four equally agreeable eating options on this plaza – a good spot away from the traffic and bustle. There's a good selection of sandwiches and salads, seafood and tajines, plus great-value couscous on Fridays.

Pâtisserie Majestic PATISSERIE €
(Map p180; cnr Rue Ammane & Ave Allal ben Abdallah; pastries from Dh12) An excellent and extremely popular patisserie, perfect for breakfast or an afternoon cake with superb coffee, and right in the centre of town.

La Dolce Vita ICE CREAM €
(Map p180; 8 Rue Tanta) Delicious homemade Italian gelato comes in a dozen flavours. It's next to the Mamma Italia restaurant.

★ **Le Petit Beur – Dar Tajine** MOROCCAN €€
(Map p180; ☑ 0537 73 13 22; 8 Rue Damas; mains Dh100; ⊙ lunch & dinner Mon-Sat; ⊜) A modest little place renowned for its excellent Moroccan food, from succulent tajines and heavenly couscous to one of the best *pastillas* in town, and it's licenced. It's quieter at lunchtime but livens up at night when the waiters double as musicians and play oud (lute) music to accompany your meal. Book ahead or get there early as it fills up quickly.

★ **Ty Potes** FRENCH €€
(Map p180; 11 Rue Ghafsa; mains from Dh80; ⊙ noon-2.45pm Tue-Sat, 11am-3pm & 7-11pm Sun) A pleasant and welcoming lunch spot and teahouse, serving an amazing range of sweet and savoury crêpes, salads and sandwiches. It's popular with well-heeled locals. The atmosphere is more European, with a deeply planted garden at the back, and the Sunday brunch (Dh105 to Dh125) is particularly well attended. Alcohol and charcuterie are served.

Mamma Italia ITALIAN €€
(Map p180; ☑ 0537 70 73 29; 6 Rue Tanta; mains from Dh70; ⊙ lunch & dinner) It looks pretty dark from the outside, but this traditionally styled bistro serves some of the best Italian food in town. Close-packed tables with plenty of candles add to the atmosphere. Some of the pasta portions can be on the small side, but the wood-fired pizzas and grilled meats will leave you planning a return visit. There's a good wine list.

La Veranda MEDITERRANEAN €€
(Map p180; ☑ 0674 84 12 44; Institut Français, 1 Rue Abou Inane; mains Dh80-130; ☺ lunch & dinner Mon-Sat) This loft-style restaurant, in a modernist villa with a pleasant garden under majestic palm trees, is the place to be at lunchtime. Run by the same owner as Le Grand Comptoir, it serves good contemporary French-Mediterranean bistro food from a changing menu written on a blackboard. The staff are young and trendy. It's just behind the church at the French Institute.

Tajine wa Tanja MOROCCAN €€
(Map p180; ☑ 0537 72 97 97; 9 Rue de Baghdad; mains Dh80; ☺ lunch & dinner Mon-Sat; ☎) Down-to-earth Moroccan dishes are the speciality at this small, friendly restaurant near the train station. Choose from a range of wood-fired grills or tajines prepared to traditional recipes, or make a special outing for the magnificent Friday couscous. It's a fairly quiet spot, and not so intimidating for women travelling alone.

L'R du Gout FRENCH €€
(Map p180; ☑ 0537 76 06 10; 8 Rue Moulay Abdel Aziz; set lunch menu Dh160; ☺ lunch & dinner) This large restaurant with a colourful interior – a blend of French bistro and Moroccan flair – is run by young Frenchmen. The menu serves traditional French brasserie food such as foie gras, veal kidneys and steak with a pepper sauce.

Cafe Weimar CAFE €€
(Map p180; 7 Rue Sana'a; pizzas Dh80) This hip cafe in the Goethe Institut is where the young and beautiful hang out for cake and coffee or lunch. It also does a simple Mediterranean menu and is a good spot for Sunday brunch. Book ahead, but there are no reservations on Friday and Saturday.

La Koutoubia MOROCCAN €€
(Map p180; ☑ 0537 70 10 75; 10 Pierre Parent; mains Dh80; ☺ lunch & dinner) Old-fashioned Moroccan restaurant with plenty of traditional *zellij* and colourful painted panels. All the classic Moroccan dishes are on the menu here, including tajines and couscous, but labour-intensive specialities like pigeon *pastilla* or *mechoui* (roast lamb) need to be ordered in advance. Good wine list.

Les Sessions du Piétri FUSION €€
(Map p180; ☑ 0537 70 91 30; Le Piétri Urban Hotel, 4 Rue Tobrouk; mains from Dh80; ☺ lunch & dinner) This newly refurbished restaurant is where the bright young things come for a drink after work, and stay on for dinner. There are live concerts on Tuesday, Friday and Saturday. An eclectic menu features everything from Asian chicken to steaks, Atlas trout to mussels, and chocolate fondue for dessert.

Le Grand Comptoir FRENCH €€
(Map p180; ☑ 0537 20 15 14; www.legrandcomptoir.ma; 279 Ave Mohammed V; mains Dh95-200; ☺ 9am-1am) Sleek, stylish and oozing the charms of a 1930s Parisienne brasserie, this suave restaurant and lounge bar woos customers with its chic surroundings and classic French menu. Candelabras, giant palms and contemporary art adorn the grand salon while a pianist tinkles in the background. A Rabat institution, and a good place to have breakfast or coffee, too.

✗ Medina & Kasbah

Restaurant el-Bahia MOROCCAN €
(Map p180; ☑ 0537 73 45 04; Ave Hassan II; mains Dh60; ☺ lunch & dinner) Built into the outside of the medina walls (a good spot for people-watching), this laid-back restaurant has the locals lapping up hearty Moroccan fare. Sit on the pavement terrace, in the shaded courtyard or upstairs in the traditional salon.

Restaurant de la Libération MOROCCAN €
(Map p180; 256 Ave Mohammed V; mains Dh60; ☺ lunch & dinner) Cheap, cheerful and marginally more classy than the string of other eateries along this road (ie it's got plastic menus and tablecloths), this basic restaurant does a steady line in traditional favourites. Friday is couscous day when giant platters of the stuff are delivered to the eager masses.

Borj Eddar SEAFOOD €€
(Map p174; ☑ 0537 70 15 00; mains Dh120; ☺ lunch & dinner) Just outside the kasbah down at the beach, this restaurant overlooking the sea has a menu of excellent fresh fish and seafood dishes. The next door Restaurant de la Plage has a similar menu and the same views, if the Borj Eddar is full. There's little to choose between them: both have glass-fronted terraces overlooking the ocean.

Riad Oudaya MOROCCAN €€€
(Map p180; ☑ 0537 70 23 92; 46 Rue Sidi Fateh; lunch/dinner set menu Dh220/330; ☺ by reservation) This lovely restaurant squirrelled away behind a wooden door in the depths of the medina is reason enough to come to Rabat. Set in a gorgeous riad, it dishes up gourmet

five-course dinners featuring anything from juicy tajines or *pastilla* to stuffed calamari.

Restaurant Dinarjat
MOROCCAN €€€

(Map p174; ☑0537 72 42 39; 6 Rue Belgnaoui; meals Dh300-400; ☺lunch & dinner) Stylish and elegant, Dinarjat is a favourite with well-heeled locals and visitors alike. It's set in a superb 17th-century Andalucian-style house at the heart of the medina, and has been carefully restored and decorated in a contemporary style but in keeping with tradition. The restaurant is an ode to the Arab-Andalucian art of living with its sumptuous architecture, refined traditional food and peaceful oud music. The tajines, couscous and salads are prepared with the freshest ingredients, using little fat, and are surprisingly light. Book in advance.

Le Ziryab
MOROCCAN €€€

(Map p180; ☑0537 73 36 36; 10 Zankat Ennajar; set menus from Dh400; ☺lunch & dinner) This chic Moroccan restaurant is in a magnificent building just off Rue des Consuls. The blend of old-world character and stylish contemporary design is reflected in the excellent menu of interesting variations on tajine, couscous, *pastilla,* and grilled meat and fish.

Agdal

Galapagos Café
CAFE €

(Map p174; 14 Blvd al-Amir Fal Ould Omar) Slick cafe-terrace with dark-wood panelling, contemporary furniture and floor-to-ceiling windows. It's popular with young professionals for its ice cream, pizzas, panini and people-watching.

Bert's
CAFE €€

(Map p174; ☑0802 00 07 07; cnr Ave de France & Rue Melouya) This very stylish cafe in smart

---

SELF-CATERING

The medina is the best place to go for self-catering supplies. The indoor fruit and vegetable market (Map p180; Ave Hassan II) has a fantastic choice of fresh produce, dried fruits and nuts. You should be able to find everything else you need (including booze) at the surrounding stalls or along Rue Souika and near Bab el-Bouiba.

You'll find Western food at the vast Hypermarché Marjane (☺7am-7pm) supermarket on the road to Salé.

Agdal dishes up a seasonal menu of vitamin-packed salads and sandwiches, very special desserts and fresh fruit juices, and they deliver from 8am to 10pm Monday to Saturday.

L'Entrecôte
FRENCH €€€

(Map p174; ☑0537 67 11 08; 74 Blvd al-Amir Fal Ould Omar; mains Dh180; ☺lunch & dinner) The menu and attitude at this upmarket, old-style restaurant in Agdal are very French, but the dark woods and rough plaster are more reminiscent of Bavaria than Bordeaux. Steak, fish and game specialities dominate the classic French menu, and to further confuse the ambience there's jazz or traditional Spanish music at night.

🍷 Drinking & Nightlife

Many Rabat bars are pretty intimidating for women. The more modern, popular joints are a safer bet.

Rabat's nightlife is a lot more limited – and subdued – than Casablanca's but there's still a fairly good range of clubs to choose from. All the large hotels have their own discos, usually fairly standard fare, and there's a few try-hard theme clubs where you might need plenty of booze to numb the decor. Expect to pay about Dh150 to Dh200 to get in and the same for drinks, and dress up or you won't even make it past the door.

Hôtel Balima
BAR

(Map p180; ☑0537 70 77 55; Ave Mohammed V) Less self-conscious than the chic town bars and an excellent place to watch Rabat go by, the leafy terrace in front of the Balima is a great place to just see and be seen. It's a relaxed place for women and pleasantly cool on summer nights, as well as being a rarity – a place to drink a beer in public.

Café Maure
CAFE

(Map p174; Kasbah les Oudaias) Sit back, relax and just gaze out over the estuary to Salé from this chilled, open-air cafe spread over several terraces in the Andalucian Gardens. Mint tea is the thing here, accompanied by little almond biscuits delivered on silver trays. It's an easy place to pass time writing postcards, and a relaxed venue for women.

Cafétéria du 7ème Art
CAFE

(Map p180; Ave Allal ben Abdallah) Set in the shady grounds of a cinema, this popular outdoor cafe attracts a mixed clientele of students and professionals. It's a relaxed place serving snacks such as pizza and panini.

El Rancho BAR

(☎0667 33 00 30; 30 Rue Mischliffen, Agdal) Tex-Mex restaurant and bar where Rabat's well-heeled go for a bite and a drink before clubbing. The atmosphere on weekends is electric, when the world-music beat gets turned up a few notches.

Le Puzzle BAR

(Map p174; ☑0537 67 00 30; 79 Ave ibn Sina, Agdal; ☺closed lunch Sun) Happening bar-restaurant in Agdal, favoured by suburban sophisticates. It has a strange mix of traditional style and modern design but pulls in the punters with half-price beer and daily live gigs (except for Wednesday and Sunday karaoke nights).

Henry's Bar BAR

(Map p180; Pl des Alaouites) If you're in search of old-time local haunts rather than squeaky-clean trendsetters, there are some dingy bars around Pl des Alaouites. Henry's is an old favourite, a staunchly male-only preserve where the smoke is thick and the alcohol neat. It's open all day but closes by about 10pm.

Amnesia CLUB

(Map p180; ☑0612 99 11 90; 18 Rue de Monastir) The hippest club in downtown Rabat, this US-themed place (complete with a diner-style back room) buzzes most nights of the week. The music is pretty standard chart pop and the young socialites who come here just lap it up.

5th Avenue CLUB

(Map p174; 5 Ave Bin al-Widane, Agdal) Another US-themed bar, this one styled on a Moroccan impression of New York, it plays a better range of music than the others and features everything from hip hop to techno to Middle Eastern.

☆ Entertainment

Rabat has a large international community and plenty of young, well-heeled and well-educated locals looking for entertainment so there's usually a good choice of events on offer. Check Ocine.ma (http://ocine.ma) for listings. Most films are dubbed in French, unless marked as '*version originale*'.

Cinéma Renaissance CINEMA

(Map p180; ☑0537 72 21 68; 266 Ave Mohammed V; orchestra/balcony Dh40/50) Large cinema complex on the main drag showing mainstream Hollywood flicks.

❶ MAPS

Rabat is one of the few places in Morocco where you can get a range of topographical Moroccan maps and town plans. The **Direction de la Cartographie** (☑0537 23 08 30; www.ancfcc.gov.ma; Ave Hassan II Km4; ☺9am-3.30pm) sells topography maps, but staff can be sensitive about selling some maps. Take your passport. Most maps need to be ordered and can be picked up 48 hours later.

Cinéma du 7ème Art CINEMA

(Map p180; ☑0537 73 38 87; Ave Allal ben Abdallah; admission Dh20) A good bet for more local offerings and art-house films, this cinema shows mainly Moroccan, Middle Eastern and European movies.

❺ Shopping

Rabat's great shopping secret is its laid-back merchants. There's little pressure to buy, so you can stroll the stalls in relative peace, but there is also less room to bargain. The souqs still have a fair selection of good handicrafts, particularly in and around Rue des Consuls in the medina and Blvd Tariq al-Marsa towards the kasbah. You'll find everything in this area from jewellery, silks and pottery to *zellij* and carved wooden furniture.

Weaving is one of the most important traditional crafts in Rabat, and the more formal, Islamic style is still favoured. On Tuesday and Thursday mornings women descend from the villages to auction their carpets to local salesmen at the carpet souq off Rue des Consuls, a great sight even though tourists are not allowed in on the action.

For fixed prices head for the **Ensemble Artisanal** (Map p174; ☑0537 73 05 05; Blvd Tariq al-Marsa), which sells a good range of crafts. For ceramics, your best bet is to head across to Salé to the Complexe des Potiers (p189).

❶ Information

EMERGENCY

SAMU (☑0537 73 73 73; ☺24hr) Private ambulance service.

SOS Médecins (☑0537 20 21 23; house call Dh400; ☺24hr) Doctors on call.

INTERNET ACCESS

Internet (Map p180; Rue Tanta; per hr Dh8; ☺9am-7.30pm) Next to the Mamma Italia restaurant.

MEDICAL SERVICES

Town pharmacies open nights and weekends on a rotational basis; check the rota posted in French and Arabic in all pharmacy windows.

Hôpital Ibn Sina/Avicennes (☑0537 67 28 71, emergencies 0537 67 44 50; Pl Ibn Sina, Agdal; ☺24hr) Medical service.

MONEY

Numerous banks (with ATMs) are concentrated along Ave Mohammed V and the parallel Ave Al-lal ben Abdallah, including Banque Populaire.

BMCE (Map p180; Ave Mohammed V; ☺8.30am-6.30pm Mon-Fri) Bank with ATM.

POST

DHL (Map p174; ☑0537 77 99 34; Ave de France, Agdal)

Main Post Office (Map p180; cnr Rue Soékarno & Ave Mohammed V; ☺8.30am-4.30pm Mon-Fri)

TOURIST INFORMATION

Office National Marocain du Tourisme (ONMT; ☑0537 67 40 13; visitmorocco@onmt.org.ma; cnr Rues Oued el-Makhazine & Zalaka, Agdal; ☺8.30am-6.30pm Mon-Fri) Smiles and vacant faces await at this bureaucratic office. A better bet is to pick up the useful tourist listing pamphlet *Clips Rabat*, available at many hotels and upmarket restaurants.

❶ Getting There & Away

AIR

Tiny Rabat-Salé Airport, 10km northeast of town, only has a clutch of international flights to Paris and Madrid. A grand taxi to the airport will cost about Dh250. There are no buses.

BUS

Rabat has two bus stations – the main **gare routière** (Map p174) where most buses depart and arrive, and the less chaotic CTM station, situated about 3km southwest of the city centre on the road to Casablanca. The main station has a **left-luggage service** (per item per day Dh5; ☺6am-11pm). To get to the town centre from either station, take bus 30 (Dh5), the tram or a petit taxi (Dh30).

Arriving by bus from the north, you may pass through central Rabat, so it's worth asking if you can be dropped off in town. Otherwise, you could save some time by alighting at Salé and taking the tram into central Rabat. Buses include:

Agadir Dh220, 10 hours, three daily

Casablanca Dh35, 1½ hours, every hour

Er-Rachidia Dh155, 10 hours, one daily

Fez Dh70, 3½ hours, nine daily

Laâyoune Dh420, 22½ hours, one daily

Marrakesh Dh130, five hours, 10 daily

Nador Dh155, 9½ hours, one daily

Oujda Dh155, 9½ hours, one daily

Tangier Dh100, 4½ hours, five daily

Tetouan Dh100, five hours, one daily

CAR

Rabat has no shortage of local car-rental agencies – most of which offer cheaper rates than these international agencies.

Avis (Map p180; ☑0537 72 18 18; 7 Rue Abou Faris al-Marini)

Budget (Map p180; ☑0530 20 05 20; Rabat Ville train station, Ave Mohammed V)

Europcar (Map p180; ☑0537 72 23 28; 25 Rue Patrice Lumumba)

Hertz (Map p180; ☑0537 70 73 66; 467 Ave Mohammed V)

City-centre parking restrictions apply from 8am to noon and 2pm to 7pm Monday to Saturday; metered parking costs Dh3 per hour. There's a convenient car park near the junction of Ave Hassan II and Ave Mohammed V.

TAXI

Grands taxis leave for Casablanca (Dh40, one hour) from just outside the intercity bus station. Other grands taxis leave for Fez (Dh60, 2½ hours), Meknès (Dh45, 90 minutes) and Salé (Dh5) from a lot off Ave Hassan II behind the Hôtel Bou Regreg.

TRAIN

Train is the most convenient way to arrive in Rabat, as the Rabat Ville train station is right in the centre of town (not to be confused with Rabat Agdal train station to the west of the city). The station has a food court and wi-fi, as well as Budget car-rental and Supratours offices.

Trains run every 30 minutes from 6am to 10.30pm between Rabat Ville and Casa Port train stations (Dh35, one hour) and Kenitra (Dh10, 30 minutes). Taking the train to Mohammed V International Airport (Dh75, 1½ hours) in Casablanca requires a change at Casa Voyageurs or at Aïn Sebaa.

On all long-distance routes there's always one late-night *ordinaire* train among the *rapide* services (see p490 for information about train classes). Second-class *rapide* services include Fez (Dh80, three hours, hourly), Marrakesh (Dh120, 4½ hours, nine daily), Meknès (Dh 65, two hours, hourly), Oujda (Dh180, nine hours, three daily) and Tangier (Dh95, four hours, eight daily).

❶ Getting Around

BUS

Some useful bus routes (Dh4):

Buses 2 & 4 Ave Moulay Hassan to Bab Zaer, for the Chellah.

Bus 3 Rabat Ville train station to Agdal.

Buses 12 & 13 Pl Melilla to Salé.

Buses 17 & 30 From near Bab al-Had to Rabat's gare routière via the map office; 17 goes on past the zoo to Temara Plage.

Bus 33 From Bab al-Had to Temara Plage.

TAXI

Rabat's blue petits taxis are plentiful, cheap and quick. A ride around the centre of town will cost about Dh15 to Dh20. There's a petit-taxi rank near the entrance of the medina on Ave Hassan II and at the train station. Note that petits taxis aren't allowed to drive between Rabat and Salé.

TRAM

The smart and efficient **Rabat-Salé tramway** (www.tram-way.ma) system is an excellent way to get around Rabat. Line 1 runs along Ave Hassan II, detouring past the Hassan Tower to Salé. Line 2 links Agdal to Salé, with handy stops at Rabat Ville and Salé Ville trains stations. Fares are Dh6, bought from ticket machines on the platforms (multiple journey tickets are also available). Services run every 20 minutes, 6am to 10pm.

Salé   سلا

POP 500,000

Still a long way from its lively counterpart and old rival on the other bank of the Oued Bou Regreg, Salé is a quiet and traditional kind of place, where time seems to have stood still. However all that is about to change with a massive project to bring the city into the 21st century that was about to be completed at the time of research: a new tramway, new bridge and a new development with apartments and shopping malls.

The centre of Salé feels more like a typical Moroccan village with its narrow alleys, old medina houses and beautiful monuments, but beyond it lies a sprawling town with characterless apartment buildings, mostly home to Rabat commuters. People are noticeably more conservative here, and the dress code is a lot tighter.

People began to settle in Salé in the 10th century and the town grew in importance as inhabitants of the older settlement at Sala Colonia began to move across the river to the new town. Warring among local tribes was still rampant at this stage and it was the Almohads who took control of the area in the 12th century, establishing neighbouring Rabat as a base for expeditions to Spain.

Spanish freebooters attacked in 1260; in response the Merenids fortified the town, building defensive walls and a canal to Bab Mrisa to allow safe access for shipping. The town began to flourish and established valuable trade links with Venice, Genoa, London and the Netherlands.

As trade thrived so too did piracy, and by the 16th century the twin towns prospered from the activities of the infamous Sallee Rovers pirates. It was here that Robinson Crusoe was brought into the town in Daniel Defoe's novel.

By the 19th century the pirates had been brought under control, Rabat had been made capital and Salé sank into obscurity.

◉ Sights

Salé is worth a day trip from Rabat. The main entrance to the medina is Bab Bou Haja, on the southwestern wall, which opens onto Pl Bab Khebaz. From here walk north to the souqs, and find the Grande Mosquée 500m further northwest along Rue Ras ash-Shajara (also known as Rue de la Grande Mosquée). Alternatively walk along the road that runs inside the city walls past Bab Bou Haja and Bab Malka for a more straightforward approach.

Grande Mosquée & Medersa   MOSQUE, MEDERSA

(medersa admission Dh10) Central to life in pious Salé and one of the oldest religious establishments in the country, the Grand Mosquée and its *medersa* are superb examples of Merenid artistry. They were built in 1333 by Almohad Sultan Abou al-Hassan Ali. The mosque is closed to non-Muslims, but the splendid *medersa* is open as a museum. Similar to those in Fez or Meknès, it takes the form of a small courtyard surrounded by a gallery. The walls are blanketed in intricate decoration, from the *zellij* base to the carved stucco and elegant cedar woodwork.

Small student cells surround the gallery on the upper floor, from where you can climb to the flat roof, which has excellent views of Salé and across to Rabat. The guardian who shows you around will expect a small tip.

Shrines   NOTABLE BUILDING

To the rear of the Grande Mosquée is the **Zawiya of Sidi Abdallah ibn Hassoun**, the patron saint of Salé. This respected Sufi died in 1604 and is revered by Moroccan

Salé

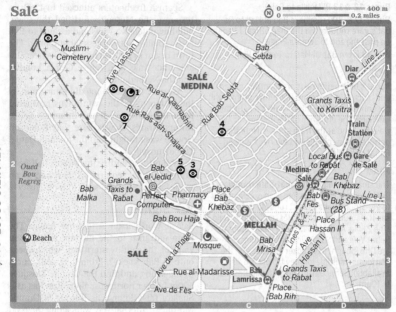

0 — 400 m
0 — 0.2 miles

travellers in much the same way as St Christopher is revered among Christians. An annual pilgrimage and procession in his honour makes its way through the streets of Salé on the eve of Mouloud (the Prophet's birthday). On this day, local fishermen dress in elaborate corsair costumes, while others carry decorated wax sculptures and parade through the streets, ending up at the shrine of the *marabout* (saint).

There are two more shrines in Salé: the **Zawiya of Sidi Ahmed Tijani**, on the lane between the mosque and *medersa*, and the white **Koubba of Sidi ben Ashir at-Taleb** in the cemetery northwest of the mosque.

Souqs
SOUQ

From the Grande Mosquée, head back to the souqs via the Rue Ras ash-Shajara, which becomes Rue Mellah el Kadim, a street lined with houses built by wealthy merchants. Shaded by trees and unchanged for centuries, the atmospheric **Souq el-Ghezel** (Wool Market) makes an interesting stop. Here, men and women haggle over the price and quality of rough white wool as it hangs from ancient scales suspended from a large tripod.

In the nearby **Souq el-Merzouk**, textiles, basketwork and jewellery are crafted and sold. Also on sale are the woven grass mats used in mosques, for which Salé is famous. The least interesting souq for travellers is the **Souq el-Kebir**, featuring secondhand clothing and household items.

🛏 Sleeping & Eating

Now that the tram has made Salé more accessible, guesthouses are opening in the medina. There are plenty of hole-in-the-wall cafes in the souqs and surrounding streets, as well as in the area just south of Pl Bab Khebaz.

The Repose
RIAD €€

(📞0537 88 29 58; www.therepose.com; 17 Zankat Talaa, Ras Chejra; ste Dh650-850; 🖥) 🏴 This traditional medina house has been carefully renovated to provide four delightfully different rooms. The leafy roof terrace is a haven of peace and very private. The knowledgeable owners will help with tours and cooking classes, and only vegetarian food is served.

ℹ Information

There are a few banks along Rue Fondouk Abd el-Handi.

Perfect Computer (Bab al-Jedid; per hr Dh4; ☺9am-10pm) Internet access.

Pharmacy (Pl Bab Khebaz)

ℹ Getting There & Away

BUS

Salé's main bus station is 1km east of the medina, but buses from Rabat also stop outside Bab Mrisa. From Rabat take bus 12, 13, 14, 16 or 34 (Dh5) from Pl al-Mellah just off Ave Hassan II, and get off at Bab Khebaz. This is also the place to take the bus back.

TAXI

Pick up a taxi in Rabat close to the Hôtel Bou Regreg, on Ave Hassan II; ask for the Bab Bou Haja or Bab Mrisa. From Salé there are departures from Bab el-Jedid and Bab Mrisa (Dh4 one way). Note that petits taxis are not permitted to travel between Rabat and Salé. Grands taxis for Kenitra leave from just north of the train station (Dh15).

TRAIN

Trains run to/from Rabat, but the tram or grands taxis are probably the simplest options. Trains north to Kenitra run every 30 minutes (Dh15).

TRAM

The easiest way to travel between Rabat and Salé is by tram (Dh6).

Around Rabat & Salé

◉ Sights

Complexe des Potiers   ARTS CENTRE

(Pottery Cooperative; ☺sunrise-sunset) The village of Oulja, 3km southeast of Salé, is home to the Complexe des Potiers, which produces a huge range of ceramics. The potters work at the back of the complex, bringing in clay from a rich seam in the surrounding hills (you'll see it on the left as you drive in), throwing and turning it on kick wheels, then glazing and firing the finished pieces in enormous kilns. A firing takes 15 hours

and reaches 900°C. Fine domestic pottery is fired in gas kilns designed to reduce environmental degradation and air pollution, but more rustic pieces are still fired in kilns fuelled by twigs and leaves from nearby eucalyptus forests.

The centre has a cafe and some workshops used by basket weavers and blacksmiths. To get here, take a petit taxi from Salé (about Dh18) or catch bus 35 or 53 (Dh4) from Bab Khebaz.

Jardins Exotiques   GARDENS

(www.jardinsexotiques; adult/child Dh10/5; ☺9am-5pm winter, to 7pm summer) Created by French horticulturist Marcel François in 1951, these gardens were declared a Natural Heritage site in 2003 and reopened in 2005 after several years of restoration. They are divided into the **Jardin Nature**, plantations that evoke the exotic vegetation the horticulturalist encountered on his many travels; the **Jardin Culture**, referring more to the philosophy of the garden in different cultures; and the **Jardin Didactique**, with birdcages, an aquarium and a vivarium.

Colour-coded paths lead through overgrown Brazilian rainforest, Polynesian jungle, Japanese pleasure grounds and an Andalucian garden. Jardins Exotiques is managed by the Mohammed VI Foundation for the Protection of the Environment.

The gardens are tranquil on weekends, and are a great place to bring children. It's also a popular spot for courting couples.

The gardens are 13km north of Rabat on the road to Kenitra. Take bus 28 from Ave Moulay Hassan in Rabat, or Bab Fès, the main gate at Salé medina.

Musée Belghazi   MUSEUM

(☎0537 82 21 78; www.museebelghazi.com; main collection Dh50, private rooms by reservation Dh100; ☺9am-7.30pm) The first museum in Morocco has a vast collection of traditional Andalucian, Jewish Moroccan and Islamic arts and crafts amassed by the Belghazi family.

Displays include measuring instruments (one of the first Belghazis was an astrologist at the Qarawiyin court in Fez), 17th-century carpets, exquisitely carved wooden *minbars* (mosque pulpits), doors and ceilings dating from the 10th century, intricate gold and silver jewellery, exceptional pottery and embroidery from Fez, and miniature copies of the Quran. There is a boutique with souvenirs and a restaurant.

The museum is 17km from Salé on the road to Kenitra. Take bus 28 from Ave Moulay Hassan in Rabat or from the main gate of the Salé medina.

Temara Plage   BEACH
There are beautiful beaches close to Rabat, such as the wild and sandy Temara Plage, 13km southwest of the city, popular with surfers and sunbathers alike. It can be reached on bus 17 from Bab al-Had in Rabat.

Plage des Nations   BEACH
The clean, sandy strip of beach at Plage des Nations, 17km north of Rabat, is a popular spot with Rabat locals. It gets some serious wave action good for surfers, but the currents can be dangerous for swimming.

Above the beach, the **Hôtel Firdaous** (☑0537 82 21 31; www.hotelfird.com; r Dh600; ☒) is remarkable for its original '70s decor. The peeling paint, rusty radiators and threadbare carpets are only just mitigated by rooms with ocean views and new bathrooms. Book in advance to have any chance of a room in summer.

To get to the beach, drive north as far as the Musée Belghazi and turn left down a road known as Sidi Bouknadel. Bus 9 or 48 from Rabat or Salé will drop you at the turn-off, from where it's a 2km walk to the beach past huge developments of holiday apartments.

Mehdiya Plage   BEACH
North along the coast, 50km from Rabat, is another strip of beach lined with holiday homes and beach bars, but here the currents are dangerous for swimmers. It gets busy with day trippers in summer but is deserted for the rest of the year. There are regular trains from Rabat to Kenitra, from where you take bus 9 or 15 to Mehdiya. Both of these buses (Dh6) and grands taxis (Dh10) leave from the corner of Rue du Souk el-Baladia and Ave Mohammed Diouri in Kenitra.

Lac de Sidi Bourhaba   OUTDOORS
Inland from Mehdiya is the beautiful freshwater Lac de Sidi Bourhaba, part of a larger protected wetland reserve. As a refuelling stop for thousands of birds migrating between Europe and sub-Saharan Africa, the lake provides some of the best birdwatching in the country, especially between October and March. It's also a great place for gentle hiking, with well-appointed walking trails in the forested hills around the lake.

More than 200 species of birds have been spotted here and many choose to winter or nest here – among them a number of rare or endangered species. This is one of the last places on earth where you can still see large numbers of marbled ducks, distinguished by the dark patch around their eyes. Other birds to look out for include the beautiful marsh owl (seen most often at dusk), the crested coot, black-shouldered kite and greater flamingo.

The **information centre** (☑0537 74 72 09; ⊙noon-4pm Sat & Sun) on the northern side of the lake is useful but has limited opening hours.

To get to the lake follow the signposts from the beach road to Mehdiya Plage, 300m past the Cafe Restaurant Belle Vue. If you're on foot, the lake is a 3.3km walk from the turn-off.

Moulay Bousselham
مولاي بوسلهام

The idyllic fishing village of Moulay Bousselham is a tranquil place, protected by the shrines of two local saints. The village is slowly expanding, as retired Europeans are starting to buy homes here. There is a sweeping beach (empty for most of the year), friendly people, good fish restaurants and an impressive, internationally important wildfowl reserve. Except for the summer months, this is a great place to spend a few days, with little more to do than birdwatching, fishing or strolling along the beach. Surfers come here for the crashing waves, but the strong currents are dangerous for swimmers. In summer the pace changes dramatically as the village becomes a low-key resort for Moroccans, and the inhabitants swell from around 1000 to 65,000 people.

Moulay Bousselham is named after a 10th-century Egyptian saint who is commemorated in one of the *koubbas* (shrines) that line the slope down to the sea, and guards the mouth of the river. Moroccans seeking a cure for psychological problems are locked into the tomb for 24 hours. Across the river is another shrine of Sidi Abd el-Galil, believed to cure sterile women. You'll find everything you need along the one main street, including a bank, post office, pharmacy and a couple of internet cafes, but there's no alcohol in town.

⊙ Sights

Merja Zerga National Park
PARK

One of the great pleasures of Morocco's Atlantic coast is to take a boat out on Merja Zerga (the Blue Lagoon), preferably with a bird guide who can bring the place to life. The 73-sq-km Merja Zerga National Park (4 sq km of water and the rest marshland) is protected by the Ramsar Convention and attracts thousands of migrant birds, including wildfowl, waders and flamingos in huge numbers, making it one of Morocco's prime birdwatching habitats. The lagoon is between 50cm and 4m deep depending on the tide. Ninety percent of the water comes from the sea, 10% is sweetwater from the Oued Dredr, south of the lagoon. At the time of research, the new tourist office was not yet open.

Although the largest flocks are present in December and January, you'll find herons, flamingos, ibises, spoonbills, plovers and egrets here as late as March or April, and there are about 100 species all year round. The calm lagoon is also a good place to see slender-billed and Audouin's gulls, and the African marsh owl. Shelducks, teals and numerous terns are frequently seen, as are marsh harriers and peregrine falcons.

There are six villages around the lake, four of which depend on agriculture, two on fishing – the men fish the lagoon and the ocean while the women gather shellfish.

Most of the fishermen take tourists around the lake as a sideline. Boat trips with the local boatmen, who have had some guide training, are easily arranged if you wander down to the small beach where the boats are moored. Expect to pay about Dh100 per hour for the boat. The only officially recognised (and by far the best) guide is **Hassan Dalil** (✆0668 43 41 10; guide half-day Dh200, plus motorboat per hr Dh100), who can also be contacted at the Café Milano (on the main road into town), where the bird log is kept. Call him rather than ask for him as several people have been known to pretend to be him in order to take his business. Otherwise ask the waiters at the Café Milano to call him. Trips can also be arranged through Villanora. The boatmen can also arrange fishing trips (Dh100 per hour, including equipment).

Hard-core birdwatchers may also want to explore **Merja Khaloufa**, an attractive lake about 8km east of Moulay Bousselham and part of the park, which offers good viewing of a variety of wintering wildfowl.

🛏 Sleeping & Eating

Hôtel Le Lagon
HOTEL €

(✆0537 43 26 50; fax 0537 43 26 49; d Dh300; ☒) The saving grace of this faded '70s hotel is its stunning location overlooking the lagoon below. The rooms are big, bright and clean, but in dire need of updating. The large terrace makes up for that. The restaurant is mediocre, and the swimming pool and nightclub are only open in July and August.

Camping Caravaning International
CAMPGROUND €

(✆0537 43 24 77; www.atlantisgatemb@yahoo.fr; 2-person tent/camping/car Dh60/70/30, extra person Dh13; ☒) An excellent site in a superb location, open all year.

Villanora
B&B €€

(✆0537 43 20 71, 0664 87 20 08; http://villanoramorocco.ifrance.com; s/d incl breakfast Dh300/400, with sea view Dh400/500; ☏) This B&B, the holiday home of an English family who fell in love with this quiet corner of Morocco, sits on top of a high dune with glorious ocean views. It's run by the Anglophile Mohammed, a family friend. There are just a few homey rooms (some with shared bathroom) where you can fall asleep to the sound of crashing waves, and breakfast is served on the terrace. Dinner is available if booked in advance – ask for the fish. Villanora is at the far northern end of town, about 2km from the main street. Booking ahead is recommended.

La Maison des Oiseaux
B&B €€

(✆061 30 10 67, 0537 43 25 43; http://moulay.bousselham.free.fr; half board per person Dh350) Another friendly guesthouse set in a lovely garden with nine simple but beautifully styled traditional rooms. There's a seminar room upstairs for visiting school groups and birdwatching excursions can be arranged for Dh200 to Dh300 for 2½ hours. The guesthouse is hidden down a maze of sandy lanes to the left as you drive into town. Ask around or call for directions.

Restaurant l'Ocean
SEAFOOD, MOROCCAN €

(✆0678 31 09 54, 0669 43 42 45; mains Dh50; ☺lunch & dinner) The road down to the seafront is lined with cafes and restaurants serving platters of grilled fish and tajines. One of the best is this small place, with a terrace, serving excellent fish, couscous, tajines and paella.

ATLANTIC COAST MOULAY BOUSSELHAM

❶ Getting There & Away

Moulay Bousselham is about 40km due south of Larache. To get here by public transport you'll need to detour to the little town of Souk el-Arba du Rhurb (grand taxi from Larache Dh35, 45 minutes), from where there are frequent grands taxis (Dh20, 45 minutes) and a few buses (Dh12, 45 minutes) to Moulay Bousselham. You can get to Souk el-Arba du Rhurb by grand taxi from Kenitra or Rabat (Dh40, 1½ hours). A private grand taxi from Larache to Moulay Bousselham costs around Dh200.

Larache   العرائش

Larache, like the other towns on this stretch of coast, is sleepy and laid-back for most of the year, bursting into life in summer when Moroccan tourists come to the beach. The charming town otherwise sees few visitors. The new town has some grand Spanish-era architecture, particularly around the central Pl de la Libération (the former Plaza de España), while the tiny crumbling medina is worth a stroll. North of the river Loukos on the edge of town sit the overgrown ruins of ancient Lixus, the legendary site of the Garden of the Hesperides.

Larache was occupied by the Spanish for most of the 17th century. The port activities were limited because of some dangerous sandbars offshore, but the locals made ships for the corsairs further south. It became the main port of the Spanish protectorate in 1911. Today the whitewashed houses with blue doors, the church, the market, the hotels and bars still reveal the strength of the Spanish influence. The town may be as picturesque as Assilah, but it gets far fewer visitors and has none of the hustle.

All Larachians seem to come out for the *paseo* (evening stroll) in the centre of town. The cafes and few restaurants fill up as the locals drink coffee, play cards and chew over the day's events, and by 10pm the streets are again deserted.

The French writer Jean Genet loved the bay of Larache and although he died in France, he was buried here.

❍ Sights

Old Town   HISTORIC SITE
Perched on a cliff top overlooking the ocean is the ruin of the kasbah (Qebibat) a 16th-century fortress built by the Portuguese and closed to visitors as it is now in a state of serious disrepair. Head south from here to the old cobbled medina, through Bab al-Khemis, a large, unmistakable Hispano-Moorish arch on Pl de la Libération. You come immediately into a colonnaded market square, the bustling Zoco de la Alcaiceria, which was built by the Spaniards during their first occupation of Larache in the 17th century. The Archaeological Museum was closed at the time of research.

Casbah de la Cigogne   LANDMARK
(Fortress of the Storks) South of the square, through the medina, is this 17th-century fortification built by the Spaniards under Philip III. Unfortunately, the building is not open to visitors.

Jean Genet's Grave   LANDMARK
To the west of town, the old Spanish cemetery is the final resting place of French writer Jean Genet (1910–86). If the gate is locked, ring the bell for the caretaker. A small tip is expected for showing you to the grave.

Galerie Afnar   GALLERY
(☏ 0613 68 14 24; www.lafnargalerie.blogspot. com; 58 Assadr Alaadam; ☉ 10am-2pm & 4-9pm) This gallery shows interesting local art and photography. The building itself is an old wheat *fondouq* (rooming house). A plaque on the outside identifies it as the site of the house of Averroes, the famous 12th-century Andalucian philosopher.

Music Conservatory   NOTABLE BUILDING
On the square northeast of the Casbah de la Cigogne and opposite the closed Archaeological Museum, you'll come across a large, remarkably ornate building with its own minaret. This is now the music conservatory and is worth a peek.

Beaches   BEACH
Larache has a small strip of sand below the town but the best beach is 7km north across the Loukos Estuary. This beach also has a huge holiday resort, Port Lixus, with a golf course, several resort hotels, villas and a luxury marina. A petit taxi will cost around Dh20, or takes buses 4 or 5 from opposite the Casbah de la Cigogne, which drop you at the Lixus turn-off, around 3km from the beach.

🛏 Sleeping

Larache has a small but decent selection of accommodation, most of which is clustered along the streets just south of Pl de la Libération.

Pension Amal
HOTEL €

(☑ 0539 91 27 88; 10 Rue Abdallah ben Yassine; s/d without bathroom Dh55/80) Dirt cheap, immaculately kept and extremely friendly, this little pension is a bargain with tiled rooms with shared facilities (hot showers are Dh10). The mattresses are renewed every year and the beds are comfortable. The owner and his son are very friendly and helpful.

Hôtel España
HOTEL €

(☑ 0539 91 31 95; http://hotelespanalarache.com; 6 Ave Hassan II; s/d Dh260/380; ❄☎) A venerable colonial-era institution, this hotel is a great place to stay. The decor is still old-style with dark wood furnishings, but the beds are comfortable, the rooms spotless and the bathrooms modernised. Rooms higher up get less noise from the square, and balcony views are great. There's no breakfast, but there are lots of cafes nearby.

Hôtel Somarían
HOTEL €

(☑ 0539 91 91 16; reservation@somarian.com; 68 Ave Mohammed Zerktouni; s/d Dh300/400) A modern hotel across the street from the covered central market. Rooms are well-presented and comfortable, with occasional cramped and crazy angles from the shape of the building. There's no breakfast; later in the day the ground-floor restaurant serves alcohol.

★ La Maison Haute
RIAD €€

(☑ 0665 34 48 88; http://lamaisonhaute.free.fr; 6 Derb ben Thami; r Dh440-550, apt Dh700-924) The most atmospheric accommodation in Larache, this wonderfully restored Hispano-Moorish house in the medina has a choice of six charming rooms with modern bathrooms. Eclectic decor, bright colours, stained-glass windows and Spanish tiled floors give this place a feeling of simplicity, warmth and tradition, while the roof terrace boasts incredible views of the ocean and market square, and offers a nice corner to read a book or sunbathe. There's dinner on request.

🍴 Eating

Eating out in Larache is cheap and cheerful with plenty of little places around Pl de la Libération and the Zoco de la Alcaiceria. The Spanish influence lingers on in the paella served in most restaurants, and the *churros* (a kind of doughnut) on the main square.

Casa Ché
SEAFOOD €

(☑ 0677 83 02 00; Ave Mohammed Zerktouni; mains around Dh50; ☻ lunch & dinner) Great-value seafood cafeteria near the covered central mar-

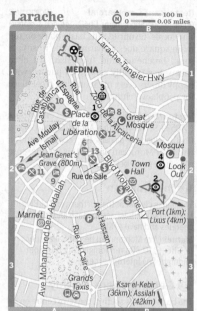

Larache

ATLANTIC COAST LARACHE

ket, bedecked with portraits of Che Guevara. Mains come with a few tapas starters and a small side of paella.

Balcón Atlantico
CAFE €

(☑ 5395 91 01 10; cnr Rue de Casablanca & Rue Tarik Ibnou Ziad; ☻ 9am-10pm) Overlooking the beach, and the nicest spot in town for a relaxed breakfast or simple lunch, this bustling cafe has plenty of outdoor seating and passable pizzas, though service is very slow.

Restaurant Commercial
MOROCCAN €

(Pl de la Libération; mains Dh40; ⊘ lunch & dinner) The locals' favourite, this basic place on the main square does a roaring trade in simple soup, brochettes and fried fish. It's ultra cheap, has friendly service, is packed with happy diners every night and is a great place for people-watching.

Restaurant Puerta Del Sol
MOROCCAN €

(☑ 0539 91 36 41; 5 Rue Ahmed Chaouki; mains Dh40; ⊘ lunch & dinner) For seafood and a choice of Moroccan dishes, this no-nonsense place is a good bet.

❶ Information

The banks cluster at the northern end of Blvd Mohammed V; most accept cash and travellers cheques and have ATMs.

Marnet (Ave Mohammed ben Abdallah; per hr Dh6; ⊘ 10.30am-midnight Sat-Thu, 3pm-midnight Fri) Internet access.

❶ Getting There & Away

The bus station is south of the town centre on Rue du Caire. Most major destinations are covered by CTM including Agadir (Dh280, 12 hours), Casablanca (Dh110, four hours, five daily), Fez (Dh85, 4½ hours, four daily), Marrakesh (Dh180, 8½ hours, daily) and Tangier (Dh35, 2½ hours, six daily).

Cheaper non-CTM buses are generally more frequent. They cover the same destinations as CTM buses, as well as Ouezzane (Dh30), Tetouan (Dh25) and Kenitra (Dh35).

Grands taxis run from outside the bus station to Ksar el-Kebir (Dh13), Assilah (Dh20), Souk el-Arba (Dh25) and Tangier (Dh35).

Lixus
الأوكوس

Set on a hill overlooking the Loukos Estuary are the Carthaginian and Roman ruins of **Lixus** FREE, a rather mysterious and neglected site that is one of the oldest inhabited places in the country. Only about a quarter of the ancient city has been excavated but the visible ruins, though badly damaged and overgrown, are impressive. Although not as extensive or as well excavated as Volubilis, the location, size and serenity of Lixus give it a lingering sense of gravitas and with a little imagination you can picture just how grand and important this city once was.

Few visitors make it here outside the summer months, and in winter your only companions will be the wind and the odd goat quietly grazing. A new **visitor centre** is under construction near the site entrance. In the meantime, there's no entrance fee, but you should tip the site guardian after your tour.

History

Megalithic stones found in the vicinity of Lixus suggest that the site was originally inhabited by a sun-worshipping people with knowledge of astronomy and mathematics. However, little more is known about the area's prehistory until the Phoenicians set up the colony Liks here in about 1000 BC. According to Pliny the Elder, it was here that Hercules picked the golden apples of the Garden of the Hesperides, thus completing the penultimate of his 12 labours. The golden apples may well have been the famous Moroccan tangerines.

In the 6th century BC the Phoenician Atlantic colonies fell to the Carthaginians. Lixus remained a trading post, principally in gold, ivory and slaves and, by AD 42, had entered the Roman Empire. Its primary exports soon changed to salt, olives, wine and *garum* (an aromatic fish paste) and its merchants also grew rich from the export of wild animals for use in the empire's amphitheatres.

The colony at Lixus rapidly declined as the Romans withdrew from North Africa, and was abandoned completely in the 5th century, after the collapse of the Roman Empire. Later, the site became known to Muslims as Tuchummus.

◉ Sights

Ruins
HISTORIC SITE

The main gate to Lixus is in the green railings that border the Larache–Tangier road. Inside the railings to the left are the remains of the *garum* factories, where fish was salted and the prized paste produced, beloved in Rome (in a neat parallel, nearby Assilah still has an anchovy paste factory today). A gravel path leads up the hill from the gate past a number of minor ruins to the **public baths** and **amphitheatre**. The amphitheatre provides impressive views of the surrounding countryside and makes a wonderful place just to sit and relax.

Most mosaics from the site were removed and are now on display at the archaeology museum in Tetouan. The Grand Temple mosaics depicting Helios, Mars and Rhea, the three Graces, and Venus with Adonis are all there. The only remaining mosaic at Lixus is that of Oceanus (the Greek Sea God). Unfortunately, it's been exposed both to the elements and to local vandalism, so is in rough shape.

Continue up the path to the main assembly of buildings, which straddle the crest of the hill. From here there are incredible views down over the Loukos Estuary and salt fields below.

The civic buildings, additional public baths and original city ramparts are here, while to the south is the striking citadel, a flurry of closely packed ruins standing stark against the sky. Although most of the antiquities are in an advanced state of decay, you should be able to make out the main temple and associated sanctuaries, an oratory, more public baths and the remains of the city walls.

❶ Getting There & Away

Lixus is approximately 4.5km north of Larache on the road to Tangier. To get there take bus 9 from outside the Casbah de la Cigogne (Dh5). A petit taxi costs about Dh25 one way; it's also on the Larache–Assilah grand taxi route.

Assilah أصيلا

The gorgeous whitewashed resort town of Assilah feels like somewhere on a Greek island, but the tapas and paella on the Spanish menus in the restaurants and the wrought-iron windows on the white houses are but a few reminders that the town was Spanish territory for a long time. Assilah is an easy and hassle-free introduction to Morocco and, with a good selection of budget hotels and restaurants plus a burgeoning art scene, the town has become a favourite stop on the traveller's trail of the North Atlantic coast.

The old medina has been seriously gentrified in the last few years as more and more houses have been bought by affluent Moroccans and Europeans, mainly Spanish. The town is sleepy for most of the year, but in the summer months the population grows from 12,000 to 110,000, when Moroccan families descend here, as elsewhere along the coast. The small town is then completely overrun, the beaches are packed and the touts come out in force. The best time to visit is in spring or autumn when the weather is still pleasant but the crowds are gone.

History

Assilah has had a turbulent history as a small but strategic port since it began life as the Carthaginian settlement of Zilis. During the Punic Wars the people backed Carthage, and when the region fell to the Romans, the locals were shipped to Spain and replaced with Iberians. From then on, Assilah was inexorably linked with the Spanish and with their numerous battles for territory.

As Christianity conquered the forces of Islam on the Iberian Peninsula in the 14th and 15th centuries, Assilah felt the knock-on effects. In 1471 the Portuguese sent 477 ships with 30,000 men, captured the port and built the walls that still surround the medina, a trading post on their famous gold route across Africa. In 1578, King Dom Sebastian of Portugal embarked on an ill-fated crusade from Assilah. He was killed, and Portugal (and its Moroccan possessions) passed into the hands of the Spanish, who remained for a very long time.

Assilah was recaptured by Moulay Ismail in 1691. In the 19th century, continuing piracy prompted Austria and then Spain to send their navies to bombard the town. Its most famous renegade was Er-Raissouli, one of the most colourful bandits ever raised in the wild Rif Mountains. Early in the 20th century, Er-Raissouli used Assilah as his base, becoming the bane of the European powers. Spain made Assilah part of its protectorate from 1911 until 1956.

◉ Sights

With more than 50 resident artists, five galleries and several artist studios and exhibition spaces, Assilah is renowned as a city of arts. It all started in 1978 when several Moroccan artists were invited to hold workshops for local children and to paint some walls in the medina as part of the town's *moussem* (saint's day celebrations). Several Zaïlachi artists and some of these children have now made their name in the contemporary-art world, among them the late Abdelilah Bououd, Brahim Jbari, Elina Atencio, Mohamed Lhaloui and several members of the Mesnani family.

Ramparts & Medina HISTORIC BUILDING, MEDINA
Assilah's largely residential medina is surrounded by the sturdy stone fortifications built by the Portuguese in the 15th century and it is these walls, flanked by palms, that have become the town's landmark.

Assilah

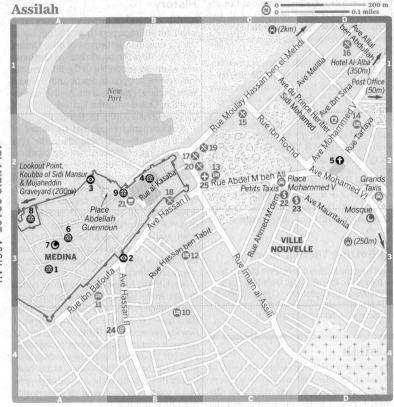

The medina and ramparts have been restored in recent years and the tranquil narrow streets lined by whitewashed houses are well worth a wander. Although the restoration work has left the medina much sanitised, the ornate wrought-iron window guards, pale-green *jalousies* (wooden, trellis-like window shutters) and colourful murals (painted each year during the Assilah Festival) give it a very photogenic quality. Craftspeople and artists have opened workshops along the main streets and invite in passers-by to see them work.

Access to the ramparts is limited. The southwestern bastion is the best spot for views over the ocean and is a popular spot at sunset. It also offers a peek into the nearby **Koubba of Sidi Mansur** (which is otherwise closed to non-Muslims) and the **Mujaheddin Graveyard.**

The southern entrance to the medina, **Bab Homar** (Ave Hassan II), is topped by the much-eroded Portuguese royal coat of arms. There are a few old **cannons** just inside the medina's seaward wall, but they are cut off from the walkway below and can only be seen from a distance. The **Bab al-Kasaba** leads to the **Great Mosque** (closed to non-Muslims) and the Centre de Hassan II Rencontres Internationales. The medina is busiest on Thursdays, Assilah's main market day.

Palais de Raissouli   HISTORIC BUILDING
Also known as the Palais de Culture (Palace of Culture) on the sea side of the medina, the palace was built in 1909 by Er-Raissouli and still stands as a testament to the sumptuous life he led at the height of his power. It has been beautifully restored, but is only open during the Assilah Festival or for temporary exhibitions, although if you can find the caretaker you may be able to persuade him to let you in. The striking building includes a main reception room with a glass-fronted terrace overlooking the sea, from where

Assilah

ATLANTIC COAST ASSILAH

Er-Raissouli forced convicted murderers to jump to their deaths onto the rocks 30m below.

Centre de Hassan II Rencontres Internationales   GALLERY
(☎0539 41 70 65; foundationdassilah@yahoo.fr; ⊙8.30am-12.30pm & 2.30-5pm, to 8pm summer) **FREE** The main exhibition space in town is just inside the medina walls. It's in a beautiful medina house and displays a revolving exhibition of international painting and sculpture in its gallery, and at times, in the nearby El-Khamra Tower, a renovated Portuguese fortification located on Pl Abdellah Guennoun.

Aplanos Gallery   GALLERY
(☎0661 99 80 30; Rue Tijara) Belgian painter Anne-Judith Van Loock created this gallery with her Moroccan husband Ahmed Benraadiya, where foreign and local artists can exhibit.

Galerie Hakim   GALLERY
(☎0661 79 95 35, 0539 41 88 96; hakimghailan@yahoo.fr; 14 Pl Sidi ben Issa) Zaïlachi artist Hakim Ghaïlan started this space and exhibits mainly young Moroccan artists.

Church of San Bartolome   CHURCH
Northwest of Pl Mohammed V (the centre of Assilah's small new town) is the Church of San Bartolome. Built by Spanish Franciscans in a typical colonial Moorish style, it is one of the few churches in Morocco allowed to ring the bells for Sunday Mass. Nearby is the marché central (central market).

Beaches   BEACH
Assilah's main beach, flanked by campsites and hotels, stretches north from town. It's a wide sweep of golden sand and although pleasant in low season, the crowds and noise from the nearby road make it much less appealing in summer. For more peace and quiet head 3km south to **Paradise Beach** at Rmilate, a gorgeous spot that really does live up to its name, though it's not cleaned much out of season. It's a pleasant walk along the coast or, alternatively, hop on one of the horse-drawn carriages that ply this route in summer. A little further on is **Rada Beach**, with a good beach cafe and bamboo bungalows.

⚜ Festivals & Events

Assilah Festival   CULTURAL
(www.c-assilah.com; ⊙Aug) The Centre de Hassan II Rencontres Internationales is the main focus for this annual festival, when artists, musicians, performers and some 200,000 spectators descend upon the town. More than 30 years old, the cultural festival features numerous workshops, public art demonstrations, concerts, exhibitions and events with participants from all over the world. A three-day horse festival, including a Moroccan *fantasia* (musket-firing cavalry charge) takes place towards the end of the three-week festival.

🛏 Sleeping

During high season (Easter week and July to September) the town is flooded with visitors so it's advisable to book well in advance. Assilah has a limited choice of budget hotels.

RASCALLY ER-RAISSOULI

Feared bandit, kidnapper and general troublemaker, Moulay Ahmed ben Mohammed er-Raissouli (or Raisuni) was one of Assilah's most legendary inhabitants. He started life as a petty crook in the Rif Mountains but saw no problem in bumping off unwilling victims and was soon renowned as a merciless murderer, and feared right across the region.

Internationally, Er-Raissouli was best known for kidnapping Westerners. He and his band held various luminaries to ransom, including Greek-American billionaire Ion Perdicaris, who was ransomed in 1904 for US$70,000.

In an attempt to control the unruly outlaw, consecutive sultans appointed him to various political positions, including governor of Assilah and later Tangier. However, Er-Raissouli continued with his wicked ways, amassing great wealth in whatever way he could. He held considerable sway over the Rif tribes and the Spanish funded his arms in the hope of keeping order in the mountains, but Er-Raissouli often used them against his benefactors.

The Spaniards eventually forced Er-Raissouli to flee Assilah after WWI, but he continued to wreak havoc in the Rif hinterland until 1925, when the Rif rebel Abd al-Krim arrested him and accused him of being too closely linked with the Spanish.

Christina's House
GUESTHOUSE €

(☑0539 41 77 88, 0677 27 64 63; christina. henshaw@btinternet.com; 26 Rue Ibn Khatib, off Blvd 16 Nov; s/d/tr/q without bathroom Dh175/400/450/500, tw with bathroom Dh550; 🕾) Christina's is a friendly guesthouse that feels more like a home than a hotel. Some rooms have shared bathrooms, but all facilities throughout are new and kept scrupulously clean. Breakfasts are taken together, either in the kitchen/dining room or on the roof terrace.

Hôtel Belle Vue
HOTEL €

(☑0539 41 77 47; Rue Hassan ben Tabit; s/d without bathroom Dh100/150, with bathroom Dh150/250) A friendly, small hotel in a quiet side street, with brightly painted wooden decor. Everything is immaculately kept, including the shared facilities. A few rooms have their own bathroom (Dh50 extra), rooms without have sinks. The rooms at the front with breezy balconies are the pick of the bunch. The rooftop terrace is a great place for an evening drink or to relax.

Hôtel Sahara
HOTEL €

(☑0539 41 71 85; 9 Rue Tarfaya; s/d/tr without bathroom Dh100/150/240) A good cheapie, this small hotel offers simple rooms set around an open courtyard. Patterned tiles and potted plants adorn the entrance, and the compact rooms are well maintained (though some have tiny windows). The sparkling shared toilets and hot showers (Dh5) are well-kept.

★ Khanfous Retreat
GUESTHOUSE €€

(☑0634 66 34 83; www.khanfousretreat.com; Bni Meslem; r with half board Dh500) In a tiny village some 15km from Assilah, the Khanfous Retreat is the perfect place to escape from it all – there's no internet or even phone signal. Chill out in the charmingly rustic house, make the 40-minute walk through the countryside to the beach, arrange a donkey trek or cookery lesson, or just unplug wonderfully from the world. It's definitely off the beaten track, but the owner will arrange transport for you.

Hotel Al-Alba
HOTEL €€

(☑0649 18 28 84; www.hotelalalba.com; 35 Ave Khalid Ibn Oualid; s Dh500-620, d Dh780-1000; ✴🕾) Don't be dismayed by the slightly cramped entrance at the Al-Alba: the rooms are fresh and cheery, with a hint of sea breeze in the decor and a warm welcome. The hotel has a decent restaurant, but the big bonus is the gorgeous in-house hammam, offering a variety of treatments to pamper yourself with (Dh185 to Dh270, non-guests welcome).

Hôtel Patio de la Luna
HOTEL €€

(☑0539 41 60 74; 12 Pl Zellaka; s/d/tr Dh350/450/450; 🕾) The only accommodation option in Assilah with any local character is this intimate, Spanish-run place secluded behind an unassuming door on the main drag. The somewhat spartan, rustic rooms have wooden furniture, woven blankets and tiled bathrooms and are set around a lovely leafy patio. The staff are friendly and it's very popular, so book ahead.

★**Dar Azaouia** RIAD €€€
(✆0672 11 05 35; www.darazaouia-asilah.com; 16 Rue 6, near Bab Homar; d Dh840-950; 🕿) This is a small but beautiful guesthouse, comfortably blending Moroccan tradition with modern French country style and the fresh salt air of the seaside. Rooms are immaculate, with lovely furnishings (the corner fireplace in one is a winner for the colder months) and a delightful roof terrace. Excellent breakfasts, with dinner on request (alcohol served). Pre-booking essential.

✖ Eating & Drinking

Assilah has a string of restaurants clustered around Bab al-Kasaba and along the medina walls on Ave Hassan II. There are a few other cheap options on Rue Ahmed M'dem near the banks on Pl Mohammed V.

Medina Wall Restaurants MOROCCAN €
(Ave Hassan II; mains from Dh40; ☺lunch & dinner) With little to choose between them, you can get cheap and quick meals at any of the restaurants along the outside of the medina walls. On offer is a selection of fish, seafood, pizza and traditional Moroccan staples.

La Symphonie II des Douceurs CAFE €
(26 Pl Zellaka; pastries from Dh12) A good place for breakfast or an afternoon sugar fix; pastries and ice cream in civilised surroundings.

Casa García SEAFOOD €€
(✆0539 41 74 65; 51 Rue Moulay Hassan ben el-Mehdi; mains from Dh80; ☺lunch & dinner) The specialities are Spanish-style fish dishes and fishy tapas at this small restaurant opposite the beach. Go for succulent grilled fish or a more adventurous menu of octopus, eels, shrimp and barnacles, served with a glass of crisp Moroccan gris wine on the large and breezy terrace. The paella is delicious, too.

Restaurant la Place MOROCCAN, SEAFOOD €€
(✆0539 41 73 26; 7 Rue Moulay Hassan ben el-Mehdi; mains Dh75; ☺lunch & dinner) Friendly, less formal and more varied than its neighbours, this licenced restaurant offers a choice of traditional Moroccan dishes as well as the ubiquitous fish and seafood. The delicious fish tajine provides the best of both worlds.

Restaurante Oceano Casa Pepe SEAFOOD €€
(✆0539 41 73 95; 8 Pl Zellaka; mains Dh80-120; ☺lunch & dinner) Black-tied waiters lure in the punters from the street at this slightly more formal dining option, where fresh seafood tops the bill. Spanish and Moroccan wine, low lighting and soft music make it a more refined atmosphere.

La Perle d'Assilah FRENCH €€€
(✆0539 41 87 58; cnr Rue Allal ben Abdallah & Ave Melilla; 2/3 courses Dh160/190; ☺noon-3pm & 7-10.30pm) Assilah's highest-end eating option, La Perle is done out like the better sort of French brasserie. The menu leans heavily on the Gallic too, with dishes such as duck in Grand Marnier, with a handful of Spanish and Asian options thrown in. The set two- and three-course menus are excellent value, or order à la carte.

Al-Madina CAFE
(Pl Abdellah Guennoun) The main attraction of this simple little cafe is its sunny seating area in the square in front of El-Khamra Tower. A great place to watch the world go by.

OFF THE BEATEN TRACK

MONOLITHS OF M'SOURA

The mysterious Monoliths of M'Soura make an interesting half-day trip from Assilah. This prehistoric site consists of a large stone circle (actually an ellipse) of about 175 stones, thought to have originally surrounded a burial mound. Although many of the stones have fallen or been broken, the circle is still impressive, its strange presence heightened by the desolation of its location. The tallest stone reaches about 5.5m in height and is known as El-Uted (The Pointer).

The stone circle is about 25km (by road) southeast of Assilah. To get there you'll need a sturdy vehicle. Head for the village of Souq Tnine de Sidi el-Yamani, off highway R417, which branches east off the main Tangier–Rabat road. Veer left in the village and follow a poorly maintained, unsealed track 6km north to the site. It can be difficult to find so you may want to ask for directions or hire a guide in the village.

Another interesting trip from Assilah is a visit to the lively Sunday market in the village of **Had Gharbia**, 16km north of town off the road to Tangier.

ℹ Information

Pl Mohammed V is crowded with banks with ATMs and change facilities. The website www. asilahinfo.com aims to collate tourist information about the town.

Cyber Haytam (197 Ave Hassan II; per hr Dh6; ⊙ 9am-midnight) Internet access.

Pharmacie l'Océan (Pl Zellaka) Pharmacy.

ℹ Getting There & Away

BUS

The bus station is on the corner of Ave Mohammed VI and the Tangier–Rabat Rd. CTM doesn't stop in Assilah but other bus companies offer various services to destinations including Casablanca (Dh80, 4½ hours), Fez (Dh60, 4½ hours), Marrakesh (Dh120, nine hours), Rabat (Dh60, 3½ hours) and Tangier (Dh15, one hour). Buses to Tangier and Casablanca leave roughly every half-hour throughout the day; long-distance buses tend to originate in Tangier, so are best booked in advance.

TAXI

Grands taxis to Tangier (Dh20) and Larache (Dh20) depart when full from Rue 2 Mars, off Ave Mohammed VI. A taxi to Tangier's airport (only 26km from Assilah) costs Dh250.

TRAIN

The train station is 3km north of Assilah (Dh10 in a green petit taxi). Destinations include Casablanca (Dh109, four hours, eight daily) via Rabat, Fez (Dh87, four hours, four daily) and Tangier (Dh16, 45 minutes, 12 daily). One overnight train goes direct to Marrakesh (Dh186, 9½ hours), but this train originates in Tangier, so buy your ticket in advance.

El-Jadida الجديدة

POP 148,000

This old Portuguese town, often known as the Cité Portugaise, has a sleepy but atmospheric Unesco World Heritage medina. A lack of investment has helped maintain the integrity of the town's rambling alleys and ramparts. For much of the year El-Jadida is a quiet backwater, disturbed only by the crowds of Moroccans flocking to its beautiful beaches and strolling its boulevards in July and August.

In 1506 the Portuguese built a fortress here to protect their ships and baptised it Mazagan, which soon developed into the country's most important trading post. Sultan Sidi Mohammed ben Abdallah seized Mazagan from the Portuguese following a siege in 1769, but the Portuguese blew up most of the fort before leaving. Most of the new settlers preferred to live in the new town and the citadel remained a ruin until the early 19th century when Sultan Abd er-Rahman resettled some of the Jews of Azemmour in old Mazagan, and renamed the town El-Jadida, 'the New One' in Arabic.

The large and influential Jewish community soon grew rich on trade with the interior, and unlike most other Moroccan cities, there was no *mellah* (Jewish quarter); the Jews mixed with the general populace and an attitude of easy tolerance was established in the city. During the French protectorate the town became an administrative centre and a beach resort, but its port gradually lost out to Safi and Casablanca.

Over the last few years, both Moroccans and foreigners have started buying up property in the old walled town, including the old colonial church. Just north of the town, on a gorgeous stretch of beach, is the recently opened tourist resort of Mazagan, which includes a golf course, casino, spa and large resort hotel. The old town of El-Jadida will be given a new, if very different, lease of life in the next few years.

⊙ Sights

Cité Portugaise   HISTORIC SITE

El-Jadida's main sight, the Cité Portugaise (Portuguese city), is a compact maze of twisting streets, surrounded by ochre ramparts. The main entrance is just off Pl Mohammed ben Abdallah and leads into Rue Mohammed Ahchemi Bahbai. Immediately on the left is the Portuguese-built Church of the Assumption, which was being restored at the time of research and will open as an upmarket hotel. Almost next door is the Grande Mosquée, which has a unique pentagonal-shaped minaret; it originally acted as a lighthouse.

Citerne Portugaise   HISTORIC BUILDING

(Portuguese Cistern; Rue Mohammed Ahchemi Bahbai; admission incl entry to ramparts Dh20; ⊙ 9am-1pm & 3-6.30pm) On the main street past the souvenir shops is a vast, vaulted cistern lit by a single shaft of light. The spectacularly tranquil spot, with a thin film of water on the floor reflecting a mirror image of the vaulted ceiling and elegant columns, was originally used to collect water. It is famous as the eerie location for the dramatic riot scene in Orson Welles' 1954 *Othello*.

El-Jadida

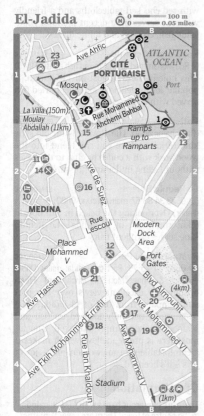

0 ——— 100 m
0 ——— 0.05 miles

El-Jadida

⊙ Sights
1 Bastion de L'Ange	B1
2 Bastion de St Sébastian	B1
3 Church of the Assumption	A1
4 Cité Portugaise	A1
5 Citerne Portugaise	A1
6 Communal Bakery	B1
7 Grande Mosquée	A1
8 Porte de la Mer	B1
9 Synagogue	B1

🛏 Sleeping
10 Hôtel de Bordeaux	A2
11 Riad Le Mazagao	A2

✕ Eating
12 Patisserie Royale	B3
13 Restaurant du Port	B2
14 Restaurant Tchikito	A2
15 Restaurante La Portugaise	A2

ℹ Information
16 @Kiltec	A2
17 Bank al-Maghrib	B3
18 BMCE	A4
19 BMCI	B4
20 Night Pharmacy	B3
21 Syndicat d'Initiative	A3

ℹ Transport
22 Grands Taxis to Sidi Bouzid & Moulay Abdallah	A1
23 Local Buses	A1

Porte de la Mer   LANDMARK
(admission free; ⊙ramparts 9am-6pm) Further down the street are the ramparts with the Porte de la Mer, the original sea gate where ships unloaded their cargo, and from where the Portuguese finally departed. To the left of the gate, through the archway, is one of the town's **communal bakeries**, where local women bring their bread to be baked.

To the right of the sea gate, a ramp leads up to the windy ramparts and **Bastion de L'Ange** (southeast corner), an excellent vantage point with views out to sea and over the new town and port. Walk along the ramparts to the left to reach **Bastion de St Sebastian** (northeast corner), from where you can see the old Jewish cemetery. Next to the bastion is the abandoned **synagogue** (originally the old prison) with its Star of David.

Beaches   BEACH
The beaches to the north and south of town are fairly clean and safe, enjoyable out of season, but packed in July and August. The beach at **Haouzia**, northeast of town, is lovely. The Mazagan resort is situated on this beach. **Sidi Bouzid**, 5km southwest of El-Jadida, is a popular spot with sunbathers and surfers.

🛏 Sleeping

A few hotels near the Cité Portugaise make El-Jadida a nice option to spend a couple of days. The hotels in the new town are more modern and comfortable but have less character.

Hôtel de Bordeaux   HOTEL **€**
(☎0523 37 39 21; 47 Rue Moulay Ahmed Tahiri; s/d without bathroom Dh100/160, with bathroom Dh180/230) The best of the cheapies, this friendly, good-value hotel in a traditional house in the medina has comfortable but compact rooms around a covered courtyard.

Only the rooms on the 1st floor have en-suite bathrooms. Rooms get cheaper the higher up you go. You'll have to use the communal shower downstairs for hot showers. The hotel is well signposted from Rue ben Tachfine.

★ **Dar al-Manar** B&B €€
(☎ 0523 35 16 45, 0661 49 54 11; www.dar-al-manar. com; r Dh800-1000; ❄ @) Outside El-Jadida overlooking the ocean is this gorgeous house with five simple but stylish and spacious rooms, in a contemporary Moroccan style. Guests can use the garden and the bright dining room. Dinner can be ordered in advance, and is cooked with vegetables from the organic garden. Call for directions; it is near the Phare Sidi Mesbah, a lighthouse, and is signposted on the road from El-Jadida north to Azemmour.

Riad Le Mazagao RIAD €€
(☎ 0523 35 01 37; www.lemazagao.com; 6 Derb el-Hajjar; d without bathroom Dh550-825; ❄) The rooms are set around the courtyard and on the roof terrace of this welcoming, atmospheric 19th-century guesthouse located in the medina. The large rooms are decorated in a warm Moroccan style with lots of tiling and local textiles, and feel very homey. Half board is obligatory if you stay more than a week. The shared bathrooms are spotless.

La Villa RIAD €€€
(☎ 0661 41 86 81, 0523 34 44 23; www.lavilladavid. com; 4 Ave Moulay Abdelhafid; r/ste Dh1100/1540; ❄ 🛜 ≋) This is a charming contemporary-style hotel in an old villa, just outside the old city and run by two Frenchmen. The rooms are set around a white courtyard. Stylish neon lights lead you upstairs, and rooms have plasma screens, wi-fi and *tadelakt* (lime plaster) bathrooms and floors. The effect is very Zen rather than high-tech. There is a little bar on the roof by the pool and the top terrace has a solarium with spectacular views over the old city. La Villa has the best restaurant in town serving inventive French-Moroccan cuisine (dinner Dh350).

✗ Eating

El-Jadida has a handful of reasonable restaurants and a thriving cafe culture.

Restaurante La Portugaise MOROCCAN €
(Rue Mohammed Ahchemi Bahbai; mains from Dh40; ⊙ lunch & dinner) Just inside the walls of the old city, this characterful little place with red-checked tablecloths and a friendly welcome serves up a decent menu of good-value fish, chicken and tajine dishes.

Restaurant Tchikito SEAFOOD €
(4 Rue Mohammed Smiha; mixed fish platter Dh40) This hole-in-the-wall, just off Pl Hansali, is popular for its delicious and cheap fried fish served with a fiery chilli sauce.

Patisserie Royale PATISSERIE €
(Pl Mohammed V) The Royale is an old-style kind of joint where you can blend into the woodwork with a coffee or chat to the locals without feeling under any pressure.

Le Requin Blue SEAFOOD €€
(☎ 0523 34 80 67; mains around Dh80; ⊙ lunch & dinner) Overlooking the beach in Sidi Bouzid (5km southwest of El-Jadida), Le Requin Blue serves excellent fish.

Restaurant du Port SEAFOOD €€
(☎ 0523 34 25 79; Port du Jadida; mains Dh80; ⊙ lunch & dinner Mon-Sat, lunch Sun) Head upstairs for excellent views over the port and ramparts from one of El-Jadida's best restaurants, naturally focused on fish and seafood, cooked simply but well. The atmosphere is pretty mellow, which makes it a comfortable spot for women, and – joy of joys – it's licenced.

❶ Information

There are numerous banks with ATMs located in the centre of town. There are several internet cafes on Ave Mohammed VI.

@Kiltec (1st fl, 62 Pl Hansali; per hr Dh6; ⊙ 9am-11pm, closed lunch Fri) Internet cafe.

Clinique Les Palmiers (☎ 0523 39 39 39; Rte de Casablanca; ⊙ 24hr) With 24-hour emergency service.

Main Post Office (Pl Mohammed V; ⊙ 8.30am-4.30pm Mon-Fri)

Night Pharmacy (off Ave Mohammed VI; ⊙ 9pm-8am)

Syndicat d'Initiative (Pl Mohammed V; ⊙ 8.30am-6.30pm Thu-Tue) This tourist office is a rarity in Morocco – it has knowledgeable and helpful staff.

❶ Getting There & Away

BUS

The **bus station** (Ave Mohammed V) is a 10-minute walk from the centre. Destinations with CTM include Casablanca (Dh40, 2 hours, four daily), Essaouira (Dh90, 4½ hours, one daily) and Safi (Dh60, 2½ hours, six daily). Cheaper local buses go to all the same destinations as well as Azemmour (Dh7), Rabat (Dh40, four hours, 12 daily) and Marrakesh (Dh45, four hours, hourly). Bus 2 for Sidi Bouzid (Dh5) and bus 6 for Moulay Abdallah (Dh5) leave from just north of the Cité Portugaise.

TAXI

Grands taxis for Azemmour (Dh10, 15 minutes) and Casablanca (Dh35, one hour) leave from the side street next to the long-distance bus station. Taxis to Oualidia (Dh25, 40 minutes) and Safi (Dh55, 90 minutes) depart from a junction on the road to Sidi Bouzid. You'll need to take a petit taxi (Dh5) to get there. The grand-taxi rank for Sidi Bouzid (Dh5) and Moulay Abdallah (Dh6) is beside the local bus station north of the Cité Portugaise.

TRAIN

El-Jadida train station is located 4km south of town. There are eight services a day to and from Casablanca (Dh35, 80 minutes). A petit taxi to the centre costs around Dh10.

Azemmour

El-Amine, one of Azemmour's most successful painters, got it right describing his favourite view of town from his roof terrace, which he has painted numerous times: the old walled medina squeezed in between the Oum er-Rbia (Mother of Spring) river and the ocean, with the fields spread beyond.

The picturesque town has inspired many artists, who have come to live here. Although it is close to the art market of Casablanca, life is still simple, with the farmers and fishermen going door-to-door with their produce. It's a sleepy backwater with a languid charm, a sturdy Portuguese medina and some wonderful accommodation options – a great place to while away a few days overlooking the river.

The Portuguese built the town in 1513 as one of a string of trading posts along the coast. The town's most famous inhabitant was Estevanico the Black. Captured and made a slave, he later became one of the first four explorers to cross the entire mainland of North America from Florida to the Pacific.

◎ Sights

The main sight is the medina, an ochre-walled town of narrow winding streets and whitewashed houses. Unlike Assilah, to the north, it is completely unadorned and still gives an authentic glimpse of life in modern Morocco. You can get up onto the **ramparts** near Pl du Souk or via steps at the northeastern corner of the medina. Walk along the walls to see **Dar el Baroud** (the Powder House), a Portuguese gunpowder store of which only the tower remains. To the north of the medina is the *mellah* and further on you'll get wonderful views over the river. All over the medina are walls painted by local artists, artists' studios including **Ahmed el-Amine** (☑ 0523 35 89 02; 6 Derb el-Hantati) and a few places selling the typical Azemmour embroidery.

🛏 Sleeping & Eating

There are lots of small restaurants outside the city walls in the new town.

Riad Azama RIAD €€
(☑ 0523 34 75 16, 0648 24 14 85; riadazama@menara.ma; 17 Impasse Ben Tahar; r incl breakfast Dh980; ☎) This is a grand 19th-century house complete with original carved woodwork and rather dark rooms surrounding a leafy courtyard. The carved, painted ceilings here are some of the finest you'll see and the rooftop terrace has great views of the medina. Dinner is available here on request.

L'Oum Errebia HOTEL €€€
(☑ 0523 34 70 71; www.azemmour-hotel.com; 25 Impasse Chtouka; s/d incl breakfast Dh600/800, with river view Dh900/1200; ☎) This place blends traditional Moroccan style with chic contemporary design. The simple rooms are delightful and the large lounge, complete with open fireplace and grand piano, acts as a modern art gallery. There's an in-house hammam (*gommage* Dh150) and treatments are available (massage Dh200). The large terrace overlooks the river and communal meals (Dh250) are served at the big dining-room table.

❶ Information

Azemmour has several banks, a pharmacy and internet access at **Capsys** (off Pl du Souk; per hr Dh7).

❶ Getting There & Away

Trains now stop nine times daily at Azemmour Halte, linking the town to El-Jadida (Dh15,15 minutes) and Casablanca (Dh31, one hour).

A grand taxi/bus from Azemmour to El-Jadida costs Dh10/7.

Oualidia

الوالدية

POP 4200

The drive from El-Jadida to Oualidia along the coastal road, where the fields come down to the wild shore of the ocean, is spectacular enough, but the view upon arrival is more than pleasing. The delightful small-scale resort of Oualidia spreads around a gorgeous crescent-shaped lagoon fringed with golden sands and protected from the wild surf by a rocky breakwater. With a good selection of accommodation and great fish restaurants (the town is particularly famous for its oysters), Oualidia is a weekend resort for Marrakshis and Casablancais.

Out of season it is still quiet, with little more to do than relax, surf, swim and eat well, but avoid the crowds in summer.

◉ Sights & Activities

The town is named after the Saadian Sultan el-Oualid, who in 1634 built the kasbah now atmospherically crumbling on the bluff overlooking the lagoon. The lagoon also attracted Morocco's royalty and the grand villa on the water's edge was Mohammed V's summer palace. Most hotels and restaurants are along the road to the beach (1km) – follow signs down beside the post office. There are no taxis on this route, but hotels will arrange transport.

Lagoon   WATER SPORTS
The safe, calm waters of the lagoon are perfect for **swimming**, **sailing** and **fishing**, while the wide, sandy beach on either side of the breakwater is good for **windsurfing** and **surfing**.

Surfland   WATER SPORTS
(☑ 0523 36 61 10; ☉ Apr–mid-Nov) Signposted left off the road to the beach, this is a well-organised surfing school run by Moroccan surf champion Noureddine Joubir. Tuition is Dh250/200 per adult/child for 1½ hours.

Maison de l'Ostréa II   TOUR
(☑ 0523 36 63 24; www.ilove-casablanca.com/os trea) Oualidia is famous for its oyster beds, which produce about 200 tonnes of oysters annually. You can visit oyster farm No 7 at Maison de l'Ostréa II to see how it all works. Oysters (per dozen Dh180) and other seafood are available at the excellent restaurant attached. If you can't tear yourself away, there are double rooms for Dh700. It's at the entrance of Oualidia on the Casablanca road.

🛏 Sleeping & Eating

All hotels listed have their own restaurants. There are some slightly cheaper places lining the road down to the beach, and other apartments and villas can be rented through numerous agencies in town. For bargain meals there is a selection of cheap eateries on the main road up in the village.

Hotel Thalassa   HOTEL €
(☑ 0523 36 60 50; s/d Dh150/200, low season Dh100/150) The only hotel on the main drag up in the town, this place is better than you might expect, with bright, airy whitewashed rooms that have old-fashioned, spick-and-span bathrooms. Good value but far from the beach.

Motel A l'Araignée Gourmande   HOTEL €
(☑ 0523 36 64 47; www.araignee-gourmande.com; s/d Dh240/280; ☎) A friendly hotel with spacious, comfortable (if a little old-fashioned) rooms. The ones over the restaurant have balconies overlooking the lagoon, while rooms in the new building next door don't. The restaurant serves up a feast of well-prepared seafood (mains from Dh80).

Hôtel-Restaurant L'Initiale   B&B €€
(☑ 0523 36 62 46; initialhotel@menara.ma; r with breakfast Dh500) This little white villa, with a warm orange interior and just six pleasant and comfortable rooms, is well equipped with new fittings, spotless bathrooms and tiny balconies. The popular licenced restaurant (mains from Dh80) is one of the best in town and serves a wide selection of fish dishes and pizzas.

L'Hippocampe   HOTEL €€€
(☑ 0523 36 61 08; hotelhippocampe@hotmail.com; d with half board Dh1400, ste with sea view Dh2600; ☎) A friendly hotel in Marrakesh pink, with seaside-fresh rooms off a magnificent garden filled with flowers, looking over the lagoon. There's an excellent fish restaurant (mains around Dh120), and steps down to the beach. It's family friendly.

La Sultana   HOTEL €€€
(☑ 0523 38 80 08; http://lasultanahotels.com/oua lidia; Parc à Huîtres No 3; r Dh2900-5300; ❀ ☎ ☒) 🌿 This spectacularly luxurious hotel has 11 rooms with fireplace, private jacuzzi and a terrace overlooking the lagoon. There's a choice of three restaurants, an indoor pool, and an infinity pool and spa – all set in beautiful landscaped gardens. It was designed to have minimal impact on the surrounding

environment; local materials were used in the building and innovative technology reduces water use.

★ Beachside Shellfish
SEAFOOD €

From late afternoon onwards, you can buy fresh shellfish on the beachfront, straight from the hauled-up boats or from crates on the backs of fishermen's scooters. Oysters, clams, razorshells and urchins are shucked as fast as you can eat them and served with a squeeze of lemon for around Dh6 a shell. Divine.

ℹ Information

You'll find a bank, CTM office and internet cafe on the main street, and a Saturday souq when people from surrounding villages come to town to sell their wares. Visit www.oualidia.info for tourist information.

ℹ Getting There & Away

Grands taxis run at irregular times to El-Jadida (Dh25, 40 minutes) and Safi (Dh25, 45 minutes). They leave from near the post office on the main road. CTM has a daily bus (Dh30) in either direction. From the main road, it's a 10-minute walk down to the lagoon and accommodation – grands taxis will ask for an extra tip to drop you downhill.

Safi آسفي

POP 285,000

An industrial centre and thriving port, Safi is a lot less picturesque than neighbouring coastal towns, but it offers an insight into the day-to-day life of a Moroccan city. Most tourists stop here en route to or from Essaouira to visit the giant pottery works that produce the typical brightly coloured Safi pottery.

The new town is pleasant enough, with tree-lined boulevards and whitewashed villas, but the alleys of the walled and fortified medina are more atmospheric to stroll through, and you often have the sights to yourself. The beaches are famous for their impressive surf.

Safi's natural harbour was known to the Phoenicians and the Romans, but in the 11th century it was a port for the trans-Saharan trade between Marrakesh and Guinea, where gold, slaves and ivory were sold. In the 14th century the town became an important religious and cultural centre, when the Merenids built a *ribat* here. The Portuguese took the city for a brief spell from 1508 until 1541, when the Saadians took it back. They built the monumental Qasr al-Bahr fortress, a cathedral and generally expanded the town, but destroyed most monuments upon their departure.

In the 16th century, Safi grew wealthy from the trade in copper and sugar, and European merchants and agents flocked to the city, but when the port at Essaouira was rebuilt in the 18th century Safi was largely forgotten.

Safi's real revival came in the 20th century when its fishing fleet expanded and huge industrial complexes were built to process the 30,000 tonnes of sardines caught annually. A major phosphate-processing complex was established south of the town and the city began to expand rapidly. Today, Safi is one of Morocco's largest ports.

◉ Sights

Colline des Potiers
LANDMARK

Outside Bab Chaba, on the hill opposite the medina gate, you can't miss the earthen kilns and chimneys of the Colline des Potiers (Potters' Hill). The skills used here are predominantly traditional and you can wander around the cooperatives and see the potters at work. If a potter invites you in to watch them at work, you'll be expected to give a small tip or buy an item or two from the shop.

Qasr al-Bahr
HISTORIC BUILDING

(Castle on the Sea; admission Dh10) The impressive castle dominates the crashing waves of the Atlantic on the rocky waterfront. The fortress was built to enforce Portuguese authority, house the town governor and protect the port. The ramp in the courtyard leads to the southwest bastion with great views. Prisoners were kept in the basement of the **prison tower**, right of the entrance, before being killed or shipped as slaves. You can climb to the top for views across the medina.

Medina
MEDINA

Across the street from the Qasr al-Bahr stands the walled medina. The main street, Rue du Souq, runs northeast from Bab Lamaasa, and you'll find most of the souqs, stalls, jewellery, clothing and food in this area. To the right of this street, down a twisting alley, are the remains of the so-called **Cathédrale Portugaise** (admission Dh10), which was never finished by the Portuguese who started it.

Safi

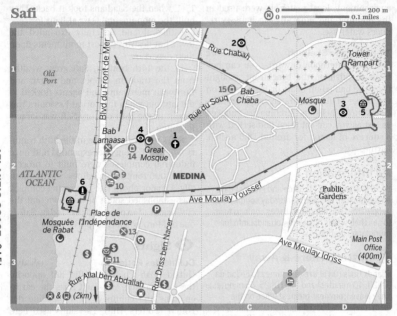

Safi

◉ Sights
1 Cathédrale Portugaise B2
2 Colline des Potiers C1
3 Kechla..D1
4 Medina...B2
5 Musée National de Céramique D1
6 Prison Tower A2
7 Qasr al-Bahr A2

🛏 Sleeping
8 Hôtel Farah C3
9 Hotel Majestic B2
10 L'Avenir Hôtel.......................................B2
11 Riad Asfi..B3

⊗ Eating
12 Café les Remparts B2
13 Restaurant Gégène...............................B3

🛍 Shopping
14 Fixed-Price Pottery Shop B2
15 Pottery Souq C1

Musée National de Céramique   MUSEUM
The **Kechla**, a massive defensive structure with ramps, gunnery platforms and living quarters, has been restored and opened as this museum. Exhibits here include pottery from Safi, Fez and Meknès, and some contemporary pieces by local artists.

🛏 Sleeping & Eating

Hotel Majestic   HOTEL
(☏0524 46 40 11; Pl de l'Indépendance; s/d/tr Dh50/100/150) A decent medina option, with large, good-value rooms, although it can be noisy. The rooms are basic and have shared bathrooms, but everything is clean and well kept, and half the rooms have ocean views. Hot showers cost Dh10.

L'Avenir Hôtel   HOTEL €
(☏0524 13 14 46; Pl de l'Indépendance; s/d Dh120/140, without bathroom Dh70/80,) One of a cluster of medina cheapies, with spartan but clean rooms and a cafe outside for breakfasts. Hot showers are Dh10.

Hôtel Farah   HOTEL €€
(☏0524 46 42 99; www.goldentulipfarahsafi.com; Ave Zerktouni; s/d/ste Dh545/600/1850; ✳🐕🖥) The best hotel in Safi, the Farah is a bargain with large and stylish rooms in pale neutrals, sparkling bathrooms, anti-allergy duvets and a minibar. There are good views from the pool terrace, plus a fitness room, hammam, restaurant and nightclub.

Riad Asfi   HOTEL €€
(☏0524 46 46 95; www.hotelriadasfi.com; 11 Pl de l'Indépendance; s/d Dh350/450; 🐕) The name flatters to deceive, as this place is a

straight-up hotel, with its only riad flourishes being its *tadelakt* plaster walls in the rooms. Nevertheless, it's a good centrally located modern standard with comfortable rooms (though you should ask for one with a balcony rather than the drearier internal-window-only options).

Open-Air Fish Restaurants SEAFOOD €
(fish, bread & sauce about Dh35; ☺ lunch & dinner)
Fish and seafood, particularly sardines, are a speciality in Safi, and the best place to sample them is at the restaurants on the hill at the *rond-point de Sidi Bouzid* (the Sidi Bouzid roundabout). Establish the price before ordering, as fish is charged by weight, or order the fish special – a plate of fish served with bread and a spicy tomato sauce. A petit taxi to get there costs around Dh10.

Café les Remparts CAFE €
(Rue du Socco; sandwiches Dh20, mains Dh50-65; ☎) A great place for people-watching on the small square leading into the medina (although the interior is a little sterile). The menu has a good selection of tajines, sandwiches and pasta dishes.

Restaurant Gégène MOROCCAN, MEDITERRANEAN €€
(☑ 0524 46 33 69; 11 Rue de la Marne; mains Dh80; ☺ dinner Mon-Sat) Old-fashioned service, tasteful decor and a surprisingly fine menu, with a wide choice of Moroccan and Mediterranean dishes from lamb tajine and pizza to Oualidia oysters, all served with a glass of wine.

Restaurant La Trattoria ITALIAN €€€
(☑ 0524 62 09 59; 2 Rue l'Aouinate; mains Dh200; ☺ 7-11pm) La Trattoria is a pleasant place with a relaxed ambience and passable Italian food. The menu has a full range of pizzas and pasta, and a good choice of fish and seafood. It's run by the same management as Restaurant Gégène, but it's more upmarket, and is located off Blvd du Front de Mer, 400m north of the medina.

🛍 Shopping

Safi is famed for its pottery, and you can find some great items here (as well as some awful tourist dross). To get a feel for prices visit the **fixed-price pottery shop** (☺ 9am-8pm) on the right-hand side of Rue du Souq as you enter the medina from Bab Lamaasa. To the left, towards the eastern end of the same street, you'll find the colourful **pottery souq**.

ℹ Information

There are plenty of banks and ATMs clustered around Pl de l'Indépendance and Pl Driss ben Nacer. Visit www.safi-ville.com for tourist information.

Main Post Office (Ave Sidi Mohammed Abdallah; ☺ 8.30am-4.30pm Mon-Fri)

Post Office (Pl de l'Indépendance; ☺ 8.30am-4.30pm Mon-Fri)

ℹ Getting There & Away

BUS

Most CTM buses stopping in Safi originate elsewhere, so consider booking in advance. Destinations include Agadir (Dh115, five hours, three daily), Casablanca (Dh95, four hours, six daily), El-Jadida (Dh60, two hours, four daily) and Essaouira (Dh50, two hours, four daily). Other operators run daily departures to the same destinations as well as to Oualidia and Tiznit.

TAXI

There are grands taxis to Marrakesh (Dh75) and Essaouira (Dh60), among other destinations, which leave from the parking lot beside the bus station. The rank for Oualidia (Dh25, 45 minutes) and El-Jadida (Dh55, 90 minutes) is a good kilometre north of town on the El-Jadida road.

TRAIN

From Safi **train station** (Rue de R'bat) there are two services per day at 5.50am and 3.50pm involving a change at Benguérir and calling at Casablanca (Dh75, 4½ hours), Rabat (Dh110, 5½ hours) and Fez (Dh185, eight hours).

ℹ Getting Around

Both the **bus station** (Ave Président Kennedy) and the train station are quite a distance south from the centre of town. A metered petit taxi from either will cost around Dh12. Local buses operate from just north of Pl Driss ben Nacer.

Around Safi

The wonderfully wild coastline north of Safi, with its dramatic cliffs sheltering gorgeous sandy coves, makes a great drive. The first stop is the headland of **Sidi Bouzid**, where you'll get a great view back over town. It's a good spot for lunch at the popular fish restaurant **Le Refuge** (☑ 0524 46 43 54; Rte Sidi Bouzid; mains Dh100; ☺ Tue-Sun).

Driving further on, you'll hit some undeveloped beaches that are up-and-coming surf spots and home to one of the longest tubular right-handers in the world. At 12km from Safi, sheltered **Lalla Fatna** is one of the nicest spots on this stretch. Take a left by the Lalla Fatna cafe down the steps to the sands beneath the cliffs. Further on you'll reach the headland and lighthouse at Cap Beddouza (23km), where there's a wide, sandy beach.

In summer (May to September) bus 15 runs along this route from Rue Driss ben Nacer in Safi.

Essaouira الصويرة

POP 70,000

Essaouira (pronounced 'essa-weera', or 'es-Sweera' in Arabic) is at once familiar and exotic with its fortified walls, fishing harbour and seagulls soaring and screaming over the town. At first it seems as though this could be a town in Brittany, France – not such a strange thought given that Essaouira was designed by the same Frenchman who designed Brittany's most famous port town, Saint-Malo. And yet once you enter the walls, it is also infinitely Moroccan: narrow alleyways, wind that reputedly drives people crazy, the smells of fish guts and damp sea air mixed with aromas of spices and thuya wood, women in white *haiks* (veils), midday palm-tree shadows on red city walls, and the sound of drums and Gnaoua singing reverberating from shops and houses.

It is the coastal wind – the beautifully named *alizee,* or *taros* in Berber – that, despite the crowds, ensures Essaouira retains its character. It blows too hard to attract sun, sand and sea tourists: for much of the year, you can't sit on the beach at all as the sand blows horizontally in your face. No surprise then that Essaouira has been dubbed 'Wind City of Africa' and attracts so many windsurfers. Sun-seekers head further south to the temperate clime of Agadir. The charm of the town is that it hasn't been entirely taken over by tourism. The fishing harbour is just as busy as it always was, the woodworkers are still amazing at their craft and the medina is just as important for locals as it is popular with tourists.

Essaouira lies on the crossroads between two tribes: the Arab Chiadma to the north and the Haha Berbers in the south. Add to that the Gnawa, who came originally from further south in Africa, and the Europeans, and you get a rich cultural mix. The light and beauty have forever attracted artists to Essaouira, and the town has a flourishing art scene. The sculptor Boujemâa Lakhdar started the local museum in the 1950s and,

in the process, inspired a generation of artists. Since then, the autodidactic *naïf* painters, who paint their dreams in a colourful palette, have earned international renown, mainly thanks to the efforts of the Galeries d'Art Damgaard.

Winter is the time to get closer to the real Essaouira, when the wind howls at its strongest and the waves smash against the city's defences. In summer the town is invaded by throngs of Moroccan tourists, the beach is crowded and it is hard to find accommodation.

History

Most of the old city and fortifications in Essaouira today date from the 18th century, but the town has a much older history that started with the Phoenicians. For centuries, foreigners had a firm grip over the town, and although Moroccans eventually reclaimed it, the foreign influence lingers on in the way the town looks and feels today.

In 1764 Sultan Sidi Mohammed ben Abdallah installed himself in Essaouira, from where his corsairs could go and attack the people of Agadir who rebelled against him. He hired a French architect, Théodore Cornut, to create a city in the middle of sand and wind, where nothing existed. The combination of Moroccan and European styles pleased the Sultan, who renamed the town Essaouira, meaning 'well designed'. The port soon became a vital link for trade between Timbuktu and Europe. It was a place where the trade in gold, salt, ivory and ostrich feathers was carefully monitored, taxed and controlled by a garrison of 2000 imperial soldiers.

By 1912 the French had established their protectorate, changed the town's name back to Mogador and diverted trade to Casablanca, Tangier and Agadir. It was only with independence in 1956 that the sleepy backwater again became Essaouira. After Orson Welles filmed *Othello* here, and following Jimi Hendrix' fleeting visit and hippies choosing Essaouira as a hang-out, the town has seen a steady flow of visitors, from artists, surfers and writers to European tourists escaping the crowds of Marrakesh.

◉ Sights

Although there aren't so many formal sights in Essaouira, it's a wonderful place for rambling. The medina, souqs, ramparts, port and beach are perfect for leisurely discovery interspersed with relaxed lunches and un-hurried coffee or fresh orange juice.

Medina
MEDINA

Essaouira's walled medina was added to Unesco's World Heritage list in 2001. Its well-preserved, late-18th-century fortified layout is a prime example of European military architecture in North Africa. For the visitor, the mellow atmosphere, narrow winding streets, colourful shops, white-washed houses and heavy old wooden doors make it a wonderful place to stroll.

The dramatic, wave-lashed ramparts that surround the medina are a great place to get an overview of the labyrinth of streets. The ramparts were famously used in the opening scene of Orson Welles' *Othello* for a panoramic shot where Iago is suspended in a cage above the rocks and sea. The easiest place to access the ramparts is at **Skala de la Ville**, the impressive sea bastion built along the cliffs. A collection of European brass cannons from the 18th and 19th centuries lines the walkway here and you'll also get great views out to sea and gorgeous sunsets.

Skala du Port
HISTORIC BUILDING

(adult/child Dh10/5; ⊙9am-5.30pm, fish auction 3-5pm Mon-Sat) Down by the harbour, the Skala offers more cannons and picturesque views over the fishing port and the Île de Mogador. Looking back at the walled me-dina from here, through a curtain of swirl-ing seagulls, you'll get the same evocative picture that is used on nearly all official literature.

The large working port is a bustling place with plenty of activity throughout the day. Along with the flurry of boats, nets being repaired and the day's catch being landed you can see traditional wooden boats being made. The boat-builders supply fishing ves-sels for the entire Moroccan coast and even as far away as France, as the design is par-ticularly seaworthy. It's also worth visiting the **fish auction**, which takes place in the market hall just outside the port gates.

Île de Mogador
ISLAND

(boats from Port du Peche) Just off the coast to the southwest is the Île de Mogador, which has some interesting structures. It's actu-ally two islands and several tiny islets – also known as the famed Îles Purpuraires (Purple Isles) of antiquity. The uninhabited islands are a sanctuary for Eleonora's falcons, which can also be easily seen through binoculars from Essaouira beach.

It is possible to arrange a private boat trip to the islands outside the breeding season, but you need to obtain a permit (free) from the port office; with that in hand, head for the small fishing boats to negotiate the trip out there. If you want to stay a few hours, fix a time for the boat to come and pick you up.

Sidi Mohammed Ben Abdallah Museum
MUSEUM

(✆0524 47 53 00; Rue Laâlouj; adult/child Dh10/5) Essaouira's beautifully refurbished museum in an old riad has a small but interesting collection of jewellery, costumes, weapons, amazing musical instruments and carpets of the region. There's a section explaining the signs and symbols used by local craftspeople and some interesting photographs of Es-saouira at the turn of the century. Note also the Roman and Phoenician objects found in the bay.

🏃 Activities

Organised horse- and camel-riding is based a few kilometres south of Essaouira in Dia-bat (p218).

Beach
BEACH

Essaouira's wide, sandy beach is a great place for walking, but the strong winds and currents mean it's not so good for sunbath-ing or swimming. Footballers, windsurfers and kitesurfers take over the town end of the beach, while fiercely competitive horse and camel owners ply the sands further on. They can be quite insistent, so be firm if you don't want to take a ride (and bargain hard if you do).

If you're walking, head south across the Ksob River (impassable at high tide) to see the ruins of the **Borj el-Berod**, an old for-tress and pavilion that's partially covered in sand. Local legend has it that this was the original inspiration for the Jimi Hendrix classic 'Castles Made of Sand' (see p214). From here you can walk inland to the village of Diabat or continue along the sands to the sand dunes of Cap Sim.

Océan Vagabond
WATER SPORTS

(✆0524 78 39 34; www.oceanvagabond.com; ⊙9am-6pm) This outfit gives two-hour surf-ing lessons (adult/child Dh385/330), as well as longer kitesurfing (Dh2310, six hours) and windsurfing (four hours, Dh1000) lessons. It also rents out equipment for all three. It has a cool cafe-restaurant on the beach, with a laid-back terrace.

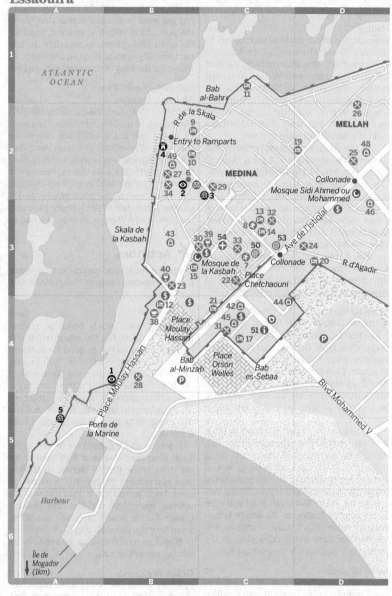

Map labels:

ATLANTIC OCEAN

Bab al-Bahr
R. de la Skala
Entry to Ramparts
MELLAH
MEDINA
Collonade
Mosque Sidi Ahmed ou Mohammed
Skala de la Kasbah
Mosque de la Kasbah
Place Chefchaouni
Ave de l'Istiqlal
Collonade
R d'Agadir
Place Moulay Hassan
Bab al-Minzah
Place Orson Welles
Bab es-Sebaa
Blvd Mohammed V
Porte de la Marine
Harbour
Île de Mogador (1km)

Hammam Lalla Mira HAMMAM
(☎0524 47 59 07; www.lallamira.net; 14 Rue d'Algerie; hammam with gommage Dh75; ☺women 9.30am-7pm, men 7-10pm) One of the oldest, this restored hammam is heated by solar energy and, although it's aimed at tourists, it has a wonderful traditional interior. Good-value massages with argan oil. If you're not staying at this guesthouse, you'll need to make a reservation for the hammam.

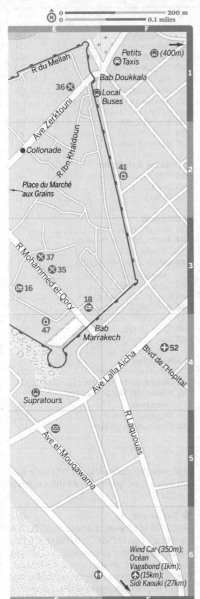

Hammam Riad el-Madina   HAMMAM

(📞0524 47 59 07; 9 Rue el-Attarine; admission Dh70, massage from Dh300; ☺women 9-10am & 3-4pm, mixed 10am-12.30pm & 4-7pm) Another good place to break a first sweat.

🎓 Courses

L'Atelier Madada   COOKING

(📞0524 47 55 12; www.lateliermadada.com; 5 Rue Youssef el-Fassi; ☺10.30am-5pm) A former warehouse is the setting for this beautifully presented cookery school with places for eight people per session. Learn the secrets of tajines and couscous in the morning (Dh450, including lunch), or Moroccan patisserie in the afternoon (Dh200). The courses are presented in English and French.

Alliance Franco-Marocaine   LANGUAGE

(📞0524 47 61 97; www.ambafrance-ma.org/in stitut/afm-essaouira/index.cfm; Derb Lâalaouj, 9 Rue Mohammed Diouri; ☺9am-12.30pm & 2.30-6.30pm Mon-Fri) Offers semester-long French classes and eight-week Arabic classes as well as regular films, exhibitions and cultural events.

👉 Tours

Ecotourisme & Randonnées   HIKING

(📞0615 76 21 31; www.essaouira-randonnees.com/; Rue Houmman El Fatouaki, Restaurant La Découverte) Offers hiking tours in the countryside outside Essaouira (Dh200/450 half-/full-day tours), including to local argan groves, the Sidi M'Bark waterfall and the Ksob River. Strong on birdwatching.

✨ Festivals

Essaouira has two major festivals that draw hoards of performers and spectators to town.

Gnaoua & World Music Festival   MUSIC

(www.festival-gnaoua.net; ☺3rd weekend Jun) Essaouira overflows every year for the celebrated Gnaoua & World Music Festival, a four-day extravaganza with concerts on Pl Moulay Hassan, Bab Doukkala and elsewhere.

Festival des Andalousies Atlantiques   MUSIC

(www.facebook.com/FestivalDesAndalousiesAtlan tiques; ☺late Oct) An eclectic mix of Andalucian music, art and dance by local and international performers.

Hammam de la Kasbah   HAMMAM

(7 Rue de Marrakesh; admission Dh10; ☺6am-8.30pm) This is the place for a more traditional, local hammam experience. Women only.

Essaouira

🛌 Sleeping

Accommodation in Essaouira isn't cheap but there's now a seemingly endless selection of properties to choose from at all price levels. Most hotels and riads are within the walls of the medina, so everything you need is within walking distance. In summer book ahead or at least arrive early in the day to find a room. As the medina gets increasingly crowded, hotels are being built along the coast further south and on the seafront.

Essaouira has a great selection of apartments and riads to rent, most of them done up in impeccable style. If you're travelling as a family or in a group, they can be an affordable and flexible option. Prices start from about Dh600 per night for a two-bed apartment. **Jack's Apartments** (☑0524 47 55 38; www.jackapartments.com; 1 Pl Moulay Hassan) has a good selection of rental options available.

★ **Dar Afram** B&B €
(☑0524 78 56 57; www.dar-afram.com; 10 Rue Sidi Magdoul; s/d from Dh150/300, tr Dh500; ☋) This extremely friendly guesthouse has simple, spotless en-suite rooms with a funky vibe. The Aussie-Moroccan owners are musicians and an impromptu session often follows the evening meals shared around a communal table. Deservedly popular.

★ **Hôtel Les Matins Bleus** RIAD €
(☑0524 78 53 63; www.les-matins-bleus.com; 22 Rue de Drâa; s/d/tr incl breakfast Dh315/490/670, ste Dh800) Hidden down a dead-end street, this charming hotel has traditionally styled rooms surrounding a central courtyard

painted in soothing grey-blues and sage. The rooms all have plain white walls, with lovely local fabrics. Breakfast is served on the sheltered terrace from where you'll get good views over the medina. Guests are offered free cookery classes.

Hôtel Beau Rivage HOTEL €

(☑0524 47 59 25; beaurivage@menara.ma; 14 Pl Moulay Hassan; s/d/tr incl breakfast Dh270/390/510; ☎) A friendly hotel in a perfect spot, overlooking the main square. The Beau Rivage has bright, cheerful rooms with modern fittings and spotless bathrooms. The rooms overlooking the square can be noisy but offer the greatest spectacle in town, while breakfast is served on the charming and quiet roof terrace with views over the port and town.

Riad Nakhla RIAD €

(☑tel/fax 0524 47 49 40; www.essaouiranet.com/riad-nakhla; 2 Rue d'Agadir; s/d/ste incl breakfast Dh230/360/500; ☎) Riad Nakhla looks like any other budget place from the outside, but inside the weary traveller is met with a beautiful courtyard, with elegant stone columns and a fountain trickling, more what you'd expect from a hotel in a higher price bracket. The well-appointed bedrooms are simple but comfortable and immaculately kept, full of local flavour with shuttered windows. Breakfast on the roof terrace with views over the ocean and town is another treat. Amazingly, the owners haven't changed their prices in years.

Riad Etoile d'Essaouira GUESTHOUSE €

(☑0524 47 20 07; www.riadetoiledessaouira.com; 2 Rue Kadissiya, Ave Sidi Mohammed ben Abdallah; s/d/tr/ste Dh385/495/660/990; ☎) Here's a newly opened guesthouse that's comfortably appointed and brightly decorated with local fabrics. It's in the *mellah* quarter of the medina. All rooms have TVs, and some are designed for families.

Dar Al-Bahar GUESTHOUSE €

(☑0524 47 68 31; www.daralbahar.com; 1 Rue Touahen; d without/with sea view Dh550/660, ste Dh880) The rooms at this lovely medina guesthouse are elegantly simple, with plain white walls, wrought-iron furniture and a contrasting touch of blue, pink, green or yellow in the traditional bedspreads and curtains. Local art adorns the walls and the views from the terrace overlooking the ocean are magnificent.

Hôtel Souiri HOTEL €

(☑0524 47 53 59; www.hotelsouiri.com; 37 Rue el-Attarine; s/d Dh250/360, without bathroom Dh150/300; ☎) A run-of-the mill budget hotel, Souiri has decent if unexciting rooms, but a handy location. Popular with tour groups.

★ Dar Adul GUESTHOUSE €€

(☑0524 47 39 10; www.dar-adul.com; 63 Rue Touahen; d Dh660-880, ste Dh1300; ☎) This lovingly restored house has just a few comfy rooms with subtle lighting, beautiful furniture and little touches that make it feel like a home rather than a hotel. The simple white walls are lifted by the brightly painted woodwork, and many colourful paintings by the owner. The staff are incredibly friendly – you'll feel more like family than a paying guest by the time you leave. Dinner is available here on request.

Lalla Mira HOTEL €€

(☑0524 47 50 46; www.lallamira.net; 14 Rue d'Algerie; s/d/ste Dh436/692/920; @) This gorgeous little place has simple rooms with ochre *tadelakt* walls, wrought-iron furniture, natural fabrics and solar-powered underfloor heating. The hotel also has a great hammam and a good restaurant (mains Dh90 to Dh120) serving a decent selection of vegetarian food.

★ Madada GUESTHOUSE €€€

(☑0524 47 55 12; www.madada.com; 5 Rue Youssef el-Fassi; r Dh1250, ste Dh1850; ☎) With five rooms and two suites, this is a stylish addition to the Essaouira accommodation scene, opting for muted greys and browns and reds. Some rooms have terraces to catch the Atlantic breeze, others have unusual semi-open-plan bedrooms-bathrooms, so are best shared with someone you already know pretty well.

Palais Heure Bleue RIAD €€€

(☑0524 47 42 22; www.heure-bleue.com; 2 Rue Ibn Batouta; d/ste Dh3300/5850; ❈☎▣) A decided hush falls as you walk through the doors of the Heure Bleue, Essaouira's top hotel. This swish riad has everything you could ever want, from a rooftop swimming pool to its own private cinema and billiard room. Chic European style and colonial charm meet in the lounge, where a grand piano sits beneath trophy heads from a long-forgotten hunting trip, and in the bedrooms where zebra prints, dark woods and marble counter tops vie for attention.

ATLANTIC COAST ESSAOUIRA

JIMI HENDRIX: CASTLES OF SAND OR PIE IN THE SKY?

There are a few stories that you might hear in Essaouira. That Jimi Hendrix lived here on and off for a few years in the 1960s. That he owned a riad that you can now stay in, or maybe it's a restaurant you can eat at. He stayed in quite a few other riads. He stayed in a campervan, or perhaps a tent. He tried to buy Île de Mogador. He composed 'Castles Made of Sand' here. He signed a photo of himself that now graces the walls of a local restaurant. He wanted to adopt a Moroccan boy. He sired various children. He shared a room with Timothy Leary.

You can hear all of these stories in Essaouira – but they're all bunkum. Hendrix did visit Morocco for about a week, once only, in July 1969, with his then girlfriend, Colette Mimram, and spent two or three days in Essaouira. But he didn't even bring a guitar. This was 18 months after the album containing the song 'Castles Made of Sand' was released.

And that photo, signed *A mon ami Sam, 63'* is quite simply a forgery!

Villa Maroc GUESTHOUSE €€€
(☑ 0524 47 61 47; www.villa-maroc.com; 10 Rue Abdallah Ben Yassine; r Dh1000-1650) Housed in a large converted 18th-century townhouse, the Villa Maroc is a model of restrained chic, with airy whitewashed rooms offset by carefully chosen wood, wicker and fabrics. The terrace offers great views, while the in-house hamman is as well-regarded for pampering as the ground-floor restaurant is for intimate dining.

✗ Eating

For morning croissants or an afternoon pastry the best places to go are **Pâtisserie Driss** (near Pl Moulay Hassan), which has a hidden seating area at the back, and **Café Faid** (near Pl Moulay Hassan). There are plenty of snack stands and hole-in-the-wall-type places along Ave Sidi Mohammed ben Abdallah, Ave Zerktouni and just inside Bab Doukkala.

Outdoor Fish Grill Stands SEAFOOD €
(port end of Pl Moulay Hassan; fish, bread & salad from Dh40) These unpretentious stands offer one of the definitive Essaouira experiences. Just choose what you want to eat from the colourful displays of freshly caught fish and shellfish at each grill, and wait for it to be cooked on the spot and served with a pile of bread and salad.

Vagues Bleus ITALIAN €
(☑ 0611 28 37 91; 2 Rue Sidi Ben Abdellah; mains Dh40-50; ⊙ noon-3.30pm & 6.30-9pm) This tiny hidden gem is unbeatable value – as well as great pasta (the lasagne is recommended), there are inventive mains like escalopes with lemon and thyme butter and crushed pota-

toes. Mains come with entrée salads and shots of fresh fruit and veggie juices.

Restaurant La Découverte MOROCCAN €
(☑ 0524 47 31 58; 8 bis, Rue Houmman El Fatouaki; mains from Dh50) A small, friendly French-run restaurant, offering a mix of Franco-Moroccan dishes. The *briouates* (stuffed filo pastry rolls) are particularly good, as are the creamy desserts.

Pasta Baladin ITALIAN €
(48 Rue Laalouj; mains from Dh65; ⊙ noon-2pm & 7-11pm Tue-Sun) Wooden bench-style seating gets you friendly with your fellow diners at this cheery Italian place. The pasta is pretty simple (a choice of four or five sauces and pastas), but it's perfectly cooked and quickly served, with plenty of parmesan on the side. Unsurprisingly popular.

Fish Souq SEAFOOD €
(off Ave de l'Istiqlal; fish, bread & salad Dh30) For a medina alternative to the fish grills near the port, visit the fish souq to buy some of the day's catch and take it to one of the grill stands in the southern corner. It'll come back cooked and served with bread and salad.

Café d'Horloge CAFE €
(Pl Chefchaouni; amlou & crêpes/bread Dh25) Set on the attractive square beneath the clocktower, this popular cafe is an excellent choice for a breakfast of *amlou* (a spread made of local argan oil, almond and honey) and crêpes or bread.

★**Elizir** MEDITERRANEAN €€
(☑ 0524 47 21 03; 1 Rue Agadir; mains Dh130-160; ⊙ 7.30-10.30pm) Elizir's unprepossessing

entrance gives way to an Aladdin's cave of 1970s Arabic junkyard chic, packed with old vinyl records, prints and cool-kitsch decor. Mains are deliciously inventive – try chicken tajine with figs and gorgonzola, or gnocchi with almond pesto and the like, with well-presented cooked Moroccan salad entrées included. Alcohol is served, and pre-booking strongly advised.

★ **Riad Al-Baraka**   MOROCCAN €€
(☑ 0524 47 35 61; 113 Rue Mohammed el-Qory; mains Dh110; ☉ lunch & dinner) Set in a former Jewish school, this hip place has several dining rooms and a bar set around a large courtyard shaded by a huge fig tree. The food is mainly Moroccan with some Middle Eastern and Jewish influences, the decor is cool, and there's live music by local bands at weekends.

La Cantina   INTERNATIONAL €€
(☑ 0524 47 45 17; 66 Rue Noutouil; ☉ 11am-7pm; ☑) Even we like a change from tajines and couscous sometimes, and if you do too try this place in the *mellah* that serves up the self-proclaimed 'best burgers in North Africa', bowls of chilli, jacket potatoes and stir-fries. Very strong on vegetarian options (veggie burgers and chilli are both highlights), and also a good place for a pot of tea and a slice of homemade cake, courtesy of the English owners.

Restaurant El-Minzah   MOROCCAN, SEAFOOD €€
(☑ 0524 47 53 08; 3 Ave Oqba ben Nafii; mains Dh85-130, set menus from Dh95; ☉ lunch & dinner) Sit on the outside terrace or in the elegant dining room inside at this popular place facing the ramparts. The menu features a good selection of international dishes with specialities such as blue shark and fresh fish, and there's lively Gnaoua music here on Saturday nights.

Restaurant Ferdaous   MOROCCAN €€
(☑ 0524 47 36 55; 27 Rue Abdesslam Lebadi; mains Dh60-80, set menu Dh105; ☉ lunch & dinner Tue-Sun) A delightful Moroccan restaurant, and one of the few places in town that serves real, home-cooked, traditional Moroccan food. The seasonal menu offers an innovative take on traditional recipes, the service is very friendly and the low tables and padded seating make it feel like the real McCoy.

Restaurante Les Alizés   MOROCCAN €€
(☑ 0524 47 68 19; 26 bis Rue de la Skala; mains Dh120; ☉ lunch & dinner) This popular place, run by a charming Moroccan couple in a 19th-century house, has delicious Moroccan dishes, particularly the couscous with fish and the tajine of *boulettes de sardines* (sardine balls). You'll get a very friendly welcome, and it's a good idea to book ahead. It's above Hôtel Smara.

La Table Madada   MEDITERRANEAN €€€
(☑ 0524 47 55 12; www.madada.com; 5 Rue Youssef el-Fassi; mains from Dh150; ☎) Long-established dinner favourite. Deep-purple seating, warm stone arches and giant lampshades dominate this trendy restaurant that serves well-cooked and original Mediterranean and Moroccan dishes. The cooking school L'Atelier Madada is attached, if you feel inspired after dinner.

La Licorne   MOROCCAN €€€
(☑ 0524 47 36 26; 26 Rue de la Skala; menu Dh160; ☉ dinner) This is a cosy place with a most un-Essaouiran feel – wooden beams and heavy chairs give it the ambience of a hunting lodge. A no-nonsense, standard Moroccan menu of tajines is served up by friendly staff.

Drinking

Essaouira isn't the hottest place for nightlife. To warm up for an evening out, you could visit the **alcohol shops** (Blvd Moulay Youssef; ☉ 9am-12.30pm & 3-6pm) just outside the medina near Bab Doukkala and take your drinks to your hotel terrace to watch the sun go down.

Le Patio   BAR
(28 Rue Moulay Rachid; ☉ dinner Tue-Sun) For something sultry, this hip bar and restaurant is a candlelit den with blood-red furnishings and a black mirror ball. You'll need to buy some tapas (Dh35) to just sit and drink or you might even be tempted by the whiff of grilled fish coming from the canopied restaurant (mains from Dh90).

Taros   BAR
(2 Rue de la Skala; ☉ noon-11pm) A great place for a sundowner, with a terrace looking over the square and port. There's often live music, too, and there's a decent fishy menu if you want to eat. It's also good for afternoon tea, or a drink at the bar.

Café Restaurant Bab Laachour   CAFE
(Pl Moulay Hassan; ☉ noon-11pm) Try the terrace here, but beer is served in the evenings only.

ESSAOUIRA ART NAÏF

Wherever you go in Essaouira, you'll see artists at work, and their paintings for sale in almost every shop. The local artists were influenced by the influx of Westerners in the 1970s and developed their own style of naive paintings, mostly using acrylics. It's a mixture of naive and modern art, often influenced by the Gnawa movement, and the artists are self-taught. The paintings are brightly coloured and often feature musicians or groups of singers.

Shopping

Essaouira has a reputation as an artists' hub, and you'll find several galleries selling works by local painters. It's a mixed bag of talent and you may need to look in all the galleries before finding something you like.

Woodcarving Workshops ARTS & CRAFTS
Essaouira is well known for its woodwork and you can visit a string of shops near the Skala de la Ville. However, the marquetry work is made from local fragrant thuya wood, which is now an endangered species – buying anything made from thuya threatens the last remaining stands of trees by increasing demand and therefore encouraging illegal logging.

Coopérative Artisanal des Marqueteurs ARTS & CRAFTS
(6 Rue Khalid ibn Oualid) Come here for fixed-price shopping.

Rafia Craft ARTS & CRAFTS
(82 Rue d'Agadir) Along with woodwork, Essaouira's other great product is its raffia work, made from the fibres of the doum palm. Much of its line is sold to European outlets.

Spice Souq FOOD & DRINK
This is the place to go for herbal Viagra, Berber lipstick, cures for baldness and exotic spices. You can also buy argan-oil products here, as well as the traditional *amlou* (about Dh40 per bottle).

Jewellery Souq JEWELLERY
A small area of jewellery shops with everything from heavy Berber beads to gaudy gold.

Galeries d'Art Damgaard ARTS & CRAFTS
(www.galeriedamgaard.com; Ave Oqba ben Nafii) This gallery is the best and oldest in town and features the work of local artists.

Association Tilal des Arts Plastiques ARTS & CRAFTS
(☑5247 47 54 24; 4 Rue de Caire) For up-and-coming artists.

Espace Othello ARTS & CRAFTS
(☑5247 47 50 95; 9 Rue Mohammed Layachi; ☻9am-1pm & 3-8pm) Up-and-coming artists.

❶ Information

DANGERS & ANNOYANCES

Essaouira is still mostly a safe, relaxed tourist town but you should be on your guard in the backstreets of the *mellah* after dark, where there are problems with drugs and drinking north of Ave Zerktouni and east of Ave Sidi Mohammed ben Abdallah, making this the least salubrious part of town.

EMERGENCIES

Medical Emergencies (☑0524 47 57 16; ☻24hr)
Police Station (☑024 78 48 80, 19; Rue du Caire) Opposite the tourist office.

INTERNET ACCESS

There are internet cafes all over town. Most open from 9am to 11pm and charge up to Dh10 per hour.
Cyber Les Remparts (12 Rue du Rif)
Mogador Informatique (5 Ave de l'Istiqlal)

MEDICAL SERVICES

Hôpital Sidi Mohammed ben Abdallah (☑0524 47 57 16; Blvd de l'Hôpital) For emergencies.
Pharmacie la Kasbah (☑0524 47 51 51; 12-14 Rue Allal ben Abdellah) Pharmacy.

MONEY

There are several banks with ATMs and exchange facilities around Pl Moulay Hassan and along the main road leading northeast to Bab Doukkala.

POST

Main Post Office (Ave el-Mouqawama; ☻8.30am-4.15pm Mon-Fri, 8am-noon Sat)
Post Office (Rue Laâlouj; ☻8.30am-4pm Mon-Fri)

TOURIST INFORMATION

The tourist office (and many hotels) can provide free maps of Essaouira, as well as the free quarterly listings mag *Guide d'Essaouira* (in English/French).

Délégation du Tourisme (☑0524 78 35 32; www.essaouira.com; 10 Rue du Caire; ☉8.30am-6.30pm)

ⓘ Getting There & Away

AIR

Daily direct flights with RAM to Casablanca leave from **Aéroport de Mogador** (☑0524 47 67 04; Rte d'Agadir), 15km south of town. There are also flights several times a week to Paris and Brussels.

BUS

The **bus station** (☑0524 78 52 41) is about 400m northeast of the medina, an easy walk during the day but better in a petit taxi (Dh10) if you're arriving/leaving late at night. The **left-luggage office** (Dh7 per item) is open 24 hours. CTM buses leave from a separate office, a Dh10 petit-taxi ride from the medina.

CTM destinations include Agadir (Dh60, 3½ hours), Casablanca (Dh150, seven hours), El-Jadida (Dh100, five hours) and Marrakesh (Dh70, 2½ hours).

Other companies run cheaper and more frequent buses to the same destinations as well as Taroudannt (Dh80, six hours) and Tan Tan (Dh130, six hours).

Supratours, the ONCF subsidiary, runs coaches to Marrakesh train station (Dh75, 2½ hours, five daily) to connect with trains to Casablanca from the station near Bab Marrakech. There's also a Dh100 'comfort plus' service once a day, and a daily departure to Agadir (Dh65, 2½ hours). Book in advance for these services, particularly in summer.

Local bus 5 to Diabat (Dh5) and Sidi Kaouki (Dh6) leaves from Blvd Moulay Youssef outside Bab Doukkala. There are about eight services a day.

TAXI

The grand-taxi rank lies immediately west of the bus station. Fares include Sidi Kaouki (Dh10, 15 minutes), Marrakesh (Dh75, 2½ hours) and Agadir (Dh70, two hours).

ⓘ Getting Around

To get to the airport take bus 2, which passes the airport turning (Dh10, 15 minutes), or a grand taxi (Dh200). The blue petits taxis are a good idea for getting to and from the bus station (Dh10) but they can't enter the medina. If you're happy to walk but don't want to carry your bags, there are plenty of enterprising men with luggage carts who will wheel your bags directly to your hotel (for about Dh20).

Cars can be hired from **Wind Car** (☑tel/fax 0524 47 28 04; Rue Princesse Lalla Amina) for around Dh450 per day. **Avis** (☑0524 47 49 26) also has an office at the airport.

ARGAN OIL

Organic argan oil is 'the new olive oil', increasingly used in hip restaurants around the world to season salads with its nutty flavour. The wrinkled argan tree is unique to this part of the world and, as a result, the argan forests of the Souss Valley and the Haha Coast south of Essaouira have been designated by Unesco as a biosphere reserve.

The tree, *Argania spinosa,* is resistant to heat and survives temperatures up to 50°C, so is an essential tool in the fight against desertification in southern Morocco. It has become vital to the local economy, providing firewood, fodder for the goats – you can see them actually climb into the branches – and oil for humans. Berber women harvest the fruits in spring. They then feed them to goats, whose digestive juices dissolve the tough elastic coating on the shell. The nuts are then recovered from the goats' dung, and the kernels are split, lightly toasted, pulped and pressed.

To produce just one litre of oil takes 30kg of nuts and 15 hours of manual labour, solely done by women. In a recent change to this tradition, some cooperatives have decided to cut the goats out of the process and are hand-picking fruits from the trees to produce a more subtle-tasting oil.

The Berbers have long used argan oil to heal, but modern research suggests that the oil may help reduce cholesterol and prevent arteriosclerosis. In the kitchen its rich and sweet nutty flavour works wonders as a salad dressing, or added to grilled vegetables or tajines. Berbers mix it with ground almonds and honey to make *amlou,* a delicacy believed to have aphrodisiac properties.

Cold-pressed oil from untoasted nuts is increasingly recognised as a prized cosmetic, particularly for the hair. The oil has a high vitamin E content, which makes it a great addition to anti-wrinkle creams.

Around Essaouira

If you have your own transport, it's worth taking a trip to one of the small women's co-operatives around Essaouira that sell argan products, natural cosmetics and foodstuffs. Try **Assafar Imitaghant** (☑0661 55 35 86), 8km from town on the road to Marrakesh, or the **Coóperative Tiguemine** (☑0524 79 01 10), 7km further on. The tourist office has a full list of places to visit. Best of all, travel south to the village of **Tamanar** to see the whole argan process at the Coopérative Amal.

Diabat الديابات

The sleepy Berber village of Diabat, just south of Essaouira, was once a dope-smoking colony popular with hippies. Today it is the site of a major new tourist development, Golf Mogador, not fully completed at the time of research. Comprising three luxury hotels and villas, the resort has a golf course designed by Gary Player. Fortunately the grey water from the complex will be used to water the course.

Activities

To try something more serious than the horse and camel rides on the beach, several companies offer cross-country trekking and multiday rides in the countryside around Essaouira. Tailor-made horse trips can be arranged through the following outfits.

Zouina Cheval   HORSE RIDING
(☑0669 80 71 01; www.zouina-cheval.com; 1hr ride Dh160, day incl picnic Dh600, treks 2/5 days Dh1900/6000) This outfit is owned and run by Najib and Sophie, highly qualified and experienced instructors who cater for all levels, including children and beginners. Longer horse trekking and camping trips are available.

La Maison du Chameau   CAMEL TREK
(☑0661 34 71 08; www.lamaisonduchameau. fr; Douar Al Arab; per hr Dh 140, per day incl lunch Dh550) This remote guesthouse is home to eight *meharis* (white Sudanese racing camels). The guesthouse offers weeklong camel-riding courses, shorter excursions and a selection of peaceful rooms decked out in vibrant fuchsia pink and electric blue. It's 7km along Rte de Marrakesh.

Ranch de Diabat   HORSE RIDING
(☑0662 29 72 03; www.ranchdediabat.com; 1hr lesson Dh165, 8-day trek incl accommodation Dh8800) Horse-riding lessons for adults and children, and excursions from an hour to wide-ranging weeklong treks. Camel rides also available.

Sleeping

Auberge Tangaro   GUESTHOUSE €€
(☑0524 78 47 84; www.aubergetangaro.com; r incl breakfast Dh600-900, ste from Dh1100; 🔊) If you want to stay in Diabat, your best bet is this rustic and remote old house in a serene location, close to the golf course. The rooms here are chic and all beautifully decorated (each has its own open fireplace) and the whole house is romantically lit by candlelight at night. Dinner is available, and there's a hammam.

Getting There & Away

To get to Diabat from Essaouira drive south on the coast road to Agadir and turn right just after the bridge about 7km out of town. Alternatively, local bus 5 leaves from outside Bab Marrakech (Dh5, every two hours).

Sidi Kaouki سيدي كاوكي

The constant blustery winds, wild beach and decent accommodation at Sidi Kaouki are fast turning it into one of Morocco's top windsurfing and surfing spots. It's not for the faint-hearted and the waters here can be dangerous for the inexperienced, but even if you don't take to the water it's a chilled escape from Essaouira.

The large building on the rocks, washed by the sea, is the final resting place of Sufi saint Sidi Kaouki who was known for his healing abilities. People still visit the shrine. You can rent a horse (Dh120 per hour) or a camel (Dh100 per hour) and ride along the long stretch of beautiful beach. For water sports, the quintessential surfers' hang-out on the beach is **Station Sidi Kaouki** (☑0672 04 40 16; www.sidi-kaouki.com), a brightly decorated cafe and restaurant with a cool vibe. You can arrange lessons and hire surfing, windsurfing and kitesurfing gear here or at **Mogasurf** (☑0618 91 04 31; www.mogasurf. com). Daily rental rates start at Dh55 (kite-surf) and Dh220 (surfboard).

A clutch of guesthouses is set back from the beachfront. They all serve dinner.

🛏 Sleeping & Eating

By the central square/parking area, there's a cluster of near-identical cafe-restaurants that serve up tajines, seafood, pasta and omelettes.

Le Dauphin Hôtel   HOTEL €
(☑0524 47 67 32; hoteldauphin@gmail.com; s/d without bathroom Dh150/200) This is a good-value backpacker option, with clean basic rooms, shared bathroom facilities and a cafe-restaurant out front.

La Pergola   HOTEL €
(☑0524 78 58 31; s/d/tr Dh200/300/500) A simple and uncluttered but fresh hotel option, with a terrace and a garden area (with restaurant) that's great for lounging. Many rooms have sea views.

Auberge de la Plage   GUESTHOUSE €€
(☑0524 47 66 00, 0661 10 26 64; www.kaouki.com; s/d/tr with bathroom incl breakfast Dh350/450/500) This delightful house has comfortable rooms with sea views. A couple of the rooms have shared bathrooms. Dinner can be ordered in advance and alcohol is served. The menu depends on what the local fishermen have caught. The garden is a shady haven, while there's nowhere better than the roof terrace to watch the sunset.

Hotel Le Kaouki   GUESTHOUSE €€
(☑0524 78 32 06; www.sidikaouki.com; s/d/tr incl half board Dh330/550/730) Decorated in bright blue with local fabrics, this is also a good choice. The staff are friendly and welcoming. There's electricity on the ground floor only, but the night-time candles give a romantic atmosphere.

Al-Vent   MOROCCAN €
(☑0623 83 66 15) A rustic setting for the chilled surfer crowd, Al-Vent serves up good breakfasts, simple lunches and seafood (and vegetarian) dinners with a minimum of fuss for maximum relaxation. Has long-term rooms for rent in the village.

ⓘ Getting There & Away

Sidi Kaouki is about 25km south of Essaouira. Bus 2 or 5 (Dh6) leaves from outside Bab Marrakech every two hours. A grand taxi will cost around Dh10 and takes 30 minutes.

ATLANTIC COAST AROUND ESSAOUIRA

Mediterranean Coast & the Rif

شاطئ‌البحر المتوسط و منطقة الرف

Best Places to Eat

➡ Art et Gourmet (p232)
➡ Club Nautique (p264)
➡ Auberge Dardara (p259)

Best Places to Stay

➡ Dar Nour (p229)
➡ Casa Perleta (p256)
➡ El Reducto (p249)

Why Go?

Northern Morocco offers a beautiful coastline, a mountainous hinterland rarely explored by visitors and just one major city. The beguiling gateway to Africa, Tangier has emerged from its shady past to become a tantalising experience. Eastward lies one of the last stretches of undeveloped Mediterranean coast with high cliffs and sandy coves.

Tetouan and Al-Hoceima reflect former Spanish protectorate days in architecture and food. More still can be found in the Spanish enclaves of Ceuta and Melilla with their medieval fortifications and spectacular architectural treasures. Ranging over the mountains inland are magnificent national parks, from the coastal Al-Hoceima to the remote Beni-Snassen, that beg to be discovered.

Go soon: the coastal highway is complete, and resorts are blooming in Martil, M'Diq and Saïdia, and these developments are changing the coastline irrevocably.

When to Go
Tangier

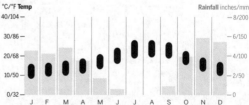

Apr Spring is perfect for trekking in the Rif or exploring national parks.

Jul Head to Chefchaouen for the annual arts festival.

Sep Mediterranean beaches await, without the crowds.

SPAIN · Tarifa

Cap Spartel

Strait of Gibraltar

Jebel Musa (842m)

MEDITERRANEAN SEA

ALGERIA

0 — 50 km
0 — 30 miles

Mediterranean Coast & the Rif Highlights

1 Dream the day away at a pavement cafe beneath the kasbah in Chefchaouen's **Plaza Uta el-Hammam** (p253)

2 Browse Tangier's myriad art galleries and stop for coffee at the **Petit Socco** (p223), haunt of the Beat poets

3 Marvel at the dragons launching from the roof of a palace in **Ceuta** (p242)

4 Wander the streets of **Melilla** (p270) and gaze at the Modernist buildings, before tapas for lunch

5 Discover Roman mosaics from Lixus in Tetouan's **Archaeology Museum** (p247)

6 Soak up the sun on the remote beaches of **Al-Hoceima National Park** (p265)

7 Take in remarkable views as you trek to Berber villages in the **Talassemtane National Park** (p266) in the Rif Mountains

WEST MEDITERRANEAN COAST

الشاطِ ءُ الغرب للبحر الأبضُّ المتوسط

Tangier

طنجة

POP 850,000

Always of huge strategic importance at the entrance to the Mediterranean, Tangier is the enthralling gateway to Africa, a tantalising introduction to a culture vastly different from that across the Strait of Gibraltar.

After WWII, Tangier became an International Zone that attracted eccentric foreigners, artists, spies and hippies. The city fell into neglect and dissolution, gaining a dismal reputation thanks to the sleaze and hustles that beset every arrival. But now the white city has turned over a new leaf, and is looking to the future with renewed vigour.

With the arrival of the new monarch in 1999 and his forward-thinking ideas about commerce and tourism, suddenly the community woke up to the potential of this great city. There's a spanking new port of enormous proportions, a new business district and a revamped airport. Buildings have been renovated, beaches cleaned up and hustlers chivvied off the streets. There's an explosion of cultural activities as well as some great places to stay and excellent restaurants.

Tangier is divided into an old walled city, or medina, a nest of medieval alleyways, and a new, modern city, the ville nouvelle. The medina contains a kasbah, the walled fortress of the sultan, which forms its western corner; the Petit Socco (also known as Socco Chico and Souq Dakhel), a historic plaza in the centre; and of course, the souqs, or markets. The much more impressive Grand Socco (officially renamed Pl du 9 Avril 1947), a pleasant square with a central fountain, is the hinge between the two sides of town, and the postcard entrance to the medina.

History

Tangier's history is a raucous tale of foreign invasion, much of it driven by the city's strategic location at the entrance to the Mediterranean. The area was first settled as a trading base by the ancient Greeks and Phoenicians (who brought the traditional Moroccan hooded robe, the jellaba, with them), and named for the goddess Tinge, the lover of Hercules, whose Herculean effort separated Europe from Africa to form the Strait of Gibraltar. Under Roman rule, it was the capital of the province of Mauretania Tingitana. The Vandals attacked from Spain in AD 429, followed by the Byzantines, and then the Arabs, who invaded in 705 and quelled the Berber tribes. Tangier passed between various Arab factions before finally coming under Almohad rule in 1149. Then the Portuguese arrived, capturing the city on their second attempt in 1471, only to hand it to the British 200 years later as a wedding gift for Charles II. Its value is difficult to assess: the English diarist Samuel Pepys called it 'the excrescence of the earth'. Moroccans

---

TANGIER IN...

One Day

Starting in the kasbah, take a wander through the **Kasbah Museum**, and a meander down the medina streets. Don't miss the treasure-trove of **Boutique Majid** before lunch at **Le Nabab**. The **Grand Socco** is the perfect place for mint tea. Wander up to **St Andrew's Church** for a spot of gravestone reading, then take in the latest art exhibition at **Centre Culturel Ibn Khaldoun** before heading to **El-Minzah Wellness** for a hammam. A drink in the **Caid's Bar** is followed by dinner at **Art et Gourmet**, before heading to **Le Tangerine** just like a Beat poet.

Two Days

Discover the vibe of the new city with breakfast at the plush **La Giralda**, where you can check the views over to Spain from **Terrasse des Paresseux**. Head to **Librairie des Colonnes** to browse the historic bookshop before a fishy lunch at **Populaire Saveur de Poisson**. A post-prandial stroll through the **Mendoubia Gardens** is perfect, followed by a photo-opportunity visit to the **fresh produce market**. Just around the corner is the **Tangier American Legation Museum** where you can seek out Morocco's *Mona Lisa*. After dinner at **La Fabrique**, have a nightcap and catch some jazz at **El Morocco Club**.

MATISSE IN TANGIER

Of the many artists who have passed through Tangier, Henri Matisse is one of the most famous. The French impressionist and leading light of the early-20th-century Fauvist movement called Tangier a 'painter's paradise'. His two visits to the city, in the spring of 1912 and again the following winter, had a profound influence on his work.

Inspired by the luminous North African light and the colour and harmony found in traditional Moroccan art, Matisse completed some 20 canvases and dozens of sketches during his time in Tangier. In them he honed the qualities that define his mature work: bold abstract lines, two-dimensional shapes and vibrant, expressive – as opposed to natural – colours.

Matisse mainly looked to the daily life of the medina for his themes. He produced several striking portraits of Zohra, a local prostitute, and a wonderful painting of a strong-featured Riffian woman sitting legs akimbo against an azure sky.

However, it is Matisse's renditions of the city that really strike a chord. Two of the most evocative are *Vue sur la Baie de Tanger* (View of the Bay of Tangier) and *La Porte de la Casbah* (Entrance to the Kasbah). Both are relatively subdued in their use of colour, but in *Paysage Vu d'une Fenêtre* (Window at Tangier) the artist hits full stride. The painting shows the view from his window in the Grand Hôtel Villa de France (p227), looking out over St Andrew's Church, with its squat tower, to the kasbah beyond. The overriding colour is a pure, sizzling Mediterranean blue.

regained control of the city under Sultan Moulay Ismail in 1679, destroying much of the city in the process. They remained in power until the mid-19th century, when North Africa once again piqued the interest of the European powers.

The modern history of Tangier begins here. While the rest of Morocco was divided between France and Spain, strategic Tangier was turned into an 'International Zone' of various sectors, similar to West Berlin in the Cold War. France, Spain, Britain, Portugal, Sweden, Holland, Belgium, Italy and the USA all had a piece of the pie, which was managed by the sultan, at least on paper. This situation lasted from 1912 until shortly after Moroccan independence, in 1956, when the city was returned to the rest of the country. During this famous Interzone period, expats flooded in, forming half the population, and a wild, anything-goes culture broke out, attracting all sorts of people, for reasons both high and low. Socialites, artists, currency speculators, drug addicts, spies, sexual deviants, exiles, eccentrics – the marginalia of humanity all arrived, giving the city a particularly sordid reputation.

When the Interzone period ended, Tangier entered a long period of decline. As the economic base moved on, so did the cultural scene. The city became a dreary port, while retaining its criminality. Having taken a dislike to it, successive monarchs cut off access to key funds. Street hustlers multiplied, turning off tourists. The numbers of expats dwindled, until there were only a few thousand left.

Since 1999, Tangier has been the site of major development with its new port, Tangier Med, and a drive towards increasing tourism across the region with Tangier the central hub.

⊙ Sights

⊙ Medina

The medina is the top attraction of Tangier, a labyrinth of alleyways both commercial and residential, contained by the walls of a 15th-century Portuguese fortress. Clean and well lit, as medinas go, the place is full of travellers' treasures, from fleeting glimpses of ancient ways of living, to the more material rewards of the souqs. The thing to do is to get lost and wander for a few hours, although there are a few sites you don't want to miss. Get as close to your destination as possible, then ask if you run into problems. Young people will be happy to take you anywhere (for a few dirhams).

★ **Petit Socco**　　　　　SQUARE, PLAZA
(Souq Dakhel; Map p226) Officially named Pl Souq ad-Dakhil, this was once the most notorious crossroads of Tangier, the site of drug deals and all forms of prostitution. Today the

Tangier

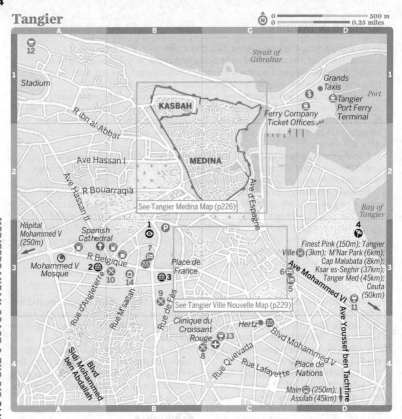

facades are freshly painted, tourists abound and it's a wonderful square for people-watching over a mint tea.

Grande Mosquée
MOSQUE

(Map p226) From the Petit Socco in the medina, Rue Jemaa el-Kebir leads east past this mosque, which at one time housed a Portuguese church. A little further on you reach a scenic lookout over the port.

★Tangier American Legation Museum
MUSEUM

(Map p226; ☑0539 93 53 17; www.legation.org; 8 Rue D'Amerique; donations appreciated; ⊙10am-1.30pm & 3-5pm Mon-Thu, 10am-noon & 3-5pm Fri) FREE This museum is a must-see: Morocco was one of the first countries to recognise the fledgling United States, and this was the first piece of American real estate abroad (look for the letter of thanks from George Washington to Sultan Moulay Suleyman). It is also the only US National Historic Land-

mark on foreign soil. The elegant five-storey mansion holds an impressive display of paintings that give a view of the Tangerine past through the eyes of its artists, most notably the Scotsman James McBey, whose hypnotic painting of his servant girl, Zohra, has been called the Moroccan *Mona Lisa*. There is a well-stocked bookshop and a wing dedicated to Paul Bowles.

Musée de la Fondation Lorin
MUSEUM

(Map p226; ☑0539 93 03 06; fondationlorin@gmail.com; 44 Rue Touahine; donations appreciated; ⊙11am-1pm & 3.30-7.30pm Sun-Fri) FREE This eclectic museum is housed in a former synagogue. Here you will find an open two-storey room with an engaging collection of black-and-white photographs of 19th- and 20th-century Tangier on the walls. Meanwhile there is likely a children's theatre going on in the centre, as the museum doubles as a workshop for disadvantaged kids, bringing life to the static display.

Tangier

⊙ Sights
1 Grand Hôtel Villa de France	B3
2 Instituto Cervantes Gallery	A3
3 Mohamed Drissi Gallery of Contemporary Art	B3
4 Town Beach	D3

⊜ Sleeping
5 Hotel El Djenina	C3
6 Marco Polo	C3
7 Pension Hollande	B3

⊗ Eating
8 Ana e Paolo	C4
9 Fès Market	B3
10 La Fabrique	B3

⊙ Drinking & Nightlife
11 Beach Club 555	D3
12 Café Hafa	A1
13 Regine Club	C4

⊜ Shopping
14 Ensemble Artisanal	B3

★ **Kasbah Museum** MUSEUM
(Map p226; ☎0539 93 20 97; Pl de la Kasbah; adult/child Dh10/3; ⊙9-11.30am & 1.30-4pm Wed-Mon) This museum is perfectly sited in Dar el-Makhzen, the former sultan's palace (where Portuguese and British governors also lived). The focus is on the history of the area from prehistoric times to the 19th century. Placards are in French and Arabic. Some highlights are pre-Roman tools; a sculpture with scenes of a bacchanalian feast; some 16th-century jewellery; an extraordinary floor mosaic from Volubilis; and a fascinating wall map of trade routes past and present. Before you leave, don't miss the exotic **Sultan's Garden** off the main courtyard, opposite the entrance. The museum is outside the medina – follow the perimeter all the way to the western end, to the highest part of the city, enter the Porte de la Kasbah, and follow the road to the museum.

Old Spanish Church CHURCH
(Map p226; 51 R as-Siaghin) Mother Teresa's Missionaries of Charity, a handful of Indian, French and Spanish nuns, work from the Old Spanish Church in the medina. They cope with heartbreaking situations: street children, disadvantaged unmarried mothers, abused children, marital violence, drugs and alcohol abuse.

⊙ Ville Nouvelle

With its Riviera architecture and colonial ambience, the area around Pl de France and Blvd Pasteur still hints at the glamour of the 1930s. It's a popular place for an early evening promenade, or a few hours sipping mint tea in one of the many streetside cafes – particularly the landmark Gran Café de Paris, whose retro facade is screaming to be captured on canvas. Where is that Tangier expat Matisse when we need him?

★ **Grand Socco** LANDMARK
(Map p226) The Grand Socco (official name Pl du 9 Avril 1947) is the romantic entrance to the medina, a large, sloping, palm-ringed plaza with a central fountain that stands before the keyhole gate Bab Fass. Once a major market, it is now the end of the line for taxis, the point at which the modern streets narrow into the past. For the best ground-floor view, climb the steps at the highest point on the circle, across from the large tan building (the police station), to what locals simply call **La Terrasse**. This is what you came for, one of those dreamy moments when you think you've entered a movie set.

The Grand Socco is also the hub of several other sights, all visible from within it. First is the Cinema Rif (p235), which stands on the circle. The brightest light on Tangier's cultural scene, it is a combination art-house cinema, cafe and archive, and is the local focal point for anything to do with film. Young locals come to soak up the ambience and use the free wi-fi.

DARNA, The Women's Association of Tangier ARTS CENTRE
(Map p226) The yellow building opposite *La Terrasse* is a small complex offering an inexpensive restaurant, a boutique shop with crafts and clothing, and a sunny courtyard, making it a popular stop for lunch or just a place to relax. Since 2002, DARNA has served as a community house to help local women in need, such as those suffering the after-effects of divorce.

Mendoubia Gardens PARK
(Map p226) Across the Grand Socco from the Cinema Rif is this large park full of strolling couples and children playing football. The Mendoubia Gardens are flanked by an elegant line of colonial buildings, perhaps the most attractive of its kind in the city. At the

Tangier Medina

MEDITERRANEAN COAST & THE RIF TANGIER

Tangier Medina

top of the central hill is a monument flanked by cannons that contains the speech given by Mohammed V asking for independence.

St Andrew's Church
CHURCH

(Map p226; Rue d'Angleterre; ⊗ services 8.30am & 11am Sun) St Andrew's Church is one of the more charming oddities of Tangier. Completed in 1905, on land granted by Queen Victoria, the interior of this Anglican church is in Moorish style, with no graven images, and the Lord's Prayer in Arabic. Behind the altar is a cleft that indicates the direction of Mecca; carved quotes are from the Quran. A real interfaith experience!

Outside in the church graveyard, there are some fascinating wartime headstones, including the fighter pilot shot while escaping (which reads 'Good Hunting, Tim') and the moving sight of entire downed aircrews, their headstones attached shoulder to shoulder. Caretaker Yassine is always on site and will let you in.

Grand Hôtel Villa de France
LANDMARK

(Map p224; Rue de la Liberté) To the north of Pl de France in the ville nouvelle, down Rue de la Liberté, stands the closed (though possibly to reopen) Grand Hôtel Villa de France. The French painter Eugène Delacroix stayed here in 1832, when it really was a grand hotel. His fellow artist and compatriot, Henri Matisse, followed in the early 1900s.

Town Beach
BEACH

(Map p224) The wide town beach has been improved – it's actually cleanest in the bustling summer. In any case, locals advise that it is still not clean enough for swimming, particularly the section closest to the port. It works well for a seaside stroll, however, and

the corniche (beachfront road) makes walking easy. It's not a great place late in the day, when muggings aren't unknown. There are plenty of attractive beaches down the nearby Atlantic Coast.

Librairie des Colonnes
LANDMARK

(Map p229; ☑ 5399 93 69 55; 54 Blvd Pasteur; ⊗ 9.30am-1pm & 4-7pm Mon-Sat) A famous landmark boasting wonderful architecture, this is Tangier's best bookshop though it has hardly any English-language books. There are frequent book readings and events, including author appearances. It was once the haunt of Paul Bowles, Jean Genet, Samuel Beckett and William Burroughs, and is an absolute institution in Tangier. Today you might bump into Tahar Ben Jelloun, Tahir Shah or Bernard-Henri Lévy.

Terrasse des Paresseux
ARCHITECTURE

(Idlers' Terrace; Map p229) The aptly named Terrasse des Paresseux provides sweeping views of the port and, on a clear day, Gibraltar and Spain. A set of ancient cannons faces the bay, symbolically warding off usurpers.

🏃 Activities

El-Minzah Wellness
SPA

(Map p229; ☑ 0539 93 58 85; www.elminzah.com; 85 Rue de la Liberté; fitness room Dh200) Pamper yourself at the luxury spa, where there's a fully equipped gym (with superb views to the sea), hammam, sauna and jacuzzi, as well as a range of massage and other therapeutic treatments.

Serenity Day Spa
SPA

(☑ 0539 37 28 28; serenity@serenityspa.ma; Rue Adolfo Fessere, in Quartier California; hammam & gommage Dh400) Here's a chance for women

MEDITERRANEAN COAST & THE RIF TANGIER

ART GALLERIES

Mohamed Drissi Gallery of Contemporary Art (Map p224; 52 Rue d'Angleterre; ⊗ 9am-1pm & 2-6pm Tue-Sun) **FREE** Housed in the former British Consulate.

Les Insolites (Map p229; ☑ 0534 59 29 83; http://lesinsolitestanger.com; 28 Rue Khalid Ibn Oualid; ⊗ 11am-8pm Mon-Sat) **FREE** Photography and books.

Galerie Conil (Map p226; ☑ 0534 37 20 54; conil.maroc@gmail.com; 7 Rue du Palmier, Petit Socco; ⊗ 11am-8pm Mon-Sat) **FREE** Contemporary art, books and clothing.

Galerie Delacroix (Map p229; 86 Rue de la Liberté; ⊗ 11am-1pm & 4-8pm Tue-Sun) **FREE** Exhibition space of the Institut Français.

Centre Culturel Ibn Khaldoun (Map p229; Rue de la Liberté; ⊗ 10am-1pm & 4-8pm) Contemporary art.

Instituto Cervantes Gallery (Map p224; Rue Belgique; ⊗ 10am-1pm & 4-8pm Tue-Sun) **FREE** Contemporary exhibitions.

to escape the all-too-male world of Morocco, at least for a few hours, and indulge the body in luxurious surroundings. This female-only hammam gets high marks from local customers. It's west of Pl de Koweit, on the road to the golf course; take a cab.

Royal Club Equestre   HORSE RIDING
(☑ 0539 93 48 84; Rte de Boubana; 30min Dh75, 1hr Dh150; ☺ 8am-noon & 3-7pm Tue-Sun) Along the road to Cap Spartel, the stables are set in the midst of forested hills, a pleasant place to explore on horseback. All riders must be accompanied by a guide, included in the price of the horse hire.

☞ Tours

To find a reputable guide, enquire at any hotel or the tourism information office. An excellent choice is Said Nacir (☑ 0671 04 57 06; www.d-destination.com). An English-speaking national guide with many years' experience, he specialises in private tours of Tangier for small parties at Dh350 per day. Another good option is Azeddine Berrada (☑ 0671 41 06 23), who offers half-day walking tours at Dh250 or a full day with a vehicle at Dh1000.

With Italian help, a series of colour-coded walks in the medina has recently been launched. There's a map on the wall of the tourist office and on medina walls in strategic spots.

Brown The kasbah

Green Rue Oued Aherdane from the kasbah to the Petit Socco

Purple Rue Dar ed-Baroud with its sea views down to the Hotel Continental

Yellow The south of the medina from the Petit Socco to the Tangier American Legation Museum

Blue Souq Dakhel: from the Petit Socco eastwards in a circle

Orange The ramparts around the medina, from the Grand Socco to the kasbah

✵ Festivals & Events

Two booklets listing events and local info, monthly *Urbain Tanger* and bi-monthly *Tanger Pocket* (both in French), are available at most hotels and online at www.urbain magazine.com and www.tangerpocket.com.

Salon International de Tanger des Livres et des Arts   CULTURAL
(☑ 0539 94 10 54; www.if-maroc.com/tanger/spip. php?rubrique59; Institut Français, 41 Rue Hassan

ibn Ouazzane; ☺ Apr) Annual weeklong book festival with varying themes.

Le Festival International de Théâtre Amateur   THEATRE
(☑ 0539 93 03 06; fondationlorin@gmail.com; 44 Rue Touahine, Fondation Lorin; ☺ May) A week of Arabic- and French-speaking theatre run by Fondation Lorin.

TANJAzz   MUSIC
(www.tanjazz.org; ☺ Sep) This ever-popular festival hosts concerts by local and international jazz musicians, including some leading names.

Festival du Court Métrage Méditerranéen   FILM
(International Mediterranean Short Film Festival; www.ccm.ma; ☺ Oct) Weeklong festival of short films from around the Mediterranean.

🛏 Sleeping

Tangier's sleeping options cater to all budgets and styles, spanning the spectrum from the ultra-cheap *pensiónes* (guesthouses) near the port to the chic hotels along the oceanfront. Most budget accommodation options are clustered around the medina and close to the port gate. They're cheap but only occasionally cheerful, so it pays to hunt around. In addition to those listed here, you can find plenty of choice in the streets around Ave Mokhtar Ahardan and Rue Magellan. Low-season travellers might get a reduced rate. Before accepting your room, however, make sure that it has not grown musty from the sea.

🛏 Medina

Melting Pot Hostel   HOSTEL €
(Map p226; ☑ 0539 33 15 08; www.meltingpot-hostels.com/tanger; 3 Rue Tsouli; dm from Dh120, d Dh360; ☎) A welcome new addition to medina sleeping options, this bright and cheerful hostel has a big, clean kitchen and plenty of chill-out space including a roof terrace with terrific views. Shared facilities are clean and the staff very friendly and helpful. Find it using the Hotel Continental as a reference point; there were no signs up yet on our visit.

Hotel Mamora   HOTEL €
(Map p226; ☑ 0539 93 41 05; 19 Ave Mokhtar Ahardan; s/d with shower Dh80/150, d with toilet Dh260) Readers enjoy this hotel in a good location near the Petit Socco with its variety

Tangier Ville Nouvelle

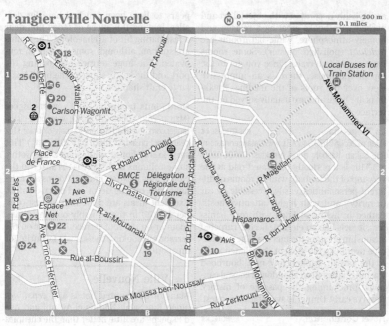

Tangier Ville Nouvelle

of rooms at different rates. It's a bit institutional, like an old school, but clean, well run and strong value for money. The rooms overlooking the green-tiled roof of the Grande Mosquée (such as room 39, from Dh220) are the most picturesque, if you don't mind the muezzin's call. Prices are always negotiable.

★ **Dar Nour** GUESTHOUSE **€€**
(Map p226; ☎0662 11 27 24; www.darnour.com; 20 Rue Gourna, Kasbah; d/ste incl breakfast from Dh720/1300; ☎) With no central courtyard, rooms here branch off two winding staircases, creating a maze of rooms and salons, each more romantic than the last. Rooms

are stylishly decorated with objets d'art and packed with books creating a relaxed and homely atmosphere, while bathrooms are *tadelakt* (polished plaster). Some rooms have a private terrace. Once you get to the top of the house, there is an impressive view over the roofs of the medina. Breakfasts are huge and are usually served on the terrace.

La Tangerina GUESTHOUSE **€€**
(Map p226; ☑ 0539 94 77 31; www.latangerina.com; Rue Sultan, Kasbah; d incl breakfast Dh600-1650; ☎) This is a perfectly renovated riad at the very top of the kasbah, with 10 rooms of different personalities, easily accessible by car (a rarity), and with highly attentive hosts. Bathed in light and lined with rope banisters, it feels like an elegant, Berber-carpeted steamship cresting the medina. The roof terrace overlooks the ancient crenellated walls of the kasbah, while below, neighbourhood washing hangs from abandoned coastal cannons, proclaiming the passage of history. Reserve early. Dinner is available on request.

Hotel Continental HOTEL **€€**
(Map p226; ☑ 0539 93 10 24; www.continental -tanger.com; 36 Rue Dar el-Baroud; s/d/tr incl breakfast Dh650/771/832; ☞☀☎) Nothing appears to have been touched here for decades, making this piece of faded grandeur a fascinating bit of archaeology. The rooms are spartan, although some have been renovated. The huge terrace overlooking the port and the sea is superb. The hotel has a large craft shop.

Nord Pinus Tanger GUESTHOUSE **€€€**
(Map p226; ☑ 0661 22 81 40; www.nord-pinus- tanger.com; Rue Riad Sultan, Kasbah; d/junior ste/ deluxe incl breakfast €150/240/290; ☀☎) This very grand house with somewhat Gothic stone columns and staircase is sister to the Nord Pinus in Arles, France. Rooms are a delight with eclectic decor and every comfort. Excellent meals are served on request (dinner Dh275) in the superbly opulent dining room or on the roof terrace. The bar on the terrace overlooking the sea is a favourite for an aperitif.

Ville Nouvelle

Many of the unrated hotels and *pensiónes* along Rue Salah Eddine el-Ayoubi and Ave d'Espagne are little better than the cheapies in the medina. This Salah/Espagne area can be dodgy at night, and questionable for women travelling alone. Following are some

---

PAUL BOWLES IN TANGIER

Perhaps the best-known foreign writer in Tangier was the American author Paul Bowles, who died in 1999, aged 88. Bowles made a brief but life-changing trip to Tangier in 1910, on Gertrude Stein's advice, then devoted the next 15 years to music composition and criticism back home. In 1938 he married Jane Sydney Auer, but they were never a conventional couple – he was an ambivalent bisexual and she was an active lesbian. After WWII Bowles took her to Tangier, where he remained the rest of his life. Here he turned to writing amid a lively creative circle, including the likes of Allen Ginsberg and William Burroughs.

During the 1950s Bowles began taping, transcribing and translating stories by Moroccan authors, in particular Driss ben Hamed Charhadi (also known by the pseudonym Larbi Layachi) and Mohammed Mrabet. He was also an important early recorder of Moroccan folk music.

Thanks partly to Bernardo Bertolucci's 1990 film, Bowles' best-known book is *The Sheltering Sky* (1949), a bleak and powerful story of an innocent American couple slowly dismantled by a trip through Morocco. His other works include *Let It Come Down* (1952), a thriller set in Tangier; *The Spider's House*, set in 1950s Fez; and two excellent collections of travel tales: *Their Heads Are Green* (1963) and *Points in Time* (1982). *A Distant Episode: the Selected Stories* is a good compilation of Bowles' short stories.

There is a dark and nihilistic undercurrent to Bowles' writing as fellow writer Norman Mailer describes: 'Paul Bowles opened the world of Hip. He let in the murder, the drugs, the death of the Square...the call of the orgy, the end of civilization'. Other commentators have tried to link aspects of Bowles' life to his writing. Bowles' autobiography *Without Stopping* (1972; nicknamed 'Without Telling') sheds little light on these matters.

The official Paul Bowles website is www.paulbowles.org.

alternatives. Nicer hotels line the Ave Mohammed VI, offering spectacular views over the Bay of Tangier and close proximity to the attractions of the city, with a couple of options right in the centre.

Hotel El-Muniria
HOTEL €

(Map p229; ☎ 0539 93 53 37; www.hotelelmuniria.com; 1 Rue Magellan; s/d Dh200/250, on terrace Dh250/300; ☎) This is your best low-end option in the ville nouvelle, and an important cut above the gloomy and often dirty competition, not to mention chock-full of Beat Generation history. French windows and bright, flowery fabrics set it apart, revealing the careful touch of a hands-on family operation. Room 4 is a great hideaway, a quiet corner double with lots of light, as is Room 8 on the terrace, a quiet double with a harbour view. Noise from Le Tangerine bar below is the only drawback.

Hotel de Paris
HOTEL €

(Map p229; ☎ 0539 93 18 77; 42 Blvd Pasteur; s/d with bathroom & breakfast Dh280/350) This reliable choice in the heart of the ville nouvelle has a classy, old-world aura in its lobby, although the breakfast area is dim. There is a variety of room types and prices depending on bathroom arrangements and balconies. All are clean and modern, but those overlooking Blvd Pasteur can get noisy. The helpful front desk makes up for the lack of service across the road at the tourist office.

Pension Hollande
HOTEL €

(Map p224; ☎ 0539 93 78 38; 139 Rue de Hollande; s/d Dh150/250, loft r without bathroom per person Dh100) Tucked away in a quiet street a short walk from Pl de France, this former hospital has sparkling whitewashed rooms and high ceilings, though the bathrooms can be claustrophobic. All rooms have a TV and a sink; doubles come with a shower. Hot water is available on demand. For a budget steal, don't miss the loft rooms up the hidden spiral staircase.

Hotel El Djenina
HOTEL €

(Map p224; ☎ 0539 92 22 44; eldjenina@menara.ma; 8 Rue al-Antaki; s/d incl breakfast Dh374/490; ☎) This somewhat characterless hotel is close to the port; rooms are bright and modern, though small. The cosy bar and restaurant with patio views to the sea are pleasant.

Marco Polo
HOTEL €€

(Map p224; ☎ 0539 94 11 24; www.marco-polo.ma; 2 Rue al-Antaki; s/d Dh462/616) This bright hotel has lots of light, sparkling marble floors and pastel walls. An excellent, central location across from the beach provides easy access to both the ville nouvelle and the medina. Undergoing refurbishment on our visit, its popular restaurant, large fitness centre, hammam and bar will no doubt continue to make it a good choice. Expect slightly higher prices. Breakfast is Dh40.

Hotel Rembrandt
HOTEL €€

(Map p229; ☎ 0539 33 33 14; www.hotel-rembrandt.com; Ave Mohammed V; s/d Dh750/780, sea view Dh870/1000; ❄ ☎ ☲) Rooms here are pretty standard and are in marked contrast to the elegant downstairs lobby, with its classic elevator and curving staircase. However, the glassed-in restaurant (set menu Dh160, alcohol served) is a welcome addition, the green garden cafe is a tranquil spot to relax, and the swank Blue Pub with its oddly purple velvet couches is a popular night spot where a beer is Dh25. Hotel breakfast costs Dh80.

El-Minzah
HOTEL €€€

(Map p229; ☎ 0539 93 58 85; www.elminzah.com; 85 Rue de la Liberté; d/ste from Dh2300/3000; ❄ ☎ ☲) The classiest five-star hotel in Tangier proper, and a local landmark, this beautifully maintained 1930s period piece offers three excellent restaurants, three equally good bars, a fitness centre, spa, pleasant gardens and even a babysitting service. It's shaped like an enormous hollow square, with a tremendous Spanish–Moorish courtyard, and has history oozing from its walls. Portside rooms offer beautiful views, but can be noisy when the wind is blowing.

SPOT THE CELEB

Sashay past the doorman at El-Minzah hotel and glide down the stairs to the beautiful Andalucian courtyard where there are dozens of photographs of celebrity visitors around the walls. Most of the photos date from the 1950s and '60s. A suave Rock Hudson, Aristotle Onassis in a white car, Jackie O too, Winston Churchill with his cigar and glitzy Rita Hayworth are just some that we spotted. Then head for the Caid's Bar (p234) for a cocktail while you decide where they'll hang your photo.

TANGIER FOR CHILDREN

For kids, **M'Nar Park** (☑0539 34 38 29; www.mnarparktanger.com; Cap Malabata; aquapark adult/child Dh100/50; ⊙8am-6pm, pool 15 Jun-15 Sep) is heaven. Located south of Cap Malabata, with great views across the Bay of Tangier, this cliffside resort offers a water park, an electronic game park, karting, a small train, a mini-football field, restaurants, a cafe and 38 residential bungalows for families.

In town and close to the Grand Socco, the Mendoubia Gardens (p225) is a park with grass for playing football and swings for letting off steam.

🍴 Eating

Tangier's 800-plus cafes are a study in local culture, and can be characterised many ways, beginning with old versus new. The former are almost exclusively male, and often shabby, while the latter are bright, modern and design-conscious, with light food, high ceilings and lots of light.

In the medina there's a host of cheap eating possibilities around the Petit Socco (Souq Dakhel) and the adjacent Ave Mokhtar Ahardan, with rotisserie chicken, sandwiches and brochettes all on offer. In the ville nouvelle, try the streets immediately south of Pl de France, which are flush with fast-food outlets, sandwich bars and fish counters.

For self-caterers, the covered markets near the Grand Socco are the best places for fresh produce, particularly on Thursday and Sunday, when Riffian women descend on the city in traditional straw hats with pompoms and candy-striped skirts to sell agricultural products. **Fès market** (Map p224), to the west of the city centre, is good for imported cheese and other treats. **Casa Pepé** (Map p229; ☑5399 93 70 39; 39 Rue ibn Rochd; ⊙9am-10.30pm) is one of several general stores in the area. You can stock up at the deli here, and buy imported foods, dry goods and liquor.

🍴 Medina

Le Salon Bleu   MOROCCAN €€
(Map p226; Pl de la Kasbah, entrance 71 Rue Amrah; mains Dh80-130; ⊙lunch & dinner) Light, bright and sea-breezy, this relaxed tearoom and restaurant owned by Dar Nour offers good,

simple food in a spectacular setting perched high above the kasbah. The roof terrace has magnificent sea views.

Le Nabab   MOROCCAN €€
(Map p226; ☑0661 44 22 20; 2 Rue al Kadiria; mains Dh110, menu Dh175; ⊙lunch & dinner Mon-Sat) This is a beautifully restored old *fondouq* (rooming house), all grey *tadelakt*, comfortable seating and swathes of airy fabrics. Dine around the huge fireplace or in a private alcove. The menu is Moroccan, the welcome friendly and it's licensed.

⭐**Art et Gourmet**   MEDITERRANEAN €€€
(Map p226; ☑0539 37 12 51; 9 Pl du 9 Avril 1947; lunch menu Dh160, mains Dh180; ⊙noon-midnight; 🎵) Overlooking the Grand Socco, the terrace of this restaurant has the best views in town. Inside, it's more formal. Menus are presented on the back of small paintings, and the *menu du jour* on a blackboard. There's lots of fish, organic vegetables and meat produced on the Boufalah farm in nearby Assilah, and fusion Moroccan dishes with a touch of Japanese. All is beautifully presented on a slate plate, and there's a good wine list. The service is excellent.

⭐**Populaire Saveur de Poisson**   SEAFOOD €€€
(Map p229; ☑0539 33 63 26; 2 Escalier Waller; fixed price menu Dh200; ⊙lunch & dinner, closed Fri; ⊝) This charming little seafood restaurant offers an excellent, filling set menu in rustic surroundings. The owner serves a four-course meal of fish soup followed by inventive plates of fresh catch, olives and various fresh breads, all of it washed down with a homemade juice cocktail made from 15 kinds of fruit. Dessert is honey and almonds. Not just a meal, a whole experience.

El Morocco Club   MEDITERRANEAN, TAPAS €€€
(Map p226; contact@elmoroccoclub.ma; 1 Rue Kashla, Kasbah; mains Dh140-195, tapas Dh40-90; ⊙dinner; 🎵) A very smart renovation of this elegant building has resulted in a stylish restaurant upstairs and a more relaxed piano bar downstairs. It's all dramatic colours and the cosy bar has some fascinating photographs on the walls. During the day, there's a cafe outside under the trees.

🍴 Ville Nouvelle

La Giralda   CAFE €
(Map p229; ☑0539 37 04 07; 1st fl, 5 Blvd Pasteur; breakfast from Dh25; ⊙7am-midnight) The

young and beautiful adore this grand cafe overlooking the Terrasse des Paresseux, with its sumptuous, Egyptian-influenced decor and intricately carved ceiling. Huge windows give great sea views. A light menu of crêpes and paninis make it a good lunch stop, too.

Fast Food Brahim   FAST FOOD €
(Map p229; 16 Ave Mexique; sandwiches from Dh22; ⊙11am-midnight) Great made-to-order sandwiches. You can't go wrong here with half a baguette filled with *kefta* (spicy lamb meatballs) and salad to eat on the hoof.

Mix Max   FAST FOOD €
(Map p229; 6 Ave Prince Héritier; meals Dh25-50; ⊙noon-2am) A trendy and popular fast-food joint, Mix Max serves up great paninis, *shwarma* and other creative fast fare.

Patisserie La Española   PATISSERIE €
(Map p229; 97 Rue de la Liberté; pastries from Dh8; ⊙7am-10.30pm winter, 7am-12.30am summer) A heavily mirrored tearoom, this cafe tempts people off the street with its pretty arrangements of cakes and pastries. Everyone seems to come here – locals and foreigners, businesspeople and courting couples.

Champs Élysées   CAFE €
(Map p229; 6 Ave Mohammed V; breakfast from Dh25; ⊙6am-10pm) This enormous cafe-in-the-round is high on opulence, with a huge central chandelier and red velour upholstery. Great sticky pastries.

Number One   MOROCCAN, FRENCH €€
(Map p229; ☑0539 94 16 74; 1 Ave Mohammed V; mains from Dh85; ⊙lunch & dinner) The rose walls and white windows in this renovated apartment provide the feel of a holiday cottage, while the red lighting, background jazz and exotic mementoes lend it an intimate, sultry allure. The Moroccan-French cuisine gets high marks from locals, who have been coming here for almost 50 years.

Eric Kayser   PATISSERIE, FRENCH €€
(cnr Rue des Amoureux & Rue Granada; mains from Dh140, dish of the day Dh120; ⊙7am-10.30pm) This renowned French *boulanger* has a bakery and restaurant in Tangier that's trendy and stylish; it's very popular for its good French cuisine.

Ana e Paolo   ITALIAN €€
(Map p224; ☑0539 94 46 17; 77 Rue Prince Héretier; mains from Dh85; ⊙lunch & dinner, closed Sun) This is a genuine, family-run Italian

---

YOU CAN'T BEAT TANGIER

The Beat Generation was a post-WWII American counterculture movement that combined visceral engagement in worldly experiences with a quest for deeper understanding. It reached its apotheosis in Tangier. Many Beat artists – writer Jack Kerouac, and poets Allen Ginsberg and Gregory Corso – were just passing through, while writers William Burroughs and Paul Bowles, and the multi-talented Brion Gysin, spent significant parts of their lives here, further inspiring a coterie of local artists. The result was a mixed bag, from the heights of artistic creativity to the lows of moral depravity. Today Beat history can still be found throughout the city:

Hotel el-Muniria (p231) William Burroughs wrote *The Naked Lunch*, his biting satire of the modern American mind, here. Originally titled *Interzone*, the book was written in the cut-up technique developed by Brion Gysin. Ginsberg and Kerouac also shacked up here in 1957.

Le Tangerine (p234) Photos of Beat customers abound on the walls of this bar (formerly the Tangier Inn) below the el-Muniria.

Café Central (p234) Burroughs' principal hang-out on the Petit Socco, where he sized up his louche opportunities.

Tangier American Legation Museum (p224) Houses a wing dedicated to Paul Bowles.

Hotel Continental (p230) Scenes from the movie version of Paul Bowles' *The Sheltering Sky* were filmed here.

Café Hafa (p234) Paul Bowles and the Rolling Stones came here to smoke hashish.

Gran Café de Paris (p234) The main literary salon during the Interzone, it also drew Tennessee Williams and Truman Capote.

MEDITERRANEAN COAST & THE RIF TANGIER

bistro with Venetian owners; it feels like you've been invited for Sunday dinner. Expect a highly international crowd, lots of cross-table conversations about the events of the day, and wholesome food including excellent charcuterie and pizzas, homemade pastas, meat and fish.

Le Pagode
CHINESE €€

(Map p229; ☑ 0539 93 80 86; Rue al-Boussiri; mains from Dh80; ⊗ noon-3pm & 7-11pm Tue-Sun) If you're tired of tajines and pasta, this realistic bit of Asia is the answer. An intimate and classy dining area, with lacquered furniture, white tablecloths and low lighting is mated with a classic Chinese menu.

La Fabrique
FRENCH €€€

(Map p224; ☑ 0539 37 40 57; Residence Salima, 7 Rue d'Angleterre; meals Dh250-350; ⊗ lunch & dinner Mon-Sat) The minimalist decor and excellent French cuisine make this restaurant just the place to be seen. The *tournedos* is legendary, though there's not much choice for vegetarians. Service is attentive and there's a good wine list. Reserve ahead.

Restaurant el-Korsan
MOROCCAN €€€

(Map p229; ☑ 0539 93 58 85; El-Minzah Hotel, 85 Rue de la Liberté; mains around Dh160; ⊗ lunch & dinner) One of Tangier's top restaurants, this chic and classy place inside the El-Minzah Hotel offers a smaller, more intimate version of the palace restaurant theme but without the bus tours. Well-presented Moroccan classics are served to soft live music, and often traditional dancing. Reservations are necessary, including one day's prior notice for lunch. Dress well.

Drinking & Nightlife

Given its hedonistic past, it's no surprise that the drinking scene is firmly entrenched in Tangerine culture. It's equally unsurprising that bars are principally the domain of men, although there are a few more Westernised places where women can take a drink. Many only get going after midnight. For coffee purists, there are three legends to visit.

Tangier's clubbing scene picks up in the summer, when Europeans arrive on the ferries. Discos cluster near Pl de France and line the beach, appealing to a wide range of clientele, from grey-haired couples to sex tourists. Cover charges vary and may be rolled into drink prices. If leaving late, have the doorman call a taxi.

Gran Café de Paris
CAFE

(Map p229; Pl de France; ⊗ 6am-10.30pm) Gravity weighs upon the grand letters of the Gran Café de Paris, reminding us of its age at the crossroads of Tangier. Facing the Pl de France since 1927, this is the most famous of the coffee establishments along Blvd Pasteur, most recently as a setting in *The Bourne Ultimatum*. In the past it was a prime gathering spot for literati.

Café Hafa
CAFE

(Map p224; Ave Hadi Mohammed Tazi; ⊗ 8.30am-11pm Mon-Fri, 8.30am-2am Sat & Sun) With its stadium seating overlooking the strait, you could easily lose an afternoon lazing in this open-air cafe, but you need good weather. Locals hang out here to enjoy a game of backgammon. There's no menu, but scrambled eggs, *b'sara* (butterbean and garlic soup) and olives are on offer.

Café Central
CAFE

(Map p226; Petit Socco; ⊗ 6am-11.30pm) The premier people-watching site in the medina, with tables on the pavement. See the local Mafiosi arrive in his new Benz, watch odd specimens of humanity drift past, hear the strange shouts echo down the alleys, and wonder what is going on upstairs. It's the perfect place to sip your coffee.

Piano Bar at El Morocco Club
BAR

(Map p226; Pl du Tabor, Kasbah; ⊗ from 8pm Tue-Sun) An atmospheric bar, this is a good place for a drink. There's usually live music at weekends.

Le Tangerine
BAR

(Map p229; 1 Rue Magellan, Hotel el-Muniria; ⊗ 10.30pm-1am, to 3am Fri & Sat) Tangier was once a gay destination, but that scene has long since departed for Marrakesh, leaving no establishments behind. Concierges report that Le Tangerine and some of the bars along the beach attract gay clientele, particularly late on weekends. Beers are Dh20.

Nord Pinus Tanger
BAR

(Map p226; Rue Riad Sultan, Kasbah; ⊗ 11am-midnight) On the top floor of this kasbah guesthouse is a bar and terrace, with fabulous views across to Spain. Sip a cocktail in the retro-chic lounge full of quirky chairs, Moroccan cushions and contemporary photography.

Caid's Bar
BAR

(El-Minzah; Map p229; 85 Rue de la Liberté; ⊗ 10am-midnight) Long the establishment's drinking hole of choice, this el-Minzah landmark is a classy relic of the grand days of international Tangier, and photos of the famous and infamous adorn the walls. Women are more than welcome and the adjacent wine bar (wine from Dh35) is equally good.

Pilo
BAR

(Map p229; cnr Ave Mexique & Rue de Fès; ⊗11am-2am) A party atmosphere pervades these two floors of local colour, underscored by some high-energy music and festive lighting. Recently redecorated, it sports red walls and year-round Christmas decorations. Women can feel comfortable here, though the working girls are upstairs.

Americain's Pub
BAR

(Map p229; Rue al-Moutanabi; ⊗noon-2am) Don't be fooled by the name: this pub is outfitted as an authentic part of the London underground, with white tiled walls, ubiquitous red trim and signage far more authentic than the Bobbies would appreciate. It's the perfect place to hide: there's no street number, and the phone is out of order.

Hole in the Wall Bar
BAR

(Map p229; Rue Prince Héretier; ⊗11am-midnight) For chuckles only, walk up Rue Prince Héretier from the Terrasse des Paresseux one-and-a-half blocks and you will see a pair of swinging black doors, Old West style. Welcome to the smallest bar in Tangier, if not the world. Beer (from Dh20) only.

Loft
CLUB

(☑0673 28 09 27; www.loftclub-tanger.com; Rte de Boubana; ⊗10pm-4am Thu & Sat) Easily Tangier's premier nightspot, this world-class, state-of-the-art club holds 2000 people and feels like an enormous silver cruise ship, with upper-storey balconies, sparkling metal railings, billowing sail-like curtains, spotlights cutting through the artificial fog – and no cover. DJ Spicy spins house and R&B. It's west of the city, near the Royal Tangier Golf Club. Go after midnight.

Beach Club 555
CLUB

(Map p224; Ave Mohammed VI; ⊗10am-3am; ☐) A beach club by day with pool, pizzeria and bar with a sports screen (admission Dh100), at night the Triple 5 morphs into one of the best discos in the city. Dance up a storm with the resident and visiting DJs.

Regine Club
CLUB

(Map p224; 8 Rue al-Mansour Dahabi; ⊗10pm-3am Mon-Sat) Welcome to the 1980s. This disco has stayed the same so long it is a museum piece, replete with glass-reflecting ball and purple velour couches. It has a great atmosphere from 1.30am, especially on weekends.

Finest Pink
CLUB

(Ave Mohammed VI; ⊗11pm-late) This gay-friendly lounge, restaurant and tapas bar opposite the Hotel Sheherazade sports a popular disco with, of course, the finest bright-pink walls.

☆ Entertainment

Films are either in Arabic or dubbed in French.

Cinema Rif
CINEMA

(Cinematheque de Tanger; Map p226; ☑0539 93 46 83; Grand Socco) In this fine, well-restored art deco building you'll find both indie and mainstream films, mostly American, Moroccan, Spanish or French (with Spanish and American films typically dubbed into Arabic).

Cinema Paris
CINEMA

(Map p229; Rue de Fès) Shows French, American and Bollywood films, the last two dubbed into French or Arabic. Tickets are Dh25 for downstairs, Dh35 for the balcony.

🔒 Shopping

🔒 Medina

The souqs of the medina are a wonderful place to spend hours shopping. Following are some unusual places you might want to check out.

Boutique Majid
ANTIQUES, JEWELLERY

(Map p226; ☑0539 93 88 92; Rue Les Almohades; ⊗10am-7pm) You can get lost for hours in this exotic antique shop, but the real gem is Majid himself. Straight out of central casting (including his red fez) he will regale you with stories of the Rolling Stones and other luminaries while showing you his amazing collection of Moroccan doors, jewellery and artefacts, clothing, fabrics and carpets.

Bleu de Fès
CARPETS, ANTIQUES

(Map p226; ☑0539 33 60 67; www.bleudefes.com; 16 Rue Les Almohades, Petit Socco; ⊗10am-7pm) Drool over stacks and stacks of Berber carpets from the Middle and High Atlas.

Bazaar of Silver Jewelry
JEWELLERY

(Map p226; ☑0539 33 62 31; 13 Rue Jamaa Jadida) The name says it all: two floors of glass cases full of silver jewellery from throughout Morocco, both new and antique, and great staff, too. Located in an obscure alley near the Café Central, Petit Socco.

Laura Wefling   ARTS & CRAFTS, CLOTHING
(Map p226; Pl de la Kasbah; ⊙11am-6pm) Next to the Kasbah Museum, this is a beautiful shop with some superb one-off pieces of clothing, bags, decor items and ceramics.

🔒 Ville Nouvelle

Bazar Tindouf   ANTIQUES
(Map p229; 72 Rue de la Liberté; ⊙10am-7pm) This shop opposite El-Minzah Hotel is bursting at the seams with antiques, glassware, brassware, ceramics, lamps, jewellery, clothing and more besides. It's definitely worth a browse.

Las Chicas   ARTS & CRAFTS, CLOTHING
(Map p226; ☑0539 37 45 10; 52 Rue Kacem Guenoun, Porte de la Kasbah; ⊙10am-7pm Mon-Sat) Just outside the kasbah, this is an eclectic mixture of a shop, stocking art pieces, homeware, cosmetics and some exquisite designer clothes, alongside a cafe. Massage is also on offer.

La Casa Barata   MARKET
(Ave Abou Kacem Sebti; ⊙9am-8pm Thu & Sun) Literally 'the cheap house', this large flea market carries everything you can imagine, from vegetables to electronics to carpets. The best opportunity to find real treasure, and an experience unto itself.

Ensemble Artisanal   ARTS & CRAFTS
(Map p224; cnr Rue Belgique & Rue M'sallah; ⊙9am-1pm & 3-7pm Sat-Thu) Undergoing renovations at the time of our visit, this government-backed arts-and-crafts centre is a good place to see the range of local crafts and watch the artisans at work. There's no haggling, as prices are fixed, but they are also much higher than in the souqs.

El Tapisero   CARPETS
(☑0539 94 56 81; www.eltapisero.com; 61 Blvd Yacoub el Mansour, Charf; ⊙9.30am-1pm & 3-7pm Mon-Thu, 9.30am-noon Fri & Sat) Make like Madonna and order a handmade carpet at El Tapisero. The team at this carpet-weaving enterprise is very creative and works with some of the big European decorators. Expect to pay about €50 to €250 per square metre.

ℹ Information

DANGERS & ANNOYANCES
As in any big city, it's best to stick to the beaten path at all times, and to take cabs point to point at night. Solo women may be subject to being hassled after about 10pm, and should avoid the port area after dark. If you have a serious problem and need help from the authorities, contact the **Brigade Touristique** (Tourist Police; Map p226; ☑177; Ave Mohammed VI, Tangier Port).

EMERGENCY
Emergency Service (☑150; ⊙24hr)

INTERNET ACCESS
There are several internet cafes in the Blvd Pasteur area.
Espace Net (Map p229; 16 Ave Mexique; per hr Dh5; ⊙9.30am-1am)

MEDICAL SERVICES
Clinique du Croissant Rouge (Red Cross Clinic; Map p224; ☑0539 94 69 76, 0539 94 69 76; 6 Rue al-Mansour Dahabi)
Hopital Mohammed V (☑0539 93 08 56; Rue Val Fleurie) On the road to the airport.
Pharmacy Anegay (Map p226; Rue as-Siaghin; ⊙8am-6pm Mon-Sat)

MONEY
Blvds Pasteur and Mohammed V are lined with numerous banks with ATMs and *bureau de change* counters. Outside of working hours, try the exchange bureaus in the big hotels.
BMCE (Map p229; Blvd Pasteur; ⊙8am-4pm Mon-Fri) One of several in this area.

POST
Main Post Office (Map p224; cnr Rue Quevada & Ave Mohammed V; ⊙8am-4pm Mon-Fri) Poste restante is at the counter furthest to the right; parcel post is on the south side of the building.

TOURIST INFORMATION
Délégation Régionale du Tourisme (Map p229; ☑0539 94 80 50; 29 Blvd Pasteur; ⊙9am-1pm & 3-6pm Mon-Fri) The recent investment in tourism infrastructure hasn't made it here. Some verbal help, but no printed material. The Hotel de Paris across the road has lots of brochures and staff are willing to help.

TRAVEL AGENCIES
The following both sell ferry and air tickets.
Carlson Wagonlit (Map p229; ☑0539 33 10 24; 91 Rue de la Liberté; ⊙9am-1pm & 3-6pm Mon-Fri)
Hispamaroc (Map p229; ☑0539 93 21 78; hispamaroc@mamnet.net.ma; 2 Rue el-Jabha el-Ouatania; ⊙9am-1pm & 3-6pm Mon-Fri)

USEFUL WEBSITES

Head to **Lonely Planet** (www.lonelyplanet.com/morocco/the-mediterranean-coast-and-the-rif/tangier) for planning advice, author recommendations, traveller reviews and insider tips.

ⓘ Getting There & Away

Tackling anywhere unfamiliar after dark is always more traumatic, so try to arrive early in the day. Remember to change money to pay the cab fare.

AIR

The Ibn Batouta International Airport (TNG) is 15km southwest of the city centre. It attracts a number of budget airlines (including easyJet from Madrid and Paris, Jetairfly from Paris, Barcelona and Rotterdam and Ryanair from London Stansted, Paris, Marseille, Brussels, Madrid, Düsseldorf and Frankfurt Hahn) as well as Iberia, British Airways and Royal Air Maroc. Check the internet for the latest service providers and schedules, as these are constantly changing.

BOAT

You have two options for crossing the Strait of Gibraltar: the fast catamaran ferries owned by **FRS** (www.frs.es) and **Balearia** (www.balearia.co.uk/), which cost Dh350 to Tarifa and take 35 minutes, or the slower ones (Dh255 to Algeciras, 2½ hours). The former are more susceptible to weather delays, which can close the port for days, but they're lifesavers for those prone to seasickness.

Ferries to and from Tarifa currently leave from Tanger Port; all other destinations are served by Tanger Med, the large terminal 48km north of the city. A shuttle bus (Dh25) leaves Tanger Med every hour on the hour for the Tanger bus station, taking 45 minutes.

Tickets are available from the company ticket booths outside the ferry terminal building at Tanger Port, in the terminal itself, or from virtually any travel agency around town; be sure to pick up an exit form so you can avoid hassles later. The main destination is the Spanish port of Algeciras, with less frequent services to Gibraltar. The Tarifa service includes a free bus transfer to Algeciras (50 minutes) on presentation of your ferry ticket. Book in advance during peak periods (particularly Easter, the last week in August and the last week in October), allow 90 minutes before departure to get tickets and navigate passport control, and remember the time difference with Spain (Morocco is one hour behind, and two hours behind during Ramadan).

Remember to get your passport stamped on the ferry before arrival in Morocco.

BUS

CTM buses depart from the **main bus station** (gare routière; ☎ 0539 94 69 28; Pl Jamaa el-Arabia), about 2km to the south of the city centre by the Syrian mosque – the distinctly un-Moroccan-looking minarets are a useful nearby landmark. Destinations include the following:

DESTINATION	COST (DH)	DURATION (HR)
Agadir	325	12½
Casablanca	140	5½
Chefchaouen	45	3
Fez	115	6
Marrakesh	230	10
Meknès	95	5
Rabat	105	4
Tetouan	20	1

Baggage is Dh10 (4kg to 10kg).

Cheaper bus companies operate from the main bus station. There are regular departures for all the destinations mentioned above, plus services to Al-Hoceima (Dh100, 10 hours) and Fnideq (Dh25, 1½ hours) – a small town 3km from the Ceuta border. The station can be busy, but pretty hassle-free, thanks to the police office in the centre. It has a **left-luggage facility** (per item per 24hr Dh5-7; ⏰ 5am-1am). A metered petit taxi to/from the town centre is around Dh10.

CAR

The major car rental agencies are at the airport. The following have in-town locations:

Avis (Map p229; ☎ 0539 93 46 46; www.avis.com/car-rental/location/AFR/MA/Tanger; 54 Blvd Pasteur; Ibn Batouta airport; ⏰ 8am-7pm Mon-Sat, 8am-noon Sun)

Budget (☎ 0531 06 09 51; Tanger Ville station; Ibn Batouta airport; ⏰ 8.30am-noon & 2.30-7pm Mon-Fri, 9am-noon & 3-6pm Sat, 9am-noon Sun)

Hertz (Map p224; ☎ 0539 32 21 65; fax 0539 94 58 30; 36 Ave Mohammed V; Ibn Batouta airport; ⏰ 8am-noon & 2.30-6.30pm Mon-Fri, 9am-noon & 3-6pm Sat, 9am-noon Sun)

A reasonably secure and convenient **car park** (42 Rue Hollande; per hr/night/24hr Dh2/15/25) is next to the Dawliz complex.

TAXI

The grand-taxi rank for places outside Tangier is across from the main bus station. The most common destinations are Tetouan (Dh30, one hour), Assilah (Dh20, 30 minutes) and Larache (Dh35, 1½ hours). For Ceuta, travel to Fnideq (Dh30, one hour), 3km from the border. There are no direct taxis to the border (Bab Sebta). Grands taxis to Tetouan also frequently wait for arriving trains at Tanger Ville train station. For destinations on the outskirts of Tangier, such as the Caves of Hercules or Cap Malabata, use the grand-taxi rank on the Grand Socco.

TRAIN

Train station Tanger Ville is hassle-free. Ten trains depart daily for Sidi Kacem, Meknès, Fez, Rabat (Ville), Casablanca (Casa Voyageurs) and Marrakesh, including a night service with couchettes, the famed *Marrakesh Express*, which should be reserved in advance (s Dh650, d per person Dh450, Dh350 with couchette). From Sidi Kacem you can get connections south to Marrakesh or east to Oujda. Schedules are best checked at www.oncf.ma. Note that the **left luggage office** (per item Dh10; ⊘7am-1pm & 2-9.30pm) only accepts locked bags. A petit taxi to/from Tangier centre should cost around Dh10.

❶ Getting Around

TO/FROM THE AIRPORT

From the port in the city to the airport, a grand taxi takes 25 minutes and costs Dh150 for the entire car. If you want to pick up a local bus from the airport, bus 17 and bus 70 run to the Grand Socco, but you'll need to walk 2km to the main road.

TO/FROM TANGER MED

A shuttle bus (Dh25) runs every hour from Tanger Med to the main bus station (45 minutes). The driver will drop you off near the train station if you ask.

BUS

Buses aren't really necessary for getting around Tangier, but two potentially useful services are bus 13, which runs from the train station via Ave Mohammed VI to Tangier Port gate, and bus 17, which links the train station and the main bus station. Tickets cost Dh8.

TAXI

Distinguishable by their ultramarine colour with a yellow stripe down the side, petits taxis do standard journeys around town from Dh8; they charge 50% more at night.

Cap Spartel كاب سبارتل

Just 14km west of Tangier lies Cap Spartel, the northwestern extremity of Africa's Atlantic Coast. It is a popular day trip with locals and tourists alike. A dramatic drive takes you through La Montagne, an exclusive suburb of royal palaces and villas, and over the pine-covered headland to the Cap Spartel Lighthouse (closed). The beaches

to the south are clean and quiet outside the summer season, so you can find your own private cove.

Below Cap Spartel, the beach Plage Robinson stretches off to the south – a great place for a bracing walk. Five kilometres further you reach the Grottes d'Hercule (admission Dh5; ⊘8am-dark), the mythical dwelling place of Hercules, next to Le Mirage hotel. Since the 1920s these caves have been quarried for millstones, worked by prostitutes and used as a venue for private parties by rich celebrities from Tangier. A much-photographed view of the Atlantic from within resembles a map of Africa. Camel rides are available here, just before the entrance to the caves on the right. A beach ride is a special treat.

🛏 Sleeping & Eating

Camping Achakkar   CAMPGROUND €
(☑0612 24 97 27; camping per person Dh25, plus per tent/car/campervan Dh25/20/45, bungalows Dh250-550) Inland from the grotto, this shady site has clean facilities and hot water (electricity Dh30, hot shower Dh20). It has a shop that stocks essentials and a spanking new cafe serving breakfast (Dh35), paninis, *shwarma* and pasta. A swimming pool was being added at the time of research.

Le Mirage   HOTEL €€€
(☑0539 33 33 32; www.lemirage-tanger.com; Cap Spartel; d from Dh2400; ❋⊛≋) One of the finest hotels in the Tangier area, with a dramatic location perched on the cliff beside the grotto, this hotel offers a view of miles of broad Atlantic beach. The bungalows are exquisite, as the price suggests, and there's a spa and golf course. Nonguests can get a taste of the opulence in the immaculate restaurant (meals around Dh500), or just stop by for a drink beneath the pergola. From the sunny terrace you can see the Roman ruins of Cotta, where fish oil was processed.

Cap Spartel Café
& Restaurant   MOROCCAN €
(☑0539 93 37 22; Cap Spartel Rd; breakfast Dh22, paninis Dh30) This restaurant next to the lighthouse is popular on weekends. Set in a lovely garden overlooking the sea, it serves good juices, crêpes both savoury and sweet, paninis and pizza.

❶ Getting There & Away

Grands taxis from Tangier are the best way of getting to Cap Spartel. A round-trip charter should cost around Dh200, including waiting time. Taxis leave from the rank in front of St Andrew's Church (p227) in Tangier.

Road to Ceuta

The scenic road from Tangier to Ceuta is worth taking: green patchwork fields, alluring mountain roads, rolling hills, rocky headlands and good sandy beaches reveal a different side to Morocco. A complete grand taxi to Fnideq, the town before the border, will cost Dh250.

The road begins at Cap Malabata, the headland opposite Tangier and some 8km from the city. There is a new corniche with expensive apartments, a golf course and hotels. Here you'll find the large M'nar Park (p232), a great place for children. It has everything from waterslides to boating, and there's a restaurant with superb views back towards Tangier.

There's no more development until Ksar es-Seghir, 25km further around the coast. This small fishing port, dominated by the remains of a Portuguese fort, has a new yacht basin and the beach is popular with locals in summer. Just beyond you'll spot Tanger Med, the massive container facility and ferry port, 48km from Tangier.

The great crag of Jebel Musa, one of the ancient Pillars of Hercules (the Rock of Gibraltar being the other), rises up 10km or so further on, and views along the pretty mountain road are spectacular, particularly as there's no development here.

Ceuta (Sebta)

سبتة

POP 84,000

Ceuta is one of a handful of Spanish possessions on the coastline of Morocco, and a real gem. Located on a peninsula jutting out into the Mediterranean, it offers a compact dose of fantastic architecture, interesting museums, excellent food, a relaxing maritime park and bracing nature walks, with A-plus traveller support at every turn. The city is particularly beautiful at night, a skyline of artfully lit buildings and bursting palms.

Ceuta served as one of the Roman Empire's coastal bases (its Arabic name, Sebta, stems from the Latin *Septem*). After a brief stint under the control of the Byzantine Empire, the city was taken in AD 931 by the Arab rulers of Muslim Spain – the basis for Spain's claim of historical rights to the land. For the next 500 years, however, this city at the tip of Africa was a prized possession, fought over and ruled successively by Spanish princes, Moroccan sultans and Portuguese kings. Things began to settle down when Portugal and Spain united under one crown in 1580, and Ceuta passed to Spain by default. When the two countries split in 1640, Ceuta remained Spanish, and has been ever since.

If entering from Morocco, Ceuta is also an eye-opener. Like the former West Berlin, it comes across as a grand social experiment concocted by rival political systems. Leaving the beggars and street hustlers behind, you cross over a grim border zone, a 400m no-man's-land of haphazardly placed barricades (part of a €30 million fence erected by the EU to prevent illegal immigration), to find yourself blinking in the light of Spanish culture, a relaxed world of well-kept plazas, beautiful buildings and tapas bars bubbling over until the wee hours. This experience alone is worth the trip and lingers thereafter.

SURVIVAL SPANISH

Hello/Goodbye	¡Hola!/¡Adios!
Yes/No	Sí/No
Please/Thank you	Por favor/Gracias
Where is...?	¿Dónde está...?
hotel	hotel
guesthouse	pensión
camping	camping
Do you have any rooms available?	¿Tiene habitaciones libres?
a single room	una habitación individual
a double room	una habitación doble
How much is it?	¿Cuánto cuesta?
What time does the next...leave?	¿A qué hora sale/llega el próximo...?
boat	barca
bus	autobús
I'd like a...	Quisiera un...
one-way ticket	billete sencillo
return ticket	billete de ida y vuelta
beer	cerveza
sandwich	bocadillo

Ceuta

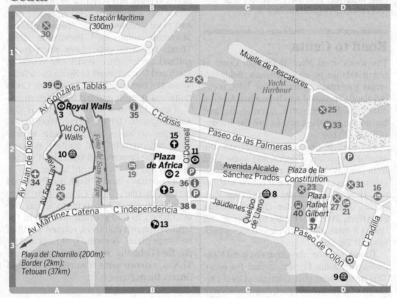

Estación Marítima
(300m)

Muelle de Pescatores

Yacht
Harbour

Av Gonzáles Tablas

Royal Walls

Old City
Walls

Av Juan de Dios

Foso de San Felipe

Plaza
de Africa

Paseo de las Palmeras

Avenida Alcalde
Sánchez Prados

Plaza de la
Constitution

Plaza
Rafael
Gilbert

C Independencia

C Edrisis

O'Donnell

Jaudenes

Queipo de Llano

Paseo de Colón

C Padilla

Av Martínez Catena

Playa del Chorrillo (200m);
Border (2km);
Tetouan (37km)

This cultural-island phenomenon is the essence of Ceuta. It explains the heavy Spanish military presence, the Moroccan immigrants, the duty-free shopping, the shady cross-border commerce and the tourism. It makes a perfect weekend getaway.

◉ Sights & Activities

Ceuta's history is outlined by the *ruta monumenta*, a series of excellent information boards in English and Spanish outside key buildings and monuments.

★ Plaza de Africa   LANDMARK
This is the charming heart of Ceuta, with manicured tropical plantings, a square of cobblestone streets and some of the city's finest architecture. Moving clockwise from the oblong Commandancia General, a military headquarters closed to visitors, you encounter the striking yellow Santuario de Nuestra Señora de Africa (◎9am-1pm & 5-9pm Mon-Sat, 9am-1pm & 6.30-9pm Sun & holidays), an 18th-century Andalucian-style church; the 19th-century Palacio de Asamblea with its elegant dome and clock, a combination palace and city hall; and finally the 17th-century, twin-spired Cathedral Santa Maria de la Asuncion

(☑0956 51 77 71; ◎9am-1pm & 6-8pm Tue-Sun, museum 10am-1pm Tue-Sat) with its museum. The centre of the plaza contains a memorial to soldiers lost in the Spanish–Moroccan War of 1860, a conflict over the borders of Ceuta.

★ Royal Walls   ARCHITECTURE
(☑0956 51 17 70; Ave González Tablas; ◎10am-2pm & 5-8pm) FREE The most impressive sight in Ceuta is the medieval Royal Walls, dating back to the 5th century. These extensive fortifications, of great strategic complexity, have been wonderfully restored, with information boards in English. The beautifully designed Museo de los Murales Reales (Ave González Tablas, inside City Walls), a gallery that houses temporary art exhibitions, lies within the walls themselves. It's a most atmospheric space, worth visiting regardless of what's on show – although if you're lucky enough to catch local artist Diego Canca, don't miss his work.

Beaches   BEACH
Easily overlooked, the two town beaches, Playa del Chorrillo and Playa de la Ribera, lie to the south of the isthmus, beneath Av Martinez Catena. They are well kept and conveniently located, although the sand is a bland grey.

Museo de la Legión   MUSEUM
(☑0956 52 64 58; Paseo de Colón; donations appreciated; ◎10am-1.30pm Mon-Sat) FREE This intriguing museum is dedicated to and run by the Spanish Legion, an army unit set up in 1920 that played a pivotal role in Franco's republican army. Loaded to the gills with memorabilia, weaponry and uniforms, not to mention glory, pomp and circumstance, it is a fascinating glimpse into the military culture that shaped the north, from the imperious statue of Franco, to the explanation of how the legion's founder, Millan Astray, lost his right eye, to the history of the legion in cinema. They even check your passport at the door. Alternatively, you can enlist at http://lalegion.es. There are guided tours in English.

Museo de Ceuta   MUSEUM
(☑0956 51 73 98; 30 Paseo del Revellín; ◎11am-2pm & 6-9pm Mon-Sat Jun-Sep) FREE This ageing municipal museum has a small collection showing the peninsula's pre-Spanish history, with all labels in Spanish. The temporary exhibitions are of more interest.

MEDITERRANEAN COAST & THE RIF CEUTA (SEBTA)

Plaza de los Reyes
LANDMARK

With its green triumphal arch (inscribed 'a monument to coexistence') and fountain, this plaza borders the twin-towered yellow Iglesia de San Francisco.

★ Casa de Los Dragones
ARCHITECTURE

(House of Dragons) The Casa de los Dragones on Plaza de los Reyes is a fantastic dream that has entered the real world. Recently restored to perfection, this former home is an extraordinary example of eclectic architecture, with Moorish arches, polished brick facades, Mansard roofs, fabulous balconies, and the pièce de résistance, four enormous dark dragons springing from the roof. Unfortunately, it's not open to the public. The intricate anagram of the Cerni Gonzalez Brothers, the builders, is emblazoned on the corner. Tip your hat.

Museo de la Basilica Tardorromana
MUSEUM

(⊙10am-1.30pm & 5-7.30pm Mon-Sat, 10am-1.30pm Sun) This superbly executed underground museum is integrated into the architectural remains of an ancient basilica discovered during street work in the 1980s, including a bridge over open tombs, skeletons included. The artefacts become a means of branching out into various elements of local history. In Spanish, but definitely worth a lap through. Enter via Calle Queipo de Llano.

Parque Marítimo del Mediterráneo
PARK

(adult/child peak season €4.80/3.70; ⊙11am-8pm Jun-Aug, casino from 10pm) This creative maritime park is one of several versions developed by the brilliant artist and architect César Manrique of the Canary Islands. He borrowed the city-walls theme to construct a huge pool deck on the sea, including a grand lagoon and two other saltwater pools, surrounded by 10 bars, pubs, restaurants, cafes and a disco. A central island holds a fortress casino. A pictorial display of Manrique's work lies just inside the entrance, 50m to the right. This is a real hit in the summer, and perfect for families.

Baños Arabes
HISTORIC BUILDING

(Calle Arrabal 16; ⊙11.30am-1.30pm & 6.30-8.30pm) Accidentally discovered during street work, these ancient Arab baths sit on a main road, an incongruous sight. There are two of them, with barrel-vaulted roofs originally covered with marble – the high-tech spa of its time.

Monte Hacho
OUTDOORS

A walk around Monte Hacho is an option on a nice day; maps are available at the tourist office or you can wing it and follow the coast. Since it's an uphill slog from town, a good option is to start by taking a cab (€15) to the Mirador de San Antonio two-thirds of the way up, which offers magnificent views over Ceuta and north to Gibraltar. The summit of the peninsula is crowned by the massive Fortaleza de Hacho, a fort first built by the Byzantines, and still an active military installation. No visitors are allowed.

Back down at the main road, you keep going clockwise until you reach the Castillo del Desnarigado (⊡0956 51 17 70; ⊙11am-2pm Sat & Sun) FREE, a small fort on the southeastern tip of the peninsula that houses a small military museum. There is a lighthouse above, and a secluded beach, Playa Torrecilla, below.

García Aldave
OUTDOORS

If you've done everything else, the García Aldave can be crossed from coast to coast along the N354, either by car or on foot (a hiking map from the tourist office will help). The route contains a series of circular neo-medieval watchtowers, closed to visitors. Several of these are visible from the excellent Mirador de Isabel II, which offers great views across the isthmus to Monte Hacho. On 1 November, the Day of the Dead, there is a mass pilgrimage here to remember the deceased.

The road ends at Benzú, a small town on the northern coast, which faces the grand sight of Jebel Musa rising across the border. The mountain is known here as the Dead Woman, as it resembles one, lying on her back. Contemplate mortality here over a cup of mint tea.

🛏 Sleeping

Ceuta isn't overrun with sleeping options, so if you're arriving late in the day an advance reservation is a good idea. Most cheap places are *pensiónes*, some of which are identifiable by the large blue-and-white 'CH' plaque.

★ Pensión La Bohemia
HOTEL €

(⊡0956 51 06 15; 16 Paseo del Revellín; per person without bathroom €30) This well-run operation, one flight above a shopping arcade, offers a bright and spotless set of rooms arranged around a central courtyard. Bathrooms are shared, with plenty of hot water and communal showers. Rooms have small TVs and fans.

Pensión Charito
HOSTEL €

(☑ 0956 51 39 82; pcharito@terra.es; 1st fl, 5 Calle Arrabal; per person €25) A bold new CH sign makes this place easier to find than before – look for the green and cream building next to the bar Bocatos José. Though a bit decrepit, the inside is clean and homey with hot showers and a small, well-equipped kitchen. If rooms are full the staff may not be present.

Hotel Ulises
HOTEL €€

(☑ 0956 51 45 40; www.hotelulises.com; 5 Calle Camoens; s/d incl breakfast €70/75; ❄ ⓦ ☎) Recently refurbished, this hotel now offers a very good deal: excellent location, parking nearby and great prices. The rooms aren't large, but come with TV and some have balconies. The cafe spills out onto the pavement and is perfect for people-watching over a drink and a few tapas.

Hostal Central
HOTEL €€

(☑ 0956 51 67 16; www.hostalesceuta.com; Paseo del Revellín; s/d/tr with bathroom €45/66/76; ❄ ⓦ) This place is in a charming location and offers a warm welcome. Rooms are airy, with nice pine furniture; the best have wrought-iron balconies overlooking the cafes of the plaza. Bathrooms and fridges are standard.

Hostal Plaza Ruiz
HOTEL €€

(☑ 0956 51 67 33; www.hostalesceuta.com; 3 Plaza Ruiz; s/d/tr with bathroom €45/66/76; ❄ ⓦ) This good-value, two-star hotel in an excellent location has ultra-modern decor and is very welcoming. Rooms are tiny but spotless, and all come with bathroom and fridge. Low-season discounts are available.

Parador Hotel La Muralla
HOTEL €€€

(☑ 0956 51 49 40; ceuta@parador.es; 15 Plaza de Africa; s/d from €101/127; ❄ ⓦ ☎) This spacious four-star hotel is perfectly situated on the Plaza de Africa. Rooms are comfortable, but not luxurious, with simple wooden doors and plain ceramic tiles. Balconies overlook a pleasant garden overflowing with palm trees. A bar-cafe adds value.

✖ Eating & Drinking

The best places to look for tapas bars are in the streets behind the post office and around Calle Millán Astray to the north of Calle Camoens. In addition to tapas, they all serve more substantial *raciones* (a larger helping of tapas) and *bocadillos* (sandwiches).

Mesón el Bache
TAPAS €

(☑ 0956 51 66 42; Sargento Mena Algeciras; tapas €2.50, raciones from €10; ⊙ 9am-3pm & 8.30pm-midnight Mon-Sat) Have your tapas in a rustic hunting lodge. The locals love it, especially for watching sport, and you get one free tapa with every drink. Just downhill from Plaza de los Reyes, looking towards the port.

Mesón el Cortijo
TAPAS €

(☑ 0956 51 19 83; 14 Calle Cervantes; tapas from €2; ⊙ lunch & dinner Mon-Sat) A classic neighbourhood gathering place heavy on tapas, *cerveza* (beer) and friendliness. Catch up on football, gossip and practise your Español.

Vincentino Pastelería
CAFE, PATISSERIE €

(Calle Alférez Bayton; sandwiches €2, bocadillos €2.50; ⊙ 8am-11pm) This place buzzes all day with people clamouring for its ice creams, sandwiches, delicious patisserie and excellent coffee. Sit inside or out.

Charlotte
CAFE €

(Plaza de los Reyes; breakfast €4; ⊙ breakfast, lunch & dinner) This is the perfect place for just about anything any time of day: they serve breakfast, a lunchtime sandwich, beer, cocktail and tapas. Swift, efficient service and a prime people-watching spot on the square make it very popular.

El Secreto de Yuste
SPANISH €

(☑ 0659 67 18 14; 1 Muralles Reales; menu €6; ⊙ lunch & dinner Mon-Sat) Here's your chance to eat inside the Royal Walls. There's a small menu of local meats and seafood enhanced by the unique atmosphere. You can sit outside by the moat.

Gran Muralla
CHINESE €

(☑ 0956 51 76 25; Plaza de la Constitution; mains from €7; ⊙ lunch & dinner) If you've had enough local food, you'll find hearty portions of Chinese standards here. Window tables have views over the plaza and out to sea.

Cala Carlota
SEAFOOD €€

(☑ 0956 52 50 61; Real Club Nautico, Calle Edrisis; mains from €8, set menu €14.50; ⊙ lunch & dinner) This simple restaurant has a prime location in the Club Nautico overlooking the yacht harbour, with outdoor seating in season. If you can see your way past the desultory service, the three-course *menú del diá* (daily set menu) is a good choice, and there are excellent fish main dishes. To get there, the underpass beneath the busy highway starts at the main tourist office, and will save you a long walk.

★ El Refectorio
SPANISH €€€

(☎0956 51 38 84; www.elrefectorio.com; Poblado Marinero; menu around €40-55; ⊗lunch & dinner) Considered by many to be Ceuta's best restaurant, El Refectorio has a good bar, and dining inside and out with magnificent sea views from the balcony. It excels at shellfish, fish and meats and has a good wine list.

Dublin
PUB

(Calle Delgado Serrano; ⊗4pm-3am Mon-Sat) It's like every other Irish pub you've ever been in, but if you need that Guinness fix (pints €5), this is the place. If the volume gets to you, you can escape to the tables outside. Go down the steps where Calle Delgado Serrano takes a 90-degree bend.

Poblado Marinero
BAR

(Seamen's Village) There are numerous bars and fast-food restaurants here.

Self-Catering

The **Supersol supermarket** (Av Muelle Cañonero Dato) is the best place to stock up on essentials and treats alike; there's a smaller branch in the city centre on Dean Navarro Acuña.

The cavernous **Central Market** (⊗8am-3pm Mon-Sat) is the local spot for fresh meat and produce, and a vibrant experience as well.

ⓘ Information

To phone Ceuta from outside Spain, dial ☎0034. Remember that Ceuta is one hour ahead of Morocco, and that most businesses will be closed on Sunday.

MEDICAL SERVICES

Instituto Gestión Sanitario (Ingesa; ☎0956 52 84 00; ⊗24hr) Next to the Royal Walls. There's another location east of the fishing port.

MONEY

Euros are used for all transactions in Ceuta. ATMs are plentiful; outside banking hours you can change money at the more expensive hotels. There are informal moneychangers on both sides of the border, although it's technically illegal to take dirhams out of Morocco.

POST

Main Post Office (Plaza de España; ⊗8.30am-8.30pm Mon-Fri, 9.30am-2pm Sat)

TOURIST INFORMATION

Main Tourist Office (☎0956 20 05 60; Baluarte de los Mallorquines; ⊗8.30am-8.30pm Mon-Fri, 9am-8pm Sat & Sun) Friendly and efficient, with good maps and brochures.

Plaza de Africa Kiosk (☎0956 52 81 46; ⊗10am-1pm & 5-8pm 15 Sep-31 May, 10.30am-1.30pm & 6-9pm 1 Jun-14 Sep) A satellite of the main tourist office.

TRAVEL AGENCIES

Av Muelle Cañonero Dato and the approach to the *estación marítima* are lined with agencies selling ferry tickets to Algeciras.

Viajes Flandria (☎0956 51 20 74; ventas@viajesflandria.com; 1 Calle Independencia; ⊗9.30am-1pm & 3.30-7pm Mon-Sat)

ⓘ Getting There & Away

MOROCCO

Buses and grands taxis to Ceuta often terminate at Fnideq, rather than at the border (Bab Sebta). If so, the border is a further 1km walk, or Dh7 by taxi. Although the border is open 24 hours, public transport is sparse from 7pm to 5am.

On the Moroccan side, you'll either fill out a departure form at the passport window, if on foot, or at the vehicle registration window. Hustlers will sell you a form for a dirham or two. If you're driving a hire car, you will be required to show proof of authorisation to take the vehicle out of the country. The 100m crossing is surprisingly disorganised, with multiple people asking for your passport. Pedestrians must frequently walk in the car lanes.

Coming the other way, there is a large grand taxi lot next to Moroccan border control. Departures are plentiful to Tetouan (Dh30, 40 minutes), from where you can pick up onward transport. Taxis to Chefchaouen or Tangier are rare, and you'll most likely have to bargain hard to hire a vehicle to yourself (Chefchaouen Dh300, 90 minutes; Tangier Dh200, one hour). A good alternative is to take a grand taxi to Fnideq (Dh7, 10 minutes), just south of the border, from where transport to Tangier (Dh30, one hour) is more frequent.

MAINLAND SPAIN

The unmissable **Estación Marítima** (Ferry Terminal; Calle Muelle Cañonero Dato) is west of the town centre. There are several daily high-speed ferries to Algeciras. Ticket offices are around the corner.

You can purchase train tickets to European destinations at the **Renfe office** (☎0956 51 13 17; 17 Plaza Rafael Gilbert; ⊗9.30am-1pm & 4.30-8.30pm Mon-Fri, 9.30am-1pm Sat) or at a travel agency. Several agencies in the ferry terminal also sell Enatcar (the main Spanish coach company) bus tickets.

❶ Getting Around

Bus 7 runs up to the border (*frontera*) every 10 minutes or so from Plaza de la Constitution (€1). If you arrive by ferry and want to head straight for the border, there's a bus stop on Ave González Tablaz opposite the entrance to the ramparts. There's also a taxi rank outside the terminal building.

If you have your own vehicle, street parking is restricted to a maximum of two hours (€1) during the day. If you are staying longer, use the **car park** (per hr €0.50, per 12hr €4) on Calle O'Donnell or the one near the Poblado Marinero (p244).

THE RIF MOUNTAINS

جبال الرّف

Tetouan

تطوان

POP 330,000

Tetouan is a jewel of a town in a striking location at the foot of the Rif Mountains, and just a few kilometres from the sea. It's unlike Tangier or the imperial cities in that it is little visited by foreign tourists. There is an air of authenticity here that adds great value to a visit. The ancient medina, a Unesco World Heritage site, looks like it has not changed in several centuries. There have been some recent upgrades – a modern bus station, restorations to the medina wall, some public gardens – but nothing like the towns along the coast. The city is poised on the edge of discovery and to the savvy traveller, this spells opportunity.

From 1912 until 1956 Tetouan was the capital of the Spanish protectorate, which encompassed much of northern Morocco. This, and the town's long relationship with Andalucia, have left it with a Hispano-Moorish character that is unique in Morocco, as physically reflected in the Spanish part of the city, known as the Ensanche (extension), whose white buildings and broad boulevards have been restored to their original condition.

The Ensanche is centred on Pl Moulay el-Mehdi and the pedestrian stretch of Ave Mohammed V, which runs east to Pl al-Jala. Here you'll find hotels, banks and places to eat. The entrance to the medina is off the grand Pl Hassan II, which faces the Royal Palace. The rest of the sprawling town has little to offer the visitor.

History

From the 8th century onwards, the city served as the main point of contact between Morocco and Andalucia. In the 14th century

---

THE CANNABIS INDUSTRY

The Rif is home to the largest acreage of cannabis cultivation in the world, an estimated 1340 sq km, or 42% of global production. Cultivation has expanded rapidly since the 1980s, in part due to increasing European demand. The cannabis trade is now the region's main economic activity, involving an estimated 800,000 people, and probably Morocco's main source of foreign currency, although rural farmers reap little from it.

Cannabis cultivation started around Ketama in the 15th century. In 1912 the right to cultivate cannabis was granted to a few Rif tribes by Spain. In 1956, when Morocco gained independence, cannabis was prohibited, but Mohammed V later condoned cultivation in the Rif after the prohibition led to conflict there.

Most large shipments of Moroccan hashish (a concentrated form of marijuana) are smuggled into Europe by boat, including small speedboats that can make a round trip to Spain in an hour. The primary departure points are Martil, Oued Laou and Bou-Ahmed, although the bigger ports of Nador, Tetouan, Tangier and Larache are also used. Traffickers also export hashish concealed in trucks and cars embarked on ferries leaving from the Spanish enclaves of Ceuta and Melilla or from Tangier. Not surprisingly, of all hashish seizures worldwide, half are made in Spain. It is now thought that terrorist groups are entering the market in order to fund operations. Traffickers have also branched out into human smuggling, to include smuggling hashish and migrants into Europe together.

To counter this illegal trade, the government, encouraged by the EU, is actively promoting rural tourism by supporting the establishment of *gîtes* and training programs for guides. Whether this will provide a sufficient alternative source of income for local people remains to be seen.

Tetouan

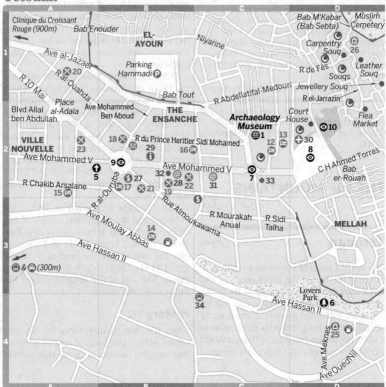

MEDITERRANEAN COAST & THE RIF TETOUAN

the Merenids established the town as a base from which to control rebellious Rif tribes, and to attack Ceuta, but it was destroyed by Henry III of Castile in 1399. After the Reconquista (the reconquest of Spain, completed in 1492), the town was rebuilt by Andalucian refugees. It prospered in part due to their skills, and to thriving pirate activity.

Moulay Ismail built Tetouan's defensive walls in the 17th century, and the town's trade links with Spain developed. In 1860, the Spanish took the town under Leopoldo O'Donnell, who extensively Europeanised it, but upon recapture two years later the Moors removed all the signs of European influence.

At the turn of the 20th century, Spanish forces occupied Tetouan for three years, claiming it was protecting Ceuta from Rif tribes. In 1913 the Spanish made Tetouan the capital of their protectorate, which was abandoned in 1956 when Morocco regained

independence. Lately the Andalucian government has provided a great cultural boost to the city by financing various restoration projects.

◎ Sights

◎ Medina

The whitewashed medina of Tetouan is an authentic time machine, and very traveller-friendly, with moped-free lanes, few street hustlers, amiable residents and a general lack of congestion, particularly in the large residential areas. In the commercial spaces, the sights and sounds of traditional life are everywhere: artisans pound brass, silk merchants offer thousands of spools of multi-coloured thread and bakers tend the public ovens. There are some 35 mosques as well, of which the **Grande Mosquée** and **Saïda Mosque**, both northeast of Pl Hassan II, are

tices traditional arts, including ornamental woodwork, silk costumes, carved plaster, intricate mosaics and decorative rifles. A fantastic central treasury holds the best of the best – don't miss the ceiling. Staff will open the treasury upon request. The building itself is of interest, set around a large courtyard, with fine doors upstairs.

Place Hassan II   LANDMARK

The broad and empty Pl Hassan II, which is mostly roped off for security reasons, links the medina to the Ensanche. It looks like it houses the Wizard of Oz, with guards standing in front of the long flat facade of the royal palace, and four somewhat bizarre columns towering all around. These are not minarets, as one might suppose, but art nouveau light towers designed by Enrique Nieto, a student of Gaudí who lived in Melilla. The large decorations on the opposite wall are abstract Hands of Fatima, a common symbol used to ward off the evil eye. There are a few cafes that are good for a rest, particularly on the 2nd floor, which allows a grander view.

◉ The Ensanche

Take in the Ensanche by walking along Ave Mohammed V from Place al-Jala to Place Moulay el-Mehdi. The broad boulevard is lined with bright white Spanish colonial architecture, with a few art deco elements, reminiscent of styles found elsewhere (eg in Casablanca and Larache) with restoration funded by the Andalucian government.

★ Archaeology Museum   MUSEUM

(Ave al-Jazaer; admission Dh10; ⊙10am-6pm Mon-Sat) A few blocks from the Pl al-Jala this extensive museum has an excellent collection of artefacts from the Roman ruins at Lixus, displayed both inside and in the gardens. Labelling is in French, Spanish and Arabic.

Iglesia de Bacturia   CHURCH

(Pl Moulay el-Mehdi; ⊙7pm daily Mass, 11am Sun Mass) This Roman Catholic church was built in 1926 and is still active. We can't think of another place in Morocco where church bells sound the hour.

★ Tetouan Museum of Modern Art   MUSEUM

(☏0666 04 60 81; www.gotetouan.com/Museums.html; Ave Al Maki Al Naciri; ⊙9am-7pm Mon-Sat) **FREE** Tetouan boasts one of only two schools of fine arts in Morocco (Casablanca has the

the most impressive, although non-Muslims are not allowed to enter. If you get lost, a few dirhams in local hands will get you to any doorstep.

The medina is bordered to the south by the pretty Lovers Park, a pleasant escape.

Ethnographic Museum   MUSEUM

(Bab el-Okla; admission Dh10; ⊙9am-4pm Mon-Sat) Just inside the picture-perfect eastern gate, Bab el-Okla, is the Ethnographic Museum. It's worth a visit for the terrace views of the Rif (ask the caretaker to open it for you, if necessary), its pleasant garden with old cannons and the display of silk wedding gowns.

★ Artisanal School   NOTABLE BUILDING

(☏0539 97 27 21; admission Dh10; ⊙8.30am-2.30pm Sat-Thu, 8.30-11.30am Fri) Just outside Bab el-Okla is the best artisan centre in northern Morocco. This is a fascinating opportunity to see masters teaching apprentices

Tetouan

other), so it's fitting that this new museum should open here. The building itself, a magnificent Spanish-castle-like structure that was once the railway station, is worth a visit. It has been carefully renovated to protect the artworks and to provide ample light inside. The museum houses contemporary Moroccan art and has visiting exhibitions.

🛏 Sleeping

Due to the rapid development of the nearby coast, the first question is whether to stay in town or not. Tetouan's port, Martil, is only an inexpensive 15-minute cab ride away; M'Diq, the classiest option, is twice that. The contrast could not be greater between the ancient medina and these modern resorts with their snazzy corniches – either jarring or a relief depending on what you're looking for. The beachfronts are very quiet outside the holiday season of July to August.

If you choose the city, your next decision is whether to stay in the medina or not. A night or two within the ancient walls is an unforgettable adventure and an opportunity to see typical Tetouan architecture and furniture, usually studded with mother-of-pearl inlay.

Pension Iberia   HOTEL €
(☏ 0539 96 36 79; 5 Pl Moulay el-Mehdi; s/d/tr without bathroom Dh60/100/150) This is the best budget option, with shuttered balconies that open out to the Pl Moulay el-Mehdi. Views of the city flowing over the hills and the fountain in the Place add a dash of romance. Room 11 is a good choice. Hot showers cost Dh10. On the 3rd floor above a bank, it has public parking (p250) nearby.

Hotel Regina   HOTEL €
(☏ 0539 96 21 13; 8 Rue Sidi Mandri; s/d/tr winter Dh100/130/180, summer Dh130/160/210) One of the larger budget choices, the Regina initially feels a bit tired, but the whitewashed walls and bright Riffian fabrics manage to wake you up. While the bathrooms are sometimes worn, everything is sparklingly clean, which makes it decent value for money. There's a cafe on the ground floor for breakfast.

Hotel Paris   HOTEL €
(☏ 0539 96 67 50; 31 Rue Chakib Arsalane; s/d Dh250/295) The simple, uninspiring rooms are clean, but the bathrooms are small. Institutional hallways accelerate you outdoors. Breakfast costs Dh40.

★ **El Reducto** RIAD €€

(☑0539 96 81 20; www.riadtetouan.com; 38 Zanqat Zawiya; s/d incl breakfast from Dh400/550; ❄️🛜) This superb house is worth a visit just to see the traditional mosaic tiles with their coppery sheen. The spotless, palatial rooms are truly fantastic, with big bathrooms (one has a Jacuzzi for two), the highest quality antique furniture and beautiful silk bedspreads. There's also a good, licensed restaurant with a Spanish touch to the menu. Climb the spiral staircase to the roof terrace for spectacular views.

Hotel Panorama Vista HOTEL €€

(☑0539 96 49 70; www.panoramavista.com; Ave Moulay Abbas; s/d incl breakfast Dh279/378; ❄️🛜) This is the best bet outside the medina. The rooms are chain-hotel style without any local ambience, but clean and with dramatic views over the Rif. The popular cafe on the 1st floor offers a strong Moroccan continental breakfast.

Blanco Riad RIAD €€€

(☑0539 70 42 02; www.blancoriad.com; 25 Rue Zawiya Kadiria; d incl breakfast from Dh660, ste Dh1760; ❄️🛜) This beautiful medina house with its typical Tetouan architecture has been carefully restored and furnished with a blend of modern and antique pieces. It offers large, comfortable rooms and a Zen-like garden. One of the salons contains a good restaurant open to nonguests.

✗ Eating

Tetouan was not known for its restaurants in the past, but things are looking up as tourism is encouraged. The best restaurants are those in medina guesthouses. Otherwise, you are restricted to grilled food and sandwiches.

Snack Taouss FAST FOOD €

(☑0533 23 11 58; 3 Rue 10 Mai; mains from Dh25; ⏰11am-11pm) Known for its burgers and chips, this little snack bar has a Syrian influence and does good felafel and delicious *shwarma* as well as inexpensive pizzas, salads, *harira* (tomato and chickpea soup), tajines and more. There's a small seating area upstairs (handy if you're waiting for a pizza), or you can eat on the move.

Birjiss FAST FOOD €

(☑0539 71 11 11; 8 Ave Mohammed Ben Aboud; panini from Dh20; ⏰noon-11pm) Made-to-order sandwiches, burgers, pizzas and *shwarma* make this a standout option. Choose from a smorgasbord of ingredients both typical and exotic.

Restaurant Albahr FAST FOOD €

(☑0533 68 96 75; 21 Rue Almoukawama; mains from Dh30; ⏰lunch & dinner) All new chrome and black decor here, with fried foods, burgers and good fish and chips on the menu. Salads are a plus, and there's couscous on Fridays (Dh50).

Restaurant Restinga MOROCCAN €

(21 Ave Mohammed V; mains from Dh45, beer from Dh20; ⏰9am-9pm) The open-air courtyard shaded by a huge ficus tree is this charming restaurant's primary attraction – along with the rare alcohol licence. A great place to duck out of the crowded boulevard for a rest and a beer, as well as some seafood from the coast.

Dallas PATISSERIE €

(☑0533 96 60 69; 11 Rue Youssef ben Tachfine; pastries from Dh4; ⏰6am-10pm) Yes, named after the TV show, but otherwise the name has no bearing on this place, a patisserie stacked to the rafters with plates of pastries. This is where local families come to load up on sweets. One block off Ave Mohammed V.

Oahda CAFE €

(☑0533 96 67 94; 16 Rue al-Ouahda; pastries from Dh4; ⏰7am-9pm, closed Fri afternoon) A female-friendly cafe popular with locals where sticky cakes are a speciality. A bit claustrophobic on the upper floor.

★ **Blanco Riad** MOROCCAN €€

(☑0539 70 42 02; 25 Rue Zawiya Kadiria; 3-course menu Dh160; ⏰dinner) The menu at this elegant riad is a cut above the usual and features some interesting fish dishes. The garden is pleasant in summer, and the dining room has both Moroccan and Western seating. Reservations essential.

El Reducto MOROCCAN €€

(☑0539 96 81 20; 38 Zanqat Zawiya; mains from Dh80; ⏰dinner) Tuck into traditional Moroccan fare in the grand surroundings of this riad. Desserts are particularly good.

Self-Catering

There's loads of fresh fruit and veg for sale in the medina on the road leading east to Bab el-Okla. The central **market** (⏰closed Fri) around the corner from Lovers Park puts on a good display, with fish brought in from the coast.

MEDITERRANEAN COAST & THE RIF TETOUAN

Drinking

As is the Moroccan norm, Tetouan's drinking establishments are firmly in the male sphere. For a drop of the hard stuff, head for the dark and smoky bars along Rue 10 Mai, northwest of Pl Moulay el-Mehdi. If you just want a beer, Restaurant Restinga (p249) is the place.

Shopping

Wood and leatherwork are the local specialties; for the latter go straight to the source at the small **tannery** (Bab M'Kabar) in the north of the medina.

Dar Lebadi   ARTS & CRAFTS, CARPETS
(☑0533 97 38 56; Jenoui section; ⊘10am-7pm) The shopping palace of the medina, this 200-year-old building, a former governor's house, has been meticulously restored, and is a clearing house for Berber artisans and Rabati carpets, with friendly staff. Worth a stop just to see the building, but be careful: you may be there for hours.

Ensemble Artisanal   ART & CRAFTS
(Ave Hassan II; ⊘8am-8pm Mon-Sat) This government-sponsored emporium is a hive of activity, with carpet weavers, leatherworkers, jewellers and woodworkers all plying their trades. Prices are fixed.

Information

INTERNET ACCESS

Cyber Friends (19 Ave Mohammed V; per hr Dh5; ⊘9am-11pm)

Remote Studios (13 Ave Mohammed V; per hr Dh9; ⊘9am-midnight)

MEDICAL SERVICES

Clinique du Croissant Rouge (Red Cross Clinic; ☑0539 96 20 20; Pl al-Hammama, Quartier Scolaire)

Main Hospital (☑0539 97 24 30; Ave Abdelkhalek Torres) About 2km out of town.

Pharmacie El-Feddan (☑0539 96 80 51; Pl Hassan II; ⊘9am-1pm & 3.30-8pm)

MONEY

There are plenty of banks with ATMs along Ave Mohammed V.

BMCE (Pl Moulay el-Mehdi; ⊘8.45am-4pm Mon-Thu, 8.45-11am Fri, 8.45am-noon Sat)

POST

Post Office (Pl Moulay el-Mehdi; ⊘8am-4pm)

TOURIST INFORMATION

Délégation Provinciale de Tourisme (☑0539 96 19 15; fax 0539 96 19 14; 30 Ave Mohammed V; ⊘10am-4pm Mon-Fri) The staff here are helpful and have lots of brochures and maps available. The 1951 murals of northern Morocco here are worth a visit, too.

TRAVEL AGENCIES

Voyages Travelmar (☑0539 71 42 37; 5 Ave Mohammed V; ⊘9am-noon & 2.30-6.30pm Mon-Sat)

Voyages Hispamaroc (fax 0539 71 33 38; 23 Ave Mohammed V; ⊘8.30am-12.30pm & 3-7pm Mon-Fri, 9am-12.30pm Sat)

Getting There & Away

AIR

The Tetouan airport opens for occasional charter flights from Paris and Brussels but has no scheduled service. Persistent rumours that a fully-fledged airport is coming may be inspired by efforts to sell foreigners real estate.

BUS

From Tetouan's modern **bus station** (cnr Ave 9 Avril & Ave Meknes) you can get to any town in the north. There's a **left-luggage office** (medium/large bag Dh6/10). Local buses serve the following destinations:

Fnideq Dh12, 1¼ hours
Martil Dh6, 25 minutes
M'Diq Dh10, one hour

CTM (☑0539 96 16 88) has its own station a five-minute taxi ride away from the main bus station. CTM has better vehicles for any long-haul destinations.

Fez Dh100, six hours
Marrakesh Dh240, 11½ hours
Rabat Dh115, four hours

TAXI

Grands taxis leave from the main bus station for Oued Laou (Dh20, 30 minutes), Al-Hoceima (Dh150, three hours), Chefchaouen (Dh30, one hour) and Tangier (Dh30, 1¼ hours).

Grands taxis leave from the CTM bus station for Fnideq (for Ceuta; Dh20, 30 minutes) and Martil (Dh7, 15 minutes).

Getting Around

Petits taxis are canary yellow but don't have meters; a ride around town should be around Dh10. If you have your own vehicle, you can keep your car at the guarded **Parking Hammadi** (Ave Al Jazaer; daytime per 4hr Dh10, per night Dh10).

Around Tetouan

While Tetouan itself sees few foreigners, in summer both local and Europe-based Moroccans flock to the golden beaches close to the town. The coast from Fnideq near Ceuta southwards to M'Diq, Cabo Negro and Martil sports two large golf resorts and swaths of holiday apartments along new corniches.

Cabo Negro & M'diq

الرأس الاسود والمضيق

Tucked into the lee of the north side of Cabo Negro is the surprising town of M'Diq. Once a small fishing village, it has rapidly grown into the classiest resort on the coast, with a grand entrance, a fine beach, good hotels, the enormous Port de Plaisance shopping centre with lots of restaurants and the yacht club. There is really little to separate this place from Florida, but if you are suffering from medina fatigue, it's the perfect stop, and only 20 minutes from Tetouan.

🛏 Sleeping & Eating

M'Diq's sleeping options tend to cater to the summer tourist trade and ignore the lower end of the price bracket. Ask for discounts outside the summer months. Given the number of new apartments, it is worth enquiring about rentals on site. There's a string of cafes and cheap eateries along the seafront.

Golden Beach Hotel   HOTEL €€
(📞 0539 97 50 77; www.goldenbeachhotel.com; 84 Rte de Sebta; s/d incl breakfast Dh478/709, incl half board Dh638/1029; 🛜🏊) This four-star, aptly named hotel right on the beach is worth the splurge. It's short on charm, but well run, well maintained and with great facilities, including a restaurant, disco, pool by the corniche and a piano bar with a most clever bar top: piano keys in marble.

Hotel Côte d'Or   HOTEL €€
(Corniche; s/d incl breakfast Dh358/486) One of several new hotels along the corniche, this one is fairly bland with simple, modern rooms. Ask for a sea view. There are also apartments that sleep five at Dh1300. It is in a superb location opposite the beach, and there's a cafe and restaurant on the ground floor.

Café Olas   SEAFOOD €
(📞 0539 66 44 33; Corniche; mains from Dh65; ⊙lunch & dinner; 🌿) You can't miss this waterfront landmark dressed up as a lighthouse, with a hopping downstairs cafe and an upstairs seafood restaurant. The decor is snappy, the rooftop views superb, and the chefs don't have to go far to get fresh catch. Located directly on the corniche car park.

La Table du Marché   SEAFOOD €€€
(📞 0661 47 85 56; Port de Plaisance; ⊙8pm-3am) Sitting at the end of a causeway in the sea, this Asian-inspired thatched-roof restaurant comes as quite a surprise. With branches in St Tropez and Marrakesh, perhaps this is the new face of Morocco. It offers seafood, sushi and Italian dishes in chic surroundings.

🛈 Getting There & Away

Grands taxis and buses travelling between Tetouan and Fnideq (3km short of the border with Ceuta) pass through M'Diq. Grands taxis to Tetouan (Dh7, 15 minutes) depart from a stand near the Narjiss Hotel on Av Lalla Nezha. Those for the border (Dh15) gather opposite the Golden Beach Hotel.

Martil   مارتل

Tetouan's port of Martil is a rapidly growing, modern beach town with a broad mountain view and a long corniche paralleled by streets full of apartment blocks, cafes, ice-cream shops and fast-food restaurants. Two

COAST ROAD FROM FNIDEQ TO MARTIL

The coast road, or Rocade, now stretches from Fnideq all the way along the Mediterranean coast to Saïdia in the far east. From Fnideq to Martil there's a spanking new corniche along the beautiful beach. While there are few hotels, a huge number of holiday apartment blocks have been completed along this stretch, and more are being built. There are resorts at Plage Riffiyenne and the Marina Smir, and the enormous Ritz-Carlton resort under construction promises golf and another marina.

If you're wondering why Moroccans prefer to holiday in apartments rather than hotels, we're told it's because they relish home cooking. Let's hope mum gets a holiday too.

golf courses and a pair of shopping centres were nearing completion at the time of research. It has year-round weekend visitors, and heaves in the summer, but is deserted the rest of the time. It's a viable base if you don't mind the 8km, 10-minute cab ride to Tetouan.

🛏 Sleeping & Eating

Hotel Etoile de la Mer
HOTEL €

(☑ 0539 97 90 58; Ave Hassan II; s/d incl breakfast Dh320/374; 🗐) With its funky design – a central, plant-filled atrium criss-crossed by stairways – and good location one block from the beach, this is Martil's best sleeping option. Riffian textiles and green paint brighten things up. The best rooms have balconies overlooking the sea, and the restaurant serves alcohol.

Camping al-Boustane
CAMPGROUND €

(fax 0539 68 88 22; Corniche; camping per person Dh20, per tent/car/campervan Dh40/20/35, electricity Dh25; ☉ office 7.30am-noon & 7-11pm; 🗐 ⛱) This secure campsite is one block from the beach, set in a pretty garden. Facilities are showing their age, but it does have a reasonable fish restaurant (mains from Dh75) and a pool in summer. There are serious drainage problems when it rains. Turn off the corniche at the fountain.

Le Guayana
MOROCCAN €

(Corniche; salads Dh35, pizzas Dh45) One of a number of restaurants on the beach, Le Guayana serves juices, decent salads and ice cream as well as the usual burgers, pizzas and paninis.

❶ Getting There & Away

Local buses to Tetouan (Dh5, 15 minutes) leave from the bus station near the water tower at the southern end of the beach. You'll find grands taxis to Tetouan (Dh7, 10 minutes) near the big mosque.

Chefchaouen
شفشاون

POP 45,000

Beautifully perched beneath the raw peaks of the Rif, Chefchaouen is one of the prettiest towns in Morocco, an artsy, bluewashed mountain village that feels like its own world. While tourism has definitely taken hold, the balance between ease and authenticity is just right. The old medina is a delight of Moroccan and Andalucian influence with red-tiled roofs, bright-blue buildings and narrow lanes converging on busy Plaza Uta el-Hammam and its restored kasbah. Long known to backpackers for the easy availability of kif (marijuana), the town has rapidly gentrified and offers a range of quality accommodation, good food, lots to do and no hassles to speak of, making it a strong alternative to a hectic multicity tour. This is a great place to relax, explore and take day trips to the cool green hills. Families take note.

Chefchaouen is split into an eastern half (the medina), and a western half (the *ciudad nueva*, or new city). The heart of the medina is Plaza Uta el-Hammam, with its unmistakable kasbah. The medina walls have recently been repaired, with Spanish funding. The principal route of the new city is Ave Hassan II, which stretches from Plaza Mohammed V, a leafy square designed by artist Joan Miró, past the western gate of Bab el-Ain, around the southern medina wall and into the medina itself. Here it dead-ends at Pl el-Majzen, the main drop-off point. The bus station is a steep 1.5km hike southwest of the town centre. The falls of Ras el-Maa lie just beyond the medina walls to the northeast.

History

Chefchaouen was originally known as Chaouen, meaning 'peaks'. Under Spanish occupation the spelling changed to Xaouen, and in 1975 the town was renamed Chefchaouen (Look at the Peaks). These days, the names are used interchangeably.

Moulay Ali ben Rachid founded Chaouen in 1471 as a base for Riffian Berber tribes to launch attacks on the Portuguese in Ceuta. The town expanded with the arrival of Muslim and Jewish refugees from Granada in 1494, who built the whitewashed houses, with tiny balconies, tiled roofs and patios (often with a citrus tree in the centre), that give the town its distinctive Spanish flavour. The pale-blue wash prevalent today was introduced in the 1930s – previously windows and doors had been painted a traditional Muslim green.

The town remained isolated and xenophobic – Christians were forbidden to enter on pain of death – until occupied by Spanish troops in 1920. When the Spanish arrived they were surprised to hear the Jewish inhabitants still speaking a variant of medieval Castilian. The Spanish were briefly thrown out by Abd al-Krim during

SPANISH MOSQUE

Looking east, you'll easily spot the so-called **Spanish mosque** on a hilltop not far from the medina. It's a pleasant walk along clear paths and well worth the effort. Start at the waterfall **Ras el-Maa**, just beyond the far northeastern gate of the medina. It's here, where the water comes gushing out of the mountain, that local women come to do their washing. The sound of the water and the verdant hills just beyond the medina wall provide a sudden, strong dose of nature.

Continuing over the bridge, you can walk to the Spanish mosque following the hillside path. The mosque was built by the Spanish in the 1920s, but never used. It fell into disrepair, but has been newly restored (by the Spanish, again) and there are plans for it to open as a cultural centre. From the hilltop minaret you'll have a grand view of the entire town sprawling over the green hills below. The mosque is a popular destination, but women may not feel comfortable there by themselves.

the Rif War in the 1920s, but they soon returned and remained until independence in 1956.

⊙ Sights

⊙ Medina

Chefchaouen's **medina** is one of the loveliest in Morocco. Small and uncrowded, it's easy to explore, with enough winding paths to keep you diverted, but compact enough that you'll never get too lost. Most of the buildings are painted a blinding blue-white, giving them a clean, fresh look, while terracotta tiles add an Andalucian flavour.

Kasbah   LANDMARK
(☏ 0539 98 63 43; Plaza Uta el-Hammam; admission incl museum & gallery Dh10; ⊙ 9am-1pm & 3-6.30pm Wed, Thu & Sat-Mon, 9am-noon & 3-6.30pm Fri) The kasbah is a heavily restored walled fortress that now contains a lovely garden, a small **Ethnographic Museum**, and an even smaller **art gallery**, currently being restored. The ethnographic museum contains some fascinating views of old Chefchaouen, including the plaza and the kasbah; the gallery promotes the work of local artists.

Grande Mosquée   MOSQUE
(Plaza Uta el-Hammam) The plaza is dominated by the red-hued walls of the kasbah and the adjacent Grande Mosquée. Noteworthy for its unusual octagonal tower, the Grande Mosquée was built in the 15th century by the son of the town's founder, Ali ben Rachid, and is closed to non-Muslims.

Plaza Uta el-Hammam   PLAZA
The heart of the medina is the shady, cobbled Plaza Uta el-Hammam, which is lined with cafes and restaurants, all serving similar fare. This is a peaceful place to relax and watch the world go by, particularly after a long day of exploration.

🏃 Activities

Ras el-Maa Riverside Walk

Exit the medina at **Bab el-Ansar** and head downhill a few metres until you cross the river. Turn right after the bridge and follow the path on the eastern side of the river, Oued Ras-el Maa. The route has been prettily landscaped, and meanders alongside the water. There are spectacular views of the medina, and it all makes a very pleasant downhill saunter of around half an hour. The path meets Ave Allal ben Abdallah where you can hail a taxi to take you back to the medina.

Spas & Hammams

Lina Ryad & Spa   SPA
(Ave Hassan I; gommage Dh300, 1hr relaxing massage Dh400; ⊙ 9am-9pm) The spa at this riad has a hammam and various forms of massage. Hydromassage is available in the heated indoor swimming pool. Have a facial, too, to complete the picture.

Douches Barakat   HAMMAM
(Onsar; hammam Dh10; ⊙ men 8am-noon, women noon-8pm) The local hammam is the traditional way to get clean – and pretty cheap, too.

Trekking

There are numerous trekking opportunities of various durations in the vast 580-sq-km

Chefchaouen

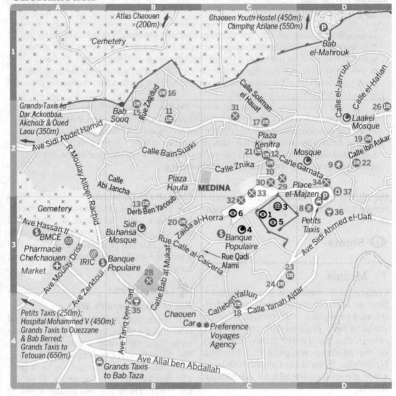

Talassemtane National Park, which begins just outside town. The name means 'cold spring' in Berber. Some popular destinations include the small villages of Kalaa and Akchour, and God's Bridge, a natural formation that looks like a stone arch. The duration of these excursions depends on how much you wish to drive versus walk.

The **Bouhachem Regional Nature Reserve** lies betweem Tetouan, Chefchaouen and Larache, and has a number of treks of various lengths visiting local villages and exploring the mountains, forests and waterfalls. There are several *gîtes* for overnight stays. The park is exceptionally beautiful and covers an enormous area of 80,000 sq km. Designated a Site of Biological and Ecological Interest, it is, along with the nearby Talassemtane National Park, one of the core areas of the Intercontinental Biosphere Reserve of the Mediterranean shared between Andalucia (southern

Spain) and Morocco. The forest has various species of oak, maritime pine and cedar. The park is home to an important number of birds (99 species), mammals (32 species including the Barbary macaque) and reptiles (17 species).

Abdeslam Mouden (☑ 0661 46 39 05; rifwalks@gmail.com; groups of up to 10 half/full day Dh250/400, lunch per person in gîte Dh85) and his team of 13 trained guides lead treks lasting from half a day to several days in both parks, with optional visits to honey production, cheese-making and organic vegetable farming projects.

Chaouen Rural (☑ 0539 98 72 67; www.chaouenrural.org; Pl el-Mazjen) offers similar treks in Talassemtane National Park, some with a focus on medicinal plants.

The **Eco-Museum** (near Camping Azilane) at the entrance to the Talassemtane National Park is well worth a visit. It has info on the park, maps of treks and an extensive display

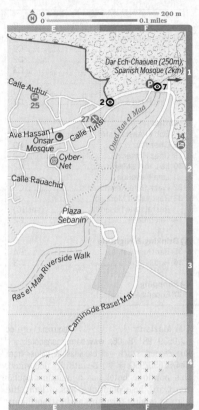

of the flora and fauna found in the park. Registration here is essential if you intend to camp during your trek.

✨ Festivals & Events

Active cultural association **Rif el-Andalus** (☎0539 98 68 00) organises two events in July. One is a large open-air art exhibition, and the other is the **Alegría**, an international music festival.

🛏 Sleeping

Chefchaouen has a large number of accommodation options. As the medina is what you'll come to Chefchaouen for, it's best to stay here, though there are some good options outside the walls. Some hotels have heating; if not, you will be sleeping beneath plenty of blankets during cold winter nights.

🛏 Medina

Hostal Guernika
GUESTHOUSE €

(☎0539 98 74 34; hostalguernika@hotmail.com; 49 Onssar; d/tr Dh200/300, d with heating Dh270) This is a warm and charming place, with a very caring and attentive owner, near the Pl el-Majzen. Most rooms are large and bright, facing the mountains. All have showers, and there's heating in winter. The terrace has spectacular views. Reserve in summer, Easter and December.

Dar Baraka
GUESTHOUSE €

(☎0614 68 24 80; www.riad-baraka.com; 12 Derb Ben Yacoub; s/d without bathroom Dh140/240, d with bathroom Dh280, q per person Dh120; 🛜) English-owned, Dar Baraka is sunny and bright. The rooms are comfortable and share spotless facilities. The terrace is one of the best, with some sun and some shade, and a comfortable lounge with lots of DVDs. There's dinner on request – it could be a curry, or if it's Sunday, Mum whips up a good roast.

Dar Terrae
GUESTHOUSE €

(☎0539 98 75 98; www.darterrae.com; Ave Hassan I; incl breakfast s/d Dh300/400, without bathroom Dh280/380; 🛜) These funky, cheerfully painted rooms are individually decorated, some with their own bathroom and fireplace, and hidden up and down a tumble of stairs and odd corners. The Italian owner prepares a fantastic breakfast spread every day, and other meals on request. It's poorly signed – if in doubt ask for the 'Hotel Italiano'.

Hotel Koutoubia
GUESTHOUSE €

(☎0668 11 53 58; Calle Andalouse; s/d/tr from Dh150/200/300; 🛜) This hotel does budget accommodation perfectly, with friendly and attentive management, a central location, traditional decor, spotless rooms and a closed-in roof terrace for those cold mornings where you can have breakfast (Dh20).

Hostal Yasmina
GUESTHOUSE €

(☎0539 88 31 18; yasmina45@hotmail.com; 12 Zaida al-Horra; r per person Dh75) For the price bracket, this place sparkles. Rooms are bright and clean, though some don't have windows. The location is a stone's throw from Plaza Uta el-Hammam, and the roof terrace is very welcoming. This bargain doesn't have many rooms, though, so it can fill up quickly.

Chefchaouen

Hotel Barcelona   GUESTHOUSE €
(☑ 0539 98 85 06; 12 Rue Targhi; d without/with bathroom Dh150/300; ☎) A friendly budget option in bright Chefchaouen blue. The fixtures and fittings are pretty basic, but the hotel is well maintained, and the rooftop terrace is wonderful.

★ Casa Perleta   GUESTHOUSE €€
(☑ 0539 98 89 79; www.casaperleta.com; Bab Souq; d incl breakfast from Dh495; ☎) This lovely house has very friendly staff. Flexible accommodation offers rooms sleeping two or three, and one suite for four. It's all muted colours and wonderful local fabrics and furniture. The cosy sitting room has a fireplace for those chilly nights, and there's central heating in all rooms and bathrooms. Topping it off is a terrace with great views.

Dar Gabriel   GUESTHOUSE €€
(☑ Spain 00 34 952 11 74 86; www.dargabriel. com; Bab Souq; d incl breakfast Dh550; ☎) The warmth of natural brick teamed with local rugs and fabrics make this a comfortable option. The cosy lounge has a fireplace, there are three roof terraces and meals can be provided. Rooms are simple and individually decorated. Excursions into the mountains are on offer.

Dar Meziana   BOUTIQUE HOTEL €€
(☑ 0539 98 78 06; www.darmezianahotel.com; Rue Zagdud; s/d/tr incl breakfast & dinner from Dh475/650/950; ❄☎) Beautifully decorated, this boutique hotel has a unique angular courtyard, lush plantings, lots of light, the highest quality furniture and extraordinary ceilings. On the edge of the medina and not signposted, but otherwise perfect. Rooms with a mountain view cost Dh300 extra.

John's House   GUESTHOUSE €€
(www.johndirkwilkinson@gmail.com; 17 Calle Autiui; for 3 per night/week Dh550/2750; ❄@) This cosiest of houses has two bedrooms, a heated bathroom and a fab terrace with a fountain large enough to dip your toes in. Owned by the British Consular warden of Chefchaouen, the Union Jack flies proudly alongside the Moroccan flag. In winter have a sing-song around the piano in front of a blazing fire.

Lina Ryad & Spa   GUESTHOUSE €€€
(☑ fax 0539 88 25 92, 0645 06 99 03; www.linariad. com; Ave Hassan I; s/d incl breakfast Dh1200/1400; ❄) The upmarket Lina Ryad is opulent and impeccably turned out. It has large, comfortable rooms with TV (and free movies) and friendly staff. The roof terraces have fabulous views. The spa boasts a small heated pool, and there's a restaurant serving both

Moroccan and international cuisine (dinner menu Dh200).

Dar Baiboo GUESTHOUSE €€€
(☑0539 98 61 53; www.casahassan.com; Rue Targhi; s/d incl breakfast Dh850/1000; ✳) This guesthouse is light and airy. Rooms open off the central courtyard and are large and comfortable.

Casa Hassan GUESTHOUSE €€€
(☑0539 98 61 53; www.casahassan.com; 22 Rue Targhi; s/d with half-board from Dh850/1000; ✳) A large guesthouse on the 2nd floor above its restaurant, this long-established choice is showing its age a bit, but has sizeable rooms with creative layouts and an in-house hammam. The terrace provides an elegant lounge, and the cosy Restaurant Tissemlal (p259) a warm hearth.

Outside the Medina

Most other accommodation options are clustered along Ave Hassan II, which runs south of the medina alongside the old city walls.

Hotel Marrakesh HOTEL €
(☑0539 98 77 74; Hotel.Marrakech1@hotmail.com; 41 Ave Hassan II; s/d incl breakfast Dh180/350, d/tr with shower Dh350/425; ☎) Set downhill from the action, the Marrakesh is a hotel with a bit of soul. Bright pastel rooms invite the fresh air in, bathrooms have powerful showers, the common room attracts with its central fireplace and carved-plaster ceiling,

and the roof terrace offers fine views over the valley. All rooms share toilets; the more expensive rooms have a shower.

Hotel Salam HOTEL €
(☑0539 98 62 39; 39 Ave Hassan II; s/d/tr Dh60/120/180) Another out-of-medina experience, the Salam has bright courtyard rooms. Shared facilities are adequate, but sinks in all rooms are a bonus.

Chaouen Youth Hostel HOSTEL €
(☑0666 90 84 42; Hay Ouatman; per person incl breakfast Dh40, per person in groups Dh30) Next to the town campsite, this hostel is bright and clean. Hot showers cost Dh20, and there's a washing machine. In season, you must produce a membership card.

Camping Azilane CAMPGROUND €
(☑0539 98 69 79; www.campingchefchaouen.com; Hay Ouatman; camping per adult Dh30, plus per tent/car/campervan Dh20/20/35, electricity Dh15; ☎) A shady setting with great views makes this site popular, although cleanliness is questionable. It is a stiff 20-minute walk from the medina. Two swimming pools were under construction on our visit. There's a small restaurant and a shop that sells some essentials, but otherwise facilities are pretty basic (hot showers Dh10). Fires and alcohol are not allowed.

Auberge Dardara INN €€
(☑0661 15 05 03, 0539 70 70 07; www.dardara.ma; Rte Nationale 2; d/tr/q incl breakfast Dh600/750/1000; ✳) This authentic

CLIMBING JEBEL EL-KELAÂ

Looming over Chefchaouen at 1616m, Jebel el-Kelaâ might initially appear a daunting peak, but with an early start, it can easily be climbed in a day if you're in reasonably good shape.

The hike starts from behind Camping Azilane, following the 4WD track that takes you to the hamlet of Aïn Tissimlane. Rocks painted with a yellow and white stripe indicate that you're on the right path. The initial hour is relatively steep as you climb above the trees to get your first views over Chefchaouen, before cutting into the mountains along the steady *piste* (track). You should reach Aïn Tissimlane within a couple of hours of setting out, after which the path climbs and zigzags steeply through great boulders for nearly an hour to a pass. Turn west along the track, which leads to the saddle of the mountain, from where you can make the final push to the summit. There's a rough path, although you'll need to scramble in places. The peak is attained relatively quickly, and your exertions are rewarded with the most sublime views over this part of the Rif.

It's straightforward and quick to descend by the same route. Alternatively, you can head north from the saddle on a path that takes you to a cluster of villages on the other side of the mountain. One of these villages, El-Kelaâ, has 16th-century grain stores and a mosque with a leaning minaret. From here, a number of simple tracks will take you back to Chefchaouen in a couple of hours.

TAGHZOUTE

Some 20km from Chefchaouen on the road to Oued Laou, **Le Caiat** (☎0666 28 87 15, 0671 85 49 97; www.caiat.com; RP 4105, Taghzoute; meals around Dh100, d Dh330-550) at Taghzoute is a wonderful mountain refuge. The Portuguese owner is a keen environmentalist and works with local Moroccans arranging treks between villages in the Talassemtane National Park. Trails of two hours to two days lead to cooling cascades and monkeys, rock pools and the rare black pine. There is a range of accommodation and a restaurant with breathtaking views across the valleys.

French *auberge* in the Moroccan countryside offers large rustic suites with TVs and fireplaces and an excellent restaurant. The 10-hectare complex includes an active farm and gardens, pool, craft shop, hammam, fitness centre, fishing, biking, mule riding, trekking and treasure hunts. Guest programs include crafts, gardening and more. It's a 10-minute taxi ride (Dh5) to Bab Taza.

Dar Zman GUESTHOUSE €€
(☎0539 98 93 46; www.darzman.net; Bab el Hammar, Ave Hassan II; d incl breakfast from Dh550; ❉🞱) A lovely, finely restored guesthouse with eight brightly painted rooms and a wonderful rooftop breakfast area, created by some ambitious young hoteliers. The faux artefacts revealed in the walls are a clever touch.

★**Dar Ech-Chaouen** GUESTHOUSE €€€
(☎0539 98 78 24; www.darechchaouen.ma; 18 Ave Ras el-Maa; d incl breakfast from Dh590, ste Dh790; ❉🞱🞱) Providing excellent accommodation, this guesthouse is close to Ras el-Maa, just outside the medina walls. It's well designed with even staircases, spacious, comfortable rooms and a shady garden terrace. There's a pool with great views, and a restaurant.

🍴 Eating

Sip a juice or mint tea while watching the world go by at the cafes on Plaza Uta el-Hammam. In the back rooms, local men play cards and smoke kif – it's worth a look,

although women won't feel particularly welcome.

Look out for the sticker in some restaurant windows announcing 'The Chefchaouen Network of Community-Involved Restaurants'. These establishments support farmers by using local organic products.

Plaza Café-Restaurants MOROCCAN €
(Plaza Uta el-Hamman; breakfast from Dh25, mains from Dh40; ⊙8am-11pm, closes earlier in winter) It's hard to make a choice between the dozen or so cafes on the main square. Menus are virtually identical – continental breakfasts, soups and salads, tajines and seafood – but the food is generally pretty good and the ambience lively.

★**Restaurant Morisco** MOROCCAN €
(☎0539 88 23 23; Plaza Uta el-Hammam; breakfast around Dh30, mains from Dh34; ⊙breakfast, lunch & dinner) The best of the Plaza restaurants, Morisco serves Chaoueni specialities. The *ftour beldi* (country breakfast) of eggs, olive oil, goat's cheese and orange juice will set you up for the day, and for dinner, try the *tahliya*: goat with almonds, raisins and honey, or the anchovy, tomato and lemon tajine. There's couscous on Fridays served with fermented milk (Dh50).

Talembote MOROCCAN €
(b'sara Dh5; ⊙breakfast & lunch) This miniscule place has no sign outside, but is worth seeking out for its delicious *b'sara* with fresh bread that makes a filling and very cheap lunch. It's at the top of the steps opposite the Hotel Parador.

La Lampe Magique MOROCCAN €
(Rue Targhi; mains from Dh45, menu Dh85; ⊙lunch & dinner) This magical place overlooking Plaza Uta el-Hammam serves delicious Moroccan staples in a grand setting. Three bright-blue floors include a laid-back lounge, a more formal dining area and a rooftop terrace. The menu – featuring favourites like lamb tajine with prunes and some great cooked salads – is much better than average, and the ambience relaxed.

Lala Mesouda MOROCCAN €
(Ave Hassan I; mains from Dh60; ⊙lunch & dinner) This restaurant serves dishes not found elsewhere in the town. Both the steak with Roquefort sauce and the chicken with cream and mushrooms are recommended, and fish is also available. The interior is comfortable

and intimate, if rather dark, and the welcome warm.

Bab el-Ansar Café
CAFE €

(Bab el-Ansar) Set into the outside wall of the medina, this cafe has a great location overlooking the falls of Ras el-Maa, with three terraces tumbling down the hill. Views are particularly nice in the late afternoon, with the sun catching the mountains opposite.

Chez Aziz
PATISSERIE €

(Ave Hassan II; pastries from Dh4) For a great selection of pastries, make your way here. Pizzas and paninis are also on the menu. They squeeze a mean juice and make good coffee too, for a quick breakfast on the run.

★ Auberge Dardara Restaurant
MOROCCAN €€

(☎ 0661 15 05 03, 0539 70 70 07; Rte Nationale 2; menu Dh120; ⊗ lunch & dinner) This is the best restaurant in the area, and worth the 10-minute drive from town (to Bab Taza, Dh5). The Tangerine owner uses only the freshest ingredients from the garden, bakes his own bread and makes his own goat's cheese. Try the superb salads, and the venison cooked with dried figs or the succulent rabbit with quince, and take along a bottle of wine.

Restaurant Tissemlal
MOROCCAN €€

(Casa Hassan; 22 Rue Targhi; menu Dh90-120; ⊗ lunch & dinner) Better known as Casa Hassan as it's part of the guesthouse (p257) of the same name, this restaurant serves the usual traditional dishes. It's particularly welcoming in winter when there's a roaring fire.

Chez Hicham
MOROCCAN €€

(Rue Targhi; mains around Dh80; ⊗ lunch & dinner) Chez Hicham has a lovely warm interior, comfortable seating and views over the kasbah from the terrace. The usual suspects are on the menu.

Self-Catering

The market off Ave Hassan II is excellent for fresh fish, meat, fruit and vegetables, and gets particularly busy on Monday and Thursday, when people come from outside Chefchaouen to sell produce.

Several local specialities are worth checking out, particularly the fragrant mountain honey and soft ewe's cheese – both served up at breakfast. Add fresh *dial makla* (a type of bread) and you have your picnic.

🍷 Drinking & Nightlife

While it's easy to find kif in Chefchaouen, it's hard to find a beer.

Bar Oum-Rabiá
BAR

(Ave Hassan II; ⊗ 10am-10pm) A very masculine option.

Hotel Parador
BAR

(☎ 0539 98 61 36; Pl el-Majzen; ⊗ 2-11pm) The soulless bar here is OK for a beer, but wine is only available if you eat in the somewhat dubious restaurant. Beers are Dh25.

Atlas Chaouen
BAR, CLUB

(⊗ 9am-11pm) The jazzy bar here is the smartest in Chefchaouen, but quite a hike. The hotel's disco (open 11pm to 3am) is the only nightclub in the area. Hotel guests are the clientele during the week, joined by locals on weekends. Beers cost Dh30.

🛍 Shopping

Chefchaouen remains an artisan centre and, as such, an excellent place to shop – especially for Riffian woven rugs and blankets in bright primary colours. Many shops have looms in situ, so you can see the blankets being made. Previously silk was the material of choice: the mulberry trees in Plaza Uta el-Hammam are a legacy of these times. Most of the weaving nowadays is with wool, one of the area's biggest products.

The largest concentration of tourist shops is around the Uta el-Hammam and Pl el-Majzen.

Well worth a visit is the **Ensemble Artisanal** (Pl el-Majzen; ⊗ 10am-2pm & 4-6pm) across from the Hotel Parador. It's one of the best we've seen in Morocco, although information boards are in Arabic and Spanish only. There are weavers at their looms, cobblers, artists, knitters and wireworkers.

ℹ Information

INTERNET ACCESS

Cyber-Net (Zanqat Sbâa; per hr Dh5; ⊗ 10am-midnight)

IRIC (Institut Raouachid pour l'Information et le Commerce; Ave Hassan II; per hr Dh5; ⊗ 8am-midnight) Next to Librairie Al-Nahj.

MEDICAL SERVICES

Hospital Mohammed V (☎ 0539 98 62 28; Ave al-Massira al-Khadra)

Pharmacie Chefchaouen (☑0539 98 61 58; Ave Moulay Driss; ☉8am-6pm Mon-Sat)

MONEY

Banque Populaire Medina (Plaza Uta el-Hammam; ☉8.45am-6pm Mon-Thu, 8.45am-noon Sat); Ville Nouvelle (Ave Hassan II, near Bab el-Ain; ☉8.45am-6pm Mon-Thu, 8.45am-noon Sat) There's an ATM at both branches.

BMCE (Ave Hassan II; ☉8.45am-6pm Mon-Thu, 8.45am-noon Sat)

POST

Post Office (Ave Hassan II; ☉8am-4pm Mon-Fri, 8-11am Sat)

TRAVEL AGENCIES

Preference Voyages Agency (☑0539 98 79 13; www.preferencevoyages.com; 39 Ave Hassan II; ☉9am-12.30pm & 3-6.30pm Mon-Fri, 9am-12.30pm Sat) This extremely helpful travel agency has tourist information and organises mountain treks with registered guides. English-speaking.

❶ Getting There & Away

BUS

Bus services from Chefchaouen originate elsewhere, so are often full on arrival. Buy the ticket for your onward journey on arrival in

OFF THE BEATEN TRACK

INTO THE RIF

Heading southeast out of Chefchaouen, the N2 road plunges into the heart of the Rif, running about 150km along the backbone of the mountains. The roads are rough, but offer spectacular views. To the southeast, Jebel Tidiquin (2448m), the highest peak in the Rif Mountains, dominates the skyline.

Issaguen appears unexpectedly from the middle of the cedar forests. A scruffy frontier town, it is one of the commercial centres of kif cultivation and smuggling (Ketama, 20km away, being the other).

Issaguen and Ketama have a notorious reputation. This is an area beyond the law. People will wonder what you are doing here, and naturally assume you are buying hashish. There is nowhere to turn if you get into trouble, and little to hold anyone back who wants some. Travellers are strongly advised to pass through and not spend the night here.

Chefchaouen to secure a seat. The bus station is 1.5km southwest of the town centre at the far end of Ave Mohammed V (Dh10 in a petit taxi from Pl el-Majzen). CTM and all other buses use the same station.

CTM (☑0539 98 76 69) serves the following destinations:

DESTINATION	COST (DH)	DURATION (HR)
Casablanca	125	6
Fez	70	4½
Nador	140	11½
Ouezzane	20	1½
Rabat	90	4½
Tangier	40	3
Tetouan	25	1½

Other companies run a number of cheaper services to the same destinations, including a daily departure for Oued Laou (Dh32, 1½ hours).

TAXI

The fixed price for a grand taxi from Tangier airport to Chefchaouen is Dh650, and from Tanger Med Dh550. Unless you can find several people to split the fare with you, it is far cheaper to go to Tangier first, then hop to Chefchaouen via Tetouan. Even if you buy two places, you will save over Dh500 and add less than an hour.

Grands taxis north leave Chefchaouen from just below Plaza Mohammed V. Most just run to Tetouan (Dh32, one hour), where you must change for Tangier or Ceuta – direct taxis are rare. From Ave Allal ben Abdallah you can catch a grand taxi to Dar Ackoubaa (Dh8, 20 minutes) from Ave Moulay Abdesalam, the junction for Oued Laou.

Grands taxis headed south gather below the central market. Catch one to Ouezzane (Dh30, one hour), where you can pick up onward transport to Fez and Meknès. There is very little transport heading east to the coast. The best option is to take a grand taxi to Dardara junction (Dh8, 15 minutes) or Bab Taza (Dh15, 30 minutes) and hope for the best from there.

❶ Getting Around

Chefchaouen's 37 blue petits taxis congregate on Pl el-Majzen and near the market. They're unmetered; most fares shouldn't top Dh10. The safe and convenient Hotel Parador **car park** (Pl el-Majzen; per night Dh10) can be used by nonguests.

Chaouen Car (☑0539 98 62 04; Ave Hassan II) This agency rents cars and also organises 4WD trips and quad bikes.

Oued Laou واد لاو

Don't let Oued Laou's dusty main street lined with slapdash construction fool you – it will all look like Martil within a few years. For now, waterfront budget rooms and cheap beer and food along the new corniche back a very long, empty beach to make it a backpacker paradise, especially in summer. There's nothing to do aside from watching the fishermen haul their boats in the morning.

The road from Chefchaouen to Oued Laou has recently been upgraded and the journey is now reduced to a little over an hour.

🛏 Sleeping & Eating

Hotel Oued Laou GUESTHOUSE €
(✉0650 18 43 38, 0655 21 37 89; Blvd Massira; s/d/tr Dh200/250/300) There are several new budget hotels to choose from, but this is the best. A new road splits it from its cafe-restaurant on the beach. Get a room with views to the sea.

Aramar SEAFOOD €
(Corniche; mains from Dh60; ☺noon-11pm, closes earlier out of season) The best of the fish restaurants along the corniche, the Aramar does a tasty platter of *poisson friture* (fried fish) for Dh80 while you watch the fishermen on the beach.

ℹ Information

Cyber Costa (per hr Dh5; ☺9am-midnight) Opposite La Plage Restaurant but unlikely to be open out of season.

ℹ Getting There & Away

If you're driving from Chefchaouen turn off the main Tetouan road at Dar Ackoubaa, 11km north of Chefchaouen. It's a wonderful drive past the large hydroelectric dam and through rolling hills and the stunning Laou Gorge. Coming from Tetouan, the Rocade N16 hugs the dramatic coastline for 140km all the way to El-Jebha.

Three buses a day connect Tetouan and Oued Laou (Dh25, two hours). There's also one bus from Chefchaouen (Dh20, 90 minutes), which continues along the coast to El-Jebha (Dh35, five hours); the return service leaves El-Jebha early in the morning. However, at Oued Laou it dumps you out by the souq, leaving you a 45-minute walk or Dh7 grand-taxi ride to town.

Grands taxis run from beside the mosque in Oued Laou to Tetouan (Dh30, one hour) via Dar Ackoubaa (Dh15, 20 minutes), where you can pick up a passing taxi for Chefchaouen.

Targa to El-Jebha
من ترگا إلى الجبهة

This stretch of the coast is very dramatic, and still remote. Pine-clad hills are interspersed with valleys of cultivated fields that roll down to the sea and beaches of grey pebbles. However, the new Rocade coastal road linking Tetouan to El-Jebha promises massive development projects with golf courses, luxury hotels and apartments.

Seventeen kilometres southeast of Oued Laou, Targa is a little village with a history of piracy. High atop an outcrop of black rock, a stone fort overlooks the village, built during the Spanish protectorate. The 13th-century mosque is associated with a local saint.

About 18km southeast of Targa, in the wide valley of Oued Bouchia, are the twin villages of Steha and Bou-Ahmed. Set back from the coast, the latter is the end point for a long-distance trek from Chefchaouen. There's an interesting souq every Tuesday, and a basic camping area in summer.

From here the road follows the coast on a splendid roller-coaster ride to the blue and white town of El-Jebha, 52km to the southeast. The rugged coastline forms a number of breathtaking and secluded bays – worth exploring if you have your own transport. Each Tuesday, the local souq draws Rif farmers from the surrounding villages. At El-Jebha you can turn south into the Rif to Issaguen, or continue on the Rocade to Al-Hoceima.

Al-Hoceima الحسيمّة

POP 283,100

Al-Hoceima is a great place to spend a few days. Quiet, safe, relaxing and hassle-free, this modern seaside resort is full of proud and genial Berbers with a surprisingly independent, Western outlook, far more than any other town in the north. In fact, if the northern Berbers had their own country, this would be its capital. There is far more of the Berber tongue, Tarifit, spoken than Spanish.

Founded by the Spanish as Villa Sanjuro, the town was built as a garrison after the Rif Wars in the early 20th century; rebel Abd al-Krim operated nearby. Independence brought the name change to Al-Hoceima, but Spanish influence remains strong in language, architecture and business.

In recent years many of Al-Hoceima's émigrés have returned and have ploughed

Al-Hoceima

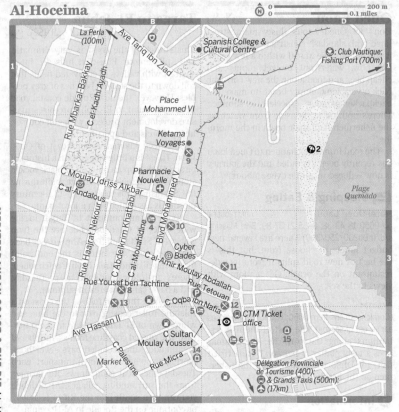

money into the town, particularly into its booming tourism industry. The wide **Pl Mohammed VI** has new fountains and a sweeping corniche follows the coast. The pretty **Pl du Rif** with its Mauresque buildings is slated to be turned into a pedestrian zone. Best of all, the wonderful **Al-Hoceima National Park** has been carefully opened to rural tourism – an opportunity not to be missed.

The town sits atop high cliffs overlooking two coves, one a beach (Plage Quemado) and the other a commercial port. Blvd Mohammed V parallels the edge from the Spanish College at one end to Pl du Rif at the other. Most of the banks, hotels and restaurants are along or close to here, with budget options clustered around Pl du Rif. The flat grid of wide streets is easy to walk and navigate. The three other town beaches lie further south, along with El Peñón de Alhucemas, one of the last bits of the Spanish protectorate.

⊙ Sights

Plage Quemado
BEACH

A pretty, steep-sided bay protects the town beach. The beach is clean enough, but the seaside resort atmosphere is marred by the port to the north and the apartment hotels that crowd the sand.

Cala Bonita, Plage Isly & Plage Asfiha
BEACH

In the summer, a good option is one of the three white sandy beaches that begin 5km south of town. During the low season they tend to be strewn with rubbish. Plage Asfiha has several ramshackle restaurants right on the beach, but will soon be overtaken by the Souani resort being built. The best way to reach these beaches is by grand taxi. For the entire taxi, reckon on about Dh50 to Cala Bonita and Dh75 to Plage Asfiha. Local buses to Ajdir and Imzouren, which pass the turn-offs for these beaches

Al-Hoceima

(Dh5 to Dh7), leave from beside the Mobil petrol station at the south end of Blvd Mohammed V.

El Peñón de Alhucemas   FORT
One of the *plazas de soberanía* (see p271), this extraordinary white island fortress can be seen a few hundred metres off Playa Asfiha, along with the uninhabited islets Isla de Mar and Isla de Tierra, which fly the Spanish flag. Spanish rule dates back to 1559, when the Saadi dynasty gave it to Spain in exchange for military assistance. In 1673, the Spanish military established a garrison there, and never left. Today, the fort hosts 60 soldiers, and cannot be visited. Spanish sovereignty has been contested by Morocco since independence in 1956.

Port   PORT
The port is mainly used for a large commercial fishing operation. It is a great place to watch the catch being unloaded, and to find dinner: take your selected fish to Club Nautique (p264) for cooking.

Sleeping

The streets between Pl du Rif and the souq are packed with ultra-cheap hotels. Some are pretty dingy, so look around before committing.

★ Hotel Villa Florido   HOTEL €
(☎0539 84 08 47; http://florido.alhoceima.com; Pl du Rif; s/d/tr Dh258/316/424; 🖳) This curvaceous art deco hotel dating from 1920, an island in the Pl du Rif, has been completely revamped in great style. Large, spotless rooms have bathrooms and satellite TV, and most have a balcony. There's a smart cafe downstairs (breakfast Dh40). The area can be noisy at night.

Hotel al-Hana   HOTEL €
(☎0666 90 32 00; 17 Calle Imzouren; s/d/tr without bathroom Dh100/160/240) With rock-bottom prices, this simple hotel is tucked into the tiny streets east of Pl du Rif. All facilities are shared, including the clean squat toilets (hot showers are free). It's well kept, and the cafe on the ground floor is full of men throwing dice.

Hotel Rif   HOTEL €
(☎0539 98 22 68; 13 Calle Sultan Moulay Youssef; s/d without bathroom Dh100/150) If your budget is really maxed-out, you'll end up in this long hallway lined with simple rooms. Bathrooms with squat toilets are shared, but you do get your own sink. Keep your door locked: the staff sleeps during the day.

La Perla   HOTEL €€
(☎0539 98 45 13; www.hotelperlamorocco.com; Ave Tariq ibn Zaid; s/d incl breakfast Dh700/850; ❂❋🖳) This modern mirrored-glass highrise business hotel has comfortable, if bland, rooms with satellite TV and large bathrooms. The tiled floors, thin walls and location on a busy corner make it quite noisy. There's a cafe on the ground floor and a restaurant upstairs.

Hotel al-Khouzama   HOTEL €€
(fax 0539 98 56 69; Calle al-Andalous; s/d Dh288/376; 🖳) Just off Blvd Mohammed V, this two-star hotel is a long-time favourite for business travellers, and is suitably comfortable, with spacious rooms (though those facing away from the street are a bit dark). All come with bathrooms and satellite TV, and the guys at reception are friendly and helpful.

Suites Hotel Mohammed V   HOTEL €€€
(☎0539 98 22 33; www.hotelsuitesmohammedv.com; Pl Mohammed VI; ste s/d Dh800/950; ℙ❋🖳❂) Al-Hoceima's most expensive option, this hotel is ultramodern and pretty characterless. It occupies a prime position perched above Plage Quemado. Rooms are

SURVIVAL TARIFIT

Hello/Goodbye	*msalkhir/baslama*
Yes/No	*wah/alla*
Please	*aafak*
Thank you	*choukrane*
Where is...?	*mani thadja (fem) or mani yadja (masc)*
hotel	*annoutir*
camping	*arihla*
Do you have any rooms available?	*maghak cha akhamane akhwane?*
a single room	*akham injnabnadam*
a double room	*akham ntnaine nyawdane*
How much is it?	*mchhar tag tha?*
What time does the next...leave?	*marmi ghayoya wanni dyouggane?*
boat	*agharabo*
bus	*toubis*
I'd like a...	*hsagh*
one-way ticket	*thawrikth ichtane waha*
return ticket	*thawrikth waakab*
beer	*berra*
sandwich	*bocadio*

spacious and comfortable and have balconies giving lovely views over the bay, but maintenance and service are questionable. There's a restaurant, bar and gym to complete the picture.

✗ Eating

Cheap restaurants cluster around Pl du Rif, serving up filling tajines, brochettes and a bit of seafood to the bus-station crowd from about Dh25 per head. There are also many snack shops around town.

★ Club Nautique   SEAFOOD €
(☑ 0539 98 14 61; Gate 2, Port d'Al-Hoceima; mains from Dh60; ☉ lunch & dinner) This is the main restaurant at the port, and a good one. After 6pm, buy your fish fresh off the boat and have them grill it for you. The 2nd floor overlooks the whole port and is a great place to relax and have a beer.

Espace Miramar   FAST FOOD €
(☑ 0531 98 42 42; Rue Moulay Ismail; mains from Dh35; ☉ lunch & dinner) It's hard to go wrong at this complex with a pizzeria, two cafes, a grill and restaurant as well as a children's playground, all perched on the cliffs overlooking the sea, and with occasional live music.

La Dolce Pizza   FAST FOOD €
(☑ 0531 98 47 52; Pl du Rif; pizza around Dh37; ☉ lunch & dinner) Also signed as DP, this cute Italian bistro thrust out into the chaos of Pl du Rif has just four tables inside and some on the pavement. Service is appallingly slow but the ambience makes it a pleasant place to people-watch and have some pizza, hamburgers or salads.

Café La Belle Vue   CAFE €
(131 Blvd Mohammed V; breakfast Dh20) Gets its name from the terrace at the back overlooking the bay. Several similar cafes on this stretch of Mohammed V have great views.

Boulangerie Patisserie Azir   PATISSERIE €
(☑ 0531 17 71 42; 14 Rue Yousef ben Tachfine; pastries from Dh4; ☉ 5am-8.30pm) This patisserie is the town favourite, with great homebaked bread and tons of different sweets.

Self-Catering
Many small general food stores are dotted around town, including **Épicerie Hassouni** (Blvd Mohammed V) and **Supermarché el-Bouayadi** (Calle Abdelkrim Khattabi).

For alcohol try **Bougamar** (near cnr of Rue Micra), the local liquor store, where bottles are dispensed from behind the counter pharmacy-style.

🍷 Drinking

Club Nautique   BAR
(Gate 2, Port d'Al-Hoceima) An atmospheric option, and the bar here usually attracts quite a crowd. Beers are Dh20.

Suites Hotel Mohammed V   BAR
(Pl Mohammed VI) A bit dingy, but the terrace has excellent views over Plage Quemado.

🛍 Shopping

There is a weekly market Monday and Tuesday in the souq.

ℹ Information

INTERNET ACCESS
Cyber Bades (Calle al-Amir Moulay Abdallah; per hr Dh5; ☉ 8am-9.30pm)

MEDICAL SERVICES

Pharmacie Nouvelle (Calle Moulay Idriss Alkbar; ⊙8.30am-12.30pm & 3-7.30pm Mon-Thu, 8.30am-noon Fri, 8am-12.30pm Sat)

MONEY

Blvd Mohammed V has several banks with ATMs, including branches of BMCE, BMCI and Banque Populaire.

POST

Post Office (Calle Moulay Idriss Alkbar; ⊙8am-4pm Mon-Fri)

TOURIST INFORMATION

Délégation Provinciale de Tourisme (Tourist Bureau; ☎0539 98 11 85; Zanqat Al Hamra, Cala Bonita; ⊙9am-1pm & 3-6pm Mon-Fri) Staff here are on the ball and have lots of information on the town and national park.

TRAVEL AGENCIES

All sell ferry tickets from Al-Hoceima in season, and from Nador year-round.

Ketama Voyages (☎0539 98 51 20; www. ktmahu@menara.ma; 146 Blvd Mohammed V; ⊙9am-1pm, 3-6pm Mon-Fri, 9am-1pm Sat)

❶ Getting There & Away

AIR

Royal Air Maroc flies from Amsterdam and in summer from Brussels to the small local airport located 12km (Dh175 by taxi) from town. Royal Air Maroc offers sporadic services from Paris and various parts of Spain, as well as Casablanca. Otherwise the best option is a flight to Nador, 150km east.

BOAT

At the time of research, there were no ferry services to Al-Hoceima.

BUS

All the bus companies have offices around Pl du Rif and at the bus station. CTM runs the following summer services:

Chefchaouen (Dh85, 5½ hours, three daily)
Nador direct (Dh65, three hours, two daily)
Oujda via Nador (Dh70, 3½ hours, one daily)

Year-round, **CTM** has the following departures:
Casablanca (Dh210, 10 hours, one daily) via Taza (Dh65, three hours)
Fez (Dh110, five hours)
Meknès (Dh130, six hours)
Rabat (Dh175, eight hours)
Tetouan (Dh110, seven hours, three daily) via Chefchaouen (Dh85, 5½ hours)

Several small companies also serve the aforementioned destinations. There are at least three buses a day to Tetouan and Tangier (Dh80 to

Dh90, 7½ hours). These stop in Chefchaouen (Dh95) only if there's enough demand. Otherwise, they'll drop you on the main road at Dardara, from where you can share a grand taxi into Chefchaouen (Dh12, 15 minutes). Heading east, there are also a couple of buses a day to Nador (Dh40, 2½ hours) and Oujda (Dh60, five hours).

TAXI

Grands taxis can be found at the bus station. The most popular destinations are Taza (Dh70, 2½ hours) and Nador (Dh60, 2½ hours). Taxis go through Nador to Melilla, not direct.

Al-Hoceima National Park

المنتزه الوطن للحس مّة

The undiscovered Al-Hoceima National Park is the hidden jewel of this region. The park extends to 485 sq km (including 190 sq km at sea). The area is dotted with Berber settlements and criss-crossed by dirt roads, making it ideal trekking and mountain-biking territory. Its isolation has helped preserve several at-risk species, from its thuya forests to an important colony of fish eagle. While a 4WD opens up your options, a 2x4 will get you through the main tracks. The park offers two regions: the central Rif bordered by the N16 in the south and west, and the coast.

At the time of research, there was no office at the park, but information brochures including a map are available from the tourist bureau in Al-Hoceima. French-speaking mountain guide Abdellah Massoudi (☎0673 22 91 22; per person per day Dh200, min Dh500) leads treks in the park of various lengths, staying overnight in *gîtes*. Visits to local artisans are encouraged.

You can also walk to El Peñón de Velez de la Gomera along the coast from Cala Iris in 1½ hours. Without your own transport, you'll need to hire a grand taxi to get there. In summer there may be enough people to share one, otherwise expect to pay Dh150 one way.

Central Rif region

Of the 15,000 people living in the park, most are of the Bokkoya tribe and live in rural communities centred around fresh water supplies. The women have good knowledge of the medicinal use of local herbs such as the abundant lavender and thyme.

A number of rare trees can be found here, such as wild carob and the endangered thuya, highly prized for its wood. Other

MEDITERRANEAN COAST & THE RIF AL-HOCEIMA NATIONAL PARK

plants include wild olive, ilex, pomegranate, ericas, bulbs and orchids. Animals include jackals, wild boar, rabbits and hares.

Coastal region

This area of the park extends out to sea and is rich in biodiversity. There are 86 species of fish and three types of dolphin. Many species represented here are rare elsewhere in the Mediterranean, such as red coral, various molluscs and algae. Among the birds, there is a considerable population of osprey (*Pandion haliaetus*).

There are several remote and scenic beaches, of which the highlight is the fantastic sight of El Peñón de Velez de la Gomera, one of the *plazas de soberanía* (p271).

Cala Iris & Torres de Alcala كالإ رّ سّ ونهر الكالا

Cala Iris now lies inside the Al-Hoceima National Park. It has a small fishing port and a beautiful sandy beach that's empty out of season – for now. Construction of an eco-resort is due to start in 2017. There's nowhere to stay here but there is a rough-looking, nameless restaurant behind the Cooperative des Marins Pecheurs that serves typical Berber food. The port is flanked by attractive beaches: Yellich (to the east) faces an island that you can walk out to; Oued Sahfa lies to the west; and an hour's hike over the hill lies Mestaza.

There are a couple of very basic shops at Torres de Alcala, 5km east. Three semi-ruined Spanish towers stand sentinel over this scruffy village, set back from a shingle beach caught between two rocky headlands.

TREKKING IN THE RIF MOUNTAINS: TALASSEMTANE NATIONAL PARK

Chefchaouen to Bab Taza شفشاون إلى باب تازة

This is the best introductory walk to the Rif Mountains. Within the Talassemtane National Park (www.talassemtane.com) and starting from Chefchaouen, it takes in some spectacular scenery, including the geologically improbable God's Bridge, a natural stone arc spanning the Oued Farda. You are also likely to meet troupes of Barbary apes.

The full trek takes five days, but there are plenty of ways to shorten the distance or duration. One option would be to arrange transport from Akchour back to Chefchaouen at the end of day two. Transport isn't too hard to find in Akchour, or you can arrange for a grand taxi from Chefchaouen to pick you up at a specified time. Alternatively, you may be able to hike back along an alternate route.

The Talassemtane National Park is one of two parks in the Rif Mountains (the other being Bouhachem). It's a largely undiscovered area and yet these mountains make perfect trekking country, blessed with magnificent ranges, gorges and valleys, with forests of cedar, cork oak and fir. Being close to the Mediterranean, the Rif are also the greenest of Morocco's mountains, and springtime, with its riot of wildflowers, is one of the most delightful times to walk here.

One thing that does deter trekkers is the region's reputation as an area of drug production. But although cannabis takes up over three quarters of cultivatable land east of Chefchaouen, trekkers have little reason to feel threatened, especially if travelling with a guide – villagers will be genuinely interested and welcoming. The trek detailed here, setting out from Chefchaouen, is well trodden and unproblematic in this respect. In a concerted effort to reduce reliance on the cannabis industry, local organisations, backed by the government, are setting up rural tourism facilities such as *gîtes* and homestays, managing routes and training guides.

The Rif Mountains rarely top more than 2500m in height, with most treks only occasionally venturing over 2000m, so altitude sickness isn't the worry it can be in other parts of Morocco.

Wildlife

The Rif's climate and proximity to Europe endows it with a Mediterranean vibe – the area closely resembles the sierras of southern Spain. Cedars make up the majority of tree species, including a rare endemic species *Abies maroccana,* a high-altitude variant of the Spanish cedar. In addition, cork oak, holm pine, wild olive, juniper and the rare carob are some that dot the limestone mountains. The stony land is hard to cultivate and thin in nutrients; deforestation is an issue here as in other parts of Morocco. Various herbs such as lavender and thyme thrive and are used by the local population as medicines.

Locals may tell you that there are wolves in the mountains, but it's a mistranslation – there are foxes. Wild boar are also native, but have a retiring nature that makes them hard to spot. The Rif's most famous mammals are the Barbary apes (known locally as *mgou*), whose range extends south into the Middle Atlas.

You'll have better luck with birdlife. Raptors easily spotted wheeling on thermals include black-shouldered kites, golden eagles and long-legged buzzards. Ravens can also be seen against the limestone cliffs.

Scorpions present a small risk in the Rif, although less so than further south. Be wary of the red scorpion; stings are extremely painful. The venomous *fer à cheval* viper (named for the horseshoe-like mark on its head) is more likely to flee from you than vice versa.

Day 1: Chefchaouen to Afeska

DURATION 5½-6½ HOURS / DISTANCE 14.5KM /
ASCENT 1200M / DESCENT 600M

An early morning start is recommended for the first day, starting on the 4WD track

The Rif Mountains

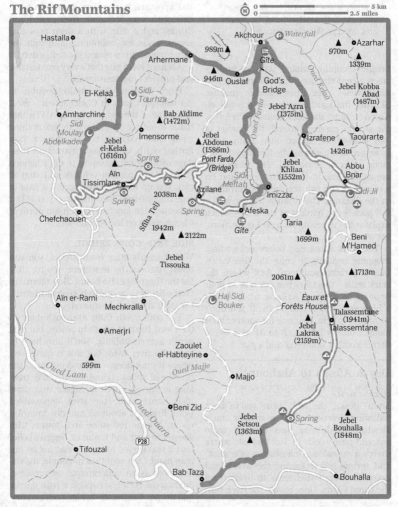

MEDITERRANEAN COAST & THE RIF CHEFCHAOUEN TO BAB TAZA

TREK AT A GLANCE

Duration four to five days

Distance 56km

Standard medium

Start Chefchaouen

Finish Bab Taza

Highest Point Sfiha Telj Pass (approximately 1700m)

Accommodation *gîtes* and camping

Public Transport yes

Summary The walking here is relatively undemanding but the mountain scenery is spectacular, the tiny Riffian villages worth a detour, and the gorges and weird geology fascinating.

behind Camping Azilane, with an initially steep ascent climbing through trees to give great views over Chefchaouen's medina. Skirting the southern slopes of Jebel el-Kelaâ (1616m), the track evens out to follow the stream passing through the hamlet of Aïn Tissimlane, before once again rising in an arc to a high pass by the jagged limestone crags of Sfiha Telj. The views here are astounding in both directions, and on a clear day you can see the Mediterranean in the distance. The climb is a killer with a full pack – the hardest of the trek – which explains the necessity for a cool early morning start.

The track turns east before descending. Stopping regularly to enjoy the fine views, take the right (southern) fork where the track splits – this takes you down in an hour or so to the village of Azilane, where there's a homestay option and a *gîte*. If you don't want to stop here, continue for another hour along a mostly level path to Afeska where there's another homestay and a *gîte*.

Day 2: Afeska to Akchour

DURATION 3½-4½ HOURS / DISTANCE 10KM / DESCENT 860M

From Afeska, the wide *piste* you've been following deteriorates to a smaller track. Heading north, you pass through more oak and pine woods to Sidi Meftah, where there's a *marabout* (mausoleum of a saint) and spring, before leaving the woods and descending the switchbacks to Imizzar on the Oued Farda. Once beside the river, turn left (away from the village, northwest), then cross the river below some impressive overhanging cliffs and continue heading northwest. You'll join a well-worn mule track that eventually leads down to Pont Farda, an ancient bridge over Oued Farda.

Cross to the west bank of the river and continue north, dwarfed by the surrounding scenery. After an hour, the trail bears left away from the river towards Ouslaf, which is overshadowed by a giant rock buttress, but keep on the same path while it bears right, descending to rejoin the river on the outskirts of Akchour (398m), which sits on the Oued Kelaâ.

Akchour is strung out along the river. As you approach it, you first come to a small cafe with very welcome river-cooled soft drinks, and a dam with a deep pool that seems made for swimming, although the water temperature means short dips only!

Akchour has a *gîte* that's very comfortable and provides excellent meals.

From Akchour, it's usually possible to get transport back to Chefchaouen – most likely one of the rugged vans or 4WDs that battle it out on the *piste*. If there's nothing going from Akchour, try Talembote, 2km further north, which has a market on Tuesdays with regular transport to Chefchaouen (Dh15). Most passing vehicles will stop to pick you up if they have space – a case of paid hitchhiking. They may drop you at Dar Ackoubaa, the junction town 10km north of Chefchaouen on the N2 highway.

SIDE TRIP: GOD'S BRIDGE

With an early start from Afeska, you can reach Akchour by lunchtime, giving time for the short hike (1½ hours, 3km return) to God's Bridge – an unlikely geological structure that shouldn't be missed.

The path south from Akchour's dam up the Oued Farda is rough in places, but well worth any scrambling. You'll also have to cross the river twice but this is quite easy where it's not deep – if you don't mind the occasional splash. (However, if you're trekking in spring, check in Afeska that snow melt hasn't made the river impassable.) God's Bridge is about 45 minutes from Akchour. A huge red stone arch towers 25m above the river and it almost beggars belief that it was carved by nature and not by human hand. Over countless millennia, the river flowed as an underground watercourse, eroding the rock and carving a path deeper and deeper, leaving the bridge high and dry.

Day 3: Akchour to Pastures above Abou Bnar

DURATION 4½-6 HOURS / DISTANCE 12KM / ASCENT 977M

An early morning start (with full water bottles, since there are no springs on the route until you reach Izrafene) sees you leaving Akchour by heading to the north, crossing the bridge over the Oued Kelaâ and then cutting right (southeast) along the track to Izrafene. It's a particularly picturesque walk as you climb up and around Jebel Azra (1375m). Your eyes lift from the steep gorges you've trekked through and out over the sweep of open mountains. If you're up for some scrambling, add half an hour to attain the peak, from where you can drink in further gorgeous views.

Having cut around the mountain, the countryside becomes gentler – rolling even – as the trail heads south. The village of Izrafene marks the halfway point of the day's trek. Just before the village, a track bears east at a col, tempting the adventurous to abandon the Bab Taza hike and walk to Taourarte (where there's a homestay and a *gîte*) and on to Bou-Ahmed on the coast, a further two to three days' walk.

From Izrafene, the track turns into a 4WD *piste* – the first since Afeska. It follows a narrow valley, gradually turning east up onto a ridge with gentle views. Where it forks, turn left, and then, just 25m later, turn right onto a trail that heads southeast to Abou Bnar through a pretty stretch of oak wood. There's little to detain you here, so continue alongside the river (not the 4WD track) through the open, grassy country to the *marabout* of Sidi Jil. This is a pretty area for camping, but if you continue for another 30 minutes, you'll come to an even more beautiful spot, set in wide pasture near the El-Ma Souka spring – an idyllic place for a night's rest.

ALTERNATIVE ROUTE: RETURN TO CHEFCHAOUEN

It's possible to trek back to Chefchaouen from Akchour in a day by an alternate route via the villages of Ouslaf, Arhermane and El-Kelaâ. El-Kelaâ is the site of fascinating Mosquée Srifi-yenne, with its strange leaning tower. This route takes a quick six hours and avoids any major climbs or descents.

Day 4: Pastures Above Abou Bnar to Talassemtane Village

DURATION TWO TO 2½ HOURS / DISTANCE 6KM / ASCENT 352M

From the campsite southwest of Abou Bnar, walk back to the 4WD track. Turn left and

---

BEFORE YOU GO: CHEFCHAOUEN TO BAB TAZA CHECKLIST

Weather Trekking is possible year-round, though it can be bitterly cold between November and March, with snow. There's frequent rain between late September and June. It's fiercely hot in summer, when some water sources dry up.

Guides Organise trekking guides through Abdeslam Mouden (p254) in Chefchaouen. Guides charge Dh400 per day.

Accommodation Many villages have simple *gîtes* that cost from Dh200 per person including dinner and breakfast. It's also possible to arrange *gîtes* in person during the trek, though there is a risk that the guardian may not be around and the *gîte* may be closed – not uncommon. Camping is not encouraged as local people don't benefit. But in some areas there are no *gîtes*, so it's the only alternative. There's one official camping site at the village of Talassemtane. Permission to camp (free) must be obtained from the Eco-Museum in Chefchaouen in advance. Staying with families en route is an option in some villages and it is possible to stop for tea with locals and to visit weaving and cheese-making cooperatives.

Maps From the government 1:50,000 topographical series, survey sheets *Chaouen* and *Bab Taza* cover the Chefchaouen to Bab Taza trek. The Eco-Museum at the entrance to the park has maps of the routes.

Equipment Where there are no *gîtes*, a tent is necessary. A decent sleeping bag is essential, and a light waterproof jacket – rain showers are common. Food and fuel supplies can be bought in Chefchaouen. Mules to carry your luggage cost from Dh250 per day including muleteer. From August to October, mules can be hard to organise as they're used for the kif harvest, and prices increase accordingly.

cross the river, and walk south into the pine woodland. You will quickly come to a T-junction, where you should keep on the right (the left goes downhill to Beni M'Hamed) where the path starts to ascend again.

Keep on the main track, ignoring further side tracks and junctions. As you rise and go through several mini-passes, the views return. To the west, the huge mass of Jebel Lakraa (2159m) dominates the countryside.

By late morning you'll reach Talassemtane village. A small sign indicates that you should turn left off the 4WD track to the house of the park's *eaux et forêts* guardian. There's an official camping site here.

SIDE TRIPS

The short walking day allows plenty of time to explore the area and watch wildlife, particularly Barbary apes.

Head north, back along the 4WD track above the *guardien's* house to a clearing and junction. Here you turn right and follow the track east into *mgou* country. Troupes are relatively common here, although they quickly retreat into the safety of the trees if you get too close. The track bends south, giving great views out across the valley to the long ridge of Jebel Taloussisse (2005m), before turning briefly east again. Here a trail on the right leads south over the spur of Talassemtane (1941m) to a football pitch – strange, but true! – on an area of flat land. From here it's possible to make a rocky traverse west, back to the campsite.

Climbing Jebel Lakraa is another alternative for gung-ho trekkers. The best approach is from the north of the mountain, trekking along the ridge to descend one of the stream gullies southeast of the summit. However, there's no fixed path and it's a scramble in places. Allow around 3½ hours return.

Day 5: Talassemtane Village to Bab Taza

DURATION 2½ TO 3½ HOURS / DISTANCE 13.5KM / DESCENT 825M

The final day is a quick descent along the 4WD track to Bab Taza, where local kif cultivation is much in evidence. The trail swings through a wide pasture and on through the cork woodland of Jebel Setsou (1363m) before revealing the sprawl of Bab Taza (or so it seems after a few days in the mountains) below.

In Bab Taza, there are quite a few cafes and a couple of grotty-looking hotels strung along the main road. The main business seems to be in huge sacks of fertiliser used for growing kif. Grands taxis leave regularly throughout the day for Chefchaouen (Dh12, 30 minutes) from the western end of town.

EAST MEDITERRANEAN COAST

الشاطئ الشرق للبحر الأبيض المتوسط

Melilla
مليلة

POP 80,800

Who would expect to find hundreds of Modernist buildings, the second-largest such collection outside Barcelona, in North Africa? Yet here they are, along with one perfectly preserved medieval fortress, several fascinating museums and nearly 50 tapas bars. The result is Melilla, a nirvana for architecture and history buffs, as well as a great place to spend the weekend.

Along with Ceuta, Melilla is one of two autonomous Spanish cities on the Moroccan coast, known as the *plazas mayores*. These cultural islands have much in common: their economies are rooted in cross-border commerce, their societies are strongly multicultural and there is a significant military presence, the result of strained relations. Melilla is nearly equally divided between Christian and Muslim, with the latter being predominantly Berber. A result of sub-Saharan immigrants trying to get in was the construction of a €33 million fence that stretches from one side of the enclave to the other. The visit of the king and queen of Spain in 2007, the first royal visit in 80 years, met with great local acclaim but was strongly reviled by the Moroccans.

Melilla is very easy on the traveller, and tourist infrastructure is excellent. While ferry-loads of visitors pour in during summer, in the low season you'll have plenty of breathing room.

Melilla oozes with history, but it is neither as broad nor as deep as you might expect. While the area has been inhabited for more than 2000 years, the old city wasn't begun until after Spanish conquest in 1496, then built up in four stages. Up until the end of the 19th century, virtually all of Melilla was contained within a single impregnable fortress. Current borders were fixed by several treaties with Morocco between 1859 and 1894, the last following an unsuccessful siege by rebellious Rif Berbers. The method involved shooting a cannonball and seeing how far it went. More fighting with rebel Berbers broke out several times in the ensuing years, until the Spanish protectorate consolidated its grip in 1927. In 1936, Franco flew here from the Canary Islands to launch the Spanish Civil War. Local politics still tips to the right.

Melilla is a semicircle of 12 sq km carved out of the Moroccan coastline. The old town, Melilla la Vieja, is a highly complex, multi-level fortress that juts out into the sea. It contains numerous museums, as well as some small residential areas. The port and major beaches lie to the south, with the ferry terminal directly east.

The 'new town' is a broken grid of streets with an attractive commercial centre full of Modernist buildings. The heart is the long triangular Parque Hernández, which ends at the circular Plaza de España. Most of the hotels, banks and restaurants are located to the north.

◉ Sights & Activities

◎ Melilla la Vieja

★ **Melilla la Vieja**   FORT
(Calle General Macías) Perched over the Mediterranean, Melilla la Vieja is a prime example of the fortress strongholds that the Portuguese and (in this case) the Spaniards built along the Moroccan littoral during the 16th and 17th centuries. Much of it has been painstakingly restored in recent years. The main entrance is **Puerta de la Marina** (Calle General Macías), fronted by a statue of Franco, from where you ascend to the summit, passing several small museums. There is a lift, too, that doesn't always work. Signage, in Spanish, French and English, is very good.

THE LAST PIECES OF EMPIRE

Some of the most fascinating places in northern Morocco are not Moroccan at all, but Spanish. When Spain recognised Moroccan independence in 1956, it retained a collection of historical oddities that had predated the Spanish protectorate. Known by the euphemism *plazas de soberanía* (places of sovereignty), they have a population of 145,000, and are divided into two groups.

The **plazas mayores** (greater places), Ceuta and Melilla, contain virtually all the people. Politically these are 'autonomous cities', with governmental powers placing them somewhere between a city and a region of Spain.

The **plazas menores** (lesser places) are inhabited by a handful of Spanish legionnaires, if that. These include three islands in the Bay of Al-Hoceima: Isla de Mar, Isla de Tierra (both deserted, apart from Spanish flags) and El Peñón de Alhucemas, a striking white fortress home to some 60 soldiers. El Peñón de Velez de la Gomera, at the end of a long canyon in the Al-Hoceima National Park, is another ancient rock fortress, connected to the mainland by a narrow spit of sand – and a guardhouse, one of the oddest national borders you'll ever see. The Islas Chafarinas, 3km from Ras el-Mar, have three small islands: Isla del Congreso, Isla del Rey and Isla Isabel II, the last with a garrison of 190 troops. Spain also owns the tiny Isla Perejil, near Ceuta, which was the cause of one of the world's smallest conflicts, when Spanish troops evicted a handful of Moroccan soldiers in 2002; and the Isla de Alborán, about 75km north of Melilla, which has a small navy garrison.

While the two fortress *peñónes* (rocky outcrops) are must-sees, none of the *plazas menores* can be entered, as they are military sites. Morocco claims them all, making their defence necessary even though their strategic importance is limited.

Recent history has been focused on problems with Spain over immigration and political sovereignty. In 2006 youths set fire to several mosques in Ceuta after a number of local Muslims were arrested on the Spanish mainland in connection with the Madrid bombings. In 2007 the king of Spain visited the city for the first time in 80 years, sparking protests from the Moroccan government. So far none of this has closed a single tapas bar. In late 2010 Moroccan youths rioted in both Ceuta and Melilla over sovereignty of the cities, sparked by a lack of jobs. Tensions continue to simmer.

Melilla

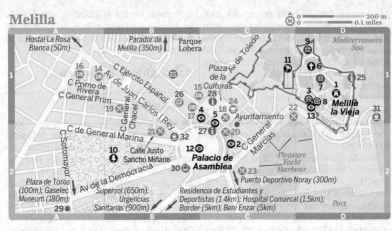

Melilla

Museo Etnográfico de la Culturas Amazigh & Sefardí
MUSEUM

(Almacenes de la Peñuelas; ☎ 0952 97 62 16; Plaza Pedro de Estopiñán; ◎10am-2pm & 5-9pm Tue-Sat, 10am-2pm Sun summer; 10am-2pm & 4-8pm Tue-Sat, 10am-2pm Sun winter) FREE This museum charts the history of the Amazigh (Berber) and Sephardic (Jewish) cultures in Melilla.

Aljibes de las Peñuelas
HISTORIC BUILDING

(◎10am-2pm & 5-9.30pm Tue-Sat, 10am-2pm Sun Apr-Sep) FREE The small door across the courtyard leads into the cave-like, other-worldly cistern that is still flowing.

Iglesia de la Purísima Concepción
CHURCH

(Parish of the Immaculate Conception; ☎ 0952 68 15 16; ◎10am-3pm & 4-9pm Tue-Sat, 10am-12.30pm Sun) This 17th-century church is worth a stop for its resplendent nave.

Las Cuevas del Conventico
HISTORIC BUILDING

(Caves of the Convent; ☎ 0952 68 09 29; admission €1.20; ◎10.30am-1.30pm & 4.30-8pm Tue-Sat,

10.30am-2pm Sun) These extensive and well-restored caves were used as a refuge during sieges, and pop out at a small beach below the cliffs. The Calle de la Concepción continues up to the baroque Iglesia de la Purísima Concepción and, just below it, the entrance to Las Cuevas del Conventico. A short film and guided tour (both in Spanish) detail the history of the caves and tunnels that lead to the cliff face. The Phoenicians first excavated the tunnels; later occupiers took turns enlarging them and they now extend over three levels. They are meticulously maintained and well lit, which sadly eliminates much of their mystery.

Museo Militar   MUSEUM
(✆0952 68 55 87; ⊙10am-2pm Tue-Sun) FREE
The history of the Spanish protectorate is dominated by military history, and this museum is the one place where you can feel the grand sweep of that violent drama, with martial music playing in the background. Don't miss the antique photographs room, where biplanes, legionnaires and Berber horsemen all fuse into a dreamy adventure novel, or the 'do not touch the cannonballs' sign, which is straight from *Dr Strangelove.*

⊙ New Town

Construction of the new part of town, west of the fortress, began at the end of the 19th century. Laid out by Gaudí-disciple Don Enrique Nieto, Melilla is considered by some to be Spain's 'second modernist city', after Barcelona. The highlight is Plaza de España, with the lovely facade of the Palacio de Asamblea facing Parque Hernández.

At the turn of the 20th century, Melilla was the only centre of trade between Tetouan and the Algerian border. As the city grew, it expressed itself in the architectural style of Modernisme (not to be confused with the cultural movement of modernism), which was then in vogue. This trend continued locally even after it went out of fashion elsewhere. The result is a living museum of hundreds of Modernist and art deco buildings. Unlike Ceuta, many of these treasures have yet to be dusted off, but the overall architectural wealth is greater.

The best way to appreciate this heritage is to stroll through the area to the north of Parque Hernández; it's known as 'the golden triangle'.

Plaza de España   LANDMARK
Several fine examples of the city's heritage are on the Plaza de España, including Nieto's Casino Militar, whose facade still depicts a republican coat of arms, and the Banco de España.

With its central fountain, the plaza is a pleasant place to sit. At the centre is an art deco military monument to campaigns in Morocco. In the distance you can see Melilla's most striking contemporary building, the new courthouse (closed to visitors), which looks like a flying saucer landed on the roof.

★Palacio de Asamblea   NOTABLE BUILDING
Nieto's art-deco Palacio de Asamblea, whose floor plan depicts a ducal crown, is an operating town hall, although the staff at the entrance are willing to show tourists around upon request. Worth seeing are two rooms on the upper floor: Salon Dorado, which

---

MODERNISME & MELILLA

Like many of the movements from which it drew its inspiration (eg the English Arts & Crafts Movement), Modernisme was a broad reaction to the material values of an industrial age, which suffused culture with a machinelike spirit. Centred in Barcelona, it was the Catalan version of art nouveau. Modernist architecture is characterised by the use of curves over straight lines, the frequent use of natural motifs (especially plants), lively decoration and rich detail, asymmetrical forms, a refined aesthetic and dynamism. Its chief proponent was Antoni Gaudí, the architect of Barcelona's famous Sagrada Família cathedral. But in Melilla, Modernism is synonymous with Enrique Nieto.

A student of Gaudí, Nieto worked on his Casa Milà in Barcelona. Wanting to escape his master's shadow, however, he left for booming Melilla in 1909 and stayed the rest of his life, becoming city architect in 1931. His work included Melilla's main synagogue, the main mosque and several buildings for the Catholic Church, representing the diversity of the city's culture. Perhaps due to the distant location of his canvas, however, this great painter in concrete is not well-known outside of Melilla.

contains a large painting of the arrival of Spaniards in Melilla in 1497, and the Sala de Plenos, where the local congress meets.

Parque Hernández
PARK

From the plaza, take a pleasant stroll down the long, palm-lined Parque Hernández. At the end, turn left down Calle Sotomayor. The Plaza De Toros, the only operating bullring in Africa, lies straight ahead.

Gaselec Museum
MUSEUM

(☎ 0952 69 55 75; Plaza Rafael Fernández de Castro y Pedrera; ☺ 6-9pm Mon-Fri, 11.30am-1.30pm & 6-9pm Sat & Sun) FREE On the other side of the park is this intriguing oddity, the passion of the former president of the local gas and electric company. It houses a museum of ancient Egypt completely composed of reproductions, including King Tut's mask and sarcophagus.

◎ Beaches

The one distressing sight in Melilla is the state of its coastline, which is everywhere strewn with plastic bottles and bags. While efforts are made to clean certain beaches, it is hard to escape this problem, particularly out of season, making you fear for the future of the Mediterranean.

There is one large beach south of the port, divided into four sections. The foul Río de Oro empties into this area, so stick to sunbathing.

An intriguing alternative is the secluded Playa de la Ensanada de los Galápagos, which is reached by taking a tunnel under the fort. It is open May to September.

🛏 Sleeping

There aren't many hotels in Melilla, so they tend to fill up even in the low season.

Hostal Residencia Cazaza
HOTEL €

(☎ 0956 68 46 48; 6 Calle Primo de Rivera; s/d €25/38) This old building with its high ceilings and small balconies has charm, and has a central location in the golden triangle. Rooms are clean and management is friendly.

Hostal La Rosa Blanca
HOTEL €

(☎ 0952 68 27 38; 7 Calle Gran Capitán; s/d with bathroom €25/35) A very basic option; the rooms are clean but vary in quality, so make sure to look before you buy. Rooms have sinks and shared bathrooms.

Residencia de Estudiantes y Deportistas
HOSTEL €

(Residence of Students & Athletes; ☎ 0952 67 00 08; Calle Alfonso X; per person incl breakfast €25, half board €30, full board €35; ☎) This is the best budget choice if you don't mind being away from the town centre. There are 87 sparkling rooms, a cafeteria, library and TV lounge. Rooms above the 2nd floor have balconies. Take local bus 3, which stops near Plaza España on Calle Marina every 10 minutes, though there are fewer services on weekends. The trip takes 10 to 15 minutes.

Hotel Anfora
HOTEL €€

(☎ 0956 68 33 40; fax 0956 68 33 44; 8 Calle Pablo Vallescá; s/d incl breakfast €46/73; ❄ ☎) This rather industrial-feeling three-star hotel is in an excellent location and offers good-sized, standard-fare rooms with TVs, fridges and balconies, as well as a gym. The rooftop restaurant serves a basic breakfast as you enjoy vistas of Melilla la Vieja and of the sea beyond.

Hotel Nacional
HOTEL €€

(☎ 0956 68 45 40; fax 0956 68 45 41; 10 Calle Primo de Rivera; s/d €35/55; ❄ ☎) This hotel has mostly compact rooms, with minibars, quaint iron furniture and modern bathrooms. Those facing inside are a bit dark, so get one looking to the street. Management is friendly, and there's a lift.

Hotel Rusadir
HOTEL €€€

(☎ 0956 68 12 40; 5 Calle Pablo Vallescá; s/d incl breakfast €71/88; ❄ ☎) This four-star hotel has been completely renovated to excellent effect, including an impressive lobby and design-conscious rooms with TVs, minibars and balconies. The restaurant puts out an impressive breakfast buffet.

Parador de Melilla
HOTEL €€€

(☎ 0956 68 49 40; www.parador.es; Ave Cándido Lobera; r €150; ❄ ☎ ▨) You'll need a vehicle to get to this very classy choice with large, grand rooms, warm use of wood throughout, a high level of quality furnishings and balconies with great views to sea. The circular dining room overlooking the city is an elegant touch. The adjacent Parque Lobera is great for kids.

🍴 Eating

Many of Melilla's restaurants are associated with hotels (like the Rusadir or the Parador), but there are plenty of others around Ave de Juan Carlos I Rey.

There are plenty of small grocery shops in the streets around Parque Hernández. For the complete supermarket experience, go to **Supersol** (Calle General Polavieja; ☺10am-10pm Mon-Sat) on the road to the frontier.

Cafetéria Militar SPANISH €
(Calle de Almovodar; mains €8; ☺1-3.30pm) A huge canteen-like affair on the side of the Palacio de Asamblea, with a few tables outside, too, this restaurant is hugely busy at lunchtime.

Café La Dolce Vita TAPAS €
(Plaza de la Culturas; raciones from €6; ☺10am-11pm) This large, buzzy cafe and tapas bar has seating all around a corner of the plaza. Have a coffee, an ice cream or a drink with tapas while people-watching.

Casa Marta TAPAS €
(Calle Justo Sancho Miñano; tapas from €2.50; ☺1-3.30pm & 8pm-1am) This is a rockin' tapas bar that brims with people of all ages both inside and out: outdoor seating is under a tent in the street. Each beer comes with free tapas, so three beers gets you a free dinner. Don't miss the *filetillo,* thin strips of beef with gravy.

Café Rossy CAFE €
(5 Calle General Prim; sandwiches from €2.50; ☺lunch & dinner) Another reliable place to grab a quick eat or while away an hour with a book and a coffee. The *bocadillos* are a perfect lunchtime snack.

Real Club Marítimo CAFE €
(Yacht Harbour; coffee & croissant €4; ☺10am-midnight) This is a private yacht club but travellers are welcome to come and sample a croissant and coffee by the sea.

★**La Pérgola** SEAFOOD €€
(☏0952 68 56 28; Calle General Marcías; mains from €10; ☺lunch & dinner) A waterfront terrace makes this classy spot a very pleasant place for a meal, or just a late afternoon drink. The speciality is barbecued seafood, and at €10 the *prix-fixe* menu cannot be beaten.

🍷 Drinking

Café Latoga CAFE
(Plaza de la Culturas; ☺10am-1am) This small bar in the lee of a grand church has a local clientele happy to sip a beer and keep an eye on the plaza.

Puerto Deportivo Noray BAR
(☺11am-2am) Look no further: this is Melilla's bar zone, with 12 different options grouped side by side on the waterfront. Enter through the car park next to the courthouse.

❶ Information

To phone Melilla from outside Spain, dial ☏0034 and drop the first zero. Melilla is one hour ahead of Morocco, and two hours ahead during Ramadan. Most shops and businesses are closed on Sunday.

INTERNET ACCESS
There are numerous internet cafes downtown.
Locutoria Dosmil (14-25 Calle Ejercito Español; per hr €2; ☺9am-2pm & 4-9pm)

MEDICAL SERVICES
Hospital Comarcal (☏0956 67 00 00; Ave de la Juventud) South side of Río de Oro.
Urgencias Sanitarias (☏0956 67 44 00; 40 Alvaro de Bazan; ☺5pm-9am Mon-Sat, 24hr Sun & public holidays) Night pharmacy.

MONEY
Euros are used for all transactions in Melilla. You'll find several banks (with ATMs) around Ave de Juan Carlos I Rey. Most will buy or sell dirham at an inferior rate to the Moroccan dealers hanging around the ferry port or the border.

On the Moroccan side of the border you can change cash at the Crédit du Maroc. There's also a Banque Populaire with an ATM 200m further into Morocco; walk straight ahead to the crossroads and it's on your left on the road to the port.

POST
Main Post Office (Calle Pablo Vallescá; ☺8.30am-8.30pm Mon-Fri, 9.30am-1pm Sat)

TOURIST INFORMATION
Fundación Melilla Ciudad Monumental (☏0952 97 62 01; www.melillamonumental. org; 13 Calle Miguel Acosta; ☺10am-2pm & 4.30-8.30pm Mon-Sat, 10am-2pm Sun) In-depth information on local architecture.

Oficina del Turismo (main) (☏0952 97 61 89; www.melillaturismo.com; Plaza de la Culturas; ☺10am-2pm & 4.30-8.30pm Mon-Sat, 10am-2pm Sun) Lots of maps and brochures and friendly, English-speaking staff. Offers special tours of religious sites. Website contains a comprehensive history and architectural tour.

Oficina del Turismo (kiosk) (☏0952 97 61 51; www.melillaturismo.com; Plaza de España; ☺10am-2pm & 4-8pm Mon-Fri) Faces the Palacio de Asamblea.

MEDITERRANEAN COAST & THE RIF MELILLA

TRAVEL AGENCIES

Viajes Melilla (☎0952 67 93 52; 1 Ave Duquesa de la Victoria; ⊗9.30am-1pm & 3.30-7pm Mon-Sat)

ℹ Getting There & Away

AIR

Air Nostrum (Iberia) (www.airnostrum.com; Melilla Airport) offers 12 daily flights between Melilla and Málaga, as well as two daily flights to Almería and Madrid, and one daily flight to Granada. The airport is a 10-minute (€6) taxi ride, and has no ATM.

BORDER CROSSING

To get to the border, you'll need to either take a taxi (€7) or catch local bus 2 (marked 'Aforos'), which runs between Plaza de España and the Beni Enzar border post (€1, every 30 minutes from 7.30am to 11pm). From where the buses stop, it's about 50m to Spanish customs and another 200m to Moroccan customs.

Before entering Morocco, fill in a white form and get your passport stamped at the booth. It's easiest to buy the form from a tout for €1. If you're driving into Morocco, remember to retain the green customs slip, which you must present when you (and your vehicle) leave the country. Large queues of vehicles entering Morocco are frequent and time-consuming; procedures for foot passengers are quick and easy.

On the Moroccan side of the border, bus 19 (usually unmarked) runs hourly to Nador (Dh28, 25 minutes). Frequent grands taxis (Dh6, 15 minutes) to Nador are tucked away in a car park to the right of this crossroad.

When entering Melilla from Morocco, fill in a white form and get your passport stamped. Some nationalities require visas to enter Spain: if they don't stop you here, they will when you try to move on to the mainland. Bus 43 goes to Plaza de España (€1).

FERRY

Melisur (☎0956 68 66 13; 8 Calle de General Marina; ⊗9am-1pm & 5-7pm Mon-Fri, 9am-noon Sat) sells Acciona (Trasmediterránea) ferry tickets to Málaga. Tickets are also available for purchase at the **estación marítima** (Ferry Port; ☎0956 68 16 33).

Ferry services to Málaga on Monday leave at noon and arrive at 7.35pm, and leave at midnight arriving at 8am on Tuesday. From Tuesday to Saturday they leave at 11.30pm.

Ferries from Málaga to Melilla leave on Sunday (7pm and 11pm) and Tuesday to Saturday (1pm). Prices begin at €45.

ℹ Getting Around

The centre of Melilla is compact and easy to walk around. Buses ply the route between Plaza de España and the border. The local **taxi service** (☎0956 68 36 21) is also useful.

Nador الناظور

POP 150,000

The Rocade (coastal road) from Al-Hoceima to Nador (130km) is a delight to travel. It passes through red cliffs, verdant gorges and, midway, an enormous sculpture of deeply eroded hills.

Within 60km of Nador there are several ramshackle, clifftop cafes that are perfect for having a mint tea as you gaze out over the sea. Don't look too closely at the deserted beaches, though, as they're knee-deep in litter.

Unfortunately Nador itself offers little when you arrive. It's a town that's in flux: a new resort is planned with a golf course, marinas and apartments around the lagoon, Marchica, but is not yet complete. There are no sights or attractions in this endless sprawl of concrete blocks. The city serves more as a transport link, with a major airport, active ferry port and train station with a service to Fez. It's best not to linger in Nador.

🛏 Sleeping

There's no shortage of hotels of all classes in Nador but be warned, many of them prefer to sell their rooms by the hour. The cheaper places are near the bus and grand-taxi stations.

Hotel Geranio   HOTEL €

(☎0536 60 28 28; 16 Rue No 20; s/d Dh160/188) Just away from the chaos of the bus station, streetside rooms here can be noisy, but the low prices make this the top budget option. Clean rooms come with tiny bathrooms. There's a ground-floor cafeteria as well.

Hotel Annakhil   HOTEL €€

(☎0536 33 58 67; 185 Blvd de Tanger; s/d incl breakfast Dh486/652; ❋⏢) The Annakhil might be overkill on decor with its orange corridors, plastic plants and bright blue bedrooms, but it's the best midrange option. There's good linen, comfortable beds, TVs and fridges in the rooms. The cafe next door serves breakfast. The bar rocks at night –

only a very brave woman would venture alone into this den.

Hotel Méditerranée
HOTEL €€

(☑0536 60 64 95; hotel.mediterranee@gmail.com; 2-4 Ave Youssef ibn Tachfine; s/d incl breakfast Dh490/650; ❄☎) Views from this hotel have been annihilated by the new Hotel Rif being constructed at the time of research. But it's still only one block back from the corniche and lagoon. The corner rooms have plenty of light, and all have TVs. There's a dull restaurant (dishes from Dh60) on the ground floor serving breakfast, omelettes and fish.

Hotel Ryad
HOTEL €€€

(☑ 0536 60 77 17; hotel-ryad@menara.ma; Ave Mohammed V; s/d Dh710/920; ❄☎) Once plush but now showing its age and somewhat overpriced, the Ryad is a large hotel with a noisy bar. The rooms have standard features and those on the top floor have views over the lagoon.

✖ Eating & Drinking

There are numerous cheap eats around the CTM bus station, serving up quick brochettes, sandwiches and tajines. Ave Mohammed V is the place for a lazy coffee, with street cafes lining the road under shady orange trees.

Café Antalya
CAFE €

(Blvd Prince Héritier Sidi Mohammed; pizzas from Dh50) All glass and chrome and spilling out onto the pavement, this smart cafe shows a new face of Nador. The pizzeria upstairs is popular with young trendies.

Restaurant Marhaba
SEAFOOD €€

(☑0536 60 33 11; Calle ibn Rochd; mains from Dh70; ☺lunch & dinner) The smartest restaurant in town, the Marhaba specialises in fish and does it very well. The main room is very large, but there's a cosier terrace at the back with fishing nets and plastic lobsters. There's no alcohol.

Café Club
CAFE

(Ave Mohammed Zerktouni; ☺8.30am-10pm) Jutting into the lagoon at the far end of Mohammed V, this island cafe is a welcome bit of maritime focus in an otherwise concrete forest. It no longer serves food, and with all the development around the lagoon, it might not survive much longer.

ⓘ Information

Credit Maroc (64 Ave Mohammed V; ☺9am-4pm Mon-Thu, 9-11am Fri, 9am-noon Sat) One of several banks on Mohammed V with foreign-exchange services and ATM.

Cyber Milano (Blvd el Massira; per hr Dh5; ☺8am-8pm)

Ketama Voyages (☑0536 60 61 91; ketamavoyage@hotmail.fr; 55 Ave Mohammed; ☺9.30am-noon & 2.30-6.30pm Mon-Fri, 9.30am-noon Sat)

Pharmacy al-Farabi (☑0536 60 60 11; Ave Mohammed V; ☺8am-6pm Mon-Sat)

Royal Air Maroc (Ave Mohammed V; ☺8.30am-12.15pm & 2.30-7pm Mon-Fri, 9am-noon & 3-6pm Sat)

ⓘ Getting There & Away

AIR
The airport is 23km south of Nador. Vueling Airlines, Royal Air Maroc and Ryanair operate numerous flights to Europe. Ryanair, Germanwings and Air Arabia fly to Germany.

BOAT
Acciona has a fast ferry service to Almería. It leaves Almería every day at 11am and arrives in Nador at 4pm, except Tuesdays when it leaves at 9am, arriving in Nador at 2pm. The return ferry leaves at 10pm, arriving the next day in Almería at 6am. The Tuesday ferry leaves Nador at 4pm and arrives at 10pm.

The port of Beni Enzar is 7km from the city but traffic makes it feel much further. The quickest way to get there is by grand taxi (Dh10, 15 minutes).

BUS
From the **CTM office** (☑0536 60 01 36; Rue Général Meziane) there are departures to all the usual suspects: Casablanca, Rabat, Meknès, Fez, Tangier, Larache, Sidi Kacem, Al-Hoceima, Chefchaouen and more. In the evening, several slightly cheaper Casablanca-bound coaches run by other companies leave from the same area. CTM has a small office in the main bus station in addition to its main office.

The main bus station is southeast of the centre. There are frequent departures:

Al-Hoceima (Dh40, three hours)

Beni Enzar (Melilla border; Dh5, 25 minutes)

Fez (Dh60, 5½ hours)

Oujda (Dh30, 2½ hours) via Berkane (Dh20, 1½ hours)

Ras el-Maa (Dh20, one hour)

Tetouan (Dh120, nine hours), some via Dardara (for Chefchaouen; Dh100, six hours)

TAXI

The huge grand-taxi lot next to the main bus station serves plenty of destinations, including the following:

DESTINATION	COST (DH)	DURATION (HR)
Al-Hoceima	65	3
Beni Enzar (the Melilla border)	6	¼
Berkane	35	1
Fez	120	5
Oujda	55	3
Taza	70	3½

TRAIN

Nador Ville train station serves the Beni Enzar/Melilla border (Dh20, 12 minutes) and Fez (Dh129, six hours, three daily).

One of these trains goes via Taourirt where you can change for Casablanca.

East of Nador

East of Nador, on the opposite side of the lagoon, the coast is a mix of salt marsh and sand dunes, which attract a wide variety of birdlife, including the greater flamingo. Two scruffy towns, Kariat Arekmane and Ras el-Maa, lie on the Rocade (N16) eastwards to Saïdia, which affords good views of the Islas Chafarinas, the last bit of Spain on the northern coast.

Arekmane has a new corniche but no further development yet. The beach, with its fishing boats, is full of rubbish, and the wetlands inland of the corniche are in danger of disappearing.

Ras el-Maa, also known as Cap de l'Eau, is faring better. The corniche has a few small restaurants and a beautiful beach.

The wetlands around the Moulouya river mouth west of Ras el-Maa are Ramsar-protected, making them a prime bird-watching area. Migrant birds from Europe include Moussier's Redstart (*Phoenicurus moussieri*), the Marbled Teal (*Marmaronetta angustirostris*) and Audouin's Gull (*Larus audouinii*). Some endemic and rare fish are also found in the wetlands here.

From the eastern side of the Moulouya River estuary, the much-vaunted Station Balnéaire (seaside resort) runs for 5km to Saïdia along a truly magnificent beach. There are hundreds upon hundreds of blocks of apartments, mostly completed. They are largely only occupied during the high season (July and August), which gives the entire development a ghostly air. The development is mostly aimed at Moroccan holidaymakers (and Moroccans returning from abroad for their holidays).

The best area of beach along this 5km stretch is at Mediterreanéa Saïdia, known as Saïdia Med, where there are several golf courses, a large shopping centre and a marina with 740 berths. Here you can hire a jet ski (per hr Dh800), a kayak (Dh40) or a motorboat (Dh1000). There are a couple of resort hotels, including the Iberostar Hotel (☑ 0536 63 00 10; www.iberostar.com; Saïdia Med; s/d full board Dh1580/2680; [P] [✳] [❄] [≋]), which offers a spa, sporting facilities and several restaurants and bars.

The next development along the coast is Perla Saïdia, so far just with apartment blocks.

Saïdia السع دّي

POP 3500

Saïdia is still the sleepy little seaside town it has always been, with holiday apartment complexes for government officials. The large developments known as the Station Balnéaire lie to the west, but the town remains quite separate.

Saïdia has a superb beach with clean yellow sand. There are loungers and umbrellas to hire, jet skis and pedalos and, most unusually, girls in bikinis. The new corniche has fast-food restaurants and clubs along it, each pumping out its own brand of music. Most, though, are closed out of season. One block back from the beach, Blvd Hassan II has some pre-existing hotels, banks, cafes and internet facilities.

🛏 Sleeping & Eating

Hotel Atlal HOTEL €€
(☑ 0536 62 50 21; atlalben@menara.ma; 44 Blvd Hassan II; d incl breakfast Dh510; [✳] [❄]) Large rooms are the order of the day at this hotel, which is run by friendly staff. There's a bar and good restaurant, too. However, noise from the basement disco can be a problem.

Restaurant Boughaz FAST FOOD €
(Corniche; pizzas from Dh30.; ⊙ 10am-10pm) One of many restaurants lining the corniche, the Boughaz serves the usual burgers, pizzas and fish. Inside it's cavernous, but there's a terrace overlooking the beach with wonderful sea views.

BENI-SNASSEN MOUNTAINS   جبال بن سناسن

Inland from the eastern Mediterranean coast, the ruggedly beautiful Beni-Snassen Mountains are a 'site of biological and ecological interest'; for all intents and purposes a national park. This is a verdant area of scenic gorges that few imagine when they think of Morocco, and even fewer visit.

The dusty modern town of **Berkane**, about 80km southeast of Nador on the road to Oujda, can serve as a handy base for exploring the mountains. While the name means 'black' in the local Berber language, Berkane is famous for its oranges and everything in the town is, well, orange: the taxis, the buildings and the wonderful statue of an orange as you enter the town. Blvd Mohammed V has a post office and plenty of ATMs, as well as a couple of hotels. The best is **Hotel Rosalina** (0536 61 89 92; www.rosalina-hotel.com; 82 Blvd Mohammed V; s/d/ste incl breakfast Dh280/360/1000).

To reach the town, CTM has an office next to Café Laetizia on the west side of the main square. There is just one early evening departure for Fez (Dh125, five hours), Meknès (Dh140, 7½ hours), Rabat (Dh180, 8½ hours) and Casablanca (Dh195, 10 hours). Long-hauls to Spain also leave from here. If you're driving your own vehicle, don't fill up with the fuel sold on the side of the road: it's contraband from Algeria and likely to be adulterated.

From Berkane, take the national road to **Taforalt** (Tafoughalt), which passes through beautiful mountain scenery. Taforalt is a somewhat haphazard settlement that arose around a former French military installation, but the northern end, which you come upon first, contains a charming strip of cafes and restaurants. One of these is the **Club Taforalt** (Apr-Oct) with a simple restaurant and swimming pool (admission Dh50) in a pretty garden. You can stay at the nearby **Auberge Taforalt** (0662 04 51 19; www.taforaltclub.com; r incl breakfast Dh350, tent Dh250).

Soon after you enter Taforalt from Berkane, turn left at the post office, then immediately turn left again and follow signs to the Infokiosk, which has a small but informative display on the natural history of the park, and an observation platform with heavenly views of a distant mesa. If you're lucky you will catch sight of a big-horned Barbary sheep from the adjacent reserve. They generally arrive around 4pm, when it is cooler.

About 2km back down the national road is a right turn signposted for two *grottes* (caves). The **Grottes des Pigeons** (1km) is the site of an active excavation by Oxford University that has revealed human remains from the Pleistocene era, including some early human jewellery (80,000 years old).

Another 5km brings you to the **Grottes de Chameau**, a multistorey cave complex with three entrances that has been closed for years due to flooding damage. Three kilometres more brings you to the pretty **Zegzel Gorge** and a beautiful serpentine drive. Don't miss the chance to sample the cumquats, a local industry. Even the Romans remarked upon them.

The source of the **Charaâ River** provides a worthwhile detour. Follow signs to the tiny hamlet of Zegzel, 2km up a side road. At the end there's a popular picnic spot near where the river gushes out of the cliff. Not far from here, a spectacular ridge road cuts east to Oujda. You'll need a 4WD vehicle, a good map and an early start.

If you don't have your own vehicle, the easiest way to access the park is to take a shared taxi from Berkane (Dh15). Alternatively hire your own taxi; the minimum fare will be in the region of Dh250 for two hours, although not all drivers will be willing to take their vehicles along the poor roads near the hamlet of Zegzel. A cheaper alternative is to take a bus or grand taxi to Taforalt and walk down. Two buses each morning make the journey from Berkane (Dh12, 30 minutes), with return services in the afternoons. Grands taxis cost Dh15, and are most frequent on market days (Wednesday and Sunday).

ⓘ Getting There & Away

The adjacent border with Algeria remains closed. While Morocco would like to reopen it, Algeria has so far refused to agree. However, there is no active conflict.

AIR

Oujda's Angad airport is 45km from Saïdia. Royal Air Maroc has two (or more in the high season) daily flights to Casablanca and direct flights to France. Ryanair operates flights to Paris, Brussels, Marseille and Düsseldorf. EasyJet, Transavia, Jetairfly and Air Arabia all have flights to Paris.

BUS

A new bus station was being built at the time of research. CTM operates an early morning bus from Nador (Dh35, two hours).

Other companies run several buses a day from Oujda to Saïdia (Dh17, one hour).

TAXI

Hiring a taxi from Oujda airport to Saïdia costs Dh150 and the journey takes an hour. A seat in a shared taxi from Oujda's bus station should cost Dh25.

Imperial Cities, Middle Atlas & the East

الامبراطوري المدن و الأطلس المتوسط و الشرق

Best Places to Eat

➡ Ruined Garden (p309)

➡ L'Amandier, Palais Faraj (p310)

➡ Marhaba Restaurant (p333)

➡ Dar Hatim (p309)

➡ Hôtel Les Cèdres (p343)

Best Places to Stay

➡ Dar Finn (p303)

➡ Funky Fes (p303)

➡ Ryad Bahia (p331)

➡ Dar Kamal Chaoui (p324)

➡ Ksar Timnay Inter-Cultures (p345)

Why Go?

If you're looking for Morocco in microcosm, this region takes the title, running the whole spectrum from imperial cities and ancient ruins to grand mountain vistas and desert oases.

The fertile plains of the north have acted as Morocco's breadbasket for centuries. The Romans left remains at Volubilis, followed in turn by Muslim dynasties who birthed Morocco's grandest imperial city: Fez.

The narrow streets of the Fez medina are a true assault on the senses. Meknès, another old imperial capital, offers a slightly more pocket-sized experience.

The Middle Atlas mountains, home to the Barbary ape, rise to the south and the area is made for hiking.

Across the mountains the distinctive kasbahs of the south begin to make an appearance. The desert isn't far away, and by the time you reach the oasis of Figuig, the olive tree has long given way to the date palm.

When to Go

Fez

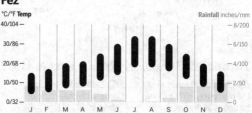

Apr Perfect spring weather and markets full of orange blossom scenting the air.

Jun Hit Fez for the Festival of World Sacred Music.

Sep Summer's heat has burned off making for perfect sightseeing conditions.

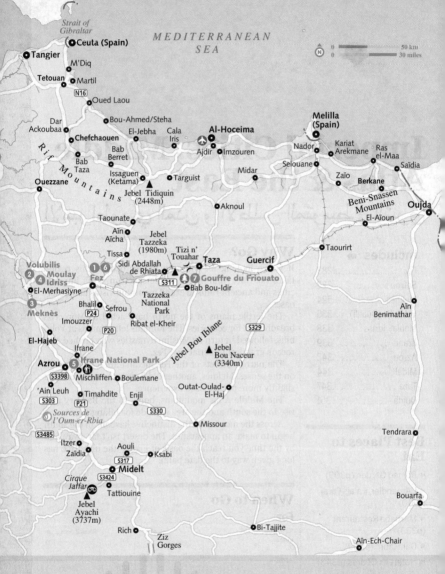

Imperial Cities, Middle Atlas & the East Highlights

1 Dive into the warren of the **medina** (p302) looking for souqs and souvenirs in ancient Fez

2 Time travel amid the mosaic-strewn Roman ruins of **Volubilis** (p336)

3 Explore the outsized imperial architecture of **Meknès** (p324)

4 Spend a day and night on pilgrimage in the holy town of **Moulay Idriss** (p338)

5 Hike in the **Ifrane National Park** (p341) in the Middle Atlas

6 Enjoy the sound of the sublime at the **Festival of World Sacred Music** (p311) in Fez

7 Make like a troglodyte in the weird caverns of **Gouffre du Friouato** (p351)

ℹ Getting There & Away

The train line connects the region's major cities to the coast, with direct links from Tangier, Rabat and Casablanca, as well as Oujda and Nador. There are also direct flights from Europe – primarily France – to Fez and Oujda. Fez and Oujda link into Royal Air Maroc's internal flight network, via Casablanca.

ℹ Getting Around

From Marrakesh and Casablanca, the train line runs east through Meknès, Fez and Taza all the way to Oujda. Travelling around the mountainous Middle Atlas, however, requires catching a bus or hiring a grand taxi.

IMPERIAL CITIES

Fez فاس

POP 1,044,000

Some 10 years ago, Fez boomed as a tourist destination. Money poured into the city, with foreigners buying up riads in the medina and new parks and fountains being established in the ville nouvelle. If you believed the travel and style pages of the Western media, Fez had become the new Marrakesh. Then the Arab Spring and similar events in other Muslim countries took their toll on tourism. Now, however, it seems that investment is on its way back, particularly apparent in the number of new hotels being built and old ones renovated in Fez.

Fassis, though, know that their city is beyond the vagaries of tourism. This is an old and supremely self-confident city that has nothing to prove to anyone. Dynasties and booms have all come and gone in the city's 1200-year existence, and Fez will be around long after the next fashion has burned itself out.

The city's allegiance, or at least submission, has always been essential to whoever held Morocco's throne. Morocco's independence movement was born here, and when there are strikes or protests, they are often at their most vociferous in Fez.

For visitors, the medina of Fès el-Bali (Old Fez) is the city's great drawcard. It's an assault on the senses, a warren of narrow lanes and covered bazaars filled to bursting with aromatic food stands, craft workshops, mosques and an endless parade of people. Old and new constantly collide – the man

driving the donkeys and mules that remain the main form of transport is likely to be chatting on his mobile phone, while the ancient skyline is punctuated equally with satellite dishes and minarets.

Years of neglect have taken their toll on the medina, however. The authorities have taken note; the city walls have been repaired and much is being done to conserve buildings. Scaffolding is everywhere. Yet for all the romance of medina life to visitors, many residents have been happy to sell up to foreigners and swap their sometimes medieval living conditions for a modern apartment in the ville nouvelle.

The trick is to dive straight in. It's initially overwhelming, but once you adjust to the pace of the city, Fez reveals its charms in the most unexpected ways. Seemingly blind alleys lead to squares with exquisite fountains, filled with the rhythmic hammer-music of copper beaters. Getting lost in Fez is where the fun really starts.

History

In AD 789, Idriss I – who founded Morocco's first imperial dynasty – decided that Oualili (Volubilis) was too small and drew up plans for a grand new capital. He died before the plans were implemented, however, so credit for the founding of Fez is given to his son, Idriss II, who carried out the will of his father. The memory of Idriss II is perpetuated in his *zawiya* (religious shrine) in the heart of Fès el-Bali.

The city started as a modest Berber town, but then 8000 families fleeing Muslim Spain and Portugal settled the east bank of the Oued Fez. They were later joined by Arab families from Kairouan (Qayrawan) in modern-day Tunisia, who took over the west bank, creating the Kairaouine quarter. The heritages of these two peoples formed a solid foundation for future religious, cultural and architectural richness. Idriss II's heirs split the kingdom, but Fez continued to enjoy peace and prosperity until the 10th century.

Over the next centuries, the fortunes of Fez rose and fell with the dynasties. Civil war and famine – incited by Berber invasions – were relieved only by the rise of the Almoravids. When that dynasty fell from power around 1154, they fled Fez and destroyed the city walls as they went. Only when the succeeding Almohad dynasty was assured of the Fassis' loyalty were the walls replaced – large sections still date from this period.

Fez continued to be a crucial crossroads, wielding intellectual rather than political influence. With the Kairaouine Mosque and University already well established, it was *the* centre of learning and culture in an empire stretching from Spain to Senegal. It recovered its political status only much later, with the arrival of the Merenid dynasty around 1250.

During the 19th century, as central power crumbled and European interference increased, the distinction between Marrakesh and Fez diminished, with both effectively serving as capitals of a fragmented country. Fez retained its status as the spiritual capital. It was here, on 30 March 1912, that the treaty introducing the French and Spanish protectorates over Morocco was signed. Less than three weeks later, rioting and virtual revolt against the new masters served as a reminder of the city's volatility.

The French may have moved the political capital to Rabat, but Fez remains a constituency to be reckoned with.

As one of Morocco's most traditional cities, Fez is generally regarded with a certain amount of awe, perhaps tinged with jealousy, by the rest of the country. Indeed, a disproportionate share of Morocco's intellectual and economic elite hail from here and it's a widely held belief (especially among Fassis) that anyone born in Fez medina is more religious, cultured, artistic and refined; that the king's wife, Princess Lalla Salma is from Fez, and the royal family spend much time here is a source of great pride for the city.

⊙ Sights

◉ The Medina (Fès el-Bali)

Travelling from the ville nouvelle to Fès el-Bali is like stepping back in time. The essential footprint of the medina hasn't changed in nearly a millennium, as the surrounding hills have constrained expansion – the last big growth of the traditional medina was in the 13th century with the construction of Fès el-Jdid. Today, around 156,000 Fassis still call this maze of twisting alleys, blind turns and hidden souqs home, while tourists call it one of the most mind-boggling places they'll visit in Morocco.

Bab Bou Jeloud in the west is the main entrance to the old city, with two main streets descending into the medina's heart. On your left as you enter is Talaa Kebira (Big Slope), with Talaa Seghira (Little Slope) on your right. Both converge near Pl an-Nejjarine, continuing to the Kairaouine Mosque and Zawiya Moulay Idriss II – the heart of the city. From here, it's uphill to reach the northern gates of Bab Guissa and Bab Jamaï, or head south towards Bab R'cif. The R'cif area has undergone a big facelift

---

THE FOUNTAINS OF FEZ

It seems like you can barely turn a corner in the Fez medina without coming across a *seqqâya* (public fountain) – Fassis have historically had something of an obsession for them. It was largely the Almoravid (1061–1147) and Almohad (1147–1248) dynasties that were the great water engineers. To supply water to their cities they diverted rivers, created lakes and constructed vast canal systems. While they did this across the country, fountain construction reached its zenith in imperial Fez.

There are well over 60 public fountains inside the medina. Along with the hammam, they are usually located near the neighbourhood mosque. Many were paid for by princes and wealthy merchants. Some of these fountains are simple basins against a wall. Most are beautifully decorated structures of coloured tiles, often under a canopy of intricately carved wood. One of the finest is the **Nejjarine fountain**. Built in the 18th century, it features *zellij* (tilework) and stucco that form patterns as delicate as lacework.

Some fountains are still used for water collection and washing by their neighbourhoods; at some, the water supply has been cut as houses gain their own water supply. The booking agency **Fez Riads** (☎0672 51 33 57; www.fez-riads.com) puts a percentage of its profits into restoring and maintaining many of the medina's most neglected fountains.

And if you think that a love of fountains is restricted to the medina, check out the ultramodern and sparkly fountains recently installed in the ville nouvelle.

with a smart new gate and refurbished square and the river is being upgraded. R'cif is likely to provide an alternate focus for the medina.

The major sights are really only a small part of the charm of the medina. It pays to give yourself a little random exploration, and simply follow your nose or ears to discover the most unexpected charms of Fez' nature. Following your nose will lead you to women with bundles of freshly cut herbs, children carrying trays of loaves to be baked in the local bakery or a cafe selling glasses of spiced Berber coffee. Around the next corner you might find a beautifully tiled fountain, a workshop making wooden hammam buckets, a camel's head announcing a specialist butcher, or just a gang of kids turning their alley into a football pitch. Everywhere, listen out for the call to prayer or the mule driver's cry 'balak!' ('look out!') to warn of the approach of a heavily laden pack animal.

Navigation can be confusing and getting lost at some stage is a certainty, but look at this as part of the adventure. A handy tip is to note the 'main' streets that eventually lead to a gate or landmark – just follow the general flow of people. Ask shopkeepers for directions, or you can fall back on the eager kids happy to rescue confused foreigners for a dirham or two.

★ Kairaouine Mosque
& University   MOSQUE
(Map p288) One of Africa's largest mosques and possibly the oldest university in the world, this mosque complex is the spiritual heart of Fez and Morocco itself. Established in 859 by Fatima el-Fihria, a Tunisian woman refugee, and expanded by the Almoravids in the 12th century, it can accommodate up to 20,000 people at prayer. It's so large that it can be difficult to actually see: over the centuries the streets and houses of the Kairaouine quarter have encroached on the building so much they disguise its true shape. The complex has recently been restored, but non-Muslims cannot enter and will have to be content with glimpses of its courtyard from the main door on Derb Boutouil. Better still, take the view from any vantage point over the medina: the huge green pyramidal roof and minaret immediately announce their presence.

★ Medersa el-Attarine   MEDERSA
(Map p288; admission Dh10; ⊙9am-6pm) Founded by Abu Said in 1325 in the heart of the me-dina, the Medersa el-Attarine was designed as an annexe to the nearby Kairaouine. The central courtyard displays the traditional patterns of Merenid artisanship, with magnificent *zellij* (tilework), carved plaster and cedar wood. Onyx columns flank the mihrab (niche facing Mecca). Slightly smaller than the Medersa Bou Inania, it has been sensitively restored.

★ Medersa Bou Inania   MEDERSA
(Map p288; admission Dh10; ⊙9am-6pm, closed during prayers) A short walk down Talaa Kebira from Bab Bou Jeloud, the Medersa Bou Inania is the finest of Fez' theological colleges. It was built by the Merenid sultan Bou Inan between 1350 and 1357. The *medersa* underwent extensive restoration a few years ago, and the results are amazing: elaborate *zellij* and carved plaster, beautiful cedar *mashrabiyyas* (lattice screens) and massive brass doors.

Whereas most *medersas* just have a simple prayer hall, the Bou Inania is unusual in that it hosts a complete mosque, including a beautiful green-tiled minaret. The mihrab has a particularly fine ceiling and onyx marble columns. It's thought that the *medersa* required a larger-scale mosque because there was none other nearby at the time.

★ Nejjarine Museum of
Wooden Arts & Crafts   MUSEUM
(Map p288; ☑0535 74 05 80; Pl an-Nejjarine; admission Dh20; ⊙10am-7pm) Opened in 1998, this museum is in a wonderfully restored *funduq* – a caravanserai for travelling merchants who stored and sold their goods below and took lodgings on the floors above. Centred on a courtyard, the rooms are given over to displays of traditional artefacts of craftsmen's tools, chunky prayer beads and Berber locks, chests and musical instruments (compare the traditional wedding furniture with the modern glitzy chairs outside in Pl an-Nejjarine). Everything is beautifully presented, although the stunning building gives the exhibits a run for their money. The rooftop cafe has great views over the medina. Photography is forbidden.

Batha Museum   MUSEUM
(Map p288; ☑0535 63 41 16; Rue de la Musée, Batha; admission Dh10; ⊙8.30am-noon & 2.30-6pm Wed-Mon) Housed in a wonderful 19th-century summer palace and converted to a

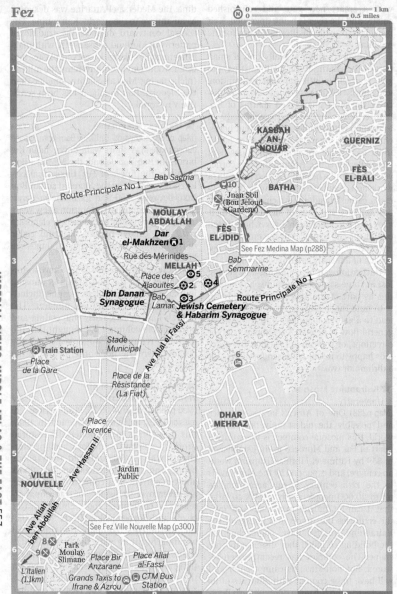

0   1 km
0   0.5 miles

IMPERIAL CITIES, MIDDLE ATLAS & THE EAST FEZ

museum in 1916, the Batha Museum houses an excellent collection of traditional Moroccan arts and crafts. Historical and artistic artefacts include fine woodcarving, *zellij* and sculpted plaster, much of it from the city's ruined or decaying *medersas*. It also has

some fine Fassi embroidery, colourful Berber carpets and antique instruments.

The highlight of the museum is the superb ceramic collection dating from the 14th century to the present. These are some fantastic examples of the famous blue pottery

Fez

of Fez. The cobalt glaze responsible for the colour is developed from a special process discovered in the 10th century.

The museum's Andalucian-style garden offers temporary respite from the bustle and noise of the medina, and the spreading holm oak provides a backdrop for the open-air concerts held here during the Sacred Music and Sufi Culture festivals.

★**Chaouwara Tanneries**   NEIGHBOURHOOD
(Map p288; Derb Chaouwara, Blida) The Chaouwara tanneries are one of the city's most iconic sights (and smells). Head east or northeast from Pl as-Seffarine and take the left fork after about 50m; you'll soon pick up the unmistakable waft of skin and dye that will guide you into the heart of the leather district (the touts offering to show you the way make it even harder to miss).

It's not often possible to get in among the tanning pits themselves, but there are plenty of vantage points from the surrounding streets, all occupied (with typical Fassi ingenuity) by leather shops. Each shop has a terrace that allows you to look over the action. Try to get here in the morning when the pits are awash with coloured dye. Salespeople will happily give an explanation of the processes involved and will expect a small tip in return or, even better, a sale. While this might feel a little commercialised, you probably won't find a better selection of leather in Morocco, and prices are as good as you'll get.

In recent years, there have been plans mooted to move the tannery out of the medina altogether and redevelop the site as a green area. However, with both the economic and cultural impact of the plans for this district of the medina remaining uncertain, it remains to be seen whether these ideas will ever leave the drawing board.

◉ Fès el-Jdid (New Fez)

Only in a city as old as Fez could you find a district dubbed 'New' because it's only 700 years old. The paranoid Merenid sultan Abu Yusuf Yacoub (1258–86) purpose-built the quarter, packing it with his Syrian mercenary guards and seeking to isolate himself from his subjects. Even today almost half of the area is given over to the grounds of the Royal Palace, still popular with Mohammed VI. Its other main legacy is the architectural evidence of its early Jewish inhabitants.

★**Dar el-Makhzen**   PALACE
(Royal Palace; Map p286; Pl des Alaouites) The entrance to Dar el-Makhzen is a stunning example of modern restoration, but the 80 hectares of palace grounds are not open to the public. Visitors must suffice with viewing its imposing brass doors, surrounded by fine *zellij* and carved cedar wood. Note the lemon trees to one side – tour guides are prone to plucking the fruit to demonstrate the juice's astringent cleaning properties on the palace gates.

Mellah   JEWISH QUARTER
(Map p286) In the 14th century Fès el-Jdid became a refuge for Jews, thus creating a *mellah* (Jewish quarter). The records suggest that the move was orchestrated to offer the Jews greater protection. And they certainly did enjoy the favour of the sultan, repaying him with their loyalty during conflict. Around 200 Jews remain in Fez, but all have now left the *mellah* in favour of the ville nouvelle. Their old houses remain, with their open balconies looking onto the streets a marked contrast to Muslim styles.

★**Jewish Cemetery & Habarim Synagogue**   CEMETERY
(Map p286; donations welcome; ⊙7am-7pm) The southwest corner of the *mellah* is home to the sea of blindingly white tombs that stretch down the hill; those in dedicated enclosures are tombs of rabbis. One of the oldest, high up against the north wall, is that

Fez Medina

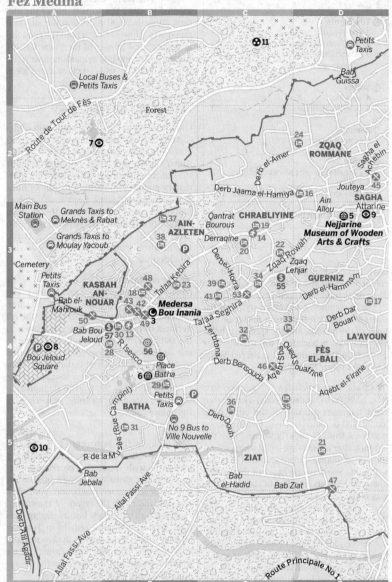

of Rabbi Vidal Hasserfaty, who died in 1600. On the slope below, the large tomb with green trimming is that of the martyr Solica. In 1834 this 14-year-old girl refused to convert to Islam or accept the advances of the governor of Tangier and subsequently had her throat slit. The cemetery is still in use.

The Habarim Synagogue, at the far end of the cemetery, now houses a museum with a whole mishmash of articles, including some poignant photos and postcards, left behind

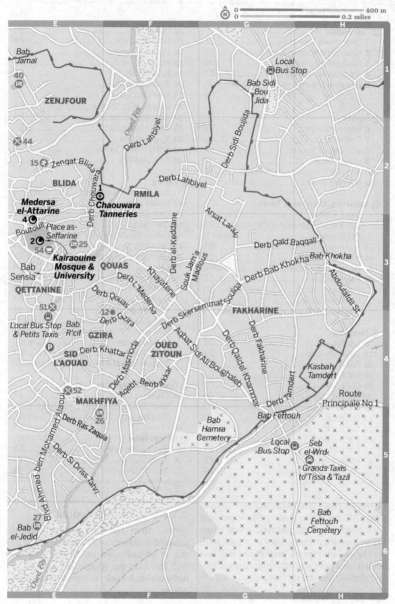

after the Jewish exodus. If the museum is locked, the gatekeeper will open it for you.

★ **Ibn Danan Synagogue** SYNAGOGUE
(Map p286; donations welcome) Located near the cemetery, this synagogue was restored with the aid of Unesco in 1999. There are no set opening times as such, but the guardian will usually let you in and point out the main features, including a *mikva* (ritual bath) in the basement.

Fez Medina

Jnan Sbil (Bou Jeloud Gardens) GARDENS
(Map p288; Ave Moulay Hassan) These gardens have been providing welcome green space for well over a century. They're a good halfway break between the *mellah* and Bab Bou Jeloud, and have recently undergone extensive renovation and replanting.

Rue des Mérinides NOTABLE BUILDING
(Map p286) This street's houses are distinguished by their wooden and wrought-iron balconies, as well as by their stucco work.

Bou Jeloud Square SQUARE
(Map p288; P) This square on the edge of the medina has a funfair at holiday times, concerts and a few storytellers.

◉ North of the Medina

Viewed from the surrounding hills, the jumbled buildings of Fez merge into a palette of white-flecked sandstone. Only here and there do the green-tiled roofs of the mosques and *medersas* provide a hint of colour.

Borj Nord VIEWPOINT
(Map p288) Head up to this lookout for one of the best panoramas of the city. Like its counterpart on the southern hills (Borj Sud), Borj Nord was built by Sultan Ahmed al-Mansour in the late 16th century to monitor the potentially disloyal populace of Fez.

STEVEN GREAVES/GETTY IMAGES ©

Medina Life

Morocco may be a rapidly modernising country, but tradition still courses strongly through its veins. With everything from dazzling crafts and ancient architecture to the best street food and shopping, you can get lost in the winding alleys of its medinas and find the heart of the country in the process.

Contents
→ Winding Lanes
→ Shopping
→ Street Eats
→ People

Above Streetside pastry vendor

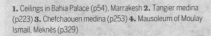

1. Ceilings in Bahia Palace (p54), Marrakesh **2.** Tangier medina (p223) **3.** Chefchaouen medina (p253) **4.** Mausoleum of Moulay Ismail, Meknès (p329)

MATTHEW SCHOLEY/GETTY IMAGES ©

2

Winding Lanes

You could happily spend days in the best medinas of Morocco – getting lost, drinking tea, and getting lost again. The serendipity of chance discoveries are all part of the charm. Magical medinas are found in every part of the country, each with its own special flavour – here are some of the most atmospheric.

Marrakesh Medina

Inside 19km of ramparts, the theatrical Djemaa el-Fna is the beating, back-flipping heart of the Marrakesh medina. Follow crazy lanes – or thoroughfares if you forgot your compass – to sights such as Bahia Palace.

Tangier Medina

Europe is just across the Strait of Gibraltar, but it feels a world away among the kasbah and souqs of the Tangier medina. Spots like Petit Socco have been given a fresh coat of paint as part of the city's makeover.

4

Chefchaouen Medina

High in the Rif Mountains, Chefchaouen medina is painted a delightful Andalucian blue, fringed with terracotta tiles and green hills. You won't get too horribly lost in this compact mini-maze.

Meknès Medina

A descendant of the Prophet Mohammed built the medina in Fez' criminally underrated neighbour. Spot balconied houses in the *mellah* (Jewish quarter), and watch the world promenade on Pl el-Hedim, the local version of Marrakesh's Djemaa el-Fna.

Fès el-Bali

Old Fez is Morocco's largest intact medina and embodies over 1200 years of history. Even old hands get lost in this maze of souqs and tanneries – you might chance upon a craft museum or a 14th-century *medersa* (theological seminary).

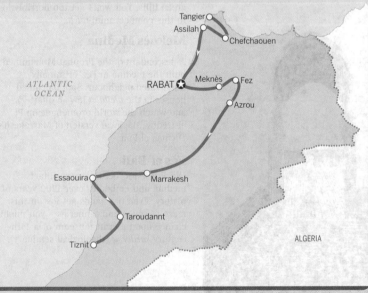

 Shopping Odyssey

3 WEEKS

Morocco's medinas have been commercial hubs for centuries, and they remain the best places to buy everything from craftwork to carrots. Pack light for Morocco – you'll need that luggage space for medina goodies.

Start your shopping expedition in **Tangier**, where the medina includes a silver jewellery bazaar and exotic antique shops. Then head for the blue-washed medina of **Chefchaouen**. The town specialises in wool, especially woven rugs and blankets.

On the Atlantic coast, pick up some contemporary art in the mural-painted medina in **Assilah**. The town thrives during its arts festival every July.

From Assilah move on to the relaxed medina in **Rabat**, with its silks, pottery and carved wooden furniture. **Meknès** is another low-pressure medina, where the local speciality is silver damascene (metalwork with intricate silver thread).

Fès el-Bali (Old Fez) is Morocco's artisanal capital. Head to the tanneries for leather goods, and converted riads and *funduqs* (merchants' hotels) for carpets; high-quality ceramics are everywhere. **Fez** is great if you want to see craft items being made by traditional methods. Near Fez, the Middle Atlas town of **Azrou** has a weekly bazaar famed for its Berber carpets.

Those same Berber motifs meet Western styles in **Marrakesh** medina. Artisanal crafts from across the country can be found here, from the most traditional styles to the best in contemporary Moroccan design, from tajine pottery to locally designed fashion.

Essaouira is another shopping must. It's best known for its woodwork – boxes and marquetry made from highly polished thuya wood – as well as palm-fibre raffia works and the bright canvases from its artists' colony. Chunky pottery from nearby Safi is also sold here in great quantities.

In the south, silver jewellery is a speciality of the Souss Valley's Chleuh tribe; pick it up in the Souq Arabe in the **Taroudannt** walled medina. **Tiznit** has a dedicated jewellery souq, with styles heavily influenced by the desert Tuareg culture.

Top: Souq, Marrakesh medina (p58)
Bottom: Ceramics worskshop, Fez medina (p304)

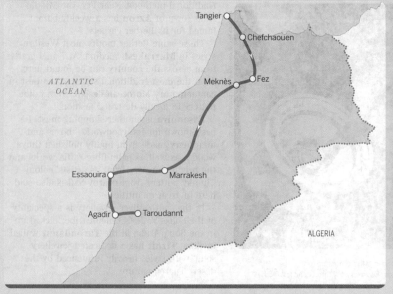

Tangier

Chefchaouen

Meknès

Fez

ATLANTIC OCEAN

Essaouira

Marrakesh

Agadir

Taroudannt

ALGERIA

Moroccan Street Eats

From hearty mountain tajines to delicate seaside ones, food reflects Morocco's many environments and historical influences. So get stuck in and let your tastebuds appreciate the country's diversity.

Your culinary tour starts in **Tangier** medina. Fill up on brochettes and fried fish – Moroccan street-food staples – but look out for local variations on Spanish tapas and paella, illustrations of the close cultural ties that span the straits.

In the Rif Mountains town of **Chefchaouen**, try out the fresh white cheese from the goats and cows that graze on the green slopes. Follow this up with lunch at the cafes on Plaza Uta el-Hammam, supplemented by the sticky pastries sold by the hawkers that circulate around the square.

Fez is known for its high Moroccan cuisine – epic dishes of couscous and the like – but offers quicker, simpler fare as well. Start the day by breakfasting on the Fassi speciality of *b'sara* (garlic and butter-bean soup), served in pottery bowls with a glug of olive oil at hole-in-the-wall eateries across the Fez medina.

Meknès is perfect for just sipping mint tea on Pl el-Hedim – and also good for sardines and sandwiches, and shopping for fresh produce in the covered market on the edge of the medina.

Hit the smoking grills and fresh orange-juice stands on the Djemaa el-Fna in **Marrakesh**, and snack with the square coursing around you. Try a *tanjia* – a Marrakchi speciality of lamb and spices in a clay pot, slow-cooked to tender perfection.

At the fishing town of **Essaouira**, between medina and port, the fish grillers will turn your pick into an outdoor feast, from sardines to shellfish bought by the handful and served with fresh bread and salad.

Head to Souq al-Had in **Agadir** for a taste of regular Morocco, where tajines bubble next to the fruit-and-veg stalls.

Put together a picnic with Souss Valley produce in the **Taroudannt** souqs.

Top: Djemaa el-Fna stalls (p73), Marrakesh
Bottom: Streetside orange stall

Animal skins being dyed in the Fez medina (p304)

People

As far as culturally diverse countries go, Morocco ticks a lot of boxes; an Arab country in Africa, with Europe as a close neighbour, and Islam tying it all together to create a national identity. Arabs, Berbers speaking several languages, European expats and sub-Saharan migrants all call Morocco home.

Street Scenes

The country's medinas are great places to make the acquaintance of locals. Pretty much the whole of Morocco passes through to sell some argan nuts or buy a mosque alarm clock. Between the milling tourists, gawking at the pre-Facebook form of human interaction seen on medina lanes, you can watch Morocco going about its daily business. You'll see people engaged in all sorts of activities, contributing to the sensory layer cake: hawking fruit and veg; stuffing mattresses; hurrying to the medersa; turning a dripping spit; juggling a mobile-phone debate and a stall teetering with dates; selecting spices for a hammam-oven-bound *tanjia*. Yes, a lot of what you'll notice will likely relate to food: navigating medinas like mighty Fez, inhabited by 150,000 Fassis and countless donkeys, is hungry work.

If your stomach's rumblings are drowning out the call to prayer, stop at one of the cafes found on every corner. Now you can join the locals in the most hallowed activity of all: drinking mint tea and watching the medina street theatre.

Merenid Tombs RUIN
(Map p288) Further up, these tombs are dramatic in their advanced state of ruin, although little remains of their fine original decoration. The views over Fez are spectacular and well worth the climb. It's best at dusk as the lights come on and the muezzins' prayer calls echo around the valley, although you shouldn't go on your own; we've received more than one account of travellers being mugged here after dark. A taxi from Bab Bou Jeloud should cost around Dh12; it's a 10-minute walk back downhill to the medina.

 Activities

For a luxury experience, there are several guesthouses that offer opulent hammam experiences.

Riad Laaroussa (Map p288; ☎0674 18 76 39; www.riad-laaroussa.com; 3 Derb Bechara; hammam & massage Dh660; ☺noon-8pm), **Riad Maison Bleue** (Map p288; ☎0535 74 18 39; www.maisonbleue.com/riad-maison-bleue; Derb el Miter, Ain-Azleten; hammam Dh500; ☺noon-8pm), **Riad Fès** (Map p288; ☎0535 94 76 10; www.riadfes.com; Derb Zerbtana; ☺1-9pm), **Palais Amani** (Map p288; ☎0535 63 32 09; www.palaisamani.com; Derb el Miter, Oued Zhoune; hammam Dh495; ☺10am-7pm) and **Le Jardin des Biehn** (Map p288; ☎0664 64 76 79; www.jardindesbiehn.com; Aqebt Sbaa, Douh; hammam Dh660; ☺9am-8pm) all have excellent private spas, with treatments starting at around Dh500.

Hammam Mernissi HAMMAM
(Map p288; Derb Serrajine; ☺women 9am-8pm, women tourist package 9am-1pm, men 6-9am & 8pm-midnight) This old hammam has recently been renovated. It's the only one in the medina that caters specifically for women tourists with a Dh150 package comprising *savon beldi* (olive oil soap) and exfoliation with a *kis* (coarse glove). A massage will cost Dh50 extra.

Hammam Rihab HAMMAM
(Map p288; 3 Chrabliyenne, Talaa Kebira; ☺women 8am-9pm, men 9pm-8am) Another ancient – but newly refurbished – hammam, this large place is clean and the staff are used to tourists. The entrance fee is Dh12, but expect to pay around Dh100 for exfoliation and a massage.

Nausikaa SPA
(☎0535 61 00 06; www.nausikaaspa.com; Ave Bahnini, Rte Ain Smen; hammam Dh100; ☺7am-9pm) In the ville nouvelle, Nausikaa offers one of the most complete packages in Fez, blending hammam traditions with a modern spa experience. A variety of sumptuous massages and therapies are on offer, along with a gym and pool.

LIFE IN THE LEATHER DISTRICT

Tanneries provide perhaps the greatest illustration of how resolutely some parts of Morocco have clung to practices developed in medieval times. Moroccan leather, and more particularly the Fassi leather produced in Fez, has for centuries been highly prized as among the finest in the world. One type of leather, a soft goatskin used mainly in bookbinding, is simply known as 'morocco'.

It's claimed that tanning leather in Morocco goes back several millennia, and little has changed since medieval times. Donkeys still labour through the narrow streets carrying skins to dye pits, which are still constructed to traditional designs (with the addition of modern ceramic tiles). Tanners are organised according to ancient guild principles, with workers typically born into the job. Unfortunately, health and safety principles are similarly old-fashioned, and health problems among the workers, who are knee-deep in chemicals all day, are not uncommon.

Rank odours abound at the tanneries, and the delicate tourists who come to view the work will often be offered a sprig of mint to hold to their noses to take the edge off the pong (rain also dampens the smell). Major components in processing the skins are pigeon poo and cow urine (for potassium) with ash; more delicate ingredients such as indigo, saffron and poppy are added later for colour.

Modern Fassi tanneries – amazingly there are about 70 tanneries in Fez – tend to use synthetic chemicals, washing pollutants into the Oued Sebou river, although the city's chrome removal plant is removing much, if not all, of the worst pollutants.

⬥ Courses

Clock Kitchen   COOKING
(Map p288; ☎ 0655 32 40 82; www.cafeclock.
com; Derb el-Magana, Talaa Kebira; half-day course
Dh600) Held in Café Clock these classes are
the place to perfect your skills in making
tajine and couscous. After planning your
menu, you shop for ingredients in the souq,
spend the morning honing your technique
and finishing up with the feast you've prepared. Other options include bread-baking
classes, patisserie workshops, making *tanjia* (slow-cooked stews) and hand-rolling
couscous.

Dar Namir Gastronomic Retreats   COOKING
(Map p288; ☎ 0677 84 86 87; www.darnamir.
com; 24 Derb Chikh el-Fouki, Fez Medina; half-
day intro from Dh660, live-in residencies per day
from Dh1650) Established food writer Tara
Stevens offers tailor-made cooking experiences in her custom-built school. Sessions
cover modern Moroccan cuisine, traditional
feasts, street food, pastry and bread baking,
as well as Sephardic and Roman cookery.
The courses also include Moroccan wine
and cheese tastings.

Fez Download   LANGUAGE
(Map p288; ☎ 0535 63 78 55; www.cafeclock.com;
Derb el-Margana, Talaa Kebira; per person incl re-
freshments Dh150) Spend a couple of hours
with the affable Khalid learning basic phrases in Moroccan Arabic, etiquette and customs. At Café Clock; minimum two people.

Arabic Language Institute   LANGUAGE
(Map p300; ☎ 0535 62 48 50; www.alif-fes.
com; 2 Rue Ahmed Hiba; 3-/6-week courses
Dh6000/10,400) Offers longer courses aimed
at foreigners, and can assist in finding accommodation for students, in apartments or
homestays. Lessons are held at the American Language Center where there's also a
superb English-language bookshop stocking
titles about Morocco.

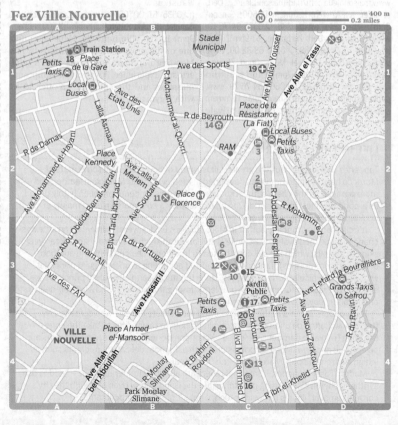

Fez Ville Nouvelle

Subul Assalam LANGUAGE
(☑0535 63 18 62; www.sacal-fez.com; 3-week group courses Dh5000, hourly lessons Dh250) This language school touts its services in cross-cultural understanding. Subul Assalam ('Pathways to Peace') can arrange homestays for its longer courses, which are offered in Darija (Moroccan Arabic), modern standard and classical Arabic, as well as Tamazight Berber.

Arabophon LANGUAGE
(☑0535 60 34 75; www.arabicstudy.com; half-/3-day courses Dh500/Dh1500, 4-week intensive course Dh4360) Intensive Moroccan and Modern Standard Arabic courses. Shorter courses are aimed at travellers: the half-day Curious Explorer and three-day Serious Explorer. There are also courses in Tamazight Berber. Lessons are offered in English, French and Spanish.

☞ Tours

There is a series of well-signed self-guided walks through the old city; each walk highlights different aspects of traditional Fez:

Fez Ville Nouvelle

Blue Knowledge and learning
Brown Monuments and souqs
Green Palaces and Andalucian gardens
Orange Walls and ramparts
Purple Fès el-Jdid
Red Artisanal crafts

The overhead signs are easy to follow, showing the direction of the next major landmark, and there are excellent English information boards at regular intervals. The *Fes Medina Thematic Tourist Circuits Guide* accompanies these self-guided walking tours marked throughout the medina, while the excellent *Fez from Bab to Bab: Walks in the Medina* by Hammad Berrada further details 11 different walks, allowing readers to discover otherwise unknown corners and courtyards amid this labyrinth.

It's well worth hiring a guide. As well as pointing out incredible architecture and clandestine corners, guides can answer cultural questions, will help overcome language barriers, and – perhaps most importantly – they will ward off other would-be guides. A full-day tour with an official guide costs from Dh350 – always ask to see their identification.

The quality of guides can vary considerably, so communication is very important to ensure that you get the best out of the experience. If you're not interested in shopping, say so firmly at the outset, although be aware that the guide who won't take a tourist to a single shop probably hasn't been born yet. It may be necessary to pay an extra Dh50 to Dh100 as a 'no shopping' supplement. If possible, arrange a guide through your hotel or guesthouse.

★ Artisanal Affairs CRAFT
(☑0645 22 32 03; http://culturevulturesfez.org; 1-2 people Dh1350) We love this in-depth, hands-on half-day tour that explores the artisanal crafts of the Fez medina. It's a chance to meet and talk to coppersmiths, tanners, mosaic tile-makers, cobblers, carpet makers and weavers. There's no shopping involved, and groups are restricted to four. The tour ends in the Artisanal School in Batha.

Plan-it Fez TOUR
(☑0535 63 87 08; www.plan-it-fez.com; 4 Arset Manjour, Batha; ☺9am-6pm Mon-Sat) Plan-it Fez provides cultural experiences including foodie adventures and cooking classes,

IMPERIAL CITIES, MIDDLE ATLAS & THE EAST FEZ

hammam packages, architectural and Islamic garden tours and excursions further afield.

Fes Rando
WALKING TOUR

(☎ 0674 79 79 83; www.fesrando.com; per person from Dh300) Day walks on Mt Zalagh above Fez and further afield into the Middle Atlas. Longer treks staying overnight in *gîtes* (trekkers' hostels) are also offered.

✯✦ Festivals & Events

Fez has several festivals that are worth considering when you're planning your trip. The Fes Festival of World Sacred Music (p311) is the city's internationally famous drawcard, but there are two newer festivals that are worth a visit. Just outside Fez, Sefrou's Cherry Festival (p324) in June is worth a day trip.

Festival of Sufi Culture
MUSIC

(www.par-chemins.org; ⊙Apr) This Sufi festival hosts a series of events each year including talks and debates, and some spectacular concerts held in the garden of the Batha Museum with Sufi musicians from across the world.

Festival of Amazigh Culture
MUSIC

(⊙Jul) This festival, which is run in association with the Institut Royal de la Culture Amazighe, aims to promote and protect Amazigh (Berber) culture. Its program includes musical performances as well as lectures and workshops.

> OFF THE BEATEN TRACK
>
> ### TISSA HORSE FESTIVAL
>
> Lying in rich arable land along the Sebou River, the prosperous farming town of Tissa is a riot of colour in spring. But by far the most interesting time to visit is for the Tissa Horse Festival, held in the second week of September. Farmers come from all around to trade their animals and celebrate with exciting *fantasias* (cavalry charges). There's not much infrastructure and dates are only set a week or two before, but the showground is to the north of town before the river bridge.
>
> To get there, take a grand taxi (Dh20) from Siham el-Wrd near Bab Fettouh in Fez.

Moussem of Moulay Idriss
RELIGIOUS

(⊙varies) Fez' biggest religious festival is also one of the country's largest. It's currently in August but the date moves according to the Islamic calendar. The *moussem* (festival in honour of a saint) of the city's founder, Moulay Idriss, draws huge crowds. Local artisans create special tributes and there's a huge procession through the medina. Traditional music is played and followers dance and shower the musicians (and onlookers) with orange-blossom water.

🛏 Sleeping

Fez doesn't lack variety in its accommodation options, with everything from simple pensions to boutique riads. Your main choice is whether to stay in the colour and chaos of the medina, or a petit-taxi ride away in the ville nouvelle (where budgets tend to go further). Room rates in Fez are in the higher (city) bracket; see p464 for details. Booking in advance is advised during high season, and especially during the Festival of World Sacred Music in June, when supplements also often apply. Note that although prices here are listed in dirham, many riads actually list (and charge) rooms in euros, so be aware of currency exchange rates when booking.

🛏 Medina

Most of the cheapest options are in touching distance of Bab Bou Jeloud, placing you right in the middle of the action. Unless noted, rooms have shared bathrooms at this price range – and don't expect hot water at the lower prices. Many midrange options in the medina, especially the riads and *dars* (small houses), edge close to the top-end price bracket. A few places offer simpler rooms at manageable prices.

★ Ziyarates Fes
HOMESTAYS €

(Map p288; ☎ 0535 63 46 67; www.ziyarates-fes.com; 35 Sidi Kjih, Talaa Seghira; s/d from Dh200/300) If you really want to experience medina life up close, there might be no better way than through this innovative homestay scheme. Around 25 Fassi families rent rooms in their homes to welcome foreign guests, while support from the regional tourism authorities ensures the quality of the places signed up. You might get to practise your Arabic, learn to cook or just help the kids with their homework in this unique cultural exchange. Exact prices vary, but all the family homes are listed (with photos) on the organisation's website.

★ Funky Fes
HOSTEL €

(Map p288; ☑ 0535 63 31 96; www.funkyfes.com; Arset Lamdisi; dm Dh130-170; ☎) Fez' first proper hostel, offering up good cheap backpacker beds close to Bab el-Jdid, this is a bright, friendly and welcome addition to the local accommodation scene. It's a youthful and social place, with more dorm beds than you might imagine, and offers local tours, activities, cooking and more.

Hôtel Cascade
HOTEL €

(Map p288; ☑ 0535 63 84 42; 26 Rue Serrajine, Bab Bou Jeloud; dm/r Dh80/180) One of the grand-daddies of the Morocco shoestring hotels, the Cascade's Bab Bou Jeloud location is hard to beat. It's exceedingly basic so adjust your expectations accordingly, but if you need to stretch your budget and meet plenty of like-minded travellers then this might be the place for you. Breakfast costs Dh20.

Hôtel Bab Boujloud
HOTEL €

(Map p288; ☑ 0535 63 31 18; www.hotelbab-boujloud.com; 49 Pl Isesco, Bab Bou Jeloud; s/d Dh200/350; ✳) Fantastically located, this hotel sits just outside Bab Bou Jeloud with all the medina action right on your doorstep. The rooms are as simple as the price tag suggests, but cosy enough and great value.

Pension Campini
HOTEL €

(Map p288; ☑ 0535 63 73 42; pensioncampini@gmail.com; Rue Campini, Batha; s/d Dh200/300; ☎) A short walk away from the Batha Museum, this is a quieter location slightly outside the medina proper. Rooms are en suite and airy. There's a small terrace, with views just over the walls of Jnan Sbil (Bou Jeloud Gardens).

Dar Bouânania
GUESTHOUSE €

(Map p288; ☑ 0535 63 72 82; darbouanania@gmail.com; 21 Derb Bensalem, Talaa Kebira; s/d/tr Dh300/400/500, without bathroom Dh200/300/400, : ☎) A popular choice with backpackers, this is a budget-style riad, giving Moroccan style while being kind to your wallet. A traditional house with courtyard, *zellij* tiles and painted woodwork, it has several well-sized rooms on a number of levels, although as all face inward they can be quite dark at times. Shared bathrooms are clean, and there's a roof terrace. Breakfast is Dh30.

★ Dar Finn
GUESTHOUSE €€

(Map p288; ☑ 0535 74 00 04; www.darfinn.com; 27 Zqaq Rowah; r Dh850-1200; P ☎ ✳) Fassi houses often surprise as they open up after passing through a dark medina doorway. Dar Finn manages the trick twice over, going from high Fassi style in the main house to an adjoining annexe with walled garden, plunge pool and a variety of terraces to relax on (there's an honesty bar for sundowner drinks). It's a clever, well-thought-out design, complemented by rooms that are decorated in a warm, subtle Moroccan style. Start the day with the generous breakfasts including homemade jams and the like.

Dar Victoria
GUESTHOUSE €€

(Map p288; ☑ 0535 63 00 03; www.darvictoria.com; 31 Rue Makhfia, R'cif; r incl breakfast Dh950-1700; ☎) Situated in a quiet street in R'cif, Dar Victoria is a lovely old restored house. The seven rooms are named after precious stones, and are decorated in chic Moroccan style in soothing colours. The bathrooms are very good. The house itself has a lot of carved plaster, which is rich in Sufi symbolism. A sanctuary, from the moment the host welcomes you with homemade cordial from an old family recipe.

Hôtel Batha
HOTEL €€

(Map p288; ☑ 0535 74 10 77; hotelbatha@menara.ma; Pl Batha; s/d incl breakfast Dh495/629; ✳ ✳) The great location, room capacity and pool keep the Batha permanently busy. It's a reasonably modern set-up, with fair rooms and cool quiet areas to retreat from the hustle of the medina. Popular with tour groups, and a convenient bar for nonguests looking for a drink in the medina. Good value.

Dar el Menia
GUESTHOUSE €€

(Map p288; ☑ 0535 63 31 64; www.medinafes.com; 7 Derb el Menia, Talaa Kebira; incl breakfast r Dh500-730, whole house from Dh1500; ☎) Dar el Menia is a compact townhouse with four rooms tucked off the main drag. It's had a sympathetic restoration job and is relatively restrained in its decor, giving an air of calm the moment you close the door. We liked the kitchen for guests' use – a great idea, especially if you fancy renting out the whole house.

Dar Iman
GUESTHOUSE €€

(Map p288; ☑ 0535 63 65 28; www.dar-iman-fez.com; 6 Derb Benazahoum, Talaa Kebira; r incl breakfast Dh730; ✳ ☎) A well-restored 400-year-old townhouse located off the main drag, run by a Moroccan-Australian couple, this is great value for the price. All the style points you'd expect are in order, from *zellij* to tall wooden doors, but it's all been put together in a laid-back manner: less is definitely more here. Only the lack of views from the terrace count against this otherwise friendly, welcoming place.

Dar Bensouda GUESTHOUSE €€

(Map p288; ☎0535 63 89 39; www.riaddarbensou da.com; 14 Zqaq Labghal, Qettanine; r incl breakfast from Dh740; ☜☷) A converted palace, Dar Bensouda is one of the most impressive medina restoration projects we've seen in Fez. Enter into a large column-flanked courtyard and admire the attention to detail here and in the immaculate rooms. A side annexe holds a small but lovely pool. The scale here is grand without being overwhelming, and the service excellent. Make sure you check out the photo album and history of the building to get a full insight into the rebuilding project.

Dar Fes Medina GUESTHOUSE €€

(Map p288; ☎0535 63 83 92; www.darfesmedina .com; Derb Mokri, Ziat; s/d/tr incl breakfast Dh550/ 660/880; ❀☜) There's a very clever trick being played here: walk through the doors and you'll think you've found yourself in a restored medina townhouse, but this *dar* is a recent build. You'll get the best of both worlds – slightly more spacious and modern rooms, but the whole thing is brushed with a pleasingly traditional veneer. Its location near Bab Ziat gives another medina rarity: taxis can drop you right outside the front door.

Dar El Hana GUESTHOUSE €€

(Map p288; ☎0535 63 58 54; www.moroccanget away.com; 22 Rue Ferrance Couicha, Chrabliyine; r incl breakfast Dh560-780; ☜) If there's a cosier and more intimate guesthouse in Fez than this *dar*, we'd like to know about it. There are just three rooms (sleeping a maximum of eight altogether), all charmingly finished and presented: we fell for the 'secret' windows allowing you to spy on the street, and the open-air shower on the terrace. This is a real home away from home, and it's possible to rent out the entire house so you can fully indulge your own fantasies of medina life.

🚶 City Walk
Mazing Medina

START BAB BOU JELOUD
END R'CIF SQ
LENGTH 3KM; TWO TO THREE HOURS

This route takes you from Bab Bou Jeloud to the Kairaouine Mosque, then south to R'cif. It could take a couple of hours or all day, depending on the number of distractions.

Unlike much of the rest of the city walls and gates, the main entry, ❶ **Bab Bou Jeloud**, is a recent addition, built in 1913. Pass through it and you come upon a hive of activity. The pavement cafes here are excellent places for people-watching.

For the tour, take the first left and then right downhill along Talaa Kebira. This part of the street is a produce market – watch out for the camel butcher displaying the heads of his wares. Where the produce ends you're at the ❷ **Medersa Bou Inania** (p285), which represents the Merenid building style at its most perfect.

Opposite the entrance to the *medersa* (above eye-level) is the famous 14th-century ❸ **water clock** designed by a clockmaker and part-time magician. Carved beams held brass bowls with water flowing between them to mark the hours, but the secret of its mechanism died with its creator.

Continuing downhill, notice the old *funduqs* (caravanserai) on both sides of Talaa Kebira. These once hosted merchants and their caravans, and have rooms on several levels around a wide courtyard for both goods and pack animals. ❹ **Funduq Kaat Smen** is particularly interesting, specialising in many varieties of honey and vats of *smen,* the rancid butter used in cooking.

About 400m from the Medersa Bou Inania, as you go around an unmistakable dogleg, you'll soon catch sight of the pretty, green-tiled minaret of the ❺ **Chrabliyine Mosque** (named for the slipper-makers who can still be found working in this area) straight ahead.

Still heading downhill, past the shoe sellers and leatherworkers, look out for a right turn onto Derb Fkahrine and a sign indicating the entrance to a tiny tree-filled

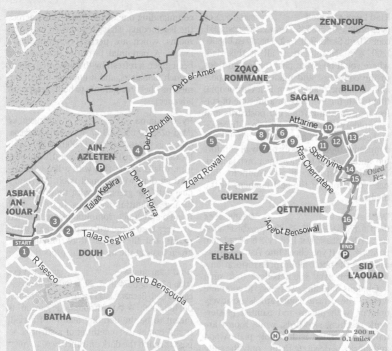

square known as the ⑥ **henna souq** – if you start walking uphill, you've gone too far. Cosmetic shops sell oils and henna. Pottery and bric-a-brac stalls abound, too.

Exiting the henna souq the same way you entered, turn left (south). After 50m a right turn brings you into ⑦ **Pl an-Nejjarine**. The lanes immediately north of the museum form part of the ⑧ **Souq an-Nejjarine** (Carpenters' Souq), where craftsmen create glittering wedding thrones.

From Pl an-Nejjarine, continue south, turning left almost immediately and ducking under the bar that prevents the passage of mules and donkeys. The lane leads between stalls piled high with candles and incense, to the entrance of the newly restored ⑨ **Zawiya Moulay Idriss II**. Non-Muslims cannot enter but can peer inside. To Fassis, this is the heart of their medina.

Afterwards, it's simplest to backtrack to Talaa Kebira. Follow the lane east – over a slight hummock and past haberdashers' stalls – until it ends at a T-junction about 100m later, where you'll find the ⑩ **Medersa el-Attarine** (p285).

On emerging from the *medersa*, turn left (south). After you've passed by the ⑪ **Pâtisserie Kortouba** the shops come to a sudden end at the walls of the great ⑫ **Kairaouine Mosque & University** (p285). The university is one of the world's oldest. Again, non-Muslims can only look through the main door.

As you proceed along the university walls clockwise, look out for the recently restored, 14th-century ⑬ **Funduq Tastawniyine**. It served for centuries as a hotel and warehouse for travelling merchants. Continue until the sound of metalworkers leads you into another small and attractive square, ⑭ **Pl as-Seffarine** (Brass-makers' Sq). With the university walls (and the entrance to its library) at your back, there is the Medersa as-Seffarine on the square's east side. Built in 1280, it is the oldest *medersa* in Fez, and the only one still in use.

Pass the *medersa* and follow the lane, turning left at the mirror stalls. Ahead is the ⑮ **Dyers' Souq**. Walk through the souq into the ⑯ **R'cif market** (p309). Explore the market, or take any left into R'cif Sq where you can catch an onward petit taxi.

Riad Lune et Soleil
GUESTHOUSE €€

(Map p288; ☑0535 63 45 23; www.riadluneetsoleil.
com; 3 Derb Skalia, Batha; r incl breakfast Dh800-
1200; ▣🔊) Hospitality is all at this riad,
where you'll be swept past the lemon trees
in the courtyard and made to feel impos-
sibly at home. Each room is a cornucopia,
filled with the evidence of a lifetime of collecting everything from old postcards and
embroidery to carvings and metalwork –
and each item with a story behind it. It's not
a museum though; there's plenty of comfort
too, and some rooms have their own jacuzzi.
You might just make it downstairs for dinner – from one of the best kitchens in the
medina.

Dar Seffarine
GUESTHOUSE €€

(Map p288; ☑0671 11 35 28; www.darseffarine.
com; 14 Derb Sbaalouyat, R'cif; r incl breakfast from
Dh780; ▣🔊) If you check into Dar Seffarine,
ask to see the photo album of its restoration –
it's the only way you'll believe that such
a fabulous building was ever a complete
wreck. The central courtyard is positively
opulent, with pillars and painted plasterwork reaching skywards, while rooms are
more understated with simple plain wood
and fabrics to decorate them – only the suite
with the painted domed ceiling makes a palatial exception. There's a pleasant terrace,
and a more intimate side courtyard off the
kitchen to relax in. The *dar* is a short walk
from Bab R'cif.

Dar Attajalli
GUESTHOUSE €€

(Map p288; ☑0535 63 77 28; www.attajalli.com;
Derb Qettana, Zqaq Rommane; r incl breakfast
Dh950-1300; ▣🔊) Dar Attajalli is a magnificent testament to the art of patient and sympathetic restoration. Everything has been
done to maintain the building's integrity,
using a minimum of modern techniques
and chemicals, while producing a supremely
comfortable guesthouse. Decoration is set
off with gently colour-themed Fassi fabrics –
colours further reflected in the planting of
the terrace roof garden, and all designed to
get you instantly relaxed (as if the organic,
locally sourced breakfasts didn't get your
day off to a good enough start).

Dar Roumana
GUESTHOUSE €€

(Map p288; ☑0535 74 16 37; www.darroumana.
com; 30 Derb el-Amer, Zqaq Roummane; r incl breakfast Dh950-1620; ▣🔊) One of those bigger-on-
the-inside townhouses, Dar Roumana will
always win fans by virtue of its beautiful
restoration job and gorgeous roof terrace

commanding one of the finest views across
the Fez medina. That's if you even leave the
rooms, which are perfect romantic hideaways. A perennial favourite, it's recently
been given a refresh by the new Australian-
French managers, and it now has one of the
medina's best restaurants to boot (reserve in
advance).

Ryad Salama
GUESTHOUSE €€

(Map p288; ☑0535 63 57 30; www.ryadsalama.
com; r incl breakfast from Dh900; 🔊▣) Well
located between Talaa Kebira and Talaa Seghira, this is a true riad with a lovely courtyard garden (with a small pool). All rooms
face onto the greenery, with those upstairs
having delightful balconies to play Fassi
Romeo and Juliet from. Rooms are finished
to a very high standard, with luxurious bathrooms, but the biggest draw remains the
green oasis at the heart of the property.

Riad Laaroussa
GUESTHOUSE €€€

(Map p288; ☑0674 18 76 39; www.riad-laaroussa.
com; 3 Derb Bechara, Talaa Seghira; r incl breakfast
Dh1400-2800; ▣🔊) Although a garden is
meant to be the defining feature of a riad,
it still comes as something of a surprise to
pass through the dark entrance here to meet
such a large green space, with its orange
trees and softly playing fountain. Instantly
relaxed, you continue to the fine rooms
decorated with modern art and unusual furniture that make it clear the owners haven't
just taken ideas from this month's Moroccan
style magazine. The new in-house hammam
is open to nonguests.

Riad Idrissy
GUESTHOUSE €€€

(Map p288; ☑0649 19 14 10; www.riadidrissy.com;
13 Derb Idrissi; r incl breakfast Dh1600; ▣🔊) Half
a dozen years in the making, this magnifi-
cently restored townhouse is a great addition to the Fez riad scene. The building
itself is grand but carries itself modestly,
while the welcome is equally warm but
understated. Central African crafts and
old Arabic vinyl records add an interesting
decorative twist. A highlight is the beautiful garden with huge papyrus and banana
trees, a green haven that's grown up among
the foundations of the building next door,
and now the appropriately named Ruined
Garden restaurant.

Riad Les Oudayas
GUESTHOUSE €€€

(Map p288; ☑0535 63 63 03; www.lesoudayas.
com; 4 Derb el-Hamiya, Ziat; r incl breakfast from
Dh1400; ▣🔊▣) The Moroccan owner is a

Paris-based designer, something that certainly shows in this riad's careful blend of traditional styles and modern design aesthetic, in everything from the downstairs salons to the chic but comfortable bedrooms. Steps lead down from street level into the courtyard garden, with a plunge pool and the riad's own hammam leading off it. Up top there's a large terrace, but if you crave privacy, two of the five rooms have private terraces.

Ryad Mabrouka
GUESTHOUSE €€€

(Map p288; ☑ 0535 63 63 45; www.ryadmabrouka. com; 25 Derb el-Mitter, Ain-Azleten; incl breakfast r Dh1150-1450, ste Dh1600-2000; ❈ 🛜 ❄) An old favourite and early player on the Fez riad scene, Mabrouka is a meticulously restored Arab-Andalucian townhouse. The courtyard, with its stucco, mosaics, magnificent cedar doors and babbling fountain, opens onto a pleasant garden of flowers and trees. There are seven rooms, decked out with tiled floors and Berber fabrics. Enjoy a simple breakfast or an all-out Moroccan feast on the verandah overlooking the medina.

Sofitel Palais Jamaï
GUESTHOUSE €€€

(Map p288; ☑ 0535 63 43 31; www.sofitel-legend. com/fes/en; Bab Guissa; s/d incl breakfast from Dh1950/2600) Once the pleasure dome of a late-19th-century vizier to the sultan, this grand hotel is set in Andalucian gardens overlooking the medina. Its rooms have had a recent makeover to keep it in line with the trendy medina guesthouses, although the occasional hint of its earlier bland international flavour still lingers. Rooms with views over the medina are great; nonguests can get a taste by visiting to enjoy a sunset drink on the terrace.

Riad Fès
GUESTHOUSE €€€

(Map p288; ☑ 0535 94 76 10; www.riadfes.com; Derb ibn Slimane, Zerbtana; r/ste incl breakfast from Dh1700/3000; ❈ 🛜 ❄) This labyrinthine riad blends ancient and modern with impressive panache. The older section shows off the best of traditional decor, while the newer quarters wouldn't look out of place in a Parisian boutique hotel yet remain unmistakably Moroccan. It has a trendy courtyard bar, restaurant, hammam and a plethora of terraces.

Riad Maison Bleue
GUESTHOUSE €€€

(Map p288; ☑ 0535 74 18 73; www.maisonbleue. com; 33 Derb el-Mitter, Ain-Azleten; r incl breakfast from Dh1700-2400; 🅿 ❈ 🛜 ❄) You have to be careful not to get lost in this riad – it's four houses knocked together and even extended across the street. Start in the orange tree–clad, Andalucian-style courtyard, then find your way to any of the 13 rooms, possibly stopping en route at the private spa, bar, dining salon and fashionably dark and plush Blue Lounge, where there is more eating and drinking on offer. If you don't want to crash in your room, chill on the terrace with its views to Borj Nord.

🛏 Ville Nouvelle

In the ville nouvelle, room rates drop considerably compared to the more popular medina, so much of the time you can get midrange service at budget prices. The ville nouvelle hotel scene is currently undergoing a mini-boom, with several new hotels opening and older ones being refurbished.

Hôtel Splendid
HOTEL €

(Map p300; ☑ 0535 62 21 48; splendid@iam.net. ma; 9 Rue Abdelkarim el-Khattabi; s/d/tr incl breakfast Dh394/512/646; ❈ ❄) Although in the budget category, this hotel makes a good claim for three stars. It's all modern and tidy, with good bathrooms and comfy beds, plus a pool for the hot days and a bar for the evenings. There's a dining room, too. Excellent value.

WHAT'S ON IN THE VILLE NOUVELLE?

Compared to the sensory overload provided by the medina, the ville nouvelle can seem boring: very modern, but with little actually going on. But for most Fassis, the ville nouvelle is the place where it's at: far more interesting and progressive than crumbling Fès el-Bali. In the last few years, huge amounts of money have been poured into the area, the benefits of which can best be seen along the long boulevard of Ave Hassan II, with its manicured lawns, palm trees, flower beds and fountains. A stroll here is a favourite evening pastime, when it's packed with families with kids, trendy teenagers and courting couples. Stop for an ice cream or just sit down on a bench and people-watch: this is the 'real' Morocco as much as any donkey-packed lane in the old city.

Hôtel Central HOTEL €

(Map p300; ☑ 0535 62 23 33; 50 Rue Brahim Roudani; per person Dh200) A bright and airy budget option that was being renovated when we visited. It's conveniently located just off busy Blvd Mohammed V. Most rooms have bathrooms, but even those without a shower have their own sinks. It's good value and popular so there's sometimes not enough rooms to go around.

Hôtel Olympic HOTEL €

(Map p300; ☑ 0535 93 26 82; fax 0535 93 26 65; cnr Blvd Mohammed V & Rue 3; s/d Dh290/340; ❄) A handy choice near the central market, this hotel has recently been refurbished. Rooms are nondescript but comfortable, and come equipped with bathroom, TV and phone. Its central location means it's often heavily booked (it's popular with tour groups), so call in advance. Breakfast is Dh35.

Youth Hostel HOSTEL €

(Map p300; ☑ 0535 62 40 85; 18 Rue Abdeslam Serghini; dm incl breakfast Dh75, d Dh170; ☺ gate open 8-10am, noon-3pm & 6-10pm) One of the better youth hostels in Morocco, the Fez branch is well looked after, and right in the centre of the ville nouvelle. Tidy rooms and facilities (including Western-style toilets) are superbly clean. There's hot water mornings and evenings.

Across Hotel HOTEL €€

(Map p300; ☑ /fax 0535 94 06 01, 0535 94 06 12; www.acrosshotels.com; 76 Blvd Chefchaouni; s/d incl breakfast Dh650/780; P ❄ 🎱 🏊) A new hotel in a convenient location, the Across ticks all the boxes for its four stars. Rooms are as you'd expect, and there's a gym, hammam, bar, restaurant and rooftop pool with amazing 360-degree views over the city.

Hôtel Mounia HOTEL €€

(Map p300; ☑ 0535 62 48 38; www.hotelmouniafes. ma; 60 Blvd Zerktouni; s/d incl breakfast from Dh551/702; ❄) A *zellij* lobby guides you into this modern and classy hotel that's popular with tour groups. Rooms are bright and tidy, with satellite TV. The restaurant is fair, and there's a smoky bar with plenty of water pipes. Rooms along corridors near the bar can be noisy. Staff are helpful, and good discounts are often available.

Hotel Sahrai HOTEL €€€

(Map p286; ☑ 0535 94 03 32; www.hotelsahrai. com; Dhar el-Mehraz; r from Dh1650; P 🅿 🏊) This new boutique hotel venture from the owners of Riad Fès is due to open in 2014. High on the southern hills overlooking the medina, it promises good things with high-end contemporary design, a Givenchy spa, restaurants and a terrace with an infinity pool and cocktail bar.

Hotel Barceló Fès Medina HOTEL €€€

(Map p300; ☑ 0535 94 88 00; www.barcelo.com; 53 Ave Hassan II; s/d Dh1760; ❄ 🎱 🏊) The four-star Hotel Barceló sweeps elegantly around a corner opposite La Fiat, affording it excellent views of the medina. Despite its name, it is in the ville nouvelle. Rooms are well designed and spacious with chic decor. There's a spa and snack bar, as well as the restaurant Le Bistrot.

🍴 Eating

Dining in Fez is something to be taken seriously. Fassi cuisine is famed across Morocco, and there are plenty of places in the medina to choose from. Popular with tour groups and their guides are the so-called 'palace restaurants' – dinner and a show in lavish surroundings, usually with plain set menus and hefty price tags. A more intimate experience can be had dining at a riad, many of which are open to nonguests and offer excellent fare. A good range of cheaper places can be found around Bab Bou Jeloud. The ville nouvelle has more options, including more non-Moroccan menus.

🍴 Medina

Café Clock CAFE €

(Map p288; ☑ 0535 63 78 55; www.cafeclock. com; Derb el-Mergana, Talaa Kebira; mains Dh55-80; ☺ 9am-10pm; 🎱 🖉) This funky place has a refreshing menu with offerings such as falafel, grilled sandwiches, some interesting vegetarian options, a monstrously large camel burger and delicious desserts. Better still, the 'Clock Culture' program includes calligraphy and conversation classes, films and sunset concerts every Sunday (Dh20), attracting a good mix of locals, expats and tourists.

Famille Restaurant Berrada MOROCCAN €

(Map p288; ☑ 0662 34 88 19; 57 Sagha el Achebine; mains around Dh40; ☺ Sat-Thu) 'Famille restaurant' says it all here – a small medina place run with much hearty cheer. Everything is very traditional, but they're used to seeing tourists too, keeping dishes turned over quickly and inviting diners into the kitchen to taste the day's selections before ordering.

Café Restaurant La Noria
MOROCCAN €

(Map p286; off Ave Moulay Hassan; menus from Dh80; ⊙7am-11.30pm) On the edge of the Jnan Sbil gardens and surrounded by crumbling city walls, this place gets the award for prettiest cafe in Fez. Its fruit trees and fountain offer respite from the medina bustle, though the *noria* (waterwheel) of its name no longer works. It serves great fruit juices, good breakfasts and reasonable meals.

Le 44
CAFE €

(Map p288; 44 Derb Bensalem, Talaa Kebira; ⊙9am-10pm; 🛜) This friendly, relaxing place down a twisty street is worth seeking out to while away a couple of hours while you check your emails over coffee or juice. There are light meals available, too.

★ Ruined Garden
MOROCCAN €

(Map p288; 📱0649 19 14 10; www.ruinedgarden.com; 13 Derb Idrissi; mains Dh120; ⊙lunch & dinner Thu-Tue; 🛜) An innovative approach to local street food is on the menu served in this delightful garden, or cosily around the fire in winter. Chef-gardener Robert Johnstone grows herbs and vegetables and smokes his own salmon. If you book ahead, they'll arrange a Sephardic feast or a traditional *mechoui:* slow-roasted lamb. Guests can be escorted to and from the house on request.

Médina Café
MOROCCAN €€

(Map p288; 📱0535 63 34 30; 6 Derb Mernissi, Bab Bou Jeloud; mains Dh70-100; ⊙8am-10pm) Just outside Bab Bou Jeloud, this small restaurant is an oasis of serenity, decorated in *tadelakt*. During the day it's a decent place to visit for a quick bite or a fruit juice; in the evening, it has a more interesting range of tajines and couscous than most places offer.

Dar Hatim
MOROCCAN €€

(Map p288; 📱0666 52 53 23; 19 Derb Ezaouia Funduk Lihoudi, Blida; 3-course menus from Dh170; ⊙lunch & dinner) A family home turned restaurant, this welcoming place pulls out all the stops in its food and service. Curiously, there are no tajines on the menu but you can order in advance. Bring along a bottle of your favourite wine. Fouad, the owner, will collect you so you won't struggle to find it.

STREET EATS

If it's just a snack you're after, you don't have to walk far in the medina to find someone selling food – tiny cell-like places grilling brochettes or cooking up cauldrons of soup, sandwich shops or just a guy with a tray selling macaroons. The top of Talaa Kebira has quite a cluster of options, otherwise follow your nose.

Bou Jeloud Restaurants (Map p288; Derb Serrajine, Bab Bou Jeloud; mains Dh30-70; ⊙8am-10pm) Walking in from Bab Bou Jeloud to the top of Talaa Seghira, you run the gauntlet of a host of restaurants touting for business. They're all pretty much alike, offering plenty of tajines, couscous and grilled meat. They're also great places to sit and people-watch over a mint tea. If you particularly want a view, try **Le Kasbah** (Map p288; Rue Serrajine; mains Dh40, set menu Dh70; ⊙8am-midnight) for its roof terrace; the cost of drinks doubles if you're not eating.

B'sara Stalls (Map p288; Talaa Kebira; soup Dh4; ⊙breakfast & lunch) Don't miss the Fassi speciality of *b'sara* (fava bean soup with garlic). Served from hole-in-the-wall places throughout the medina, our favourites are at the top of Talaa Kebira and in Achebine. Perfect fuel for exploring the city, the soup is ladled into rough pottery bowls and served with a hunk of bread, a dash of olive oil and a sprinkling of chilli.

Snail Stand (Map p288; cnr Talaa Seghira & Derb el-Horra; snails Dh5; ⊙5-10pm) This permanent stand is a good place to fill up on a molluscan snack – the ultimate in prepackaged fast food. Grab a pin to pluck the beasts out of their shells, then slurp down the aromatic broth. Delicious!

R'cif Market (Map p288; inside Bab R'cif; ⊙8am-8pm Sat-Thu; 📱) Those who shop for fresh produce in the medina know that R'cif is the best place to go – its traders always have the freshest fruit, vegetables and meat.

Talaa Kebira Market (Map p288; ⊙8am-8pm Sat-Thu) Tucked inside Bab Bou Jeloud, this is a good choice, and ideally located.

Le Chameau Bleu MOROCCAN €€
(Map p288; ☑ 0535 63 89 91; 1 Derb Tariana; mains Dh55-130; ☺ lunch & dinner) Well-signed just off Talaa Kebira, Chameau Bleu is a converted medina house on several levels, with tables all the way up to the roof terrace. We found the grilled meat and Atlas trout dishes to be particular winners; we've also had good reports about the pasta on offer.

★**Restaurant Dar Roumana** MEDITERRANEAN €€€
(Map p288; ☑ 0535 74 16 37; 30 Derb el-Amer; 2/3 courses Dh275/350; ☺ 7.30-9.30pm Tue-Sun; ☑) French chef Vincent Bonnin offers a menu that's Mediterranean with a Moroccan slant, making the best of local produce. There are innovative salads and excellent fish and meat dishes. Vegetarians won't go hungry. Eat in the courtyard or on the wonderful terrace in fine weather. Alcohol is served. When booking, you can ask for an escort to and from the restaurant.

Fez Café FRENCH, MOROCCAN €€€
(Map p288; ☑ 0664 64 76 79; 13 Akbat Sbaa, Douh; mains around Dh150; ☺ 11am-11pm; ☎☑) A charming restaurant set in a wonderful garden once owned by a pasha. The set-up is relaxed bistro-style, with a summery verandah and inside dining. Chef Hicham presents dishes that are a delicious seasonal mix of French and Moroccan. Fish is particularly good, and vegetarians will feel at home. Alcohol is served.

Tours Around Fez PICNICS €€€
(☑ 0535 74 00 04, 0655 01 89 75; into@darfinn. com; dinner per person Dh800; ☺ mid-May–end Sep) Here's your opportunity to look down on Fez from afar while dining. Relax on carpets under the olive trees on Mt Zalagh while your hosts prepare a three-course sunset dinner. The maximum group size is eight (at which point prices drop to Dh600 per guest, including transport), the minimum two. Bookings essential.

L'Amandier, Palais Faraj MOROCCAN €€€
(Map p288; ☑ 0535 63 53 56; www.palaisfaraj.com; Bab Ziat; mains from Dh150; ☺ dinner from 7.30pm) Excellent Moroccan cuisine is served in the restaurant or on the terrace of this new hotel, with spectacular views across the medina. All the classics are here, from an excellent pigeon *pastilla* (savoury-sweet pie) to golden lamb with almonds and onion jam, all served with attention to detail in the subtle spicing. A most elegant choice for dinner.

Restaurant Riad al Andalib MOROCCAN €€€
(Map p288; ☑ 0535 76 45 65; www.riadandalib. ma; Ave Ahmed Ben Mohamed Alaoui, R'cif; mains around Dh150; ☺ lunch & dinner) This large place in R'cif attracts a lunchtime crowd. While the menu is traditional Moroccan fare, the food is delicately spiced and thoughtfully presented. Service is attentive, and alcohol is served.

✗ Ville Nouvelle

For quick, filling meals, there are a few cheap eats on or just off Blvd Mohammed V, especially around the central market. You'll also find a good choice of sandwich places around Pl Florence.

Chicken Mac MOROCCAN €
(Map p300; Ave Lalla Meriem; mains around Dh40; ☺ 9am-11pm) Several eateries seem to run into each other along this strip in a continuously busy row of tables and chairs on the street. Chicken Mac is the last one away from Hassan II, and quickly serves up generous plates of rotisserie chicken, fried fish, bowls of *harira* (lentil soup) and other cheap, filling meals.

Restaurant Marrakech MOROCCAN €
(Map p300; ☑ 0535 93 08 76; 11 Rue Omar el-Mokhtar; mains from Dh70; ☺ lunch & dinner) A charming restaurant that goes from strength to strength behind thick wooden doors. Red *tadelakt* walls and dark furniture, with a cushion-strewn salon at the back, add ambience, while the menu's variety refreshes the palate, with dishes such as chicken tajine with apple and olive, or lamb with aubergine and peppers (there's also a three-course set menu).

Crémerie Skali CAFE €
(Map p300; ☑ 5356 65 09 92; Blvd Mohammed V; breakfast around Dh20; ☺ 6am-10pm) With a good corner location, this is an ideal stop for breakfast – one that's popular with office workers and families alike. As well as pastries and juice, it can rustle up some pretty good scrambled eggs.

L'Italien ITALIAN €€
(☑ 0535 94 33 84; contact@restaurantitalien. ma; Residence Longchamp, Ave Omar Ibn Khattab, Champs de Courses; pizza & pasta from Dh85, mains Dh120; ☺ lunch & dinner Wed-Mon; ☎) As the name suggests, Italian food is on the menu here, from a wide range of pizzas cooked in a wood-fired oven to steaks and

fish. The trendy industrial-themed decor and pleasant service make it a good choice for a change of pace. Wine is available.

Kaï Taï
ASIAN €€
(Map p286; ☑0535 65 17 00; 12 Rue Ahmed Chaouki; sushi Dh50-105, mains Dh80; ☺lunch & dinner) This is not going to be the best Asian food you have ever eaten, but the sushi, Vietnamese and Thai dishes on offer in suitably minimalist surroundings add a chilli-zing to palates jaded by one tajine too many.

MB Restaurant Lounge
MEDITERRANEAN €€€
(Map p286; ☑0535 62 27 27; 12 Rue Ahmed Chaouki; mains Dh130-230; ☺lunch & dinner) Making a strong bid for Fez' classiest restaurant, MB is all about cool stylish minimalism with modern furniture and rough-hewn stone. Food has a strong French influence. Retire to the upstairs bar at the end of the evening or swing by in the middle of the day for the Dh200 lunch menu.

Central Market
SELF-CATERING
(Map p300; Blvd Mohammed V; ☺8.30am-noon) If you're in the ville nouvelle and you're in need of fresh fruit and veggies, spices, nuts, olives or a parcel of delicious dates, you can't beat the new town's central market. It also has a couple of good cheese stalls and there are alcohol shops around the corner.

Borj Fes
SELF-CATERING
(Map p300; Ave Allal el Fassi; ☺9am-9pm) The first-ever shopping centre in Fez (with the first-ever escalator), this new centre has a large supermarket with a wider range of foodstuffs than you'll find in the medina, and an alcohol section.

🍷 Drinking

It can seem as if the main occupation in the ville nouvelle is sitting in cafes nursing a *nus-nus* (coffee with milk). Blvd Mohammed V and Ave Hassan II have the greatest concentration, but you don't have to go far to grab a table, order a drink and watch the day unfold. In the medina, many of the restaurants around Bab Bou Jeloud double as cafes.

Riad Fès
BAR
(Map p288; 5 Derb ibn Slimane; ☺10am-midnight) The classiest place for a drink in the whole city, the courtyard Alcazar bar of Riad Fès is a delight. Stucco columns catch the light reflected off the central pool, and soft music plays while you sit at the glass bar or sink into the cushions. There's a good range of beer and spirits, plus wine available by the glass. Open to the elements, it's a little cold in winter, but fashionably cool in summer. The Riad now has a new wine bar next to the swimming pool.

Mezzanine
BAR
(Map p286; 17 Kasbah Chams; ☺noon-1am) Scoring highly on the fashion meter and for late opening, this bar is more Ibiza than Moulay Idriss, and popular with the hip young Fassi crowd. The terrace overlooking Jnan Sbil gardens is a good place to chill with a beer or cocktail, and there's tapas too if you want some finger food.

Hôtel Batha
BAR
(Map p288; Pl Batha; ☺11am-11pm) There are a couple of options for drinks in this handily located medina hotel. The Churchill Bar is inside the hotel and in winter even features a log fire to warm yourself. At the back of the hotel (side entrance), the outside Consul Bar

FÈS FESTIVAL OF WORLD SACRED MUSIC

The **Fès Festival of World Sacred Music** (☑0535 74 06 91; www.fesfestival.com; ☺Jun) brings together music groups and artists from all corners of the globe, and it has become one of the most successful world music festivals around. Based on the idea that music can engender harmony between different cultures, the festival has attracted big international stars such as Ravi Shankar, Youssou N'Dour and Salif Keïta. Concerts are held in a variety of venues, including the Batha Museum, various riads and Bou Jeloud Sq. While the big names are a draw, equally fascinating are the more intimate concerts held by Morocco's various *tariqas* (Sufi brotherhoods). Fringe events include art exhibitions, films and debates. The festival has been praised by the UN as a major event promoting dialogue between civilisations. Tickets can go like hot cakes and accommodation books up far in advance (often attracting a festival premium) – so organise as far ahead as possible if you plan on attending.

is a more relaxed place for late-night drinks, and has its own disco until midnight (closed Monday).

MB BAR

(Map p286; 12 Rue Ahmed Chaouki; ⏰11am-2am) Dark leather, stylishly rough stone walls and a well-stocked bar make this place the perfect ville-nouvelle retreat for a classy drink or two, served with tapas.

Cremerie La Place CAFE

(Map p288; Pl as-Seffarine; ⏰7.30am-8pm) Put a cafe in one of the most interesting spots in the medina, and you have a near-perfect combination. Over juice, tea, coffee and pastries, the parade passes before you, accompanied by the tapping of the square's coppersmiths.

☆ Entertainment

Live-music buffs know the best time to visit Fez is festival time. Café Clock has regular Sunday sunset concerts worth checking out.

Institut Français (Map p300; ☎0535 62 39 21; www.institutfrancaisfes.com; 33 Rue Loukili) organises a packed program of films, concerts, exhibitions and plays.

🛍 Shopping

Fez is the artisanal capital of Morocco. The choice of crafts is wide, quality is high and prices are competitive, so take your time to shop around. As usual, it's best to seek out the little shops off the main tourist routes (principally Talaa Kebira and Talaa Seghira in the medina).

For leather, the area around the tanneries, unsurprisingly, has the best selection of goods.

In the medina, there are many well-restored riads and *funduqs* that have been converted into carpet showrooms. While they certainly offer a great opportunity to sit with a mint tea in spectacular surroundings and look at some fabulous rugs, the hard sell is like no other place in Morocco. You can pick up some wonderful pieces, but also pay over the odds for factory-made rubbish.

ℹ Information

DANGERS & ANNOYANCES

Although Fez is safe in comparison to Western cities of the same size, it's not really safe to walk on your own in the medina late at night, especially for women. Knife-point robberies are not unknown. Hotels and many restaurants are usually happy to provide an escort on request if you're out late.

Fez has long been notorious for its *faux guides* (unofficial guides) and carpet-shop hustlers, all after their slice of the tourist dirham. *Faux guides* tend to congregate around Bab Bou Jeloud, the main western entrance to the medina, although crackdowns by the authorities have greatly reduced their numbers and hassle.

Even many official guides will suggest visitors turn their tour into a shopping trip, and the pressure to buy can be immense. Fez' carpet sellers are masters of their game. If you really don't want to buy, it might be best not to enter the shop at all: once the parade of beautiful rugs begins, even the hardest-minded of tourists can be convinced to buy something they didn't really want (honeyed words suggesting that you could always sell the carpet later on eBay at vast profit should be treated with extreme scepticism). It's also worth remembering that any time you enter a shop with a guide, the price of the goods immediately goes up to cover their commission. Shopping in Fez needn't be a battle – indeed it's best treated as a game – but it's worth being prepared.

Beware the touts who board trains to Fez, often at Meknès. They can be very friendly, approaching you claiming to be students or teachers returning to Fez – they'll often have 'brothers' who have hotels, carpet shops or similar.

INTERNET ACCESS

Wi-fi is common across most midrange accommodation and above, and is sometimes available at cafes and restaurants.

FASSI POTTERY

Ceramics seem to be everywhere in Fez – from the distinctive blue-glaze pottery to the intricate mosaics decorating fountains and riads. **Art Naji** (☎0535 66 91 66; www.artnaji.net; Ain Nokbi; ⏰8am-6pm) is the place to go to buy the real deal. You can see the entire production process, from pot-throwing to the painstaking hand painting and laying out of *zellij* (tilework) – it's a joy to behold. The potteries are about 500m east of Bab el-Ftouh, an easy trip in a petit taxi – look for the plumes of black smoke produced by olive pits, which burn at the right temperature for firing the clay. You can even commission a mosaic and arrange for it to be shipped home.

MINT IMAGES - ART WOLFE/GETTY IMAGES ©

Natural Landscapes

Morocco's landscapes are incredibly diverse – you could spend a lifetime exploring the country and only ever scratch the surface. For those with shorter timeframes, pick up your hiking pack or saddle up your camel and prepare to get lost in the wilderness.

Contents

Above Camel caravan in the Sahara

SIMON MONTGOMERY/GETTY IMAGES ©

Mountain Ranges

Visible from both the Mediterranean and the Sahara, Morocco's mountains are as iconic as medinas and tajines – and they've been around much longer. They offer some of the best trekking landscapes in the world, from easy day walks to full-on expeditionary hikes.

Rif Mountains

Close to the Mediterranean coast, the Rif is Morocco's greenest range, and is covered in wildflowers in spring.

High Atlas

The High Atlas rolls from snow-covered peaks such as Jebel Toubkal to the Dadès and Todra Gorges. Those in good physical condition can climb Toubkal, but if grands taxis are your preferred mode of transport, the High Atlas is still memorable. Roads pass crumbling kasbahs and Berber villages, and wind up the Tizi n'Test and Tizi n'Tichka passes.

1. Chefchaouen (p252), Rif Mountains **2.** Tizi n'Tichka (p109), High Atlas **3.** The road from Imilchil (p140), Middle Atlas

Middle Atlas

You might think you're in the Alps when walking among the flowerbeds of Ifrane, a Middle Atlas alpine resort.

Anti Atlas

Closer to the Sahara, the Anti Atlas is a land of jagged peaks such as quartzite Jebel L'Kest, with oasis villages in the valleys. The wild, arid Jebel Saghro is home to the seminomadic Aït Atta.

Top Mountain Treks

Rif Mountains From Chefchaouen through Talassemtane National Park.

M'Goun Traverse Prehistoric rock forms, ridges, escarpments and river gorges.

Jebel Toubkal The two-day ascent of North Africa's highest peak.

Jebel Saghro Palm and almond groves beneath twisted volcanic pinnacles.

Anti Atlas Unexplored trails among ochre cliffs and saffron fields.

Deserts & Oases

Morocco sits on the edge of the great Sahara, and its dunes and oases are a huge draw for travellers. Follow the paths of the old camel caravans that once trekked across the desert, carrying salt and gold from Timbuktu.

Erg Chebbi & Erg Chigaga

The dunes at Erg Chebbi (p148) and Erg Chigaga (p125), respectively rising to 160m and 300m, are Morocco's greatest desert sights. These are the places to disappear into the desert, accompanied by a camel and blue-robed guide, to see the sand sea by moonlight and sleep in a nomad camp.

Desert Valleys

Coming from Marrakesh, there are more accessible glimpses of the desert in the Drâa Valley, where a sign once advised desert caravans that Timbuktu was only 52 days away, and oases remain the region's lifeblood. In Ouarzazate the desert stretches to the foot of the Atlas, and palms can be spotted through slit windows in the Taourirt kasbah.

1. Dunes at Erg Chebbi (p148) **2.** *Palmerie* outside N'Kob (p151) **3.** Desert mountains outside Ouarzazate (p112)

The Deep South

Largely overlooked by travellers, the *hammada* (flat, stony desert) of the far south runs through the Western Sahara. It's a stark environment, mainly crossed by overlanders en route to Mauritania.

Top Oases

Figuig Seven traditional desert villages amid 200,000 date palms.

N'Kob Mudbrick castles overlook the *palmeraie* (palm grove).

Skoura The Unesco-protected 'Oasis of 1000 Palms'.

Afella-Ighir Rocky red gorges tower above the palms.

Ameln Valley Village *palmeraies* beneath Jebel L'Kest.

Tata Treetops are a welcome sight in this Saharan outpost.

Paradise Valley *Palmeraies,* oleanders and beehives line the gorge.

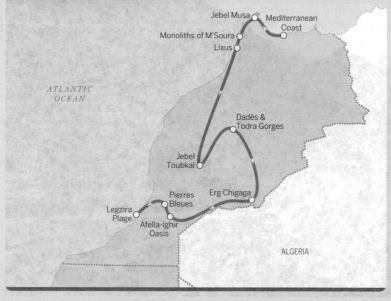

Mediterranean Coast

Jebel Musa

Monoliths of M'Soura

Lixus

ATLANTIC OCEAN

Dadès & Todra Gorges

Jebel Toubkal

Pierres Bleues

Erg Chigaga

Legzira Plage

Afella-Ighir Oasis

ALGERIA

Moroccan Landmarks

3 WEEKS

Strike out from urban Morocco with this tour of pillars, peaks and other natural landmarks. It samples the country's biggest mountain range, the fringes of the Sahara and the Atlantic surf.

The best way to appreciate the landscape of Morocco is to arrive by boat rather than plane; overlanders get to spy a landmark before they even step off the ferry from Europe: the **Mediterranean coast**, backed by the Rif Mountains, is an exciting first glimpse of Africa. The great crag of **Jebel Musa** outside Tangier is one of the ancient Pillars of Hercules that stand on either side of the Straits of Gibraltar.

The impact of the ancients is also on display on the coast. Half-abandoned in rolling countryside, the **Monoliths of M'Soura**, near Assilah, stand in a circle on a mysterious, prehistoric site. They're near the landmark left by the Romans at hilltop **Lixus**.

Head into the High Atlas, Morocco's greatest mountain range. **Jebel Toubkal** is North Africa's highest peak, but there are plenty of classic vistas to see without trekking to the top, including the rocky **Dadès Gorge** and the high drama of **Todra Gorge**.

Cross into the south of Morocco, where the mountains dwindle into the sands of the Sahara. **Erg Chigaga** is a landmark in this corner of the great desert, with 40km of dunes rising to 300m – plenty to explore from the saddle of a camel, and to sleep among while under a blanket of stars.

There's more to the Sahara than just dunes, of course. The desert theme continues at **Afella-Ighir**, a quintessential oasis occupying red-rock gorges. Nearby, a landscape artist created an Anti Atlas attraction when he daubed the **Pierres Bleues** (Painted Rocks).

Finish on the Atlantic coast, where natural stone arches reach out to sea at **Legzira Plage**, strange giant sculptures that bookend the trip – or act as tempting gateways to the great empty expanses of the deep south.

Top: Ruins at Lixus (p194)
Bottom: Todra Gorge (p138)

Fishing boats, Essaouira (p208)

Coastal Delights

Screeching seagulls, seafood tajines, Berber fishing villages, uncrowded beaches, salt-encrusted ramparts: the Moroccan coast is an unsung glory. Just as epic as the well-publicised mountains, it stretches from Mediterranean coves and cliffs to anglers' huts by the long, empty coastal highway through the Western Sahara.

Assilah

Tangier might have all the bustle of a modern port city, but the quieter charms of Assilah lie just a short hop south along the coast. The whitewashed walls of its compact seaside medina are daily freshened by the Atlantic breeze, and enlivened every year with new colourful murals that pop up during the annual Assilah Festival.

Essaouira

The sea walls of Essaouira's medina have been standing against the surf and spray for centuries. Inside, alleys lead to artists' galleries and craft workshops, while at the town's harbour fishermen sell the catch of the day, from silvery sardines and wide, flat rays to inky-black lobsters, prickly sea urchins and tentacled squid – all ready to be cooked up for a perfect seafood dinner.

Wildlife Wetlands

Away from the crashing waves, Morocco's coast also offers up plenty of quieter moments. Some of the best are its coastal national parks, which provide great opportunities for bird-watching. The best places are Merja Zerga near Larache, and Souss-Massa in the deep south. Both are perfect places to spot migratory species, as well as flamingos and, at Souss-Massa, the rare bald ibis.

Cyber Batha (Map p288; Derb Douh; per hr Dh10; ⊘9am-10pm) Has English as well as French keyboards.

Cyber Club (Map p300; Blvd Mohammed V; per hr Dh6; ⊘9am-10pm)

Teleboutique Cyber Club (Map p300; Blvd Mohammed V; per hr Dh7; ⊘9am-11pm) Above the *téléboutique* (telephone office) on the corner.

MEDICAL SERVICES

Clinique al-Kawtar (⌨0535 61 19 00; Ave Mohamed el-Fassi, Route d'Immouzzer) Large modern hospital in the ville nouvelle, just off the main road to the airport.

Night Pharmacy (Map p300; ⌨0535 62 34 93; Ave Moulay Youssef; ⊘9pm-6am) Located in the north of the ville nouvelle; staffed by a doctor and a pharmacist.

MONEY

There are plenty of banks (with ATMs) in the ville nouvelle along Blvd Mohammed V, all offering foreign exchange. In the medina there is an ATM at the post office and at banks on Blvd Ahmed ben Mohamed Alaoui in R'cif, as well as these useful spots:

Banque Populaire (Map p288; Talaa Seghira; ⊘8.45am-6pm Mon-Thu, 8.45am-noon Sat)

Société Générale (Map p288; Bab Bou Jeloud; ⊘8.45am-6pm Mon-Thu, 8.45-11am Fri, 8.45am-noon Sat)

POST

Main Post Office (Map p300; cnr Ave Hassan II & Blvd Mohammed V; ⊘8am-4pm Mon-Fri, 8.30am-noon Sat) Poste restante is next door on the left, at the Amana office.

Post Office (Map p288; Pl Batha; ⊘8am-4pm Mon-Fri) Located in the medina; it also has an ATM.

TOURIST INFORMATION

There is no tourist bureau in the medina.

Délégation Régionale de Tourisme (Tourist Information Office; Map p300; ⌨0535 62 34 60; Pl Mohammed V; ⊘8.30am-4.30pm Mon-Fri) On our visit, this office had no information, maps or brochures.

TRAVEL AGENCIES

Carlson Wagonlit (Map p300; ⌨0535 62 29 58; fax 0535 62 44 36) Behind Central Market; useful for flights and ferries.

USEFUL WEBSITES

Culture Vultures (www.culturevulturesfez.org) For arty Fez happenings including artisanal projects, tours, workshops, residencies, arts and culture.

View From Fez (www.theviewfromfez.com) News-and-views blog for keeping up to date with what's happening in Fez.

❶ Getting There & Away

AIR

Fez airport (⌨0535 67 47 12) is 15km south of the city, at Saïss. **RAM** (Map p300; ⌨0535 62 55 16; 54 Ave Hassan II) operates daily flights to Casablanca, as well as connections to Europe. At the time of research, the airport was being expanded.

BUS

The main bus station for **CTM buses** (Map p286; ⌨0535 73 29 92; www.ctm.ma) is near Pl Atlas in the southern ville nouvelle. In high season, buy tickets in advance, particularly to Tangier, Marrakesh and Chefchaouen. Services can be reduced out of season.

CTM runs nine buses a day to Casablanca (Dh95, 4½ hours) via Rabat (Dh75, three hours) between 1.15am and 7.15pm, and eight buses to Meknès (Dh25, one hour) between midnight and 11pm. There are three evening buses for Marrakesh (Dh165, 9½ hours); the 8pm bus arrives at 5.45am.

Heading north and east, there are three overnight buses for Tangier (Dh115, six hours), two for Chefchaouen (Dh70, four hours), four for Tetouan (Dh100, five hours), one overnight for Al-Hoceima (Dh120, five hours), four for Nador (Dh115, five hours) and four for Oujda (Dh120, five hours).

International services to Spain and France with Eurolines also depart from the CTM bus station.

Non-CTM buses depart from the **main bus station** (Map p288; ⌨0535 63 60 32) outside Bab el-Mahrouk on the edge of the medina, or from the streets immediately surrounding the bus station. Fares are slightly lower than CTM, and reservations can be made for popular routes. It has a **left-luggage facility** (⊘6am-midnight).

At least six buses run daily to Casablanca, Chefchaouen, Er-Rachidia, Marrakesh, Meknès, Midelt, Oujda, Rabat, Tangier and Tetouan. Less frequent buses go to Rissani (Dh100, eight hours), Tinerhir (Dh147, 16 hours) and Ouarzazate (Dh192, 13 hours).

Locally, there are frequent departures to Azrou (Dh20, 1½ hours), Ifrane (Dh16, 1½ hours), Moulay Yacoub (Dh10, 30 minutes), Sefrou (Dh10, 40 minutes), Taza (Dh30, three hours, hourly) and Ouezzane (Dh30, three hours, twice daily).

CAR

There are several guarded car parks around the medina: on Pl Bou Jeloud close to Bab Bou Jeloud, in Batha, north of Talaa Kebira at Ain Azleten and in the south at R'cif. In the ville nouvelle there's a guarded car park in front of the central market. **Chriftrans** (⌨0615 45 01 28;

chriftrans@gmail.com) is a reliable transport and vehicle-hire company, offering services from airport pick-ups to day trips from Fez and longer hires.

TAXI

There are several grand taxi ranks dotted around town. Taxis for Moulay Yacoub (Dh10, 20 minutes), Meknès (Dh22, one hour) and Rabat (Dh60) leave from in front of the main bus station (outside Bab el-Mahrouk). Taxis for Tissa (Dh20, 45 minutes) and Taza (Dh50, 2½ hours) depart from Seb el-Wrd on the hill opposite Bab Fettouh, the medina's southeastern gate. The rank for Sefrou (Dh12, 30 minutes) is located at Slaiki, southeast of Pl de la Résistance in the ville nouvelle. Azrou (Dh33, one hour) and Ifrane (Dh28, 45 minutes) taxis wait at a parking lot to the west of the CTM bus station in the south of the ville nouvelle.

Grands taxis outside the train station don't have specific destinations so cannot be shared.

TRAIN

The **train station** (📞 0535 93 03 33) is in the ville nouvelle, a 10-minute walk northwest of Pl Florence. To take advantage of the **left-luggage office** (Map p300; per item Dh10; ⏰ 6am-8pm), bags must be locked or padlocked.

Trains depart every hour between 4.50am and 6.50pm to Casablanca (Dh165, four hours), via Rabat (Dh120, three hours) and Meknès (Dh30, 30 minutes). There are four additional overnight trains. Ten trains go to Marrakesh (Dh295, eight hours) and four go to Tangier (Dh155, five hours) direct (two more via Sidi Kacem and one via Mechra Bel Ksiri). Direct trains for Oujda (Dh160, 5½ hours) via Taza (Dh56, two hours) leave four times daily.

ⓘ Getting Around

TO/FROM THE AIRPORT

There is a regular bus service (bus 16) between the airport and the train station (Dh20, 25 minutes), with departures every half-hour or so. Grands taxis from any stand charge a set fare of Dh120.

BUS

Fez has a reliable local bus service. At certain times of day, however, the buses are like sardine cans and are notorious for pickpockets. The standard fare is Dh2.50. Some useful routes:

No 9 Pl Atlas via Blvd Chefchaouni (both in the ville nouvelle) to near the Batha Museum (Fès el-Bali); the bus returns via Pl de la Résistance, Ave Hassan II and Ave des FAR.

No 10 Train station via Bab Guissa (northern Fès el-Bali) to Bab Sidi Bou Jida (northeastern Fès el-Bali).

No 19 Train station via Ave Hassan II (both in ville nouvelle) and Bab el-Jdid (southern Fès el-Bali) to Pl R'cif (central Fès el-Bali).

No 47 Train station to Bab Bou Jeloud (Fès el-Bali).

TAXI

Drivers of the red petits taxis generally use their meters without any fuss, but we have recently experienced hassles with touts at the train station. Insist on the meter, or walk further to hail a taxi. Expect to pay about Dh10 from the train or CTM station to Bab Bou Jeloud. As usual, there is a 50% surcharge after 8pm. You'll find taxi ranks outside all the gates of the medina. Only grands taxis go out to the airport.

Sefrou صفرو

The small Berber town of Sefrou, just 30km southeast of Fez, is a picturesque place situated on the edge of the Middle Atlas. It has a small but interesting medina that was designated on Unesco World Heritage Site in 2013. As such, the medina walls have been restored and some *funduqs* are being rebuilt. Sefrou once hosted one of Morocco's largest Jewish communities (as many as 8000 people, according to some accounts), and it was here that Moulay Idriss II lived while overseeing the building of Fez. It's an easy day trip from Fez, ideal if you need to escape the big city.

◎ Sights & Activities

Medina   MEDINA

Sefrou's medina is a manageable place to get around, especially compared to Fez. The Oued Aggaï flows through its centre, opening the place up and giving it more of an airy feeling than many old medinas. The best point of entry is northerly Bab el-Maqam. Follow the main flow of people downhill to the southeast and pass two mosques. Cross over the river and continue up the main shopping street to where the road splits: straight ahead takes you to Bab Merba, in the medina's southern wall, next to another mosque; the right fork brings you to the beginning of the *mellah*.

Mellah   NEIGHBOURHOOD

The *mellah* stretches from here northwest along the river. Although its Jewish population has gone, the district still retains a few distinctive wooden-galleried houses and lanes so narrow two people can only just pass. In its heyday, the *mellah* was so dark

Sefrou

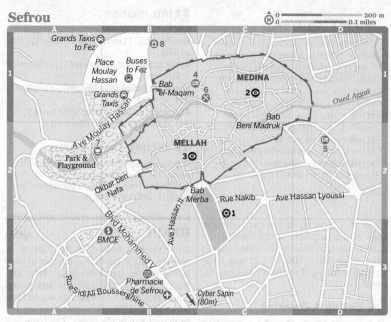

and crowded that street lamps had to be lit even in the middle of the day. Today it has an edgy feel: some buildings are derelict and there have been reports of muggings.

Jewish School
JEWISH

Just south of Bab Merba, this former Jewish school with its own prayer room is now closed. Knock and the guardians will probably let you in for a small donation.

Cascades
WATERFALL

A 1.5km walk west of town are the Cascades, a modest waterfall. Follow the signs from Ave Moulay Hassan around Al-Qala' (a semi-fortified village) and along the river's lush valley.

Rural Textile Trail
CRAFT

(☑ 0645 22 32 03; http://culturevulturesfez.org; 2 people per day incl lunch Dh2500) Local artist Jessica Stephens will weave you through the spinners, thread shops, tailors and jellaba (garment) button makers of Sefrou, ending at the women's carpet cooperative in a nearby mountain village.

🛏 Sleeping

Dar Attamani
GUESTHOUSE €€

(☑ 0535 96 91 74; www.darattamani.com; 414 Bastna, Medina; s/d/tr from Dh260/440/550; 🛜)

This lovely old Jewish house is tucked right in the heart of the medina. The owner has taken a great deal of attention to styling, and each room has a different look, giving the place an idiosyncratic style. Some rooms are en suite, others have shared bathrooms, and for shoestringers there are beds on the roof terrace (Dh110). Half board is also available.

La Maison des Lallas
GUESTHOUSE €€

(☑ 0535 66 11 16; www.lamaisondeslallas.com; 304 Derb El Miter; r from Dh352; 🛜) This pretty

IMPERIAL CITIES, MIDDLE ATLAS & THE EAST SEFROU

CHERRY FESTIVAL

Sefrou is a sleepy place on the whole, except in mid-June when the annual Cherry Festival (Festival des Cerises; www.festival-cerises-sefrou.com) fills the streets for four days to celebrate the local cherry harvest. There's plenty of folk music, along with displays by local artists, parades, *fantasias* and sports events, as well as the crowning of the Cherry Queen. Sefrou lays claim to the longest-running town festival in Morocco – it celebrated its 90th year in 2010.

house in a quiet street has five bedrooms, each with a bathroom, and a lovely courtyard that's traditionally decorated. Jamila can provide dinner (Dh132) and even a picnic basket (Dh44) if you're heading into the hills.

🍴 Eating & Drinking

There's a string of cafes and a bar along Blvd Mohammed V, all fairly masculine places to drink coffee. There are a few cheap eats with soup, kebabs and tajines in the medina.

Restaurant Farah MOROCCAN €
(Haddadine Sq; meals about Dh30; ⊙11am-9pm) The best of the bunch is the Restaurant Farah. It doesn't have its name outside, but it's easy to find opposite the knife-grinders and blacksmith with his fiery anvil (*Haddadine* means ironmongers). Here you can enjoy delicious spit-roast chicken with harissa for dipping, spiced chickpeas or *loubia* (beans), chips, bread and salad.

Café Zahra el-Jebal CAFE
(Town Park; ⊙9am-10pm) Women will feel comfortable at this lovely cafe spread along the shady riverbank in the park. It's known for its good milkshakes.

🛍 Shopping

You might snap up a bargain at the market held every Thursday.

Ensemble Artisanal HANDICRAFTS
(Rte de Fès) The usual selection of rugs, pots, clothes and leather are available here at fixed prices.

ℹ Information

BMCE (Blvd Mohammed V; ⊙8.45am-6pm Mon-Thu, 8.45-11am Fri, 8.45am-noon Sat) Has an ATM.

Cyber Sapin (Blvd Mohammed V; per hr Dh4; ⊙9am-9pm)

Main Post Office (Blvd Mohammed V; ⊙8am-4pm Mon-Fri)

Pharmacie de Sefrou (Blvd Mohammed V; ⊙8.30am-6pm Mon-Sat) Pharmacy.

ℹ Getting There & Away

Regular buses (Dh8, 40 minutes) and grands taxis (Dh11, 30 minutes) run between Sefrou and Slaiki in Fez. For Azrou, take a grand taxi to Immouzzer (Dh12) and change.

Bhalil بهاليل

This curious village, 5km from Sefrou, is worth a visit. It contains a number of troglodyte houses (cave dwellings) built into the picturesque mountainside and picked out in pastel hues of pink, yellow and blue. Some go so far as to utilise caves for the primary room of the house. The result is a cool, spacious room, usually used as a salon, while bedrooms and private areas are built above. A grand taxi from Sefrou to Bhalil costs Dh4.

Kamal Chaoui and his wife Béatrice offer very comfortable accommodation at **Dar Kamal Chaoui** (📞0678 83 83 10, 0535 69 27 37; www.kamalchaoui.com; 6 Kaf Rhouni; s & d from Dh605; 🖥), and Naima cooks delicious dinners (Dh175). Decorated in local Berber style, it has a relaxing roof terrace with sweeping views. Kamal is a mine of information on the area and can arrange mountain excursions, including a visit to the troglodyte caves for tea with the inhabitants (Dh275).

Meknès مكناس

POP 1,000,000

Of the four imperial cities, Meknès is the most modest by far – neither capital (Rabat), trendy tourist hub (Marrakesh) or home to a famed medina (Fez). In fact, Meknès, which receives fewer visitors than it really should, is rather overshadowed because of its proximity to Fez. Quieter and smaller than its grand neighbour, it's also more laid-back with less hassle, yet still has all the winding narrow medina streets and grand buildings

Meknès

0.5 miles
1 km

VILLE NOUVELLE

Main Train Station

CTM Bus Station

Ave de la Gare

Rue de Rabat

Ave Hassan I

Rue de la Gare

Rue Emir Abdelkader

El-Amir Abdelkader Train Station

Blvd Allal ben Abdallah

Rue Ghana

Place de l'Istiqlal (Place Batha)

Central Market

See Meknès Ville Nouvelle Map (p329)

Ave Moulay Mohammed

Rue ben Dough

Ave des FAR

Hôpital Moulay Ismaïl

Route 21

Oued Bou Fekrane

Ave Moulay Hafid

Sharia Benghazi

Sharia al-Ouma al Moutahida

R Ferhat Hachad

Institut Français

Ave Moulay Ismaïl

Blvd Abderrahmane ben Zidane

Royal Palace

Blvd Circulaire

Lahboul Gardens

R Rouamzine

Cemetery

Bab er-Rih

Royal Golf Course

R al-Andalous

MEDINA

Place Berdaine

Bab el-Jedid

Bab Berrima

Place Lalla Aouda

DAR EL-KBIR

Place el-Hedim

Bab Berdaine

Cemetery

Cemetery

OLD MELLAH

Bab el-Khemis

Bab Berrima

See Meknès Medina Map (p326)

R d'Agouraï

NEW MELLAH

that it warrants as a one-time home of the Moroccan sultanate. Sultan Moulay Ismail, the architect of Meknès' glory days, might be a little disgruntled at the city's current modesty, but visitors will find much to be enchanted by.

Encircled by the rich plains below the Middle Atlas, Meknès is blessed with a hinterland abundant with cereals, olives, grapes, citrus fruit and other agricultural products that remain the city's economic backbone. In the midst of this agricultural region sit the Roman ruins at Volubilis and the hilltop tomb of Moulay Idriss, two of the country's most significant historic sites. If you base yourself in Meknès you'll find plenty to keep you busy.

The valley of the (usually dry) Oued Bou Fekrane neatly divides the old medina in the west and the French-built ville nouvelle in the east. Moulay Ismail's tomb and imperial city are south of the medina.

History

The Berber tribe of the Meknassis (hence the name Meknès) first settled here in the 10th century. Under the Almohads and Merenids, Meknès' medina was expanded and some of the city's oldest remaining monuments were built.

It wasn't until the 17th century that Meknès really came into its own. The founder of the Alawite dynasty, Moulay ar-Rashid, died in 1672. His successor and brother, Moulay Ismail, then made Meknès his capital, and he would reign from here for 55 years.

Ismail endowed the city with 25km of imposing walls with monumental gates and an enormous palace complex that was never completed. That he could devote the time and resources to construction was partly due to his uncommon success in subduing all opposition in Morocco and keeping for-

Meknès Medina

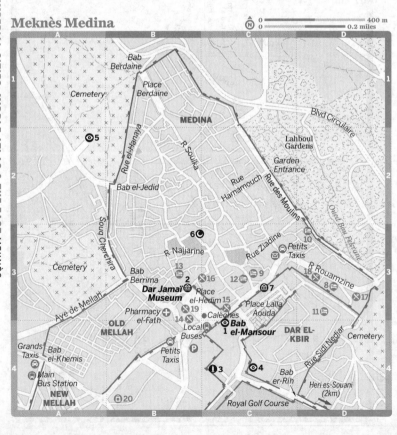

eign meddlers at bay, mainly because of his notorious Black Guard.

The death of Ismail in 1727 also struck the death knell for Meknès. The town resumed its role as a backwater, as his grandson Mohammed III (1757–90) moved to Marrakesh. The 1755 earthquake that devastated Lisbon also dealt Meknès a heavy blow. As so often happened in Morocco, its monuments were subsequently stripped in order to be added to buildings elsewhere. It has only been in the past few decades, as the town's tourist potential has become obvious, that any serious restoration attempts have taken place.

In 1912 the arrival of the protectorate revived Meknès as the French made it their military headquarters. The army was accompanied by French farmers who settled on the fertile land nearby. After independence most properties were recovered by the Moroccan government and leased to local farmers.

Meknès Medina

◉ Sights

◉ The Medina

The heart of Meknès medina is Pl el-Hedim, the large square facing Bab el-Mansour. Built by Moulay Ismail and originally used for royal announcements and public executions, it's a good place to sit and watch the world go by – kids playing football, hawkers selling miracle cures, and promenading families. There's always something going on, and you get the sense that the city authorities would love for it to turn into the local equivalent of Marrakesh's Djemaa el-Fna. One edge is lined with cafes and restaurants; behind these is an excellent, covered produce market.

To the south, the impressive monumental gateway of Bab el-Mansour leads into Moulay Ismail's imperial city. The narrow streets of the old *mellah* are in the west of the medina – look for the old balconied houses so distinctive of the Jewish quarter.

The easiest route into the souqs is through the arch to the left of the Dar Jamaï Museum on the north side of Pl el-Hedim. Plunge in and head northwards, and you'll quickly find yourself amid souvenir stalls and carpet shops.

Markets MARKET
There are many *qissariat* (covered markets). A couple of these are devoted to textiles and carpets, which are noisily auctioned off on Sunday mornings. **Okchen Market** specialises in fine embroidery. On Rue Najjarine, you'll pass stalls of *babouches* (leather slippers) in multicoloured rows and **Qissariat ad-Dahab**, the jewellery souq. Outside of the city wall, you'll find a colourful souq selling spices, herbs and nuts, and a lively **flea market**.

★ Dar Jamaï Museum MUSEUM
(Map p326; ☏ 0555 53 08 63; admission Dh10; ◷ 9am-noon & 3-6.30pm Wed-Mon) Overlooking Pl el-Hedim is Dar Jamaï, a palace built in 1882 by the powerful Jamaï family, two of whom were viziers to Sultan Moulay al-Hassan I. When the sultan died in 1894, the family fell foul of court politics and lost everything, including the palace, which was passed on to the powerful Al-Glaoui family. In 1912 the French commandeered the palace for a military hospital.

Since 1920 the palace has housed the Administration des Beaux Arts and one of

Morocco's best museums. Exhibits include traditional ceramics, jewellery, rugs and some fantastic textiles and embroidery. Look out for the brocaded saddles, and some exquisite examples of Meknasi needlework (including some extravagant gold and silver kaftans). The *koubba* (domed sanctuary) upstairs is furnished as a traditional salon complete with luxurious rugs and cushions. The museum also has a fine collection of antique carpets, representing various styles from different regions of Morocco.

The exhibits are well constructed; explanations are in French, Arabic and sometimes English. The museum's Andalucian garden and courtyard are shady, peaceful spots amid overgrown orange trees.

Musée de Meknès   MUSEUM

(Meknès Museum; Map p326; Route Dar Smen; admission Dh10; ⊙9am-noon & 3-6.30pm Wed-Mon) Housed in the gracious old Tribunal building, this new museum features metalwork, farming implements, clothing, jewellery, carpets and ceramics. Look out for the remarkable set of armour made of copper and encrusted with coral beads, turquoise studs and coins. This warrior was well protected with helmet, breastplate and gauntlets.

Medersa Bou Inania   MEDERSA

(Map p326; Rue Najjarine; admission Dh10; ⊙9am-noon & 3-6pm) Opposite the Grande Mosquée, the Medersa Bou Inania is typical of the exquisite interior design that distinguishes Merenid monuments. It was completed in 1358 by Bou Inan, after whom a more lavish *medersa* in Fez is also named. This *medersa* is a good display of the classic Moroccan decorative styles – the *zellij* base, delicate stucco midriff and carved olive-wood ceiling.

Students aged eight to 10 years once lived two to a cell on the ground floor, while older students and teachers lived on the 1st floor. Anyone can climb onto the roof for views of the green-tiled roof and minaret of the Grande Mosquée nearby, but the *medersa* is otherwise closed to non-Muslims.

Mausoleum of Sidi ben Aïssa   MAUSOLEUM

(Map p326) Sidi ben Aïssa gave rise to one of the more unusual religious fraternities in Morocco, known for their self-mutilation and for their imperviousness to snake bites. His followers gather here at his mausoleum in April from all over Morocco and further afield. The mausoleum is closed to non-Muslims.

THE ALMIGHTY MOULAY

Few men dominate the history of a country like the towering figure of Sultan Moulay Ismail (1672–1727). Originating from the sand-blown plains of the Tafilalt region, his family were sherifs (descendants of the Prophet Mohammed) – a pedigree that continues to underpin the current monarchy.

Ruthlessness as well as good breeding were essential characteristics for becoming sultan. On inheriting the throne from his brother Moulay ar-Rashid, Moulay Ismail set about diffusing the rival claims of his 83 brothers and half-brothers, celebrating his first day in power by murdering all those who refused to submit to his rule. His politics continued in this bloody vein with military campaigns in the south, the Rif Mountains and Algerian hinterland, bringing most of Morocco under his control. He even brought the Salé corsairs to heel, taxing their piracy handsomely to swell the imperial coffers.

The peace won, Moulay Ismail retired to his capital at Meknès and began building his grandiose imperial palace, plundering the country for the best materials, and building city walls, kasbahs and many new towns. This cultural flowering was Morocco's last great golden age.

Moulay Ismail also considered himself a lover. Although he sought (but failed to receive) the hand in marriage of Louis XIV of France's daughter, he still fathered literally hundreds of children. Rather foolishly, however, he did nothing to secure his succession. When he died the sultanate was rocked by a series of internecine power struggles, from which the Alawites never fully recovered.

Nevertheless, his legacy was to be the foundation of modern Morocco. He liberated Tangier from the British, subdued the Berber tribes and relieved the Spanish of much of their Moroccan territory. Moulay Ismail sowed the seeds of the current monarchy and beneath his strong-arm rule the coherent entity of modern Morocco was first glimpsed.

Meknès Ville Nouvelle

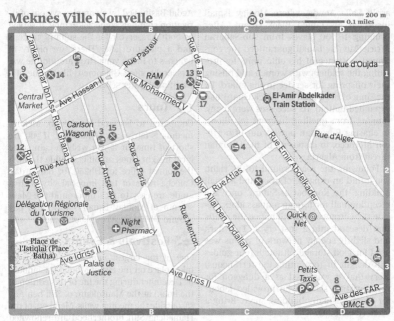

◎ Imperial City

★ Bab el-Mansour
GATE

(Map p326) The focus of Pl el-Hedim is the huge gate of Bab el-Mansour, the grandest of all imperial Moroccan gateways. The gate is well preserved with lavish (if faded) *zellij* and inscriptions across the top. It was completed by Moulay Ismail's son, Moulay Abdallah, in 1732. You can't walk through the *bab* itself (although it's sometimes open to host exhibitions), but instead have to make do with a side gate to the left.

Mausoleum of Moulay Ismail
MAUSOLEUM

(Map p326; donations welcome; ◎8.30am-noon & 2-6pm Sat-Thu) Diagonally opposite the Koubbat as-Sufara' is the resting place of the sultan who made Meknès his capital in the 17th century. Moulay Ismail's stature as one of Morocco's greatest rulers means that non-Muslim visitors are welcomed into the sanctuary. Entry is through a series of austere, peaceful courtyards meant to induce a quiet and humble attitude among visitors, an aim that's not always successful in the face of a busload of tourists. The tomb hall is a lavish contrast and showcase of the best of Moroccan craftsmanship. Photography

Meknès Ville Nouvelle

🛏 Sleeping
1 Hôtel Akouas	D3
2 Hôtel Bab Mansour	D3
3 Hôtel de Nice	A2
4 Hôtel Majestic	C2
5 Hôtel Malta	A1
6 Hôtel Palace	A2
7 Hôtel Rif	A2
8 Hôtel Volubilis	D3

🍴 Eating
9 Central Market	A1
10 Le Pub	B2
11 Marhaba Restaurant	C2
12 Palais de Poulet	A2
13 Promenade Palace	B1
14 Restaurant Gambrinus	A1
15 Restaurant Pizza Roma	B2

🍷 Drinking & Nightlife
16 Café Opera	B1
17 Café Tulipe	C1

is permitted, but non-Muslims may not approach the tomb itself.

Koubbat as-Sufara'
MONUMENT

(Map p326; admission Dh10; ◎9am-noon & 3-6pm) South of Bab el-Mansour lies the *mechouar* (parade ground), now known as Pl Lalla Aouda, where Moulay Ismail inspected his famed Black Guard. After bringing 16,000 slaves from sub-Saharan Africa, Moulay Ismail guaranteed the continued existence of his elite units by providing the soldiers with women and raising their offspring for service in the guard. By the time of his death, the Black Guard had expanded tenfold. Its successes were many, ranging from quelling internal rebellions, to chasing European powers out of northern Morocco, to disposing of the Ottoman threat from Algeria.

Following the road around to the right, you'll find an expanse of grass and a small building, the Koubbat as-Sufara', once the reception hall for foreign ambassadors. Beside the entrance, you will notice the shafts that descend into a vast crypt. This dark and slightly spooky network of rooms was used for food storage, although tour guides will delight in recounting the (erroneous) story that it was used as a dungeon for the Christian slaves who provided labour for Moulay Ismail's building spree. Bring a torch (flashlight).

★ **Heri es-Souani** RUIN

(admission Dh10; ☺9am-noon & 3-6.30pm) Nearly 2km southeast of the mausoleum, Moulay Ismail's immense granaries and stables, Heri es-Souani, were ingeniously designed. Tiny windows, massive walls and a system of underfloor water channels kept the temperatures cool and air circulating. The building provided stabling and food for an incredible 12,000 horses, and Moulay Ismail regarded it as one of his finest architectural projects.

The roof fell in long ago, but the first few vaults have been restored. They're impressive, but overly lit which robs them of much of their ambience – seek out the darker, more atmospheric corners. Those beyond stand in partial ruin, row upon row across a huge area.

In summer it's a long hot walk here from Moulay Ismail's mausoleum, so you might want to catch a taxi or calèche (horse-drawn carriage). If you do decide to walk, follow the road from the mausoleum south between the high walls, past the main entrance of the Royal Palace (no visitors) and a campsite, to find the entrance straight ahead.

Agdal Basin LAKE

Immediately north of the granaries and stables lies an enormous stone-lined lake, the Agdal Basin. Fed by a complex system of irrigation channels some 25km long, it served as both a reservoir for the sultan's gardens and a pleasure lake. There are plenty of benches to break your stroll around the waters, and a giant Giacometti-like statue of a traditional water seller.

☞ Tours

Compared to Fez and Marrakesh, Meknès medina is fairly easy to navigate. If you are short of time, or if you wish to gain some local insight, book an official guide through the tourist office for Dh250 for half a day. Calèche rides of this imperial city with a guide are easy to pick up around the Mausoleum of Moulay Ismail – expect to pay around Dh150 for a couple of hours.

✯✯ Festivals & Events

One of the largest *moussems* in Morocco takes place on the eve of Moulid (in January or December during the life of this edition of the book) at the Mausoleum of Sidi ben Aïssa, outside the medina walls. Members of the Hamadcha Sufi brotherhood are renowned for trances that make them impervious to pain, but public displays of glass-eating, snake bites and ritual body piercing are no longer allowed (though you'll see pictures about town). It's a busy and popular festival with *fantasias* (musket-firing cavalry charges), fairs and the usual singing and dancing.

🛏 Sleeping

Most accommodation is located in the ville nouvelle, with the exception of a cluster of ultrabudget options and a number of new riads.

🛏 Medina

Most of Meknès' cheapies cluster along Rue Dar Smen and Rue Rouamzine in the old city. In the high season and during festivals, they can fill up quickly. To be on the safe side, get here early in the day or reserve a room.

Hôtel Maroc HOTEL €

(Map p326; ☎0535 53 00 75; 7 Rue Rouamzine; per person Dh100, roof terrace Dh50) A perennially popular shoestring option, the Maroc has kept its standards up over the many years we've been visiting. Friendly and quiet, rooms (with sinks) are simple, and the shared bathrooms are clean. The terrace and courtyard filled with orange trees add to the ambience.

★Ryad Bahia GUESTHOUSE €€

(Map p326; ☏0535 55 45 41; www.ryad-bahia. com; Derb Sekkaya, Tiberbarine; s/d incl breakfast from Dh400/650; ❄☎) This charming riad is just a stone's throw from Pl el-Hedim. The main entrance opens onto a courtyard (also hosting a great restaurant). Rooms are pretty and carefully restored, and the owners (keen travellers themselves) are eager to swap travel stories as well as guide guests in the medina, especially as Bouchra is a licensed guide.

Riad d'Or GUESTHOUSE €€

(Map p326; ☏0641 07 86 25; www.riaddor.com; 17 Derb el-Anboub; r Dh495-935; ❄☎☒) Recently refurbished, this riad is spread over two townhouses, with 11 rooms tumbling around unexpected courtyards and staircases. Many rooms can sleep four or more people. There's a good restaurant, too. The biggest surprise is hidden on one of the roof terraces: who expected to find a swimming pool there?

Riad Safir GUESTHOUSE €€

(Map p326; ☏0535 53 47 85; www.riadsafir. com; 1 Derb Lalla Alamia; s/d/tr incl breakfast Dh550/660/770; ❄☎) This delightful, intimate guesthouse comes in two halves: the original Safir is a homely confection that swaps the traditional *zellij* and plaster of some places for swathes of soft fabrics and carpets in creams and warm oranges, and plenty of wood. Next door is all ultramodern chic, with stylishly restrained colours and artful decoration. An unexpected, but winning, contrast.

Riad Lahboul GUESTHOUSE €€

(Map p326; ☏0535 55 98 78; www.riadlahboul.com; 6 Derb Ain Sefli, Rouamzine; r from Dh600; ❄☎) This family-friendly guesthouse is run by a Moroccan-English couple. You enter into a salon in high-Moroccan style, but above this the six rooms are positively cosy; one is a large apartment. Dining in is a good option as the food is excellent, and the location puts you on the edge of the medina across from the peaceful Lahboul Gardens.

Riad Meknès GUESTHOUSE €€

(Map p326; ☏0535 53 05 42; www.riadmeknes. com; 79 Ksar Chaacha, Dar el-Kabir; s/d/tr incl breakfast Dh440/660/770; ❄☎☒) This large, airy riad is located amid the ruins of the Palais Ksar Chaacha, in a quiet area full of lawyers' offices and public scribes. Rooms are tastefully decorated in a traditional-meets-modern style. It is noted for its food (the restaurant is open to the public), and there are a couple of salons for dining, or you can just relax by the chic plunge pool and cactus garden.

Le Jardin de Ryad Bahia GUESTHOUSE €€€

(☏0535 55 45 41; www.lesjardinsderyadbahia.com; r Dh800-1000; ❄☎☒) The owners of Ryad Bahia have also opened this large, airy house in the countryside 5km west of Meknès. The lovely garden has a large pool, and there's a hammam, sauna and jacuzzi. The house has nine bedrooms with balconies, and relaxing living spaces. Cooking classes are a speciality (Dh400 per person). This is the place for a breath of fresh air if you're all medina-ed out, especially as you can just go for the day (transport provided).

🛏 Ville Nouvelle

The ville nouvelle also has some decent budget options, as well as more expensive establishments.

Hôtel Majestic HOTEL €

(Map p329; ☏0535 52 20 35; 19 Ave Mohammed V; s/d incl breakfast Dh287/374) Open for business since 1937, the Majestic is one of the best deco buildings in Meknès. Rooms are comfortable, if old-fashioned, and there's plenty of character to go around from the dark-wood dado to the original deco light fittings. A quiet courtyard, roof terrace and friendly management top things off, making this a hard budget option to beat.

Hôtel Palace HOTEL €

(Map p329; ☏0535 40 04 68; fax 0535 40 14 31; 11 Rue Ghana; s/d Dh180/230; ☒) Looking very dour from the street, this hotel turns out to be surprisingly good value, offering large airy rooms with attached bathrooms, many with balcony. The mezzanine sofas give an extra option for chilling out. It's frequently full, so call in advance.

Hôtel Volubilis HOTEL €

(Map p329; ☏0535 52 50 82; Ave des FAR; s/d/tr Dh242/289/376) This is a reasonable option, with fair rooms and en-suite bathrooms. Try to avoid the rooms at the front above the main road, as they can stay pretty noisy throughout the night.

Hôtel de Nice HOTEL €€
(Map p329; ☑0535 52 03 18; www.hoteldenice
-meknes.com; cnr Rue Accra & Rue Antserapé; s/d
incl breakfast from Dh425/530; ❋) This hotel
continues to fly the flag for quality and
service. It's modern, efficient and ever-so-
slightly shiny, so it's a surprise that room
rates aren't a good Dh100 more than they
actually are. Rooms are nicely decorated
and well sized, and there's a bar and restaurant too.

Hôtel Rif HOTEL €€
(Map p329; ☑0535 52 25 91; hotel_rif@menara.
ma; Rue Accra; s/d incl breakfast Dh666/832; ❋🔊
❋) The four-star Hôtel Rif is a consistent
performer in the upper midrange hotel
stakes. The hotel interior has a slightly
funky modernist ambience, and we love
the concrete-chocolate confection of the
exterior. The courtyard pool is good for dipping your toes in, but as it's overlooked by
the bar, female bathers will feel enormously
exposed.

Hôtel Akouas HOTEL €€
(Map p329; ☑0535 51 59 67; 27 Rue Emir Abdelkader; s/d/tr Dh341/422/543; ❋❋) This
friendly, family-run three-star hotel has
a little more local colour than its rivals.
Rooms, while not huge, are modern, serv-
iceable and very fairly priced. The place
also has a decent restaurant and a nightclub.

Hôtel Bab Mansour HOTEL €€
(Map p329; ☑0535 52 52 39; hotel_bab_man-
sour@menara.ma; 38 Rue Emir Abdelkader; s/d
Dh396/521; ❋🔊) It's a fine line between
tasteful and characterless and, while comfortable enough, the Bab Mansour never
quite seems to develop much of a personality – the famous *bab* is depicted in tiles in
the bathrooms, but it's more DIY store than
Moroccan *zellij*. That said, it's well run, with
everything you'd expect in a tourist-class
hotel.

Hôtel Malta HOTEL €€€
(Map p329; ☑0535 51 50 20; www.hotel-malta.
ma; 3 Rue Charif Idrissi; s/d Dh726/1000; ❋🔊)
The Malta sets its aim a little higher in its
service than most of the hotel options in
Meknès, with pleasing results. The spacious rooms may never win any design
awards, but they're comfy to relax in, and
there's satellite TV, a restaurant and a
plush piano bar.

 Eating

Medina

Restaurant Oumnia MOROCCAN €
(Map p326; ☑0535 53 39 38; 8 Ain Fouki Rouamzine; set menu Dh95; ⊙noon-3pm & 7-10pm)
This is less a formal restaurant and more
like a few rooms of a family home converted into dining salons, and the emphasis here is on warm service and hearty
Moroccan fare. There's just a three-course
set menu, but it's a real winner, with delicious *harira*, salads and a choice of several
tajines of the day.

Pavillon des Idrissides CAFE €
(Map p326; 147 Dar Smen Lahdim; mains from Dh55;
⊙8.30am-10pm) An ideal spot for a quick coffee or a lazy meal, this cafe-restaurant has
scooped all the others in finding a great view
overlooking Bab el-Mansour. The food is an
unsurprising mix of grills, tajines and couscous – perfectly decent, but the setting is
really the thing here.

Restaurant Mille et Une Nuits MOROCCAN €
(Map p326; ☑0535 55 90 02; off Pl el-Hedim;
mains Dh55-95; ⊙noon-3pm & 7.30-10pm) Easily located off Pl el-Hedim, this is another
converted house, whose owners have leant
towards the more showy 'palace' restaurant
style of surroundings. You'll find all the Moroccan standards and classics on a reasonably priced menu.

Sandwich Stands FAST FOOD €
(Map p326; Pl el-Hedim; sandwiches around Dh30;
⊙7am-10pm) Take your pick of any one of
the stands lining Pl el-Hedim, and sit at the
canopied tables to watch the scene as you
eat. There are larger meals like tajines, but
the sandwiches are usually quick and excellent, while a few places nearer the medina
walls do a good line in sardines.

Rue Rouamzine Eateries FAST FOOD €
(Map p326; Rue Rouamzine; meals Dh30-60; ⊙11am-
10pm) Particularly handy for the cheap hotels
on the edge of the medina proper, this street
has plenty of good eating places serving up
sandwiches, kebabs, tajines, grilled chicken,
fruit juices and ice cream.

Ryad Bahia MOROCCAN €€
(Map p326; ☑0535 55 45 41; www.ryad-bahia.
com; Derb Sekkaya, Tiberbarine; mains Dh80-130;
⊙noon-3pm & 7-10pm) Nonresidents are welcome to eat at the restaurant of this riad

(book in advance), and it makes a pleasant evening dining spot with its tables around the courtyard. The menu is typically Moroccan, but everything is tasty and served and presented nicely.

Restaurant Riad Meknès MOROCCAN €€
(Map p326; ☑ 0535 53 05 42; 79 Ksar Chaacha; mains from Dh60, set menus Dh110-160; ☺ noon-3pm & 7-10pm) While all the riads in Meknès medina have lovely restaurants, this is a great option for nonguests. Set around a lush green courtyard, it's a great place to relax, and while the menu of salads, tajines and couscous is simple, it's all delicious and served with care and attention.

Dar Sultana MOROCCAN €€
(Map p326; ☑ 0535 53 57 20; Derb Sekkaya, Tiberbarine; mains from Dh75, 3-course set menu Dh110; ☺ noon-3pm & 7-10pm) Also going under the name Sweet Sultana, this is a small but charming restaurant located in a converted medina house. The tent canopy over the courtyard gives an intimate, even romantic, atmosphere, set off by walls deocrated with henna designs and bright fabrics. The spread of cooked Moroccan salads is a highlight.

Covered Market SELF-CATERING
(Map p326; Pl el-Hedim; ☺ 7.30am-9pm) This is *the* place in Meknès to get fresh produce, and is virtually a tourist attraction in itself, with its beautifully arranged pyramids of sugary sweet delicacies, dates and nuts, olives and preserved lemons in glistening piles. There's good-quality fruit and veg here, as well as meat – the faint-hearted may choose to avoid the automated chicken-plucking machines at the rear of the hall.

✗ Ville Nouvelle

Promenade Palace MOROCCAN €
(Map p329; ☑ 0535 52 61 72; cnr Rue de Tarfaya & Sahat Lahri; breakfast Dh25, pizza Dh35; ☺ 8am-11pm; ☎) Spanking new with lots of shiny chrome and set over two floors as well as the pavement, this cafe-restaurant is just the place to try a Moroccan breakfast of *khlii* (preserved meat) and eggs. For later in the day, there's a range of pizzas, pastas and crêpes both sweet and savoury.

Palais de Poulet FAST FOOD €
(Palais Hassani; Map p329; Rue Tetouan; mains from Dh30; ☺ noon-10pm) Looking down from the Hôtel Rif towards Ave Hassan II, this is one of several good and cheap rotisserie places where you can fill up quickly on chicken, chips, bread and salad. Although you order from the table, pay at the counter inside.

Marhaba Restaurant MOROCCAN €
(Map p329; 23 Ave Mohammed V; tajines Dh25, Fri couscous Dh35; ☺ noon-10pm) This canteen-style place – the essence of cheap and cheerful – is hugely popular. While you can get tajines and the like, do as everyone else does and fill up on a bowl of *harira*, a plate of *makoda* (potato fritters) with bread and hard-boiled eggs – and get change from Dh15. We defy you to eat better for cheaper.

Restaurant Gambrinus MOROCCAN €
(Map p329; ☑ 0535 52 02 58; Zankat Omar ibn Ass; mains around Dh60, set menu Dh77; ☺ noon-3pm & 7-10pm) A good place for Moroccan food in colourful surroundings in the ville nouvelle, which is something of a surprise when you discover that the original Gambrinus was a Czech immigrant in 1914. It's perennially popular with locals, who come for the good range of tajines.

Restaurant Pizza Roma MOROCCAN €
(Map p329; Rue Accra; mains from Dh20; ☺ noon-10pm) Although the name suggests that pizzas are the speciality here, you could do far worse than load up on a filling plate of rotisserie chicken with rice and chips. An unassuming place, it's popular with female diners.

Le Pub FUSION €€
(Map p329; ☑ 0535 52 42 47; 20 Blvd Allal ben Abdallah; mains Dh90-150; ☺ 11am-midnight) If you don't mind stepping back into the '80s with disco music and coloured lights in the cave-like interior, Le Pub is a welcome change. The menu is split in two – half offering continental dishes, the other a Moroccan take on Asian food. We preferred the Asian dishes, but there are some good steaks too. As befits the name, alcohol is served.

Central Market SELF-CATERING
(Map p329; Ave Hassan II; ☺ 7am-noon) A good place to shop in the ville nouvelle, with a variety of fresh-food stalls, alcohol shops and various imported foodstuffs.

🍺 Drinking

It's a popular adage that Meknès has more bars than any other Moroccan city, and if all you're after is a quick bottle of Flag beer, then you won't lack for options (in the ville nouvelle, that is). Many are grouped around Blvd Allal ben Abdallah, but are generally pretty seedy affairs, designed for serious drinking and smoking, with women not at all welcomed.

The hotel bars are often more amenable, as well as licensed restaurants. Le Pub is, appropriately, one of the nicer places to get a drink – slump in a comfy chair, drink at the bar itself, or head downstairs to smoke a sheesha and catch some live music on weekends.

The ville nouvelle is the place to go for relaxed cafe culture, especially on and around Ave Mohammed V and the pedestrianised area around Cinema Camera. Those following are female-friendly as far as Moroccan cafes go.

Café Tulipe
CAFE

(Map p329; Rue de Tarfaya; ⊗7am-10pm; ☎) Just off the main road, the Tulipe has a large shady terrace and modern interior; it's one of the most pleasant cafes in which to kill an hour or two.

Café Opera
CAFE

(Map p329; 7 Ave Mohammed V; ⊗7am-10pm) Airy and old-fashioned, this grand cafe is a classic, and among the most popular for Moroccan men to sip their mint tea. Sitting outside and people-watching is a great breakfast pastime.

☆ Entertainment

The Institut Français (Map p325; ☎0535 51 58 51; inst.fr.mek@aim.net.ma; Rue Ferhat Hachad; ⊗8.30am-noon & 2.30-6.30pm Mon-Sat) is the centre of Meknès' cultural life, with films, plays, concerts and exhibitions.

🔒 Shopping

While the souqs of Meknès aren't as extensive as those of Fez or Marrakesh, the lack of hassle can make them a relaxed place to potter around looking for souvenirs. A particular speciality of Meknès is silver damascene, where metalwork is intricately inlaid with silver wire.

Centre Artisanale
ARTS & CRAFTS

(Map p326; Ave Zine el-Abidine Riad; ⊗9am-1pm & 3-7pm Mon-Sat) This is the place to go if you want to get an idea of what to look for and how much to spend. Quality is high, but prices are fixed.

Pottery Stalls
ARTS & CRAFTS

(Map p326; ⊗9am-10pm) Set up on the western side of Pl el-Hedim.

Pavillon des Idrissides
ARTS & CRAFTS

(Map p326; ⊗10am-10pm) The ground floor is set over for handicrafts, and is good for browsing.

ℹ Information

INTERNET ACCESS

Quick Net (Map p329; 28 Rue Emir Abdelkader; per hr Dh6; ⊗9am-10pm)

MEDICAL SERVICES

Hôpital Moulay Ismail (Map p325; ☎0535 52 28 05; off Ave des FAR)

Night Pharmacy (Map p329; Rue de Paris; ⊗6pm-9am)

Pharmacy el-Fath (Map p326; Pl el-Hedim; ⊗8.30am-6pm Mon-Thu & Sat, 8.30am-noon Fri)

MONEY

There are plenty of banks with ATMs both in the ville nouvelle (mainly on Ave Hassan II and Ave Mohammed V) and the medina (Rue Sekkakine).

BMCE (Map p329; 98 Ave des FAR; ⊗9am-4pm) An after-hours exchange office on the southeast side of the ville nouvelle.

POST

Main Post Office (Map p329; Pl de l'Istiqlal; ⊗8am-4pm) The parcel office is in the same building, around the corner on Rue Tetouan.

Post Office (Map p326; Rue Dar Smen; ⊗8am-4pm) In the medina.

TOURIST INFORMATION

Délégation Régionale du Tourisme (Map p329; ☎0535 52 44 26; Pl de l'Istiqlal; ⊗8.30am-4.30pm Mon-Fri, 8-11.30am Sat) Limited tourist information and pamphlets.

TRAVEL AGENCIES

Carlson Wagonlit (Map p329; ☎0535 52 19 95; 1 Rue Ghana) A source for air, ferry and coach tickets.

RAM (Map p329; ☎0535 52 09 63; 7 Ave Mohammed V) Handles tickets for all major airlines.

ℹ Getting There & Away

BUS

The CTM bus station (Map p325; ☎0535 52 25 85; Ave des FAR) is about 500m east of the junction with Ave Mohammed V. The main bus station lies just outside Bab el-Khemis, west of the medina. It has a left-luggage office and the usual snack stands.

CTM departures include Casablanca (Dh90, four hours, six daily) via Rabat (Dh55, two hours), Fez and Marrakesh (Dh155, eight hours, twice daily), Tangier (Dh90, five hours, five daily), Oujda (Dh130, 7½ hours, daily) via Taza (Dh70, three hours), Er-Rachidia (Dh120, 5½ hours, three daily), and two buses to Nador (Dh130, five hours).

Slightly cheaper than CTM, other buses serve the following destinations from numbered windows in the main bus station:

No 2 Midelt, Er-Rachidia, Ouarzazate and Rissani (daily)

No 4 Rabat and Casablanca (hourly 5.30am to 4pm)

No 6 Tangier (seven daily), Tetouan via Chefchaouen (four daily), Ouezzane (two daily)

No 7 Fez (hourly 5am to 6pm), Taza (one daily), Oujda (four daily) and Nador (four daily)

No 8 Moulay Idriss (hourly 8am to 6pm)

TAXI

The principal grand-taxi rank is a dirt lot next to the bus station at Bab el-Khemis. There are regular departures to Fez (Dh20, one hour), Ifrane (Dh28, one hour), Azrou (Dh28, one hour) and Rabat (Dh50, 90 minutes). Grands taxis for Moulay Idriss (Dh15, 20 minutes) leave from opposite the Institut Français – this is also the place to organise round trips to Volubilis.

TRAIN

Although Meknès has two train stations, head for the more convenient El-Amir Abdelkader, two blocks east of Ave Mohammed V. There are 15 daily trains to Fez (Dh20, 45 minutes), four of which continue to Taza (Dh56, 3½ hours) and three to Oujda (Dh130, 6½ hours). Twelve go to Casablanca (Dh90, 3½ hours) via Rabat (Dh65, 2¼ hours). There are eight direct services to Marrakesh (Dh174, seven hours). For Tangier, there are three direct trains (Dh85, four hours), or take a westbound train and change at Sidi Kacem or Mechra Bel Ksiri.

ⓘ Getting Around

BUS

Overcrowded city buses ply the route between the medina and ville nouvelle. The most useful are bus 2 (Bab el-Mansour to Blvd Allal ben Abdallah, returning to the medina along Ave Mohammed V) and bus 7 (Bab el-Mansour to the CTM bus station). Tickets are Dh3.

TAXI

Urban grands taxis (silver-coloured Mercedes Benz with black roofs) link the ville nouvelle and the medina, charging Dh2.50 per seat or Dh15 for the whole taxi. Pale-blue petits taxis use the meter: from El-Amir Abdelkader train station to the Bab el-Mansour expect to pay around Dh10.

A more touristy way to get around the medina is by calèche, available for hire on Pl el-Hedim and outside the Mausoleum of Moulay Ismail. They charge around Dh70 per hour.

Volubilis (Oualili)   وليلي

The Roman ruins of Volubilis sit in the middle of a fertile plain about 33km north of Meknès. The city is the best preserved archaeological site in Morocco and was declared a Unesco World Heritage Site in 1997. Its most amazing features are its many beautiful mosaics preserved in situ. The new Visitor Centre & Museum was on the point of opening at the time of our visit.

Volubilis can easily be combined with nearby Moulay Idriss to make a fantastic day trip from Meknès. The guides on site conduct good one-hour tours for around Dh150. Most speak decent enough English to explain the site in detail. Many official guides in Fez and Meknès are also knowledgable about the site.

In the heat of a summer day, the sun can be incredibly fierce at Volubilis, so bring a hat and plenty of water. Spring is the ideal season, when wildflowers blossom amid the abandoned stones, and the surrounding fields are at their greenest. The best time to visit is either first thing in the morning or late afternoon, when you're more likely to have the place to yourself, with just the guardian's donkey grazing among the ruins. At dusk, when the last rays of the sun light the ancient columns, Volubilis is at its most magical.

History

Excavations indicate that the site was originally settled by Carthaginian traders in the 3rd century BC. One of the Roman Empire's most remote outposts, Volubilis was annexed in about AD 40. According to some historians, Rome imposed strict controls on what could and could not be produced in its North African possessions, according to the needs of the empire. One result was massive deforestation and the large-scale planting of wheat around Volubilis. At its peak, it is estimated that the city housed up to 20,000 people. The site's most impressive monuments were built in the 2nd and 3rd centuries, including the triumphal arch, capitol, baths and basilica.

Volubilis

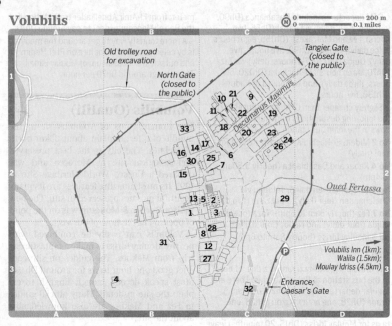

As the neighbouring Berber tribes began to reassert themselves, so the Romans abandoned Volubilis around 280. Nevertheless, the city's population of Berbers, Greeks, Jews and Syrians continued to speak Latin right up until the arrival of Islam. Moulay Idriss found sanctuary here in the 8th century, before moving his capital to Fez. Volubilis continued to be inhabited until the 18th century, when its marble was plundered for Moulay Ismail's palaces in Meknès, and its buildings were finally felled by the Lisbon earthquake of 1755.

◎ Sights

Roman Ruins   RUINS
(admission Dh10; ☺8am-sunset) Only about half of the 40-hectare site has been excavated. A major on-site museum displaying Volubilis' most celebrated finds was about to open when we visited, and will eventually house the prized discoveries (including some fine bronzes) currently in Rabat's archaeology museum.

Although parts of certain buildings are roped off, you are free to wander the site at will. Bar a couple of vague signboards, there's little in the way of signposting or information on what you're actually seeing. It's well worth considering taking a guide,

especially if you're pressed for time. If you prefer to wander on your own, allow at least two hours to see the essentials, and up to a full day for the real enthusiast.

The better-known monuments are in the northern part of the site, although the entrance is in the south. Once over the Oued Fertassa, the path leads onto the ridge and through the residential quarter.

➡ Ancient Volubilis

Although the least remarkable part of the site, the **olive presses** here indicate the economic basis of ancient Volubilis, much as the plentiful olive groves in the surrounding area do today. Wealthy homeowners had private olive presses.

➡ Buildings

Next to the **House of Orpheus** are the remains of **Galen's Baths**. Although largely broken, they clearly show the highly developed underfloor heating in this Roman hammam. Opposite the steam room are the communal toilets – where citizens could go about their business and have a chat at the same time.

The capitol, basilica and 1300-sq-metre forum are, typically, built on a high point. The **capitol**, dedicated to the Triad of Jupiter, Juno and Minerva, dates back to AD 218; the **basilica** and **forum** lie immediately

Volubilis

to its north. The reconstructed columns of the basilica are usually topped with storks' nests – an iconic Volubilis image if the birds are nesting at the time of your visit. Around the forum is a series of plinths carved with Latin inscriptions that would have supported statues of the great and good. Keep your eyes out for the carved stone drain-hole cover – an understated example of Roman civil engineering.

The marble **Triumphal Arch** was built in 217 in honour of Emperor Caracalla and his mother, Julia Domna. The arch, which was originally topped with a bronze chariot, was reconstructed in the 1930s, and the mistakes made then were rectified in the 1960s. The hillock to the east provides a splendid view over the entire site.

➡ Houses with Mosaics

The **House of Orpheus** is the finest and largest of the homes, containing a mosaic

of Orpheus charming animals by playing the lute, and a dolphin mosaic in the dining room. Note that the private hammam has a caldarium (hot room) with visible steam pipes, a tepidarium (warm room) and a frigidarium (cold room), as well as a solarium.

On the left just before the triumphal arch are a couple more roped-off mosaics. One, in the **House of the Acrobat**, depicts an athlete being presented with a trophy for winning a desultory race, a competition in which the rider had to dismount and jump back on his horse as it raced along.

From the arch, the ceremonial road, **Decumanus Maximus**, stretches up the slope to the northeast. The houses lining it on either side contain the best mosaics on the site. The first on the far side of the arch is known as the **House of the Ephebus** and contains a fine mosaic of Bacchus in a chariot drawn by panthers.

Next along, the **House of the Columns** is so named because of the columns around the interior court – note their differing styles, which include spirals. Adjacent to this is the **House of the Knight** with its incomplete mosaic of Bacchus and Ariadne. The naked Ariadne has suffered somewhat from the attentions of admirers.

The next three houses are named for their excellent mosaics: the **House of the Labours of Hercules**, the **House of Dionysus and the Four Seasons** and the **House of the Nymphs Bathing**. The first is almost a circular comic strip, recounting the Twelve Labours. Several of Hercules' heroic feats were reputed to have occurred in Morocco, making him a popular figure at the time.

The best mosaics are saved until last. Cross the Decumanus Maximus and head for the lone cypress tree, which marks the **House of Venus**, home of King Juba II. There are two particularly fine mosaics here, appropriately with semi-romantic themes. The first is the **Abduction of Hylas by the Nymphs**, an erotic composition showing Hercules' lover Hylas being lured away from his duty by two beautiful nymphs. The second mosaic is **Diana Bathing**. The goddess was glimpsed in her bath by the hunter Acteon, whom she turned into a stag as punishment. Acteon can be seen sprouting horns, about to be chased by his own pack of hounds – the fate of mythical peeping toms everywhere. A third mosaic from this house,

IMPERIAL CITIES, MIDDLE ATLAS & THE EAST VOLUBILIS (OUALILI)

of Venus in the Waves, can be seen in the Kasbah Museum in Tangier.

🛏 Sleeping & Eating

Oualila
GUESTHOUSE €

(📱0662 52 81 05; www.walila.com; Oualili; 6 people Dh750; 🅿) This historic old house is let as a whole and has three bedrooms; new rooms and a restaurant are currently being built. It's all set on a farm with orchards, vegetables and animals. You can get your hands dirty helping out, ride mules into the hills and tuck into the home-grown food at dinnertime.

Volubilis Inn
HOTEL €€€

(📱0535 54 44 05; hotelvolubilisinn@gmail.com; Rte de Meknès; d incl breakfast from Dh1050; 🅿✳🎇) On a rise above the Roman site, this huge four-star hotel has rooms with good views to the Volubilis ruins and countryside. There are several terraces with a couple of restaurants (mains from Dh85) and a noisy bar – the common parts are quite grand although rooms lapse into 'airport hotel' mood, and lack atmosphere. Ask for reductions out of season.

❶ Getting There & Away

The simplest and quickest way to get here from Meknès is to hire a grand taxi for the return trip. A half-day outing should cost Dh350, with a couple of hours at the site and a stop at Moulay Idriss (worth an overnight stay in itself).

A cheaper alternative is to take a shared grand taxi from near Meknès' Institut Français to Moulay Idriss (Dh10) and then hire a grand taxi to take you to Volubilis (Dh40 complete hire). If the weather isn't too hot, it's a lovely 45-minute walk between Moulay Idriss and Volubilis.

There are no buses to Volubilis.

Moulay Idriss مولاي ادريس

The picturesque whitewashed town of Moulay Idriss sits astride two green hills in a cradle of mountains slightly less than 5km from Volubilis, and is one of the country's most important pilgrimage sites. It's named for Moulay Idriss, a great-grandson of the Prophet Mohammed, the founder of the country's first real dynasty, and Morocco's most revered saint. His tomb is at the heart of the town, and is the focus of the country's largest *moussem* every August.

Moulay Idriss fled Mecca in the late 8th century in the face of persecution at the hands of the recently installed Abbasid caliphate, which was based in Baghdad. Idriss settled at Volubilis, where he converted the locals to Islam, and made himself their leader, establishing the Idrissid dynasty.

Moulay Idriss' holy status kept it closed to non-Muslims until the mid-20th century, and its pious reputation continues to deter some travellers. However, the embargo on non-Muslims staying overnight in the town has long disappeared, and local family-run guesthouses have started to open to cater to visitors. Those who do stay are invariably charmed – it's a pretty and relaxed town with a centre free of carpet shops and traffic, and offers a chance to see Morocco as Moroccans experience it.

The main road leading from the bus/grands-taxis stand to the square (Pl Mohammed VI) has a Banque Populaire ATM, and a couple of internet cafes.

⊙ Sights

Mausoleum of Moulay Idriss   MAUSOLEUM

Although this twin-hill town is a veritable maze of narrow lanes and dead ends, it is not hard to find the few points of interest. The first is the Mausoleum of Moulay Idriss, the object of veneration and the reason for the country's greatest annual *moussem* in late August. An important pilgrimage for many, including the royals, it is accompanied by *fantasias,* markets and music. It's said locally that five pilgrimages to Moulay Idriss during the *moussem* equals one haj to Mecca.

From the main road (where buses and grands taxis arrive), head uphill and bear right where the road forks. You'll quickly find yourself on the wide square of Pl Mohammed VI, lined with cafes – a great place to sit and watch the pace of life. At the top of the square is the entrance to the mausoleum via a three-arched gateway at the top of some steps, surrounded by shops selling religious goods to pilgrims. Not far inside there's a barrier, beyond which non-Muslims cannot pass. Moulay Ismail created this pilgrimage site by building the mausoleum and moving the body of Moulay Idriss, in a successful attempt to rally the support of the faithful.

From here, head left up into the maze of streets to find your way to a couple of vantage points that give good panoramic views of the mausoleum, the town and the surrounding country. Plenty of guides will offer their services – you can get an informative, entertaining tour for as little as Dh30.

If you don't feel like being guided, head back to the fork and take the road heading uphill, signposted to the Municipalité. Near the top of the hill, just before the Agfa sign, take the cobbled street to the right. As you climb up you'll notice the only **cylindrical minaret** in Morocco, built in 1939. At the top of the hill ask a local for the **grande terrasse** or **petite terrasse**. These terraces provide vantage points high above the mausoleum and most of the town.

🛏 Sleeping & Eating

Rooms are at a premium during the *moussem*, so book in advance. The cheap food stands around the main square are all good for a quick snack. The grilled chicken with salad is something of a local speciality.

Dar Zerhoune GUESTHOUSE €
(📞 0535 54 43 71; www.buttonsinn.com; 42 Derb Zouak Tazgha; s/d/tr incl breakfast Dh200/300/500; 🛜) To the right uphill from the mausoleum, this gem of a guesthouse has a welcoming flavour. There are a variety of rooms and a couple of terraces (including a view to Volubilis), where you can take lazy breakfasts and opt in for a delicious home-cooked lunch or dinner. Tours, bike hire and cooking lessons are also offered.

Dar Al Andaloussiya Diyafa GUESTHOUSE €
(📞 0535 54 47 49; www.maisondhote-volubilis.com; Derb Zouak Tazgh; s/d incl breakfast Dh200/300; ✳) 'Diyafa' means hospitality, and you'll certainly find it at this friendly house. There's plenty of traditional decor and fabrics, as well as family photos: look out for the one of King Mohammed VI inaugurating the house. Rooms are generous and good value. A dinner menu is available from Dh75.

Hotel Diyar Timnay HOTEL €
(📞 0535 54 44 00; amzday@menara.ma; 7 Aïn Rjal; s/d/tr incl breakfast Dh160/240/300; ✳) Near the grands-taxis stands, this is the town's only hotel. It's unexpectedly large when you get inside, with good but unflashy rooms. Most are en suite, although a few have separate (but still private) bathrooms. The restaurant (mains Dh50 to Dh60) does a roaring lunchtime trade with tour groups visiting Volubilis, and has great views to the archaeological site.

La Colombe Blanche GUESTHOUSE €
(📞 0535 54 45 96; www.maisondhote-zerhoune.ma; 21 Derb Zouak Tazgha; s/d incl breakfast Dh205/325; ✳🛜) A traditional home turned guesthouse – the family occupies the ground floor while guests are up above. It also bills itself as a restaurant, with home-cooked meals available on request (menu Dh85). In good weather eat on the terrace, with views to Volubilis. At the mausoleum, turn right uphill and follow the signs.

⭐ **Dar Ines** GUESTHOUSE €€
(📞 0535 54 49 07; www.dar-ines.com; 57 Hay Tazga, Derb Amjout; d incl breakfast from Dh440; 🛜) 🍃 This grand house on the edge of the medina has been beautifully renovated and has wonderful views. There are seven rooms around two staircases, with plenty of nooks and crannies for relaxing. All rooms have solar-heated showers and there's a hammam and restaurant. The owners offer craft courses as well as trekking in the nearby mountains.

ℹ Getting There & Away

Grands taxis (Dh15, 20 minutes) to Moulay Idriss leave Meknès from outside the Institut Français, and buses (Dh8) leave from the Meknès bus station every hour from 8am to 6pm. Taxis leave Moulay Idriss from a stand at the bottom of town on the main road.

If you have your own transport, you might consider continuing to Fez via Nzala-des-Béni-Ammar, or to Meknès via the village of El-Merhasiyne. Both routes have wonderful views and eventually join back up with the main roads. As the road surfaces are very rough, these drives are really only possible in summer unless you have a 4WD.

MIDDLE ATLAS

Ifrane   ا فران

As foreign tourists head to the medinas for a taste of the 'real' Morocco, Moroccan tourists find more favour with places like Ifrane. Tidy, ordered and modern, it feels more like Switzerland relocated to the Middle Atlas than North Africa.

The French built Ifrane in the 1930s, deliberately trying to recreate an alpine-style resort. It has neat red-roofed houses, blooming flower beds and lake-studded parks, all kept impeccably tidy. Many major employers (including the government) maintain apartment complexes here for their vacationing workers, and it's a popular summer day trip for picnickers. In the winter, the affluent flock here to ski, and hoi polloi come for the pure fun of throwing snowballs at each other. Outside the holiday season, Ifrane's population is boosted by the rich, trendy students of the town's prestigious Al-Akhawayn University.

The main road from Meknès is called Blvd Mohammed V and it runs through Ifrane from west to east. This is where you will find the bus station, west of the centre, and the tourist office, at the intersection with Ave des Tilluels. Most of the cafes and hotels are clustered in the centre along Rue de la Cascade and Ave de la Poste.

⊙ Sights

Al-Akhawayn University UNIVERSITY
The campus of Al-Akhawayn University is at the northern end of town, and is a squeaky-clean showcase of Moroccan education. It was founded in 1995 by Morocco's King Hassan II and King Fahd of Saudi Arabia, and aims to promote tolerance between faiths. For now, only the rich and beautiful need apply – the car parks are full of flash cars, and the air trills with the most fashionable of mobile-phone ring tones. Lessons in English are based on the American system and there are US staff and exchange students. You can wander into the well-kept grounds – weekday afternoons are the best, as there are plenty of students who are usually willing to show you around.

Stone Lion MONUMENT
Ifrane's other landmark is the stone lion that sits on a patch of grass near the Hôtel Chamonix. It was carved by a German soldier during WWII, when Ifrane was used briefly as a prisoner-of-war camp, and commemorates the last wild Atlas lion, which was shot near here in the early 1920s. Having your picture taken with the lion is something of a ritual for day-trippers.

🛌 Sleeping

Hotel prices in Ifrane reflect the town's affluence, and its year-round popularity means demand for rooms runs high.

Campsite CAMPGROUND €
(☑ 0535 56 60 25; Blvd Mohammed V; camping per person D10, plus per car/tent/campervan Dh10/30/50; ⊙ closed winter) Leafy campsite just west of the bus station.

Hôtel Chamonix HOTEL €€
(☑ 0535 56 60 28; contact@lechamonix. com; Ave de la Mare Verte; s/d/tr incl breakfast Dh468/535/690; 🌐🛰) This three-star place is well maintained and centrally located. Rooms are bright and spacious, if a little bland, with attached bathrooms and central heating. There's a decent restaurant and bar (which turns into a nightclub on weekends), and the hotel can rent out ski equipment.

Hotel les Tilleuls HOTEL €€
(☑ 0535 56 66 58; hoteltilleuls@gmail.com; cnr Ave des Tilleuls & Rue de la Cascade; s/d Dh300/450) 🏷 The cheapest hotel in Ifrane is this old institution on the corner of the main square. The rooms are large and come with bathroom and TV, but it's all very run down.

★ Hôtel Perce-Neige HOTEL €€€
(☑ 0535 56 64 04; fax 0535 56 71 16; Rue des Asphodelles; s/d/tr Dh650/810/960; 🌐) A pretty accommodation option situated about 200m southeast of the centre in garden surroundings. The rooms could be a bit bigger, but they're very comfortable and come with satellite TV and bathroom. Some have a balcony, and those at the front can be a bit noisy. The licensed restaurant is a good dining option (set menus Dh150). The shop in the lobby sells paintings by local artists.

Michlifen Ifrane LUXURY HOTEL €€€
(☑ 0535 86 40 00; www.michlifenifrane.com; r from Dh4000; 🅿🌐🛰📶) Overlooking Ifrane from the north, this oversized ski lodge is one of Morocco's most luxurious hotels. Local cedar is evident throughout the rather dark interior, with rooms echoing a luxury chalet. The attention to detail goes as far as the carefully selected art decorating the walls. There are two pools: one on the terrace for summer, and another indoors for winter, along with a spa, gym and tennis courts.

🍴 Eating & Drinking

Several cafes and cheap eats cluster around the bus station area, where you'll also find the market for fresh produce.

Café Restaurant la Rose MOROCCAN €
(☑ 0555 56 62 15; 7 Rue de la Cascade; mains around Dh80, pizzas Dh60; ⊙ noon-3pm & 7-10pm) This small restaurant has always been popular in town for its Middle Atlas trout and traditional Moroccan fare.

IFRANE NATIONAL PARK

This 500-sq-metre park encompasses Ifrane and Azrou as well as numerous Berber villages. It is known for its Atlas cedar trees and the Barbary macaque, an endangered species, and some 30 other mammals. Birdlife is exceptional and includes red kite, marbled teal, and common kestrel. Two Ramsar wetland sites and the lakes **Dayet Ifrah** and **Dayet Aoua** support ruddy shelduck and various coots.

The **Ifrane National Park Office** (Direction Provinciale des Eaux et Fôrets et de la Lutte contre la Désertification; ☑0535 56 12 96; Blvd Hassan II, Azrou; ☻9am-4.30pm Mon-Fri) is in Azrou and if it's manned, you can pick up a map and information.

Lakes Circuit (Route des Lacs)

A pretty diversion north of Ifrane is the lake circuit around Dayet Aoua. Signposted off the main Fez road 17km north of Ifrane, the route winds for 60km through the lake country between the P24 and P20. If you don't have your own vehicle, hiring a grand taxi in Ifrane for a tour of a couple of hours should cost around Dh300. That said, the joy of the area is to get out and walk along the lake shore and enjoy the tranquillity of the scenery. This is an area made for hikers and mountain bikers.

Dayet Aoua is surrounded by woodlands, and the whole area is notably rich in bird life. Keep an eye out in particular for raptors, including booted eagles, black and red kites and harriers. The lake attracts significant numbers of ducks and waders, including crested coot, woodpeckers, tree creepers and nuthatches, which flit among the trees around the southeastern end of the lake.

The lake is a popular picnic destination for families on weekends, but during the week you'll get the place largely to yourself. Beyond Dayet Aoua, the road loops east and then south, skirting past Dayet Ifrah and the even smaller lake of Dayet Hachlaf. The road is decent, but is liable to be snowbound in winter.

If you want to linger longer, there's a good sleeping option at Dayet Aoua: the delightfully rustic **Le Gîte Dayet Aoua** (☑0535 61 05 75; www.gite-dayetaoua.com; r Dh300; ☒) offers comfortable rooms with bathroom, all decorated in local Berber style. Have a few days of internet detox (there's no w-ifi here) and go cycling, horse-riding or walking with a guide. There's a pool, too. Food is Amazigh cuisine (lunch Dh120).

Exploring the Azrou Area

'**Ain Leuh** is a pretty village 25km southwest of Azrou within the Ifrane National Park. The drive here is through thick forest of cedar and holm oak, so you might just be tempted to stop your vehicle anywhere and hit the trail. Instead, take in the large Tuesday weekly souq (the best day to get public transport), which attracts market-goers from around the region, particularly from the Beni M'Guild Berbers. It's a pleasant climb through the rough streets of flat-roofed houses to a waterfall in the hills above.

Around 20km south of 'Ain Leuh, an even more picturesque walk leads to the water-falls at the **Sources de l'Oum-er-Rbia**. Leave the road at Lac Ouiouane and follow the path down past a number of farmhouses to a small valley, where a bridge crosses the Rbia river. From here, it's about a 15-minute walk to the gorge where several dozen springs break out of the rocks to form a series of waterfalls. There are a couple of cafes where you can take a rest.

It's possible to incorporate these walks into a much longer circuit trek of up to six days from 'Ain Leuh. For more information, contact official local mountain guides, brothers **Boujmaa & Saleh Boudaoud** (☑0663 76 08 25) of the Association des Guides de Montagnes du Moyen Atlas. A one-day walk with a guide costs Dh600 per person including a picnic lunch, and prices drop if there are more in the group. For two to seven days, count on Dh1000 per person for the guide and a mule to carry baggage and equipment. *Gîtes* and homestays (Dh300 to Dh700 per person) within the park provide ample opportunity to experience the local cuisine and Berber way of life.

La Paix
CAFE €

(Ave de la Mare Verte; ⊕9am-10pm) La Paix is situated just up from the Hôtel Chamonix. Among its features is a wide glass frontage, perfect for people-watching over a breakfast of croissants and coffee.

Complexe Touristique
Aguelman
CAFE, MOROCCAN €

(Ave Hassan II; entrance Dh5; meals Dh80-100; ⊕9am-midnight) Overlooking the artificial lake on the main road and opposite the lion statue, this is a huddle of options under one roof, aimed squarely at the local tourist market. There's a more formal dining room with Moroccan dishes for the evenings, a bar, and a simple diner with pizza, pasta, omelettes and sandwiches. In fine weather, eat at the tables outside overlooking the water.

❶ Information

BMCE (Ave de la Mare Verte; ⊕8.30am-4pm) One of several banks with ATMs on this road.

Délégation Provinciale du Tourism (Tourism Office; ☑0535 56 68 21; Ave Prince Moulay Abdallah; ⊕8.30am-4.30pm Mon-Fri)

Pharmacie Mischliffen (Rue de la Cascade; ⊕8.30am-6pm)

Post Office (Ave de la Poste; ⊕8am-4pm) Has an ATM.

❶ Getting There & Away

The bus station is next to the market, west of the town centre. There's also a brand-new bus station south of town that was not yet in use at the time of our visit, but it's here the grands taxis congregate. They go to Fez or Meknès (Dh28) and Azrou (Dh8).

Each morning and evening, CTM buses leave for Marrakesh (Dh155, eight hours) via Beni Mellal. There's a daily 9am departure for Casablanca (Dh120, five hours) via Meknès (Dh25, one hour) and Rabat (Dh90, 3½ hours).

Non-CTM buses are more frequent but Ifrane is not a regular stop: ask to be dropped off.

Azrou
أزرو

The Berber town of Azrou is an important market centre sitting at the junction of the roads to Fez, Meknès, Midelt and Khenifra. Deep in the Middle Atlas it sits amid stunning scenery, with sweeping views of cedar and pine forests, and high meadows that burst into flower every spring. Thoroughly unhurried, it's a relaxing spot to wind down if you've had too much of big cities.

Azrou (Great Rock) takes its name from the outcrop marking the town's western boundary. The big **Ennour mosque**, beautifully finished with local cedar, provides another handy landmark.

Azrou hosts one of the region's largest weekly souqs, and is particularly known for its Berber carpets, so timing your visit for market day (Tuesday) is a good idea. A museum of the Middle Atlas has been under construction for some years, yet its final opening seems permanently delayed. It's probably better instead to just head out of town to enjoy the surrounding countryside; there are plenty of day walks that take in the mountain air and great views. You might even spot a few of the local Barbary apes.

🛏 Sleeping

For its size, Azrou has a surprising number of sleeping options, with more being added out of town along the Fez road (look out for the Disneyland-esque 'castle' that attracts Emirati tourists).

Hôtel Les Cèdres
HOTEL €

(☑0535 56 23 26; Pl Mohammed V; s/d/tr Dh75/105/160, with bathroom Dh115/160/220; ☎) Built in 1925, this hotel still has plenty of interesting period features and a hint of deco styling in its fixtures. It's clean and simple, and has a certain faded charm. Rooms are good value – all have sinks, and some have en-suite bathrooms. The verandah is a great place to relax with mint tea, and there's a good restaurant.

Auberge du Dernier Lion de
l'Atlas
GUESTHOUSE €

(☑0535 56 18 68; www.dernierlionatlas.ma; 16 Rte de Meknès; s/d/tr Dh225/300/400; ☎) A bit of a way from the centre of Azrou, this is nonetheless a good option, with pleasant rooms and a friendly atmosphere. If you're basing yourself in the Middle Atlas area, the owner is a mine of local information. Breakfast (Dh25) and evening meals (Dh70) are available. There's no signpost, so look out for a large green villa on the right travelling from town.

Hôtel le Panorama
HOTEL €

(☑0535 56 20 10; www.hotelpanorama.ma; Hay Ajelabe; s/d/tr Dh274/330/435) Built in a grand alpine-chalet style, Azrou's most comfortable hotel is in a quiet wooded spot a short walk northeast of town, with a pleasant gar-

Azrou

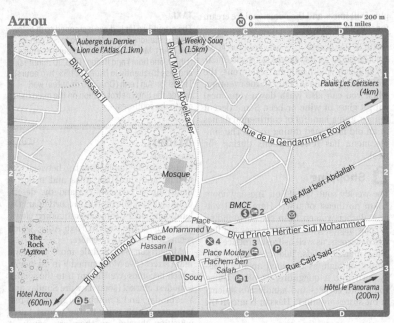

N   0 ———————— 200 m
     0 ———————— 0.1 miles

Auberge du Dernier Lion de l'Atlas (1.1km)

Weekly Souq (1.5km)

Blvd Hassan II

Blvd Moulay Abdelkader

Palais Les Cerisiers (4km)

Rue de la Gendarmerie Royale

Mosque

Rue Allal ben Abdallah

BMCE $ 2

Place Mohammed V

Blvd Prince Héritier Sidi Mohammed

Place Hassan II

8 4

3

P

The Rock 'Azrou'

Blvd Mohammed V

MEDINA

Place Moulay Hachem ben Salah

Rue Caid Said

Souq

1

Hôtel Azrou (600m)

5

Hôtel le Panorama (200m)

den. Rooms are compact with balconies, but it's all in need of a revamp. The restaurant is fair.

Hôtel Salame   HOTEL €

(☑ 0535 56 25 62; salame_hotel@yahoo.fr; Pl Moulay Hachem ben Salah; s/d Dh150/200) This small hotel is an exceedingly pleasant place to stay. Small, cute rooms are nicely presented with a smattering of traditional Berber decoration, and you will be made welcome by the friendly staff. Shared bathrooms are kept constantly clean, with 24-hour hot showers (Dh10).

Hôtel Beau-Séjour   HOTEL €

(☑ 0535 56 06 92; beau-sejour-hotel@yahoo.fr; 45 Pl Moulay Hachem ben Salah; s/d/tr Dh70/100/180, cold/hot showers Dh5/10) Another decent budget option, rooms here are pretty simple and unaffected. The roof terrace has good views across Azrou.

Palais des Cerisiers   HOTEL €€€

(Rue Cedre Gouraud btwn Azrou & Ifrane; d incl breakfast & dinner from Dh1250, ste/family apt Dh1800; P ❄ 🛜 🏊) A smart upmarket choice, this hotel is surrounded by cherry blossoms in spring. Rooms are spacious and comfortable with heating, and suites have a fireplace.

Azrou

🛏 Sleeping

1	Hôtel Beau-Séjour	C3
2	Hôtel Les Cèdres	C2
3	Hôtel Salame	C3

🍴 Eating

4	Café Boulangerie Bilal	C3
	Hôtel Les Cèdres	(see 2)

🛍 Shopping

5	Ensemble Artisanal	A3

There's a tennis court, gym and spa, and an elegant restaurant.

✖ Eating

Hôtel Les Cèdres   MOROCCAN €

(☑ 0535 56 23 26; Pl Mohammed V; mains around Dh50; ☉ noon-3pm & 7.30-10pm) A hotel restaurant with a 1920s dining room and log fire, and our favourite eating place in Azrou. The local trout is always good, plus there are some more unusual dishes like rabbit tajine.

Café Boulangerie Bilal   CAFE €

(Pl Mohammed V; sandwiches Dh25; ☉ 8am-10pm) This is an always-busy cafe with upstairs seating, good sandwich and tajine options,

IMPERIAL CITIES, MIDDLE ATLAS & THE EAST   AZROU

plus fruit juices and the occasional ice cream for the hot weather.

Hôtel le Panorama
MOROCCAN, EUROPEAN €

(☑0535 56 20 10; Hay Ajelabe; set menu Dh130; ⊘7.30-10pm) Another hotel restaurant, the Hôtel le Panorama is better in the evenings, when you can also wash down your meal with a glass of wine or beer. Some decent tajines, and a handful of continental dishes in an old-fashioned dining room. The simple menu has fewer options during the week.

Shopping

The weekly souq is held on Tuesday about 1.5km northeast of town. Here you'll witness Berber women from the surrounding villages haggling with dealers over the flatweave carpets, as well as fresh produce and other market goods. Take care if it's been raining though, as the souq area can easily turn into a quagmire. At other times, you'll find carpets and handicrafts aplenty in the stores around Pl Hassan II and in the medina.

Ensemble Artisanal
ART, CRAFTS

(Blvd Mohammed V; ⊘8.30am-noon & 2.30-6pm Sat-Mon) This showroom has the usual fixed-price shop but also a number of craftspeople working on the premises – look out for the Middle Atlas carpets. There's a cafe on the roof terrace, too.

ℹ Information

BMCE (Pl Mohammed V; ⊘8.45am-6pm Mon-Thu, 8.45-11am Fri, 8.45am-noon Sat) *Bureau de change* and one of several ATMs on the square.

Post Office (Blvd Prince Héritier Sidi Mohammed; ⊘8am-4pm Mon-Fri)

ℹ Getting There & Away

Azrou is a crossroads, with one axis heading northwest to southeast from Meknès to Er-Rachidia, and the other northeast to Fez and southwest to Marrakesh.

BUS

CTM offers daily departures from the bus station on Blvd Moulay Abdelkader to Beni Mellal (Dh75, 4½ hours), Casablanca (Dh130, six hours), Fez (Dh40, 1½ hours), Marrakesh (Dh145, eight hours) and Meknès (Dh30, two hours).

Other cheaper companies have frequent daily departures to Fez (Dh20), Meknès (Dh18), Ifrane (Dh8), Midelt (Dh32) and Er-Rachidia (Dh75).

TAXI

The grand-taxi lot is down a stepped path below the bus station. Regular taxis go to Fez (Dh30, one hour), Meknès (Dh30, one hour), Khenifra (Dh30, one hour) and Ifrane (Dh8, 10 minutes), and less frequently to Midelt (Dh55, two hours). Those for 'Ain Leuh (Dh15, 20 minutes) wait beside the Shell petrol station on the main road out to the southwest.

Midelt
ميدلت

POP 47,000

Midelt sits in apple country between the Middle and the High Atlas and makes a handy break between Fez and the desert. Coming from the north in particular, the landscape offers some breathtaking views, especially of the eastern High Atlas, which seems to rise out of nowhere.

Midelt consists of little more than one main street (Ave Mohammed V in the north, which becomes Ave Hassan II to the south), a modest market (souq days are Sunday and Wednesday) and a number of oversized restaurants, which cater to the tourist buses whistling through on their way south. It makes a good base for some off-*piste* exploring of the Jebel Ayachi region.

◎ Sights

Kasbah Myriem
ARTS CENTRE

(Atelier de Tissages et Borderie; ☑0664 44 73 75; ⊘8am-noon & 2-6pm Mon-Thu & Sat & 9-11am Fri) If you're in the mood for carpets, this workshop, about 1.5km out of town, is worth a look. It assists Berber women develop their embroidery and weaving. The workshop provides looms and materials, as well as a simple place to work. Local girls – aged 15 or so – come here in order to learn these skills from more experienced women. Literacy lessons are also offered. Follow the signs from the main road, then enter behind the clinic.

While you are here, you may wish to peek into the monastery (⊘services 7.15am daily & 10am Sun), which is home to a few Franciscan monks. The grounds and chapel are a peaceful place to collect your thoughts. Ring the bell at the gate to the right of the workshop.

Kasbah des Noyers
KASBAH

The village of Berrem, 6km west of Midelt, is also known as the Kasbah des Noyers for the ancient walnut trees shading its environs. There's not much going on here, but the quaint village, with its colourful mosque and ancient earthen walls, makes a good destination for a day hike from Midelt. Follow the main path through the kasbah to the scenic overlook of the **Gorges des Berrem**. Hiring a grand taxi from Midelt costs about Dh50.

🛏 Sleeping

Auberge Jaafar
HOTEL €

(☑ 0535 58 34 15; Berrem; d incl breakfast Dh300, apt for up to 6 Dh500; P 🏊) This peaceful kasbah-style complex is about 6km west of Midelt through apple orchards, just past the village of Berrem. Rooms of all shapes and sizes are set up around terraces and blooming courtyards. Order during the day if you're going to eat in.

Hôtel Atlas
HOTEL €

(☑ 0535 58 29 38; 3 Rue Mohammed el-Amraoui; s/d/tr Dh60/120/150) This friendly pension is a fair budget option, with home-cooked food on request. Rooms are predictably simple, but clean, as are the shared bathrooms with squat toilets (hot showers cost Dh10).

★ Ksar Timnay Inter-Cultures
RESORT €€

(☑ 0535 58 34 34; www.ksar-timnay.com; btwn Zaida & Midelt; s/d half board Dh340/540, Riad Mimouna half board Dh450/650; P 🏊 🛜 🏊) Set in large leafy grounds with its own park and lake, this complex offers a wide range of accommodation from rooms to family apartments, some in the fancier Riad Mimouna, as well as camping and caravanning. Rooms are large and comfortable with air-conditioning, central heating and TV. There's superb birdwatching in the vicinity (Dupont's Larks being shy residents with a distinctive song). The owners are passionate about the region and offer excursions at Dh300 per person per day, as well as trekking to Jebel Masker (3265m) and Jebel Ayachi (3737m).

Riad Villa Midelt
GUESTHOUSE €€

(☑ 0535 36 08 51; www.hotel-riad-villa-midelt.com; 1 Pl Verte; s/d incl breakfast Dh450/600; P 🏊 🛜) In a garden setting, this large villa south of town offers spacious rooms, some with balconies. Breakfasts are enormous, and the friendly staff will whip up dinner for Dh350.

Hôtel Kasbah Asmaa
HOTEL €€

(☑ 0535 58 04 05; s/d half board Dh450/600; 🏊 🏊 🏊) About 3km south of Midelt, this large kasbah-style hotel announces that you're on the road south. It has fair rooms that were being refurbished on our visit, and an invit-

Midelt

ing pool at the bottom of the property, far away from the rooms so as not to be overlooked. The licensed restaurant is worth eating at, even for nonguests.

🍴 Eating

As usual, cheap eats and snacks are plentiful in the area around the bus station. There's also a produce market here.

Fast Food Tati-Sou
FAST FOOD €

(Rue Ezzerqutouni; meals Dh30; ⊙ noon-3pm, 7-9pm) Don't be fooled by the name: this is Midelt's best chicken. Dh30 gets you a quarter chicken with salad.

Complexe Touristique Le Pin
MOROCCAN €€

(☑ 0535 58 35 50; Ave Hassan II; mains Dh80; ⊙ noon-5pm year-round plus 7-10pm Apr-Aug; 🛜) This large lunchtime restaurant draws the coach groups, but you can easily escape the crowds in the garden, and the sizeable turnover ensures fresh meals, all served in generous portions. Alcohol is served. In the summer months it's open in the evenings for drinks and ice creams, and is a favourite with families.

ℹ Information

BMCI (Ave Hassan II; ☺8.45am-6pm Mon-Thu, 8.45-11am Fri, 8.45am-noon Sat) One of several banks with ATMs on this street.

Cybernet (Ave Hassan II; per hr Dh6; ☺8am-midnight)

Ksar Timnay Inter-Cultures (✆0535 58 34 34; www.ksar-timnay.com; Rte de Zaidia; ☺8am-8pm) About 15km north of Midelt, this is the best source of information – including trekking guides and 4WD rental – in the eastern High Atlas.

Post Office (off Ave Hassan II; ☺8am-4pm) South of the internet centre.

ℹ Getting There & Away

Midelt has two bus stations: one off Ave Mohammed V in town, and the new one 2km to the east of town. CTM services mostly run at night. There's an evening departure to Casablanca (Dh155, seven hours) via Rabat (Dh125, five hours), and to Rissani (Dh85, four hours) via Er-Rachidia (Dh50, two hours) and Erfoud (Dh75, 3½ hours). There are also night-time services for Azrou (Dh55, two hours), Meknès (Dh70, three hours) and Fez (Dh75, four hours).

Other buses cover the same routes at more sociable hours – Fez (Dh55, five hours) is serviced by six departures through the day.

Grands taxis run to Azrou (Dh45, two hours) and Er-Rachidia (Dh60, two hours).

Around Midelt

Midelt's location on the cusp of the eastern High Atlas makes it a great base for exploring. Off the main routes, roads are rough *pistes*, with many only really negotiable between May and October and even then only by 4WD. It's heaven for mountain bikers, as well as ideal hiking country. Ksar Timnay Inter-Cultures in Midelt will rent you a 4WD (with driver) for around Dh1000 – good value if there's a group of you.

Cirque Jaffar

The Cirque Jaffar winds through the foothills of Jebel Ayachi, 25km southwest of Midelt. It's a rough *piste*, and regular cars will grumble on the route in all seasons but the height of summer. The scenery is wonderful though – the dramatic crests of the Atlas, carpeted in places with cedar forest, and studded with tiny Berber mountain villages.

From Midelt, take the Zaïdia road for about 10km and turn off at the signpost for the village of Aït Oum Gam. Then follow the signs to Matkan Tounfit. After that the route loops back through Tattiouine and on to Rte S3424 back to Midelt. Allow a day for the whole 80km circuit. Ksar Timnay Inter-Cultures offers this day trip for Dh350 per person including meals.

If walking is more your thing, and you have a tent, it's possible to strike out from Timnay to the Cirque Jaffar on foot. A two-day round trip gives you a good taste of the area. From Timnay you can walk to the village of Sidi Amar, which is surrounded by apple orchards and is particularly colourful during the souq that's each Wednesday. Camp further along at Jaffar, located in the valley in the centre of the spectacular circle. On day two, return to the Timnay complex via the impressive river gorges. A guide isn't strictly necessary, but one can be organised via Ksar Timnay Inter-Cultures. An equally good companion is the guidebook *Grand Atlas Traverse* by Michael Peyron.

Gorges d'Aouli

An interesting road trip takes you 25km northeast of Midelt along the S317 road to the Gorges d'Aouli. A series of cliffs carved by the Moulaya, they were until recently mined extensively for lead, copper and silver. The abandoned workings can be clearly seen – many halfway up the cliff face – although the mine entrances themselves are blocked off for safety reasons. Nevertheless, the place exudes a slightly creepy ghost-town feel, especially with the dipping sun at the end of the day.

Further along the road, the small village of Aouli sits against the spectacular backdrop of the river gorge. This is a great stretch to explore by mountain bike – it's about two hours' ride from Midelt, if you're up to the gruelling uphill ride back. Note that the road deteriorates to rough *piste* at some points. A round trip by grand taxi to Aouli from Midelt should cost no more than Dh250.

THE EAST

Taza

تازة

At first glance, Taza seems to fulfil all the criteria of a sleepy provincial capital. The rush of activity common in Moroccan towns of comparable size seems entirely absent here, while its sprawling layout gives it a slightly abandoned air. But it makes an interesting break in a journey: climb the newly-restored fortifications of Taza Haute, and the panoramic views of the Rif to the north and the Middle Atlas to the south are breathtaking. Taza also provides a handy base for exploring the eastern Middle Atlas, including Gouffre du Friouato (one of the most incredible open caverns in the world) and Tazzeka National Park.

Taza is divided neatly in two: the ville nouvelle (also called Taza Bas, or Lower Taza), centred on Pl de l'Indépendance, and the walled medina (Taza Haute), occupying the hill 2km to the south. Local buses and sky-blue petits taxis (Dh6) run regularly between the two.

History

The fortified citadel of Taza is built on the edge of an escarpment overlooking the only feasible pass between the Rif Mountains and the Middle Atlas. It has been important throughout Morocco's history as a garrison town from which to exert control over the country's eastern extremities.

The Tizi n'Touahar, as the pass is known, was the traditional invasion route for armies moving west from Tunisia and Algeria. This is, in fact, where the Romans and the Arabs entered Morocco. The town itself was the base from which the Almohads, Merenids and Alawites swept to conquer lowland Morocco and establish their dynasties.

All Moroccan sultans had a hand in fortifying Taza. Nevertheless, their control over the area was always tenuous because the fiercely independent and rebellious local tribes continually exploited any weakness in the central power in order to overrun the city. Never was this more so than in the first years of the 20th century, when 'El-Rogui' (Pretender to the Sultan's Throne) Bou Hamra held sway over most of northeastern Morocco.

The French occupied Taza in 1914 and made it the main base from which they fought the prolonged rebellion by the tribes of the Rif Mountains and Middle Atlas.

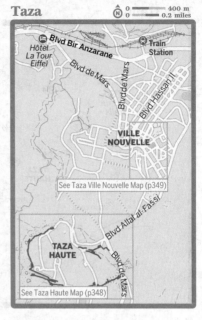

⊙ Sights & Activities

★ **Medina Walls** RAMPARTS
(Map p348) The medina walls, around 3km in circumference, have recently been restored. They are a legacy from when Taza served briefly as the Almohad capital in the 12th century. The **bastion** (Map p348) – where the walls jut out to the east of the medina – was added 400 years later by the Saadians. The most interesting section of wall is around **Bab er-Rih** (Gate of the Wind; Map p348), from where there are superb views over the surrounding countryside. Look southwest to the wooded slopes of Jebel Tazzeka in the Middle Atlas, and then to the Rif in the north, and it's easy to see the strategic significance of Taza's location.

Grande Mosquée MOSQUE
(Map p348) Not far from Bab er-Rih is the Grande Mosquée, which the Almohads began building in 1135; the Merenids added to it in the 13th century. Non-Muslims are not allowed to enter, and it's difficult to get much of an impression from the outside of the building. From here the main thoroughfare wriggles its way southeast to the

Taza Haute

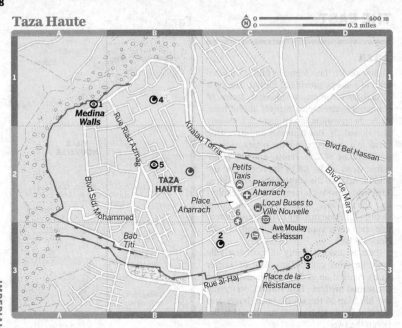

far end of the medina. Keep your eye out for occasional examples of richly decorated doorways and windows high up in the walls, guarded by old, carved cedar screens.

Souqs   MARKETS
(Map p348) The souqs and **qissariat** (covered markets) start around the Mosquée du Marché, offering mats and carpets woven by the Beni Ouarain tribe in the surrounding mountains. It's a great chance to observe the workings of a Berber market.

Andalous Mosque   MOSQUE
(Map p348) At the end of the main street, close to the *mechouar,* is this mosque that was constructed in the 12th century.

Hammam   HAMMAM
(Map p348; Pl Aharrach; admission Dh10; ⊙ men 5am-noon & 7pm-midnight, women noon-7pm) A good hammam to visit to scrub away the cares of the road.

🛏 Sleeping

Taza has only a handful of hotels, and the amount of business they do can be gauged by the general readiness there is to offer discounts of up to 25% if you stay more than a night.

Hôtel de l'Étoile   HOTEL €
(Map p348; ☎ 0535 27 01 79; 39 Ave Moulay el-Hassan; s/d Dh40/60) This Spanish-owned cheapie next to Pl Aharrach is easy to miss (the sign is hidden under the arcaded front), but inside, the strawberry-pink paint job is hard to escape. Friendly enough, it's as basic as the tariff suggests – rooms are fine for the money, with shared toilets. All have sinks and there are new showers with constant hot water (Dh10).

Grand Hôtel du Dauphiné
HOTEL **€**
(Map p349; ☑ 0535 67 35 67; Pl de l'Indépendance; s/d Dh185/290) Ideally located on the main square, the Dauphiné is good value in the budget category. Rooms are hardly exciting, but most are generously sized, and those at the front have small balconies. On the ground floor there's a bar and restaurant (dinner only).

Hôtel La Tour Eiffel
HOTEL **€€**
(☑ 0535 67 15 62; tourazhar@hotmail.com; Blvd Bir Anzarane; s/d incl breakfast Dh347/424; ❄ 🤖 🛜) Stuck on the road out of town, the Tour Eiffel is named for its high aspirations. Past the cramped lobby, a lift swishes you up to well-sized and fairly comfy rooms, many with great views out towards the mountains. The house restaurant has good juices and is noted for its seafood.

✖ Eating & Drinking

There aren't really any restaurants in the medina, just snack stalls selling kebabs and the like, although there is plenty of fresh produce in the souqs. In the ville nouvelle, the street souq just off Pl de l'Indépendance also has produce and lots of tasty snack stands that really come to life in the evening. Ave Mohammed V is well supplied for grocery stores. If you're waiting for onward transport and are in need of sustenance, there's a row of fast-food places where the buses stop on the Fez–Oujda road (Blvd Bir Anzarane).

Mou Mou
FAST FOOD **€**
(Map p349; Ave Moulay Youssef; tajines Dh25, pizzas from Dh30; ☹ noon-3pm & 7-10pm) If you've been lulled into thinking that Taza is a sleepy place, hit this packed-out corner joint, with happy customers spilling out of the door. Tasty fast food is the order of the day here: great *shwarma*, paninis, pizzas and juices.

Les Deux Rives
MOROCCAN, MEDITERRANEAN **€**
(Map p349; ☑ 0535 67 12 27; 20 Ave Mohammed VI; mains around Dh30; ☹ noon-3pm & 7-10pm) This fresh and cosy little restaurant is a good option. The menu is a mix of Moroccan and continental – some tajines, couscous and a good *pastilla*, with a smattering of pizzas and grilled meat thrown in.

Café Amsterdam
BREAKFAST **€**
(Map p349; Ave Moulay Youssef; pastries from Dh8; ☹ 8am-noon) This is a great breakfast stop with its own patisserie so you're never short of sticky pastry options. Sadly there's no

outside seating, but the interior is crisply decorated.

La Casa
MOROCCAN **€**
(Map p349; Ave Mohammed V; mains Dh24; ☹ 8am-10pm) One of a rash of very modern places full

Taza Ville Nouvelle

Taza Ville Nouvelle

of chrome and black tiles, this place has a cafe at the front and restaurant at the back. They do the usual paninis, burgers and wraps.

Grand Hôtel du Dauphiné   MOROCCAN €€
(Map p349; ☑ 0535 67 35 67; Pl de l'Indépendance; meals Dh80; ⊗ 7-10pm) On the ground floor of the hotel, the Dauphiné serves up the usual range of Moroccan standards (with some good fish), plus a handful of continental dishes thrown in. It's pretty tasty and efficiently served, but the big dining room could use a little atmosphere.

Café la Joconda   CAFE
(Map p349; Ave Mohammed VI; ⊗ 8am-10pm) Another good modern cafe with plenty of pavement seating, and one that's not threatened by the concept of female customers.

❶ Information

Attajariwafa Bank (Map p349; Ave Moulay Youseff; ⊗ 8.45am-4pm Mon-Thu, 8.45-11am Fri, 8.45am-noon Sat) Has an ATM.

BMCI (Map p349; Pl de l'Indépendance; ⊗ 8.45am-4pm Mon-Thu, 8.45-11am Fri, 8.45am-noon Sat) Has an ATM.

Cyber Attoraya (Map p349; Rue Allal ben Abdullah; per hr Dh5; ⊗ 24hr)

Cyber Friwato (Map p349; cnr Ave Mohammed VI; per hr Dh4; ⊗ 9am-11pm)

Main Post Office (Map p349; off Rue de Maré; ⊗ 8am-4pm)

Pharmacy Aharrach (Map p348; Pl Aharrach; ⊗ 8am-6pm)

Post Office (Map p348; Ave Moulay el-Hassan; ⊗ 8am-4pm) Opposite the main square.

❶ Getting There & Away

BUS

Few buses actually originate in Taza, but plenty pass through on their way between Oujda and points west of Taza such as Fez, Tangier and Casablanca, as well as to the coast.

The **CTM office** (Map p349; ☑ 0535 67 30 37; Place de l'Indépendance) is located in the ville nouvelle. There's a morning departure for Casablanca (Dh175, seven hours), stopping at Fez (Dh50, two hours), Meknès (Dh75, 3½ hours) and Rabat (Dh145, 4½ hours). Three buses leave for Tangier (Dh175, 8½ hours). There are also morning services for Oujda (Dh75, three hours) and Nador (Dh70, three hours).

Non-CTM buses servicing these same destinations stop near the new Fez–Oujda highway next to the grand-taxi lot. It's all a bit random, so ask around the day before as to what's expected – and jump in a grand taxi if the wait seems too long.

TAXI

Most grands taxis congregate near the train station. They depart fairly regularly for Fez (Dh35 on the old road; Dh40 on the highway, 2½ hours). Less frequently, taxis head for Oujda (Dh100, three hours) and Al-Hoceima (Dh75, three hours). A grand taxi return trip to the Gouffre du Friouato costs Dh300.

TRAIN

Taza's location on the train line makes rail the best transport option. Three trains run to Fez (Dh56, two hours). Four continue to Meknès (Dh82, three hours), and three to Rabat (Dh165, 5½ hours) and Casablanca (Dh204, 6½ hours). There is one direct train to Tangier (Dh212, seven hours), and three changing at Sidi Kacem or Fez. In the opposite direction, three trains go to Oujda (Dh111, 3½ hours).

Jebel Tazzeka Circuit

It's possible to make an interesting day trip of a circuit around Jebel Tazzeka, southwest of Taza. The Hôtel La Tour Eiffel (p349) has a good hand-drawn map. This takes in the Cascades de Ras el-Oued at the edge of Tazzeka National Park, the cave systems of Gouffre du Friouato and the gorges of the Oued Zireg. The scenery is grand, although the road is very narrow and twisty in parts, with plenty of blind corners from which grands taxis can unexpectedly speed around.

If you don't have a vehicle, expect to pay around Dh600 for a grand taxi for the day from Taza, although a few direct grands taxis to the Gouffre du Friouato can sometimes be found near the train station.

THE FIRST LEG

The first stop is the Cascades de Ras el-Oued, 10km from Taza. A popular picnic site, they're at their grandest in the early spring, flushed with rain and snow melt – by the end of summer the flow is just a trickle. Just above the waterfalls is the village of Ras el-Mar, where there's a small cafe below the road, with great mountain views. The entry to Tazzeka National Park is also near here. With its stands of cork oak you could conceivably spend a day walking here.

Leaving the waterfalls, continue along the right fork onto the plateau and up to a small pass. On your left you'll see the strange depression of the Daïa Chiker, a dry lake bed. In early spring, however, a shallow lake often forms as a result of a geological curiosity associated with fault lines in the calciferous rock structure.

GOUFFRE DU FRIOUATO

Further along, 25km from Taza, the **Gouffre du Friouato** (📞 0668 57 61 94, 0666 01 47 90; admission Dh5, guide Dh200, protective clothing & headlamp Dh50; ⊙ 8am-6pm) is well signposted and up a very steep road. The cavern is the main attraction of this circuit. At over 20m wide and 230m deep, it is said to be the deepest cavern in North Africa, and the cave system is possibly the most extensive. It was first investigated in 1935 and access is via 520 precipitous steps (with handrails) that lead you to the floor of the cavern. It's a strenuous climb back up, but there's talk of installing a lift. At the bottom, you can squeeze through a hole to start exploring the fascinating chambers that are found 200 more steps below. It's dark and dirty and eerily beautiful. The most spectacular chambers, full of extraordinary formations, are the **Salle de Lixus** and the **Salle de Draperies**. They do indeed resemble thin sheets of curtains, frozen and calcified. Allow at least three hours there and back. Speleologists have explored to a depth of 300m, but they believe there are more caves another 500m below.

The admission fee allows you to enter the cavern mouth at a depth of 160m. Beyond that, a guide is needed to go further underground to the grandest chambers. Bank on the occasional scramble, and squeezes through narrow sections; not recommended for claustrophobes. Overalls, nonslip overshoes and a helmet with lamp must be rented.

BACK TO TAZA

Beyond the Gouffre du Friouato, the road climbs into coniferous forests past **Bab Bou-Idir**. Abandoned for much of the year, in summer holidaymakers fill its campsite and tiled alpine-style houses. This is a good base for day hikes in the area. There's a new national park information office, and several marked trails from an easy 1.4km to a more strenuous 17.3km. The forests contain wild boar and deer, and Barbary sheep are being reintroduced.

About 8km past Bab Bou-Idir, a rough track branches off to the right 9km up to **Jebel Tazzeka** (1980m). A *piste* goes to the summit, and it's a tough climb. At the top is a TV relay station, and great panoramic views out to the Rif and the Middle Atlas.

After 38km, the main road joins the main Fez–Taza road at Sidi Abdallah de Rhiata.

On the way you will wind around hairpin bends through some dense woodland and then down through the pretty gorges of the **Oued Zireg**. From the intersection at Sidi Abdallah de Rhiata, take the main highway back east to Taza, pausing at **Tizi n'Touahar** on the way for more views.

Oujda وجدة

POP 450,000

Oujda is the largest city in eastern Morocco, and its modern facade belies its millennium-old age. It's a relaxed place that seems surprised to see foreign travellers, but it wasn't always like this. A quick survey of the map and recent history gives the reason. Oujda is the terminus of the train line, it has good links to the rest of the country, and was once near the busiest border crossing with Algeria, making it popular with traders and tourists alike. When the border closed in 1995, Oujda's economy took a major hit. However, recent tourism development along the nearby Mediterranean coast and the consequent rise in importance of the airport are having a positive knock-on effect on the city. In addition, Oujda's important university remains a mainstay of the economy and the city's intellectual life.

Despite few attractions, it's hassle-free so you can catch your breath after heading down from the Rif Mountains or before travelling on to Figuig and the Sahara.

History

Oujda lies on the main axis connecting Morocco with the rest of North Africa (the Romans built a road through here). Like Taza, it occupied a key position in controlling the east and was often seen as a vital stepping stone for armies aiming to seize control of the heartland around it.

Founded by the Meghraoua tribe in the 10th century, Oujda remained independent until the Almohads overran it a century later. Under the Merenids, Algerian rulers based in Tlemcen took the town on several occasions, and in the 17th century it fell under the Ottoman in Algiers.

Moulay Ismail put an end to this in 1687, and Oujda remained in Moroccan hands until 1907, when French forces in Algeria crossed the frontier and occupied the town in one of a series of similar 'incidents'. The protectorate was still five years away, but the sultan was powerless to stop it.

Oujda

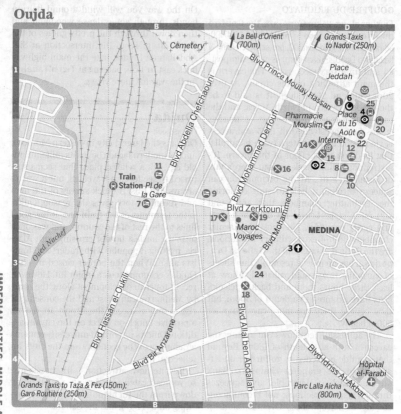

The French soon expanded Oujda, which is still burgeoning as a provincial capital.

◉ Sights

Medina
MEDINA

Oujda's medina isn't large but the walls and several surrounding squares have been rebuilt. Enter through the eastern gate, **Bab el-Ouahab**. It is chock-full of food stalls (Oujda olives are well regarded) and street cafes. Bustling without being overwhelming, it's a great slice of tradition and modernity. From Pl el-Attarine, head north through the souqs past the 14th-century **Grande Mosquée** built by the Merenids, popping out near Pl du 16 Août, the centre of the ville nouvelle.

Central Oujda
NOTABLE BUILDING

Although full of new buildings, a few deco structures survive in the side streets of central Oujda. Walking south along Blvd Mo-

hammed V, note the 1930s **clock tower**, the fine sandstone **mosque**, and the impressive French neo-Moorish **Banque al-Maghrib**, before arriving at the **Church of St Louis** (Pl 9 Juillet; ⊙ Mass 6.30pm Sat, 9am Sun), with nesting storks on its towers.

Parc Lalla Aicha
PARK

(Ave Yacoub Al-Mansour; ⊙ 7am-7pm) This beautiful park is worth a stroll. There's a swimming pool (summer only, admission Dh20), cafe, tennis and horse riding.

⭐ Festivals & Events

Oujda is renowned for its music: a cross-cultural mix of Algerian, Andalucian and Moroccan.

International Gharnati Festival

(⊙ Jul) Gharnati is Algerian music from Andalusia (the name is derived from Granada) and is particularly renowned in nearby Tlemcen.

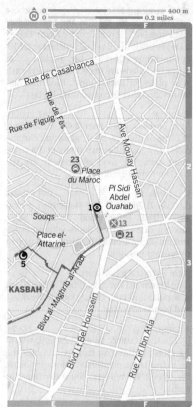

Oujda

◎ Sights
1 Bab el-Ouahab E2
2 Banque al-Maghrib D2
3 Church of St Louis C3
4 Clock Tower D1
5 Grande Mosquée E3
6 Mosque D1

◎ Sleeping
7 Atlas Terminus B2
8 Hôtel Afrah D2
9 Hotel Al Manar C2
10 Hôtel Angad D2
11 Hôtel Ibis Moussafir B2
12 Hôtel Tlemcen D2

◎ Eating
13 Argana F3
14 Café Pâtisserie Colombe D2
15 L'Excellence D2
16 Restaurant Le Comme Chez Soi C2
17 Restaurant Nacional C3
18 Rihab C3
19 Trocadero C3

◎ Transport
20 CTM Office D2
21 Local Buses F3
22 Petits Taxis D2
23 Petits Taxis E2
24 RAM C3
25 Trans Ghazala Ticket Office D1

IMPERIAL CITIES, MIDDLE ATLAS & THE EAST OUJDA

Oujda International Rai Festival
(☉Aug) Rai music developed in Algeria in the 1930s as a form of protest folk music.

Moussems of Sidi Yahia Ben Younes
(☉Aug & Sep) This is held 6km south of Oujda. Patron saint of the city and venerated by Moroccans, Sidi Yahia is also thought to be John the Baptist or perhaps a Castilian rabbi. Thousands of pilgrims flock to the celebrations. The trees around the shrine (closed to non-Muslims) are festooned with rags, tied to receive blessings – a throwback to pre-Islamic fertility beliefs. To get to Sidi Yahia, take bus 1 (Dh6) from outside Bab el-Ouahab in Oujda. A petit taxi should cost around Dh30.

◎ Sleeping

Hôtel Angad   HOTEL €
(☏0536 69 14 51; hotelangad@hotmail.fr; Rue Tafna; s/d Dh160/200, with air-con Dh200/240;

☏) The top pick of the budget hotels is this affordable two-star. Rooms are basic, with large bathroom and TV; get a room at the back as streetside can be noisy. The downstairs cafe does breakfast and pizza.

Hôtel Tlemcen   HOTEL €
(☏0536 70 03 84; 26 Rue Ramdane el-Gadhi; s/d/tr Dh90/180/270) This friendly little place offers excellent value, and has a grand-looking lobby. Quarters are small but bright, with bathroom and TV. Air-conditioning was being installed at the time of research, so expect slightly higher prices.

Hôtel Afrah   HOTEL €
(☏0536 68 65 33; 15 Rue Tafna; s/d Dh70/120; ☏) The tiles and plasterwork in the lobby lend some traditional Moroccan flavour here. Self-contained rooms are a bit boxy, but otherwise this is a good budget choice.

Hotel Al Manar   HOTEL €€
(☏0536 68 88 55; hotelalmanara@menara.ma; 50 Blvd Zerktouni; s/d Dh360/420; ❀☏) Centrally located, the Al Manar is suitably towering

SOLAR SAHARA

One thing the desert has in copious amounts (apart from sand) is sunshine, and in November 2009 Morocco revealed a US$9 billion investment plan to generate 20% of its energy from solar energy by the year 2020. Much of it will be produced in the Moroccan Orient, the region running along the Algerian border from the Mediterranean to Figuig. The upgrading of infrastructure on the highway south of Oujda (proclaimed from dozens of roadside billboards) points to the money pouring into the region. In addition, a great deal of investment is earmarked for the Ouarzazate region.

The programs are being financed by private investors as well as the World Bank, the European Investment Bank, and Spain, France, Germany and Saudi Arabia.

for its name. Functional and practical decor: rooms are fine value, although avoid the darker, small-windowed interior rooms.

Hôtel Ibis Moussafir HOTEL €€
(☑0536 68 82 02; www.ibishotel.com; Pl de la Gare; s/d Dh612/684; ✷ ᐧ ᐧ) Bang in front of you as you leave the train station, the Ibis has all the up-to-the-minute facilities and comfortable rooms you'd expect from this international hotel chain – you could be anywhere (or nowhere) in the world.

Atlas Terminus HOTEL €€€
(☑0536 71 10 10; www.hotelsatlas.com; Pl de la Gare; s/d incl breakfast Dh1310/1500; ✷ ᐧ ᐧ) Sitting imperially, the Atlas Terminus is very grand. Rooms and service are the best quality, with three restaurants, bar and nightclub, pool and spa.

🍴 Eating

We asked a resident the best thing about the city. 'It has plenty of cafes', was the reply. It's true: people-watching over coffee or mint tea is a major occupation for locals (well, the men). There's a rash of new, modern cafes, and many serve good food.

In the medina, the stalls inside Bab el-Ouahab offer more traditional fare, including *kefta* (spiced meatballs), bowls of *harira* and boiled snails.

★ Restaurant Nacional MOROCCAN €
(☑0536 70 32 57; 107 Blvd Allal ben Abdallah; meals from Dh25; ☉noon-3pm & 7-10pm) This is a Oujda institution: people queue for tables at lunchtime (there's a big, packed salon upstairs). Salads are great, and waiters rush with plates of grilled meat, fried fish and tajines, and there's couscous on Fridays.

Trocadero CAFE, ITALIAN €
(Blvd Zerktouni; mains from Dh40; ☉8am-10pm; ᐧ) One of the new black, glass and chrome cafes, Trocadero has two floors and a pavement area. The food is excellent: try the chicken florentina or risotto.

L'Excellence CAFE, ITALIAN €
(☑0536 71 28 18; 30 Blvd Mohammed V; pizza around Dh40; ☉8am-10pm) Another large, modern cafe over two floors with an excellent patisserie around the corner and a pizza restaurant upstairs.

Café Pâtisserie Colombe CAFE €
(Blvd Mohammed V; croissants Dh2; ☉8am-10pm) A popular and busy cafe, good for breakfast and people-watching.

Argana CAFE €
(Pl Sidi Abdel Ouahab; tajines Dh25; ☉9am-9pm) Join lots of Moroccan families and take the lift to this large, plant-filled cafe overlooking the square. There's (very loud) live music at night.

La Belle d'Orient SEAFOOD €€
(☑0536 70 59 61; 65 Blvd Ahfir; mains from Dh75; ☉lunch) An excellent choice if you're in the mood for fish fresh from the coast. Sardines are grilled on the barbecue outside, there's a fish tajine (Dh100) or a platter of fish *friture* (Dh75). Pizzas are also available.

Rihab CAFE, ITALIAN €€
(☑0536 70 51 51; cnr Blvd Idriss Al-Akbar & Allal ben Abdallah; mains from Dh95; ☉8am-11pm; ᐧ) Amy Winehouse would have sung 'yes, yes, yes' to this Rihab. The ground and 1st floors are a swish, modern cafe, ice-cream parlour and excellent *boulangerie*, while on the 8th floor there's a good restaurant with a wide range of fish and Italian dishes.

Restaurant Le Comme Chez Soi FRENCH €€
(☑0536 68 60 79; 8 Rue Sijilmassa; mains around Dh110) This licensed restaurant has a French-influenced menu, with some good meat and fish dishes, plus a smattering of pastas.

ℹ Information

There are numerous banks with ATMs and *bureaux de change* located along Blvd Mohammed V.

Delegation Provinciale du Tourisme (Pl du 16 Août; ⊙9am-4pm Mon-Thu, 9am-noon Fri) As usual, this is just an administrative office, but it does have a good map of the city.

Hôpital el-Farabi (☑0536 68 27 05; Ave Idriss el-Akbar)

Internet (Blvd Mohammed V; per hr Dh5; ⊙9am-10pm) Above the *téléboutique*.

Main Post Office (Blvd Mohammed V; ⊙8am-4pm)

Maroc Voyages (☑0536 68 39 93; 110 Blvd Allal ben Abdallah; ⊙9am-6pm Mon-Thu, 9am-noon Fri & Sat)

Pharmacie Mouslim (Blvd Mohammed V; ⊙8am-6pm)

Police Station (Blvd Mohammed Derfoufi)

FIGUIG فجيج

In the days of cross-border tourism, Figuig (fig-eeg) was popular with travellers. Few people make it here now, which is a shame because it is one of Morocco's best oasis towns: seven traditional desert villages amid 200,000 date palms fed by artesian wells. Once a historic way station for pilgrims travelling to Mecca, Figuig now sleeps, only waking for the autumn date harvest.

Figuig has an upper and lower town. The main road, Blvd Hassan II, runs through the upper (new) town, where there are ATMs, a post office and pleasant municipal gardens.

Where the road passes the Figuig Hotel, it drops downhill towards the lower town – the basin of palms and *ksour* (mudbrick castles) that make up the old part of Figuig. This ridge provides a handy landmark as well as views over the *palmeraie* (oasis) and into Algeria; the best views are from Azrou, where the path leads towards Ksar Zenaga, or from the terrace of the Figuig Hotel.

The seven *ksour* that make up the town each control an area of *palmeraie* and its all-important supply of water. The largest and most rewarding is **Ksar Zenaga**, south below the ridge splitting the oasis. Take the paths following irrigation channels past palm trees and gardens, then suddenly you're among a warren of covered passages. As you tunnel between the houses, look out for some marvellous, ancient wooden doors, and watch out – you may find yourself in someone's backyard.

The crumbling state of many *ksour* lets you see their clever construction: palm-tree trunks plastered with pisé (rammed earth), and ceilings made of palm fronds. It's cool and dark and often eerily quiet. You may meet married women swathed in white robes, with the startling exception of one uncovered eye. It's easy to get lost; village children will happily guide you for a few dirham.

Closer to the upper part of town, to the west of the main road, **Ksar el-Oudahir** is home to a lovely octagonal minaret built in the 11th century. It's known as the *sawmann al-hajaria* (tower of stone), and its design is quite unlike anything you'll see anywhere else in Morocco, instead echoing the minarets of Mauritania and the Sahel.

One of the best ways to taste traditional Figuigi life is to stay at the **Auberge Oasis** (☑0536 89 92 20; www.auberge-oasis.com; Rue Jamaa, Ksar Zenaga; s/d Dh100/170, incl full board Dh300/600; @), a family home built of adobe in a *ksar*. Rooms are traditionally decorated (and with en suite), and you can relax in the rooftop Berber tent. The home-cooked meals are excellent.

Arriving in Figuig, buses stop at the 'bus station' – little more than a junction and three ticket offices – at the north end of town. They then continue on to the lower town, terminating at Tachraft Sq in Zenaga.

Always check out transport options the day before travelling. There are two buses a day to Oujda (Dh93, seven hours), and one every other day with CTM (Dh100). All stop at Bouarfa, where you can change for connections to Er-Rachidia.

The border with Algeria is closed, but in the unlikely event of it reopening, it's 3km from Figuig to Moroccan customs, and a further 4km to the Algerian town of Béni Ounif.

ℹ️ Getting There & Away

AIR

Oujda's **Angad Airport** (📞 0536 68 32 61) is 15km north of the town off the road to Saïdia. Grand-taxi fares are set at Dh150, but any bus to Nador, Berkane or Saïdia can drop you on the main road for a few dirham.

RAM (📞 0536 68 39 09; 45 Blvd Mohammed V) has two (or three) daily flights to Casablanca and direct flights to France. Ryanair operates flights to Paris, Brussels, Marseille and Düsseldorf. EasyJet, Transavia, Jetairfly and Air Arabia all have flights to Paris.

BORDER CROSSING

Few anticipate the Algerian border will be re-opening soon.

BUS

The main bus station sits in the shadow of the huge Mohammed VI Mosque. The **CTM office** (📞 0536 68 20 47; Rue Sidi Brahim) has a suboffice just off Pl du 16 Août selling tickets to Casablanca (Dh210, nine hours overnight), Taza (Dh65, 3½ hours), Fez (Dh120, five hours), Meknès (Dh120, six hours), Rabat (Dh180, 7½ hours), and Tangier (Dh210, 11 hours) also via Taza, Fez and Meknès. There is also a service every other day to Figuig (Dh100, six hours).

Trans Ghazala runs several daily services to Casablanca via Taza, Fez, Meknès and Rabat.

You can also buy tickets for these services at the **Trans Ghazala ticket office** (📞 0536 68 53 87; Rue Sidi Brahim).

Numerous other companies with ticket offices in the bus station offer frequent departures for Taza, Fez and Meknès as well as Berkane (Dh16, 20 minutes) and Nador (Dh35, three hours). There are two daily buses to Bouarfa (Dh66, five hours) and Figuig (Dh93, seven hours). There are also several buses a day to Saïdia (Dh17, one hour) and Al-Hoceima (Dh79, six hours). There are also two daily buses to Tangier (Dh195, 10 hours) via Tetouan (Dh137, nine hours).

TAXI

Grands taxis leave regularly from the main bus station to Taza (Dh80, three hours). Change here for onward connections. Grands taxis heading north to Nador (Dh60, three hours), Saïdia (Dh25, one hour) and Berkane (Dh25, one hour) congregate north of town near the junction of Rue ibn Abdelmalek and Blvd Mohammed Derfoufi.

TRAIN

Oujda's train station is at the west end of Blvd Zerktouni. Three trains leave daily for Casablanca (Dh305, 10 hours) and three for Tangier (two via Sidi Kacem, Dh320, 10 hours). All stop at Taza (Dh111, 3½ hours), Fez (Dh160, six hours) and Meknès (Dh190, 6½ hours).

Southern Morocco & Western Sahara

جنوب المغرب والصحراء الغربي

Best Places to Stay

➡ Palais Oumensour (p371)

➡ Les 3 Chameaux (p390)

➡ Ksar Massa (p367)

➡ La Maison Anglaise (p371)

➡ Tizourgane Kasbah (p377)

Off the Beaten Track

➡ Anti Atlas trekking (p382)

➡ Afella-Ighir oasis (p380)

➡ Ameln Valley (p380)

➡ Id-Aïssa (p395)

➡ Oases and *agadirs*, Tata (p381)

Why Go?

The Souss Valley, where goats climb argan trees beneath the sun-baked Anti Atlas, draws a line across Morocco. South of this fertile valley, the pace of life in mountain villages and Saharan gateways is seductively slow, free from the hassles of mass tourism and modern existence.

A sense of somewhere really fresh and undiscovered gusts through the region like the spring winds – and you'll want to savour it. On elegantly wrecked seafronts, sip a mint tea and gaze at the wild Atlantic Coast. When trekking, mountain biking or driving through wrinkled Anti Atlas foothills, stop before the next oasis village and appreciate the silence.

The locals, from Chleuh Berbers in the Souss to the Saharawi in the Western Sahara, seem determined to complement the landscapes. Their light robes flutter under desert skies, and their dark herds dot rocky hillsides.

Head south: you'll be surprised.

When to Go
Agadir

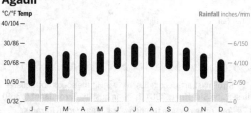

Feb Trek the Anti Atlas and hit the Atlantic Coast for winter sun and surf.

Mar See almond trees blossom, celebrated by Tafraoute's harvest festival.

Nov Catch Taliouine's saffron festival and Immouzzer des Ida Outanane's olive harvest.

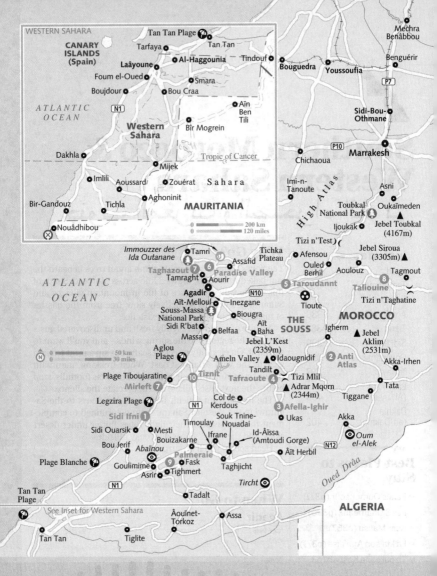

Southern Morocco & Western Sahara Highlights

1. Stroll past art-deco relics in seaside **Sidi Ifni** (p390)

2. Trek, drive or cycle through the **Anti Atlas** (p375)

3. Explore the oasis of **Afella-Ighir** (p380)

4. Visit traditional Berber houses and cycle around **Tafraoute** (p375)

5. Hit the souqs and squares in bustling **Taroudannt** (p369)

6. Meander up **Paradise Valley** (p368), an accessible part of the western High Atlas

7. Hang loose in the surf spots of **Mirleft** (p389) and **Taghazout** (p367)

8. Taste saffron and argan oil in **Taliouine** (p374)

9. Put your feet up on the Sahara's fringes in the **palmeraie accommodation** (p394) around Goulimime

10. Shop for silver in **Tiznit medina** (p384)

Climate

Southern Morocco divides into three distinct geographical areas, each with its own microclimate. The semitropical, verdant Souss Valley is hot and humid, with temperatures ranging between 22°C and a steamy 38°C, when water vapour rises like a mist from the huge citrus groves that fill the valley. The valley is also prone to heavy winds in spring. The climate of the barren Anti Atlas veers between freezing winters and hot, dry summers. The deep southern coast enjoys a more constant year-round sunny climate.

Language

Arabic remains the lingua franca of major cities in the south. The Chleuh tribes who dominate the Souss speak Tashelhit, a Berber dialect, most noticeable in the Anti Atlas. French is widely spoken and Spanish is still heard in some of Spain's former territories.

THE SOUSS VALLEY

Agadir اكادير

POP 679,000

Agadir feels unlike anywhere else in Morocco. A busy port and beach resort sprawling beneath its kasbah, the city was completely rebuilt following a devastating earthquake in 1960. It is now the country's premier destination for sun, sand, pubs and pizza. Laid out as a large grid of downtown streets, surrounded by spacious residential suburbs, Agadir's concrete-covered inland quarters are ugly and sterile. However, the city hits its stride on the beachfront promenade, where Moroccan street life comes with a refreshing sense of space. Arching south of the shiny white marina, the sheltered sandy beach offers clean water and 300 sunny days a year.

Agadir caters mainly to package-tour holidaymakers, and will appeal less to independent travellers with an interest in Moroccan culture. Families will also enjoy relaxing on the beach and wandering around the handful of sights. If you do not have children in tow, however, we recommend heading elsewhere to make the most of a visit to Morocco.

The city spreads over a large area, both along the coast and inland from the huge swath of beach. From the northern end of the beach, near the marina and port, three parallel streets – 20 Août, nearest the ocean, Mohammed V and Hassan II – run through the main tourist area.

History

Named after the *agadir* (fortified granary) of the Irir tribe, Agadir has a long history of boom and bust. It was founded in the 15th century by Portuguese merchants wanting to develop trade links with the Saharan caravans. From the mid-16th century, as the Saadian empire expanded, the port became prosperous from the export of local sugar, cotton and saltpetre, and products from Saharan trade, which the Moroccans then controlled. But this prosperity ended in the 1760s, when the Alawite sultan Sidi Mohammed ben Abdullah diverted the trade to Essaouira.

The French colonists went some way towards redeveloping Agadir in the 20th century, but the earthquake on 29 February 1960 completely destroyed the city. As many as 18,000 people perished – around half of the population. The authorities, unable to cope with the apocalyptic aftermath of death and disease, sprayed the area with lime and DDT, and left the dead where they had been buried, in the collapsed city. The mound this created is now known as Ancienne Talborjt.

Since its reconstruction, Agadir has developed into an important port, with a large fishing fleet helping to make Morocco the world's largest exporter of tinned sardines. Agadir has also become Morocco's top beach resort, and the luxury marina complex signals ambitions to move upmarket.

◉ Sights

Mémoire d'Agadir   MUSEUM
(cnr Ave du Président Kennedy & Ave des FAR; adult/child Dh20/10; ⏱9am-12.30pm & 3-6pm Mon-Sat) This small museum in the southwest corner of Jardin de Olhão, entered from outside the park, is dedicated to the 1960 earthquake. Displays include interesting photos of Agadir since the 1920s, while others show the effects of the quake.

Jardin de Olhão   PARK
(Ave du Président Kennedy; ⏱2.30-6.30pm Tue-Sun) FREE A cool, relaxing garden created in 1992 to mark the twinning of Agadir with the Portuguese town of Olhão.

Agadir

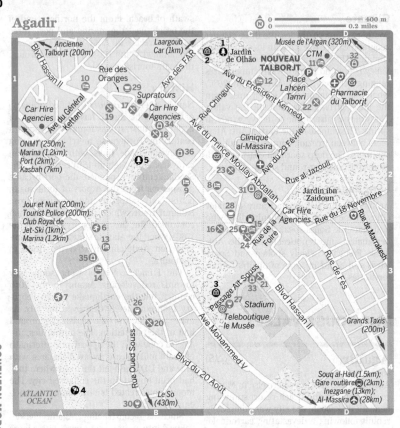

Musée du Patrimoine Amazigh
MUSEUM

(☎0528 82 16 32; Passage Aït Souss; adult/child Dh20/10; ⏰9.30am-12.30pm & 2-5.30pm Mon-Sat) 🖉 With an excellent display of Berber artefacts, especially jewellery, the museum is a great place to learn about the traditional life and culture of the region's Berber people.

Vallée des Oiseaux
PARK

(Valley of the Birds; ⏰11am-6pm) **FREE** A leafy city-centre retreat in the dry riverbed running down from Blvd Hassan II to Blvd du 20 Août, with a shaded children's playground, an aviary and a small zoo.

Kasbah
KASBAH

(off Ave al-Moun) The hilltop kasbah, 7km northwest of the centre and visible from much of the city, is a rare survivor of the 1960 earthquake. The views from up here of the port, marina and Agadir are fantastic.

Built in 1541 and restored in the 1740s, the kasbah once provided housing for nearly 300 people. All that remains is the outer wall, though traces of the dwellings can still be made out. The inscription over the entry arch in Dutch and Arabic ('Believe in God and respect the King') is a reminder of the beginning of trade with the Low Countries.

The walk up to the kasbah is long, hot and uncomfortable: get a taxi (about Dh25) and walk back down.

Ancienne Talborjt
HISTORIC SITE

(off Ave al-Moun) The grassy area below the kasbah covers the remains of old Agadir town and constitutes a mass grave for all those who died in the 1960 earthquake.

Marina
MARINA

(☎0661 21 57 46; off Ave Mohammed V) The city's newest attraction is a billion-dirham pleasure port between the beach and commercial port. As well as mooring for your floating palace, the complex of faux white kasbahs

Agadir

has holiday apartments, shops (mostly international brands), cafes, restaurants and boat trips for groups.

Activities

Beaches

Agadir's glory is its crescent beach, which usually remains unruffled when the Atlantic winds are blustering elsewhere. It's clean and well maintained, spotlit at night and patrolled by lifeguards and police during peak periods (mid-June to mid-September). There is a strong undertow.

The beach is mostly hassle-free, but single females or families will have a more relaxed time at one of the private beaches near the marina, or in front of the big hotels around Sunset Beach and Palm Beach. Facilities here include showers, toilets and kids' play areas; deckchairs and umbrellas can be hired (Dh20).

The shops on the promenade just south of the marina sell bodyboards for about Dh130. Many larger beach hotels and surf clubs rent out windsurfing equipment, jet skis, bodyboards and surfboards.

At sunset and into the evening, Agadir's activity of choice is strolling along the promenade that runs south from the marina.

Club Royal de Jet-Ski   WATER SPORTS
(☑ 0665 95 24 35; www.agadiradventure.com) Offers jet-skiing and flyboarding on the beach near the marina.

Hammams

Several big hotels, including the Royal Atlas, have spas offering hammam, massage and a range of treatments.

Musée de l'Argan   HAMMAM
(☑ 0528 84 87 82; www.lemuseedelargan.com; Ave Moulay Youssef; hammam & scrub Dh150; ⊙10am-9pm) Geared towards tourists, this unisex hammam offers massages and argan-based treatments.

👉 Tours

Petit Train d'Agadir   TOUR
(Blvd du 20 Août; adult/child Dh18/12; ⊙every 40min from 9.15am) This chain of buggies snakes around the city centre for 35 minutes.

Festivals & Events

Music Festivals   MUSIC
(www.festival-timitar-agadir.blogspot.com) Festival Timitar attracts Moroccan and international musicians and DJs to Agadir every June, and the Concert for Tolerance takes place on the beach in October/November.

SOUTHERN MOROCCO & WESTERN SAHARA AGADIR

🛏 Sleeping

Agadir has set its sights on the midrange and top-end visitor, but if you move away from the beach, you will find budget and lower midrange options. High season in Agadir includes Easter, summer and the Christmas period, when European holiday-makers fly out on package tours. During these times, it's best to book ahead.

Midrange and top-end hotels often offer discounts during low season; budget prices fluctuate less, but deals are available online. Many luxury hotels along the seafront are geared towards package tours, but discounts on their published rates are sometimes available to independent travellers.

A strip of luxury beachfront hotels and resorts runs south of the centre on Rue Oued Souss and Chemin des Dunes, including Riu Tikida and Sofitel properties. Luxurious riads and kasbahs are found on the outskirts of Agadir – in the hills inland or to the south en route to Inezgane.

🛏 Centre & Seafront

Hôtel Petite Suède   HOTEL €
(☑0528 84 07 79; www.petitesuede.com; cnr Blvd Hassan II & Ave du Général Kettani; s/d incl breakfast Dh205/330; 🕾) Readers recommend this simple but perfectly located hotel, five minutes' walk from the beach, with good service and a roof terrace for breakfast and ocean views. One of Agadir's more Moroccan-styled hotels, with an attractive, rug-scattered interior.

Hotel Atlantic   HOTEL €€
(☑0528 84 36 61; www.atlantichotelagadir.com; off Blvd Hassan II; s/d/tr incl breakfast Dh510/620/880; 🕸🕾🌊) The three-star Atlantic is one of the best deals in Agadir, offering comfortable rooms and, in the cool and breezy reception, professional service. It has a spa, a lovely little pool, and tours on offer.

Hôtel Kamal   HOTEL €€
(☑0528 84 28 17; www.hotel-kamal.com; Blvd Hassan II; s/d/tr/q Dh404/465/569/673; 🕾🌊) A popular and well-run downtown hotel in a white block overlooking Pl de L'Esperance, the Kamal manages to appeal to a range of clients, from package tourists to travelling Moroccans. Rooms are tired, but the staff are helpful, the pool is large enough to swim laps and there is a bar. Breakfast (Dh36) is dull and overpriced; go downstairs to Dolce & Caffe. Discounts are offered online.

Studiotel Afoud   APARTMENT €€
(☑0528 84 39 99; www.studiotel-afoud.com; Rue de la Foire; s/d Dh630/740; 🕸🕾🌊) If you would like to self-cater, these studios are simple but pleasant, each featuring a kitchen with hob and fridge, and a balcony overlooking the peeling neighbouring buildings. On the ground floor is a restaurant, grocery booth and bookcase of paperback novels.

Royal Atlas   HOTEL €€€
(☑0528 29 40 40; www.hotelsatlas.com; Blvd du 20 Août; s/d incl breakfast Dh1428/1657; 🕸@🕾🌊) This beachfront colossus ticks all the five-star boxes with a Moroccan flourish. Carpets and antiques dot the tiled floors leading to the palm-fringed bar and pool area, and the 350 rooms and suites. Facilities include a nightclub, gym, Daniel Jouvance spa, private beach, Italian and Moroccan restaurants, and all the extras you would expect.

Kenzi Europa   HOTEL €€€
(☑0528 82 12 12; www.kenzi-hotels.com; Blvd du 20 Août; s/d Dh1700/1800; 🕸🕾🌊) This Kenzi hotel is about the most stylish and restrained thing in tacky Agadir. Curvy lamp-shades and flat surfaces abound in the calm, minimal rooms; facilities include a spa, restaurant and bar; and a band tinkles away in the lobby. Only the plastic octopus and dolphins in the children's pool detract from the overall smoothness. Specials are offered.

🛏 Nouveau Talborjt

The best area for budget options is away from the ocean in Nouveau Talborjt, where there are three budget hotels on Pl Lahcen Tamri. The all-night bus activity ensures that most hotel receptions here are open 24 hours; the area is a little seedy.

Hotel Sindibad   HOTEL €
(☑0528 82 34 77; sinhot@menara.ma; Pl Lahcen Tamri; s/d Dh300/350; 🕸🕾🌊) This blue-and-white building, above a patisserie on the square, has small en-suite rooms. The star attraction is the pint-sized rooftop pool.

Hotel Tamri   HOTEL €
(☑0528 82 18 80; Ave du Président Kennedy; s/d Dh90/120) This modern, friendly and clean hotel has turquoise balconies overlooking the palms in the tiled courtyard, and pictures of old Agadir in reception. Rooms have basins, and the shared bathrooms have squat toilets.

✖ Eating

Self-caterers should check out **Marché Central** (off Blvd Hassan II), which has a fresh food market on the ground floor, or **Uniprix** (Blvd Hassan II), a supermarket that stocks everything from cheese and biscuits to beer, wine and spirits.

✖ Centre & Nouveau Talborjt

Daffy   MOROCCAN €
(Rue des Oranges; mains Dh50; ☉ lunch & dinner) This popular unlicensed tourist restaurant offers tastes of Moroccan cuisine, including couscous (on Friday) and tajines, as well as seafood and salads.

La Tour de Paris   MOROCCAN, INTERNATIONAL €
(Blvd Hassan II; mains Dh60; ☉ lunch & dinner) One of the less pizza-orientated eateries in this area, La Tour de Paris has a pleasant terrace and art-nouveau stylings. Inside, the televised soccer and keyboard player are less impressive, but the menu features couscous, *pastilla* (pie), tajines, seafood, steaks and pasta.

La Siciliana   PIZZERIA €
(Blvd Hassan II; mains Dh70; ☉ lunch & dinner) In a line of Italian eateries, this unlicensed restaurant is the most atmospheric of the lot. Between noon and 5pm weekdays, its pizza and pasta deals (Dh30 to Dh60) are popular.

Dolce & Caffe   CAFE, ICE CREAM €
(Blvd Hassan II; snacks Dh30; ☉ 8am-10pm) One of Agadir's coolest cafes, serving delectable gâteaux, tarts, ice cream, crêpes, light meals and breakfasts with an R&B soundtrack.

Tafarnout   PATISSERIE €
(Blvd Hassan II; snacks Dh30; ☉ 10am-10pm) Agadir's smartest patisserie, with indoor and outdoor seating and a wide range of gâteaux, tarts, croissants, crêpes and biscuits.

SOS Poulet & Pizza   FAST FOOD €
(Ave du Prince Moulay Abdallah; half chicken Dh48, pizza Dh35-65; ☉ lunch & dinner) These adjoining snack bars are popular for their rotisserie chicken and pizzas.

★ Côte Court   SEAFOOD, MEDITERRANEAN €€
(☑ 0528 82 65 33; off Blvd Hassan II; mains Dh90-170; ☉ noon-11.30pm) This restaurant at the Royal Tennis Club occupies a lovely outdoor area, which is equal parts chichi garden and nomad camp, with up-lit trees, basket lamps and the pizza oven flickering away. The service is attentive and the menu features some

unusual dishes such as calamari risotto with chorizo chips. A children's menu (Dh45) is available.

Mezzo Mezzo   ITALIAN €€
(☑ 0677 19 73 79; Blvd Hassan II; mains Dh90; ☉ lunch & dinner; ☏) A shining beacon among Agadir's many stodgy pizzerias, Mezzo Mezzo offers a good range of pizzas, daily specials and wine by the glass. The kitchen also produces pasta and fish dishes, and there's a smooth European sophistication to the decor and service.

Le P'tit Dôme   MOROCCAN, INTERNATIONAL €€
(☑ 0528 84 08 05; Blvd du 20 Août; mains Dh100; ☉ lunch & dinner) In a line of tourist restaurants, Le P'tit Dôme offers good service, black-and-white decor and a touch more class than its neighbours. The usual pizza, meat, seafood and Moroccan dishes are served, with a three-course set menu (Dh120) and children's menu (Dh60) offered. The food is unexciting, but the outdoor seats are a pleasant dining environment.

✖ Marina

The upmarket marina at the northern end of the seafront promenade has a concentration of midrange and top-end restaurants and cafes, where you can dine in style on international food.

Les Blancs
SEAFOOD, SPANISH **€€**

(☑ 0528 82 83 68; mains Dh130; ⊘ lunch & dinner) Occupying a series of elegant white blocks by the beach at the entrance to the marina, Les Blancs serves seafood and meat dishes including paella, the house speciality (two people minimum). In season, book ahead to score an outside table. For a sunset snack, pizza (Dh90) is served in the terrace bar.

33 Yacht Adress
SEAFOOD, MOROCCAN **€€€**

(☑ 0529 90 09 00; mains Dh160; ⊘ lunch & dinner) This upmarket restaurant is an excellent spot for sundowners, with superb views down the beach. The menu, prepared by three French chefs, is a good mix of seafood (sole, lobster, bouillabaisse) and meat dishes (chicken *pastilla,* shoulder of lamb).

La Madrague
MEDITERRANEAN, SEAFOOD **€€€**

(☑ 0528 84 24 24; mains Dh110-280; ⊘ lunch & dinner) This stylish restaurant occupies a quiet corner of the marina, with a view of the kasbah above the boats. It specialises in dishes such as pasta, risotto, crab and prawns, and offers a three-course weekday lunch special (Dh180).

Drinking & Nightlife

There's a great choice of cafes and patisseries, where you can start the day with coffee and pastries or recover from the rigours of the beach. Many open midmorning, but the best time to hit the caffeine is late afternoon, when Agadiris return to consciousness after the hot afternoon and catch up with friends.

Blvd du 20 Août, inland from Sunset Beach, is good for bars and nightclubs, especially around the top of Rue Oued Souss. At the marina and along the promenade leading to it, there are also plenty of cafes and bars. Beers are typically Dh5 to Dh10 more expensive at night, but many bars extend their daytime prices during early-evening happy hours. Many also offer the dubious pleasure of karaoke or crooning entertainers.

The restaurants in Agadir are generally licensed.

There is a decent range of nightclubs, mostly glitzy, Westernised affairs scattered along Blvd du 20 Août and Rue Oued Souss, and attached to the big hotels. Top choices are **Papa Gayo** (Chemin des Dunes), **Le So** (Sofitel Royal Bay, Chemin des Dunes) and **Actors** (Royal Atlas, Blvd du 20 Août).

La Truite Irish Bar
PUB, CAFE

(Passage Aït Souss; ⊘ noon-late; 🐾) As its name suggests, this place is confused even by the standards of its genre, with more pictures of King Mohammed VI than shamrocks. Nonetheless, it offers outside tables, draught beer, English breakfasts and soccer broadcasts.

Jour et Nuit
CAFE

(Rue de la Plage; ⊘ 24hr) A popular spot for a seafront sundowner. The newer of the two neighbouring branches has a panoramic terrace.

Orange Café
CAFE

(Rue des Oranges; ⊘ 10am-8pm; 🐾) This cool little courtyard cafe, with chilled Arabic electronica on the stereo and a fountain gurgling away, serves coffee and light meals (Dh15 to Dh25).

Uniprix Cafe
BAR, CAFE

(Blvd Hassan II; ⊘ 11am-9pm) The outside tables are a prime spot for people-watching.

La Verandah
CAFE

(Immeuble Oumlil, Blvd Hassan II; ⊘ 9am-8pm) This meeting point offers strong coffee and light meals on its glassed-in verandah.

English Pub
PUB

(Blvd du 20 Août; mains Dh75; ⊘ noon-late) Come to this Union Jack–festooned bar for Stella Artois, all-day breakfasts and karaoke.

Cafe III
SHEESHA

(off Rue de la Foire; ⊘ 6pm-late) Hip young locals of both sexes come here to smoke sheesha beneath flatscreen TVs.

Shopping

Souvenirs are often trucked into Agadir from other parts of Morocco and tend to be of low quality, although Marrakshi vendors

---

WORTH A TRIP

SOUQ AL-HAD

Leave the seafront to shop with the locals at **Souq al-Had** (Blvd Abderrahim Bouabid; ⊘ Tue-Sat), which slaps a big, messy dollop of Moroccan atmosphere onto concrete Agadir. Stalls sell everything from jellabas (a popular flowing garment) to fish, including some good handicrafts, leatherwork and lanterns. Among the lines of fresh fruit and veg from the Souss Valley, look out for Berber apothecaries selling herbal incense, lipstick and potions that have all sorts of effects on the bowels.

have started to outsource production here. The options in the centre are unatmospheric but low-pressure environments offer easy shopping.

Librairie Papetrie (Passage Aït Souss) and **Al Mouggar Bookshop** (cnr Ave du Prince Moulay Abdallah & Ave du 29 Février) sell books in English.

Ensemble Artisanal   ARTS & CRAFTS
(Ave du 29 Février; ⊙10am-12.30pm & 2.30-5pm Mon-Sat) Some of the best craftwork found in Agadir.

Marché Central   ARTS & CRAFTS
(off Blvd Hassan II; ⊙8am-4pm Mon-Sat) Pick up presents ranging from chessboards to leatherwork in and around this concrete building.

Uniprix   SUPERMARKET
(Blvd Hassan II; ⊙9am-6pm Mon-Sat) Sells swimwear, holiday essentials and some handicrafts.

Tafoukt Souq   SOUVENIRS
(Blvd du 20 Août; ⊙9.30am-12.30pm & 2-6pm) A touristy bazaar with everything from Berber jewellery to football tops.

ℹ Information

EMERGENCY

Police (☑19; Rue du 18 Novembre) There's also a Nouveau Talborjt office on Pl Lahcen Tamri, and a **Tourist Police** (Rue de la Plage) post on the promenade.

INTERNET ACCESS

There are internet cafes all over the centre and Nouveau Talborjt.
Adrar Net (Ave du Prince Moulay Abdallah; per hr Dh5; ⊙9am-10pm)
Teleboutique le Musée (Passage Aït Souss; per hr Dh5; ⊙10.30am-11pm)

MEDICAL SERVICES

Most of the larger hotels are able to recommend reliable, English-speaking doctors. Pharmacy windows display a list of that week's '*pharmacies de garde*', which open 24 hours on a rotating basis.
Clinique al-Massira (Ave du 29 Février; ⊙24hr) Medical clinic.
Pharmacie du Talborjt (off Pl Lahcen Tamri; ⊙9am-12.30pm & 2.30-5pm Mon-Sat)

MONEY

There are banks all over the centre, most with ATMs and exchange facilities, and exchange booths and ATMs at the airport. Large hotels change cash and travellers cheques.

POST

Main Post Office (Ave Sidi Mohammed; ⊙8.30am-4.30pm Mon-Fri)
Post Office (Ave du 29 Février; ⊙8.30am-4.30pm Mon-Fri)

TOURIST INFORMATION

Information Booth (☑0528 83 91 02; Al-Massira Airport; ⊙24hr)
ONMT (Délégation Régionale du Tourisme; ☑0528 84 63 77; Immeuble Ignouan, Ave Mohammed V; ⊙8.30am-4.30pm Mon-Fri) In the blue building next to DHL; not particularly helpful.

TRAVEL AGENCIES

There are many travel agencies around the junction of Blvd Hassan II and Ave des FAR, variously representing major airlines and offering tours and day trips.

ℹ Getting There & Away

AIR

Al-Massira Airport (☑0528 83 91 02; www.onda.ma; N10), mainly served by Royal Air Maroc (RAM) and European charter flights and budget airlines, is 28km southeast of Agadir en route to Taroudannt. Facilities include a post office, bag-wrap service, cafes, souvenir shops and wi-fi hot spots.

BUS

Although a good number of buses serve Agadir, it is quite possible you'll end up in Inezgane, 13km south, the regional transport hub. Check before you buy your ticket. Plenty of grands taxis (Dh5) and local buses (Dh8) shuttle between there and Agadir.

All the major bus companies, and plenty of smaller companies, serve the massive circular **gare routière** (bus station; Blvd Abderrahim Bouabid), past Souq al-Had. If you want to travel on a specific bus, it is worth booking ahead.

CTM (☑0528 82 53 41), which has a Nouveau Talborjt ticket office off Pl Lahcen Tamri, has several daily departures to these destinations:

DESTINATION	COST (DH)	DURATION (HR)
Casablanca	210	8
Dakhla	370	20
Essaouira	70	3½
Laâyoune	230	11½
Marrakesh	105	3½
Rabat	230	9
Tangier	325	13½
Taroudannt	35	2
Tiznit	40	1¾

Supratours (0528 84 12 07), which has a city-centre ticket office on Rue des Oranges, offers similar services.

CAR & MOTORCYCLE

The distances involved in touring southern Morocco make it worthwhile considering car rental. It is cheapest to book a vehicle online in advance; www.economycarrentals.com offers good deals in Agadir and at Al-Massira Airport. Local agencies charge from about Dh300 for a small car for one day, though there's usually room for haggling.

Local agencies are clustered in the arcade across Ave du Prince Moulay Abdallah from the bottom of Ave du 29 Février; around the junction of Ave des FAR and Blvd Hassan II; and at the corner of Ave Mohammed V and Ave du Général Kettani. Avis, Budget, Europcar and Hertz have offices both in the latter location and at the airport, where Thrifty and Sixt also have desks. Some accommodation options, such as Hôtel Petite Suède (p362), also offer car hire.

Scooters and motorbikes are also available, but you should check the state of the machines carefully.

TAXI

The main grand-taxi rank is located at the south end of Rue de Fès. Destinations include Essaouira (Dh80), Inezgane (Dh5) and Tarou-dannt (Dh32).

Getting Around

TO/FROM THE AIRPORT

The easiest option is to organise a transfer through your accommodation or hire a grand taxi.

Bus 37 runs from outside the airport (about 500m straight out on the road) to Inezgane (Dh8; every 40 minutes or so between 6.45am and 10.15pm), from where you can continue to

Agadir and destinations throughout southern Morocco.

You can also catch a shared grand taxi from outside the airport gates to Aït-Melloul (starting price Dh30; haggle hard), from where you can continue to Inezgane or Agadir.

BUS

Journeys within Agadir cost Dh4 and you can buy tickets on the bus. Buses run along Ave Mohammed V between the port and Inezgane.

TAXI

Orange petits taxis run around Agadir. Prices are worked out by meter; ask for it to be switched on. It costs about Dh10 to cross town.

Souss-Massa National Park منتزه سو ماسه الوطني

One of Morocco's most significant national parks and bird reserves, Souss-Massa (0528 33 38 80; www.tinyurl.com/ohwlnjs; Biougra) stretches down the coast from Inezgane, a block of over 330 sq km of protected land between the main north–south highway and the beach. It is a spectacular and wild place of cliffs, sand dunes, farmland, coastal steppes and forests.

The park was created in 1991 in recognition of its importance as a feeding ground for birds. The Souss estuary, at the northern end of the park, and in particular the Massa coastal lagoon, near the southern end, are popular with birdwatchers. The best times for birdwatching are March to April and October to November. Birds found here include ospreys, marbled ducks, cormorants, greater flamingos, flocks of sandgrouse and warblers. But the biggest attraction is the northern bald ibis. These birds, revered in ancient Egypt and once widespread in central Europe, North Africa and the Middle East, are an endangered species, with the world's only sizeable population found on this stretch of coast. Tourism development is an ongoing threat to the four local breeding grounds, which remain off-limits, but you can spot ibises around Oued Massa or at the mouth of the Tamri River.

The park is also a great place for walking. Animals such as jackals, red foxes, wild cats, genets and Eurasian wild boars are found here, while a large fenced area in the north of the park contains species that have disappeared from the south, including Dorcas and dama gazelles, addaxes, red-necked ostriches and scimitar-horned oryxes.

ℹ AIRPORT TAXIS

You can catch a taxi straight from Al-Massira Airport to numerous destinations. Tariffs for private hire, which are displayed at the airport information booth:

Agadir or Inezgane Dh200

Essaouira or Goulimime Dh1000

Mirleft Dh700

Tafraoute Dh900

Taghazout Dh300

Taroudannt or Tiznit Dh450

Guides can be arranged in the village of Massa, some 60km south of Agadir (signposted from the N1). From there, a track leads along the river to the estuary mouth (5km) and a tarred road leads to Sidi R'bat (8km). This tiny village has two claims to fame. Supposedly it is where the biblical Jonah was vomited up by a whale, and also where Uqba bin Nafi, the 7th-century Arab conqueror of Morocco, rode his horse triumphantly into the sea and called on God to witness that he could find no land left to conquer.

★Ksar Massa (☏0661 28 03 19; www.ksarmassa.com; Sidi R'bat; s/d/tr incl breakfast Dh1411/1962/2693, tent s/d Dh700/1100, lunch/dinner Dh170/300; ❋⛫⛭) , spectacularly located on Sidi R'bat beach, is a fantastical destination in itself. The terracotta-and-blue contemporary kasbah is a wonderful place to unwind, with hazy ocean views from its perch above the pale sands. Luxuriously spacious rooms and suites are painted in bright colours and meals are sumptuous affairs with multiple dishes. Management can arrange guided trips into the park and throughout the region. To get there, follow the signs from Massa or 3km south of Belfaa.

Next to Ksar Massa, La Dune (☏0666 80 78 24; www.ladune.de; Sidi R'bat; s/d/tr incl breakfast Dh400/500/650, tent per person incl breakfast from Dh100, dinner Dh70; ❋) has basic two- and four-person Berber tents, a pleasantly cool tented restaurant and African-themed, occasionally garish rooms with balconies.

ℹ Getting There & Away

From Agadir and Inezgane, Tiznit-bound local buses and grands taxis will drop you in Belfaa or Massa (about Dh20). From either, a grand taxi to Sidi R'bat costs about Dh200. Accommodation options in Sidi R'bat also offer transfers to/from Agadir airport (about Dh400). From Massa, it is about an hour's walk to Oued Massa river mouth; 4WDs also head into the park, but both Oued Massa and Oued Souss are usually accessible by 2WD (or grand taxi).

North of Agadir

Despite the villas, fun parks, golf courses and development projects colonising the coast around Agadir, if you're looking for surf and less crowded beaches, head north. There are sandy coves every few kilometres.

ℹ Getting There & Away

Grands taxis travel between Agadir and Taghazout (Dh10) via Aourir and Tamraght.

Tamraght & Aourir طمرات و اوريد

Aourir and Tamraght are known collectively as Banana Village because of the banana groves alongside Oued Tamraght, which separates the villages. Respectively some 12km and 14km north of Agadir, they share Banana Beach, which can be good for beginner surfers at its southern end. Aourir has facilities including a petrol station, a post office and banks.

At Rocher du Diable, round the headland to the north of Banana Beach, Imourane Surf Island (☏0614 12 20 00; www.imouranesurfisland.com; wetsuit/board rental per day Dh50/100, 2½hr lesson Dh200) offers surfboard rental and lessons. As in Taghazout, various companies offer accommodation and surf packages.

At the southern end of Banana Beach, Villa Mandala (☏0528 31 47 73; www.surfmaroc.co.uk; Aourir; r per person incl breakfast Dh400-500; ⛫⛭) is run by Surf Maroc and geared towards surfers. The decor mixes traditional and contemporary, with a curvy pool and white, rug-scattered interior.

The kitschy Hotel Littoral (☏0528 31 47 26; www.hotellittoral.com; Rte d'Essaouira, Aourir; s/d/tr/q/apt incl breakfast Dh240/328/477/686/987; ⛫⛭) is basic but comfortable, with a bar-restaurant and well-equipped en-suite rooms.

At the northern end of the beach, Banana Beach (Tamraght; mains Dh70; ⊙breakfast & lunch) is the perfect spot to while away a few hours, offering sunloungers on the sands and seafood, omelettes, sandwiches and cold beer. Chez Brahim (Rocher du Diable; mains Dh70; ⊙lunch & dinner) is smarter, serving hearty fish or meat platters (from Dh150) on its seafront terrace.

Taghazout تاغزوت

Six kilometres from Tamraght, the laid-back fishing village of Taghazout, once famous for calamari and hippies, is now considered Morocco's premier surfing destination for both pros and learners. Surf breaks such as Hash Point, Panorama, Anchor Point, La Source, Killer Point and Mysteries surround the village. The surf is most reliable from October to April.

If you just want to hang out, haul your hammock elsewhere; the scruffy roadside village is a mixed-up place, a dry tourist town where surf culture dominates. The main beach is great for swimming, but during and after the Moroccon summer holiday, the influx of domestic tourists overwhelms the village's infrastructure.

Taghazout has internet cafes and a pharmacy, but most facilities are in Aourir.

Run by a group of British surfers, Surf Maroc (☑ 0528 20 02 72, 0675 46 06 37, in UK 0044 1794 322 709; www.surfmaroc.co.uk; 🖳) offers accommodation, guiding, lessons, yoga, equipment and car hire, appealing to experts and learners alike. Accommodation comes with splashes of surf cool at Taghazout Villa (☑ 0528 20 03 68; www.surfmaroc.co.uk/taghazoutvilla; r per person incl breakfast Dh350; 🖳) and L'Auberge (☑ 0528 20 02 72; www.surfmaroc.co.uk/auberge; r per person incl breakfast Dh250; 🖳); at the time of writing, Surf Maroc was set to open a boutique hotel with a pool, hammam and licensed restaurant in late 2014.

Numerous locals have followed in Surf Maroc's wake, offering accommodation and surf packages. Taghazout Surf Hostel (☑ 0676 06 94 95; www.taghazoutsurfhostel.com; r incl breakfast from Dh330; 🖳), run by the friendly Yassine, has basic double, twin, quadruple and six-bed rooms with shared bathrooms. Locals also rent out apartments and rooms, which may be your only option in summer if you have not booked ahead. Taghazout Bay Apartments (☑ 0671 63 89 83; www.taghazoutsurfcars.com; per person Dh150) offers tidy self-catering accommodation and car hire.

There are several cafes and snack bars (all unlicensed) on the main road. At the foot of the lanes leading to the beach, the cafe at L'Auberge (mains Dh60; ⊙ breakfast, lunch & dinner) is a funky hangout serving Moroccan and international food, including recommended fruit juices and Moroccan chicken stew.

Immouzzer des Ida Outanane
ايموزار ادو اوتنان

This thoroughly recommended detour takes you about 60km (two hours' drive) northeast of Agadir, into the High Atlas foothills. On the way you pass through the aptly named Paradise Valley, an oleander- and palm-lined gorge, and a popular picnic and swimming spot. Local producers have formed a route du miel (honey route), and stalls sell the sweet stuff as well as argan oil. Signs by the road point to walking trails.

The famous cascades of Immouzzer are one of North Africa's most beautiful waterfalls. The calcium-rich water flows most strongly between February and August, although recent droughts have frequently reduced it to a trickle. Given the stream of tourist stalls and *faux guides* (unofficial guides) leading to the falls, you may prefer Paradise Valley.

When it's flowing, water falls off the edge of the plateau in several chutes, running down one cliff face known as the Bride's Veil. The path to the foot of the falls finishes at an iridescent blue plunge pool with overhanging rocks and foliage. If you can cross the river here, you can climb to a plateau and see the top plunge pool, and caves once inhabited by hippies. The steep, 4km road from Immouzzer village down to the falls is one of many walks in the region.

The area turns white in February and March when the almond trees blossom. There is a honey harvest and festival in July and August, and around late November you may be lucky enough to witness the olive harvest. Locals climb into the trees to shake olives from the branches and oil is pressed in the village. Thursday is souq day.

🛏 Sleeping & Eating

There are cafes at the bottom of the path to the falls, and on the way up. The hotels in Paradise Valley are spread out about 30km from Aourir.

★ Auberge le Panoramic   HOTEL €
(☑ 0528 21 67 09; www.auberge-le-panoramic.com; Paradise Valley; s/d/tr incl half-board Dh280/500/750; ❄ 🖳) The new block at this friendly stop on the *route du miel* is the pick of Paradise Valley's accommodation, with almost vertigo-inducing views from the en-suite rooms' balconies. The restaurant serves tajines, omelettes, brochettes and a breakfast featuring three honeys, produced by the beehives on the slopes below.

Hotel Tifrit   HOTEL €
(☑ 0528 21 67 08; www.hotel-tifrit.net; Paradise Valley; s/d incl half board Dh300/450; ❄ 🖳) Right by the river in the *palmeraie* (palm grove), near the waterfall of the same name, Tifrit has six en-suite rooms with big windows overlooking the palms.

Auberge Bab Immouzer
HOTEL €

(☑ 0670 13 10 06; www.aubergebabimouzer.com; Paradise Valley; r Dh250-300; ❄ ☷) Well kept but low on atmosphere, Bab Immouzer has six en-suite rooms and a series of terraces overlooking the neighbouring *palmeraie* and valley. Poolside rooms have balconies with a view.

Hôtel des Cascades
HOTEL €€

(☑ 0528 82 60 23; www.cascades-hotel.net; s/d Dh460/572; ❄ ☷) In a wonderful location on the edge of Immouzer village, perched high above the valley, this hotel is set in a riotous garden with tennis courts. Flower baskets and artwork decorate the terrace and corridors; the 27 rooms have small balconies, and there's a licensed restaurant (mains Dh75). Paths descend 4km from the garden to the cascades. The hotel also has a self-catering house 20km away, en route to Essaouira.

❶ Getting There & Away

Buses and grands taxis run between Aourir and Immouzzer (Dh25) until about 4pm. From Agadir, it is hard to visit the falls in a day by public transport; you can visit on a tour or hire a grand taxi. Thursday, when Immouzzer's weekly market takes place, is a good day to pick up a lift but a bad time to drive as the narrow road is busy. Between October and May, the river sometimes destroys the road.

Taroudannt
تارودانت

POP 70,000

Taroudannt (also spelled Taroudant) is sometimes called 'Little Marrakesh', but that description doesn't do the Souss Valley trading centre justice. Hidden by magnificent red-mud walls, and with the snowcapped peaks of the High Atlas beckoning beyond, Taroudannt's souqs and squares have a healthy sprinkling of Maghrebi mystique. Yet it is also a practical place, a market town where Berbers buy the produce of the rich and fertile Oued Souss plain.

There aren't any must-see sights. Instead, the medina is a place to stroll and linger. The two souqs are well worth a browse, more laid-back than Marrakesh but with an atmosphere of activity that is missing in Agadir. With the little-explored western High Atlas, the Anti Atlas and the coast all nearby, the town makes a good base for trekking and activities. Just 65km inland from Al-Massira Airport, it is a more atmospheric staging post to/from the airport than Agadir.

History

Taroudannt was one of the early bases of the Almoravids, who established themselves here in AD 1056, at the beginning of their conquest of Morocco. In the 16th century, the emerging Saadians made it their capital for about 20 years. By the time they moved on to Marrakesh, they had turned the Souss Valley, in which the city stands, into the country's most important producer of sugar cane, cotton, rice and indigo; all valuable trade items on the trans-Saharan trade routes the dynasty was keen to control. The Saadians constructed the old part of town and the kasbah, though most of it was destroyed and the inhabitants massacred in 1687 by Moulay Ismail, as punishment for opposing him. Only the ramparts survived. Most of what stands inside them dates from the 18th century.

Taroudannt continued to be a centre of intrigue and sedition against the central government well into the 20th century, and indeed played host to El-Hiba, a southern chief who opposed the Treaty of Fès, the 1912 agreement that created the French Protectorate.

◉ Sights

Ramparts
HISTORIC SITE

The 7.5km of ramparts surrounding Taroudannt are among the best-preserved pisé walls in Morocco. Their colour changes from golden brown to deepest red depending on the time of day. They can easily be explored on foot (two hours), preferably in the late afternoon; or take a bike or horse-drawn calèche and see the walls by moonlight.

Gates
HISTORIC SITE

Built in the 16th and 17th centuries, a string of mighty defensive towers create the gates of the city. Considered the main gate, the triple-arched **Bab el-Kasbah** (also known as Bab Essalsla) is approached via an avenue of orange trees. Steps lead to the top of the tower, where you can walk along the ramparts. Near Bab el-Kasbah, **Bab Sedra** (cyclists and pedestrians only) leads to the kasbah.

Kasbah
KASBAH

The old kasbah quarter, originally a fortress built by Moulay Ismail, is today a poor but safe residential area, where winding lanes and low archways lead to tiny squares and dead ends. The governor's palace, on the

Taroudannt

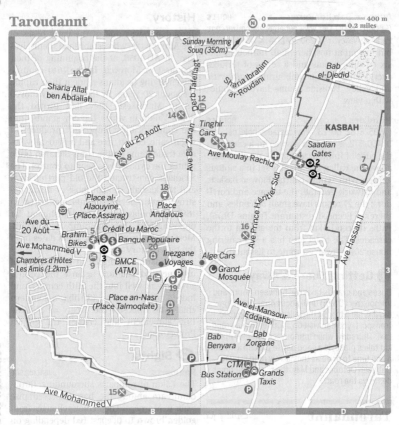

eastern side of the kasbah, now forms part of Hôtel Palais Salam.

Place al-Alaouyine   SQUARE

(Place Assarag) During Moroccan holidays, the *grand place* is like Marrakesh's Djemaa el-Fna in miniature, with storytellers, snake charmers, escapologists and performers working the crowds.

🏃 Activities

★ La Maison Anglaise   CULTURAL TOUR

(☑ 0661 23 66 27, 0528 55 16 28; www.sites.google.com/site/cecumaisonanglaise/activities; 422 Derb Afferdou) Excellent guides and activities including trekking, Berber village visits and homestays, wildlife trips, cookery lessons, and visits to the soap-making and beekeeping cooperatives they support. Day trips to the valley at Afensou in the High Atlas involve walking through olive groves to a swimming hole.

Calèche   CARRIAGE TOUR

You can tour the ramparts in a calèche. The horse-drawn carriages gather just inside Bab el-Kasbah, on Pl al-Alaouyine and at other prominent spots. A one-way trip across town should cost roughly the same as by petit taxi, although the driver may disagree; don't pay more than Dh20. For a one-hour tour, including the medina, a circuit of the ramparts and a small tannery, don't pay more than Dh100.

Trekking   TREKKING

Taroudannt is a great base for trekking in the western High Atlas region, including the secluded Tichka Plateau, a delightful area of highland meadows and hidden gorges (two days minimum). The Afensou and Tizi n'Test areas are ideal for day walks. Agencies in town offer treks; insist on travelling with a qualified guide. Charges start at about Dh350 per person per day, including transport and picnic. In addition to the

Taroudannt

trekking guides available through accommodation, **Abdellatif Abassi** (☏0670 59 13 88; abdelroudana@gmail.com) is uncertified but recommended by readers, and can organise mules and village homestays.

🛌 Sleeping

Budget hotels on and around the two central squares offer basic accommodation and roof terraces, good for sunbathing and people-watching, while the midrange hotels listed below offer pick-ups from Agadir Al-Massira Airport (Dh400) and can organise activities.

Hotel Saadiens   HOTEL €

(☏0528 85 25 89; hotelsaad@menara.ma; Ave du 20 Août; s/d Dh220/280; 🛜❄) Signposted from all over town, Saadiens has aged but spacious rooms with reasonable en-suite bathrooms, stripy bedspreads and Berber designs on the doors. Despite the gloomy, echoing corridors, it is a central retreat from the medina, with a 1st-floor lounge and mountain views from the roof terrace. Ave

du 20 Août is a thoroughfare, so ask for a room at the rear. Half-board is available.

Hôtel Taroudannt   HOTEL €

(☏0528 85 24 16; Place al-Alaouyine; s/d/tr from Dh160/200/300; ❄) In this central option, tiled corridors lead past a restaurant and jungly courtyard to rooms with simple bathrooms. The drawbacks are the noise from Pl al-Alaouyine and the popular courtyard bar, which may make women feel uncomfortable.

Chambres d'Hôtes des Amis   MAISON D'HÔTE €

(☏0667 60 16 86; www.chambresdesamis.com; Sidi Belkas; s/d incl breakfast Dh80/160; 🛜) This good-value guesthouse has aged but big rooms, basic bathrooms with intermittent hot water, a couple of salons, and a roof terrace for breakfast. It's 800m west of Bab Taghount (on the west side of the ramparts) at the beginning of the open countryside, although street noise and the nearby mosque overwhelm any suburban tranquillity. The proprietor, Said Dayfollah, offers bike hire, trekking and activities, pick-ups from Al-Massira Airport (Dh300) and meals on request (Dh70).

Hôtel el-Warda   HOTEL €

(☏0528 85 27 63; Pl an-Nasr; s/d/tr Dh80/100/130) This ultra-cheapie has a *zellij* (tilework) terrace overlooking Pl an-Nasr and basic 2nd-floor rooms with shared toilets and showers. Solo female travellers might find the alley entrance and male-dominated 1st-floor cafe difficult.

★Palais Oumensour   BOUTIQUE HOTEL, RIAD €€

(☏0528 55 02 15; www.palaisoumensour.com; Al Mansour Borj Oumensour Tadjount; r/ste incl breakfast Dh770/990; ❄🛜❄) Tasteful, tranquil and good value, Palais Oumensour hides away on a medina lane by the Catholic church garden. Above the central courtyard with its jade pool, the four doubles and six suites are a winning mix of modern comforts and traditional materials, with Georges Braque prints and *tadelakt* (polished lime plaster) walls. In the elegant public spaces is a hammam, a massage room, a roof terrace with High Atlas views, two Jacuzzis and a bar.

★La Maison Anglaise   GUESTHOUSE €€

(☏0661 23 66 27, 0528 55 16 28; www.sites.google.com/site/cecumaisonanglaise; 422 Derb Afferdou; s/d incl breakfast Dh350/550; ❄@🛜) On a quiet street north of Taroudannt's central hubbub, this Green Key–certified medina house makes a comfortable and welcoming base, run by a brilliant team of lovely locals. As well as nine en-suite rooms, there is a kitchen for self-catering, a roof terrace with views of the High and Anti Atlas, informative displays in the tiled corridors, and a small library. Breakfast and meals are feasts, too. What really makes this British-owned option special is the staff, who help you get to grips with local culture, whether on their tours (p370) or by just pointing you in the right direction. As the name suggests, English is spoken.

Ryad Tafilag BOUTIQUE HOTEL €€
(☎0528 85 06 07; www.riad-tafilag.com; Derb Tafellagt; s/d/tr incl breakfast from Dh550/605/770;) Consisting of a few medina houses joined together, this creative and original hotel is a warren of spiral staircases, terraces, lounges, hidey holes and a hammam. You may feel like Alice in Wonderland exploring its corners, or just feel irritated when you forget your camera and face a multistorey expedition to fetch it. The eight relaxing rooms and suites, three of which have private terraces, place guests' needs above the dictates of design, managing to be unfussily artistic throughout. Free bikes are offered to guests.

Hôtel Palais Salam KASBAH €€
(☎0528 85 25 01; www.hotel-palais-salam-taroudant.com; kasbah; s/d/ste incl breakfast from Dh582/674/1424;) This former pasha's residence, entered through the east wall of the kasbah, lives up to its palatial name, with gardens, pools, courtyards and fountains (one inhabited by turtles) on various levels. With their traditional decor, the older, ground-floor rooms have an authentic feel, but the newer rooms, behind pink walls and blue shutters, are more spacious. Rooms and bathrooms are disappointing compared with newer options, as is the service, but it remains a wonderful environment, with a bar and Moroccan and international restaurants.

Eating

The hotel cafes and touristy eateries on Pl al-Alaouyine are good for breakfast on the square, and serve tajines and simple grills later in the day. The best place to look for cheap eats is around Pl an-Nasr and north along Ave Bir Zaran, where you will find the usual tajines, *harira* (lentil soup) and salads.

Putting together a picnic is easy in Taroudannt. In addition to stalls in the souqs, there's a **fruit and vegetable market** (Ave du 20 Août) at the northern end of Ave Bir Zaran. La Maison Anglaise (p371) also makes picnics (Dh50) for nonguests.

★ **L'Agence** MOROCCAN, FRENCH €
(☎0528 55 02 70; Ave Prince Héretier Sidi Mohammed; mains Dh50, set menu Dh110; ⊙lunch & dinner) Behind the Grand Mosquée, this delightful little restaurant serves dishes from the French-Moroccan proprietors' homelands, with mains such as chicken *pastilla* and goat tajine on offer. The starters include delicious tasting plates, which you can enjoy among lanterns hanging from wooden beams and artworks in alcoves.

Chez Nada MOROCCAN €
(☎0528 85 17 26; Ave Moulay Rachid; mains Dh55-95, set menu Dh80; ⊙lunch & dinner) This 60-year-old restaurant specialises in tajines, including one with pigeon (or chicken), prunes and grilled almonds. Above the male-dominated ground-floor cafe and elegant white 1st-floor dining room, the roof terrace has views over public gardens. *Pastilla* and royal couscous (Dh75 to Dh95) should be ordered two hours ahead.

Mehdi Snack FAST FOOD €
(off Ave Moulay Rachid; set menu & pizza Dh20-70; ⊙10am-11pm) Located at the back of Chez Nada, and run by the same family, this snack bar sells burgers, pizzas, brochettes and salads.

Jnane Soussia MOROCCAN €€
(☎0528 85 49 80; Ave Mohammed V; mains Dh80; ⊙lunch & dinner) This recommended garden restaurant has tented seating areas set around a large swimming pool adjacent to the ramparts. The house specialities include *mechoui* (whole roast lamb) and pigeon *pastilla,* which have to be ordered in advance, but the chicken tajine with lemon and olives is good for a light lunch and everything is decent.

Drinking & Nightlife

There is a line of fresh **orange-juice stands** on Pl an-Nasr. Hôtel Palais Salam and Hôtel Taroudannt have bars.

Cafe Andalous JUICE BAR
(Pl Andalous; smoothies Dh10) Beneath a dentist's sign on a small square adjoining Ave

Bir Zaran, this cheerful place is good for a mixed-fruit smoothie.

Shopping

Taroudannt is the central Chleuh city of the Souss, so it is a good place to look for the quality silver jewellery for which this tribe is renowned. The jewellery is influenced both by Saharan tribes and by the Jewish silversmiths who formed a significant part of the community until the late 1960s.

★ Souq Arabe ARTS & CRAFTS
The main souq, also known as the *grand souq,* has antique and souvenir shops hidden in the quiet streets. The area southwest of the mosque is good for present shopping, with a small square of jewellery shops just off Ave Bir Zaran.

Souq Berbère ARTS & CRAFTS, CARPETS
Also known as the *marché municipal,* this souq on the south side of Pl an-Nasr sells carpets, jewellery, argan oil, musical instruments, lamps, leatherwork and ceramics – past the trainers and mobile phones on the central thoroughfare.

Sunday Morning Souq FOOD & DRINK
This large market, held outside Bab el-Khemis north of the kasbah, brings in people from the whole region.

Information

Taroudannt has no 'European' quarter or ville nouvelle (new town). Most facilities are found on and around the two central squares, Pl al-Alaouyine (formerly Pl Assarag) and Pl an-Nasr (formerly Pl Talmoqlate).

Banks on Pl al-Alaouyine have ATMs, money-changing facilities and visa services. Internet cafes are found along Aves Bir Zaran and Mohammed V.

Hospital (Ave Moulay Rachid)

Inezgane Voyages (☑0528 55 06 46; Pl an-Nasr; ☺9am-12.30pm & 2.30-5pm Mon-Sat) Represents airlines including RAM.

Post Office (Ave du 20 Août; ☺8.30am-4.30pm Mon-Fri)

ℹ Getting There & Away

BUS
Buses depart from the station outside Bab Zorgane. **CTM** (☑0528 85 38 58; Bab Zorgane) has the most reliable buses, with at least one daily service to each of the following:

DESTINATION	COST (DH)	DURATION (HR)
Agadir	35	3
Casablanca	195	8
Marrakesh	100	4
Ouarzazate	105	5

Other companies serve Agadir and Inezgane (Dh25, 1½ hours, hourly), Taliouine (Dh70, 1½ hours, daily) and Tata (Dh80, five hours, daily).

CAR
The best option is to hire a car from one of the major companies operating at Agadir Al-Massira Airport.

There are local agencies in Taroudannt, including **Alge Cars** (☑0615 09 04 13; algecars@yahoo.fr; Ave Prince Héretier Sidi Mohammed, opposite mosque; per day Dh300) and **Tinghir Cars** (☑0661 19 02 89; Ave Moulay Rachid).

ARGAN COUNTRY

As you travel along the N10 east of Taroudannt you will see frizzy argan trees, beloved of local goats and international chefs, growing near the road.

In a restored 19th-century mansion on the edge of the Berber village of Ouled Berhil, some 45km northeast of Taroudannt, is **Hôtel Palais Riad Hida** (☑0528 53 10 44; www.riadhida.com; s/d incl half-board Dh638/1067; ❄☎☀). Accommodation is in nondescript bungalows, but it's a special environment from the moment you cross the tiled threshold and clap eyes on the central courtyard, with its towering palms and long pools.

Some 10km further on from Ouled Berhil, a signpost indicates the Tizi n'Test road, one of the most spectacular and perilous passes in the country, leading northeast over the High Atlas to Marrakesh.

Approaching the mountains, this secondary road leads through a lush state-run argan preserve – a dream destination for mountain goats accustomed to slim pickings in the High Atlas. Stop here to picnic in the shade among frolicking kids, or stake out the herds for the ultimate Anti Atlas postcard shot: a goat casually balanced on a treetop, munching on sun-ripe argan nuts.

TAXI

Grands taxis gather just outside Bab Zorgane. Destinations include the following:

Agadir (Dh30)

Inezgane (Dh26) Change here for frequent services to Agadir.

Marrakesh (Dh130) To travel via the Tizi n'Test, you will need to hire the entire taxi (Dh700 to Dh1000).

ⓘ Getting Around

Taroudannt is a good place to cycle; bikes can be rented at **Brahim Bikes** (☑ 0662 74 10 91; Pl al-Alaouyine; per hr/day Dh10/60). Petits taxis charge Dh7 per trip (Dh10 after 8pm).

Taliouine تالوين

POP 6000

The straggling village of Taliouine, halfway between Taroudannt and Ouarzazate, is dominated by hills and the impressive Glaoui kasbah.

Taliouine is the African centre of *l'or rouge* (red gold) – saffron, the world's most expensive spice. Numerous shops and boutiques sell it here for about Dh35 to Dh40 per gram. The purple *Crocus sativus* flower, from which the spice comes, grows only above 1200m. It flowers between mid-October and mid-November, when a festival is held to celebrate the harvest and you can see locals picking the flowers around villages 12km east of Taliouine.

Beware 'counterfeit saffron'; the genuine article should stain your fingers yellow (rather than red), taste bitter (rather than sweet) and carry a spicy price tag.

The village comes to life during the Monday souq, near Auberge le Safran.

◉ Sights & Activities

Activities can be arranged through **Zafrani** (☑ 0613 88 05 26; www.zafrani.ch; Taliouine), as well as through accommodation. The Swiss-Moroccan company specialises in trekking, but it organises a range of cultural tours and activities including star-gazing, skiing and meditation, catering to people and families of all ages.

★**Coopérative Souktana du Safran**　MUSEUM

(☑ 0528 53 44 52; www.souktanadusafran.org; ⊗ 8.30am-6.30pm) 🖉 Founded in 1979, the largest and oldest of Taliouine's saffron cooperatives has 160 members (four are women). The centre is well worth visiting for the museum, calligrapher and informative employees. They can explain saffron production, give you a tasting and sell you the spice, plus related products including chocolates, cosmetics and calligraphy ink.

Dar Azaafaran　MUSEUM

(☑ 0528 53 44 13; www.darazaafaran.com; ⊗ 8am-7pm) This modern information centre is devoted to *l'or rouge,* with a small museum, saffron for sale by local cooperatives and a display of the current going rate.

Calligraphie Tifinaghe　ARTS CENTRE

(☑ 0601 35 31 51; www.molidaz.blogspot.com) An Amazigh poet and calligrapher, Moulid Nidouissadan paints Berber proverbs and colourful compositions.

Kasbah　KASBAH

Gazing at the brown hills, the kasbah is mostly disintegrating, but it makes a pleasant sunset stroll.

Trekking　TREKKING

Taliouine is a popular trekking centre for nearby **Jebel Siroua**, which offers some of the finest walking in the Anti Atlas. The village is one of the best places in the region to find trekking guides; in addition to accommodation and Zafrani, try **Maroc Inedit** (☑ 0666 36 25 42; www.maroc-inedit.com) and **Siroua Discovery** (☑ 0617 03 07 03; www.siroua-discovery.com).

🛏️ Sleeping & Eating

For dinner, ask for half-board at your accommodation or try Auberges le Safran or Souktana. At the west end of the main drag near the *gare routière* (bus station), grills smoke away, and you can get a tajine (Dh50), made with saffron, at Auberge Siroua. In addition to the following, there are cheap hotels on the main street.

Auberge le Safran　HOTEL €

(☑ 0668 39 42 23; www.auberge-safran.com; d/tr/ste from Dh170/210/300; ❋ 🛜 🐾) Le Safran has basic, colourful en-suite rooms, with two budget doubles on the roof terrace and a spacious four-person suite. The salon looks across the fields at the kasbah, and downstairs is a Berber tent on the patio. The hotel harvests its own saffron, which it sells in the on-site shop-museum and uses in the delicious meals. The road noise is irritating, but the service is professional. Owner Mahfoud offers activities including trekking, hammam visits, saffron-based cookery courses, and a saffron and argan producers tour.

Auberge Souktana
HOTEL €

(☑0528 53 40 75; souktana@menara.ma; rooms s/d/tr/q Dh180/220/300/360, bungalows s/d Dh100/160, tents 1/2 people Dh50/80; 🕾) At this trekking-orientated auberge, guests consult maps in the relaxing communal area, and owner Ahmed can offer advice and arrange guides. Half-board is available (per person Dh220) and the colourful rooms are pleasantly decorated in traditional style. It's east of the village, across the N10 from the kasbah with great views of the crumbling fort.

Chez Souad
MAISON D'HÔTE €

(☑0671 05 68 46; moradchoukri@yahoo.fr; r per person from Dh60) Overlooking a dusty soccer pitch behind Dar Azaafaran, this sprawling family home has a rooftop terrace with views of the kasbah and town. There are eight rooms accommodating up to four people each, three with private bathroom. Half-board is available (per person Dh160) and Souad's brother, Morad Choukri, is a trekking guide.

★ Escale Rando
MAISON D'HÔTE €€

(☑0662 54 78 28; www.escalerando.fr; s/d without bathroom Dh242/330, with bathroom Dh330/440; 🕾) Abutting the kasbah, this is a romantic little spot centred on a courtyard with gardens, lights, fountains and tortoises. There are four high-ceilinged rooms, a fully equipped kitchen and, for hot nights, a terrace where guests can sleep alongside the kasbah battlements. Half-board is an extra Dh55 per person and activities can be arranged.

Auberge Tobkal
CAMPGROUND, APARTMENT €€

(☑0528 53 43 43; www.maghrebtourism.com/aubergetoubkal; camping Dh60, bungalow per person incl half-board Dh220, apt Dh800-1200; 🕾🎱) This tidy campground, on the main road 500m east of the turn-off for the kasbah, also has bungalows with en-suite bathrooms and four new apartments.

ℹ Information
On the main road near Dar Azaafaran are banks and an internet cafe.

ℹ Getting There & Away
The N10 east of Talioune crosses a beautiful and immense landscape, before joining the N9 (the main Marrakesh–Ouarzazate road) near the turn-off to Aït Benhaddou.

BUS
Talioune has a small *gare routière* (bus station). There are not always seats available on the buses passing through town, so grands taxis, also found at the bus station, are a better option.

TAXI
Ouarzazate Direct taxis are rare; you will normally have to change at Tazenakht (Dh30).

Taroudannt There are direct taxis, but it will likely be quicker to change at Ouled Berhil (Dh28).

THE ANTI ATLAS
الأطلس الصغير

The Anti Atlas remains one of the least visited parts of Morocco's mountainscape, which is surprising, as it is beautiful and close to Agadir. The mountains are the stronghold of the Chleuh tribes, who live in a loose confederation of villages strung across the barren mountains, some of them still far beyond the reach of any central authority. Living in areas moulded by the demanding landscape of granite boulders and red-lava flows, the Chleuh have always been devoted to their farms in the lush oasis valleys, now some of the country's most beautiful *palmeraies*.

Tafraoute
تافراوت

POP 5000

Nestled in the gorgeous Ameln Valley, the village of Tafraoute is surrounded on all sides by red-granite mountains. Despite its unassuming appearance, the area is quite prosperous due to the hard-earned cash sent home by relatives working in the big cities or abroad. It is a pleasant and relaxed base for exploring the region.

☆ Activities
The best way to see the beautiful surrounding countryside is by walking or cycling, and several companies and guides offer mountain-biking and trekking trips. Operators have booths west of Hôtel Salama. **Tafraoute Aventure** (☑0528 80 13 68; www.tafraout-aventure.com; bike hire per day Dh50) has useful colour maps of the area; you can pick up photocopies elsewhere. Tafraoute Aventure offers information and guides for most activities, although there are also some excellent specialists.

Tafraoute

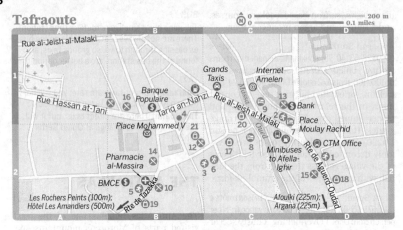

Cycling

The palm-filled Aït Mansour Gorges, leading towards the bald expanses of the southern Anti Atlas, and the Pierres Bleues (p379) are great destinations. Several places rent out bikes of varying quality; expect to pay about Dh50/80 per day for a road/mountain bike with a helmet, pump and puncture-repair kit.

Maison de Vacances   BICYCLE RENTAL
(☑ 0528 80 01 97; maison_vacances@yahoo.fr; per day Dh80) Has good mountain bikes.

Tafraoute VTT   BICYCLE RENTAL
(☑ 0670 40 93 84; www.tafraout-vtt.cla.fr; per day Dh50-80) Has bike racks for cars – useful for a drive-and-cyle trip to Aït Mansour.

Trekking & Climbing

Tafraoute and the Anti Atlas offer numerous climbing routes and trekking possibilities, though most of the walks are strenuous.

Au Coin des Nomades   CLIMBING, HIKING
(☑ 0661 62 79 21; starsmoons@outlouk.fr) Houssine Laroussi, a respected climber, is a good source of trekking and climbing information, guides, books and topograpical maps. He can also organise village homestays.

Tawada   HIKING, CLIMBING
(☑ 0661 82 26 77; www.guide-tafraout.com) Accredited English-speaking guide Brahim Bahou offers information and guided treks lasting from one day upwards, and can organise mules.

Hammams

Tafraoute is a good place for an authentic hammam experience as some houses here still lack water. There are three in town; massages are available at the **new hammam** (Dh10; ☺ men 7am-10pm, women to 7pm) behind Auberge Les Amis, although the male-only **old hammam** (Dh10; ☺ men 7am-10pm), just behind the market, is more authentic.

✽✽ Festivals & Events

Almond Blossom Festival FESTIVAL
(☉Mar) The Tafraoute area celebrates its almond harvest at the Almond Blossom Festival.

🛏 Sleeping

There are two campgrounds 1km west of town on the Tiznit road (R104).

★ Hôtel Salama HOTEL €
(✆0528 80 00 26; www.hotelsalama.com; s/d/tr Dh178/256/314, half-board per person Dh208; ✱❄) Readers recommend this hotel mixing local materials and modern standards, with Berber artefacts decorating the corridors and helpful staff, who speak some English. The roof terrace has mountain views and some rooms have balconies overlooking the market square, which the cafe-restaurant (breakfast/set menu Dh23/65) opens out onto.

Les Rochers Peints HOTEL €
(✆0528 80 00 32; www.hotelrocherspeints-tafraout.com; s/d/tr Dh200/300/350) The former Riad Tafraout lives up to its name with its profusion of colourful stained glass, artworks, carvings, furniture, rugs, textiles, Berber decor and vintage French posters. Located on the edge of town, it has a wraparound terrace with good mountain views and an airy cafe in reception. The only letdown is the 10 en-suite rooms, which are small and stuffy.

Argana MAISON D'HÔTE, HOSTEL €
(✆0528 80 14 96; www.argana-tafraout.com; s/d incl breakfast from Dh120/200; ✱❄) Recommended by readers, Argana has comfortable backpacker-style rooms of various sizes with shared bathrooms. Also on offer is a laundry service, good breakfast, lounge, terraces, and advice from the helpful owner Mustapha, an English-speaking trekking afficionado.

Auberge Les Amis HOTEL €
(✆0528 80 19 21; auberge.lesamis@yahoo.fr; r without bathroom incl breakfast Dh170, s/d with bathroom incl breakfast Dh130/200; ✱❄) Overlooking Pl Moulay Rachid, Les Amis has nine basic rooms on three floors, and a Berber tent (per person Dh60) on the roof terrace. The bathrooms are slightly whiffy but the carpet bedheads give a pleasant Berber ambience.

Hôtel Tanger HOTEL €
(✆0528 80 01 90; s/d Dh40/80) A small, friendly hotel with nine basic rooms, reasonable shared bathrooms and toilets, and a roof terrace. The ground-floor cafe serves breakfast (Dh25), tajines (Dh35) and the usual dishes.

Afoulki MAISON D'HÔTE €
(✆0528 80 14 92; www.maisondhotes-afoulki.com; s/d Dh100/200) Above its cafe-restaurant (breakfast/set menu Dh20/75), Afoulki's white rooms are bland but large and clean, with shared bathrooms and a roof terrace.

Hôtel Les Amandiers HOTEL €€
(✆0528 80 00 88; www.hotel-lesamandiers.com; s/d Dh318/436; ✱❄🐾) This kasbah-like hilltop pile has 60 reasonably attractive rooms with small balconies making the most of the incredible views of the rock formations ringing Tafraoute. The pool and restaurant (set menu Dh140) share the views; the bar is tucked away in a corner without any vistas, but you can take drinks outside. The furniture is rather tired and the hotel needs a renovation, but you may have the place to yourself.

WORTH A TRIP

TIZOURGANE KASBAH

Overlooking the main road roughly 65km from Tafraoute and 100km from Agadir, this stunning renovated 13th-century kasbah (✆0661 94 13 50; www.tizourgane-kasbah.com; Rte d'Agadir, Idaougnidif; per person incl half-board Dh330; ❄) would make an atmospheric last night before catching the plane home. The kasbah was essentially a fortified town, enclosing 25 houses, a mosque, granary and prison, and thick stone walls tower above the passages around the ancient structure. Rooms are simply decorated, with carpets, stripy bedspreads, fans and shared bathrooms, but derive extra romance from the setting. There's a hammam and a terrace restaurant surveys the wrinkled hillsides, scattered villages and Jebel L'Kest. If you're just passing, you can tour the kasbah for Dh10. Buses on the Aït Baha route to Agadir can drop you here.

✕ Eating & Drinking

Plenty of small food stores sell basic picnic supplies to supplement the fruit, veg and olives available in the markets. For a sunset beer, head to the panoramic terrace at Hôtel Les Amandiers.

Café-Restaurant Atlas
CAFE €

(meal Dh40; ☺ lunch & dinner) The covered terrace at Atlas is a popular local hang-out, with cheese omelettes, brochettes, tajines and sandwiches on the broad menu.

Cafe-Restaurant Panorama
CAFE €

(mains Dh60; ☺ lunch & dinner; 🖥) Recommended locally, this terrace eatery dishes up tajines, omelettes, large glasses of fruit juice and mountain views.

L'Étoile d'Agadir
CAFE €

(breakfast Dh30; ☺ 8am-6pm) Recommended by readers, this is Tafraoute's favourite cafe for a continental breakfast in the morning sun. After serving breakfast, L'Étoile remains open for drinks throughout the day.

★ Restaurant La Kasbah
REGIONAL, MOROCCAN €€

(☎ 0672 30 39 09; mains Dh70, set menu Dh90; ☺ breakfast, lunch & dinner) Decorated with rugs, lanterns and jewellery, this licensed restaurant serves dishes including tajines, *harira* and the house speciality, nomad tortilla: *kalia* (minced mutton with tomato, peppers, egg, onion and 44 spices served in a tajine). Argan oil and spices abound in all the dishes.

Restaurant L'Étoile du Sud
MOROCCAN €€

(☎ 0528 80 00 38; set menu Dh90; ☺ lunch & dinner) L'Étoile du Sud serves a good set menu in a rather kitsch Bedouin-style tent. You may have to share the place with tour groups, particularly at lunchtime, but the service is professional and on warm nights it's one of the best places to eat.

🛍 Shopping

Several slipper shops around the market area sell the traditional leather slippers (yellow for men, red for women). Look out, too, for people selling local argan and olive oil. Numerous shops around the post-office square sell Berber jewellery, argan products and souvenirs, and shopping here is less pressurised than in the cities.

★ Maison du Troc
CARPETS, CRAFT

(☺ 10am-8pm Mon-Sat & by appointment) A good range of Berber and Tuareg products, including pottery, jewellery, cactus-silk blankets and camel-wool kilims (carpets), some made by local village women.

Au Coin des Nomades
CRAFT, SOUVENIRS

Berber handiwork and local souvenirs at reasonable prices. Hours are sporadic.

Maison Tuareg
CARPETS, CRAFT

(☺ 9am-12.30pm & 2.30-6pm Mon-Sat & by appointment) Stocks Berber and Tuareg carpets, jewellery and souvenirs from the Atlas, Rif and Sahara. Has a booth opposite Hôtel Salama.

Souq
CARPETS

(☺ Tue & Wed) A lively weekly souq takes place near Hôtel Salama. Small dealers sometimes sell Berber carpets here.

ℹ Information

There are numerous banks with ATMs and exchange facilities in the centre. For tourist information and local events, visit www.tafraout.info.

Internet Amelen (off Rue al-Jeish al-Malaki; per hr Dh5; ☺ 8.30am-10pm)

Pharmacie al-Massira (☎ 0528 80 01 60; Pl al-Massira; ☺ 8am-8.30pm)

Post Office (Pl Mohammed V; ☺ 8.30am-4.30pm Mon-Fri) Has a bureau de change and pay phones.

ℹ Getting There & Away

BUS

Buses depart from outside the various company offices, mostly on Rue al-Jeish al-Malaki.

CTM (☎ 0528 80 17 89; Rte Aguerd-Oudad) has a morning bus to the following places:

DESTINATION	COST (DH)	DURATION (HR)
Agadir	70	6
Casablanca	245	12
Inezgane	70	6
Marrakesh	145	8½
Tiznit	40	3

For destinations to the south, change in Tiznit.

TAXI

Station wagons and Land Rovers do the rounds of various villages in the area, mostly on market days. They hang around the post-office square, and on Rue al-Jeish al-Malaki by the Afriquia petrol station at the bottom of Tariq an-Nahzi. Grands taxis leave for Tiznit (Dh40) in the morning from the latter location.

Around Tafraoute

Renting a mountain bike is a great way to get to most of the sights around Tafraoute.

Tazekka

The closest of the easily accessible examples of prehistoric rock engravings found in the Tafraoute area, the Carved Gazelle is 2km away on the edge of the village of Tazekka. It's a simple carving on the top face of a fallen block. The easiest way to find it is to walk along Rte de Tazekka, then make enquiries when you reach the village. It's not far from Camping Tazka on the Tiznit road (R104), so you could, alternatively, ask for directions there.

★ **Maison Traditionnelle**
(☏ 0673 82 90 54; Maisonberbere30@yahoo.fr; adult Dh15; ☺ 8am-6pm) This place stands in the largely uninhabited old hilltop village, where bulging boulders have been incorporated into the pisé walls of the centuries-old houses. You can visit the Carved Gazelle as part of a tour of the four-floor dwelling, where the knowledgeable proprietor Mahfoud's family once lived. It's possible to stay the night here (per person including breakfast/half-board Dh150/230) and Mahfoud, a

trekking guide, offers Berber music soirées and tea ceremonies.

Tirnmatmat

To find the rock engravings at Tirnmatmat, take the Tiznit road (R104), then after 14km turn north at Tahala towards Aït Omar. Just before the village, an unmarked *piste* (track) leads to Tirnmatmat, where you will find the *gravures* (engravings) along the riverbed (the local kids will lead you there, or engage a guide from Tafraoute). The village sits in a lovely spot and there are excellent walks in all directions.

Le Châpeau de Napoléon & the Pierres Bleues

The village of Aguerd-Oudad, 3km south of Tafraoute, makes for a nice stroll or bike ride. From the roundabout by the Afriquia petrol station in Tafraoute, take the road to Tiznit via Izerbi. On the way you will see the unmistakable rock formation known as Le Châpeau de Napoléon (Napoleon's Hat).

Some 7km south of Tafraoute, 500m past the foot of the road to the Afella-Ighir oasis, a *'touristique piste'* leads uphill to the right to the Pierres Bleues (Painted Rocks), the work of Belgian artist Jean Verame.

Around Tafraoute

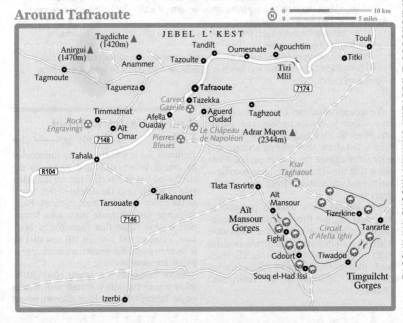

AFELLA-IGHIR

Southeast of Tafraoute is the pretty oasis of Afella-Ighir. Leave Tafraoute on the Aguerd–Oudad road, turning left a few kilometres south of the village, and travel roughly 25km over a mountain pass through Tlata Tasrirte to the start of the dramatic Aït Mansour Gorges. You can see the Pierres Bleues from the road up to the pass, which is often foggy and sometimes snowed over in winter.

You can drive through the gorges in a normal car if it hasn't rained, but walking or mountain biking is the best way to appreciate this atmospheric area, where red cliff faces tower above the palms. In the village of Aït Mansour at the beginning of the gorges and oasis, Auberge Aït Mansour (☏ 0676 73 51 98; www.auberge-ait-mansour-hanane-blogspot.com; r/half-board per person Dh80/170) offers mattresses on the floor and squat toilets. Owner Abdou can guide you to the old village nearby for oasis views. A little further on, Chez Messaoud (☏ 0670 79 35 67, 0528 21 83 38; half-board per person Dh150) is equally basic, although there are flush toilets. It serves tea and sells water and basic provisions. Breakfast (Dh40) and meals (Dh60) are available if you book ahead.

Follow the road through a string of villages perched above the oasis, until you reach the T-junction in Gdourt after about 8km. Turn right here for Tiznit or to loop back to Tafraoute. Turning left, the next village is Souq el-Had Issi, a rather depressing settlement that accommodates workers from the nearby gold mine. From Souq el-Had Issi, the road leads south to Aït Herbil. After about 12km, there are some impressive rock carvings in Ukas, although you need a guide to find them.

A turn-off 1km beyond Souq el-Had Issi leads 5km northeast to the village of Tiwadou, where the family-run Auberge Sahnoun (☏ 0667 09 53 76, 0528 21 83 65; maisonsahnoun@gmail.com; r per person incl half-board Dh150) is on the edge of a *palmeraie* (palm grove). It has three basic but cosy rooms, with mattresses on the floor and a good shared bathroom with hot water, and a roof terrace. The auberge's late owner, Mohamed Sahnoun, was involved in village development projects.

In a 4WD, you can continue from Tiwadou through the Timguilcht Gorges to Tlata Tasrirte (about 20km). At the time of writing, it was not possible to drive this circuit in a 2WD vehicle, as the road disintegrates after Tanrarte; the tarred road is being extended, so it should be possible in the future.

Daily minibuses run through the villages to Tafraoute (Dh25), leaving Tiwadou at about 5am and returning around 11am.

Tafraoute Aventure (p375) offers a 4WD day trip incorporating walks in Aït Mansour and Timguilcht Gorges, Ukas and lunch in Tiwadou (Dh1200 for the vehicle, including driver and fuel).

Verame spray-painted the smooth, rounded boulders in shades of blue, red, purple and black in 1984 and, although the rocks have a faded air, they remain strange and impressive against the landscape. Local lore has it that the villagers give these incongruous tourist attractions a fresh coat of paint every year.

The packed earth track is passable in a normal car, but this is prime mountain-biking territory. You can see the rocks after a couple of kilometres, then ride or drive right up to them some 5km away. The track leads 9km to the village of Afella Ouaday, 5km from Tafraoute on the Tiznit road (R104).

Ameln Valley & Jebel L'Kest جبل لكست و اميلن وادي

Tafraoute lies in a basin, largely surrounded by craggy brown cliffs and rocks. To the northwest lies one such ridge, on the other side of which runs the Ameln Valley. North of the valley is Jebel L'Kest (2359m). From Tafraoute you can make out a rock formation in this range that resembles a lion's face. Villagers will jokingly tell you that he is there to guard the women while their husbands are away working.

From Tafraoute, the Agadir road (R104) takes you to the valley, dotted with picturesque Berber villages. Four kilometres out of Tafraoute, the road forks with the right branch turning east up the valley towards Agadir.

⭐ **Maison Traditionnelle** MUSEUM
(📞0666 91 81 45; Oumesnate; admission Dh10; ⊙8am-sunset) At Oumesnate, 6km from Tafraoute, follow the signs through the village and then the footpath to this mountainside museum house. The three-storey granite, palm and argan house, some 400 years old, was inhabited by 20 family members – three generations – until 1982. The blind owner, Abdesslam, or one of his sons, will take you on a fascinating tour, telling tales of traditional life.

🛏 Sleeping & Eating

The villages have numerous basic *gîtes* (trekkers' hostels), *maisons d'hôte* and homestays; Au Coin des Nomades (p376) can organise a stay. The following are mostly in Tandilt, 4km from Tafraoute, and Oumesnate. These accommodation options are the only places to eat in the villages.

⭐**Oumesnate Maison d'Hôte** GUESTHOUSE €
(📞0666 91 77 68; maisondhote@gmail.com; Oumesnate; s/d incl half-board Dh250/400; ❄) Staying in the six-room guesthouse next to Oumesnate's Maison Traditionnelle, run by the same family, is a wonderful way to get an insight into Berber village life. If you don't have a pressing need for internet access and, ideally, you have a car, spending a night here would be more interesting than Tafraoute. Rooms have en-suite bathrooms, and meals (Dh70) are available with notice. Abdesslam's English-speaking son Rachid organises trekking and 4WD and bike tours.

Yamina GUESTHOUSE €
(📞0670 52 38 83, 0528 21 66 21; www.yamina-tafraout.com; Tandilt; per person incl breakfast/half-board Dh150/209; ❄🛜) 🅿 At the top of the village, Yamina is run by a Berber woman and her French husband, who have created a unique cross between a comfortable guesthouse and a *maison traditionnelle* (traditional house). Reached along terraces, courtyards and earthen walkways with low ceilings, the simple rooms are beautifully decorated with cheery paintwork on the walls and beams.

L'Arganier d'Ammelne HOTEL, CAMPGROUND €
(📞0528 80 00 69; www.arganierammelne.com; Rte d'Agadir, Tandilt; s/d/f incl half-board Dh250/360/750; ❄🛜) This hotel's pleas-

ant pink, yellow and pisé rooms open onto a flowery garden. The terrace restaurant (meals/set menu Dh40/75) serves delicious dishes including local specialities and the recommended beef tajine with apricots, almonds and prunes.

Chez Amaliya HOTEL €€
(📞0528 80 00 65; www.chezamaliya.com; Tazoulte; s/d/tr incl breakfast from Dh330/500/750; ❄🛜❄) A few hundred metres past the turning for Tandilt, Oumesnate and Agadir, this Dutch-owned hotel is one of the valley's grandest options. A Berber tent and Jebel L'Kest's lion face rise above the pool, and paintings and local maps decorate the lobby. It has a bar, souvenir shop and smart restaurant (mains Dh70) serving Moroccan and Western dishes; readers recommend the chicken *pastilla*. Rooms are gloomy but comfortable, and there is a six-person rooftop apartment (Dh1000).

ℹ Getting There & Away

Minibuses (Dh5) and grands taxis (Dh8) head along the main road between the villages and Tafraoute.

Tata طاطا
POP 40,000

Situated on the Saharan plain at the foot of Jebel Bani, Tata was an oasis settlement along the trade route from West Africa. Its name, which roughly means 'take a break' in Tashelhit, recalls those days of Saharan caravans, as do the turban-wrapped men sipping tea in the shade. Close to the Algerian border, the small town has a garrison feel, with four types of police and military stationed here, and you may be questioned on your way into town. With good infrastructure and less hassle than other Saharan spots, Tata is poised to become more of a destination for travellers.

The palmeraie is well worth exploring. You can drive a 7km circuit of it, or catch a local bus (Dh5). Above the village at the far end of the *palmeraie* is a white hilltop *marabout* (saint's tomb), which you can see from Tata.

Tata is best as a base for off-the-beaten-track excursions, such as desert camping; Akka oasis, kasbah and *agadir;* and the rock engravings at Tiggane, Oum el-Alek and Tircht, among the finest in Morocco. Helpful multilingual Berber guide Isam, based at souvenir shop Maison du Patrimoine (☎ 0613 24 13 12; issam3599@hotmail.com; Ave Mohammed V), charges about Dh350 per day for one or two people (Dh900 including 4WD).

On Ave Mohammed V is a post office, an internet cafe, banks with ATMs and money-changing facilities, and the seldom-open Délégation Régionale du Tourisme (☎ 0528 80 20 76; crt-guelmim.com/prevince-tata-en.html).

🛏 Sleeping & Eating

There are basic hotels and cafes on Ave Mohammed V near Maison du Patrimoine. Full- or half-board at one of the following would be the best option.

Hôtel La Renaissance　　HOTEL €
(☎ 0528 80 22 25; larenaissance1982@gmail.com; Ave des FAR; s/d Dh150/210; 🖥) This central stalwart with *palmeraie* views has small but comfortable rooms and a pleasant lounge and breakfast area. The only downsides are the cramped bathrooms and occasional unsavoury character in the bar.

Hotel Les Relais des Sables　　HOTEL €
(☎ 0528 80 23 01; Ave des FAR; s/d/tr from Dh210/250/363; 🕸🖥🖥) Popular with tour groups and overlanders; the pool, bar, restaurant and gardens are more impressive than the service and small en-suite rooms in stuffy bungalows.

Oasis Dar Ouanou　　MAISON D'HÔTE, CAMPGROUND €
(Akka Izankad; per tent incl shower from Dh70, s/d/f incl breakfast Dh300/350/600; 🖥) By the N12 3km southwest of Tata, this ramshackle but clean building has cool rooms, a courtyard with fountains and palms, and oasis and mountain views from the roof terrace.

Municipal Campsite　　CAMPGROUND €
(Ave Mohammed V; per tent incl shower from Dh30) Next to the dry river, with a reasonable ablutions block with flush toilets.

Maison d'Hôte Hayat　　CAMPGROUND, GUESTHOUSE €€
(☎ 0668 37 52 27; assamedeta_tata@yahoo.fr; Indfiane; per tent incl shower from Dh80, r per person Dh200) In the process of opening when we visited Tata, Hayat occupies a scenic riverside spot in a village on the outskirts of Tata, with lanterns lighting the walkway and views of the old fort. On an ecological farm run by a local environmental, cultural and tourism association, the property will offer campsites, nomad tents (per person Dh200), basic rooms in a *maison traditionnelle* and an outdoor restaurant.

Dar Infiane　　MAISON D'HÔTE €€€
(☎ 0661 61 01 70, 0528 80 21 04; www.darinfiane.com; Indfiane; r incl breakfast Dh884-1860, meals Dh200; 🕸) Tata's old kasbah, perched above the *palmeraie,* has been turned into a Green Key guesthouse. Off a carpet-strewn central courtyard lie 10 rooms, in which the French owners have kept the original eccentricities such as low beams intact. The *dar* (house) has both fans and detractors, with some guests raving about magical evenings on the rooftop terrace in the still of the Sahara night, while others criticise the service.

🛈 Getting There & Away

BUS

Tata's bus station is in the centre near Pl de la Marche Verte, but will be relocated to near Hotel Les Relais des Sables. CTM and Supratours do not serve Tata; **Satas** (☎ 0672 31 18 43; Pl de la Marche Verte; ⊙ 8.30am-12.30pm & 2-6pm Mon-Sat) has the following daily departures:

Agadir Dh80, eight hours
Goulimime Dh60, five hours
Marrakesh Dh140, 10 hours
Taroudannt Dh80, five hours
Tiznit Dh70, 6½ hours
Zagora Dh120, eight hours

TAXI

Grands taxis leave from Pl de la Marche Verte to the following destinations:

Agadir Dh140
Akka-Irhen For Taliouine; Dh25
Bouizakarne For Tiznit; Dh100
Goulimime Dh110
Igherm For Tafraoute; Dh40
Ouarzazate Dh130
Taroudannt Dh80

TREKKING IN THE ANTI ATLAS

The last significant mountains before the Sahara, the arid, pink- and ochre-coloured Anti Atlas are little visited by trekkers, and yet they offer some wonderful trekking opportunities. Taliouine is well set up for trekking, and Tafraoute is the centre of the region. The quartzite massif of Jebel L'Kest (2359m), the 'amethyst mountain', lies about 10km north of Tafraoute, and the twin peaks of Adrar

Mqorn (2344m) are 10km southeast. Beneath the jagged mass of these peaks lie lush irrigated valleys and a string of oases.

At the eastern end of the Anti Atlas near Taliouine, almost due south of Jebel Toubkal, Jebel Siroua (3305m) rises starkly above the landscape. This dramatic volcano makes an excellent centrepiece to varied long-distance treks.

For further advice, and to arrange guides, mules and gear, contact the operators listed under Tafraoute (p375), Taliouine (p374) and Taroudannt (p369).

Around Tafraoute

Morocco has such a wealth of trekking options that perhaps it is not surprising that an area with the potential of Tafraoute has not yet been fully exploited. The adventurous trekker will find here, as elsewhere in the Moroccan south, many challenging and rewarding treks. Because of local depopulation caused by movement to the cities, and the decline in the use of mules for agriculture, many paths are partially abandoned and nature is particularly wild here. Trekkers might spot Cuvier's gazelles, wild boars, Barbary sheep and rich endemic vegetation.

This is a tougher area than the M'Goun Massif or Tichka Plateau and trekkers will need to cope with a lack of facilities and the harsh climate. This close to the Sahara, summer (June until mid-September) is blisteringly hot, and winter sees the occasional snowfall on the high passes and peaks, so the region is best walked at the end of winter. Late February is ideal. Daytime temperatures may be 20°C, but at night it can drop below freezing.

Other than the odd small store, you won't find many supplies in the area, so the great challenge is carrying enough food and water to keep you going. As with other remote Moroccan areas, it is often possible to stay in village houses, but you must still be prepared to camp and to carry food and water.

The best way of doing this is by hiring a guide and mules; there are trekking guides – and *faux guides* – in Tafraoute. As ever, insist on seeing a guide's ID card before you start discussing possibilities. As a rule, trained mountain guides do not tout for business in the street. Mules are rarely found around Tafraoute, but you may be able to arrange this through your guide.

Jebel L'Kest and the approaches from Tafraoute are covered by the 1:50,000 map sheets *Had Tahala* and *Tanalt*, while the whole area is covered by 1:100,000 sheets *Annzi, Tafrawt, Foum al-Hisn* and *Taghjijt*. You should be able to find these maps in Au Coin des Nomades (p376), in specialist bookshops (p35), or in good big-city bookshops in Morocco.

This part of the Atlas is not well developed for tourism, and transport is an issue throughout. *Camionettes* (pick-up trucks) and minibuses provide a reliable though infrequent service to some villages and grands taxis run on souq days, but at other times you may need to hire one to get to trailheads.

Jebel L'Kest

The area's star attraction is this massive quartzite ridge that stretches away northwest of Tafraoute. Despite the harshness of the landscape, the Berbers who live in local villages manage to grow the mountain staples of wheat, barley, olives, figs and almonds. The village of Tagdichte is the launching point for a day ascent of Jebel L'Kest (2359m). Tagdichte can be accessed by minibus or taxi, and homestay accommodation can be arranged there.

Ameln Valley

There are some 26 villages neatly spaced out through the Ameln Valley, which runs along the south side of Jebel L'Kest, and they make for a great walk. You'd need weeks to do a full circuit, but a stunningly beautiful and suitably stretching five-day walk would start in Oumesnate, take in several villages, and head up to Tagdichte for an ascent of Jebel L'Kest. Alternatively, the ascent could be tackled as part of a gentle trek east through the valley from, say, Tirnmatmat to Oumesnate, both just off the road. You could also base yourself at Oumesnate Maison d'Hôte (p381) and go on treks from there.

Adrar Mqorn & Around

Southeast of Tafraoute the possibilities are also exciting. The scramble up Adrar Mqorn (2344m) is hard but worthwhile. Due south of its twin peaks are the palm-filled gorges of Aït Mansour and Timguilcht, which make up Afella-Ighir oasis (p380).

Jebel Aklim

Jebel Aklim (2531m) sits in an even remoter area than Jebel L'Kest, yet is surrounded by Berber villages in valleys guarded by old kasbahs. From the top there are great views over to the High Atlas and Jebel Siroua. It makes a great focal point for a four- or five-day walk out of Igherm, which is roughly equidistant from Tafraoute (to the southwest), Taroudannt, Taliouine and Tata.

Jebel Siroua

Some way south of the High Atlas, at the eastern edge of the Anti Atlas, the isolated volcanic peak of Jebel Siroua (3305m) offers unique trekking opportunities. Remote villages, tremendous gorges, a tricky final ascent and some dramatic scenery all make this an excellent place for trekkers in search of solitude, stark beauty and a serious walk.

The Jebel Siroua ascent is the most obvious walk, but, as ever in Morocco, lasting memories will be found elsewhere: in the beauty of lush valleys, in the hospitality shown in Berber homes, in the play of light on rock and in the proximity of the Sahara. So if you don't fancy the climb to the summit, the mountain circuit still makes a wonderful trek, with diverse scenery, traditional activities in the villages and beautiful, well-maintained agricultural terraces.

Mules can also be hired at short notice (often the next day) at villages around the mountain.

The 1:100,000 *Taliwine* and 1:50,000 *Sirwa* maps cover the route. In winter it can be fiercely cold here, so the best times to trek are autumn, when the saffron harvest takes place, and spring. You should be able to find these maps in Au Coin des Nomades (p376), in specialist bookshops (p35), or in good big-city bookshops in Morocco.

If you need supplies, there are small stores in Taliouine and Tazenart, and weekly markets take place in Taliouine, Aoulouz, Askaoun, Tazenakht and Igli.

Routes

There's a challenging, weeklong trek that allows you to walk out of Taliouine along a gentle dirt trail, which heads eastward up the Zagmouzen Valley to Tagmout. The route then heads northeast through Atougha, from where the summit of Jebel Siroua is best reached in two days, with a night at Tegragra. Walking at a regular pace, you'll ascend the summit on the morning of the fourth day.

After descending into the gorges, you'll reach the extraordinary cliff village of Tizgui, where you can spend the night, before continuing to Tagouyamt on the fifth day. The village has limited supplies and, in case you can't find a room, a good place to camp in the amazing Tislit Gorge. From Tislit, the valley continues to Ihoukarn, from where you can head south to the Taliouine-Ouarzazate road at Tizi n'Taghatine (organise beforehand in Taliouine to be picked up here); or complete the circuit by walking west back to Taliouine (two days from Tislit via Tagmout and the Zagmouzen Valley).

An alternative circuit that is even less trekked starts at the village of Tamlakout, where there is a classified *gîte,* and takes in Aït Tigga, the Assif Mdist and the foot of Jebel Siroua. It then ascends the mountain, continues to Aziouane and exits via the Amassines. Some of the trek is strenuous but no one day should involve more than six hours' walking.

Taliouine and Anezale (for Tamlakout) are both on the main Taroudannt to Ouarzazate road, regularly served by grands taxis and buses.

SOUTHERN ATLANTIC COAST

Tiznit تزنيت

POP 53,600

South of the Souss Valley and at the western end of the Anti Atlas, Tiznit is an old walled medina town surrounded by modern development. It was originally the site of a cluster of forts that were encircled in the 19th century by some 5km of pisé wall. It quickly became a trade centre and remains a provincial capital and centre for Berber jewellery, with a souq devoted to the silver stuff. This slow-paced and authentic spot, with its dusty medina lanes and conservative but friendly inhabitants, is a convenient stopoff en route between the Anti Atlas and Atlantic Coast.

History

In 1881 Sultan Moulay al-Hassan (1873–94) founded Tiznit as a base from which to

BEYOND THE GLITTER

Berber jewellery serves a much wider purpose than simple adornment. A woman's jewellery identifies her as a member of a clan or tribe, is a sign of her wealth, reflects cultural traditions, and has power beyond the visual – to protect her from the evil eye.

A woman will receive jewellery from her mother until she marries. For her marriage, her future husband will commission his mother or sister to provide jewellery. These pieces will be kept by her as a dowry and added to throughout her life; they will always be made of silver, as gold is considered evil.

Necklaces are important; the traditional assemblage in the southern oasis valleys sometimes features talismans of silver, pink coral, amazonite, amber, Czech glass and West African ebony beads. Women will also own bracelets, *fibulas* (elaborate brooches, often triangular, used for fastening garments), anklets, earrings and headdresses. Some jewellery will be worn every day, while the finest pieces will be saved for occasions such as festivals, pilgrimages and funerals.

Jewellery's protective, medicinal and magical properties are extremely important. The necklaces contain charms bought from magicians or holy men, offering protection against the evil eye, disease, accidents and difficulties in childbirth. Silver is believed to cure rheumatism; coral symbolises fertility and is thought to have curative powers; amber is worn as a symbol of wealth and to protect against sorcery (it's also considered an aphrodisiac and a cure for colds); amazonite and carnelian stones are used in divining fortunes; and shells traded from East Africa symbolise fertility.

Talismans feature stylised motifs of animals, the sun, moon and stars, which are all believed to have supernatural powers. A common symbol to ward off the evil eye is the hand of Fatima, daughter of the Prophet Mohammed. Any depiction of the hand (which represents human creative power and dominance) or of the number five is believed to have the same effect as metaphorically poking your fingers into the evil eye with the words *khamsa fi ainek* (five in your eye).

assert his authority over the rebellious Berber tribes of the south. To do this, he built the town's perimeter walls. Jewish silversmiths were moved into the town and they gave it a reputation for silver workmanship.

However, Tiznit remained embroiled in local sedition, and was a centre of dissent against the 1912 treaty that turned Morocco into a French and Spanish protectorate. This resistance movement was led by El-Hiba, the so-called 'Blue Sultan' from the Western Sahara, who earned his nickname for always wearing his Saharawi veil.

Following Sultan Moulay Hafid's capitulation to the French at the Treaty of Fès, El-Hiba proclaimed himself sultan here in 1912. The southern tribes rose to support him and El-Hiba marched north at the head of an army of men from the Tuareg and Anti Atlas tribes. They were welcomed as liberators in Marrakesh, but much of the army was slaughtered by the French as it moved towards Fez. El-Hiba retreated to Taroudannt, then Tiznit, then up into the Anti Atlas, where he pursued a campaign

of resistance against the French until his death in 1919.

◉ Sights & Activities

Tiznit medina is a sleepy place where it is fun to wander around spots such as the jewellery souq and Rue Imzilne, a street of leather-sandal shops. The Berber traders here are tough salesmen, but it is still worth trying to strike a bargain. Things liven up considerably on Thursday, which is market day.

City Walls   HISTORIC SITE
It's possible to climb onto sections of the 5km-long city walls, which have some 30 towers and nine gates. On the northern side of the medina, Bab Targua overlooks a *palmeraie* with a natural spring, used as a laundry by local women.

Grande Mosquée   MOSQUE
The minaret of the Grande Mosquée (closed to non-Muslims) is studded with jutting wooden sticks. Local legend suggests this is where the souls of the dead congregate. More likely, these were left in place by the masons who built the minaret to help them

Tiznit

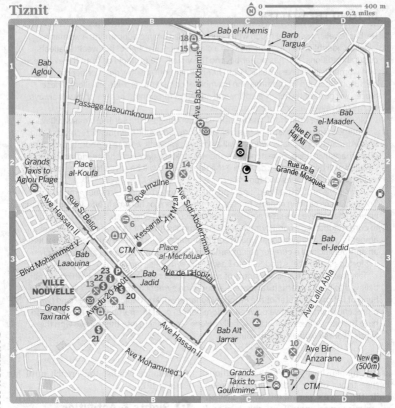

climb up and replaster. A similar arrangement is used on minarets across the Sahara in Mali and Niger.

Source Bleue
HISTORIC SITE

The original town spring is now a shallow, stagnant pool, green rather than blue. Legend has it that a woman of ill repute, Lalla Zninia, stopped to rest here at what was then plain desert. She spent the next three days repenting her wicked ways, and God was so impressed that he showed forgiveness by having a spring gush beneath her feet. Her name was thus given to the village that preceded Sultan Moulay al-Hassan's 19th-century fortress town.

🛏 Sleeping

Hotels are gathered around the large roundabout to the southeast of Bab Oulad Jarrar, with a few options in the medina.

Bab el Maader
GUESTHOUSE €

(☎ 0673 90 73 14; www.bab-el-maader.com; 132 Rue El Haj Ali; r Dh330; ⊗ Sep-Jun) This traditional house in the medina is Tiznit's best address, a five-room guesthouse with a courtyard, plenty of great decorative touches and good use of Moroccan fabrics and materials. The French-Moroccan team can give pointers and arrange trips in the region.

Riad Le Lieu
GUESTHOUSE €

(☎ 0528 60 00 19; www.riadlelieu-tiznit.com; 273 Impasse Issaoui; r/ste/apt Dh220/290/320; 🖥) Five double rooms and suites and a four-person apartment share this former courthouse with the restaurant of the same name. One suite has a private shower, but otherwise the rooms and suites share bathrooms. Rooms are poky, but the warm welcome and copious breakfast (Dh30) make this a relaxing haven in the medina.

Tiznit

◉ Sights
1 Grande Mosquée C2
2 Source Bleue C2

⊟ Sleeping
3 Bab el Maader D2
4 Camping Municipal.............................. C4
5 Hôtel de Paris.. C4
6 Hôtel des Touristes B3
7 Hotel Tiznit C4
8 Riad Janoub... D2
9 Riad Le Lieu B2

⊗ Eating
10 Complex Tiznit Essaada C4
11 Food Market B3
12 Idou Tiznit Supermarket...................... C4
13 La Ville Nouvelle.................................... A3

Riad Le Lieu.................................. (see 9)
14 Snack Stands... B2

⊜ Drinking & Nightlife
15 Cafe Panoramique B1

⊙ Shopping
16 Ensemble Artisanal A4
17 Jewellery Souq....................................... B3
18 Trésor du Sud B1

ⓘ Information
19 Bank B2
20 Banque Populaire.................................. B3
21 BMCE A4
22 BMCI A3
23 Tiznit Voyages B3

Hôtel des Touristes HOTEL €
(☑0528 86 20 18; http://hoteltouristetiznit.voila
.net; Pl al-Méchouar; s/d/tr/q from Dh50/90/120/
140; �) Abdul and Mohammed's spotless,
welcoming 1st-floor hotel is a dependable,
central budget option. Rooms are entered
from a quiet, cheerful communal area with
a book exchange; those overlooking Pl al-
Méchouar have small balconies, but all lack
fans. The room next to the flush toilet is particularly hot and noisy.

Hotel Tiznit HOTEL €
(☑0528 86 24 11; tiznit–hotel@menara.ma; Ave
Bir Anzarane; s/d Dh247/310; ☐) Set in leafy
grounds with a large pool, Tiznit is unexciting and a little run-down but comfortable
and welcoming. The pink rooms are reasonably spacious with TV and small bathroom.

Hôtel de Paris HOTEL €
(☑0528 86 28 65; www.hoteldeparis.ma; Ave Hassan II; s/d/tr Dh140/180/250; ☐) This hotel
would be fine if you hit town feeling as tired
as the decor of the en-suite rooms and just
wanted to crash between buses. There's a
cafe-restaurant downstairs.

Camping Municipal CAMPGROUND €
(☑0528 60 13 54; Bab Oulad Jarrar; camping per
person Dh36) The municipal campground is
next to the old walls.

Riad Janoub MAISON D'HÔTE €€
(☑0679 00 55 10; www.riadjanoub.com; 193 Rue
de la Grande Mosquée; r incl breakfast from Dh748;
☐) French couple Gilbert and Clau-
dine are attentive hosts in this modern riad,
which has Moroccan and European salons,

a massage room, hammam and roof terrace,
all overlooking the pool and garden. The six
comfortable rooms, including a wheelchair-
accessible option, have soft colour schemes,
rugs and traditional trimmings.

✖ Eating & Drinking

Food Market MARKET
(Ave du 20 Août; ⊙9am-4pm Mon-Sat) A good
option for picnic supplies.

Idou Tiznit Supermarket SUPERMARKET
(Bab Oulad Jarrar; ⊙9am-12.30pm & 2.30-6pm
Mon-Sat) Behind the hotel of the same name,
selling a range of local and imported food.

La Ville Nouvelle CAFE, MOROCCAN €
(17 Ave du 20 Août; mains Dh35-55; ⊙breakfast
& lunch) At this popular multistorey cafe,
brisk waiters serve classic salads, brochettes,
tajines and *kefta* (spiced meatballs).

Complex Tiznit Essaada FAST FOOD, SEAFOOD €
(Ave Lalla Abla; mains Dh35-55; ⊙breakfast, lunch
& dinner) On this strip, snack bars serve
dishes such as brochettes and rotissserie
chicken. Look out for Tiznit Essaada, which
also offers *shwarma*, paninis, pizza and fish
dishes on its covered terrace.

Snack Stands FAST FOOD €
Along Ave Sidi Abderhman, the main road
through the medina.

★Riad Le Lieu MOROCCAN €€
(☑0528 60 00 19; www.riadlelieu-tiznit.com; 273
Impasse Issaoui; mains Dh32-95; ⊙breakfast, lunch
& dinner; ☐) Charming Aïcha attracts locals
and tourists alike with daily specials, typically

including tomato and goats' cheese salad, *pastilla* and camel, beef or sardine tajine. The intimate setting is a courtyard with foliage and lanterns overhead. There are just four tables, so book ahead in high season.

Cafe Panoramique CAFE
(Ave Sidi Abderhman; ⊙8.30am-6pm) Panoramique has views of the city walls and surrounding countryside from its roof terrace.

🛍 Shopping

★ Jewellery Souq JEWELLERY
With its long history of silversmiths, the jewellery souq has some of the best work in southern Morocco. It's a pleasant place to wander, with blue-doored shops and windows full of silverware. Some of the jewellery is made in Tiznit, and some bought from Saharan tribes to the south. You will need time to look around and bargain to get the best prices.

Trésor du Sud JEWELLERY
(www.tresordusud.com; Bab el-Khemis, Ave Sidi Abderhman; ⊙9am-5pm Mon-Sat & by appointment) Jewellery shops are found along Ave Sidi Abderhman, the main road through the medina. At the top, Trésor du Sud is not the cheapest, but the work is good and it deals in hallmarked solid silver.

Ensemble Artisanal JEWELLERY
(Ave du 20 Août; ⊙9am-12.30pm & 2.30-5pm Mon-Sat) Artisans ply their wares in a hassle-free environment.

ⓘ Information

There are internet cafes around Pl al-Méchouar. Most banks with ATMs and exchange facilities are in the ville nouvelle, but there are banks in the medina.

Main Post Office (Ave du 20 Août; ⊙8.30am-4.30pm Mon-Fri) In the ville nouvelle.

Post Office (Ave Sidi Abderhman; ⊙8.30am-4.30pm Mon-Fri) In the medina.

Tiznit Voyages (☑0528 86 21 17; www.tiznitvoyages.com; Ave Hassan II; ⊙9am-12.30pm & 2-5pm Mon-Sat) This RAM agent also organises excursions and has local maps.

ⓘ Getting There & Away

BUS

Buses leave from the new bus station just off the Tafraoute road, past the Thursday souq site. CTM has another office closer to the centre on the same road, and one on Pl al-Méchouar. Cheap bus-company offices are clustered on

Ave Lalla Abla, just northeast of the roundabout near Bab Oulad Jarrar. CTM serves the following destinations:

DESTINATION	COST (DH)	DURATION (HR)
Agadir	40	2
Dakhla	350	20
Goulimime	40	2½
Laâyoune	190	9
Tafraoute	40	2½
Tan Tan	80	4½

TAXI

Unless mentioned otherwise, taxis leave from the main grand-taxi rank, opposite the main post office in the western part of town:

Agadir D32

Aglou Plage Dh5; from a stand on Ave Hassan II.

Goulimime Dh37; from a stand just south of the roundabout near Bab Oulad Jarrar, across Rte de Goulimime from the Total garage.

Inezgane Dh27

Mirleft Dh15

Sidi Ifni Dh27

Tafraoute Dh40

ⓘ Getting Around

Red petits taxis charge Dh7 for a journey (Dh10 after 7.30pm).

Aglou Plage   اكلو بلاج

Aglou Plage, 14km northwest of Tiznit, is a long beach with good surf, although the strong undertow makes it dangerous for swimming most of the time. When the Atlantic winds start blustering, it's a wild and woolly sort of place. Development is taking its toll, but the settlement has some charm, with a raised walkway for promenading between the seafront cafes.

If you're driving from Tiznit to Mirleft, the route via Aglou Plage takes you along a beautiful stretch of coastline.

At the south end of Aglou beach, signposted from the highway, French-Moroccan Le Chant du Chameau (☑0667 90 49 91; www.chantduchameau.com; per person incl breakfast/half-board Dh275/385) has five rooms in a rust-red house, with a tented restaurant and a terraced garden where prickly pears grow among the rocks. Excursions in the area and a weeklong course in *tadelakt*, the local plaster-work, are offered.

Grands taxis serve Aglou Plage from Tiznit (Dh5), but not Mirleft.

Mirleft

ميرلفت

POP 6500

One of the region's most beautiful roads runs south of Aglou Plage, offering wonderful views of the ocean, rugged hills and the occasional empty cove. Then comes Mirleft, with a burgeoning surf scene and beckoning cafes under the arches on its main street. Historically popular with artists, musicians and overlanders recovering from Saharan crossings, this cosmopolitan little spot is developing as fans of water and wind sports discover the area. Mirleft also has a healthy share of the best coastal accommodation south of Essaouira. The climate is gentle, the air clear, the views magnificent – and the fledgling tourism development has largely been the work of individuals, rather than corporations or chains.

◎ Sights & Activities

Stroll down the arcaded main street, which resembles the set of a cowboy film. Under the pink-and-blue arches you will find arts and crafts, argan products, souvenirs, carpets, surfboards, beach-tennis sets and two small vegetable markets.

If at first the scruffy village seems uninspiring, the gentle bustle soon becomes contagious. A social morning coffee is followed by a trip to the beach – choose from the village's largest beach, Imin Tourga (also known as *la grande plage*), Fish Beach, Camping Beach, Coquillage Beach, Aftas Beach, Plage Sauvage and Marabout's Beach. The last is the most dramatic, with its *marabout* tomb and savage-looking rocks.

There are plenty of activities to keep you busy, with six surf schools, mostly located on the road to Imin Tourga. The beach is good for surf casting (fishing), and hotels and guides can organise trips from trekking to desert excursions. Many of the following operators offer packages including accommodation, food, transfers and hire-car.

★ **Surf en Marruecos**   SURFING
(☎0615 99 04 70; www.surfenmarruecos.com) The Spanish-owned surf school has spearheaded Mirleft's development as a surf destination, organising an international longboard competition here every August.

Spot-M   SURFING
(☎0610 41 90 46; www.spot-m.com) A British-owned surf specialist.

Mirleft Ride   SURFING
(☎0661 44 19 33; www.mirleftride.com) Runs surf schools and organises fishing trips and treks into the hills.

Paraglide Morocco   PARAGLIDING
(☎0676 31 86 55; www.paraglidemorocco.com) The British-owned outfit is geared towards seasoned paragliders, but tandem flights (Dh550) are available.

Le Nid d'Aigle   PARAGLIDING
(☎0671 66 85 05; www.nidaigle.com) Offers paragliding.

🛏 Sleeping

There are plenty of short-let apartments available in Mirleft, costing from about Dh200 per night; ask at the entrance to the village.

Hôtel Abertih   HOTEL €
(☎0528 71 93 04; www.abertih.com; s/d incl breakfast with bathroom Dh200/300, without bathroom Dh150/200; 🐾) Looking like it popped out of a Cubist painting, blue-and-yellow Abertih is equally colourful inside, where open courtyards lead to 11 rooms above the licensed ground-floor restaurant. The French-owned hotel offers half-board and hire-car packages, making it popular with paragliding groups.

Hotel Atlas   HOTEL €
(☎0528 71 93 09; atlasmirleft@gmail.com; s/d/tw incl breakfast without shower Dh120/240/240, s/d incl breakfast with shower Dh200/300, meals from Dh16; 🐾) French-owned Atlas' palatial roof terrace is Mirleft's top party spot, a popular fixture on the southern surf circuit. The blue-shuttered rooms, entered from a corridor open to the elements, are pleasantly rustic and the hotel has a 1st-floor balcony and ground-floor restaurant.

Hotel du Sud   HOTEL €
(☎0528 71 94 07; www.hotel-mirleft.fr; s/d/q Dh130/170/250; 🐾) Up a pink staircase from Franco-Amazigh restaurant La Bonne Franquette, the basic rooms are simply but tastefully decorated, with colourful bedspreads and vintage postcards. Rudimentary shared bathrooms have showers in stalls. The turquoise patio and roof terrace are cool refuges on hot days.

Sally's Bed & Breakfast   GUESTHOUSE €€
(☎0528 71 94 02; www.sallymirleft.com; Les Amicales; r incl breakfast Dh550-1250; 🐾) Created by a horse-loving Englishwoman, Sally this

gorgeous cliff-top villa above Imin Tourga, one of Mirleft's largest and cleanest beaches, has breathtaking views up the coast. With six en-suite rooms and antiques decorating the lounge, it's a stylish and comfortable hideaway.

★ **Les 3 Chameaux**   MAISON D'HÔTE €€€
(☑ 0528 71 91 87; www.3chameaux.com; s/d/ste incl half-board Dh1186/1472/1672; ❄ 🖥 ☀) High on the hill, in a renovated 1930s military fort, is Mirleft's best address, a lovely guesthouse with fabulous views over the village to the sea beyond. It's worth paying extra for one of the suites, which have balconies and bathroom windows surveying the sea or the valley behind the property. The rooms are less impressive, without TV or air-conditioning. Facilities include a pool (heated during the winter), hammam, licensed restaurant and boutique. The only sound is the roar of the surf far below, and you'll feel yourself unwinding as soon as you arrive.

Dar Najmat   BOUTIQUE HOTEL €€€
(☑ 0528 71 90 56; www.darnajmat.com; s/d incl half-board Dh1078/1485, apt Dh1705; ❄ 🖥 ☀) With its infinity pool seemingly melting into Marabout's Beach, Dar Najmat's view is up there with the best on the Moroccan coast. You'll want to start taking photos as soon as you pull off the road, 2km south of Mirleft. The decor in the seven rooms and the two-bedroom apartment has been perfectly judged, with Moroccan materials achieving a contemporary look and harmonious feel.

✖ Eating

Apart from excellent restaurants at the above hotels, cafes on the main street serve up some of the tonnes of fresh fish that get caught here.

Restaurant Tigmi   MOROCCAN €
(☑ 0670 70 60 43; meals Dh60; ☺ lunch & dinner) Readers recommend this friendly, family-run restaurant with a small terrace near Hôtel Abertih. Dishes include dromedary rib steak and octopus tajine.

Restaurant Ayour   BERBER €
(☑ 0528 71 91 71; meals Dh65; ☺ lunch & dinner) Next to Hotel du Sud, cosy Ayour is one of Mirleft's best stand-alone restaurants. It's slightly overpriced, but tajines, spaghetti and fish dishes are all on the menu.

ⓘ Getting There & Away

Grands taxis run to Sidi Ifni (Dh13) and Tiznit (Dh15). The daily Trans Kam (p393) bus between Ifni and Marrakesh stops here.

Sidi Ifni   سيدي إفني

POP 40,000

Returned to Morocco by the Spanish as late as 1969, Sidi Ifni adds a dash of Gabriel García Márquez to the usual Moroccan tajine. The slowly decaying art-deco buildings on the hilly streets are a haunting reminder of colonial ambitions. At the heart of what was the Spanish Sahara, Ifni was once a base for slave-trading operations and later a large exporter of fish to the Spanish mainland. When the sun sets on the esplanade and dilapidated *calles* (streets), and the Atlantic mist gives everything a soft focus, Ifni seems an eerie outpost.

The locals have painted the town blue and white, and continue the colour scheme in their turbans and robes. They support Spanish football teams, they take siestas and they're more likely to greet travellers with *hola* than *bonjour*. You might hear Bob Dylan blaring from a cafe or get into a philosophical conversation; it's an intellectual spot, where the expats and local cafe crowd are laid-back even by Moroccan standards.

History

Spain acquired the enclave of Sidi Ifni after defeating the Moroccan forces in the war of 1859. They christened their new possession Santa Cruz del Mar Pequeña, but seem to have been uncertain what to do with it as they did not take full possession until 1934. Most of Ifni dates from the 1930s and features an eclectic mix of art deco and traditional Moroccan styles.

On Moroccan independence in the late 1950s, Spain refused to withdraw, citing the fact that some 60% of the town's population was Spanish. The protracted dispute over territorial rights included the Ifni War, in which the town was besieged. The dispute eventually ended in 1969, when the UN brokered an agreement for Spain to cede the enclave back to Morocco. Santa Cruz was renamed Sidi Ifni, after a holy man buried in the town in the early 1900s. Ifni still celebrates 'Independence Day' (30 June) with a festival on the abandoned airfield.

Sidi Ifni

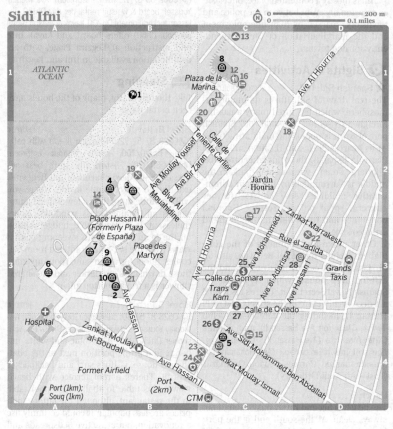

Sidi Ifni

◎ Sights
1	Beach	B1
2	Cine Avenida	B3
3	Former Spanish Consulate	B2
4	Law Courts (Former Church)	B2
5	Letterbox	C4
6	Lighthouse	A3
7	Royal Palace	A3
8	Ship House	C1
9	Town Hall	B3
10	Twist Club	B3

◎ Activities, Courses & Tours
11	Ifni Surf	C1
12	Sahara Surf Shop	C1

◎ Sleeping
13	Camping Sidi Ifni	C1
14	Hôtel Bellevue	A2
15	Hôtel Ère Nouvelle	C4
16	Hôtel Suerte Loca	C1
17	Xanadu	C2

◎ Eating
18	Café-Restaurant Azta	C2
19	Café-Restaurant Mar Pequeña	B2
20	Chez Sofia	C1
21	Eddib	B3
22	Fruit & Vegetable Market	D3
23	Gran Canaria	C4
24	Municipal Market	C4

◎ Drinking & Nightlife
	Hôtel Bellevue	(see 14)

◎ Information
25	Attijariwafa Bank	C3
26	Banque Populaire	C4
27	BMCE	C3
28	Hassan Cyber	D3

Ifni is mostly a contented place, but clashes occasionally erupt between the police and townsfolk, sparked by high unemployment and the marginalisation of the independently spirited town.

◉ Sights & Activities

★ Spanish Sidi Ifni — HISTORIC BUILDINGS

The real draw of Sidi Ifni is its unique atmosphere, which has lured many a passing foreigner to settle. The small old Spanish part of town is one of the main attractions. At its heart is Pl Hassan II (often still called Plaza de España), the colonial centrepiece. The large square with a small park in the middle is surrounded by the main administrative buildings: law courts (former church), royal palace, former Spanish consulate and town hall, mostly in grand art-deco style.

Other interesting remnants of the colonial era include the Hôtel Bellevue, also on Pl Hassan II, a nearby lighthouse and the cliff-top ship house, which served as the Spanish Naval Secretariat. There's also some art-deco architecture in the streets east of Pl Hassan II, including the derelict nightclub Twist Club (off Ave Hassan II) and cinema Cine Avenida (Ave Hassan II). The post office still has a letterbox (Ave Mohammed V) outside marked 'Correos – Avion/Ordinario' (Post – Air Mail/Ordinary).

Beach — BEACH

The beach is big and rarely busy, though not always clean. At the south end is the port: Ifni's economy is based on small-scale fishing, with most of the catch sold in Agadir. The odd construction just offshore is the remains of an old land-sea conveyor, which was used to take cargo from ships to the old Spanish port.

Surfing — WATER SPORTS

There's some excellent surfing around Ifni. The knowledgeable Ahmed at Dik Surf School (☏0671 62 12 26; www.diksurfschool.wordpress.com; board & wetsuit rental per day Dh120, 2hr lesson incl equipment Dh125), a good source of information about local waves, teaches and has boards for hire. Sahara Surf Shop (☏0528 87 53 50; suerteloca36@yahoo.com; Plaza de la Marina; board & wetsuit rental per day Dh150, 2hr lesson incl equipment Dh180), another good place to pick up local knowledge, offers board and bike hire, instruction and packages including bed and breakfast at the affiliated Hôtel Suerte Loca. Ifni Surf

(☏0662 53 37 17; www.ifnisurf.com; Ave Moulay Youssef; board & wetsuit rental per day Dh150, 2hr lesson incl equipment Dh200, kayak & wetsuit rental per hour Dh60) offers board and kayak hire and instruction at Legzira Plage, with accommodation available in Ifni and Legzira.

🛏 Sleeping

Like the rest of Ifni, many of the hotels have seen better days.

Hôtel Bellevue — HOTEL €

(☏0528 87 52 72; Pl Hassan II; s/d with bathroom Dh170/200, s/d/tr without bathroom Dh105/130/150) Historically Ifni's best address, the art-deco charms of the Bellevue's exterior do not continue inside, where you will find little more than a few stylised lampshades and stained-glass windows. Nonetheless, it is a reasonable budget option on the main square, with sweeping coastal views from the bar-restaurant and room balconies. Shoot for an en-suite room upstairs; those downstairs are darker and the shared shower is a frugal rooftop affair.

Hôtel Suerte Loca — HOTEL €

(☏0528 87 53 50; suerteloca36@yahoo.com; Ave Moulay Youssef; s/d without shower Dh80/125, with shower Dh150/200) This blue-and-white auberge, in a prime position next to the boat-shaped house, is Ifni's surf and backpacker central. There's a roof terrace with beach views, plus table football and a pool table in the restaurant, although the latter's high prices are less popular. It could certainly use a renovation, but attractive bedspreads and balconies feature in the simple rooms.

Hôtel Ère Nouvelle — HOTEL €

(☏0528 87 52 98; Ave Sidi Mohammed ben Abdallah; s/d Dh35/70) Above a local restaurant, this central cheapie has spartan rooms with narrow beds. The shared bathrooms sport that classic shower/squat toilet combination. However, it's welcoming and secure, and the breakfast of bread, honey and snow-white butter is delicious.

Camping Sidi Ifni — CAMPGROUND €

(☏0528 87 67 34; off Ave Al Hourria; tent/caravan/room Dh35/75/85) Next to the outdoor swimming pool at the north end of the beach.

★ Xanadu — MAISON D'HÔTE €€

(☏0528 87 67 18; www.maisonxanadu.com; 5 Rue el Jadida; s/d incl breakfast Dh360/550; @ 🛜) Tucked away on a lane off Ave Mohammed V, this restored house offers a contemporary take on the Ifni aesthetic, with soothing colours pervading the five rooms. Breakfast on the roof is a pleasure and the book-filled lounge is ideal for whiling away an evening. The charming French host, Patrick, speaks some English, and offers guided hikes and 4WD excursions.

Eating

There's a covered fruit and vegetable market off Zankat Marrakesh. A souq is held on Sundays, 1km out of town on the road to the port.

★ Café-Restaurant Mar Pequeña
SEAFOOD, MOROCCAN €

(☑0655 58 04 32; 20 Blvd Al Mouahidine; set menu Dh50-100; ☺lunch & dinner; ✐) Less male-dominated than the neighbouring cafes, this good-value family-run restaurant is at the top of the seafront steps. The Tanani clan is full of smiles, the surrounds intimate and perfect for people-watching, and the broad menu includes tajines, couscous, *pastilla,* grills, a good vegetable selection and numerous seafood dishes. The hearty fish tajine is recommended. When we visited, the Tananis were setting up a nearby fish and grill cafe, Chez Sofia (Calle de Teniente Carlier; ☺lunch & dinner).

Municipal Market
SEAFOOD, SELF-CATERING €

(cnr Ave Mohammed V & Ave Hassan II) In addition to the fish market, fruit and vegetable market and surrounding cafes, look out for the courtyard of smoking grills. In this atmospheric outdoor spot, where cooks fan the coals and call out to punters, you can get grilled seafood – including sardines (Dh15), fish (Dh40) and prawns – served with salad and bread.

Eddib
PIZZERIA €

(Ave Hassan II; pizza Dh30-50; ☺lunch & dinner) Eddib's small range of pizzas have toppings such as tuna, minced meat, olives and egg. The covered outdoor seats have views of art-deco buildings and takeaway is available.

Gran Canaria
INTERNATIONAL, SEAFOOD €

(Ave Mohammed V; mains Dh40–70; ☺lunch & dinner) With pavement seats and views down the main street from its roof terrace, Gran Canaria's dishes range from fish tajine and fish *pastilla* to pizza and paella.

Café-Restaurant Azta
SEAFOOD, MOROCCAN €€

(☑0528 78 07 67; Ave Al Hourria; set menu Dh100; ☺breakfast, lunch & dinner; ☎) Relaunched and renamed in 2013 by new owners Aziz and Tarik, this garden restaurant's specialities include fresh grilled fish, lamb or chicken crêpes, and lamb tajine with prunes and apricots. Western dishes are also offered, as is a buffet and musical soirée on Saturday and Moroccan cookery courses (minimum six people).

☕ Drinking & Nightlife

Cafes line Ave Hassan II, with views of Pl Hassan II and the airfield.

Hôtel Bellevue
BAR

(Pl Hassan II) On a terrace above the beach, the bar at Hôtel Bellevue is a pleasant spot for a beer.

❶ Information

Good websites include www.ifniville.com and www.visit-sidiifni.blogspot.com. Head to Ave Mohammed V for pharmacies and for banks offering currency exchange and ATMs.

Hassan Cyber (Ave Hassan I; per hr Dh4; ☺10am-2pm & 5pm-midnight Sat-Thu, 5pm-midnight Fri) Internet access.

❶ Getting There & Away

BUS

CTM (☑0661 80 18 98; majid.ifni@hotmail.com; Ave Hassan II) Daily departures to destinations including Casablanca (Dh260, 12 hours), Marrakesh (Dh160, 7½ hours), Agadir (Dh70, four hours) and Laâyoune (Dh165, eight hours).

Trans Kam (☑0601 07 33 10; Ave Mohammed V) Daily bus to/from Marrakesh at 5am/1pm (eight hours, Dh110).

GRAND TAXI

The grand-taxi station is on the east side of town. Taxis serve Goulimime (Dh25), Legzira Plage (Dh13), Mirleft (Dh13), Tiznit (Dh27) and Agadir (Dh60).

Around Sidi Ifni

Hotels will advise on the many walks to be done in the countryside around Sidi Ifni.

Legzira Plage

El Gzira, usually called Legzira Plage, is a superb secluded bay 10km north of Ifni with excellent sand and two dramatic natural stone arches reaching over the sea. It's accessible from Rte 104 but better reached by walking along the beaches and cliffs. Tourism development is slowly spreading down the access road from Rte 104, but the beach itself remains pristine and undeveloped.

At the foot of the access road, a cluster of hotels and auberges overlook the beach. **Beach Club** (✆0670 52 28 00; www.legzira beachclub.com; s/d from Dh175/275) has the best rooms, some with shared sea-facing balconies.

Sable d'Or (✆0661 30 24 95; eddibmo-hamed2@yahoo.se; r Dh150-300) has small but comfortable rooms, opening onto terraces with sea views. Its public areas were being renovated when we visited.

The hotels offer half-board (about Dh250 per person) and you can get a simple lunch of grilled fish at the neighbouring beach cafes (about Dh60).

Grands taxis stop on Rte 104 en route between Sidi Ifni (Dh10) and Mirleft (Dh15).

Sidi Ouarsik

The fishing village of Sidi Ouarsik, 18km south of Sidi Ifni along the coast, has a great beach. Overlooking it from the bare hillside, **Auberge Figue de Barbarie** (✆0672 69 08 13; www.aubergefiguedebarbarie. com; s/d Dh150/200), named after the surrounding prickly pears, occupies a beautifully restored farmhouse with green lizards painted on the walls. The four rooms are simple, traditional affairs with small salons and shared bathrooms, but certainly aren't lacking in style. The auberge was previously a ruin and there are idiosyncrasies – high winds sometimes knock out the electricity – but it's a great place to savour the countryside. Half-/full board are an extra Dh100/150 per person. The owners, who can help organise activities including fishing, biking and day trips, also offer a restored pisé house in Ifni (Dh1500/3000 per week/month).

Mesti

This Berber village is 25km southeast of Sidi Ifni on the road through the prickly-pear-covered hills to Goulimime. At the turnoff for Mesti and the back road to Tiznit, you can do a tasting at the shop of honey cooperative **Miel Afoulki** (✆0661 47 24 33). It sells some extraordinary local flavours, including orange and euphorbia. In the village, the **Tafyoucht Cooperative** (✆0528 21 84 16; tafyouchte.com) is a women's cooperative producing oil and cosmetic products (Dh35 to Dh250) from the versatile argan tree, with a shop for tastings.

Goulimime   كَلْميم

POP 96,000

Once the 'Gateway of the Sahara', dusty Goulimime (or Guelmim) sprang up as a border town where farmers from the fertile Souss traded with nomads from the south. If you have come from the north, you will still recognise Goulimime as a border town: for the first time, you will see Saharawis in the majority.

The main reason to stop here is the Saturday-morning souq, which includes a camel market and takes place a few kilometres from town on the Tan Tan road. A weeklong *moussem* (festival) and camel fair is held here around the end of July.

🛏 Sleeping

You will only want to stay in Goulimime if necessary, as many hotels are basic and some may not appeal to women. If you have transport, there is better accommodation outside town.

Hôtel Ijdiguen   HOTEL €

(✆0528 77 14 53; Blvd Ibnou Battouta; s/d Dh75/150) Across the road from the grand-taxi station, Ijdiguen ('Ichdigen') is clean and welcoming, with tiled corridors, reasonable rooms and shared showers.

Hôtel Hamza   HOTEL €€

(✆0528 87 39 75; hotelhamza.webs.com; off Rte d'Agadir; s/d/tr/ste Dh360/460/520/900; ☀@🅿🌐) In this quiet and welcoming caravanserai located behind the tourist office, expansive corridors lead to cool and spacious rooms with bathrooms of varying quality.

Hôtel Adil Moussafir   HOTEL €€

(✆0528 77 29 30; www.hoteladilmoussafir.com; off Rte d'Agadir; s/d/tr/ste Dh480/550/700/1000; 🌐) Goulimime's grandest option, the Adil Moussafir has a restaurant (mains Dh70) and spacious, comfortable rooms with slightly tired bathrooms.

🍴 Eating

Around the bus station and north of the post office are good areas for cafes and restaurants.

AROUND GOULIMIME

Tighmert oasis makes a scenic drive from Goulimime, with views of the distant Anti Atlas. You can drive a circuit of this *palmeraie* (palm grove)in an hour or two on Rte d'Asrir, returning to town along the Goulimime–Assa road.

There are a few basic guesthouses in the oasis, mostly located some 20km southeast of Goulimime off Rte d'Asrir. Maison d'Hôtes Nomades (☎ 0667 90 96 42; www.darnomade.com; off Rte d'Asrir; d/tr from Dh200/250, breakfast/dinner/picnic Dh30/80/50) is a family-run guesthouse deep in the oasis (there are some tight corners on the drive there), with rugs and farming implements decorating the pisé walls and simple rooms with shared or private bathroom. Accommodation is also available in a Berber tent (per person Dh60) and dinner features dishes such as dromedary tajine. Camel rides and other activities are offered, but you may prefer to just lounge on the roof terrace taking in the views.

For a grand taxi to Tighmert from Goulimime (Dh10), take a petit taxi (day/night Dh5/9) to the grand-taxi station near the central market, 800m south of Pl Bir Anzarane at the start of the road to Assa and Asrir.

Accessed from the N12 between Goulimime and Tata (or along back roads from the Anti Atlas), the oasis village of Id-Âïssa, also known as Amtoudi after the gorge it occupies, has walking trails to two *agadirs,* a waterfall and cave paintings. One of the *agadirs* is particularly impressive, towering above the village on a spindly outcrop. Beneath the gorge's towering cliffs, French-owned guesthouse On Dirait le Sud (☎ 0528 21 85 69; ondiraitlesud@yahoo.fr; s/d/tr with bathroom from Dh255/260/315, without bathroom Dh155/160/215, dm per person Dh55, breakfast Dh35, dinner Dh80-100) has four simple whitewashed rooms adorned with rugs. It is well set up for trekking, with information and maps in the salon, and two- to 16-day guided treks offered in the Anti Atlas. In the second half of September, a festival and fantasia takes place in the nearby village of Âït Herbil, also known for its rock engravings.

Id-Âïssa is 30km from the N12, signposted from near the village of Taghjicht. To get there by grand taxi from Goulimime, you will likely have to change in Bouizakarne and Souk Tnine-Nouadai. A shared/private taxi from Bouizakarne costs about Dh35/210. From Tata, pick up a ride to Goulimime or Bouizakarne and alight in Taghjicht, from where a private taxi costs Dh120.

On the other side of Goulimime, French resort Fort Bou-Jerif (☎ 0528 87 30 39; www.fortboujerif.com; campsite from Dh70, incl half-board s Dh490-600, d Dh800-1000, khaïma per person incl half-board Dh320;) offers a taste of the desert, 40km northwest of town via the Sidi Ifni and Plage Blanche roads (it's well signposted). The last 9km is rough *piste*, passable in a normal vehicle at glacial pace. Built near a ruined French Foreign Legion fort, the compound has a range of sleeping options, from hotel and motel rooms to *khaïmas* (nomad tents) and camping. There is also a bar-restaurant (set menu Dh180), where the speciality is dromedary tajine. Owner Pierre offers activities including 4WD trips to Plage Blanche, a little-visited and unspoiled stretch of beach 40km southwest of Bou-Jerif.

La Plage Blanche MOROCCAN €
(Ziz garage, Rte d'Agadir; meals Dh60; ⊙breakfast, lunch & dinner) Near Pl Bir Anzarane, this Westernised snack bar serves dishes ranging from pizzas, burgers and spaghetti to tajines and *pil-pil* prawns. On Friday, join the locals and treat yourself to the couscous, while the masses pray outside the mosque across the road.

ℹ Information

Pl Bir Anzarane is the centre of town, and near here you'll find banks, internet cafes and the post office.
Tourist Office (☎ 0528 87 29 11; www.crt-guelmim.com; 3 Résidence Sahara, Rte d'Agadir; ⊙8.30am-4.30pm Mon-Fri) Follow the sign for Hôtel Hamza and turn immediately left.

ⓘ Getting There & Away

AIR

RAM (www.royalairmaroc.com) flies between Goulimime Airport and Casablanca five times a week (Dh600). **Canary Fly** (www.canaryfly.es) flies weekly to/from Gran Canaria (€130) in Spain's Canary Islands. Laâyoune-based travel agent El Sahariano (see p400) sells tickets for both.

BUS

The bus station is a 10-minute walk north of Pl Bir Anzarane.

CTM (Blvd Ibnou Battouta) and Supratours have at least one daily departure to the following places:

DESTINATION	COST (DH)	DURATION (HR)
Agadir	85	5
Casablanca	280	12
Dakhla	315	16
Laâyoune	155	7½
Marrakesh	180	7½
Rabat	305	13½
Tan Tan	40	2
Tiznit	40	2¾

Daily **Satas** (☑ 0528 87 22 13; Gare Routière) buses are a cheaper option:

DESTINATION	COST (DH)
Agadir	50
Inezgane	40
Laâyoune	130
Tan Tan	30
Tiznit	30

TAXI

You can catch grands taxis from behind the bus station to Inezgane (Dh70), Laâyoune (Dh200), Sidi Ifni (Dh25), Tan Tan (Dh50) and Tiznit (Dh35).

Tan Tan & Tan Tan Plage طانطان

POP 50,000

South of Goulimime, across the dry Oued Drâa, you enter the cauldron of the Sahara proper. The 130km of desert highway to Tan Tan is impressive for its bleak emptiness and harsh *hammada* (flat, stony desert).

If you weren't stopped by security on the way in, you could probably drive along the N1 (known as Ave Hassan II within Tan Tan's boundaries) without realising you were in the town, which spreads mostly south of the highway. The majority of the inhabitants are nomads who settled here, and blue robes are a big feature. The army and police presence is also noticeable, due to the proximity of the disputed Western Sahara. Look out for the middle-of-the-roundabout stop sign west of town; the police at the post beyond are not shy of issuing a ticket or pocketing a *petit cadeau* (little present) to overlook the infraction.

Tan Tan was founded in the 1940s during the Spanish Protectorate, but had its moment in 1975, when the area was the departure point for the Green March (p424). It's a run-down place with tough but not unfriendly inhabitants. The Sunday souq is held 1.5km south of town and a Unesco-protected *moussem* (www.moussemdetantan.org/en) takes place in September, featuring camel racing and music.

Tan Tan Plage, also known as Al-Ouatia, 25km west of Tan Tan, is a dilapidated seaside resort overlooking a long, windswept beach. The town only briefly comes to life during the Moroccan summer holiday, but staying here is nonetheless preferable to Tan Tan.

🛏 Sleeping & Eating

🍴 Tan Tan

There are cheap eateries on Ave Hassan II, Ave Mohammed V and around the *gare routière* (bus station), although many close at lunchtime or take a while to rustle up food. Hôtel Sable d'Or is a popular choice for a meal or *café au lait*. Cheap hotels overlook the *gare routière*.

Hôtel Sable d'Or HOTEL €
(☑ 0528 87 80 69; sabledor@gmail.com; Ave Hassan II; s/d Dh150/200; 🐾) Next to the banks on the main road, this friendly family-run hotel has comfortable en-suite rooms with flatscreen TV. Ask for a room at the rear, away from the main road. There's a cafe-restaurant with a pool table.

Hôtel Bir Anzarane HOTEL €
(☑ 0528 87 78 34; hotelbiranzarane@hotmail.fr; Ave Hassan II; s/d/tr Dh80/100/180; 🐾) A worn but clean place, next to the royal palace (soldiers patronise the cafe here) on the west side of the river. Above the breezy cafe, the small but neat rooms share bathrooms with squat and flush toilets.

SOUTHERN MOROCCO & WESTERN SAHARA TAN TAN

Tan Tan Plage

There are seafront hotels and campgrounds on the port road.

Hôtel Belle Vue HOTEL €
(☑0528 87 91 33; s/d from Dh100/200; ☎) This appropriately named family-run seafront hotel has basic en-suite rooms, reached along white corridors hung with cheery paintings. The cafe-restaurant (breakfast and meals Dh25 to Dh90) is one of Tan Tan Plage's best, serving tajines, omelettes, sardines and calamari.

Hôtel Hagounia HOTEL €
(☑0528 87 90 20; www.hotel-hagounia.com; s/d incl breakfast from Dh200/300, ste Dh500/600; ☎) The Hagounia has gloomy but comfortable rooms, featuring small balconies with beach or port views, and a sea-facing cafe-restaurant.

❶ Information

TAN TAN

Telephone boutiques and banks with ATMs and exchange facilities are clustered around the junction of Aves Hassan II and Mohammed V.
Club Internet (off Ave Hassan II; per hr Dh3; ☺9am-midnight) Next to Samir Oil petrol station.
Post Office (Pl de la Mare Verte)

TAN TAN PLAGE

A post office and two banks with ATMs and exchange facilities.

❶ Getting There & Away

AIR

RAM (www.royalairmaroc.com) flies between Tan Tan Airport and Casablanca five times a week (Dh600).

BUS

CTM (☑0528 76 58 86; Ave Hassan II) in Tan Tan has daily departures including the following:

DESTINATION	COST (DH)	DURATION (HR)
Agadir	125	6
Dakhla	290	14
Goulimime	40	1½
Laâyoune	120	5
Tiznit	80	3½

Supratours (☑Tan Tan Plage 0528 87 96 65, 0528 87 77 95; Ave Hassan II), which stops in Tan Tan and also at its office in Tan Tan Plage op-

posite the Dubai Hotel, operates similar services at slightly higher prices.

Other, cheaper companies, all serving the same destinations, use Tan Tan **gare routière** (bus station; Pl de la Marche Verte), off Ave Mohammed V about 1km south of Ave Hassan II.

TAXI

From Tan Tan *gare routière*, grands taxis head to Agadir (Dh100), Goulimime (Dh50), Inezgane (Dh100), Laâyoune (Dh150), Tan Tan Plage (Dh11), Tarfaya (D150) and Tiznit (Dh70).

Grands taxis to Tan Tan Plage also leave from the top of Blvd el-Amir Moulay Abdallah, a few hundred metres south of Ave Hassan II.

Tarfaya طرفايه
POP 6000

The small fishing port of Tarfaya was the centre of the Spanish Protectorate of Cap Juby, now known as the Tarfaya Strip. A Scottish trader, Donald Mackenzie, created the original settlement in the late 19th century, building a small trading post on a rock just offshore, which he called Port Victoria. When the Spanish took over, they appropriated the building, now known as Casa Mar (p398). The area gained independence from Spain in 1958.

The Moroccan government upgraded Tarfaya's municipal status to provincial centre in 2009, and the town is on the cusp of big developments. A wind farm is being constructed 25km away and a new port is planned, with hopes for the relaunch of the ferry connection to the Canary Islands and greater tourist numbers. New beachfront promenades and restaurants are also on the drawing board. For now, however, Tarfaya's charm remains; it's a friendly outpost with a seductively remote feel to the sand blowing between its crumbling colonial relics.

The town will forever be associated with the French pilot and writer Antoine de Saint-Exupéry. In 1926 he began flying in the airmail service between France and Senegal, and Cap Juby was one of the stops. In 1927 he was appointed station manager for Cap Juby and he spent a couple of years here, writing his first novel *Courrier Sud* (Southern Mail), in which an airmail pilot dies south of Boujdour in the desert of Rio de Oro. He also picked up inspiration for his most famous story, *Le Petit Prince* (The Little Prince), which features a pilot lost in the desert.

◉ Sights & Activities

There are some good fishing, surfing and kitesurfing spots around Tarfaya. Ask your accommodation or Les Amis de Tarfaya about organising an expedition.

★ Historic Sites   HISTORIC SITES

Numerous dilapidated buildings recall the days when Saint-Exupéry and the chaps touched down here. The Casa Mar is abandoned but still standing, and can be easily reached at low tide. At the north end of the beach, a monument honours Saint-Exupéry's memory: a dinky green Bréguet 14 biplane, the sort he used to fly. Nearby, the Spanish fort now houses military barracks, and behind the museum is the 1930s cinema; in the same area, swashbucklers swapped anecdotes between flights at Bar des Pilotes. The wrecked Armas ferry Assalama, 2km south of town, put paid to the short-lived connection between Tarfaya and Fuerteventura when it went down in 2008.

Musée Saint-Exupéry   MUSEUM

(☎ 0661 07 94 88; admission Dh10; ⊘ 8.30am-4.30pm Mon-Fri, by appointment Sat & Sun) Tells the stories (in French) of Saint-Exupéry, the airmail service's founder Pierre-Georges Latécoère, and the incredible service itself, which eventually became part of Air France.

Festivals & Events

Rallye Toulouse Saint-Louis   FESTIVAL

(www.rallyetoulousesaintlouis.com; ⊘ late Sep or early Oct) The airmail service is remembered when light aircraft fly from France to Senegal and back, landing in Tarfaya en route.

🛏 Sleeping & Eating

There are numerous self-catering apartments in Tarfaya, including Residence Armas (☎ 0673 54 66 47; ste Dh350; 🖎), which has four suites sleeping up to three people each. Les Amis de Tarfaya can help you find an apartment.

Numerous cafes on the main street serve cheap dishes such as grilled fish.

Residence Hotelière Addoyouf   PENSION €€

(Hotel Cap Juby; ☎ 0665 43 58 92; alisalemtarfaya@gmail.com; s/d Dh188/376) This blue-and-yellow building at the northern entrance to town has five rooms on the 1st floor, with a shared bathroom, kitchen and terrace. Meals are available and an adjoining booth sells basic provisions.

Casa Mar   HOTEL €

(☎ 0528 89 53 26; casamarhotel@gmail.com; s/d without bathroom from Dh100/120, with bathroom Dh180/250; 🖎) Just outside the port entrance, Casa Mar's cafe-restaurant (breakfast/mains Dh25/70) serves a good selection of seafood dishes, ranging from mixed grilled fish to calamari tajine. The cafe, a popular meeting point, is a good place to check your emails and watch local characters stroll in. Rooms in the hotel's old section are terrible, but a new extension was being built when we visited, with spacious en-suite rooms and port views.

Hotel Aoudate   HOTEL €€

(☎ 0528 89 58 68; per person incl breakfast from Dh250; 🖎) The builders were finishing this hotel when we visited, and it promised to be Tarfaya's most comfortable. Available with or without balcony and private bathroom, the 35 rooms have attractive checkered bedding and satellite TV, with sea views from the upper floors. A Spanish restaurant was set to join the ground-floor cafe.

ℹ Information

Tarfaya has a medical centre, pharmacies, an internet cafe, a laundrette and banks with ATMs and exchange facilities.

Les Amis de Tarfaya (☎ 0661 07 94 88; sadat@yours.com) Information is available from the English-speaking Sadat at this local tourism association, based at Musée Saint-Exupéry.

ℹ Getting There & Away

Bus companies, including CTM, stop in Tarfaya, but **Supratours** (☎ 0528 89 52 84; Rte du Port) has the only reliable office. It has the best buses and so is the best option anyway, given the brutal journey times in the Sahara. Daily Supratours departures head for the following places:

DESTINATION	COST (DH)	DURATION (HR)
Agadir	180	8
Dakhla	220	10
Goulimime	130	6
Laâyoune	40	2
Marrakesh	250	13
Tan Tan	80	3
Tiznit	150	7

Grands taxis go to Laâyoune (Dh40) and Tan Tan (Dh80). Tarfaya has petrol stations, car-washing services and mechanics.

WESTERN SAHARA
الصحراء الغربية

Ask any Moroccan about the status of the Western Sahara and they will insist it belongs to their country, yet the UN is clear that this is still under dispute. Local maps may show this region as a seamless continuation of the *hammada* around Tarfaya, but many outside Morocco disagree.

This area largely comprises the former colonies of Spanish Sahara and part of the Tarfaya Strip. Crossing the vast tracts of desert here, one does marvel at the dispute. The towns are merely administrative centres, and the terrain stretching away from the N1 is featureless, arid, inhospitable and uninviting. Despite this distinct lack of postcard prettiness, this environment has phosphate, oil and fishing potential – significant factors in the dispute.

It's one of the world's most sparsely populated territories, and despite the 1991 ceasefire in the war between Morocco and the separatist Polisario Front, the Moroccan military sometimes seems to outnumber the civilians. If you want to appreciate the Sahara and see oases and dunes, the likes of Merzouga, Figuig and Tata are better choices: more scenic, safer and reached via less gruelling journeys from central Morocco. For travellers who need to cross the Western Sahara to reach Mauritania, bear in mind that this is a disputed area and read our safety guidelines.

Due to the volatile situation in the Western Sahara while this book was being researched, the information on Laâyoune and Dakhla has been updated remotely via phone and internet.

History

Despite its windswept desolation, the Western Sahara has a long and violent history. Islamic missionaries started to spread Islam

---

SAFE TRAVEL IN THE WESTERN SAHARA

Given the ongoing tensions in the Western Sahara, travelling to the region is inadvisable. If you need to cross the area to reach Mauritania, it is recommended that you avoid Laâyoune in particular; the city was the focus of the violent clashes in November 2010 and remains volatile. While there is the obvious danger of being caught in a riot or a confrontation between Moroccans and Saharawis, dealing with the Moroccan authorities at the numerous roadblocks actually poses more risks.

In engineering a media blackout, the Moroccans are determined to keep journalists from the region. Following the violent raid of the Gadaym Izik camp near Laâyoune in 2010, reporters were prevented from boarding planes to Laâyoune, and Spanish journalists who reached the city were detained and deported. Spain has been most critical of Morocco's occupation, so Spanish travellers are likely to field most questions from Moroccan officials.

However, everyone should treat the checkpoint stops seriously, tedious though they are, as there is a small risk of travellers being taken for a journalist or Polisario sympathiser. Even as you approach the Western Sahara, entering and travelling between towns such as Tarfaya, Tan Tan, Goulimime and Tata, foreigners are invariably asked about their profession, next destination and purpose in the region. Sometimes these questions will quickly dissolve into enquiries about your soccer allegiances, and you will be waved on. In the Western Sahara, your passport and visa details will be noted down, along with your vehicle details if you are driving. If you're on a bus, often you can stay in your seat while the police take your ID and write down your particulars; sometimes you will be summoned to speak to a head honcho in a hut.

Occupations that are likely to ring alarm bells at police posts are journalism or working in aid. If police confirm that you work in an occupation of that nature, you could be followed, detained, sent back to Morocco proper or even deported to a nearby location such as the Canary Islands. The authorities are generally more wary of travellers visiting Laâyoune than Dakhla or Tarfaya.

Once in Laâyoune and Dakhla you will be aware of the military and police, both of which are sensitive to photography around military installations. Similarly, they will not take too kindly to you photographing or trying to visit the refugee camps around both cities, where many Saharawis still live.

among the Zenata and Sanhaja Berber tribes here in the 7th century. A second wave of Arab settlers, the Maqil from Yemen, migrated to the desert in the 13th century, and the whole region became predominantly Arabic.

In the 19th century, the Spanish grabbed the Western Sahara and renamed it Rio de Oro. In reality, Sheikh Ma El-Ainin and his son El-Hiba controlled the desert and the nomadic tribes well into the 20th century. From the 1930s, an uneasy colonial peace prevailed until Moroccan independence in the late 1950s, when new nationalist fervour saw the genesis of the Polisario Front and a guerrilla war against the Spanish.

When it was abandoned by Spain in 1975, Morocco and Mauritania both raised claims to the desert region, but Mauritania soon bailed out. In November 1975 King Hassan II orchestrated the Green March – 350,000 Moroccans marched south to stake Morocco's historical claim to the Western Sahara.

Over the following years, Rabat poured in 100,000 troops to stamp out resistance, and gained the upper hand. The UN brokered a ceasefire in 1991, but a promised referendum, in which the indigenous Saharawis could choose between independence and integration with Morocco, has yet to materialise.

Ever since, Morocco has strengthened its hold on the territory, pouring money into infrastructure projects, particularly offshore oil exploration, and attracting Moroccans from the north to live here tax-free. Until late 2010, the troubled area seemed to be lying dormant, with the dispute largely forgotten by the world beyond this remote region. However, on 8 November 2010, Moroccan security forces stormed the Gadaym Izik camp near Laâyoune, in an attempt to break up the 15,000-strong protest camp. Both sides incurred fatalities in the ensuing clashes, which turned into riots and engulfed the city, with 700-plus Saharawi injuries, and scenes of fire and destruction in the international media. Laâyoune and Dakhla have both seen several clashes and riots since then, and Africa's longest-running territorial dispute continues.

For the most up-to-date information on the Western Sahara, or the Saharawi Arab Democratic Republic (as the separatist government calls the occupied territory), check ARSO (www.arso.org), BBC (www.tinyurl.com/37j6p8n), CIA World Factbook (www.tinyurl.com/38nkck), Global Voices (www.globalvoicesonline.org) and UN (www.un.org).

Climate

Beyond the foothills of the Anti Atlas lies a parched hinterland starved of moisture. Here temperatures can exceed 45°C during the day and plunge to 0°C at night, while an annual rainfall of less than 125mm gives a suffocating aridity hovering between 5% and 30% – dry enough to mummify corpses. The desert wind, known locally as the *chergui*, *irifi* or *sirocco*, adds to the harsh conditions. From March to April, sandstorms also plague the desert, making driving inadvisable.

It is important to carry a good supply of water. In winter it is also essential to carry a warm sleeping bag and some warm clothing as desert nights can be bitterly cold.

Language

In the Western Sahara, Arabic and French are spoken almost universally. As a previous Spanish Protectorate, the more common second language was, until recently, Spanish, a habit that lingers in the older generation. English is also spoken, due to the UN presence.

❶ Getting There & Away

There is no officially designated border between Morocco and the Western Sahara, and Morocco treats the region as an integrated part of the country.

Flights link both Laâyoune and Dakhla with Agadir, Casablanca and Gran Canaria. In addition to the airlines, Laâyoune-based travel agent **El Sahariano** (☑ 0528 98 12 12; www.elsahariano.com; Blvd de Mekka) sells tickets for these flights.

Supratours and CTM both operate buses to Laâyoune and Dakhla. Given the brutal journey times in the Western Sahara, it is best to stick with these reliable companies.

One of the benefits of the area's tax-free status is that petrol costs a couple of dirham less per litre than in the rest of Morocco. The first of the Atlas Sahara petrol stations is just south of Tarfaya. For car hire, Dakhla-based **Laargoub Car** (☑ 0528 93 04 47; www.laargoubcar.com; Ave Ahmed Bahnini) also covers Laâyoune, Agadir, Essaouira and Marrakesh, with one-way rental available.

Laâyoune (Al-'Uyun) العيون

POP 200,000

The Spanish created Laâyoune as an outpost from which to administer the nearby Bou Craa phosphate mines. The Moroccans had bigger ambitions and spent more than US$1

Laâyoune

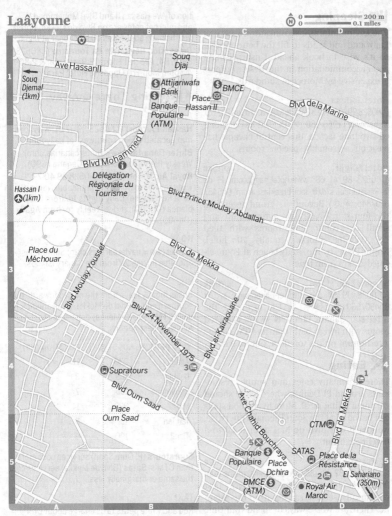

billion turning it into the principal city of the Western Sahara. Now neither Saharawi nor Spanish, its population is mostly Moroccans, lured from the north by the promise of healthy wages and tax-free goods.

A government centre and military garrison with UN Land Cruisers drifting along its drab avenues, Laâyoune is not worth a visit. Indeed, given the tensions in the Western Sahara's largest and most volatile city, we recommend you avoid stopping here, as there's nothing to justify the risk of police hassle or getting caught in a riot. Whether you're heading north or south, distances are

Laâyoune

Sleeping
1 Hôtel Jodesa	D4
2 Hôtel Nagjir	D5
3 Sahara Line Hotel	B4

Eating
4 Le Poissonier	D3
5 Pizzeria la Madone	C5

so great that you may have to stop here, but try to plan your trip so you pause in Tarfaya or Dakhla instead.

🛏 Sleeping

The UN maintains a significant presence in Laâyoune and tends to fill the better hotels, so it's wise to book ahead. Unsurprisingly, good accommodation in this desert outpost is expensive by Moroccan standards.

Hôtel Jodesa HOTEL €

(📞0528 992064; 223 Blvd de Mekka; s/d Dh120/170, with shower Dh165/180; 📶) Behind its dilapidated two-tone facade, this central cheapie has basic but reasonably spacious rooms.

Hôtel Nagjir HOTEL €€

(📞0528 89 41 68; www.hotel-nagjir.com; Pl de la Résistance; s/d/tr incl breakfast from Dh545/670/845; ❄📶) Beyond its grand reception, the four-star Nagjir has a restaurant and small but comfortable rooms with tiled floors. It has another, equally '70s hotel, Nagjir Plage, by the sandy beach at Foum el-Oued, 22km from town.

Sahara Line Hotel HOTEL €€

(📞0528 99 54 54; Blvd el-Kairaouane; s/d/tr Dh450/560/670; ❄📶) A UN favourite, the three-star Sahara Line has swish, carpeted rooms with fridge, bathroom and TV. There's a restaurant on the top floor, but no bar.

🍴 Eating

There are many cafes and simple restaurants around Pl Dchira, where Dh30 should get you a filling meal. More lively food stalls can be found at the Souq Djemal. Otherwise, wander down Blvd de Mekka or head to a hotel restaurant.

Le Poissonier SEAFOOD €

(📞0528 99 32 62; 183 Blvd de Mekka; mains from Dh50; ⏰lunch & dinner) One of the city's best restaurants, serving catches from the Atlantic. There are worse ways to spend your time in Laâyoune than over a fish soup or lobster here.

Pizzeria la Madone ITALIAN €

(📞0528 99 32 52; 141 Ave Chahid Bouchraya; pizzas Dh45-70; ⏰lunch & dinner) A cosy place to eat, although it also does a brisk takeaway trade, la Madone specialises in pasta dishes and thin-crust pizzas.

ℹ Information

The city's showpiece is the vast Pl du Méchouar, but there is no obvious centre. The post office, banks and most hotels are along Ave Hassan II and Blvd de Mekka. There are several banks with ATMs and exchange facilities near the intersection of Ave Hassan II and Blvd Mohammed V, and internet cafes are on Blvd de Mekka. Bored youths hang about at Pl du Méchouar at night.

Délégation Régionale du Tourisme (📞0528 89 16 94; Ave de l'Islam; ⏰9am-noon & 2.30-4.30pm Mon-Fri) Opposite Hôtel Parador.

ℹ Getting There & Away

AIR

Hassan I Airport (📞0528 89 37 91; www.onda.ma) Located 1.5km southwest of Laâyoune.

Binter Canarias (www.bintercanarias.com) Weekly flights to/from Gran Canaria (€90).

Royal Air Maroc (RAM; 📞0528 89 40 77; www.royalairmaroc.com; Immeuble Nagjir, Pl de la Résistance) Daily flights to/from Casablanca (Dh800); thrice weekly to/from Agadir (Dh600).

BOAT

Armas (www.navieraarmas.com) Sometimes operates ferries to/from the Canary Islands.

BUS

Buses mostly leave from the offices towards the southern end of Blvd de Mekka. Book ahead for daily **CTM** (Blvd de Mekka) departures to the following destinations:

DESTINATION	COST (DH)	DURATION (HR)
Agadir	230	11
Dakhla	165	8
Goulimime	155	7
Marrakesh	325	14
Tan Tan	120	5
Tiznit	190	9

Supratours (Pl Oum Saad) services cost more than CTM's; **Satas** (Blvd de Mekka) services cost the same or marginally less.

TAXI

Red and white petits taxis charge about Dh5 to take you across town, including to the main grand-taxi station, located about 2km east of the centre along Blvds Prince Moulay Abdallah and Abou Bakr Seddik. Grand-taxi services include Tan Tan (Dh150), Goulimime (Dh200), Inezgane (for Agadir; Dh250) and Dakhla (Dh180).

Dakhla (Ad-Dakhla) الداخلة

POP 60,000

Established by the Spanish in 1844 and formerly called Villa Cisneros, Dakhla lies just north of the Tropic of Cancer on a sandy peninsula, stretching out 40km from the main coastline. It's a very lonely 500km drive from Laâyoune (more than 1000km from Agadir) through endless *hammada*. After so many hours on the road, it is tempting to imagine that you are arriving at the end of the earth. It is certainly the end of Morocco, or at least the last major settlement, closer to Nouâdhibou (Mauritania) than Laâyoune.

And yet Dakhla feels less remote than many southern towns and certainly more prosperous, with a selection of good hotels and restaurants. The whitewashed, arcaded streets are a little soulless, but are refreshing after some of the run-down backwaters to the north. Although Western Saharan tensions lurk under the carefree, sea-breeze surface – fishing rights are a touchpaper between the Saharawi and Moroccan settlers – Dakhla's inhabitants appear relatively modern and progressive. Money continues to find its way along the peninsula, with investments made by the Moroccan government and developers, and workers tempted from the north. New apartment blocks stretch the town boundaries and the huge port is home to Morocco's largest fishing fleet.

Dakhla is reasonably easy to get around; hotels, cafes, bus offices and most of the main facilities are within walking distance of each other in the centre.

🛏 Sleeping

Hôtel Erraha   HOTEL €
(☑ 0528 89 88 11; Ave Banchekroune; s/d/tr Dh275/330/550; 🛜) The Erraha's spacious rooms have hot water and balconies overlooking the new Edderhem Mosque and its green square. The staff are a genial bunch and there's a cafe. The location, about 1km southwest of the centre, is a little out of the way, but convenient for grands taxis and the SAT and Supratours offices.

Hôtel Aigue   HOTEL €
(☑ 0528 89 73 95; Ave Sidi Ahmed Laaroussi; s/d Dh85/125) In a tall, narrow building, the Aigue is one of the central budget hotels overlooking the pedestrianised shopping lanes just southwest of the Supratours office. It has basic, pokey rooms with shared showers and squat toilets, but it's clean, secure and central.

Hôtel Sahara   HOTEL €
(☑ 0528 89 77 73; Ave Sidi Ahmed Laaroussi; r Dh85-210) The Sahara's rooms have little balconies. The basic options share showers and squat toilets; the better-value en-suite rooms have sit-down toilets and TVs.

Hotel Tafoudart   HOTEL €
(☑ 0668 72 27 39; Ave Beuchekroune; s without/ with shower & TV Dh65/125, d Dh85/175) This friendly hotel is about 10 minutes' walk east of the grands-taxis station. Recommended if you want a comfortable, secure night with no frills.

★ Bab al-Bahar   BOUTIQUE HOTEL €€€
(☑ 0528 93 14 40; www.bab-al-bahar.com; Ave Mohammed V; s/d incl breakfast from Dh900/1400; ❄ @ 🛜) A relaxing waterfront choice, from the mini Zen garden on the reception desk to the 35 delightful rooms with window seats. Activities including kitesurfing and 4WD excursions in the dunes are offered. Next to the lapping water, the stylish Italian restaurant (set menu Dh150) offers pasta, pizzas, lighter meals and a Saturday-night seafood buffet (Dh180).

Sahara Regency   RESORT €€€
(☑ 0528 93 15 55; www.sahararegency.com; Ave al-Walae; r/ste incl breakfast from Dh945/1365; ❄ 🛜 🛜) Entered through archways, the four-star Sahara Regency's rooms are mini-apartments, but the furniture and fittings are aged. Nonetheless, the overall package is good, with a rooftop pool and ground-floor tearoom and restaurant. Tours and activities including kitesurfing are offered.

🍴 Eating & Drinking

For an alcoholic drink with your meal before entering dry Mauritania, head to the restaurants at Bab al-Bahar and the Sahara Regency.

Café Restaurant
Samarkand   SEAFOOD, MOROCCAN €
(☑ 0528 89 83 16; Ave Mohammed V; mains Dh50-60; ⏰ lunch & dinner) This waterfront terrace restaurant has views of the white cliffs of Africa from its pergolas. The menu features a wide range of fish and other dishes; order in advance for couscous or fish *pastilla*.

Café-Restaurant Bahia   SEAFOOD, SPANISH €€
(☑ 0528 93 00 62; 16 Ave Mohammed V; meals Dh90; ⏰ lunch & dinner) A good, unlicensed fish restaurant serving catches including calamari and octopus.

Hassan Fruits   JUICE BAR
(Ave al-Walae) Across the pedestrian crossing from the Dakhla peninsula monument, this is popular for a slice of gâteau and a mixed fruit cocktail (Dh15).

🛍 Shopping

A pedestrianised shopping lane runs north from Ave Sidi Ahmed Laaroussi between Hôtels Sahara and Aigue. Vendors here sell goods ranging from argan oil to bright *mlahfa* (fine, colourful Saharan fabrics).

Ensemble Artisanal JEWELLERY, SOUVENIRS
(Ave el-Moukouama) Marrakesh medina it ain't, but you can find last-minute gifts here, particularly Saharan jewellery.

ℹ Information

Internet cafes and banks with ATMs are found in the centre of town and next to Hôtel Erraha.
Post Office (Ave el-Moukouama)

ℹ Getting There & Around

AIR

Dakhla Airport (☏ 0528 93 06 30; www.onda.ma) About 200m west of the Sahara Regency.
Canary Fly (www.canaryfly.es) Weekly flights to/from Spain's Gran Canaria (€100).
Royal Air Maroc (RAM; ☏ 0528 89 70 49; www.royalairmaroc.com) Daily flights to/from Casablanca (Dh1000); twice weekly to/from Agadir (Dh800).

BUS

CTM (☏ 0528 89 81 66; Blvd 4 Mars) and **Supratours** (Ave Mohammed V) have offices in the centre. Companies including Supratours and SAT have offices on and around Ave Banchekroune, between the grands-taxis station and the Edderhem Mosque.

Book ahead for daily services to these destinations (details given below are for travel on CTM buses):

DESTINATION	COST (DH)	DURATION (HR)
Agadir	370	20
Laâyoune	165	8½
Marrakesh	460	23
Tan Tan	290	13½

CAR

There are plenty of mechanics, mostly in the newer part of town to the southwest, who can service vehicles before a trek south.

TAXI

White-and-turquoise petits taxis whiz around town (day/night Dh5/6). The grand-taxi station is in Al-Messira, southwest of the centre. Destinations include Inezgane (for Agadir; Dh400) and Laâyoune (Dh180).

Understand Morocco

Morocco Today

Morocco is taking increasingly confident steps into the 21st century. Although global recession and regional politics resulted in a downturn in tourist numbers in recent years, the economy is slowly rebounding through its close ties to the EU and USA. While the perennially thorny issue of Western Sahara shows no sign of immediate resolution, some deft political manoeuvring by its savvy king helped the country avoid the regional turmoil of the Arab Spring.

Best on Film

Casanegra Nour-Eddine Lakhmari's film about growing up and confronting the darker side of Casablanca.

La Grande Villa Latif Lahlou's tale of a couple relocating from Paris to Casablanca.

A Thousand Months Faouzi Bensaïdi's family epic. Winner of the 2003 Premier Regard at Cannes.

Marock Laïla Marrakchi's film about a Muslim girl and a Jewish boy who fall in love. Winner of the Un Certain Regard at Cannes in 2005.

Best in Print

The Sacred Night Tahar ben Jelloun's tale of a Marrakesh girl raised as a boy won France's Prix Goncourt.

Dreams of Trespass: Tales of a Harem Girlhood Fatima Mernissi's memoirs of 1940s Fez blend with other women's stories.

The Polymath Bensalem Himmich's novel about 14th-century scholar and exile Ibn Khuldun.

Welcome to Paradise Mahi Binebine's novel exploring the promise and trauma of emigration.

Renovations in Progress

Wherever you go in Morocco, you'll see work in progress. Massive infrastructure projects are improving the transport network; signs announce new women's artisan associations in mountain hamlets; a mosaic *mâalem* (master artisan) hunkers in a niche in a palace wall with a tiny chisel, tapping out a zigzag shape to match a gap in the *zellij* (tilework). Development schemes, self-help organisations and economic liberalisation are attempting to move the country on from cycles of poverty and official censorship of expression – or as Driss ben Hamed Charhadi described it in his 1964 book of the same name, 'a life full of holes'.

Social rifts are not easy to fill. While economic growth sits around 3% to 4%, unemployment hovers around 45% for youth, and a 2011 cafe bombing in Marrakesh's cosmopolitan Djemaa el-Fna tragically underlined economic and cultural tensions. Two popular magazines were forced to cease publication in 2010: *Nichane* after a mildly irreverent article about Moroccan humour, and *Le Journal Hebdomadaire* after publishing a poll citing only a 91% approval rating for the king.

Yet as you can tell from the centuries-old stone minarets and remarkably intact mudbrick castle towers that dot its rugged landscape, Morocco has already weathered adverse conditions over the past millennium without crumbling. With all available means – vibrant local organisations, plucky media, resilient senses of humour, a tiny chisel if necessary – Moroccans are fashioning a modern society on the foundations of an ancient one.

Rise of the Tourism Economy

Your arrival is hotly anticipated in Morocco. The government's 'Vision 2010' of welcoming 10 million visitors by 2010 may have fallen shy of achieving its goal, due to recession in Europe, but tourism has more than doubled since 2002, low-cost European airlines are servicing more Moroccan airports, and the new 'Plan Azur' to create six coastal resort magnets for tourism is well under way. In the past decade, tourism has handily overtaken agriculture and fishing as Morocco's main occupation, and services represent over half of Morocco's GDP, ahead of industry (mainly textile production) and phosphate mining (mostly in Western Sahara).

All this has changed everything and nothing about Morocco, which has been a crossroads culture for 1000 years. In the souqs, you'll still hear carpet-sellers delivering their best one-liners – but now they're in Arabic, Berber, French, Spanish, English, Italian, Portuguese, German and Russian. Many historic family homes in Moroccan medinas have been converted into guesthouses, where the mint tea is ceremoniously poured for new arrivals with time-honoured hospitality.

With tourism still developing, your choices shape Morocco's future. Tourism could mean more golf courses that strain local resources, or cultural tourism that rewards communities for conservation of local landmarks and traditions. Spending a day in Morocco's pristine countryside is even more helpful. The UN estimates that for every eight to 10 tourists who visit an urban area, one job is created locally, while in rural areas those tourists represent six or seven essential new job opportunities. Even short visits have an outsized impact, since the average traveller expenditure for a splashy Marrakesh weekend is equivalent to three or four months' salary for most Moroccans (about Dh900). For the 50% of Morocco's population that's under 25, opportunities to interact with visitors and practise foreign languages are key preparations for joining Morocco's increasingly competitive and cosmopolitan workforce.

Morocco's Tangled Web

Royal rose gardens are lined with internet kiosks, cybercafe screens shield couples smooching via Skype, and commentators discuss breaking news in Egypt via Twitter: welcome to Morocco, home of techie trendsetters.

Social-media adoption has accelerated across Morocco, often outpacing political controls. With periodic restrictions on services like YouTube and Skype and arrests of local bloggers, Morocco's 2013 ranking on Reporters Without Borders' Press Freedom Index sits at 136 out of 178 countries.

Yet as Morocco's new National Press Syndicate reported in 2010, Moroccans' preferred information source is now the internet. Don't be surprised to sit next to a smartphone status–updating Moroccan on a rural bus ride.

AREA: **446,550 SQ KM**

POPULATION: **32.6 MILLION**

GDP PER CAPITA: **US$5200**

UNEMPLOYMENT: **9%**

LIFE EXPECTANCY: **76.3 YEARS**

ADULT LITERACY: **67%**

if Morocco were 100 people

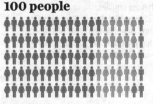

66 would be 15-64 years old
28 would be 0-14 years old
6 would be 65 years and older

ethnicity
(% of population)

60
Amazigh (Berber)

39
Arab/Other

1
European

population per sq km

MOROCCO   ALGERIA   UK

≈ 15 people

Do

Conserve water Water is a scarce and valuable resource in this pre-Saharan country.

Cover knees and shoulders Whether you're a man or woman; it shows your respect for your Moroccan hosts.

Learn basic greetings A few words in Darija or Berber will delight your hosts, who will also make an effort to speak your language.

Don't

Give money, sweets or pens to children It encourages begging and shames families.

Eat in public during Ramadan Or drink alcohol within view of a mosque.

Skip pleasantries Say hello before asking for help or prices.

Reforms & Challenges

At the urging of human-rights advocates, the extreme measures of King Hassan II's 'Years of Lead' have been curbed by King Mohammed VI. But public demand for greater democratic participation, poverty alleviation and press freedoms has outpaced government reform efforts.

Clever manoeuvring by Mohammed VI saw Morocco sidestep the upheavals of the Arab Spring. The student-led 20 February movement protesting institutional corruption and abuses of the Makhzen – the elite that surrounds the royal court and dominates the political and business life of the country – was largely neutered by the announcement of a new constitution offering more political accountability. Approved by popular referendum, it made Berber an official language of Morocco, as well as offering the government more executive powers. However, politics in Morocco still remains almost entirely under the patronage of the crown, and speaking out against the king is a social taboo.

Morocco continues to be buffeted by the world economic downturn. In 2013, a survey revealed that 42% of young Moroccans wanted to emigrate. As Morocco attempts to redefine itself for the 21st century, the challenges – and opportunities – are myriad.

History

Before there were dunes, mosques, or even carpet dealers in Morocco, this region was under water. In the Atlas Mountains and Saharan steppes, strata mark the geologic time and place where tectonic plates shifted billions of years ago and civilisation surfaced from a rugged seabed. The earliest evidence of human settlement in Morocco dates from 75,000 to 125,000 BC, when the stone tools used locally were advanced technology. But the ice age wasn't kind to these proto-Moroccan 'pebble people', and left the country wide open for settlement when the weather warmed around 5000 BC.

Live Free or Die Trying: The Berbers

The fertile land revealed after the great thaw was a magnet for near-eastern nomads, early ancestors of Morocco's Amazigh (plural Imazighen, loosely translated as 'free people') who may have been distant cousins of the ancient Egyptians. They were joined by Mediterranean anglers and Saharan horse-breeders around 2500 BC, with Phoenicians showing up fashionably late around 800 BC and East Africans around 500 BC.

When the Romans arrived in the 4th century, they didn't know quite what to make of this multicultural milieu. The Romans called the expanse of Morocco and western Algeria 'Mauretania' and the indigenous people 'Berbers', meaning 'barbarians'. The term has recently been reclaimed and redeemed by the Berber Pride movement, but at the time it was taken as quite a slur.

The ensuing centuries were one long lesson for the Romans in minding their manners. First the Berbers backed Hannibal and the Carthaginians against Rome in a protracted spat over Sicily known as the Punic Wars (264–202 BC). Fed up with the persistently unruly Berbers, the new Roman emperor Caligula finally declared the end of Berber autonomy in the Maghreb (northwest Africa) in AD 40.

Defying Orders under Roman Noses

True to his ruthless reputation, Caligula divided relatively egalitarian Berber clans into subservient classes of slaves, peasants, soldiers and Romanised aristocrats. This strategy worked with Vandals and Byzantines,

> The emblem on the Berber flag is the Tifinagh letter 'yaz' – it symbolises a free person (*amazigh*), the Berbers' name for themselves.

TIMELINE	Origin	248,000–73,000 BC	5000–2500 BC
	According to Amazigh folklore, the earth's first couple birthed 100 babies and left them to finish the job of populating the planet.	Precocious 'pebble people' begin fashioning stone tools far ahead of the European Stone Age technology curve.	Once the ice age melts away, the Maghreb becomes a melting pot of Saharan, Mediterranean and indigenous people. They meet, mingle and merge into a diverse people: the Amazigh.

Pre-Islamic Sites

Carved Gazelle, Tafraoute

Roman Diana mosaics at Volubilis

Phoenician/Roman ruins at Lixus

Prehistoric petroglyphs, Oukaïmeden

Roman Sala Colonia, Chellah

but Berbers in the Rif and the Atlas drove out the Romans with a campaign of harassment and flagrant disregard for Roman rules. Many Berbers refused to worship Roman gods, and some practised the new renegade religion of Christianity in open defiance of Roman rule. Christianity took root across North Africa; St Augustine himself was a Berber convert.

Ultimately Rome was only able to gain a sure foothold in the region by crowning local favourite Juba II king of Mauretania. The enterprising young king married the daughter of Mark Antony and Cleopatra, supported scientific research and performing arts, and helped foster Moroccan industries still vital today: olive-oil production from the region of Volubilis (near Meknès), fishing along the coasts, and vineyards on the Atlantic plains.

The Roman foothold in Mauretania slipped in the centuries after Juba II died, due to increasingly organised Berber rebellions inland and attacks on the Atlantic and Mediterranean coasts by the Vandals, Byzantines and Visigoths. But this new crop of marauding Europeans couldn't manage Mauretania, and neither could Byzantine emperor Justinian. Justinian's attempt to extend his Holy Roman Empire turned out to be an

WHEN PURPLE WAS PURE GOLD

The port that is today called Essaouira was hot property in ancient times, because it had one thing everyone wanted: the colour purple. Imperial purple couldn't be fabricated, and was the one colour strictly reserved for Roman royalty. This helps explain the exorbitant asking price, which according to Aristotle was 10 to 20 times its weight in gold. The natural dye came from the spiky murex marine snails that clung to the remote Purpuraire (Purple) Islands – as though that could save them from the clutches of determined Roman fashionistas.

Technically the Phoenicians were there first and discovered the stuff, but everyone wanted purple power. Savvy King Juba II established a coastal dye works in the 1st century BC to perform the tricky task of extracting murex dye from the vein of the mollusc, and kept his methods a closely guarded secret. The hue became wildly popular among royal celebrities of the day; Cleopatra loved the stuff so much that she dyed the sails of her royal barge purple to meet Mark Antony.

But violet soon turned to violence. Legend has it that Juba's son Ptolemy was murdered by Emperor Caligula for having the audacity to sport a purple robe, making trendy Ptolemy possibly the world's first fashion victim. The bright, nonfading dye was never successfully produced commercially, and the secret extraction methods were assumed lost in the siege of Constantinople in 1453. But in Essaouira the stuff is mysteriously still available, for a price. The mysteries of the colour purple are still passed down from one generation of murex collectors to the next, and are jealously guarded.

1600 BC	950 BC	800–500 BC	4th–1st century BC
Bronze Age petroglyphs in the High Atlas depict fishing, hunting and horseback riding – a versatile combination of skills and cultures that would define the adaptable, resilient Amazigh.	Amazigh rebuff Rome and its calendar year, and start tracking Berber history on their own calendar on 13 January; it's maintained for centuries after the Muslim Hejira calendar is introduced.	The Maghreb gets even more multiculti as Phoenicians and East Africans join the Berbers, making the local population as complex a mix as a *ras al-hanout* spice blend.	Romans arrive to annex Mauretania, and 250 years later they're still trying, with limited success and some Punic Wars to show for their troubles.

unholy mess of treaties with various Berber kingdoms, who played their imperial Byzantine connections like face cards in high-stakes games. The key history of Morocco would be defined by such strategic gamesmanship among the Berbers, whose savvy, competing alliances helped make foreign dominion over Morocco a near-impossible enterprise for more than a millennium.

Islam Arrives in Morocco

By the early 7th century, the Berbers of Morocco were mostly worshipping their own indigenous deities, alongside Jewish Berbers and a smattering of local Christian converts. History might have continued thus, but for a middle-aged man thousands of miles away who'd had the good fortune to marry a wealthy widow, and yet found himself increasingly at odds with the elites of his Arabian Peninsula town of Mecca. Mohammed bin Abu Talib was his given name, but he would soon be recognised as the Prophet Mohammed for his revelation that there was only one God, and that believers shared a common duty to submit to God's will. The polytheist ruling class of Mecca did not take kindly to this new religion, which assigned them shared responsibilities and took away their minor-deity status, and kicked the Prophet out of town on 16 July AD 622.

This Hejira (exile) only served to spread the Prophet Mohammed's message more widely. By the Prophet's death in 632, Arab caliphs – religious leaders inspired and emboldened by his teachings – were carrying Islam east to Central Asia and west to North Africa. But infighting limited their reach in North Africa, and it took Umayyad Arab leader Uqba bin Nafi until 682 to reach the Atlantic shores of Morocco. According to legend, Uqba announced he would charge into the ocean, if God would only give him the signal. But the legendary Algerian Berber warrior Queen al-Kahina would have none of Uqba's grandstanding, and with her warriors soon forced Uqba to retreat back to Tunisia.

Although an armed force failed to win the Berbers over to Islam, force of conviction gradually began to succeed. The egalitarian premise of Islam and its emphasis on duty, courage and the greater good were compatible with many Berber beliefs, including clan loyalty broadly defined to include almost anyone descended from the Berber equivalent of Adam and Eve. Many Berbers willingly converted to Islam – and not incidentally, reaped the benefits of Umayyad overland trading routes that brought business their way. So although Uqba was killed by his Berber foes before he was able to establish a solid base in Morocco, by the 8th century his successors were able to pull off this feat largely through diplomatic means.

Key Islamic Sites Open to Non-Muslims

Tin Mal Mosque, High Atlas

Medersa Bou Inania, Fez

Zawiya Nassiriyya, Tamegroute

Hassan II Mosque, Casablanca

Ali ben Youssef Medersa, Marrakesh

Queen al-Kahina had one distinct advantage over the Umayyads: second sight. The downside? She foretold her own death at the hands of her enemy.

HISTORY ISLAM ARRIVES IN MOROCCO

---

49 BC	**25 BC–AD 23**
North African King Juba I supports Pompey's ill-fated power play against Julius Caesar. Rome is outraged – but senators pick up where Pompey left off, and assassinate Caesar.	Rome gets a toehold in Mauretania with farms, cities and art, thanks to Juba II. He expands Volubilis into a metropolis of 20,000 residents, including a sizeable Jewish Berber community.

JOHN ELK/GETTY IMAGES ©

➡ Ruins at Volubilis (p335)

Islam Stays, but Umayyads Must Go

The admiration between the Berbers and the Arab Umayyads was not always mutual, however. While the Umayyads respected Jews and Christians as fellow believers in the word of a singular God, they had no compunction about compelling polytheist Berbers to pay special taxes and serve as infantry (read: cannon fodder). The Umayyads greatly admired Berber women for their beauty, but this wasn't necessarily advantageous; many were conscripted into Umayyad harems.

Even the Berbers who converted to Islam were forced to pay tribute to their Arab overlords. A dissident school of Islamic thought called Kharijism critiqued the abuses of power of the Umayyads as a corruption of the faith, and called for a new moral leadership. In the mid-8th century, insurrections erupted across North Africa. Armed only with slings, a special force of Berbers defeated the elite Umayyad guard. The Umayyads were soon cut off from Spain and Morocco, and local leaders took over an increasingly lucrative trade in silver from the Western Sahara, gold from Ghana and slaves from West Africa.

A Death-Defying Dynasty: The Idrissids

Looking back on early Berber kingdoms, the 14th-century historian Ibn Khuldun noted a pattern that would repeat throughout Moroccan dynastic history. A new leadership would arise determined to do right, make contributions to society as a whole and fill the royal coffers, too. When the pursuit of power and royal comforts began to eclipse loftier aspirations, the powers that be would forfeit their claim to moral authority. A new leadership would arise determined to do right, and the cycle would begin all over again.

So it was with the Idrissids, Morocco's first great dynasty. A descendant of the Prophet Mohammed's daughter Fatima, Idriss I fled Arabia for Morocco in AD 786 after discovering ambitious Caliph Haroun ar-Rashid's plan to murder his entire family. But Idriss didn't exactly keep a low profile. After being proclaimed an imam (religious leader) by the local Berbers, he unified much of northern Morocco in the name of Islam. Just a few days after he'd finally settled into his new capitol at Fez in 792, Haroun ar-Rashid's minions finally tracked down and poisoned Idriss I. Yet death only increased Idriss I's influence; his body was discovered to be miraculously intact five centuries later, and his tomb in the hillside town of Moulay Idriss remains one of the holiest pilgrimage sites in Morocco.

His son Idriss II escaped Haroun's assassins and extended Idrissid control across northern Morocco and well into Europe. In perhaps the first (but certainly not the last) approximation of democracy in Morocco,

Key Moroccan Dynasties

Idrissid –
8th-10th century

Almoravid –
11th-12th century

Almohad –
12th-13th century

Merenid –
13th-15th century

Saadian –
16th-17th century

Alawite –17th
century-present

200–429	533	662–682	711
Vandals and Visigoths take turns forcing one another out of Spain and onto the shores of Morocco, until local Rif warriors convince them to bother the Algerians instead.	Justinian ousts the last Vandals from Morocco, but his grand plans to extend the Holy Roman Empire are soon reduced to a modest presence in Essaouira, Tangier and Salé.	Arabs invade the Maghreb under Umayyad Uqba bin Nafi, introducing Islam to the area. Berber warriors eventually boot out the Umayyads, but decide to keep the Quran.	Northern Morocco and most of Spain come under Umayyad control, and Berbers are strategically settled throughout Andalusia.

BERBER PRIDE & PREJUDICE

Despite a rich tradition of poetry, petroglyphs, music and art dating as far back as 5000 BC, the Amazigh were often misconstrued as uneducated by outsiders, because no standard written system had been consistently applied to their many distinct languages. The Romans tried for 250 years to take over Amazigh territory and institute Roman customs – and when that failed they bad-mouthed their adversaries, calling them 'Berbers', or Barbarians. The name stuck, and so did anti-Amazigh prejudice.

The protectorate established French as the official language of Morocco to make it easier to conduct (and hence control) business transactions and affairs of state. Complex Amazigh artistic symbolism and traditional medicine were dismissed as charming but irrelevant superstition by those not privy to the oral traditions accompanying them, and the educated classes were encouraged to distance themselves from their Berber roots. But Amazigh languages and traditions have persisted in Morocco, and the Berber Pride movement has recently reclaimed 'Berber' as a unifying term.

After independence (1955–56), Arabic was adopted as the official language, though French continues to be widely spoken among the elite, and Darija is the commonly understood Moroccan Arabic dialect. As recently as the 1980s, the use of Berber script was subject to censure in Morocco. But with the backing of King Mohammed VI – who is part Berber himself – the ancient written Tifinagh alphabet that first emerged around the time of Egyptian hieroglyphics was revived in 2003, and a modernised version is now being taught in some schools as a standardised written Berber.

More than 60% of Moroccans now call themselves Amazigh or Berber, and Berber languages are currently spoken by some 8.5 to 10 million Moroccans. Berber Pride is now mainstream in Morocco, with the introduction of the official Moroccan broadcaster Chaîne Amazigh, offering TV and radio broadcasts in three Amazigh languages. Yet Human Rights Watch reported that in 2010, parents who gave their children Amazigh names were told the names were rejected by state bureaucrats as 'not recognizably Moroccan'. After a public outcry, the policy was reversed, so babies too can show Berber Pride in Morocco.

Idriss II's 13 sons shared power after their father's death. Together they expanded Idrissid principates into Spain and built the glorious mosques of Fez: the Kairaouine and the Andalous.

Warriors Unveiled: The Almoravids

With religious leaders and scholars to help regulate trade, northern Morocco began to take shape as an economic entity under the Idrissids. But the south was another story. A dissident prophet emerged near Salé brandishing a Berber version of the Quran, and established an apocryphal Islam called Barghawata that continued to be practised in the region for centuries. The military strongmen who were left in control of

788–829	8th century	1062	1069
Islam takes root in Morocco under Idriss I and Idriss II, who make Fez the epitome of Islamic art, architecture and scholarship and the capital of their Idrissid empire.	Through shared convictions and prudent alliances, Arab caliphates control an area that extends across the Mediterranean and well into Europe, just 320km shy of Paris.	With the savvy Zeinab as his wife and chief counsel, Berber leader Youssuf ben Tachfine founds Marrakesh as a launching pad for Almoravid conquests of North Africa and Europe.	The Almoravids take Fez by force and promptly begin remodelling the place, installing mills and lush gardens and cleaning up the city's act with running water and hammams.

trading outposts in the Atlas Mountains and the Sahara demanded what they called 'alms' – bogus religious nomenclature that didn't fool anyone, and stirred up resentments among the faithful.

From this desert discontent arose the Sanhaja, the pious Saharan Berber tribe that founded the Almoravid dynasty. While the Idrissid princes were distracted by disputes over Spain and Mediterranean Morocco, the Sanhaja swept into the south of Morocco from what is today Senegal and Mauritania. Tough doesn't do justice to the Sanhaja; they lived on camels' meat and milk instead of bread, wore wool in the scorching desert and abstained from wine, music and multiple wives. Their manly habit of wearing dark veils is still practised today by the few remaining Tuareg, the legendary 'Blue Men' of the desert (and the many tourists who imitate them in camel-riding photo-ops). When these intimidating shrouded men rode into Shiite and Barghawata outposts under the command of Yahya ibn Umar and his brother Abu Bakr, they demolished brothels and musical instruments as well as their opponents.

From Marrakesh to Barcelona, the Ultimate Power Couple

After Yahya was killed and Abu Bakr was recalled to the Sahara to settle Sanhaja disputes in 1061, their cousin Youssef ben Tachfine was left to run military operations from a campsite that would become Marrakesh the magnificent. To spare his wife the hardships of life in the Sahara, Abu Bakr divorced brilliant Berber heiress Zeinab en-Nafzawiyyat and arranged her remarriage to his cousin. Though an odd romantic gesture by today's standards, it was an inspired match. It would be Zeinab's third marriage: before marrying Abu Bakr, she was the widow of one of the leading citizens of Aghmat, and had considerable fortune and political experience at her command. Between Ben Tachfine's initiative and Zeinab's financing and strategic counsel, the Almoravids were unstoppable.

The Almoravids took a while to warm up to their new capital of Marrakesh – too many mountains and rival Berbers around, and too few palm trees. To make themselves more at home, the Almoravids built a mud wall around the city, 8m high and 19km long, and set up the ingenious *khettara* underground irrigation system that still supports the *palmeraie* – a vast palm grove outside Marrakesh now dotted with luxury villas. The Jewish and Andalucian communities in Fez thrived under Ben Tachfine, a soft-spoken diplomat and, like his wife, a brilliant military strategist. His Spanish Muslim allies urged him to intercede against Christian and Muslim princes in Spain, complaining bitterly of extortion, attacks and debauchery. At the age of almost 80, Ben Tachfine launched successful campaigns securing Almoravid control of Andalusia right up to the Barcelona city limits.

Berber Languages in Morocco

Tashelhit – Central Morocco

Tamazight – Middle Atlas

Tarifit – Rif

Tuareg (Tamashek) – Sahara

In Morocco's second parliamentary elections in 2007, 34 women were elected, representing 10.4% of all seats – that's just behind the US at 12.5% female representation after 110 elections.

1082

Almoravid control stretches south to Ghana and Timbuktu, east to Algiers, and north from Lisbon to Spain's Ebro River, near Barcelona.

1121–30

Almohad spiritual leader Mohammed ibn Tumart loudly condemns Almoravid indulgence in music and wine, but also champions scientific reasoning and political organisation based on a written constitution.

⇒ A Berber nomad making a traditional mud oven

SARA-JANE CLELAND/GETTY IMAGES ©

Sticks & Stones: The Almohads

Youssef ben Tachfine was a tough act to follow. Ali was his son by a Christian woman, and he shared his father's commitments to prayer and urban planning. But while the reclusive young idealist Ali was diligently working wonders with architecture and irrigation in Marrakesh, a new force beyond the city walls was gathering the strength of an Atlas thunderstorm: the Almohads.

Almohad historians would later fault Ali for two supposedly dangerous acts: leaving the women in charge and allowing Christians near drink. While the former was hardly a shortcoming – after all, his stepmother's counsel had proved instrumental to the Almoravids – there may be some merit in the latter. While Ali was in seclusion praying and fasting, court and military officials were left to carry on, and carry on they did. Apparently, Almoravid Christian troops were all too conveniently stationed near the wine merchants of Marrakesh.

The Hard Knocks of Ibn Tumart

None of this sat well with Mohammed ibn Tumart, the Almohad spiritual leader from the Atlas who'd earned a reputation in Meknès and Salé as a religious vigilante, using his walking stick to shatter wine jars, smash musical instruments and smack men and women with the audacity to walk down the street together. Ibn Tumart finally got himself banished from Marrakesh in the 1120s for knocking Ali's royal sister off her horse with his stick.

But though Ibn Tumart died soon after, there was no keeping out the Almohads. They took over Fez after a nine-month siege in 1145, but reserved their righteous fury for Marrakesh two years later, razing the place to the ground and killing what was left of Ali's court (Ali died as he lived, quietly, in 1144). Their first projects included rebuilding the Koutoubia Mosque – which Almoravid architects, not up on their algebra, had misaligned with Mecca – and adding the soaring, sublime stone minaret that became the template for Andalucian Islamic architecture. The Tin Mal Mosque was constructed in the High Atlas to honour Ibn Tumart in 1156, and it remains a wonder of austere graces and unshakable foundations.

Almohad Demolition & Construction Crews

A bloody power struggle ensued between the sons of Ibn Tumart and the sons of his generals that wouldn't be settled definitively until 1185, when Abu Yusuf Yacoub, the young son of the Muslim governor of Seville and Valencia, rode south into Morocco and drove his foes into the desert. But

An incisive look at religious life on opposite ends of the Muslim world, anthropologist Clifford Geertz's groundbreaking *Islam Observed: Religious Development in Morocco and Indonesia* reveals complex variations within the vast mosaic of Islam.

1147	1199	1276	1324–52
The Almohads finally defeat the Almoravids and destroy Marrakesh after a two-year siege, paving the way for Yacoub el-Mansour and his architects to outdo the Almoravids with an all-new Marrakesh.	A vast swath of prime Mediterranean commercial real estate from Tripoli to Spain is consolidated under Almohad control.	Winds of change blow in from the Atlas with the Zenata Berbers, who oust the Almohads and establish the Merenid dynasty with strategic military manoeuvres and even more strategic marriages.	Tangier-born adventurer Ibn Battuta picks up where Marco Polo left off, travelling from Mali to Sumatra and Mongolia and publishing *Rihla* – an inspired though not entirely reliable travel guide.

he also kept and expanded his power base in Spain, winning so many victories against the princes of Spain that he earned the moniker El-Mansour, 'the victorious'. He modelled Seville's famous La Giralda after Marrakesh's Koutoubia minaret, and reinvented Marrakesh as an Almohad capital and learning centre to rival Fez.

Yacoub el-Mansour's urban-planning prowess also made Fez arguably the most squeaky-clean city of medieval times, with 93 hammams, 47 soap factories and 785 mosques complete with ablutions facilities. Yacoub el-Mansour was also a patron of great thinkers, including Aristotle scholar Ibn Rashid – whose commentary would help spark a Renaissance among Italian philosophers – and Sufi master Sidi Bel-Abbes. However, Yacoub's enlightenment and admiration of architecture was apparently not all-encompassing; several synagogues were demolished under his rule.

Defeated by Bulls & Betrayal

Similar thinking (or lack thereof) prevailed in 12th-century Europe, where a hunt for heretics turned to officially sanctioned torture under papal bulls of the egregiously misnamed Pope Innocent IV. Bishop Bernard of Toledo, Spain, seized Toledo's mosque, and rallied Spain's Castilian Christian kings in a crusade against their Muslim rulers.

The Almohads were in no condition to fight back. When Yacoub's 16-year-old son was named caliph, he wasn't up to the religious responsibilities that came with the title. Instead, he was obsessed with bullfighting, and was soon gored to death.

Yacoub el-Mansour must've done pirouettes in his grave around 1230, when his next son tapped as caliph, Al-Mamun, allied with his Christian persecutors and turned on his fellow Almohads in a desperate attempt to hang onto his father's empire. This short-lived caliph added the ultimate insult to Almohad injury when he climbed the Koutoubia *minbar* (pulpit) and announced that Ibn Tumart wasn't a true Mahdi (leader) of the faithful. That title, he claimed, rightfully belonged to Jesus.

In *The Conquest of Morocco*, Douglas Porch describes a controversial colonial war promoted as a 'civilising mission' and supported by business interests – a chapter of Middle Eastern history since repeated, as Porch observes in the 2005 edition.

By Marriage or Murder: The Merenids

When Zenata Berbers from the Anti Atlas invaded the Almohad capital of Marrakesh in 1269, the Almohad defeat was complete. The Zenata had already ousted the Almohads in Meknès, Salé and Fez and along most of the Atlantic Coast. To win over the devout, they promised moral leadership under their new Merenid dynasty. Making good on the promise, the Merenids undertook construction of a *medersa* (school of religious learning) in every major city they conquered, levying special taxes on Christian and Jewish communities for the purpose. In exchange, they allowed these communities to practise key trades, and hired Christian

1348	1377	1415	1480–92
Bubonic plague strikes Mediterranean North Africa; Merenid alliances and kingdoms crumble. Rule of law is left to survivors and opportunists to enforce, with disastrous consequences.	At Kairaouine University in Fez, Ibn Khaldun examines Middle Eastern history in his groundbreaking *Muqaddimah*, explaining how religious propaganda, taxation and revisionist history make and break states.	In search of gold and the fabled kingdom of Prester John – location of the Fountain of Youth – Portuguese Prince Henry the Navigator begins his conquests of Moroccan seaports.	Ferdinand and Isabella conquer Spain, and persecution of Muslims and Jews escalates.

mercenaries and Jewish policy advisors to help conduct the business of the Merenid state.

But this time the new rulers faced a tough crowd not easily convinced by promises of piety. Fez revolted, and the Castilian Christians held sway in Salé. To shore up their Spanish interests, the Merenids allied with the Castilian princes against the Muslim rulers of Granada. Once again, this proved a losing strategy. By the 14th century, Muslim Spain was lost to the Christians, and the Strait of Gibraltar was forfeited. The Merenids also didn't expect the Spanish Inquisition, when over one million Muslims and Jews would be terrorised and forcibly expelled from Spain.

Without military might or religious right to back their imperial claims, the Merenids chose another time-tested method: marriage. In the 14th century, Merenid leaders cleverly co-opted their foes by marrying princesses from Granada and Tunis, and claimed Algiers, Tripoli and the strategic Mediterranean port of Ceuta.

Death by Plague & Office Politics

But the bonds of royal marriage were not rat-proof, and the Merenid empire was devastated by plague. Abu Inan, son of the Merenid leader Abu Hassan, glimpsed opportunity in the Black Death, and proclaimed himself the new ruler despite one minor glitch: his father was still alive. Abu Hassan hurried back from Tripoli to wrest control from his treacherous son in Fez, but to no avail. Abu Inan buried his father in the royal Merenid necropolis outside Rabat in 1351, but he too was laid to rest nearby after he was strangled by one of his own advisors in 1358.

The Merenids had an unfortunate knack for hiring homicidal bureaucrats. To cover his tracks, Abu Inan's killer went on a royal killing spree, until Merenid Abu Salim Ibrahim returned from Spain and terminated this rampaging employee. Abu Salim's advisor sucked up to his boss by offering his sister in marriage, only to lop off Abu Salim's head after the wedding. He replaced Abu Salim with a Merenid patsy before thinking better of it and strangling the new sultan, too. This slippery advisor was assassinated by another Merenid, who was deposed a scant few years later by yet another Merenid – and so it continued for 40 years, with new Merenid rulers and advisors offing the incumbents every few years. While the Merenids were preoccupied with murderous office politics in Meknès and Fez, the Portuguese seized control of coastal Morocco.

Victory Is Sweet: The Saadians

Much of Portugal (including Lisbon) had been under Muslim rule during the 12th century, and now the Portuguese were ready for payback – literally. The tiny, rugged kingdom needed steady supplies of food for its people and gold to fortify its growing empire, but Morocco stood in

A Travellers History of North Africa by Barnaby Rogerson is a handy and accessible guide that puts Morocco amid the wider currents of regional history.

1497–1505	1498	1525	1578
Moroccan ports are occupied by English, Portuguese and Spanish forces and sundry pirates, from Mediterranean Melilla to Agadir on the Atlantic Coast.	Church Inquisitors present European Muslims and Jews with a choice: a) conversion and persecution; or b) torture and death. Many choose c) none of the above, and escape to Morocco.	Like a blast of scorching desert wind, the Beni Saad Berbers blow back European and Ottoman encroachment in Morocco, and establish a new Saadian dynasty in Marrakesh.	The Saadians fight both alongside and against Portugal at the Battle of Three Kings, ending with 8000 dead, a scant 100 survivors and the decimation of Portugal's ruling class.

the way. No nation could wrest overland Saharan trade routes from the savvy Berber warriors who'd controlled key oases and mountain passes for centuries. Instead, the Portuguese went with tactics where they had clear technical advantages: naval warfare and advanced firearms. By systematically capturing Moroccan ports along the Mediterranean and Atlantic coasts, Portuguese gunships bypassed Berber middlemen inland, and headed directly to West Africa for gold and slaves.

Sugar Caravans

Once trade in the Sahara began to dry up, something had to be done. Entire inland communities were decimated, and formerly flush Marrakesh was wracked with famine. The Beni Saad Berbers – now known to history as the Saadians – from the Drâa Valley took up the fight against the Portuguese. With successive wins against European, Berber and Ottoman rivals, the Saadians were able to reinstate inland trade. Soon the Saadians were in control of such sought-after commodities as gold, slaves, ivory, ostrich feathers and the must-have luxury for trendy European royals: sugar.

The Saadians satisfied European sugar cravings at prices that make today's oil and cocaine cartels look like rank amateurs. With threats of full-scale invasion, the Saadians had no problem scaring off customers and suppliers. The most dangerous sugar-dealer of all was Saadian Sultan Ahmed al-Mansour ed-Dahbi, who earned his names Al-Mansour (the Victorious) for defeating foes from Portugal to the Sudan, and Ed-Dahbi (the Golden) for his success in bilking them. This Marrakshi Midas used the proceeds to line his Badi Palace in Marrakesh from floor to ceiling with gold and gems. But after the sultan died, his short-lived successor stripped the palace down to its mudbrick foundations, as it remains today. The Saadian legacy is most visible in the Saadian Tombs, decked out for a decadent afterlife with painted Carrara marble and gold leaf. The Saadians died as they lived: dazzling beyond belief and a touch too rich for most tastes.

The Rise of Mellahs

Under the Saadians, Jewish communities also took up crucial roles as dealers of the hottest Moroccan commodities of the time: salt and sugar. While European Jewish communities faced the Inquisition, forced conversions and summary executions, the comparatively tolerant Saadian dynasty provided Jewish communities with some security, setting aside a section of Marrakesh next to the royal kasbah as a Jewish quarter, or *mellah* – a name derived from the Arabic word for salt. This protection was repaid many times over in taxes levied on Jewish and Christian businesses, and the royally flush Saadians clearly got the sweet end of the

Global Voices Morocco provides a roundup of Moroccan news and opinion online, including English translations of bloggers' responses to Moroccan news at www.global voicesonline. org/-/world/ middle-east-north-africa/ morocco.

Historic Moroccan Mellahs

Tamnougalt

Demnate

Fez

Zagora/Amezrou

Essaouira

Marrakesh

1591	1610–14	1659–66	1662
With 4000 European mercenaries, Ahmed al-Mansour ed-Dahbi crosses the Sahara and defeats a 40,000-strong army for control of the fabled desert caravan destination of Timbuktu.	Oxford graduate and erstwhile lawyer Henry Mainwaring founds the Masmouda Pirates Republic near Rabat, pillaging Canadian cod, French salt-fish and Portuguese wine. He is later elected to Britain's parliament.	The Alawites end years of civil war, and even strike an uneasy peace with the Barbary pirates controlling Rabati ports.	Portugal gives Tangier to the British as a wedding present for Charles II. After a lengthy siege, it is eventually returned to Moroccan control in 1684.

deal. Yet several Jewish Moroccans rose to prominence as royal advisors, and in the Saadian Tombs of Marrakesh, trusted Jewish confidantes are buried closer to kings than royal wives.

By day, Jewish merchants traded alongside Christian and Muslim merchants, and were entrusted with precious salt, sugar and gold brought across the Sahara; by night they were under official guard in their quarters. Once the *mellahs* of Fez and Marrakesh became overcrowded with European arrivals, other notable *mellahs* were founded in Essaouira, Safi, Rabat and Meknès, and the traditions of skilled handicrafts that flourished there continue to this day. The influence of the *mellahs* spread throughout Morocco, especially in tangy dishes with the signature salted, pickled ingredients of Moroccan Jewish cuisine.

Moulay Ismail was pen pals with England's James II and Louis XIV of France, and tried to convert the Sun King to Islam by mail.

Pirates & Politics: The Early Alawites

The Saadian dynasty dissolved in the 17th century like a sugar cube in Moroccan mint tea, and civil war prevailed until the Alawites came along. With illustrious ancestors from the Prophet Mohammed's family and descendents extending to the current King Mohammed VI, the Alawites were quite a change from the free-wheeling Saadians and their anarchic legacy. But many Moroccans might have preferred anarchy to the second Alawite ruler, the dreaded Moulay Ismail (1672–1727).

A despot whose idea of a good time included public disembowelments and amateur dentistry on courtiers who peeved him, Moulay Ismail was also a scholar, dad to hundreds of children and Mr Popularity among his royal European peers. European nobles gushed about lavish dinner parties at Moulay Ismail's palace in Meknès, built by conscripted Christian labourers. Rumour has it that when these decidedly non-union construction workers finished the job, some were walled in alive. The European royal party tab wasn't cheap, either, but Moulay Ismail wasn't worried: piracy would cover it.

Whatever happened to Barbary pirates? How did Islam mesh with Berber beliefs? And why was Morocco the exception to Ottoman rule? Jamil Abun-Nasr unravels these and other Moroccan mysteries in *A History of the Maghreb in the Islamic Period*.

In Her Majesty's Not-So-Secret Service: Barbary Pirates

Queen Elizabeth I kicked off the Atlantic pirate trade, allying against her arch-nemesis King Phillip II of Spain with the Saadians and specially licensed pirates known as privateers. The most notoriously effective hires were the Barbary pirates, Moriscos (Spanish Muslims) who'd been forcibly converted and persecuted in Spain and hence had an added motivation to shake down Spaniards. James I outlawed English privateering in 1603, but didn't seem to mind when his buddy Moulay Ismail aided and abetted the many British and Barbary pirates who harboured in the royal ports at Rabat and Salé – for a price.

1672	18th century	1757–90
The Alawite Moulay Ismail takes the throne. One of the greatest Moroccan sultans, he rules for 55 years and the Alawite succession lasts to the present day.	The Alawites rebuild the ancient desert trading outpost of Sijilmassa, only to lose control of it to Aït Atta Berber warriors, who raze the town. Only two not-so-triumphal arches remain.	Sidi Mohammed III makes a strategic move to the coast, to rebuild Essaouira and regain control over Atlantic ports. Inland imperial cities of Fez and Meknès slip into decline.

→ Saadian Tombs (p55), Marrakesh

HUW JONES/GETTY IMAGES ©

But pirate loyalties being notoriously fickle, Barbary pirates attacked Ireland, Wales, Iceland and even Newfoundland in the 17th century. Barbary pirates also took prisoners, who were usually held for ransom and freed after a period of servitude – including one-time English allies. Captives were generally better off with Barbary pirates than French profiteers, who typically forced prisoners to ply the oars of slave galleys until death. Nevertheless, after pressure from England secured their release in 1684, a number of English captives were quite put out about the whole experience, and burned the port of Tangier behind them. But other English saw upsides to piracy and kidnapping: when the Portuguese were forced out of Essaouira in the 17th century, a freed British prisoner who'd converted to Islam joined a French profiteer to rebuild the city for the sultan, using free labour provided by European captives.

Impress Moroccans with your knowledge of the latest developments in Moroccan society, Amazigh culture and North African politics, all covered in English at www.magharebia.com.

Troubled Waters for Alawites

After Moulay Ismail's death, his elite force of 50,000 to 70,000 Abid, or 'Black Guard', ran amok, and not one of his many children was able to succeed him. The Alawite dynasty would struggle on into the 20th century, but the country often lapsed into lawlessness when rulers overstepped their bounds. Piracy and politics became key ways to get ahead in the 18th and 19th centuries – and the two were by no means mutually exclusive. By controlling key Moroccan seaports and playing European powers against one another, officials and outlaws alike found they could demand a cut of whatever goods were shipped through the Strait of Gibraltar and along the Atlantic Coast.

In the late 18th century, when Sidi Mohammed ben Abdullah ended the officially condoned piracy of his predecessors and nixed shady side deals with foreign powers, the financial results were disastrous. With added troubles of plague and drought, Morocco's straits were truly dire.

With Friends Like These: European Encroachment

For all their successful European politicking, the early Alawites had apparently forgotten a cardinal rule of Moroccan diplomacy: never neglect Berber alliances. Sultan Moulay Hassan tried to rally support among the Berbers of the High Atlas in the late 19th century, but by then it was too late. France began to take an active interest in Morocco around 1830, and allied with Berbers across North Africa to fend off the Ottomans. After centuries of practise fighting Moroccans, Spain took control of areas of northern Morocco in 1860 – and generated lasting resentment for desecrating graveyards, mosques and other sacred sites in Melilla and Tetouan. While wily Queen Victoria entertained Moroccan dignitaries and

1767–1836	1777	1830	1860
Cash-strapped Morocco makes extraordinary concessions to trading partners, granting Denmark trade monopolies in Agadir and Safi, and France and the US license to trade in Morocco for a nominal fee.	A century after the English leave Tangier a royal wreck, Morocco gets revenge and becomes the first country to recognise the breakaway British colony calling itself the United States of America.	France seizes the Algerian coast, increasing pressure on the Moroccan sultan to cede power in exchange for mafia-style protection along Morocco's coasts from the advancing Ottomans.	If at first you don't succeed, try for seven centuries: Spain takes control of a swath of northern Morocco reaching into the Rif.

pressed for Moroccan legal reforms, her emissaries were busy brokering deals with France and Spain.

Footloose & Duty-Free in Tangier

Order became increasingly difficult to maintain in Moroccan cities and in Berber mountain strongholds, and Moulay Hassan employed powerful Berber leaders to regain control – but accurately predicting Moulay Hassan's demise, some Berbers cut deals of their own with the Europeans. By the time Moulay Hassan's teenage successor Sultan Moulay Abdelaziz pushed through historic antidiscrimination laws to impress Morocco's erstwhile allies, the Europeans had reached an understanding: while reforms were nice and all, what they really wanted were cheap goods. By 1880, Europeans and Americans had set up their own duty-free shop in

TWO THOUSAND YEARS OF MOROCCAN JEWISH HISTORY

By the 1st century AD, Jewish Berber communities that were already well established in Morocco included farmers, metalworkers, dyers, glassblowers and bookbinders. The Merenids established the first official *mellah* (Jewish quarter) in Fez, where Jewish entrepreneurs excluded from trades and guilds in medieval Europe were able to conduct business. Jewish Moroccans were taxed when business boomed for the ruling dynasty and sometimes blamed when it didn't, yet they managed to flourish under the Merenids and Saadians, while European Jews faced the Inquisition and persecution.

Under Alawite rule in the 17th to 19th centuries, the official policy toward Jewish Moroccans was one of give and take: on the one hand they had opportunities as tradespeople, business leaders and ambassadors to England, Holland and Denmark in the 19th century; on the other hand they were subjected to taxes, surveillance and periodic scapegoating. But in good times and bad, Jewish Moroccans remained a continuous presence.

By 1948, some 300,000 Jewish Moroccans lived in Morocco. Many left after the founding of the states of Morocco and Israel, and today only an estimated 3000 to 8000 remain, mostly in Casablanca. A Jewish community centre in Casablanca was a bombing target in 2003, and though no one was harmed at the community centre, trade-centre blasts killed 33 and wounded 100. Yet the Casablanca community remains intact, and Casablanca is home to the recently expanded Moroccan Jewish Museum.

Under the current king, Jewish schools now receive state funding, and a few Jewish expatriates have responded to a royal invitation to return, contributing to the revival of Essaouira's *mellah*. Yet the everyday champions of Jewish heritage in Morocco remain ordinary Moroccans, the one million people worldwide of Moroccan Jewish heritage, and culturally engaged travellers, who together ensure Moroccan Jewish customs, festivals and landmarks get the attention they deserve.

1880	1906	1912	1921–26
France, Britain, Spain and the US meet in Madrid and agree that Morocco can retain nominal control over its territory – after granting themselves tax-free business licenses and duty-free shopping.	The controversial Act of Algeciras divvies up North Africa among European powers like a *bastilla* pigeon pie, but Germany isn't invited – a slight that exacerbated tensions among European powers.	The Treaty of Fez hands Morocco to the French protectorate, which mostly protects French business interests at Moroccan taxpayer expense with the ruthless assistance of Berber warlord Pasha el-Glaoui.	Under the command of Abd al-Krim, Berber leaders rebel against Spanish rule of the Rif, and Spain loses its foothold in the mountains.

Tangier, declaring it an 'international zone' where they were above the law and beyond tax collectors' reaches.

But the lure of prime North African real estate proved irresistible. By 1906, Britain had snapped up strategic waterfront property in Egypt and the Suez; France took the prize for sheer acreage from Algeria to West Africa; Italy landed Libya; Spain drew the short stick with the unruly Rif and a whole lot of desert. Germany was incensed at being left out of this arrangement and announced support for Morocco's independence, further inflaming tensions between Germany and other European powers in the years leading up to WWI.

France Opens a Branch Office: The Protectorate

Whatever illusions of control Morocco's sultanate might have been clutching slipped away at the 1906 Conference of Algeciras, when control of Morocco's banks, customs and police force was handed over to France for 'protection'. The 1912 Treaty of Fez establishing Morocco as a French protectorate made colonisation official, and the French hand-picked a new sultan with all the backbone of a sock puppet. More than 100,000 French administrators, outcasts and opportunists arrived in cities across Morocco to take up residence in French villes nouvelles (new towns).

Résident-Général Louis Lyautey saw to it that these new French suburbs were kitted out with all the mod cons: electricity, trains, roads and running water. Villes nouvelles were designed to be worlds apart from adjacent Moroccan medinas (historic city centres), with French schools, churches, villas and grand boulevards named after French generals. No expense or effort was spared to make the new arrivals feel right at home – which made their presence all the more galling for Moroccans footing the bill through taxes, shouldering most of the labour and still living in crowded, poorly serviced medinas. Lyautey had already set up French colonial enterprises in Vietnam, Madagascar and Algeria, so he arrived in Morocco with the confidence of a CEO and a clear plan of action: break up the Berbers, ally with the Spanish when needed and keep business running by all available means.

Nationalist Resistance

Once French-backed Sultan Yusuf died and his French-educated 18-year-old son Mohammed V became sultan, Lyautey expected that French business in Morocco would carry on as usual. He hadn't counted on a fiery young nationalist as sultan, or the staunch independence of ordinary Moroccans. Mining strikes and union organising interfered with France's

According to the 2010 Human Development Index, 28.5% of Moroccan households are poor, and another 11.4% are at risk. Moroccan officials dispute the validity of these statistics, placing the poverty figure nearer 9%.

1942	1943–45	1944–53	1955–56
In defiance of Vichy France, Casablanca hosts American forces staging the Allied North African campaign. This move yields US support for Moroccan independence and the classic Humphrey Bogart film *Casablanca*.	When the Allies struggle in Italy, US General Patton calls in the Goums, Morocco's elite force of mountain warriors. With daggers and night-time attacks, they advance the Allies in Tuscany.	Moroccan nationalists demand independence from France with increasing impatience. Sultan Mohammed V is inclined to agree, and is exiled to Madagascar by the protectorate for the crime of independent thought.	Morocco successfully negotiates its independence from France, Spain cedes control over most of its colonial claims within Morocco, and exiled nationalist Mohammed V returns as king of independent Morocco.

most profitable colonial businesses, and military attention was diverted to force Moroccans back into the mines. Berbers had never accepted foreign dominion without a fight, and they were not about to make an exception for the French. By 1921 the Rif was up in arms against the Spanish and French under the leadership of Ibn Abd al-Krim al-Khattabi. It took five years, 300,000 Spanish and French forces and two budding Fascists (Francisco Franco and Marshal Pétain) to capture Ibn Abd al-Krim and force him into exile.

The French won a powerful ally when they named Berber warlord Thami el-Glaoui pasha of Marrakesh, but they also made a lot of enemies. The title gave the pasha implicit license to do as he pleased, which included mafia-style executions and extortion schemes, kidnapping women and children who struck his fancy, and friendly games of golf at his Royal Golf Club with Ike Eisenhower and Winston Churchill. The pasha forbade talk of independence under penalty of death, and conspired to exile Mohammed V from Morocco in 1953 – but Pasha Glaoui would end his days powerless, wracked with illness and grovelling on his knees for King Mohammed V's forgiveness.

Although the French protectorate of Morocco was nominally an ally of Vichy France and Germany in WWII, independent-minded Casablanca provided crucial ground support for the Allied North African campaign. When Morocco's Istiqlal (Independence) party demanded freedom from French rule in 1944, the US and Britain were finally inclined to agree. Under increasing pressure from Moroccans and the Allies, France allowed Mohammed V to return from exile in 1955. Morocco successfully negotiated its independence from France and Spain between 1956 and 1958.

A Rough Start: After Independence

When Mohammed V died suddenly of heart failure in 1961, King Hassan II became the leader of the new nation. Faced with a shaky power base, an unstable economy and elections that revealed divides even among nationalists, Hassan II consolidated power by cracking down on dissent and suspending parliament for a decade. With heavy borrowing to finance dam-building, urban development and an ever-expanding bureaucracy, Morocco was deep in debt by the 1970s. Attempts to assassinate the king underscored the need to do something, quickly, to turn things around – and then in 1973, the phosphate industry in the Spanish-controlled Western Sahara started to boom. Morocco staked its claim to the area and its lucrative phosphate reserves with the Green March, settling the area with Moroccans while greatly unsettling indigenous Saharawi people agitating for self-determination.

The most comprehensive Berber history in English is *The Berbers* by Michael Brett and Elizabeth Fentress. The authors leave no stone carving unturned, providing archaeological evidence to back up their historical insights.

Read firsthand accounts of Morocco's independence movement from Moroccan women who rebelled against colonial control, rallied and fought alongside men in Alison Baker's *Voice of Resistance: Oral Histories of Moroccan Women*.

1961	1975	1981	1984
When Mohammed V dies suddenly, Hassan II becomes king. He transforms Morocco into a constitutional monarchy in 1962, but the 'Years of Lead' deal heavy punishments for dissent.	The UN concludes that the Western Sahara is independent, but Hassan II concludes otherwise, ordering the Green March to enforce Morocco's claims to the region and its phosphate reserves.	After the Casablanca Uprising, the military rounds up dissenters and unionists nationwide. But demands for political reforms increase, and many political prisoners are later exonerated.	Morocco leaves the Organisation of African States (now the African Union) in protest against the admission of Saharawi representatives. It remains the only African state outside the body to this day.

Years of Lead

Along with the growing gap between the rich and the poor and a mounting tax bill to cover Morocco's military spending in the Western Sahara, King Hassan II's suppression of dissent fuelled further resentment among his subjects. By the 1980s, the critics of the king included journalists, trade unionists, women's-rights activists, Marxists, Islamists, Berbers advocating recognition of their culture and language, and the working poor – in other words, a broad cross-section of Moroccan society.

The last straw for many came in 1981, when official Moroccan newspapers casually announced that the government had conceded to the International Monetary Fund to hike prices for staple foods. For the many

MARCHING TO THE KING'S TUNE

Talk of 'Greater Morocco' began in the 1950s, but in the 1970s it became the official explanation for Morocco's annexation of phosphate-rich Spanish Sahara. There was a snag: the Popular Front for the Liberation of Sagui al Hamra & Río di Oro (Polisario – Saharawi pro-independence militia) declared the region independent. Putting his French legal training to work, Hassan II took up the matter with the International Court of Justice (ICJ) in The Hague in 1975, expecting the court would provide a resounding third-party endorsement for Morocco's claims. Instead the ICJ considered a counter-claim for independence from the Polisario, and dispatched a fact-finding mission to Spanish Sahara.

The ICJ concluded that ties to Morocco weren't strong enough to support Moroccan sovereignty over the region, and the Western Sahara was entitled to self-determination. In a highly creative interpretation of this court judgment, Hassan II declared that Morocco had won its case and ordered a celebratory 'peace march' of more than 350,000 Moroccans from Marrakesh into the Western Sahara in 1975 – some never to return. This unarmed 'Green March' was soon fortified by military personnel and land mines, and was vehemently resisted by armed Polisario fighters.

The Green March is no longer the symbol of national pride it once was; Green March murals that once defined desert-cafe decor have been painted over with apolitical dunescapes. Meanwhile, phosphate profits have dwindled, due to falling prices, mining sabotage and spiralling costs for Moroccan military operations, exceeding US$300 million annually by 1981.

A truce was finally established in 1991 between Morocco and the Polisario, but Morocco's 2010 raid of the Gadaym Izik protest camp of 15,000 displaced Saharawis resulted in at least a dozen deaths and hundreds of injuries, according to the BBC, plus more than 100 detentions of activists, as reported by Human Rights Watch. The actions haven't altered Polisario's demand for a referendum, while Rabat maintains that it will grant the Western Sahara autonomous status, but not a referendum. So the status of the Western Sahara remains unresolved – a rallying cry for many Saharawis, and an awkward conversation nonstarter for many deeply ambivalent Moroccan taxpayers.

1994	1999	2002–07	2004–05
Years of poor relations between Morocco and Algeria, primarily over the Western Sahara issue, lead to the permanent closure of the border between the two countries.	Soon after initiating a commission to investigate abuses of power under his own rule, Hassan II dies. All hail Mohammed VI, and hope for a constitutional monarchy.	Historic reforms initiated under King Mohammed VI include regular parliamentary and municipal elections across Morocco, plus the Mudawanna legal code offering unprecedented protection for women.	Equity and Reconciliation Commission televises testimonies of the victims of Moroccan human-rights abuses during the 'Years of Lead'; it becomes the most watched in Moroccan TV history.

Moroccans subsisting on the minimum wage, these increases meant that two-thirds of their income would be spent on a meagre diet of sardines, bread and tea. When trade unions organised protests against the measure, government reprisals were swift and brutal. Tanks rolled down the streets of Casablanca and hundreds were killed, at least 1000 wounded, and an estimated 5000 protesters arrested in a nationwide *laraf*, or roundup.

Far from dissuading dissent, the Casablanca Uprising galvanised support for government reform. Sustained pressure from human-rights activists throughout the 1980s achieved unprecedented results in1991, when Hassan II founded the Equity and Reconciliation Commission to investigate human-rights abuses that occurred during his own reign – a first for a king. In his very first public statement as king upon his father's death in 1999, Mohammed VI vowed to right the wrongs of the era known to Moroccans as the Years of Lead. The commission has since helped cement human-rights advances, awarding reparations to 9280 victims of the Years of Lead by 2006.

New Regime, New Hopes

As Moroccans will surely tell you, there's still room for improvement in today's Morocco. The parliament elected in 2002 set aside 30 seats for women members of parliament, and implemented some promising reforms: Morocco's first-ever municipal elections, employment non- discrimination laws, the introduction of Berber languages in state schools, and the Mudawanna, a legal code protecting women's rights to divorce and custody. But tactics from the Years of Lead were revived after the 2003 Casablanca trade-centre bombings and a 2010 military raid of a Western Sahara protest camp, when suspects were rounded up – in 2010 Human Rights Watch reported that many of them had been subjected to abuse and detention without counsel. Civil society is outpacing state reforms, as Moroccans take the initiative to address poverty and illiteracy through enterprising village associations and non-governmental organisations.

Talk Morocco offers frank, irreverent commentary about Moroccan identity, democracy, red tape, gender relations and more at www. talkmorocco.net.

2004	2006	2011	2013
Morocco signs free-trade agreements with the EU and the US, and gains status as a non-NATO ally.	Morocco proposes 'special autonomy' for the Western Sahara, and holds the first direct talks with Polisario in seven years – which end in a stalemate.	Pro-democracy revolutions in Tunisia and Egypt inspire Morocco's 20 February Movement; in response the king announces limited constitutional reform, passed by national referendum.	Morocco continues to be governed by the king and a coalition led by Prime Minister Abdelilah Benkirane of the moderate Islamist Justice and Development Party (PJD).

A Day in the Life of Morocco

Forget the glossy travel brochures about Marrakesh, movies filmed in the Moroccan Sahara, urban legends about decadent Tangier. As anyone who's been there knows, the best way to get to know Morocco is through Moroccans. So to introduce you to Morocco, meet Driss, Fatima, Rashid and Amina, four characters who are composites of people you might encounter during a day in Morocco. The way each of these characters spends the day illustrates the tremendous variation and some major recurring themes in Moroccan daily life.

Morning: Meet Driss

Moroccan girls account for almost two-thirds of the half-million Moroccan kids under 15 who work instead of getting an education.

Six days a week, Driss wakes at 6am to ride his scooter from his family's apartment in a Marrakesh suburb to the riad (courtyard house, converted into a guesthouse) where he works. He knows enough English to explain the riad's breakfast menu to guests and speaks fluent Moroccan Arabic, French and classical Arabic (mostly from watching the news on Al-Jazeera) – plus his native Berber language, Tashelhit. Driss takes computer courses on his weekly morning off. His father approves: he owns a small *hanout* (corner grocery) and doesn't read or write that well himself, but insisted that Driss and his four siblings attend school.

Driss knows his parents will start pressuring him to get married now that he's pushing 30, but he's in no rush and not especially interested in the village girls they have in mind. He'd rather have a girlfriend in the city first, and take things from there.

Noon: Meet Fatima

Nineteenth-century Swiss adventurer Isabelle Eberhardt dressed as a Berber man, became a Sufi, smoked kif, operated as a triple agent, married an Algerian dissident and wrote her memoir *The Oblivion Seekers* – all before the age of 30.

It's been a long, hot morning cracking argan nuts at a fair-trade women's cooperative near Agadir, and Fatima is ready for her lunch break. She's not really hungry – now that she has a steady hourly income through the cooperative, she doesn't go hungry anymore – but she could use a breather, and likes to chat. She speaks Tashelhit at home, gets by in Moroccan Arabic, and can say 'hello' and 'welcome' in French and English to foreigners who sometimes visit the argan cooperative, but she doesn't read or write.

Her five grandchildren do, though, and she's very proud of that fact. Fatima lives frugally, saving most of her income to cover their school fees. All her four children are married, and she always has stories and treats for her grandchildren when they visit. When she goes into town to visit her daughter, she's truly shocked by the prices and she's surprised by how informal young people are towards their elders, though not offended – she thinks it's good for young people to think for themselves.

As Fatima stands, she feels a pang of arthritis. She worries about the family that has largely depended on her since her husband passed away a few years ago. She thanks God she can work, and is determined that in two years she'll make the pilgrimage to Mecca, *inshallah* (God willing).

Afternoon: Meet Rashid

Looking for lizards, Rashid almost bumps into a trekker along the 4km mountain path from school. Last year's drought hit their Middle Atlas village hard. His family had to sell their donkey, and make tough choices about who they could spare this harvest season. Eleven-year-old Rashid is a better student and worse goatherd than his sisters, so he gets to go to school – for now, anyway.

He likes to surprise his sisters by bringing something home from school: one time, a foreign trekker for tea. His family served their best bread and butter, and though no one understood a word the guy was saying, he wasn't bad at *koura* (football). The postcard the trekker sent through the village association is on the family-room shelf, and Rashid is sure that if he can go to the regional middle school, one day he'll write back in perfect English.

Evening: Meet Amina

It's 6.30pm, and though Amina just got back from her French literature class at university, she's ready to go out again. Not that there's anything special on the agenda: a stroll, maybe the library or an internet cafe so she can chat with friends.

She'll have Facebook responses from her cousins in France; her uncle there is funding her education. Amina studies hard, and hopes to work in the Moroccan government like her dad – maybe even the foreign service, though she's never been outside Morocco, and rarely gets a chance to leave their suburb of Rabat. But she's hooked on world news, keeping up in French, Arabic and English through the internet and satellite TV.

Tonight she'll make plans for the weekend, maybe going out to a restaurant with friends. Amina doesn't drink alcohol personally, but some people she knows do, and she doesn't judge them for it. As far as dating goes, she's not ready to settle down yet – there's too much else to do first.

Social Norms

Family Values

As different as Driss, Fatima, Rashid and Amina may seem, they all show a profound attachment to family. While they each have ambitions and

More than 10% of the winners in Morocco's second parliamentary elections in 2007 were women, and women have been elected to municipal offices across the country: including lawyer Fatima Zahra Mansouri, elected mayor of Marrakesh in 2009 at age 33.

THE FOREIGNERS NEXT DOOR

With an attractive climate and exchange rate, Morocco has 100,000 foreign residents – and counting. Many Moroccan emigrants from Europe and the US are returning to Morocco to live, retire or start businesses, creating a new upper-middle economic class. The carefree spending of returnees is a source of revenue and a certain amount of resentment for Moroccans, who grumble openly about returnees driving up costs and importing a culture of conspicuous consumption that's unattainable and shallow.

An international vogue for riads has seen many Europeans buying and restoring historic structures – and sometimes pricing Moroccans out of the housing market and leaving medina neighbourhoods strangely empty and lifeless off-season. It's a double-edged sword: maintenance and restoration of centuries-old medina houses is often beyond the reach of the families who live in them, and who grab with both hands the chance to upgrade to homes with modern amenities in the villes nouvelles (new towns). At the same time, others grumble that the European influx brings to mind colonial-era enclaves.

Travellers can make the exchange more equitable by venturing beyond riad walls to explore Moroccan culture, meet Moroccans on their own turf and ensure Moroccans benefit from tourism.

DRESSING TO IMPRESS IN MOROCCO

A common question is 'how best to dress as a visitor in Morocco?'

Women aren't expected to cover their head in Morocco. Some Moroccan women do and some don't wear the hijab (headscarf). Some wear it for religious, cultural, practical or personal reasons, or alternate, wearing a head covering in the streets but taking it off at home and work. A full face-covering veil is unusual in cities, and even rarer among rural women working in the fields.

That said, your choice of attire may be perceived as a sign of respect for yourself and Moroccans alike. For both men and women, this means not wearing shorts, sleeveless tops or clingy clothing. If you do, some people will be embarrassed for you and the family that raised you, and avoid eye contact. So if you don't want to miss out on some excellent company – especially among older Moroccans – dress modestly.

ideas of their own, their aspirations are tied in some way to family – a much-admired trait in Morocco.

Even major status symbols (like Driss' motor scooter and the satellite TV at Amina's house) are valued less as prized possessions than as commodities benefiting the family as a whole. This is beginning to change, as the emerging middle class Driss represents moves out of large family homes and into smaller apartments in the suburbs, where common property is not such a given. But family connections remain paramount in Morocco, and remittances from Moroccans living abroad to family back home represent as much as 20% of GDP.

Since family is a focal point for Moroccans, expect related questions to come up in the course of conversation: where is your family? Are you married, and do you have children? How are they doing? This might seem a little nosy, and a roundabout way of finding out who you are and what interests you. But to Moroccans, questions about where you work or what you do in your spare time are odd ice-breakers, since what you do for a living or a hobby says less about you than what you do for your family.

For a millennia-old civilisation, Morocco looks young. Half the population is under 25, almost a third is under 15, and less than 5% is over 65.

Education

Next to family, education is the most important indicator of social status in Morocco. Driss and Amina read and write, like 56% of Morocco's adult population. But even with her college degree, Amina may find her employment options limited: 40% of Moroccan humanities graduates were unemployed in 2008.

Rashid's ability to read makes him an exception in rural Morocco – in rural areas, less than 50% of first-graders complete primary school. This is even lower for girls, and 72% of rural women cannot read or write. Schooling to age 14 is now officially mandated, and local initiatives have dramatically improved opportunities for education in the Moroccan countryside. But for vulnerable rural families like Rashid's, just getting the children fed can be difficult, let alone getting them to school. Around a quarter of Moroccans are judged to live in near or absolute poverty, and suffer from food insecurity (living in fear of hunger).

Best-selling Moroccan author and academic Fatima Mernissi exposes telling differences and uncanny similarities in the ideals of women in Europe and the Middle East in Scheherazade Goes West: Different Cultures, Different Harems.

Shifting Gender Roles

A decade or two ago, you might not have met Fatima or Amina. Most of the people you'd see out and about, going to school, socialising and conducting business in Morocco would have been men. Women were occupied with less high-profile work, such as animal husbandry, farming, childcare, and fetching water and firewood.

As of 2004, Morocco's Mudawanna legal code guarantees women crucial rights with regard to custody, divorce, property ownership and child support, among other protections. Positive social pressure has greatly reduced the once-common practice of hiring girls under 14 years of age as domestic workers, and initiatives to eliminate female illiteracy are giving girls a better start in life. Women now represent nearly a third of Morocco's formal workforce, forming their own industrial unions, agricultural cooperatives and artisans' collectives.

The modern Moroccan woman's outlook extends far beyond her front door, and women visitors will meet Moroccan women eager to chat, compare life experiences and share perspectives on world events. Male-female interactions are still somewhat stilted by social convention – though you'll surely notice couples meeting in parks, at cafes and via webcam. Young Moroccan women are on the move, commuting to work on motor scooters, taking over sidewalks on arm-in-arm evening strolls, and running for key government positions.

Social Behaviour

As you will probably notice in your travels through Morocco, behaviour that is considered unacceptable outdoors, in full public view – such as drinking alcohol, or making kissy faces at someone of the opposite sex – is often tolerated in the relative privacy of a restaurant terrace, riad or internet cafe. In this context, Amina's views on drinking and internet dating are not so radical, and Driss may stand a chance with his cybercafe cutie. While there are still laws in Morocco restricting the consumption of alcohol in view of a mosque, sex outside marriage and homosexuality, enforcement of these laws is rare. With proper discretion, there is plenty of latitude when it comes to socially acceptable behaviour.

Religion

Morocco is 99% Muslim. Christian and Jewish communities have existed here for centuries, but in recent years their numbers have dwindled.

The Five Pillars of Islam

Soaring minarets, shimmering mosaics, intricate calligraphy, the muezzin's call to prayer: much of what thrills visitors in Morocco today is inspired by a deep faith in Islam. Islam is built on five pillars: *shahada,* the affirmation of faith in God and God's word entrusted to the Prophet Mohammed; *salat,* or prayer, ideally performed five times daily; *zakat,* or charity, a moral obligation to give to those in need; *sawm,* the daytime fasting practised during the month of Ramadan; and *haj,* the pilgrimage to Mecca that is the culmination of lifelong faith for Muslims.

JOKES

Catch Moroccan Arabic jokes you might otherwise miss with *Humour and Moroccan Culture,* a treasury of Moroccan wit in translation, collected by American expat Matthew Helmke.

MOROCCAN SOCIAL GRACES

Many visitors are surprised at how quickly friendships can be formed in Morocco, and often a little suspicious. True, carpet-sellers aren't after your friendship when they offer you tea, but notice how Moroccans behave with one another, and you'll see that friendly overtures are more than a mere contrivance. People you meet in passing are likely to remember you and greet you warmly the next day, and it's considered polite to stop and ask how they're doing. Greetings among friends can last 10 minutes, as each person enquires after the other's happiness, well-being and family.

Moroccans are generous with their time, and extend courtesies that might seem to you like impositions, from walking you to your next destination to inviting you home for lunch. To show your appreciation, stop by the next day to say hello, and be sure to compliment the cook.

Shiites & Sunnis

While all Muslims agree on the basic tenets received by the Prophet Mohammed, doctrinal disagreements ensued after his death. The Umayyads challenged his son-in-law Ali's claim to the title of caliph, or leader of the faithful. Some Muslims continued to recognise only successors of Ali; today they are known as Shiites. But in numerical terms, the Umayyad caliphate's Sunni Muslim practice is more common today.

Morocco is mostly Sunni, and follows the Maliki school of Sunni thought. Historically this school has been less strict, with Maliki *qaids* (judges) applying the sharia (religious code) according to local custom instead of absolutist rule of law.

To avoid conflict, French Resident-Général Lyautey banned non-Muslims from mosques in Morocco. Moroccans appreciated the privacy so much that they ousted the French from Morocco, and kept the ban.

Marabouts & Zawiyas

An important Moroccan tradition is the custom of venerating *marabouts* (saints). *Marabouts* are devout Muslims whose acts of devotion and professions of faith were so profound, their very presence is considered to confer *baraka* (grace) even after their death. Moroccans go out of their way to visit *marabout* mausoleums and *zawiyas* (shrines).

This practice of honouring *marabouts* is more in line with ancient Berber beliefs and Sufi mysticism than orthodox Islam, which generally discourages anything resembling idol worship. Visits to *zawiyas* are side trips for the many devout Moroccans who spend a lifetime preparing and planning for the *haj*.

Prospects for the Future

Economic Mobility

Fatima, Driss and Amina would be considered very fortunate in Morocco, where steady income is a rarity and 35% of the average Moroccan income covers basic foodstuffs. Only 10% of Moroccans can afford imported foods at the supermarket, let alone eating at restaurants occasionally like Amina. While the gap between rich and poor is growing in Morocco, Driss and Fatima represent an emerging middle class – though on average, Moroccans make much less in a day than Europeans do in an hour.

Career Opportunities

Driss, Amina and Fatima's incomes come from foreign trade, tourism, farming and remittances from relatives living abroad – broadly representative of the country as a whole. Social security is provided by the family in Morocco, not the government, so like Fatima, most Moroccans cannot afford to consider retirement. With fierce competition for limited employment opportunities and spots in state-sponsored universities, even star students like Amina must rely on family for help – and some take extreme risks to seek opportunities abroad.

Farida ben Lyzaid's film *A Door to the Sky* tells the story of an émigré's return to Morocco, and her delicate balancing act between activism and tradition.

Like many Moroccans born and raised in rural villages, 11-year-old Rashid probably won't be able to stay home much longer. Since 55% of rural Moroccan families struggle to meet subsistence-level needs, rural teens often must move to larger towns and cities to find work and educational opportunities.

Your visit to Morocco can have a positive impact on future prospects for Moroccans like Driss, Amina and Fatima, but especially Rashid – tourism in rural areas makes it possible for youth to remain with their families, and avoid an at-risk existence in the city. While Moroccans are working hard to extend their welcome to visitors, tourism can be a strain on local resources; your choice of sustainable alternatives can help reverse that pattern, and make tourism a net benefit for Morocco.

Moroccan Cuisine

Moroccan cuisine is the stuff of myth and legend – and sometimes sheer befuddlement, thanks to seemingly indecipherable menus. The most important take-home message? It's more than just couscous and tajines. Have no fear of the salad course, since these vegetable dishes are mostly cooked or peeled and among Morocco's finest culinary offerings. Dessert is a temptation you won't want to resist, and includes flaky pastries rich with nuts and fragrant traces of orange-flower water. *B'saha* – here's to your health.

Food

The food you find in Morocco is likely to be fresh, locally grown and homemade, rather than shipped in from Brazil, microwaved and served semi-thawed. Most Moroccan ingredients are cultivated in small quantities the old-fashioned way, without GMOs (genetically modified organisms), chemical fertilisers, pesticides or even mechanisation. These technologies are far too costly an investment for the average small-scale Moroccan farmer, as is organic certification and labelling – so though you may not see a label on it to this effect, much of the Moroccan produce you'll find in food markets is chemical- and GMO-free.

Produce

The splendid appearance, fragrance and flavour of Moroccan market produce will leave you with a permanent grudge against those wan, shrivelled items trying to pass themselves off as food at the supermarket. There's a reason for this: Moroccan produce is usually harvested by hand when ripe, and bought directly from farmers in the souqs. Follow the crowds of Moroccan grandmothers and restaurant sous-chefs to the

Food Facts: Morocco's Farmers

47% of Morocco's population lives in rural areas

40% of the country is involved in food production, mostly small-scale

19% of Morocco's land is arable

EATING DURING RAMADAN

During Ramadan, most Moroccans observe the fast during the day, eating only before sunup and after sundown. Dinner is eaten later than usual – around 11pm – and many wake up early for a filling breakfast before dawn. Another popular strategy is to stay up most of the night, sleep as late as possible, and stretch the afternoon nap into early evening. Adapt to the local schedule, and you may thoroughly enjoy the leisurely pace, late-night festivities and manic feasts of Ramadan.

Although you will not be expected to observe the fast, eating in public view is generally frowned upon. Hence many restaurants are closed during the day until *lftour*, the evening meal when the fast is broken – though if you call ahead to restaurants in tourist areas, you may have luck. With a little planning, there are plenty of other workarounds: load up on snacks in the market to eat indoors, make arrangements for breakfast or lunch in the privacy of your guesthouse, and ask locals about a good place to enjoy *lftour*.

Lftour comes with all the traditional Ramadan fixings: *harira* (a hearty soup), dates, milk, *shebbakia* (a sweet, coiled pastry that's guaranteed to shift your glucose levels into high gear) and *harsha* (buttery bread made of semolina and fried for maximum density). You may find that *harira* is offered free; even Moroccan McDonald's offers it as part of their special Ramadan Happy Meal.

HOW MUCH FOR A MEAL?

Eating reviews are ordered by preference. Price ranges are based on the cost of an evening main course, excluding drinks and tips:

€ Up to Dh70

€€ Dh70 to Dh150; a set meal including wine would typically cost Dh250 to Dh400

€€€ More than Dh150; a set meal including wine would typically cost more than Dh400

Midrange and top-end restaurants are mostly found within the ville nouvelle of large cities, with a few notable exceptions in Fez and Marrakesh.

A service charge may automatically be added to your bill in better restaurants. A TVA tax (similar to value-added tax), usually around 10%, may also be charged, but generally this is built into the price of your meal.

carts and stalls offering the freshest produce. Just be sure to peel, cook or thoroughly wash produce before you eat it, since your stomach may not yet be accustomed to local microbes.

Meats

Carnivores and sustainability-minded eaters can finally put aside their differences and enjoy dinner together in Morocco. As you may guess, watching sheep and goats scamper over mountains and valleys in Morocco, herds live a charmed existence here – at least until dinnertime. Most of the meat you'll enjoy in Morocco is free-range, antibiotic-free and raised on a steady diet of grass and wild herbs. If you wonder why lamb and mutton is so much more flavourful in Morocco than the stuff back home, you'll find your answer scampering around the High Atlas foothills.

Seasonal Variations

If there is one food you adore or a dish you detest, you might want to plan the timing of your visit to Morocco accordingly. Morocco offers an incredible bounty of produce, meats and fish, but these vary seasonally. The country's relative lack of infrastructure and hard currency can be advantageous to visitors – hence the picturesque mountain villages that seem untouched by time, and the jackpot of dirhams you get for your euros – but this also makes importing produce tricky. This means that if you're visiting in autumn, you may have to enjoy fresh figs instead of kiwi fruit (not exactly a hardship).

When you consider your menu options, you'll also want to consider geography. Oualidia oysters may not be so fresh by the time they cross mountain passes to Ouarzazate, and Sefrou cherries can be hard to come by in Tiznit. So if your vacation plans revolve around lavish seafood dinners, head for the coasts; vegetarians visiting desert regions in autumn should have a high tolerance for dates.

Quitting While You're Ahead

One final and important Moroccan dining tip: pace yourself. Moroccan meals can be lengthy and generous, and might seem a bit excessive to an unyielding waistband. Take your time and drink plenty of water throughout your meal, especially with wine and in dry climates, instead of pounding a drink at the end. There are better ways to end a meal than dehydration and bloating – namely, a dessert *bastilla* (multilayered pastry) with toasted almonds, cinnamon and cream. Your Moroccan hosts may urge you on like a cheerleading squad in a pie-eating contest, but

What's in Season in Morocco?

Autumn – figs, pomegranates, grapes

Spring – apricots, cherries, strawberries, peaches

Summer – watermelon, wild artichokes, tomatoes

Winter – oranges, mandarins, onions, beets, carrots, potatoes, other root vegetables

Year-round – almonds, walnuts, bananas, squash, pumpkin, fava beans, green beans, lentils, eggplant, peppers, lemons (fresh and preserved)

obey your instincts and quit when you're full with a heartfelt *'alhamdu-lallah!'* (Thanks to God!).

Al-Ftour (Breakfast)

Even if your days back home begin with just coffee, it would be a culinary crime to skip breakfast in Morocco. Whether you grab yours on the go in the souq or sit down to a leisurely repast, you are in for a treat. Breakfasts are rarely served before 9am in guesthouses and hotels, so early risers in immediate need of coffee will probably have to head to a cafe or hit the souqs.

Street Eats

Sidewalk cafes and kiosks put a local twist on Continental breakfast, with Moroccan pancakes and doughnuts, French pastries, coffee and mint tea. Follow your nose and rumbling stomach into the souqs, where you'll find tangy olives and local *jiben* (fresh goat's or cow's milk cheese) to be devoured with fresh *khoobz* (Moroccan-style pita bread baked in a wood-fired oven until it's crusty on the outside, yet fluffy and light on the inside). *Khoobz* can be found wrapped in paper at any *hanout* (cupboard-sized corner shops found in every neighbourhood).

In the souqs, you can't miss vendors with their carts piled high with fresh fruit. They're right: you'll never know how high oranges can be stacked or how delicious freshly squeezed *aseer limoon* (orange juice) can be until you pay a visit to a Moroccan juice-vendor's cart. Drink yours from a disposable cup or your own water bottle, because the vendor's glasses are rinsed and reused dozens of times daily.

One savoury southern breakfast just right for chilly mornings is *bessara* (a steaming-hot fava-bean purée with cumin, olive oil and a dash of paprika), best when mopped up with *khoobz* still warm from the communal oven right down the street. For a twist on the usual French breakfast pastries, try *rghaif* (flaky, dense Moroccan pastries like flattened croissants), typically served with warm honey, apricot jam, or if you're

---

TOP TIPS FOR ENJOYING STREET FOOD & STAYING HEALTHY

Make a beeline for busy stalls Moroccans are sticklers for freshness, and know which places consistently deliver. *Snak* stalls have better turnover of fresh ingredients than most fancy restaurants, where you can't typically check the meat and cooking oil before you sit down to dinner.

Check out the cooking oil Is it extremely smoky, pungent or murky? Hold out for fresher, cleaner cooking oil.

Always look over the ingredients Check the food on display, especially if you'll be ordering meat or seafood. This is no time to get squeamish. Are the fish eyes still bright, the hearts bloody and the snails alive? That's a good sign for adventurous foodies who want to try fried fish, skewered, grilled lamb hearts, and steaming snail soups.

Clean your hands right before eating Much of what we call 'food poisoning' is actually illness caused by bacteria transferred from hand to mouth while eating.

Use your bread to scoop up food This is how Moroccans eat, and it makes sense. If you're using utensils briefly rinsed in cold water, hygiene-wise, you're sharing a rather intimate moment with the stranger who used them before you.

Stick to your own purified or bottled water It takes time adjusting to local water, so it's better to drink purified or bottled stuff – and never drink out of rinsed-and-reused stall glasses.

Wait until your second-to-last night If your stomach is skittish, hold out for that street food adventure. If dinner goes down a treat – as it should – you'll be back tomorrow.

lucky, nutty *tahalout* (date syrup). The truly adventurous can start their day with a rich stew of lamb's head or calves' feet, generously ladled into an enamel bowl from a huge vat precariously balanced on a makeshift gas burner.

Breakfast of Champions

As a guest in a Moroccan home, you'd be treated to the best of everything, and the best guesthouses scrupulously uphold this Moroccan tradition each morning. You'll carb-load like a Moroccan marathoner, with some combination of the following to jumpstart your day:

Hold the hot sauce: dousing your tajine with *harissa* (capsicum-pepper sauce) is generally done in Tunisia, Morocco's chief rival in the kitchen and on the football field.

Ahwa (Coffee) *Ahwa* is one option, but also *café au lait* (coffee with milk), *thé b'na na* (tea with mint) or *thé wa hleb* (tea with milk), *wa* (with) or *bla* (without) *sukur* (sugar).

Aseer limoon (Orange juice)

Bayd (Eggs) Cooked in omelettes, with a dash of *kamun* (freshly ground cumin) or *zataar* (cumin with toasted sesame seeds).

Beghrir Moroccan pancakes with an airy, spongy texture like crumpets, with honey or jam.

French pastries Croissants, *pain au chocolat* and others.

Khoobz Moroccan-style pita bread baked in a wood-fired oven, usually served with butter and jam or olive oil and *zataar*.

Rghaif Flat, buttery Moroccan pastries.

Sfenj Moroccan doughnuts (sometimes with an egg deep-fried in the hole).

El-Ghda (Lunch)

Lunch is traditionally the biggest meal of the day in Morocco, followed by a nice nap through the heat of the day. The lunch hour here is really a three- to four-hour stretch from noon to 3pm or 4pm, when most shops and facilities are closed, apart from a few stores catering to tourists.

For speed eaters this may seem inconvenient, but especially in summer it's best to do as the locals do, and treat lunchtime as precious downtime. Tuck into a tajine, served à la carte with crusty bread, or upgrade to a *prix fixe* (three-course restaurant lunch). Afterwards, you'll have a whole new appreciation for mint tea and afternoon naps.

SEXY SEKSU

Berbers call it *seksu*, *New York Times* food critic Craig Claiborne called it one of the dozen best dishes in the world, and when you're in Morocco, you can call couscous lunch. You know that yellowish stuff that comes in a box, with directions on the side instructing you to add boiling water and let stand for three minutes? That doesn't count. What Moroccans call couscous is a fine, pale, grain-sized, hand-rolled pasta lightly steamed with aromatic broth until toothsome and fluffy, served with a selection of vegetables and/or meat or fish in a delicately flavoured reduction of stock and spices.

Since preparing and digesting a proper couscous takes a while, Moroccans usually enjoy it on Fridays, when many have the day or the afternoon off after Friday prayers. Couscous isn't a simple side dish but rather the main event of a Moroccan Friday lunch, whether tricked out Casablanca-style with seven vegetables, heaped with lamb and vegetables in Fez, or served with tomatoes, fish and fresh herbs in Essaouira. Many delicious couscous dishes come without meat, including the pumpkin couscous of Marrakesh and a simple yet savoury High Atlas version with stewed onions. But scrupulous vegetarians will want to enquire in advance whether that hearty stock is indeed vegetarian. Sometimes a couscous dish can be ordered à la carte, but usually it's a centrepiece of a multicourse lunch or celebratory *diffa* – and when you get a mouthful of the stuff done properly, you'll see why.

Snak Attack

If you're still digesting your lavish guesthouse breakfast come lunchtime, try one of the many *snak*s (kiosks) and small restaurants offering lighter fare – just look for people clustered around sidewalk kiosks, or a sign or awning with the word *snak*. Many hard-working locals do not take afternoon siestas, and instead eat sandwiches on the go. At the risk of stating the obvious, always join the queue at the one thronged with locals: Moroccans are picky about their *snak*s, preferring the cleanest establishments that use the freshest ingredients.

Here's what you'll find on offer:

Brochettes Kebabs rubbed with salt and spices, grilled on a skewer and served with *khoobz* and *harissa* (capsicum-pepper sauce), cumin and salt. Among the most popular varieties are lamb, chicken, *kefta* (spiced meatballs of ground lamb and/or beef) and the aggressively flavourful 'mixed meat' (usually lamb or beef plus heart, kidney and liver).

Merguez Hot, spicy, delicious homemade lamb sausage, not to be confused with *teyhan* (stuffed spleen; like liver, only less bitter and more tender) – *merguez* is usually reddish in colour, while *teyhan* is pale.

Pizza Now found at upscale *snak*s catering to the worldly Moroccan middle class. Look for *snak*s boasting wood-fired ovens, and try tasty local versions with olives, onions, tomatoes, Atlantic anchovies and wild thyme.

Shwarma Spiced lamb or chicken roasted on a spit and served with *tahina* (sesame sauce) or yoghurt, with optional onions, salad, *harissa* and a dash of *sumac* (a tart, pickle-flavoured purple spice; highly recommended).

Tajines The famous Moroccan stews cooked in conical earthenware pots that keep the meat unusually moist and tender. The basic tajines served at a roadside *snak* are usually made with just a few ingredients, pulled right off a camping stove or *kanun* (earthenware brazier), and plonked down on a ramshackle folding table. Often you can pick your tajine; point to one that's been bubbling for an hour or two, with nicely caramelised onions and well-reduced sauce. Don't let appearances fool you: this could be one of the best tajines you'll eat in Morocco. Pull up a stool and dig in, using your *khoobz* as your utensil instead of rinsed-and-reused flatware.

The Moroccan Power Lunch

Some upscale Moroccan restaurants that serve an evening *diffa* (feast) to tourist hordes serve a scaled-down menu at lunch, when waitstaff are more relaxed and the meal is sometimes a fraction of the price you'd pay for dinner. You might miss the live music and inevitable belly dancing that would accompany a fancy supper – but then again, you might not. Three courses may seem a bit much for lunch, but don't be daunted: what this usually means is a delightful array of diminutive vegetable dishes, followed by a fluffy couscous and/or a small meat or chicken tajine, capped with the obligatory mint tea and biscuits or fruit.

Mezze (Salad course) This could be a meal in itself. Fresh bread and three to five small, usually cooked vegetable dishes that might include lemony beet salad with chives, herbed potatoes, cumin-spiked chickpeas, a relish of roasted tomatoes and caramelised onions, pumpkin purée with cinnamon and honey, and a roasted, spiced eggplant dip so rich it's often called 'aubergine caviar'.

Main The main course is usually a tajine and/or couscous – a quasi-religious experience in Morocco not to be missed, especially on Fridays. The most common tajine choices are *dujaj mqalli bil hamd markd wa zeetoun* (chicken with preserved lemon and olives, zesty in flavour and velvety in texture); *kefta bil matisha wa bayd* (meatballs in a rich tomato sauce with a hint of heat from spices and topped with a sizzling egg); and *lehem bil berquq wa luz* (lamb with prunes and almonds served sliding off the bone into a saffron-onion sauce). If you're in Morocco for a while, you may tire of these classic tajine options – until you come across one regional

Moroccan Snacks

fresh or dried fruit

roasted almonds, chickpeas, and pumpkin and sunflower seeds

hard-boiled eggs with fresh cumin

roasted corn fresh off the brazier

sandwiches of brochettes or merguez with cumin, salt and harissa

escargot (snails) in hot, savoury broth

ice cream

patisseries (Moroccan or French)

Top chefs consult Paula Wolfert's *Couscous and Other Good Food from Morocco*, which includes 20 tantalising recipes for the titular dish; it won the 2008 James Beard Cookbook Hall of Fame Award.

variation that makes all your sampling of chicken tajine with lemon and olives worthwhile. That's when you cross over from casual diner to true tajine connoisseur, and fully appreciate the passionate debates among Moroccans about such minutiae as the appropriate thickness of the lemon rind and brininess of the olives. Variations on the classics are expected, but no self-respecting Moroccan restaurant should ever serve you a tajine that's stringy, tasteless, watery or overcooked.

Dessert At lunchtime, dessert is usually sweet mint tea served with almond cookies. You may not think you have room, but one bite of a dreamy *kaab el-ghazal* (crescent-shaped 'gazelle's horns' cookie stuffed with almond paste and laced with orange-flower water) will surely convince you otherwise. A light, refreshing option is the tart-sweet *orange á canelle* (orange slices with cinnamon and orange-flower water).

L'Asha (Dinner)

Dinner in Morocco doesn't usually start until around 8pm or 9pm, after work and possibly a sunset stroll. Most Moroccans eat dinner at home, but you may notice young professionals, students and bachelors making a beeline for the local *snak* or pizzeria. In winter you'll see vendors crack open steaming vats of *harira* – a hearty soup with a base of tomatoes, onions, saffron and coriander, often with lentils, chickpeas and/or lamb. Dinner at home may often be *harira* and lunch leftovers, with the notable exception of Ramadan and other celebrations.

Diffa

With enough hard currency and room in your stomach, you might prefer restaurants to *snak* fare for dinner. Most upscale Moroccan restaurants cater to tourists, serving an elaborate *prix fixe* Moroccan *diffa* (feast) in a palatial setting. This is not a dine-and-dash meal, but an

Moroccan Sauces

*Mhammar –
paprika, cumin and
butter*

*Mqalli – saffron, oil
and ginger*

*Msharmal –
saffron, ginger and
a dash of pepper*

*Qadra – smen
(seasoned butter)
with vegetable
stock, chickpeas
and/or almonds.*

VEGETARIANS: YOUR MOROCCAN MENU

Breakfast Load up on Moroccan pastries, pancakes, fresh fruit and fresh-squeezed juice. Fresh goat's cheese and olives from the souq are solid savoury choices with fresh-baked *khoobz* (Moroccan-style wood-fired pita bread). *Bessara* is a delicious bean soup that's typically meat-free, but steer clear of bubbling roadside vats if you're squeamish – they may contain snails or sheep's-head soup.

Lunch Try the *mezze* of salads, which come with fresh bread and may range from delicate cucumbers in orange-blossom water to substantial herbed beets laced with kaffir lime. Vegetarians can sometimes, but not always, order a Berber vegetable tajine or Casablanca-style couscous with seven vegetables. Ingredients are bought fresh daily in small quantities and the chef may not have factored vegetarians into the restaurant's purchases – so call ahead if you can. Pizza is another widely available and inexpensive menu option, best when spiked with local herbs and olives.

Snacks Market stalls feature cascades of dried figs, dates and apricots alongside towering cones of roasted nuts with salt, honey, cinnamon, cane sugar or hot pepper. Chickpeas and other pulses are roasted, served hot in a paper cone with cumin and salt, and are not to be missed. Tea-time menus at swanky restaurants may feature *briouats* (cigar-shaped pastries stuffed with goat's cheese or egg and herbs), plus finger sandwiches, pastries and cakes. If that's not enough, there's always ice cream, and mint tea with cookies or nuts are hardly ever more than a carpet shop away.

Dinner For a hearty change of pace from salads and couscous, try a vegetarian pasta (anything with eggplant is especially tasty) or omelette (usually served with thick-cut fries). If you're staying in a Moroccan guesthouse, before you leave in the morning you can usually request a vegetarian tajine made to order with market-fresh produce. Pity you can't do that at home, right?

TASTY BEAST: MECHOUI

Special occasions call for Morocco's very best beast dish: *mechoui,* an entire slow-roasted lamb. The whole beast is basted with butter, garlic, cumin and paprika, and slow-roasted in a special covered pit until it's ready to melt into the fire or your mouth, whichever comes first. Local variations may include substituting a calf instead, or stuffing the lamb with some combination of almonds (or other nuts), prunes (or other dried fruit) or couscous. Sometimes *mechoui* is accompanied by kebabs or *kwa* (grilled liver kebabs with cumin, salt and paprika). Other than Moroccan weddings, the best place to have *mechoui* is right off Marrakesh's Djemaa el-Fna around lunchtime, served with olives and bread in Mechoui Alley. Do not attempt to operate heavy machinery or begin a whirlwind museum tour post-*mechoui;* no amount of post-prandial mint tea will make such exertions feasible without a nap.

evening's entertainment that often includes live music or belly dancing and wine or beer.

Fair warning about palace restaurants: your meal may come with a side order of kitsch. Many palace restaurants appear to have been decorated by a genie, complete with winking brass lamps, mirrors, swagged tent fabric and tasselled cushions as far as the eye can see. Often it's the ambience you're paying for rather than the food, which can vary from exquisitely prepared regional specialities to mass-produced glop. Here's a rule of thumb: if the place is so cavernous that your voice echoes and there's a stage set up for a laser show, don't expect personalised service or authentic Moroccan fare.

Whether you're in for a *diffa* at a Moroccan home (lucky you) or a restaurant, your lavish dinner will include some combination of the following:

Mezze Up to five different small salads (though the most extravagant palace restaurants in Marrakesh and Fez boast seven to nine).

Briouat Buttery cigar-shaped or triangular pastry stuffed with herbs and goat's cheese, savoury meats or egg, then fried or baked.

Pastilla The justly famed savoury-sweet pie made of *warqa* (sheets of pastry even thinner than filo), painstakingly layered with pigeon or chicken cooked with caramelised onions, lemon, eggs and toasted sugared almonds, then dusted with cinnamon and powdered sugar.

Couscous Made according to local custom; couscous variations may be made of barley, wheat or corn.

Tajine Often your choice of one of a couple of varieties.

Mechoui Slow-roaste lamb; or some regional speciality.

Dessert This may be *orange á canelle,* a dessert *bastilla* (with fresh cream and toasted nuts), *briouat bil luz* (briouat filled with almond paste), *sfaa* (sweet cinnamon couscous with dried fruit and nuts, served with cream) or *kaab el-ghazal.*

Drinks

To wash your *diffa* down and stay hydrated, you'll need a good amount of liquid. Day and night, don't forget to drink plenty of bottled or purified water. Vying to quench your thirst are orange-juice vendors loudly singing their own praises, and water vendors in fringed tajine-shaped hats clanging brass bowls together.

Moroccan tap water is often potable, though not always – so stick with treated water or local mineral water. Best bets are Sidi Ali and sparkling Oulmes; others have a chalky aftertaste.

For Moroccan recipes, a glossary of Arabic ingredients and Moroccan cooking tips and anecdotes, surf Moroccan Gateway's foodie links at www.al-bab.com/maroc/food.htm.

Vitamin-rich Moroccan argan oil is popular as a cosmetic, but also as a gourmet treat: the toasted-hazelnut flavour makes an intriguing dipping oil and exotic salad dressing.

If you're offered Moroccan mint tea, don't expect to bolt it and be on your way. Mint tea is the hallmark of Moroccan hospitality, and a sit-down affair that takes around half an hour. If you have the honour of pouring the tea, pour the first cup back in the teapot to help cool it and dissolve the sugar. Then starting from your right, pour each cup of tea from as high above the glass as you can without splashing. Your hosts will be most impressed.

Moroccan mint tea ('Berber whiskey') may be ubiquitous after meals, but you can find a mean cup of coffee in Morocco, too. Most of it is French-pressed, and delivers a caffeine wallop to propel you through the souqs and into the stratosphere.

> More than 186 reader-rated Moroccan recipes from foodie magazines *Gourmet* and *Bon Appétit* are online at www.epicurious.com, including quick and healthy options and suggested wine pairings.

Moroccan Beer, Wine & Spirits

Yes, you can drink alcohol in Morocco without offending local sensibilities, as long as you do it discreetly. Serving alcohol within many Moroccan medinas or within view of a mosque may be frowned upon, and liquor licences can cost an astronomical Dh20,000 – but many Moroccan guesthouses and restaurants get around these hurdles by offering booze in a low voice, and serving it out of sight indoors or on a terrace. So if you're in the mood for a beer and don't find it on the menu, you might want to ask the waiter in a low voice, speakeasy-style.

One point of caution: quality assurance is tricky in a Muslim country where mixologists, micro-brewers and licensed sommeliers are in understandably short supply, and your server may not be able to make any personal recommendations from the wine menu. Since wines are subject to unpredictable heat exposure in transit and storage, be sure to taste your wine before the server leaves the table – red wines are especially subject to spoilage. Don't hesitate to send back a drink if something about it seems off; your server will likely take your word for it.

> Before dinner, your host may appear with a pitcher and a deep tray. Hold out your hands, and your host will pour rosewater over them.

Beer

Casa A fine local pilsner beer
Flag A faintly herbal second-best
Flag Special Affordable and the most popular beverage in Morocco (25 million units consumed annually)

BEEN THERE, EATEN THAT

Eat your way across Morocco, north to south, with these outstanding regional dishes:

Casablanca *Seksu bedawi* (couscous with seven vegetables)

Chefchaouen *Djaj bil berquq* (chicken with prunes)

Demnate *Seksu Demnati* (couscous made with corn or barley instead of semolina)

Essaouira *Hut mqalli* (fish tajine with saffron, ginger and preserved lemons); *djej kadra toumiya* (chicken with almonds, onions and chickpeas in buttery saffron sauce)

Fez *Kennaria* (stew with wild thistle or artichoke, with or without meat); *hut bu'etob* (baked shad filled with almond-stuffed dates)

High Atlas *Mechoui* (slow-roasted stuffed lamb or beef)

Marrakesh *Bessara* (fava beans with cumin, paprika, olive oil and salt); *tanjia* (crock-pot stew of seasoned lamb cooked for eight to 12 hours in the fire of a hammam)

Meknès *Kamama* (lamb stewed with ginger, seasoned butter, saffron, cinnamon and sweet onions)

Southern Coast *Amlou* (argan-nut paste with honey and argan oil)

Tangier Local variations on tapas and paella

Wine

White Moroccan white wines are a solid bet, including the crisp, food-friendly Larroque; well-balanced, juicy Terre Blanche, a Chardonnay/Viognier/Sauvignon Blanc blend; citrusy, off-dry Cuveé du Président Sémillant; and Siroua S, a cool coastal Chardonnay.

Gris & Rosé These are refreshing alternatives, especially not-too-fruity Medaillon Rosé de Syrah; peachy-keen Eclipse Grenache/Cinsault blend; fresh, fragrant Domaine Rimal Vin Gris; the juicy, aptly named Rosé d'un Nuit d'Eté (Summer's Night Rosé) of Grenache/Syrah; and the crisply top-range Volubilia.

Red Reliable reds include the admirable Burgundian-style Terre Rouge from Rabati coastal vineyards; well-rounded Volubilia from Morocco's ancient Roman wine-growing region; and spicier Merlot/Syrah/Cabernet Sauvignon Coteaux Atlas. Guerrouane Rouge is a heavy red at the cheaper end of the scale, while Morocco's Jewish community has bequeathed the country an interesting selection of kosher wines.

Spirits

Creative cocktails Mojitos, caipirinhas and negronis are three imported cocktails that become local nightclub favourites when made with (respectively) Moroccan mint, local kaffir lime and orange-blossom water. These Moroccan twists can make even low-end alcohol seem top-shelf...at least until tomorrow morning.

Local eau de vie Mahia is a Moroccan spirit distilled from figs that's around 80% proof, with a flavour somewhere between Italian grappa and Kentucky moonshine. You won't find it on most menus, because it's usually made in home distilleries for private consumption. If you're staying at a guesthouse, your hosts may know where you can get some, but they may try to warn you off the stuff – *mahia* hangovers are legendary.

Cooking at guesthouses is usually done by *dadas,* who are champions of Morocco's culinary traditions, cooking feasts with whatever's freshest in the market, usually without a recipe or a measuring cup. If a *dada's* delights impress you, ask to thank her personally – it's good form, and good *baraka* (blessings) besides.

Music

Any trip to Morocco comes with its own syncopated soundtrack: the early evening *adhan* (call to prayer), and the ubiquitous donkey-cart-drivers' chants of '*Balek!*' – fair warning that since donkeys don't yield, you'd better, and quick. Adding to the musical mayhem are beats booming out of taxis, ham radios and roadside stalls, and live music performances at restaurants and weddings, on street corners and headlining at festivals year-round. For a memory bank of Maghrebi music any DJ would envy, sample these varieties.

Classical Arab-Andalucian Music

No, that's not a musical rugby scrum: the *haidous* is a complex circle dance with musicians in the middle, often performed in celebration of the harvest.

Leaving aside the thorny question of where exactly it originated (you don't want to be the cause of the next centuries-long Spain-Morocco conflict, do you?), this music combines the flamenco-style strumming and heartstring-plucking drama of Spanish folk music with the finely calibrated stringed instruments, complex percussion and haunting half-tones of classical Arab music. Add poetic lyrics and the right singer at dinner performances, and you may find that lump in your throat makes it hard to swallow your *pastilla* (pigeon pie).

You'll hear two major styles of Arab-Andalucian music in Morocco: Al-Aala (primarily in Fez, Tetouan and Salé) and Gharnati (mostly Oujda). The area of musical overlap is Rabat, where you can hear both. Keep an eye out for concerts, musical evenings at fine restaurants and classical-music festivals in Casablanca and Fez, and look especially for performances by Gharnati vocalist Amina Alaoui, Fatiha El Hadri Badraï and her traditional all-female orchestras from Tetouan, and Festival of World Sacred Music headliner Mohamed Amin el-Akrami and his orchestra.

MOROCCAN MUSIC FESTIVALS

Dates and locations may vary, so check www.maghrebarts.ma/musique.html for updates.

March Rencontres Musicales de Marrakesh (classical); Tremplin (urban music), in Casablanca

April Festival of Sufi Culture (www.par-chemins.org), in Fez; Jazzablanca (www.jazzablanca.com), in Casablanca

May Jazz aux Oudayas, in Rabat; L'Boulevard (www.boulevard.ma), in Casablanca; Mawazine Festival of World Music (www.festivalmawazine.ma), in Rabat

June Festival of World Sacred Music (www.fesfestival.com), in Fez; Gnaoua & World Music Festival (www.festival-gnaoua.net), in Essaouira; Jazz au Chellah, in Rabat

July Marrakesh Festival of Popular Arts (www.marrakechfestival.com); Voix des Femmes (Women's Voices), in Tetouan; Festival Timitar (Amazigh music), in Agadir; Festival du Desert (www.festivaldudesert.ma), in Er-Rachidia

September TANJAzz (www.tanjazz.org), in Tangier

October Festival des Andalousies Atlantiques (www.facebook.com/FestivalDesAndalousiesAtlantiques), in Essaouira; Jazz in Riad Festival, in Fez

Gnaoua

Joyously bluesy with a rhythm you can't refuse, this music may send you into a trance – and that's just what it's meant to do. The brotherhood of Gnaoua began among freed slaves in Marrakesh and Essaouira as a ritual of deliverance from slavery and into God's graces. A true Gnaoua *lila,* or spiritual jam session, may last all night, with musicians erupting into leaps of joy as they enter trance-like states of ecstasy that can send fez-tassels spinning and set spirits free.

Join the crowds watching in Marrakesh's Djemaa el-Fna or at the annual Gnaoua and World Music Festival in Essaouira, and hear Gnaoua on Peter Gabriel's Real World music label. Gnaoua *mâalems* (master musicians) include perennial festival favourites Abdeslam Alikkane and his Tyour Gnaoua, crossover fusion superstar Hassan Hakmoun, rising star *mâalem* Saïd Boulhimas and his deeply funky Band of Gnawas, Indian-inflected Nass Marrakech and reggae-inspired Omar Hayat. Since Gnaoua are historically a brotherhood, most renowned Gnaoua musicians have been men – but the all-women Sufi group Haddarates plays Gnaoua trances traditionally reserved for women, and family acts include Brahim Elbelkani and La Famille Backbou.

To explore Amazigh music in a variety of styles, languages and regions, check out samples, musician bios and CDs from basic bluesy Tartit to '70s-funky Tinariwen at www.azawan.com.

Berber Folk Music

There's plenty of other indigenous Moroccan music besides Gnaoua, thanks to the ancient Berber tradition of passing along songs and poetry from one generation to the next. You can't miss Berber music at village *moussems* (festivals in honour of a local saint), Agadir's Timtar Festival of Amazigh music, the Marrakesh Festival of Popular Arts and Imilchil's Marriage Festival, as well as weddings and other family celebrations.

The most renowned Berber folk group is the Master Musicians of Joujouka, who famously inspired the Rolling Stones, Led Zeppelin and William S Burroughs, and collaborated with them on experimental fusion with lots of clanging and crashing involved. Lately the big names are women's, including the all-woman group B'net Marrakech and the bold Najat Aatabou, who sings protest songs in Berber against restrictive traditional roles. For more women vocalists, head to Tetouan for the Voix des Femmes (Women's Voices) festival.

From Marock to Hibhub

Like the rest of the Arab world, Moroccans listen to a lot of Egyptian music, but Moroccopop is gaining ground. A generation of local DJs with cheeky names like Ramadan Special and DJ Al Intifada have mastered the art of the unlikely mashup. And so have some of the more intriguing talents to emerge in recent years: Hoba Hoba Spirit, whose controversy-causing, pop-punk *Blad Skizo* (Schizophrenic Country) addresses the contradictions of modern Morocco head-on; Moroccan singer-songwriter Hindi Zahra, Morocco's answer to Tori Amos, with bluesy acoustic-guitar backing; Darga, a group that blends ska, Darija rap and a horn section into Moroccan surf anthems; and the bluntly named Ganga Fusion and Kif Samba, who both pound out a danceable mix of funk, Berber folk music, reggae and jazz. For something completely different, check out the burgeoning Megadeth-inspired Moroccan metal scene at Casa's annual L'Boulevard festival.

But ask any guy on the street with baggy cargo shorts and a T-shirt with the slogan MJM (*Maroc Jusqu'al Mort;* Morocco 'til Death) about Moroccan pop, and you'll get a crash course in *hibhub* (Darija for hip hop). Meknès' H-Kayne rap gangsta-style, while Tangier's MC Muslim raps with a death-metal growl, and Fez City Clan features a talented but

Check out Morocco's latest Top 10 hits and hear Darija DJ stylings on RealPlayer audio at Radio Casablanca online: www.maroc.net/newrc.

FOR THOSE ABOUT TO MO'ROCK, WE SALUTE YOU

Not since Ozzy bit a live bat onstage has hard rock caused such an uproar. In 2003, police, who didn't appreciate being rocked like a hurricane, arrested 11 Moroccan metalheads for making their audiences 'listen, with bad intent, to songs which contravene good morals or incite debauchery'. Despite widespread protests that authorities were driving the crazy train, the rockers were ultimately sentenced to one year in jail for 'employing seductive methods with the aim of undermining the faith of a Muslim'.

But diehard Moroccan metalheads got organised, calling all rockers to the mosh-pit in Sidi Kacem, an inland agricultural centre near Meknès better known for braying donkeys than wailing guitars. The second Sidi Rock festival was held in February 2008, showcasing bands from the area with names sure to warm any true metalhead's heart, if not a mullah's, including Despotism from Casablanca and Sidi Kacem's own Damned Kreation (now Putrid Cadavers). Far from pleather-clad '80s hair bands, these Moroccan groups write their own rebellious lyrics and rock hardcore in black jeans and torn T-shirts.

The metal scene has since outgrown its Sidi Kacem venue, storming the stage at L'Boulevard, Casablanca's free festival of urban music held at the Casa stadium in May, and at L'Boulevard's March showcase for emerging artists, Tremplin (Trampoline), held at the coolest-ever rock venue: Casa's *anciens abbatoirs* (old slaughterhouses). Past editions of the festivals have focused on hip-hop and electronica, but there's a jittery excitement when the metal bands take the stage, and the police reinforcements brought in to monitor the mosh-pits look distinctly nervous.

With the 2010 editions of L'Boulevard and Tremplin featuring metal headliners and attracting 30,000 spectators over four days, the mainstreaming of Mo'rock raises another question: once metal goes legit, what's a Moroccan rebel to do? The answer seems obvious: go emo'rocco.

annoying kid rapper and an Arabic string section. The acts that consistently get festival crowds bouncing are Agadir's DJ Key, who remixes hip-hop standards with manic scratching and beat-boxing, and Marrakesh's Fnaire, mixing traditional Moroccan sounds with staccato vocal stylings. Rivalling 'Blad Skizo' for youth anthem of the decade is Fnaire's 'Ma Tkich Bladi' (Don't Touch My Country), an irresistibly catchy anthem against neocolonialism with a viral YouTube video.

Marock on Film

This Is Maroc (2010) Hat Trick Brothers' road trip.

I Love HipHop in Morocco (2007) H-Kayne, DJ Key, Bigg and other hip-hop groups struggle to get gigs.

International musicians find themselves attracted to Morocco with increasing frequency. The Festival of World Sacred Music held in Fez attracts an ever-more diverse range of headline acts, from Björk to Patti Smith, while Rabat's Mawazine Festival of World Music brings in the pop mainstream from Beyoncé to Elton John. The latter highlighted the sometimes delicate nature of the position of music in Morocco – while the government defended Elton John's homosexuality against Islamist criticism Moroccan musicians have to tread a finer line, especially if commenting on social issues. In 2012, and following the Arab Spring, rapper El Haked was imprisoned for a year for 'undermining the honour' of public servants when the video for his song 'Klab ed-Dawla' (Dogs of the State) pictured corrupt police wearing the heads of donkeys. El Haked had previously been jailed for criticising the monarchy.

Literature & Cinema

Morocco's rich oral tradition has kept shared stories and histories alive. Watch the story-tellers and singers in Marrakesh's Djemaa el-Fna in action and you'll understand how the country's literary tradition has remained so vital and irrepressible, despite press censorship. More recently, novelists like Tahar ben Jelloun have brought their rich prose to bear on the national experience. Moroccan cinema is younger still, but the country is actively moving beyond being a glitzy film location to a producer in its own right.

Literature

A Different Beat

The international spotlight first turned on Morocco's literary scene in the 1950s and '60s, when Beat Generation authors Paul and Jane Bowles took up residence in Tangier and began recording the stories of Moroccans they knew. *The Sheltering Sky* is Paul Bowles' most celebrated Morocco-based novel, while the nonfiction *Their Heads Are Green and Their Hands are Blue* is a valuable travelogue. Following exposure from the Beats, local writers broke onto the writing scene. Check out Larbi Layachi's *A Life Full of Holes* (written under the pseudonym Driss ben Hamed Charhadi), Mohammed Mrabet's *Love With a Few Hairs* and Mohamed Choukri's *For Bread Alone*. Like a lot of Beat literature, these books are packed with sex, drugs and unexpected poetry – but if anything, they're more streetwise, humorous and heartbreaking.

In *Moroccan Folk Tales*, Jilali El Koudia presents 31 classic legends ranging from a Berber version of Snow White to a tale of a woman who cross-dresses as a Muslim scholar.

Coming up for Air

Encouraged by the outspoken 'Tangerine' authors, Moroccan poet Abdellatif Laâbi founded the free-form, free-thinking poetry magazine *Anfas/Souffles* (Breath) in 1966, not in the anything-goes international zone of Tangier, but in the royal capital of Rabat. What began as a journal became a movement of writers, painters and filmmakers heeding Laâbi's outcry against censorship: '*A la poubelle poème/A la poubelle rythme/A la poubelle silence*' ('In the trash, poetry/In the trash, rhythm/In the trash, silence'). *Anfas/Souffles* published 21 more daring issues, until the censors shut it down in 1972 and sent Laâbi to prison for eight years for 'crimes of opinion'. Government censorship notwithstanding, the complete French text of *Anfas/Souffles* is now available online at http://clic-net.swarthmore.edu/souffles/sommaire.html.

The literary expression Laâbi equated to breathing has continued unabated. In 1975, *Anfas/Souffles* cofounder and self-proclaimed 'linguistic guerrilla' Mohammed Khaïr-Eddine published his confrontational *Ce Maroc!*, an anthology of revolutionary writings. A Souss Berber himself, Khaïr-Eddine called for the recognition of Berber identity and culture in his 1984 *Legend and Life of Agoun'chich*, which served as a rallying cry for today's Berber Pride movement.

Author Tahir Shah moved his family from London to Casablanca to become a Moroccan storyteller groupie, collecting tales for his *In Arabian Nights: In Search of Morocco Through Its Stories and Storytellers*.

Living to Tell

Still more daring and distinctive Moroccan voices have found their way into print over the past two decades, both at home and abroad.

Among the most famous works to be published by a Moroccan author are *Dreams of Trespass: Tales of a Harem Girlhood* and *The Veil and the Male Elite: A Feminist Interpretation of Women's Rights in Islam,* both by Fatima Mernissi, an outspoken feminist and professor at the University of Rabat. In Rabati author Leila Abouzeid's *Year of the Elephant* and *The Director and Other Stories from Morocco,* tales of Moroccan women trying to reinvent life on their own terms become parables for Morocco's search for independence after colonialism.

The past several years have brought increased acclaim for Moroccan writers, who have continued to address highly charged topics despite repeated press crackdowns. Inspired by *Anfas/Souffles,* Fez-born expatriate author Tahar ben Jelloun combined poetic devices and his training as a psychotherapist in his celebrated novel *The Sand Child,* the story of a girl raised as a boy by her father in Marrakesh, and its sequel *The Sacred Night,* which won France's Prix Goncourt. In *The Polymath,* 2009 Naguib Mahfouz Prize–winner Bensalem Himmich reads between the lines of 14th-century scholar and political exile Ibn Khaldun, as he tries to stop wars and prevent his own isolation. Several recent Moroccan novels have explored the promise and trauma of emigration, notably Mahi Binebine's harrowing *Welcome to Paradise,* Tahar ben Jelloun's *Leaving Tangier* and Laila Lalami's celebrated *Hope and Other Dangerous Pursuits.*

In *Stolen Lives: Twenty Years in a Desert Jail,* Malika Oufkir describes her demotion from courtier to prisoner after her father's plot to assassinate King Hassan II. Unsurprisingly, it was initially banned in Morocco on its publication.

Cinema
On Location in Morocco

Until recently Morocco has been seen mostly as a stunning movie backdrop, easily stealing scenes in such dubious cinematic achievements as *Sex and the City 2, Prince of Persia, Alexander, Ishtar, Troy* and *Sahara.* But while there's much to cringe about in Morocco's IMDb filmography, the country had golden moments on the silver screen in Hitchcock's *The Man Who Knew Too Much,* Orson Welles' *Othello* and David Lean's *Lawrence of Arabia.*

Morocco has certainly proved its versatility: it stunt-doubled for Somalia in Ridley Scott's *Black Hawk Down,* Tibet in Martin Scorsese's *Kundun* and Lebanon in Stephen Gaghan's *Syriana,* and *Inception's* Kenyan

MOROCCO'S LANDMARK CINEMA REVIVAL

Despite Morocco's creative boom, cinephiles have begun to fear for Morocco's movie palaces, since ticket prices can't compete with cheap pirated DVDs. In 2007, only 5% of Morocco's population went to the movies, while more than 400,000 pirated DVDs were symbolically seized from souq stalls in Rabat and Casablanca. Thirty years ago, there were 250 cinemas in Morocco; in 2010, only 30 were left.

Moroccan cinema buffs are rallying with **Save Cinemas in Marocco** (savecinemas inmarocco.com), an initiative that is preserving and promoting Morocco's historic movie palaces as architectural wonders and key modern landmarks in Morocco's ancient storytelling tradition. Tangier's 1930s Cinema Rif reopened in 2006 as Cinematheque de Tanger, a nonprofit cinema featuring international independent films and documentaries. Cinema Camera in Meknès – possibly Morocco's most glorious art-deco picture house – continues to thrive on mainstream Egyptian, Hollywood and Bollywood fare. Check out its fabulous 'Golden Era Hollywood' mural as its stairs sweep up to the auditorium.

The Moroccan government is showing initiative, too: in 2008, the state launched Aflam, a new, free, national TV channel showcasing Moroccan-made movies, and films dubbed or subtitled in French, Darija and Tamazight. With the runaway success of the Marrakesh International Film Festival, state-sponsored movie festivals are springing up across Morocco; check www.maghrebarts.ma/cinema.html for schedules.

dreamscape was actually Tangier. Morocco also stole the show right out from under John Malkovich by playing itself in Bernardo Bertolucci's *The Sheltering Sky,* and untrained local actors Mohamed Akhzam and Boubker Ait El Caid held their own with Cate Blanchett and Brad Pitt in the 2006 Oscar-nominated *Babel.*

Morocco's Directorial Breakthrough

Historically, Morocco has imported its blockbusters from Bollywood, Hollywood and Egypt, but today, Moroccans are getting greater opportunities to see films shot in Morocco that are actually by Moroccans and about Morocco. The home-grown film industry produced 18 feature films and 80 shorts in 2010, compared with four features and six shorts in 2004.

Moroccan filmmakers are putting decades of Ouallywood filmmaking craft and centuries of local storytelling tradition to work telling epic modern tales, often with a *cinéma vérité* edge. Morocco's 2010 Best Foreign Film Oscar contender was Nour-Eddine Lakhmari's *Casanegra,* about Casablanca youth thinking fast and growing up faster as they confront the darker aspects of life in the White City. Other hits include Latif Lahlou's 2010 *La Grande Villa,* tracking one couple's cultural and personal adjustments after relocating from Paris to Casablanca.

Euro-Moroccan films have already become mainstays of the international festival circuit, notably Faouzi Bensaïdi's family-history epic *A Thousand Months,* winner of the 2003 Cannes Film Festival Le Premier Regard, and Laïla Marrakchi's *Marock,* about a Muslim girl and Jewish boy who fall in love, which screened at Cannes in 2005. With their stylish handling of colliding personal crises in 2006's *Heaven's Doors,* twentysomething Spanish-Moroccan directors Swel and Imad Noury hit the festival circuit with *The Man Who Sold the World,* a Dostoyevsky-existentialist fable set in Casablanca.

Thanks to critical acclaim and government support, new voices and new formats are emerging in Moroccan cinema. Young directors are finding their voices through a new film school in Marrakesh and short-film showcases, including back-to-back short-film festivals in Rabat and Tangier in October. A 2009 film-festival favourite, Hakim Belabbes' feature-length documentary *Ashlaa* (In Pieces) collages 10 years of footage of the director's extended family into a compelling family portrait. Women directors have stepped into the spotlight, from Farida Benlyazid's 2005 hit *The Dog's Life of Juanita Narboni,* a Spanish expat's chronicle of Tangier from the 1930s to the 1960s, to rising star Mahassine El Hachadi, who won the short-film prize at the 2010 Marrakesh International Film Festival while still in film school. Leila Kilani's *Les Yeux Secs* (2003) broke further ground by not only being filmed in Amazigh rather than Arabic, but tackling hard subjects like female trafficking and prostitution. The use of social critique and even occasional nudity has brought criticism from Moroccan Islamists – with film-makers unafraid to push back in the name of artistic freedom.

LITERATURE & CINEMA CINEMA

None of the 1942 classic *Casablanca* was actually shot in Casablanca. It was filmed on a Hollywood back lot, and the Rick's Café Américain set was based on the historic El-Minzah Hotel in Tangier.

How big is Bollywood in Morocco? In 2005, more than a third of the movies shown in Morocco were Bollywood films, and a 2008 Casablanca screening of *Chalte Chalte* starring Shahrukh Khan with an in-person appearance by co-star Rani Mukerji drew 50,000 devoted fans.

Art & Crafts

The usual arts and crafts hierarchy is reversed in Morocco, where the craft tradition is ancient and revered, while visual art is a more recent development. Ornament is meant to be spiritually uplifting, while nonfunctional objects and representational images have traditionally been viewed as pointless – or worse, vanity verging on idolatry. While Morocco's contemporary visual-arts scene remains small, its many beautiful crafts – from carpets and leather to pottery and metalwork – make the quintessential souvenir of any trip.

Visual Art

Moroccan Art Stars

Mahi Binebine – ethereal figures in beeswax, colliding, pulling apart, not seeing one another

Hassan Echair – objects hanging in tenuous balance: white fence-posts, charcoal, twigs wrapped in string

Larbi Cherkaoui – gestural and seemingly urgent calligraphic flourishes on goatskin

Perhaps because it has been relegated to a marginal position, Moroccan contemporary art has particular poignancy and a sense of urgency, expressing aspirations and frustrations that can be understood instinctively – while eluding media censorship.

The new artworks emerging from Morocco are not kitschy paintings of eyelash-batting veiled women and scowling turbaned warriors, though you'll still find these in tourist showrooms. These form a 19th-century French Orientalist tradition made largely for export, and contemporary Moroccan artists like Hassan Hajjaj are cleverly tweaking it. Hajjaj's provocative full-colour photographs of veiled women are not what you'd expect: one tough lady flashing the peace sign wears a rapper-style Nike-logo veil, emblazoned with the slogan 'Just Do It' across her mouth.

Morocco's visual-art scene put down roots in the 1950s and '60s, when folk artists in Essaouira and Tangier made painting and sculpture their own by incorporating Berber symbols and locally scavenged materials. Landscape painting became a popular way to express pride of place in Essaouira and Assilah, and abstract painting became an important means of poetic expression in Rabat and Casablanca.

Marrakesh's art scene combines elemental forms with organic, traditional materials, helping to ground abstract art in Morocco as an indigenous art form. The scene has taken off in the past decade, with the **Marrakech Biennale** (www.marrakechbiennale.com) launched in 2005, the first School of Visual Arts MFA program two years later, and Morocco's first International Art Fair in 2009.

Calligraphy

To find out more about where those splendid traditional designs originated and learn to trace a few yourself, check out *The Splendour of Islamic Calligraphy* by Abdelkebir Khatibi and Mohammed Sijelmassi.

Calligraphy remains Morocco's most esteemed visual art form, practised and perfected in Moroccan *medersas* (theological colleges) over the last 1000 years. In Morocco, calligraphy isn't just in the Quran: it's on tiled walls, inside stucco arches, and literally coming out of the woodwork. Look carefully, and you'll notice that the same text can have an incredibly different effect in another calligraphic style. One calligrapher might take up a whole page with a single word, while another might turn it into a flower, or fold and twist the letters origami-style into graphic patterns.

The style most commonly used for Qurans is Naskh, a slanting cursive script introduced by the Umayyads. Cursive letters ingeniously interlaced to form a shape or dense design are hallmarks of the Thuluth style, while high-impact graphic lettering is the Kufic style from Iraq. You'll see three main kinds of Kufic calligraphy in Morocco: angular, geometric letters are square Kufic; ones bursting into bloom are foliate Kufic; and letters that look like they've been tied by sailors are knotted Kufic.

Lately, contemporary artists have reinvented calligraphy as a purely expressive art form, combining the elegant gestures of ancient scripts with the urgency of urban graffiti. Farid Belkahia's enigmatic symbols in henna and Larbi Cherkaoui's high-impact graphic swoops show that even freed of literal meanings, calligraphy can retain its poetry.

Crafts

For instant relief from sterile modernity, head to your nearest Moroccan souq to admire the inspired handiwork of local *mâalems* (master artisans). Most of Morocco's design wonders are created without computer models or even an electrical outlet, relying instead on imagination, an eye for colour and form, and steady hands you'd trust to take out a tonsil.

All this takes experience. In Fez, the minimum training for a ceramic *mâalem* is 10 years, and it takes a *zellij* mosaic maker three to four months to master a single shape – with 360 shapes to learn, mastery is a lifelong commitment. When you watch a *mâalem* at work, it's the confidence of the hand movements, not the speed, that indicates a masterwork is in the making. Techniques and tools are handed down from one generation to the next, and friendly competition among neighbours propels innovation.

Instead of sprawling factory showrooms, *mâalems* work wonders in cubby holes lining souqs, each specialising in a traditional trade. But artisans in rural areas are not to be outdone: many Moroccan villages are known for a style of embroidery or a signature rug design. Most of the artisans you'll see in the souqs are men, but you're likely to glimpse women *mâalems* working behind the scenes knotting carpets in Anti Atlas and Middle Atlas villages, weaving textiles along the Southern coast and painting ceramics in Fez, Salé and Safi.

Carpets

If you manage to return from Morocco without a carpet, you may well congratulate yourself on being one of few travellers to have outsmarted the wiliest salespeople on the planet.

The most reliable resource in English on Moroccan carpets is (the aptly named) *Moroccan Carpets,* by Brooke Pickering, W Russell Pickering and Ralph S Yohe. It's packed with photos to help pinpoint the origins and style of any carpet that mysteriously followed you home.

TOP CARPET-BUYING TIPS

➡ Know your limits. Namely, how much blank wall and floor space you actually have, your airline's luggage weight limit, the cost of shipping and duty, and purchase price.

➡ Tread cautiously with antique rugs. Few genuine antique rugs are left in Morocco. New rugs are aged by being stomped on, bleached by the sun or otherwise treated.

➡ Inspect the knots. You'll be asked to pay more for carpets with a higher number of knots per sq cm, which you'll begin to discern by examining the back of carpets to look for gaps between knots. Some carpets are washed in hot water to bind the wool together more tightly, but you can often distinguish these shrunken rugs by their misshapen, irregular borders.

➡ Get plenty of vegetables. Prices are often higher for carpets whose wool is coloured using vegetable dyes (which tend to fade faster) instead of synthetics; you can usually tell these by their muted tones, and the carpet-seller may be able to tell you what plant was used to make the dye.

➡ Enjoy the transaction. Banter before you bargain, keep your sense of humour, come back tomorrow, and drink mint tea so sweet you'll want to brush your teeth twice. Besides fond memories, at the end of it all you should have a carpet that suits you.

Moroccan carpets hook travellers almost every time because there's a right carpet for almost everyone – and if that sounds like something your mother once said to you about soul mates, it's not entirely a coincidence. Women in rural Morocco traditionally created carpets as part of their dowries, expressing their own personalities in exuberant colours and patterns, and weaving in symbols of their hopes for health and married life. Now carpets are mostly made as a way to supplement household income, but in the hands of a true *mâalem,* a hand-woven carpet brings so much personality and *baraka* (blessings) underfoot, it could never be mistaken for a mere doormat.

Carpets you see in the souqs may already have been bought and sold three or four times, with the final price representing a hefty mark-up over what the weaver was paid for her work. Consider buying directly from a village association instead: the producer is more likely to get her fair share of the proceeds, you'll get a better deal without extensive bargaining, and you may meet the artisan who created your new rug.

Fair-Trade Carpet

Jemaite Tifawin Carpet Cooperative, Anzal

Cooperative Feminin de Tissage Aït Bououli, Aït Bououli

Kasbah Myriem, Midelt

Coopérative de Tissage, Ouarzazate

Ensemble Artisanales in cities nationwide

Textiles

Anything not nailed down in Morocco is likely to be woven, sewn or embroidered – and even then, it might be upholstered. Moroccan women are the under-recognised *mâalems* of Moroccan textiles, and the tradition they've established has recently helped attract emerging fashion enterprises and global brands to Morocco. One-third of Moroccan women are employed in Morocco's industrial garment industry, but for meticulous handiwork with individual flair, check out traditional textile handicrafts.

Embroidery

Moroccan stitchery ranges from simple Berber designs to minutely detailed *terz Fezzi,* the elaborate nature-inspired patterns stitched in blue upon white linen that women in Fez traditionally spend years mastering for their dowries. Rabati embroidery is a riot of colour, with bold, graphic flowers in one or two colours of silk thread that almost completely obscures the plain-cotton backing. But the ladies of Salé also deserve their

---

CARPET CATEGORIES

Rabati carpets Plush pile carpets in deep jewel tones, featuring an ornate central motif balanced by fine detail along the borders. Many of the patterns may remind you of a formal garden, but you may see newer animal motifs and splashy modern abstract designs. Rabati carpets are highly prized, and could run you Dh2000 per sq metre.

Chichaoua rugs Simple and striking, with spare zigzags, asterisks, and enigmatic symbols on a variegated red or purple background. About Dh700 to Dh1000 per sq metre.

Hanbels or kilims These flat-woven rugs with no pile make up for a lack of cushiness with character. Some *hanbels* include Berber letters and auspicious symbols such as the evil eye, Southern Cross and Berber *fibule* (brooch) in their weave. Ask the seller to explain them for you – whether it's folklore or fib, the carpet-seller's interpretation adds to the experience. About Dh700 to Dh900 per sq metre.

Zanafi or glaoua Kilims and shag carpeting, together at last. Opposites attract in these rugs, where sections of fluffy pile alternate with flat-woven stripes or borders. These are usually Dh1000 to Dh1750 per sq metre.

Shedwi Flat-woven rugs with bold patterns in black wool on off-white, so au naturel you can still feel the lanolin between your fingers when you rub it. For as little as Dh400 for a smaller rug, they're impressive yet inexpensive gifts.

due for their striking embroidery in one or two bold colours along the borders of crisp white linen.

Passementerie

What's that guy doing with a blow-dryer and silk thread down a medina side alley? That would be a *passementerie* (trims) *mâalem* at work, using a repurposed blow-dryer to spin thread from a nail stuck in the wall until it's the perfect width and length to make into knotted buttons, silken tassels and snappy jellaba trim. In a cupboard-sized Moroccan *passementerie* shop, you'll find enough gold braid to decorate an army of generals and more tassels than a burlesque troupe could spin in a lifetime – but you'll also find a jackpot of small, portable gifts. Moroccan *mâalems* have made a stand-alone art of trimming, wrapping wire and washers with silk thread to create mod statement necklaces, napkin-ring holders, knotted keychains and curtain-pulls.

Felt

Handmade felt hats, slippers, coats, pillows, bags or floor coverings really put wool through the wringer: it's dyed, boiled and literally beaten to a pulp. Instead of being woven or sewn, felt is usually pounded with *savon noir* (natural palm soap), formed into the intended shape on a mould and allowed to dry gradually to hold its shape. Felt makers are usually found in the wool souq in major cities.

Weaving

Beyond the sea of imported harem pants and splashy synthetic jellabas in the souqs, hand-woven Moroccan fabrics with exceptional sheen and texture may catch your eye: nubby organic cotton from the Rif, shiny 'cactus silk' *(soie végétale)* woven with cotton and rayon from the south, sleek Marrakesh table linens and whisper-soft High Atlas woollen blankets. Some lesser-quality knock-offs are industrially produced, but connoisseurs seek out the plusher nap, tighter weave and elegant drape of hand-woven Moroccan fabrics.

In souqs, village cooperatives and Ensemble Artisanal showrooms, you might glimpse two to four women at a time on a loom, working on a single piece. Men work larger looms for jellaba fabric, pushing the shuttle with arms as they pound pedals with their feet – producing one metre of fabric this way is a workout equivalent to running several miles while dribbling a basketball. You can buy linens and clothing ready-made or get hand-woven fabric by the bolt or metre, and have Moroccan decor and couture custom-made to your specifications. Tailors can be found in every major city, but be sure to leave enough time for the initial consultation plus two fittings for clothing.

Leatherwork

Now that there's not much call for camel saddles anymore, Moroccan leather artisans keep busy fashioning embossed leather book covers and next season's must-have handbags with what look like medieval dentistry tools. Down medieval *derbs* (alleys), you'll discover freshly tanned and dyed lime-green leather sculpted into fashion-forward square pouffes (ottomans), yellow pompoms carefully stitched onto stylish fuchsia kidskin gloves, or shocking silver leather stretched and sewn into flouncy bedroom slippers. Along these leather souqs, you might spot artisans dabbing henna onto stretched goatskin to make 'tattooed' leather candle holders, lampshades or stand-alone artworks. If you're in town for a couple of days, you might even commission an artisan to make you a custom-made bag, lambskin leather jacket or jodhpurs.

ART & CRAFTS CRAFTS

Emerging Art Talents

Khadija Kabbaj – basketry tables, mummified Barbies and other subversively applied traditions

Hicham Benohoud – self-portraits with faces obliterated by shredded paper, sticky notes, corks

Hassan Hajjaj – mock fashion photos of women in Louis Vuitton veils and Moroccan-flag jellabas

The Art of the Islamic Tile, by Gerard Degeorge and Yves Porter, celebrates the splendours of ceramics across the Middle East, from Istanbul to Fez.

If it's an authenticity trip you're after, for men you'll prefer the traditional yellow *babouche*s (slippers) or 'Berber Adidas', leather slippers with soles made from recycled rubber tyres. Women's *babouche*s come in a broader range of colours and designs, and you may see vats of vibrant dye used for them in tanneries in Fez. But as colourful as they may look from afar, the tanneries give off a putrid stench – many medina residents would prefer to see them outside the city limits.

Plain terracotta cooking tajines are oven safe, fine for stovetop cooking and cost less than Dh80. Wrap them well against breakages on the trip home.

Ceramics

Moroccan ceramics are a delight, and excellent value – a decorative tajine may run you Dh150 to Dh400, depending on size and decoration. Different regions have their own colour schemes: Meknès ceramics tend to be green and black, Safi offers black and white Berber patterns, and Tamegroute makes a distinctive green glaze from oxidised copper. Salé is strong on yellow and turquoise, geometric patterns and intricate dot-patterned dishes. Marrakesh specialises in monochrome ceramics in red, graphite or orange instead of elaborate decoration. Many rural areas specialise in terracotta crockery, with plain, striking shapes and Berber good-luck symbols painted in henna.

Zellij

To make a Moroccan fountain, grab your hammer and chisel, and carefully chip a glazed tile into a geometrically correct shape. Good job – now only 6000 more to go to finish your water feature. Then again, you might leave it to the Moroccan mosaic masters to spiff up your foyer with glittering *zellij* end tables, entryway mirrors and fountains of all sizes. Fez has a reputation for the most intricate, high-lustre *zellij,* and the historic fountains around town dating from the Middle Ages are convincing advertisements for Fassi masterworks.

Brass, Copper & Silver

Tea is a performance art in Morocco, requiring just the right props. As though tea poured from over your head wasn't dramatic enough, gleaming brass teapots and copper tea trays are hammered by hand to catch the light and engraved with calligraphy to convey *baraka* on all who partake. Pierced brass lamps and recycled tin lanterns add instant atmosphere – and if all else fails to impress, serve your guests a sliver of cake with an inlaid knife from Morocco's dagger capital, Kelaâ M'Gouna.

Most 'silver' tea services are actually nickel silver, and should cost accordingly – about Dh50 to Dh250 for the teapot, and usually more for the tray (depending on size and design).

Jewellery

Not all that glitters is gold in Morocco, since Berbers traditionally believe gold to be a source of evil. You may see some jewellers with magnifying glasses working a tricky bit of gold filigree, but most gold you see in the souqs is imported from India and Bali. Sterling will be marked with 925, and is often sold by weight rather than design. Morocco's mining operations are more concerned with phosphates and fossils than with precious gems, but you will see folkloric dowry jewellery and headdresses with semiprecious stones, including coral, agate, cornelian and amber.

Lots of the 'amber' you'll see in the souqs is plastic. The genuine article will have a faint incense smell when you light a match near it, and a slightly waxy feel.

But Moroccan *mâalems* don't need precious materials to create a thing of beauty. Ancient ammonite and trilobite fossils from Rissani make fascinating prehistoric amulets, and striking Berber *fibales* (brooches) in silver are Tiznit's speciality. Layered wood, nickel silver and brightly coloured enamel make groovy cocktail rings in Marrakesh, and desert Tuareg talismans in leather and silver are fitting gifts for a man of the world.

BUYING SUSTAINABLE SOUVENIRS

Most Sustainable: Tyre Crafts

Used tyres don't biodegrade, and burning them produces toxic fumes – but when cleverly repurposed by Moroccan artisans, they make fabulous home furnishings. Tyre-tread mirrors make any entryway look dashingly well-travelled and inner-tube tea trays are ideal for entertaining motorcycle gangs. For the best selection, visit the tyre-craft *mâalems* (master artisans) lining the south end of Rue Riad Zitoun el-Kedim in Marrakesh.

Quite Sustainable: Argan Oil

The finest cosmetic oil to ever pass through the business end of a goat. Outside Essaouira and in the Anti Atlas, goats climb low argan trees to eat the nuts, digesting the soft, fuzzy outer layer and passing the pit. Traditionally, women then collect the dung, and extract, clean and crack the pit to remove the nut, which is then pressed to yield the orange-tinted oil rich in vitamin E. This is arduous handwork, and buying from a collective is the best way to ensure that the women are paid fairly.

Possibly Sustainable: Berber Carpets & Blankets

Berber blankets are often made with wool so natural that you can feel the lanolin on them. Most weavers use a combination of natural and artificial dyes to achieve the desired brilliance and lightfastness. Some cooperatives card and dye their own wool for natural colours, but for bright colours it's better that they source their wool from reputable dyers instead of handling and disposing of chemical dyes themselves. For associations advancing best environmental practices and paying women weavers fairly, visit Kasbah Myriem (p344), Cooperative Feminin de Tissage Aït Bououli (p93), Jemaite Tifawin Carpet Cooperative (p127) and Association Gorge du Dadès (p136).

Not so Sustainable: Thuya Wood

The root of a juniper that grows only in Morocco, this caramel-coloured knotty burl is at risk of being admired to extinction. Buy carved thuya bowls and jewellery boxes only from artisans' collectives more likely to practise responsible collection and reforesting, such as the Cooperative Artisanal des Marqueteurs (p216) and the Cooperative Artisanale des Femmes de Marrakesh (p79).

Woodwork

The most pleasingly scented part of the souq is the woodworkers' area, aromatic from the curls of wood carpeting the floors of master-carvers' workshops. These are the *mâalems* responsible for the ancient carved, brass-studded cedar doors and those carved cedar *muqarnas* (honeycomb) domes that cause wonderment in Moroccan palaces. Tetouan, Meknès and Fez have the best reputations for carved wood ornaments, but you'll see impressive woodwork in most Moroccan medinas.

For the gourmets on your gift list, hand-carved orangewood *harira* (soup) spoons are small ladles with long handles that make ideal tasting spoons. Cedar is used for ornate jewellery boxes and hefty chip-carved chests are sure to keep the moths at bay. The most prized wood is thuya wood, knotty burl from the roots of trees indigenous to the Essaouira region. Buy from artisans' associations that practise responsible tree management and harvesting.

Answers to your every 'how'd they do that?' are on display at state-run Ensemble Artisanales, where you can watch *mâalems* at work and purchase their handiwork at fixed (if somewhat stiff) prices.

Architecture

Stubbed toes come with the territory in Morocco: with so much intriguing architecture to gawp at, you can't always watch where you're going. Some buildings are more memorable than others – as in any developing country there's makeshift housing and cheap concrete – but it's the striking variation in architecture that keeps you wondering what's behind that wall, down the block and over the next mountain pass. Here's some Moroccan landmarks likely to leave your jaw on tiled floors, and your toes in jeopardy.

Deco Villas

Top Deco

Villa des Arts,
Casablanca

Jardin Majorelle,
Marrakesh

Cinematheque,
Tangier

Plaza de España,
Melilla

El-Minzah Hotel,
Tangier

When Morocco came under colonial control, villes nouvelles (new towns) were built outside the walls of the medinas, with street grids and modern architecture imposing strict order. Neoclassical facades, mansard roofs and high-rises must have come as quite a shock when they were introduced by the French and Spanish.

But one style that seemed to bridge local Islamic geometry and streamlined European modernism was art deco. Painter Jacques Majorelle brought a Moroccan colour sensibility to deco in 1924, adding bursts of blue, green and acid yellow to his deco villa and Jardin Majorelle.

Author Tahir Shah's relocation to Casablanca and restoration of a historic home inspired *The Caliph's House,* including this observation: 'There can be no country on earth better suited to buying decorations than Morocco. Every corner of the kingdom has its own unique styles, each one perfected through centuries of craftsmanship.'

In its 1930s heyday, Casablanca cleverly grafted Moroccan geometric detail onto whitewashed European edifices, adding a signature Casablanca Mauresque deco look to villas, movie palaces and hotels, notably Marius Boyer's 1930 Cinéma Rialto and the 1922 Hôtel Transatlantique. Tangier rivalled Casablanca for Mauresque deco decadence, with its 1940s Cinematheque and 1930s El-Minzah Hotel – the architectural model for Rick's Cafe Américain in the 1942 classic film *Casablanca.* Mauresque elements can be seen in cities all over Morocco.

Funduqs

Eight of the world's leading Islamic architectural scholars give you their best explanations in *Architecture of the Islamic World: Its History and Social Meaning* by Oleg Grabar et al.

Since medieval times, these creative courtyard complexes featured ground-floor artisans' workshops and rented rooms upstairs – from the nonstop *funduq* flux of artisans and adventurers emerged cosmopolitan ideas and new inventions. *Funduqs* once dotted caravan routes, but as trading communities became more stable and affluent, most *funduqs* were gradually replaced with private homes and storehouses. Happily, 140 *funduqs* remain in Marrakesh, including historic *funduqs* near Pl Bab Fteuh, several lining Rue Dar el-Bacha and one on Rue el-Mouassine featured in the film *Hideous Kinky*. In Fez, an exemplary *funduq* dating from 1711 underwent a six-year renovation to become the spiffy Nejjarine Museum of Wooden Arts & Crafts. The state is investing Dh40 million to spruce up 98 more *funduqs,* so now's the time to see them in all their well-travelled, shop-worn glory.

Hammams

These domed buildings have been part of the Moroccan urban landscape since the Almohads, and every village aspires to a hammam of its own – often the only local source of hot water. Traditionally they are built of mudbrick, lined with *tadelakt* (satiny hand-polished limestone plaster that traps moisture) and capped with a dome with star-shaped vents to let steam escape. The domed main room is the coolest area, with side rooms offering increasing levels of heat to serve the vaguely arthritic to the woefully hung-over.

The boldly elemental forms of traditional hammams may strike you as incredibly modern, but actually it's the other way around. The hammam is a recurring feature of landscapes by modernist masters Henri Matisse and Paul Klee, and Le Corbusier's International Style modernism was inspired by the interior volumes and filtered light of these iconic domed North African structures. *Tadelakt* has become a sought-after surface treatment for pools and walls in high-style homes, and pierced domes incorporated into the 'Moroccan Modern' style feature in umpteen coffee-table books. To see these architectural features in their original context, pay a visit to your friendly neighbourhood hammam – there's probably one near the local mosque, since hammams traditionally share a water source with ablutions fountains.

Historic Hammams

Hammam Dar el-Bacha, Marrakesh

Hammam Lalla Mira, Essaouira

Douches Barakat, Chefchaouen

Hammam Bab Doukkala, Marrakesh

Archaeological excavations, Aghmat

Kasbahs

Wherever there were once commercial interests worth protecting in Morocco – salt, sugar, gold, slaves – you'll find a kasbah. These fortified quarters housed the ruling family, its royal guard, and all the necessities for living in case of a siege. The *mellah* (Jewish quarter) was often positioned within reach of the kasbah guard and the ruling power's watchful eye. One of the largest remaining kasbahs is Marrakesh's 11th-century kasbah, which still houses a royal palace and acres of gardens, and flanks Marrakesh's *mellah*. Among the most photogenic northern kasbahs are

HAMMAM ETIQUETTE

Visiting a hammam (traditional bathhouse) is infinitely preferable to cursing under a cold shower in a cheap hotel. They're busy, social places, where you'll find gallons of hot water, and staff available to scrub you clean. They're also good places to meet the locals and, especially for women, somewhere to escape street hassle.

Every town has at least one hammam, often a modern, white-tiled and spacious affair. Often there are separate hammams for men and women; others open to either sex at different hours or on alternate days.

Some hammams are unmarked and others simply have a picture of a man or woman stencilled on the wall outside; locals will happily direct you. Most hammams are welcoming, but a few (often those close to a mosque) are unwilling to accept foreign visitors.

Bring your own towels (in a waterproof bag), a plastic mat or something to sit on, and flip-flops (thongs). Some hammams sell toiletries; look out for *ghassoul* (clay mixed with herbs, dried roses and lavender), *el-kis* (coarse glove), black soap made from the resin of olives (which stings if you get it in your eyes) and henna (used by women).

You'll be given a bucket and scoop; remember to use the communal bucket when filling yours with water. Most hammams have showers.

Hammam admission is typically around Dh10 (more in tourist areas), plus the optional extras of *gommage* (scrub) and massage.

A few midrange and top-end hotels have more expensive hammams, which normally require advance notice to heat up, and a minimum of four or five people.

ENDANGERED MONUMENTS: GLAOUI KASBAHS

The once spectacular Glaoui kasbahs at Taliouine, Tamdaght, Agdz and especially Telou-et have been largely abandoned to the elements – go and see them now, before they're gone. These are deeply ambivalent monuments: they represent the finest Moroccan artistry (no one dared displease the Glaoui despots) but also the betrayal of the Alawites by the Pasha Glaoui, who collaborated with French colonists to suppress his fellow Mo-roccans. But locals argue Glaoui kasbahs should be preserved, as visible reminders that even the grandest fortifications were no match for independent-minded Moroccans.

the red kasbah overlooking all-blue Chefchaouen, and Rabat's white-washed seaside kasbah with its elegantly carved gate, the Bab Oudaia.

Unesco World Heritage designations saved Taourirt kasbah in Ouarza-zate and the rose-coloured mudbrick Aït Benhaddou, both restored and frequently used as film backdrops. To see living, still-inhabited kasbahs, head to Anmiter and Kasbah Amridil in Skoura Oasis.

Ksour

The location of *ksour* (mudbrick castles; singular *ksar*) are spectacularly formidable: atop a rocky crag, against a rocky cliff, or rising above a palm oasis. Towers made of metres-thick, straw-reinforced mudbrick are el-egantly tapered at the top to distribute the weight, and capped by zigzag *merlon* (crenellation). Like a desert mirage, a *ksar* will play tricks with your sense of scale and distance with its odd combination of grandeur and earthy intimacy. From these watchtowers, Timbuktu seems much closer than 52 days away by camel – and in fact, the elegant mudbrick architecture of Mali and Senegal is a near relative of Morocco's *ksour*.

To get the full effect of this architecture in splendid oasis settings, visit the *ksour*-packed Drâa and Dadès Valleys, especially the fascinating ancient Jewish *ksar* at Tamnougalt and the pink/gold/white *ksar* of Aït Arbi, teetering on the edge of the Dadès Gorge. Between the Drâa Valley and Dadès Valley, you can stay overnight in an ancient *ksar* in the castle-filled oases of Skoura and N'Kob, or pause for lunch at Ksar el-Khorbat and snoop around 1000-year-old Ksar Asir in Tinejdad.

In 2009, Dh230 million was set aside to restore *ksour* and kasbahs, with top priorities in Er-Rachidia, Erfoud and Rissani.

Caravan stops are packed with well-fortified *ksour*, where merchants brought fortunes in gold, sugar and spices for safekeeping after 52-day trans-Saharan journeys. In Rissani, a half-hour circuit will lead you past half a dozen splendid ancient *ksour*, some of which are slated for restora-tion. Along caravan routes heading north through the High Atlas toward Fez, you'll spot spectacular *ksour* rising between snowcapped mountain peaks, including a fine hilltop tower that once housed the entire 300-person community of Zaouiat Ahansal.

Medersas

More than schools of rote religious instruction, Moroccan *medersas* have been vibrant centres of learning for law, philosophy and astronomy since the Merenid dynasty. For enough splendour to lift the soul and distract all but the most devoted students, visit the *zellij*-bedecked 14th-century Medersa el-Attarine in Fez and its rival for top students, the intricately carved and stuccoed Ali ben Youssef Medersa in Marrakesh. Now open as museums, these *medersas* give some idea of the austere lives students led in sublime surroundings, with long hours of study, several roommates, dinner on a hotplate, sleeping mats for comfort and one bathroom for up to 900 students. While other functioning *medersas* are closed to non-Muslims, Muslim visitors can stay overnight in some Moroccan *med-*

ersas, though arrangements should be made in advance and a modest donation is customary.

Mosques

Even small villages may have more than one mosque, built on prime real estate in town centres with one wall facing Mecca. Mosques provide moments of sublime serenity in chaotic cities and on busy village market days, and even non-Muslims can sense their calming influence. Towering minarets not only aid the acoustics of the call to prayer, but provide a visible reminder of God and community that puts everything else – minor spats, dirty dishes, office politics – back in perspective.

Mosques in Morocco are closed to non-Muslims, with two exceptions that couldn't be more different: Casablanca's sprawling Hassan II Mosque and austere Tin Mal Mosque nestled in the High Atlas. The Hassan II Mosque was completed in 1993 by French architect Michel Pinseau with great fanfare and considerable controversy: with room for 25,000 worshippers under a retractable roof and a 210m-high laser-equipped minaret, the total cost has been estimated at €585 million, not including maintenance or restitution to low-income former residents moved to accommodate the structure (the cases are still apparently pending). At the other end of the aesthetic spectrum is the elegant simplicity of Tin Mal Mosque, built in 1156 to honour the Almohads' strict spiritual leader, Mohammed ibn Tumart, with cedar ceilings and soaring arches that lift the eye and the spirits ever upward.

Muslims assert that no Moroccan architecture surpasses buildings built for the glory of God, especially mosques in the ancient Islamic spiritual centre of Fez. With walls and ablutions fountains covered in lustrous green and white Fassi *zellij* (ceramic tile mosaic), and mihrabs (niches indicating the direction of Mecca) swathed in stucco and marble, Fez mosques are purpose-built for spiritual glory. When vast portals are open between prayers, visitors can glimpse (no photos allowed) Fez' crowning glory: Kairaouine Mosque and Medersa, founded in the 8th century by a Fassi heiress. Non-Muslims can also see Morocco's most historic *minbar* (pulpit): the 12th-century Koutoubia *minbar,* inlaid with silver, ivory and marquetry by Cordoba's finest artisans, and housed in Marrakesh's Badi Palace.

Ramparts

Dramatic form follows defensive function in many of Morocco's trading posts and ports. The Almoravids took no chances with their trading capital, and wrapped Marrakesh in 16km of pink pisé (mudbrick reinforced with clay and chalk), 2m thick. Coastal towns like Essaouira and Assilah have witnessed centuries of piracy and fierce Portuguese-Moroccan trading rivalries – hence the heavy stone walls dotted by cannons, and crenellated ramparts that look like medieval European castle walls.

Riads

Near palaces in Morocco's major cities are grand riads, courtyard mansions where families of royal relatives, advisors and rich merchants whiled away idle hours gossiping in *bhous* (seating nooks) around arcaded courtyards paved with *zellij* and filled with songbirds twittering in fruit trees. Not a bad set-up, really, and one you can enjoy today in one of the many converted riad guesthouses in Marrakesh and Fez.

So many riads have become B&Bs over the past decade that 'riad' has become a synonym for 'guesthouse' – but technically, an authentic riad has a courtyard garden divided in four parts, with a fountain in the centre. A riad is also not to be confused with a *dar,* which is a simpler,

The only fully active mosque non-Muslims are allowed to visit in Morocco is Casablanca's Hassan II Mosque. It's the world's fifth-largest mosque, so you won't be cramping anyone's style.

In addition to ancient fortress walls, 3m- to 6m-high border barriers wrap the Mediterranean towns of Ceuta and Melilla. Spain and Morocco dispute their sovereignty, and local architecture does nothing to resolve the conflict: the Spanish point out Andalucian elements, which Moroccans will certainly remind you developed under Almohad rule.

LOST IN THE MEDINA MAZE? FOLLOW SOUQ LOGIC

In labyrinthine Moroccan medinas, winding souqs hardly seem linear, but they do adhere to a certain logic. Centuries ago, market streets were organised by trade so that medieval shoppers would know where to head for pickles or camel saddles. More than other medinas, Fez souqs maintain their original medieval organisation: kiosks selling silver-braided trim are right off the kaftan souq, just down the street from stalls selling hand-woven white cotton for men's jellabas. What about wool? That's in a different souq, near stalls selling hand-carved horn combs for carding wool. The smelliest, messiest trades were pushed to the peripheries, so you'll know you're near the edge of the medina when you arrive at tanneries, livestock markets and egg souqs. In Marrakesh, the saddle-making souq is at the northeast end of the souq, not far from the tanneries.

*Medinas:
Morocco's Hidden
Cities* explores
the shadows of
ancient Moroccan
walled cities, with
painterly images
by French photographer Jean-Marc
Tingaud and
illuminating commentary by Tahar
ben Jelloun.

smaller house constructed around a central light well – a more practical structure for hot desert locales and chilly coastal areas. With more than 1000 authentic riads, including extant examples from the 15th century, Marrakesh is the riad capital of North Africa.

From outside those austere, metre-thick mudbrick walls, you'd never guess what splendours await beyond brass-studded riad doors: painted cedar ceilings, ironwork balconies and archways dripping with stucco. Upkeep isn't easy, and modernising mudbrick structures with plumbing and electricity without destabilising the foundations is especially tricky. But for all its challenges, this ancient material may be the building material of the future. Mudbrick insulates against street sound, keeps cool in summer and warm in winter, and wicks away humidity instead of trapping it like mouldy old concrete – no wonder green builders around the world are incorporating it into their constructions.

Souqs

In Morocco, souqs – the market streets of a medina – are often covered with palm fronds for shade and shelter, and criss-crossed with smaller streets lined with food stalls, storerooms and cubby-hole-sized artisans' studios carved into thick mudbrick walls. Unlike souqs, these smaller streets often do not have names, and are together known as a *qissaria*. Most *qissariat* are through streets, so when (not if) you get lost in them, keep heading onward until you intersect with the next souq or buy a carpet, whichever happens first.

Top Souqs

*Okchen Market,
Meknès*

*Souq Sebbaghine
(Dyers' Souq),
Marrakesh*

*Souq an-Nejjarine
(Carpenters'
Souq), Fez*

*Souq el-Ghezel
(Wool Souq), Salé*

*Marché Central,
Casablanca*

Zawiyas

Don't be fooled by modest appearances or remote locations in Morocco: even a tiny village teetering off the edge of a cliff may be a major draw across Morocco because of its *zawiya* (shrine to a *marabout*). Just being in the vicinity of a *marabout* (saint) is said to confer *baraka* (a state of grace). Zawiya Nassiriyya in Tamegroute is reputed to cure the ill and eliminate stress, and the *zawiya* of Sidi Moussa in the Aït Bougomez Valley is said to increase the fertility of female visitors.

To boost your *baraka* you can visit the Tamegroute and Aït Bougomez *zawiyas* as well as the *zawiya* of Moulay Ali ash-Sharif in Rissani, which is now open to non-Muslims. Most *zawiyas* are closed to non-Muslims – including the famous Zawiya Moulay Idriss II in Fez, and all seven of Marrakesh's *zawiyas* – but you can often recognise a *zawiya* by its ceramic green-tiled roof and air of calm even outside its walls. In rural areas, a *marabout's* shrine (often confusingly referred to as a *marabout* rather than *zawiya*) is typically a simple mudbrick base topped with a whitewashed dome – though in the Ourika Valley village of Tafza you can see a rare red-stone example.

Natural Wonders

Morocco's geographical variety can come as a surprise. A day's journey can take you from Atlantic beaches through rich farmland, and over high mountain passes to the Sahara itself. The human landscape is no less fascinating – half of all Moroccans still live in rural areas, and everywhere you'll spot people working this extraordinary land, harvesting barley on tiny stone-walled terraces hewn from cliffsides, tending to olive and argan groves, or leading their flocks of sheep to mountain pastures.

Coastline

When the Umayyads arrived in Morocco, they rode their horses onto Atlantic beaches and dubbed the country *Al-Maghreb* (where the sun sets), knowing that the sea marked the westernmost limit of their conquests. The coast has played a central role in Moroccan history, from the Barbary pirates to the Allied landings of WWII, but it's learning to relax: King Mohammed VI's Plan Azur is currently developing stretches of Moroccan coastline into shiny new tourist hubs complete with holiday villas, beach resorts and golf courses. Luckily for nature lovers, there's still pristine coastline in between, with rare shorebirds and cliff's-edge vistas.

Fishing and international trade have defined the Atlantic coastal economy ever since the Phoenicians and Romans established their port at Lixus. But the Atlantic also has its wild side, with raw, rocky beaches around whitewashed Assilah, and wetland habitats, such as the lagoon of Merja Zerga National Park, attracting flamingos and rare African wildfowl. South of Casablanca are the ports of Oualidia and Essaouira, former pirate coves where rare wildlife still flourishes and Morocco's best seafood is served port-side. South of the commercialised boardwalks of Agadir, resort beaches empty into great sandy expanses stretching through Western Sahara to Mauritania. Morocco's southern Atlantic coast has recently reprised its notorious pirate ways, smuggling sub-Saharan African immigrants to the Canary Islands.

By contrast, the craggy Mediterranean coast has remained relatively undeveloped until recently, despite a spectacular coastline of sheltered coves and plunging cliffs. Tangier and the port towns of Ceuta and

If you're going for a dip, be aware that the Atlantic rollers can hide some fearsome riptides, and once you're in the waters there's nothing between you and the Americas (or at best, the Canary Islands).

DUST-UP IN THE DESERT

To see the desert the way nature intended, take a dromedary instead of an all-terrain vehicle. The 4WDs break up the surface of the desert, which is then scattered into the air by strong winds. By one estimate, the annual generation of dust has increased by 1000% in North Africa in the last 50 years – a major contributor to drought, as dust clouds shield the earth's surface from sunlight and hinder cloud formation. What happens in the desert has far-reaching consequences: dust from the Sahara has reached as far away as Greenland. If you travel by camel instead, desert wildlife won't be scared off by the vibrations, and you're much more likely to spot small, sensitive and rather adorably big-eared desert creatures like the fennec fox, jerboa and desert hedgehog.

Melilla make the best of their advantageous positions, with scenic overlooks and splendid coastal villas. The major barrier to the east is the Rif Mountains, rugged terrain inhabited by staunchly independent Riffian Berbers who effectively resisted colonial control and speak their own language (Tarifit). The Rif has remained politically marginalised, which has one highly debatable advantage: kif (cannabis) is widely grown in the region east of Tetouan. But lack of access to essential services has compounded local poverty, and it's taken huge government investment to improve access to schooling and medicine via new infrastructure. Well-graded roads make exploring the Rif coastline more possible than ever before.

Mountains

Three mountain ranges ripple diagonally across a topographical map of Morocco: the Rif in the north, the Middle Atlas (south of Fez) and the High Atlas (south and northeast of Marrakesh), with the southern sub-chain of the Anti Atlas slumping into the desert. The monumental force of plate tectonics brought these ranges into existence. Around 60 million years ago, a dramatic collision of African and Eurasian plates lifted up the High Atlas, while closing the Strait of Gibraltar and raising the Alps and Pyrenees. More recently, the mountains have provided shelter for self-sufficient Berbers, a safe haven for those fleeing invaders and a strategic retreat for organising resistance against would-be colonisers.

When hiking in the Rif, try not to step on the kif. Morocco is the one of the world's largest producers of cannabis, most of it destined for markets in western Europe.

In the north, the low Rif Mountains form a green, fertile arc that serves as a natural coastal barrier. Even the Vandals and Visigoths were no match for independent-minded Riffian Berbers, who for millennia successfully used their marginal position to resist incursions from Europe and Africa alike.

The Middle Atlas is the Moroccan heartland, a patchwork of farmland that runs from Volubilis to Fez and gradually rises to mountain peaks covered with fragrant forests of juniper, thuya and cedar. This sublime trekking country is also home to the Barbary ape, Morocco's only (non-human) primate. Running northeast to southwest from the Rif, the range soars to 3340m at its highest point.

But the real drama begins east of Agadir, where foothills suddenly rise from their crouched position to form the gloriously precipitous High Atlas Mountains. South of Marrakesh, the High Atlas reach dizzy heights at Jebel Toubkal, North Africa's highest summit (4167m). On the lower flanks, the mountains are ingeniously terraced with orchards of walnuts, cherries, almonds and apples, which erupt into bloom in spring. The High Atlas hunkers down on the southeast into the Anti Atlas range, which protects the Souss Valley from the hot winds of the rising Sahara Desert.

Desert

No landscape is more iconic in Morocco than the desert, with rolling dunes and mudbrick *ksour* (fortified strongholds) rising majestically from hidden palm oases. But most of the desert is neither oasis nor dune, and it's virtually uninhabitable. Vast tracts of barren, sun-bleached *hammada* (stony desert) are interrupted by rocky gorges, baked over millions of years by the desert's ovenlike heat until the blackened surface turns glassy. The desert forms still-disputed borders east and south to Algeria and Mauritania. South of the Anti Atlas, the barren slopes trail off into the stony, almost trackless desert of Western Sahara.

Even today, the sight of an oasis on this desolate desert horizon brings a rush of elation and wonder – but when ancient caravans emerged after a gruelling 52-day trans-Saharan journey with final stretches of dunes at

Erg Chigaga and Tinfou, the glimpse of green on the horizon at Zagora was nothing short of life-saving. From Zagora, caravans heading to the Middle Atlas laden with gold proceeded warily through the Drâa Valley from one well-fortified *ksar* to the next, finally unloading the camels and packing up mules at Skoura oasis.

Some caravans passed through the ancient desert gates of Sijilmassa (near Rissani), though there was no easy route: one approach was via the rose-gold dunes of Erg Chebbi at Merzouga, while the other led past formidable Jebel Sarhro, inhabited by equally formidable seminomadic Aït Atta warriors. Today the mood in oases is considerably more relaxed, with a slow pace in the daytime heat and sociable evenings as visitors and locals gather around a warming fire.

Wildlife

Even after millennia of being inhabited, farmed and grazed, Morocco still teems with wildlife – a testament to sustainable traditional practices and careful resource management handed down through generations. Today Morocco's 40 different ecosystems provide a habitat for many endemic species, including flora and fauna that are rare elsewhere. Industrialisation has put considerable pressure on Morocco's delicately balanced natural environments, and while steps are being taken to create wildlife reserves for Morocco's endangered species, visitors can do their part to preserve natural habitats by staying on marked *pistes* (dirt tracks) and taking out waste.

Coastal Species

Away from the urban sprawl of port cities and resort complexes are long stretches of rugged Moroccan coastline, where people are far outnumbered by abundant bird populations and marine mammals such as dolphins and porpoises. Along beaches, you'll spot white-eyed gulls, Moroccan cormorants and sandwich terns. Seabirds and freshwater birds thrive in preserves such as Souss-Massa National Park, where you might spy endangered bald ibis along with the ducks and waders who migrate here from Europe for the winter. On Morocco's Mediterranean coast, you

One less-than-charming fact about snake charming: to prevent them from biting handlers, snakes' mouths are sometimes stitched closed. This often causes fatal mouth infections and leaves snakes unable to feed. To discourage this practice, don't pose with or tip snake charmers handling snakes whose mouths are stitched shut.

THE BARBARY LION – BACK FROM THE DEAD?

When Morocco's national football team – the Atlas Lions – take to the pitch, they're honouring one of the country's most iconic animals, albeit one that has long been on the extinct species list.

The Barbary Lion was North Africa's top predator. It was the largest and heaviest of all lion subspecies, with the males famed for their thick black manes. They were hunted by the Romans to provide sport for the gladiatorial combats of the Colosseum, while Moroccan sultans later gave them as diplomatic gifts. Slowly exterminated across the region through hunting and habitat loss, the lions persisted in heavily forested parts of Morocco's Atlas and Rif Mountains well into the 20th century. The last wild lion is thought to have been shot in 1942, although recent research suggests that populations survived into the 1960s – no doubt aided by their naturally solitary behaviour, rather than living in prides as lions do in the rest of Africa.

Remnant lion populations of mixed heritage survived in zoos across the world, including the personal zoo of the current king of Morocco. In recent years, a captive breeding program, coupled with the latest genetic fingerprinting techniques, has been attempting to recreate a genetically pure and viable population of the big cats. The ultimate aim of the International Barbary Lion Project is to create a protected reserve in the Atlas Mountains large enough to allow a limited reintroduction program. While this is a long way off – and the willingness of locals to share land with a top predator remains unknown – perhaps the last roar of this magnificent animal is yet to be heard.

might spot one of the world's most endangered animals: the Mediterranean monk seal. Only 450 to 600 remain, and a few have been sighted taking refuge in sheltered Moroccan coves.

Desert Habitats

The Sahara may seem like a harsh place, but it's home to numerous creatures, including several furry, cuddly ones: several varieties of fluffy gerbils; long-eared, spindly-legged, cartoonish jerboas; and the world's tiniest hedgehog, the desert hedgehog, tipping the scales at 300g to 500g. The delightful fennec fox has fur-soled feet and huge batlike ears to dissipate Sahara heat; pups look like Chihuahuas, only fuzzier. This desert fox is stealthy and nocturnal, but if you're travelling by dromedary and staying overnight in the desert, you might catch a brief glimpse.

While desert heat makes most humans sluggish, many desert creatures are elegant and swift. Dorcas gazelles are common, and you might also catch a glimpse of a rare, reddish Cuvier's gazelle. Lizards you might see darting through the desert include skinks and spiny-tailed lizards, and you might catch sight of the devilish-looking (though not especially poisonous) horned viper. Golden jackals are the most common predator in the Sahara, though in the more remote parts of the Western Sahara a few desert-adapted cheetahs may yet survive.

Mountain Wildlife

Forested mountain slopes are Morocco's richest wildlife habitats, where it's easy to spot sociable Barbary macaques (also known as Barbary apes) in the Rif and Middle Atlas, especially around Azrou. Less easy to track are mountain gazelles, lynx and the endangered mouflon, or Barbary sheep. The mouflon are now protected in a High Atlas preserve near the Tizi n'Test, where its only predator is the critically endangered Barbary leopard – the last population of leopards in North Africa.

Golden eagles soar in Atlas mountain updrafts, and High Atlas hikes might introduce you to red crossbills, horned larks, acrobatic booted eagles, Egyptian vultures, and both black and red kites. In springtime, butterflies abound in the mountains, including the scarlet cardinal and bright-yellow Cleopatra.

National Parks

With cities encroaching on natural habitats, the Moroccan government is setting aside protected areas to prevent the further disappearance of rare plant and animal species. Toubkal National Park in the High Atlas Mountains was the first national park to be created in 1942. After the vast Souss-Massa National Park was founded in 1991 outside Agadir, Morocco created four new national parks in 2004: Talassemtane (589 sq km) in the Rif; Al-Hoceima (485 sq km) in the Mediterranean, with outstanding coastal and marine habitats along the Mediterranean that include one of the last outposts of osprey; Ifrane National Park (518 sq km) in the Middle Atlas, with dense cedar forests and Barbary macaques; and the Eastern High Atlas National Park (553 sq km).

Today Morocco's 14 national parks and 35 nature reserves, forest sanctuaries and other protected areas overseen by Morocco's Direction des Eaux et Forêts are conserving species and advancing natural sciences. Park staff are tracking the region's biodiversity through botanical inventories, bird censuses, primate studies and sediment analyses. These studies are critical to understanding the broader causes of habitat loss, in Morocco and beyond; the Spanish and American Park Services have studied Morocco's parklands to better understand biodiversity concerns.

Sahara: A Natural History, by Marq de Villiers and Sheila Hirtle, is a highly readable account of the Sahara's wildlife, its people and geographical history.

The endangered Houbara bustard is making a comeback with the release of 5000 captive-bred birds into a 40,000-sq-km protected zone in Morocco's eastern desert – among the largest reintroductions of any endangered species in the world. Bustards are notoriously difficult to breed in captivity due to their intricate mating behaviour and nervous disposition.

NOTABLE NATIONAL PARKS

NATIONAL PARK	LOCATION	FEATURES	ACTIVITIES	BEST TIME
Toubkal National Park (p100)	near Marrakesh	highest peak in North Africa	hiking, climbing	May-Jun
Souss-Massa National Park (p366)	south of Agadir	coastal estuaries & forests; 275 species of birds, including endangered bald ibis, mammals & enclosed endangered species	wildlife-watching, birdwatching, hiking	Mar-Oct
Lac de Sidi Bourhaba (p190)	Mehdiya	lake & wetlands; 200 migratory bird species, including marbled duck, African marsh owl & flamingo	hiking, swimming, birdwatching	Oct-Mar
Merja Zerga National Park (p191)	Moulay Bousselham	lagoon habitats; 190 species of waterfowl, including African marsh owl, Andouin's gull, flamingo & crested coot	wildlife-watching	Dec-Jan
Talassemtane National Park (p266)	Chefchaouen	cedar & fir forests; Barbary macaque, fox, jackal & bats in the cedar forest	wildlife-watching, hiking	May-Sep
Bouarfa Wildlife Sanctuary	Bouarfa	red rock steppe	hiking, climbing	Apr-Oct
Tazzeka National Park (p350)	near Taza	oak forests & waterfalls	hiking	Jun-Sep
Al-Hoceima National Park (p265)	Al-Hoceima	thuya forest, limestone escarpments, fish eagles	birdwatching, hiking	May-Oct

Parks have proven a boon to local wildlife, but a mixed blessing for human residents. While national parks protect local ecosystems and attract tourist revenue, access for local communities to water, grazing land and wild plants harvested for food and medicine has been limited or cut off entirely. But by conserving parkland, the Ministries of Tourism and Agriculture aim to help local ecosystems flourish, gradually restore arable land and ultimately benefit local communities with ecotourism that provides a profitable alternative to kif cultivation. In the near future, fees for park admission may be instituted to support the parks' conservation, scientific and community missions. Meanwhile, the best sights in Morocco are still free and visitors can show their appreciation to local communities by supporting local NGOs along their route.

Creative Conservation

The only thing more natural than the wonders of Morocco is the impulse to preserve them. Morocco is in a fortunate position: to envision a more sustainable future, it can look to its recent past. Ancient *khettara* irrigation systems, still in use, transport water from natural springs to fields and gardens in underground channels, without losing precious water to evaporation. Although certification is still a novel concept, most small-scale Moroccan farming practices are organic by default, since chemical fertilisers are costly and donkey dung pretty much comes with the territory. Community hammams use power and water for steamy saunas more efficiently than individual showers or baths. Locally made, detergent-free *savon noir* ('black soap' made from natural palm and olive oils) is gentle enough for a shave and effective as laundry soap, without polluting run-off – and leftover 'grey water' can be used for gardens and courtyard fountains. With Morocco's traditional mudbrick architecture, metre-thick walls provide natural insulation against heat in summer and chill in winter, eliminating most street noise and the need for air-con and central heating.

Morocco is also thinking on its feet, becoming an early adopter of resource-saving new technologies. The pioneering nation is already harnessing wind power in the Rif, and Ouarzazate now produces a combined 500,000 megawatts of electricity at five sites, making it one of the world's largest solar-electricity generators.

To tackle challenges still ahead, Morocco will need all the resourcefulness it can muster – and all the support it can get from visitors. Due to the demands of city dwellers and tourist complexes, 37% of villages around Marrakesh now lack a reliable source of potable water. Damming to create reservoirs frequently strips downstream water of valuable silts needed to sustain farms and coastal wetlands. Forests are also under threat, with around 250 sq km of forest lost each year, including Moroccan pine, thuya and Atlas cedar. Pollution is a weighty concern, literally: Morocco's cities alone produce an annual harvest of 2.4 million tonnes of solid waste.

The Sahara Conservation Fund (www.sahara conservation. org) is dedicated to preserving the wild creatures of the Sahara, and provides a preview of wildlife you might spot in this vibrant desert ecosystem.

While Morocco is considering legislation on a host of environmental measures from wetlands protection to mandating biodegradable plastic bags, changes are already afoot in communities nationwide. Everywhere you travel in the country, you'll notice minor modifications that collectively make major savings in scarce resources – and you're invited to participate. Solar water heaters provide instant hot water for showers in the afternoon and evening, so taking showers at those times saves water that might otherwise be wasted by running the tap while gas heaters warm up. Reforestation programs are helping prevent erosion, and you can help by staying on marked mountain paths and supporting local NGO reforestation initiatives. Organic gardens provide fresh ingredients for meals, reducing the dependence on food transported over long distances – and ordering local, seasonal specialities provides positive reinforcement for local food sourcing. Morocco's Green Key program also certifies hotels and guesthouses that institute a range of resource-conserving measures, from low-flow toilets to environmentally friendly cleaning products, although it has received criticism from some quarters for granting certificates to hotels with distinctly high-impact facilities like swimming pools.

Add these traditional, national and local resource-saving practices together, and Morocco is poised not only to make the switch to sustainable tourism, but to show Europe how it's done.

Survival Guide

Directory A–Z

Accommodation

A wide range of accommodation options is available in Morocco.

The rates quoted here are for high season (November to April) weekends and, unless otherwise mentioned, exclude breakfast. Reviews are ordered by preference, and price ranges are based on the cost of a double room:

Budget (€) Up to Dh400

Midrange (€€) Dh400 to Dh800

Top end (€€€) More than Dh800

Exceptions to these price ranges are Casablanca, Essaouira, Fez, Marrakesh, Rabat and Tangier. For these places, the following price ranges apply:

Budget (€) Up to Dh600

Midrange (€€) Dh600 to Dh1200

Top end (€€€) More than Dh1200

In the listings here, the official, government-assigned rates (including taxes) are quoted, although these are intended as a guide only.

Discounts Many hotels will offer 'promotional discounts' from their advertised rates, especially in large resorts like Agadir or during the low season (May to October). It is always worth asking when you book.

Seasons Accommodation is often scarce during Easter week and August, popular times for Spanish and French tourists to visit Morocco. Another busy time, particularly in Marrakesh, is Christmas and New Year.

Solo travellers Outside the cities, the rates in many places are per person rather than per room, and single occupancy of rooms is rarely a problem. However, in riads, the limited accommodation means that discounts on single occupancy are fairly minimal.

Apartments

➡ If travelling in a small group or as a family, consider self-catering options, particularly in low season, when prices can drop substantially.

➡ Agadir, nearby Taghazout, Essaouira, Assilah and the bigger tourist centres on both coastlines have a fair number of self-catering apartments and houses,

sometimes in tourist complexes.

➡ **Airbnb** (www.airbnb.com) offers good rental options in many Moroccan cities.

Camping

➡ You can camp anywhere in Morocco if you have permission from the site's owner.

➡ There are many official campsites.

➡ Most official sites have water and electricity; some have a small restaurant, grocery store and even a swimming pool.

➡ Most of the bigger cities have campsites, although they're often some way from the centre.

➡ Such sites are sometimes worth the extra effort to get to, but often they consist of a barren and stony area offering little shade and basic facilities.

➡ Particularly in southern Morocco, campsites are often brimming with enormous campervans.

COSTS

➡ At official sites you'll pay around Dh10 to Dh20 per person, plus Dh10 to Dh20 to pitch a tent and about Dh10 to Dh15 for small vehicles.

➡ Parking a campervan or caravan typically costs around Dh20 to Dh30, although this can rise as high as Dh45.

BOOK YOUR STAY ONLINE

For more accommodation reviews by Lonely Planet authors, check out http://lonelyplanet.com/hotels/. You'll find independent reviews, as well as recommendations on the best places to stay. Best of all, you can book online.

PRACTICALITIES

Weights & Measures

➡ Morocco uses the metric system.

Newspapers & Websites

➡ For Moroccan newspapers online, visit www.onlinenewspapers.com/morocco.htm.

➡ French-language dailies include the semi-official **Le Matin** (www.lematin.ma), and the opposition **Libération** (www.libe.ma), **L'Opinion** (www.lopinion.ma) and *Al-Bayane*.

➡ Major European, British and American papers (or their foreign editions) and magazines are available in most of the main cities.

➡ English-language websites include the **Morocco Board News Service** (www.moroccoboard.com), **Morocco Newsline** (www.morocconewsline.com) and **Agence Maghreb Arabe Presse** (www.map.ma/en). **Maghrebarts** (www.maghrebarts.ma) has arts and media coverage.

Radio

➡ Most Moroccan radio stations broadcast in Arabic or French on AM or FM.

➡ Broadcasting across North Africa and Europe from Tangier, you can listen to the Maghrebi affairs and music station Médi 1 via radio (105.3MHz in Marrakesh and 95.3 or 101 in Tangier) and www.medi1.com.

➡ State-run **SNRT** (www.snrt.ma) has regional and national stations, including the urban Chaine Inter, available via radio (98.8MHz in Marrakesh and 90MHz in Casablanca) and www.chaineinter.ma.

Television & DVD

➡ Satellite dishes are everywhere, and pick up foreign stations.

➡ The major TV station, 2M, is partly state-owned and broadcasts in languages including Arabic and French via satellite, analogue and www.2m.ma.

➡ Médi 1's news and current-affairs broadcasts are available via satellite and www.medi1tv.com.

➡ Moroccan DVDs share region 5 with much of Africa and Asia (North America is region 1, Europe is mostly region 2 and Australia is region 4).

➡ Electricity generally costs another Dh10 to Dh15.

➡ A hot shower is about Dh5 to Dh10.

➡ Many campsites have basic rooms or self-catering apartments.

Gîtes d'Étape, Homestays & Refuges

➡ *Gîtes d'étape* are homes or hostels, often belonging to mountain guides, which offer basic accommodation (often just a mattress on the floor) around popular trekking routes in the Atlas and Rif Mountains.

➡ *Gîtes* have rudimentary bathrooms and sometimes hot showers.

➡ Larger than *gîtes*, mountain refuges offer Swiss-chalet-style accommodation.

➡ Accommodation at refuges is usually in dormitories with communal showers, and often includes a lively communal dining/living room.

➡ **Club Alpin Français** (CAF; ☎0522 27 00 90; http://cafmaroc2011.ffcam.fr; 50 Blvd Moulay Abderrahman, Quartier Beauséjour, Casablanca) runs refuges in the High Atlas.

➡ If you are trekking in the High Atlas or travelling off the beaten track elsewhere, you may be offered accommodation in village homes.

➡ Many homestays won't have running water or electricity, but you'll find them big on warmth and hospitality.

➡ You should be prepared to pay what you would at *gîtes d'étape* or mountain refuges.

Hostels

Part of Hostelling International, **Fédération Royale Marocaine des Auberges** de Jeunes (☎0522 47 09 52; http://tinyurl.com/373omvl) has reliable youth hostels in Casablanca, Fez, Marrakesh, Meknès, Ouarzazate and Rabat.

➜ If you're travelling alone, hostels are among the cheapest places to stay (Dh30 to Dh60 a night), but many are inconveniently located.

➜ Some offer kitchens, family rooms and breakfast.

➜ If looking for a budget hostel, beware of individuals' houses converted in the dead of night without the appropriate licences.

Hotels

➜ You'll need your passport number (and entry-stamp number) when filling in a hotel register.

➜ Some hotels in more isolated regions offer half-board (demi-pension), which means breakfast and dinner are included, or full-board (pension), also including lunch. This can be a good deal.

BUDGET

➜ You'll find cheap, unclassified (without a star rating) or one-star hotels clustered in the medinas of the bigger cities.

➜ Some are bright and spotless; others haven't seen a mop for years.

➜ Cheaper prices usually mean shared washing facilities and squat toilets.

➜ Many budget hotels don't supply soap in the bathrooms, so bring a bar or some gel.

➜ Occasionally there's a gas-heated shower, for which you'll pay an extra Dh5 to Dh10.

➜ Where there is no hot water at all, head for the local hammam.

➜ Many cheap hotels in the south offer a mattress on the roof terrace (Dh25 to Dh30); others also have traditional Moroccan salons, lined with banks of seats and cushions, where you can sleep for a similar price.

MIDRANGE

➜ Midrange hotels in Morocco are generally of a high standard.

➜ Options range from hotels offering Western-style rooms, which are modern if a little soulless, to riads and maisons d'hôtes (small hotels), which capture the essence of Moroccan style with comfort and character.

➜ In this price range, you should expect an en-suite room with shower.

➜ In cheaper areas such as the south, you may find midrange standards at budget prices.

TOP END

➜ Hotels in this bracket are similar to midrange places but with more luxurious levels of comfort and design.

➜ In resorts such as Agadir, many top-end hotels are self-contained holiday complexes, offering features such as golf courses, nightclubs and multiple restaurants.

Riads, Dars & Kasbahs

For many guests, the chance to stay in a converted traditional house is a major drawcard of a trip to Morocco. These midrange and top-end options are the type of accommodation that the term 'boutique hotel' could have been invented for, and no two are alike. Service tends to be personal, with many places noted for their food as much as their lodgings.

Locations Marrakesh is the most famous destination for riads (there are several hundred); Fez, Meknès, Essaouira and Rabat are also noteworthy. With their popularity seemingly unassailable, you can increasingly find riads in the most unexpected corners of the country.

Riads and dars Although the term riad is often used generically, a riad proper is a house built around a garden with trees. You'll also come across plenty of dars (traditional townhouses with internal courtyards).

Kasbahs Often functioning as hotels, kasbahs (old citadels) are found in tourist centres in central and southern Morocco. Rooms in kasbahs are small and dark, due to the nature of the building, but are lovely and cool in summer.

Booking Most riads operate on advance bookings, and it's worth planning ahead, as most only have a handful of rooms and can fill quickly. Advance booking often means that someone from the riad will be sent to meet you outside the medina when you arrive: labyrinthine streets conspire against finding the front door on your first attempt.

Rates Room rates are generally comparable to four- or five-star hotels. Many riads list their online rates in euros, rather than dirham, at exchange rates favourable to themselves, so always double check the prices when booking.

Customs Regulations

Importing or exporting dirham is forbidden, although checks are rare so don't worry about the loose change you may have at the end of a drink.

Forbidden items include 'any immoral items liable to cause a breach of the peace', such as 'books, printed matter, audio and video cassettes'.

Duty-free allowances are as follows:

➜ up to 200 cigarettes, or 25 cigars, or 250g of tobacco

➜ 1L of alcoholic drink

➜ 150ml of perfume

➜ presents or souvenirs worth up to Dh2000

Electricity

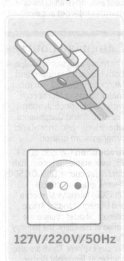

127V/220V/50Hz

Embassies & Consulates

The **Moroccan Ministry of Foreign Affairs and Cooperation** (www.diplomatie.ma/en) has a list of embassies and consulates in Morocco. Most embassies and diplomatic representation are in Rabat, and open from about 9am until noon, Monday to Friday. Rabat embassies include the following:

Algerian Embassy (Map p174; ☑0537 76 54 74; http://consulatalgerie-casablanca.com; 46-48 Ave Tariq ibn Zayid) Also has a consulate-general in Casablanca and consulate in Oujda.

Canadian Embassy (☑0537 68 74 00; www.rabat.gc.ca; 13 Rue Jaafar as-Sadiq, Agdal)

Dutch Embassy (Map p174; ☑0537 21 96 00; http://marokko.nlambassade.org; 40 Rue de Tunis) Also has a consulate-general in Casablanca.

French Embassy (Map p174; ☑0537 68 97 00; www.ambafrance-ma.org; 3 Rue Sahnoun, Agdal) Also has consu-

lates in Agadir, Casablanca, Fez, Marrakesh, Rabat and Tangier.

German Embassy (Map p180; ☑0537 21 86 00; www.rabat.diplo.de; 7 Rue Madnine) Also has a consulate in Rabat and honorary consulates in Agadir and Casablanca.

Mauritanian Embassy (☑0537 65 66 78; www.mauritania.mr/fr; 6 Rue Thami Lamdaouar, Soussi)

Spanish Embassy (Map p174; ☑0537 63 39 00; www.exteriores.gob.es/embajadas/rabat; Ave Annasr) Also has consulates-general in Agadir, Casablanca, Larache, Nador, Rabat, Tangier and Tetouan.

UK Embassy (Map p174; ☑0537 23 86 00; www.gov.uk/government/world/organisations/british-embassy-rabat; 17 Blvd de la Tour Hassan) Also has honorary consulates in Agadir, Marrakesh and Tangier.

US Embassy (Map p174; ☑0537 76 22 65; http://rabat.usembassy.gov; 2 Ave de Mohammed El Fassi) Also has a consulate-general in Casablanca.

The following countries do not have embassies in Morocco:

Australia (http://tinyurl.com/248erss) The Australian

embassy in Paris is responsible for Morocco. The Canadian embassy in Rabat provides consular assistance to Australians.

Ireland (www.dfa.ie/embassies/irish-embassies-abroad/europe/portugal) The Irish embassy in Lisbon is responsible for Morocco. Has honorary consulates in Agadir and Casablanca.

New Zealand (www.nzembassy.com/spain) The New Zealand embassy in Madrid is responsible for Morocco.

Gay & Lesbian Travellers

➡ Homosexual acts (including kissing) are illegal in Morocco, and carry a potential jail term of up to three years and/or a fine.

➡ In practice, although not openly admitted or shown, sex between men is not uncommon, even if few actively self-identify as gay.

➡ Platonic affection is freely shown among Moroccans, more so between men than women.

➡ For travellers, discretion is the key in most places. Avoid public displays of affection – aggression

---

GOVERNMENT TRAVEL ADVICE

For the latest travel information log on to the following websites:

www.auswaertiges-amt.de German Federal Foreign Office.

www.fco.gov.uk/travel UK Foreign & Commonwealth Office.

www.minbuza.nl Dutch Ministry of Foreign Affairs.

www.mofa.go.jp Japanese Ministry of Foreign Affairs.

www.safetravel.govt.nz New Zealand Ministry of Foreign Affairs and Trade.

www.smartraveller.gov.au Australian Government's travel advice and consular information.

www.travel.state.gov US Department of State's Bureau of Consular Affairs.

www.voyage.gc.ca Canadian Consular Services Bureau.

towards gay male travellers is not unheard of.

➡ Some towns are more gay-friendly than others, with Marrakesh winning the prize, followed by Tangier.

➡ There are no dedicated gay destinations, although 'gay' bars can be found here and there; nightlife in the bigger cities includes something for everybody.

➡ The pressures of poverty mean many young men will consider having sex for money or gifts. Exploitative relationships form an unpleasant but real dimension of the Moroccan gay scene.

➡ Lesbians shouldn't encounter any problems, though it's commonly believed by Moroccans that there are no lesbians in their country.

Websites

Useful websites that give the low-down on local laws and attitudes to homosexuality include the following:

Kif Kif (www.kifkifgroup.org/) Moroccan civil society organisation promoting lesbian, gay, bisexual and transsexual rights.

Gay & Lesbian Arab Society (www.glas.org) Resources on homosexuality in the Arab world.

Global Gayz (www.global-gayz.com) A useful resource with good links on Morocco.

Insurance

A travel-insurance policy to cover theft, loss and, in particular, medical problems is strongly recommended for all visitors to Morocco.

Activities Some policies specifically exclude 'dangerous activities', which can include scuba diving, motorcycling, skiing and even trekking, so ensure your policy covers these if needed.

Driving Make sure you have adequate travel medical insurance and any relevant car insurance if you're driving.

Extensions If you need to extend your cover on the road, do so before it expires or a more expensive premium may apply.

Flights Paying for your airline ticket with a credit card often provides some travel-accident insurance, but take note of exclusions. You may be able to reclaim the payment if the operator doesn't deliver.

Online insurance Worldwide travel insurance is available at www.lonelyplanet.com/travel_services. You can buy, extend and claim online any time – even if you're already on the road.

Purchase Buy travel insurance as early as possible. Buying just before you leave home may mean you're not covered for delays to your flight caused by strike action that began, or was threatened, before you took out the insurance.

Internet Access

➡ Moroccan internet cafes are common, efficient and cheap (Dh3 to Dh10 per hour), usually with reasonable connection speeds.

➡ Two irritants for many travellers are the widespread French and Arabic (nonqwerty) keyboards, and Moroccan men's common use of internet cafes to view pornographic websites and similar.

➡ The internet icon (@) is used for reviews where accommodation options offer a computer with internet for guest use.

➡ The wi-fi icon (📶) indicates that a business has a wireless network.

➡ Wi-fi is widely available in midrange and top-end accommodation and in many of the better budget options. It is slowly becoming more widespread in destinations that host lots of foreigners.

➡ If you're bringing a laptop, check the power-supply voltage and bring a universal adapter. USB modems

are widely available from mobile-phone shops, and cost around Dh200 for one month's internet access.

Language Courses

There are courses in Arabic – both Modern Standard and Moroccan (Darija) – in most major towns in Morocco, with a high concentration in Fez, Rabat and Casablanca, where long- and short-term programs are offered.

Arabophon (☎0535 60 34 75; www.arabicstudy.com; half-day/3-day course Dh500/1500; 4-week intensive course Dh4360) Intensive Moroccan and Modern Standard Arabic courses. Shorter courses are aimed at travellers: the half-day Curious Explorer and three-day Serious Explorer. There are also courses in Tamazight Berber. Lessons are offered in English, French and Spanish.

Jeunesse des Chantiers Marocains (http://perso.menara.ma/youthcamps) Offers language and cultural-immersion programs in Marrakesh.

Legal Matters

Drugs Moroccan law (p473) prohibits the possession, offer, sale, purchase, distribution and transportation of cannabis (known locally as kif). The penalties for possessing even small amounts of drugs are severe, and include up to 10 years' imprisonment, with no remission for good behaviour, heavy fines and confiscation of your vehicle or vessel. Acquittals in drug cases are rare.

Help & advice If you get into trouble, your first call should be to your embassy or consulate; remember that it's not unknown for local police to be in on scams. The London-based **Fair Trials International** (FTI; ☎4420-7762 6400; www.fairtrials.net) provides legal assistance and advocacy to individuals facing criminal charges in a foreign country.

Police If you get arrested by the Moroccan police, you won't have much of a legal leg to stand on. It's unlikely that any interpreter on hand will be of sufficient standard to translate an accurate statement that will, nonetheless, play a vital part in subsequent judicial proceedings. According to some human-rights groups, physical abuse while in custody is not unknown.

Maps

Few decent maps of Morocco are available in the country itself, so get one before leaving home.

Michelin's No 742 (formerly No 959) map of Morocco is arguably the best. It has the following features:

➡ The 1:4,000,000 scale map of the whole country includes the disputed Western Sahara.

➡ Features a 1:1,000,000 enlargement of Morocco.

➡ Features 1:600,000 enlargements of Marrakesh and the High Atlas, Middle Atlas and Fez areas.

➡ Shows sites of weekly markets, kasbahs and *marabouts* (holy mausoleums of local saints).

➡ Notes particularly scenic roads.

➡ Available in major Moroccan cities.

The GeoCenter World Map *Morocco* is preferred by many and has similar, often clearer, detail. Features:

➡ Shows Morocco at a handy 1:800,000 scale (and the Western Sahara at 1:2,500,000).

➡ Occasionally available in Morocco.

Additionally, several maps include Morocco as part of northwestern Africa. An overlanding classic, Michelin's No 741 (formerly Nos 953 and 153) map covers all of west Africa and most of the Sahara. It has a scale of 1:4,000,000.

Soviet survey maps of Morocco, with scales ranging from 1:100,000 to 1:1,000,000, are available online and at good map shops worldwide. They often have to be ordered and can take up to six weeks to arrive.

Money

➡ The Moroccan currency is the dirham (Dh), which is divided into 100 centimes.

➡ You will find notes in denominations of Dh20, Dh50, Dh100 and Dh200.

➡ Coins come in denominations of Dh1, Dh2, Dh5 and Dh10, as well as, less frequently, 10, 20 and 50 centimes.

➡ Break big notes whenever possible. Moroccans guard their small change jealously (taxi drivers *never* seem to have any), and so should you. The Dh20 note is the most useful note in your wallet.

➡ The dirham is a restricted currency, meaning that it cannot be taken out of the country and is not available abroad.

➡ The dirham is fairly stable, with no major fluctuations in exchange rates.

➡ Euros, US dollars and British pounds are the most easily exchanged currencies.

ATMs

➡ ATMs (*guichets automatiques*) are the easiest way to access your money in Morocco.

➡ A common sight even in the smallest towns, virtually all accept Visa, MasterCard, Electron, Cirrus, Maestro and InterBank cards. Most banks charge you for withdrawing money from foreign cash machines; check before travelling.

➡ BMCE (Banque Marocaine du Commerce Extérieur), Crédit du Maroc, Banque Populaire, BMCI (Banque Marocaine pour le Commerce et l'Industrie),

Société Générale and Attijariwafa Bank all offer reliable service.

➡ ATMs sometimes run dry on weekends.

➡ The amount of money you can withdraw from an ATM generally depends on the conditions attached to your card; many machines will dispense no more than Dh2000 at a time.

Black Market

The easy convertibility of the dirham leaves little room for a black market, but you'll find people in the streets asking if you want to exchange money, especially in Tangier, Casablanca and on the borders of (and just inside) the enclaves of Ceuta and Melilla. Avoid these characters; there's no monetary benefit to be had from such transactions and scams are common.

Cash

You'll need to carry some cash with you. Some riads accept payment in euros, but often at less preferential rates than you can get at the bank.

➡ Keep a handful of small denomination notes in your wallet, or just in a pocket (but never a back pocket), for day-to-day transactions.

➡ Put the rest in a money belt or another safe place.

➡ If you're travelling in out-of-the-way places, make sure you have enough cash to last until you get to a decent-sized town.

➡ Keep an emergency stash of euros in small denominations.

➡ The endless supply of small coins may be annoying, but they're handy for taxis, tips, guides and beggars.

Credit Cards

➡ Major credit cards are widely accepted in the main tourist centres.

➡ They often attract a surcharge of around 5% from Moroccan businesses.

➤ The main credit cards are MasterCard and Visa; if you plan to rely on plastic cards, the best bet is to take one of each.

➤ Most large bank branches will give you cash advances on Visa and MasterCard. Take your passport with you.

Moneychangers

➤ Any amount of foreign currency may be brought into the country.

➤ It is illegal to import and export dirham.

➤ Banks and exchange bureaus change most currencies, but Australian, Canadian and New Zealand dollars are often not accepted. You'll occasionally be asked for ID when changing money.

➤ Moroccan banking services are reasonably quick and efficient.

➤ Rates do not vary much from bank to bank, although it doesn't hurt to look around.

➤ Travellers cheques are becoming harder to change. If banks accept them, you'll need to take your passport along to change them (plus the travellers cheque receipt in some places).

➤ Hang on to all exchange receipts. They show you changed money legally, and you'll need them to convert leftover dirham at

most Moroccan banks and *bureaux de change*.

CEUTA & MELILLA

➤ In the Spanish enclaves of Ceuta and Melilla the currency is the euro.

➤ The Moroccan banks on the enclaves' borders exchange cash only.

➤ Banks in Ceuta and Melilla deal in dirham, but at rates inferior to those offered in Morocco.

Tipping

➤ Tipping is an integral part of Moroccan life; almost any service can warrant a tip. You'll hear the word *baksheesh*. Although frequently taken to mean a bribe, it generally means money paid for a service rendered, and can include tipping.

➤ Don't be railroaded, but the judicious distribution of a few dirham for a service willingly rendered can make your life a lot easier.

➤ Bear in mind that unskilled workers in Morocco earn less than Dh100 per day.

Travellers Cheques

➤ Travellers cheques are not recommended in Morocco – even large city banks often do not accept them.

➤ If you want to carry some anyway, as a fallback in the event of theft, American Express (Amex), Visa and Thomas Cook cheques

are the most useful, and have efficient replacement policies.

➤ Keeping a record of the cheque numbers and those you have used is vital when it comes to replacing lost travellers cheques.

➤ Make sure you keep this record separate from the cheques themselves.

➤ Almost all banks charge commission on travellers cheques.

➤ Normally the commission is around Dh10 to Dh20 per cheque; check before changing.

Opening Hours

Although a Muslim country, for business purposes Morocco follows the Monday to Friday working week. Friday is the main prayer day, however, so many businesses take an extended lunch break on Friday afternoon. During Ramadan the rhythm of the country changes, and office hours shift to around 10am to 3pm or 4pm.

Hours often vary between medinas and villes nouvelles (new towns): most businesses close on Sundays in villes nouvelles, whereas those in the medinas usually open continuously from about 9am to 7pm except on Fridays.

Medina souqs and produce markets in the villes nouvelles tend to wind down on Thursday afternoon and are usually empty on Friday. Business hours are highly variable for cafes and snack stands, which can be both seasonal and subject to to the owner's mood.

Souqs in small villages start early and generally wind down before the onset of the afternoon heat.

In cities, pharmacies open all night on a rotating basis. All pharmacies should have a list in their window of that week's night pharmacies.

TIPPING IN MOROCCO

SERVICE	TIP
Restaurant	10%
Cafe	Dh2
Museums guides	DH3-5
Porters	Dh3-5
Public-toilet attendants	Dh2-3
Baggage handlers	Dh3-5
Petrol-pump attendants	Dh3-5
Car-park attendants	Dh3-5; Dh10 for overnight parking

In the main tourist cities, *bureaux de change* (foreign-exchange bureaus) often open until 8pm and over the weekend.

Téléboutiques (private telephone offices) and internet cafes often stay open late into the night, especially in cities.

Banks 8.30am to 6.30pm Monday to Friday

Post offices 8.30am to 4.30pm Monday to Friday

Government offices 8.30am to 6.30pm Monday to Friday

Restaurants noon to 3pm and 7pm to 10pm

Bars 4pm till late

Shops 9am to 12.30pm and 2.30pm to 8pm Monday to Saturday (often closed longer at noon for prayer)

Tourist offices 8.30am to noon and 2.30pm to 6.30pm Monday to Thursday, 8.30am to 11.30am and 3pm to 6.30pm Friday

Photography

➡ Morocco is a photographer's dream, but never point your camera at anything that's vaguely military or could be construed as 'strategic'. This includes airports, bridges, government buildings and members of the police or armed forces.

➡ Hide your camera when going through checkpoints in and near the Western Sahara.

➡ It is common courtesy to ask permission before taking photographs of people. Urban Moroccans are generally easygoing about it. Women, older people and rural folk often don't want to be photographed. Respect their right to privacy and don't take photos.

➡ Memory cards and batteries for digital cameras are quite easy to find in photography shops in major cities (especially Marrakesh and Casablanca).

➡ A USB memory stick is useful for backing up photos, but most internet cafes can burn you a CD if needed.

➡ Kodak and Fuji colour negative film (35mm and APS), as well as video tapes, are readily available in bigger cities and towns.

➡ They are marginally more expensive than in Europe. Slide film is more difficult to come by.

➡ If you buy film in Morocco, check expiry dates.

➡ Professional photo labs offer the most professional processing services.

➡ Lonely Planet's *Travel Photography* provides comprehensive advice on taking terrific photos when you're on the road.

Post

➡ Offices of **Poste Maroc** (www.bam.net.ma) are distinguished by a yellow 'PTT' sign or the 'La Poste' logo.

➡ *Tabacs*, the small tobacco and newspaper kiosks scattered about city centres, often sell stamps, and have shorter queues.

➡ The postal system is fairly reliable, if not terribly fast.

➡ It takes at least a week for letters to reach European destinations, and two weeks to get to Australia and North America.

➡ Sending post from a city normally gives mail a head start.

➡ Worldwide postcards cost around Dh13 to send, and letters around Dh18.

Sending Parcels

➡ The parcel office, indicated by the sign 'colis postaux', is generally in a separate part of the post-office building.

➡ A 1kg package costs around Dh140 to send via airmail to the UK, Dh140 to the USA and Dh240 to Australia.

➡ Parcels should not be wider, longer or higher than 2m; weight limit varies according to the destination, but it's typically 30kg.

➡ To ship goods home, buy a box and a shipping form at the post office and take them to the shop where you purchased your wares.

➡ The shopkeeper knows the product and can wrap and pack the pieces well with newspaper and cardboard.

➡ If you've purchased carpets, the vendor should have rolled and bound them in plastic sacks; if not, return and ask them to do so.

➡ Label the outside of the package in several places with a waterproof pen.

➡ Be very clear about the destination country; marking it in French as well as English helps.

➡ Indicate the value of the contents if you like, but you may be charged taxes at the receiving end.

➡ Don't seal the box! Customs officers at the post office need to view the contents.

➡ Your packages will be weighed and you will be charged Par Avion (air) freight rates unless you specify that you prefer the items shipped by land.

➡ The overland service is considerably less expensive but can take three months.

➡ Valuable speciality items such as large furniture may involve customs clearance.

➡ Shopkeepers should be able to arrange clearance and shipping for you, but make sure you keep copies of all documentation in case the goods never arrive.

Express Mail & Couriers

➡ There is usually an Express Mail Service (EMS), also known as Poste Rapide, in the same office as parcel post.

➡ In Morocco the service is run by **Chronopost International Maroc** (www. chronopost.ma).

➡ A 500g package costs from Dh320 to send to the UK or Europe, and Dh330 to North America or Australia.

➡ Private courier companies, with offices in the major cities, are faster and more expensive. International couriers with offices throughout Morocco include **DHL** (www.dhl-ma.com) and **TNT** (www.tnt.com).

Receiving Mail

➡ Having mail addressed to 'Poste Restante, La Poste Principale' of any big town should not be a problem.

➡ Some offices only hang on to parcels for a couple of weeks before returning them.

➡ You'll need your passport to claim mail and you'll be charged Dh3.50 for collection.

➡ An alternative way to receive letters is through Amex (if you are an Amex client). **Amex** (www. americanexpress.com) is represented by the travel agency Voyages Schwartz, which has branches in Casablanca, Tangier and Marrakesh. You will usually be asked to produce a passport for identification purposes and there may be a charge if you're not an Amex client.

Public Holidays

Banks, post offices and most shops will shut on the main public holidays, although transport still runs.

New Year's Day (1 January)

Independence Manifesto (11 January) Commemorates the publication in Fez of the Moroc-

can nationalist manifesto for independence.

Labour Day (1 May)

Feast of the Throne (30 July) Commemorates King Mohammed VI's accession to the throne.

Allegiance of Oued Eddahab (14 August) Celebrates the 'return to the fatherland' of the Oued Eddahab region in the far south, a territory once claimed by Mauritania.

Anniversary of the King's and People's Revolution (20 August) Commemorates the exile of Mohammed V by the French in 1953.

Young People's Day (21 August) Celebrates the king's birthday.

Anniversary of the Green March (6 November) Commemorates the Green March 'reclaiming' the Western Sahara in November 1975.

Independence Day (18 November) Commemorates independence from France.

MAJOR ISLAMIC HOLIDAYS

The rhythms of Islamic practice are tied to the lunar calendar, which is slightly shorter than its Gregorian equivalent, so the Muslim calendar begins around 11 days earlier each year.

The following principal religious holidays are celebrated countrywide, with interruptions and changes of time to many local bus services and increased pressure on transport in general. Apart from on the first day of Ramadan, offices and businesses close.

Moulid (or Mouloud) an-Nabi celebrates the birth of the Prophet Mohammed. Children are often given presents.

Eid al-Fitr (Feast of the Breaking of the Fast), also known as Eid as-Sagheer (the Small Feast), is the end of Ramadan. The four-day celebration begins with a meal of *harira* (lentil soup), dates and honey cakes, and the country grinds to a halt during this family-focused period.

Eid al-Adha (Feast of the Sacrifice) sees sheep traded for the ritual sacrifices that take place throughout the Muslim world during this three-day celebration. Also known as the Eid al-Kabeer (Grand Feast), it commemorates Ibrahim's sacrifice. The sheep sacrifice is often a very public event – be prepared for the possibility of seeing blood running in the gutters and sheep heads being flamed over fires in the street.

Because the precise date of an Islamic holiday is in doubt until a few days before the start of that month, the dates below are only approximate.

HOLIDAY	2014	2015	2016	2017
Moulid an-Nabi	13 Jan	3 Jan	12 Dec	1 Dec
Ramadan begins	28 Jun	18 Jun	6 Jun	27 May
Eid al-Fitr	27 Jul	17 Jul	5 Jul	25 Jun
Eid al-Adha	4 Oct	23 Sep	11 Sep	1 Sep
New Year begins	25 Oct	14 Oct	2 Oct	21 Sep

TRAVEL DURING RAMADAN

Ramadan Mubarak! (Happy Ramadan!) Ramadan is a lunar month dedicated to *sawm* (fasting) – from sun-up to sundown, the faithful abstain from food, drink, tobacco and sex to concentrate on spiritual renewal – and *zakat* (charity).

Many businesses operate with limited hours and staff, so try to book accommodation, transport and tours in advance. Call offices to ensure someone will be there. Most restaurants close by day; pack lunches or reserve at tourist restaurants. Stores often close in the afternoon; bargaining is better before thirst is felt in the midday heat. During the lifetime of this edition of the guide, Ramadan falls in the summer, so be prepared for long, hot days.

Sunset streets fill with Ramadan finery, light displays, music, tantalising aromas and offers of sweets. After an *iftar* (fast-breaking meal) of dates, soup or savoury snacks, people gobble sweets until the late-night feast. More visits and sweets follow, then sleep, and an early rise for the *sahur* (meal before the sunrise).

Travellers are exempt from fasting; it's hard enough at home under controlled conditions. To show support, avoid eating, drinking or smoking in public, and grant people privacy at prayer times. Taxi drivers don't appreciate being flagged down minutes before the evening call to prayer announcing *iftar*.

When a new friend offers you sweets or invites you to a feast, you honour by accepting; refusal is crushing. You're not obliged to return the favour or eat the sweets; reciprocate the *zakat* by giving to a local charity perhaps.

Safe Travel

Morocco is one of the safest African countries for travellers. The great majority of Moroccans are friendly and honest, but like anywhere there are traps for the unwary.

Drugs

➡ Morocco's era as a hippie paradise, riding the Marrakesh Express and all that, has been consigned to history.

➡ Plenty of dope (known as kif) may be grown in the Rif Mountains, but drug busts are common and you wouldn't want to investigate Moroccan prison conditions from the inside.

➡ Always bear in mind that it's illegal to buy, sell or consume hashish in Morocco. If you're going to smoke kif, don't do it in public and be extremely circumspect about who you buy it from.

➡ If caught, you may be looking at a fine and, in the worst case, a prison sentence.

➡ Hashish is sometimes referred to as 'chocolate', the Spanish slang, or more often just as 'something special' or 'shit', which you will definitely be in if you get caught.

➡ Although some locals continue to smoke as a recreational pastime, as a tourist you're more vulnerable.

SCAMS & HASSLE

The vast majority of Moroccan stories of extortion and rip-offs are drug-related. Recent legislation and a hard government line may have forced dealers to give up their more aggressive tactics, but the hassle has not disappeared.

A common ploy is to get you stoned, force you to buy a piece of hash the size of a brick and then turn you over to the police (or at least threaten to). Once you've purchased hash, or even just smoked some, you're unlikely to call the cops, and the hustlers know it.

HOT SPOTS

➡ Associating with Tangier's lowlife is for the initiated

only. New arrivals should ignore late-night offers of hashish and grass. These dealers have a sixth sense for greenness, and won't miss an opportunity to squeeze ridiculous amounts of money out of frightened people.

➡ Watch out for similar scams in Tetouan, Assilah, Casablanca and Marrakesh.

➡ Issaguen (Ketama) and the Rif Mountains are Morocco's kif-growing heartland. Issaguen in particular can be a bag-load of trouble, and is best avoided unless you're accompanied by a reliable guide.

MAJOUN

➡ You may occasionally be offered *majoun*, a sticky, pasty mass (not unlike molasses) made of crushed marijuana seeds.

➡ A small ball of *majoun* can send you reeling (see Paul Bowles' *Their Heads Are Green* or *Let It Come Down* for descriptions).

➡ Anyone with a slight tendency to paranoia when smoking dope should be aware that this is a common reaction among first-time *majoun* munchers.

SPAIN

Although the Spanish police have a relaxed attitude towards small amounts of cannabis for private use, Spanish customs will come down hard on people entering the country from Morocco in possession of the drug, and you could be done for trafficking.

➡ If you're taking a car across, the chances that it will be searched are high.

➡ *Never* carry parcels or drive vehicles across borders for other people.

Getting Lost

➡ A minor irritation is the ever-changing street names in Moroccan cities.

➡ For years, there's been a slow process of replacing old French, Spanish and Berber names with Arabic ones.

➡ The result so far is that, depending on whom you talk to, what map you use or which part of the street you are on, you're likely to see up to three different names.

➡ The general Arabic word for street is *sharia*, or *derb* in medinas (*zankat* for smaller ones).

➡ The French avenue, boulevard and *rue* are still common. In the north and far south you'll still find the Spanish *calle* and *avenida*.

➡ In some cases the Arabic seems to have gained the upper hand. This is reflected in listings here, in which some streets appear as *sharia* or *zankat* if local usage justifies it.

MEDINAS

➡ Street names won't help much in the labyrinthine medinas, although in theory a compass might.

➡ If you feel you're getting lost, stick to the main paths (which generally have a fair flow of people going either way) and you'll soon reach a landmark or exit. Kids will sometimes offer to direct you for a few dirhams; corner shops are better places to ask for directions.

Plumbing

➡ Patience can be required when it comes to Moroccan plumbing.

➡ In cheap, unclassified hotels without star ratings, trickling cold water and squat toilets are common.

➡ Sometimes hot water is enthusiastically promised, but it may be tepid at best and only available at certain times of the day.

➡ In rural areas, water is sometimes heated by a wood fire, but this comes at an environmental cost. Wood is expensive, water is often in short supply and deforestation is a major problem in Morocco.

➡ In small towns and rural areas the hammam may be a better bet.

Smoking

➡ Smoking is a national pastime in Morocco and nonsmoking restaurants and hotels are rare.

➡ This generally affects popular places rather than top-end restaurants and hotels, where you may find nonsmoking areas.

➡ Most popular eateries and cafes have outdoor seating, so the problem is reduced.

➡ Only the very top-end hotels and some riads have a nonsmoking policy.

WOMEN

➡ In Muslim countries, it is often considered unacceptable for women to smoke. This is a cultural rather than religious dictate.

➡ Particularly outside the big cities, you'll seldom see women smokers.

➡ Although most religious leaders condemn smoking, like drinking, as *haram* (forbidden), only during daylight hours of the holy month of Ramadan is the habit seriously eschewed.

➡ This shouldn't affect foreigners too much, although women may wish to refrain from smoking within local homes and be discreet elsewhere.

Theft

On the whole, theft is not a huge problem in Morocco. Travellers can minimise risk by being vigilant (but not paranoid) in the major cities and taking some basic precautions. As the saying goes: 'Trust in God, but tie your camel.'

➡ When wandering around the streets, keep the valuables you carry to a minimum.

➡ Keep what you must carry around with you well hidden.

➡ Be particularly careful when withdrawing money from ATMs.

➡ External money pouches attract attention. Neck pouches or moneybelts worn under your clothes attract less attention. They are better places to keep your money, passport and other important documents, but keep a small amount of everyday cash easily accessible to avoid having to flash your stash.

➡ If you prefer to keep things in your room (preferably locked inside your suitcase), nine times out of 10 you'll have no trouble.

➡ Rooms in top-end hotels often have safes.

➡ Other hotels sometimes have a safe at reception, where you could stow valuables such as a camera.

➡ Leaving anything in a car, even out of sight, is asking for trouble.

➡ In the large cities, notably Casablanca, there are some desperate people, and physical attacks on foreigners occasionally occur.

➡ Treat the medinas with particular caution at night.

➡ The medinas in Marrakesh, Casablanca and Tangier have a particular reputation for petty theft. A common tactic is for one person to distract you while another cleans out your pockets.

Touts, Guides & Hustlers

Morocco's notorious hustlers and *faux guides* (unofficial guides) remain an unavoidable part of the Moroccan experience.

➡ *Brigades touristiques* (tourist police) were set up in the principal tourist centres, and anyone suspected of trying to operate as an unofficial guide could face jail and/or a huge fine. This has greatly reduced, but not eliminated, the problem.

➡ Hustlers are often desperate to make a living, and they can be persistent and sometimes unpleasant.

➡ You'll generally find them hanging around the entrances to the big cities' medinas, and outside bus, train and ferry stations.

➡ Having a siege mentality would be an overreaction. Indeed, when arriving in a place for the first time, you might benefit from the services of a guide, official or otherwise.

➡ Although high unemployment rates drive the numbers of *faux guides*, not all are complete imposters. Many are very experienced and speak half a dozen languages.

➡ Sometimes their main interest is the commission gained from certain hotels or on articles sold to you in the souqs.

DEALING WITH GUIDES

➡ Agree a price before setting off on a tour.

➡ Set some parameters on what you expect to see and the number of shops you're taken to. If you don't want a shopping expedition included in your tour, make this clear beforehand.

➡ Unofficial guides charge around Dh50 to Dh100 per day. Rates should always be per guide, not per person.

➡ A few dirham will suffice if you want to be guided to a specific location (like a medina exit).

➡ Whatever you give, you'll often get the 'you can't possibly be serious' look. The best reply is the 'I've just paid you well over the odds' look.

➡ Maintain your good humour and, after a couple of days in a place, the hassle tends to lessen considerably.

➡ Official guides can be engaged through tourist offices and some hotels at the fixed price of around Dh250/300 per day (plus tip) for a local/national guide.

➡ It's well worth taking a guide when exploring Fez and Marrakesh medinas. The guide can help you find interesting sights and shops in the melee, stop you from getting lost and save you from being hassled by other would-be guides.

DRIVING & TRANSPORT

➡ Drivers should note that motorised hustlers operate on the approach roads to Fez and Marrakesh. These motorcycle nuisances are keen to find you accommodation and so on, and can be just as persistent as their counterparts on foot.

➡ Travellers disembarking from (and embarking on) the ferry in Tangier may receive some hassle from touts and hustlers.

➡ Arriving by train in cities like Fez and Marrakesh, you may run into 'students' or similar, with the uncanny knowledge that your preferred hotel is closed or full, but they just happen to know this great little place...

Telephone

➡ Within Morocco, always dial the local four-digit area code even if you are dialling from the same town or code area.

➡ You can make calls from *téléboutiques* (private

THANKS BUT NO THANKS

Faux-guides abound in tourist hot-spots, hustling to 'help' you and earn some commission from souvenir shops. To avoid being hounded to within an inch of your life in the medina, and to help prevent nervous breakdowns and embarrassing incidents of 'medina rage', the following are useful tactics:

➡ Politely decline all offers of help you don't want, and exchange a few good-humoured remarks (preferably in Arabic), but don't shake hands or get involved in any lengthy conversation.

➡ Give the impression that you know exactly where you're going, or explain that you employed a guide on your first day and now you'd like to explore on your own.

➡ Wear dark sunglasses and retreat to a cafe, restaurant or taxi if you're beginning to lose your cool.

➡ In extreme situations, use the word 'police' and look like you mean it.

telephone offices) and public payphones.

→ Attendants at *téléboutiques* will usually change small notes into coins.

→ Most payphones are card-operated.

→ You can buy *télécartes* (phonecards) at *tabacs* and *téléboutiques*.

→ Payphones have easy-to-follow instructions.

→ Calling from a hotel normally doubles the cost of your call.

→ Moroccan landline numbers start with 05.

International Calls

→ International calling cards are available from telecommunication shops such as Méditel.

→ If you can find a reasonable internet connection, a Skype call will likely be cheaper. Computers in internet cafes normally have headsets.

→ Méditel's Dawlia card offers rates starting at Dh1.75 per minute. To use the Dawlia card, call the 10-digit card number prefixed with 133, then type in the four-digit PIN number and follow the voice prompts.

→ France, Spain and Italy are the cheapest countries to call, and rates are lower between 8pm and 8am, at weekends and on public holidays.

Mobile Phones

→ Morocco has three GSM mobile-phone networks: Méditel (www.meditelecom. ma), Maroc Telecom (www. iam.ma) and Inwi (www.inwi. ma).

→ Coverage is excellent, apart from in the mountains and desert.

→ If your mobile phone is unlocked, buying a prepaid mobile SIM card (around Dh20) will likely be cheaper than using your phone on roaming.

→ Domestic calls cost from Dh1.20 per minute, international calls from Dh2.50 per minute.

→ Calls are cheaper between 8am and 8pm.

→ You need to show a passport or other form of identification when buying a SIM card.

→ *Téléboutiques*, news-stands and grocery stores sell scratch cards for topping up your credit. Look out for special offers for extra credit.

→ Moroccan mobile numbers start with 06.

Time

Standard Moroccan time is on GMT/UTC.

Daylight saving Daylight saving runs from the end of March to the end of October. The exception is during Ramadan, when Morocco reverts to GMT, but it does go back again to daylight saving afterwards. Daylight saving almost always causes confusion in Morocco; watch out for 'city time' and 'medina time' – many people in medinas don't bother to change their clocks.

Spain If you're travelling to/from Spain (including Ceuta and Melilla), note that Morocco's clocks run one hour behind Spain's for half the year except during daylight saving, when

there is no time change between the countries.

Local attitudes Time is something that most Moroccans seem to have plenty of; they're not in nearly as much of a hurry to get things done as most Westerners. Rather than getting frustrated by this, learn to go with the flow a little.

Toilets

→ Flush toilets are a luxury in a country struggling with water shortages. Outside midrange and top-end hotels and restaurants, toilets are mostly of the squat variety.

→ Squat toilets feature a tap, hose or container of water for sluicing – the idea being to wash yourself (with your left hand) after performing.

→ There's often no toilet paper (*papier hygiénique*) so keep a supply with you.

→ Don't throw the paper into the toilet as the plumbing is often dodgy; instead discard it in the bin provided.

→ Women who have their period will need to take along a plastic bag for disposing of used tampons and pads.

→ Public toilets are rare outside the major cities.

→ If you find a public toilet, you'll need to bring a tip for the attendant, stout-soled shoes, and very often a nose clip.

Tourist Information

Cities and larger towns have tourist offices, which are normally repositories of brochures run by uninformed staff and, as such, usually best avoided. Often the receptionist in your hotel or another local will be more helpful than such bureaus. The best tourist offices are found in smaller destinations that are trying to promote themselves.

USEFUL NUMBERS

Morocco country code ☏212

International access code from Morocco ☏00

Directory enquiries ☏160

Spain country code (including Melilla & Ceuta) ☏34

DIFFERENCES FROM STANDARD MOROCCAN TIME

COUNTRY	CAPITAL CITY	DIFFERENCE FROM MOROCCO
Australia	Canberra	+11hr
Canada	Ottawa	-5hr
France	Paris	+1hr
Germany	Berlin	+1hr
Japan	Tokyo	+9hr
Netherlands	Amsterdam	+1hr
New Zealand	Wellington	+13hr
Spain	Madrid	+1hr
UK	London	0hr
USA	Washington DC	-5hr

L'Office National Marocain du Tourisme (ONMT; www.visitmorocco.com) The Moroccan National Tourist Office runs most tourist offices.

Travellers with Disabilities

Morocco has few facilities for the disabled, but the country is not necessarily out of bounds for travellers with a physical disability and a sense of adventure. Some factors to be aware of:

➡ The awkward nature of narrow medina streets and rutted pavements can make mobility challenging at times even for the able-bodied.

➡ Not all hotels (almost none of the cheaper ones) have lifts, so booking ground-floor hotel rooms ahead of time is essential.

➡ Only a handful of the very top-end hotels have rooms designed for the disabled.

➡ Travelling by car is probably the best transport, though you'll be able to get assistance in bus and train stations (a tip will be required).

➡ Many tour operators can tailor trips to suit your requirements.

➡ Vision- or hearing-impaired travellers are poorly catered for. Hearing loops, Braille signs and talking pedestrian crossings are nonexistent.

Organisations

Organisations that disseminate information, advice and assistance on world travel for the mobility impaired include the following:

Access-able Travel Source (www.access-able. com) An information provider for travellers with mobility problems.

Apparleyzed (www.apparleyzed.com) For paraplegic and quadriplegic people and others with spinal-cord injuries, featuring travel information.

Disabled Travelers Guide (www.disabledtravelersguide. com) A general guide for travellers with disabilities.

Mobility International USA (MIUSA; www.miusa. org) Promoting the inclusion of people with disabilities in international programs, with a page of air-travel tips.

Society for Accessible Travel & Hospitality (SATH; www.sath.org) Has news, tips and members' articles and blogs.

Visas

➡ Most visitors to Morocco do not require a visa and are allowed to remain in the country for 90 days on entry.

➡ In all cases, your passport must be valid for at least six months beyond your date of entry.

➡ Nationals of Israel and many sub-Saharan African countries (including South Africa) must apply in advance for a three-month visa (single/double entry about US$30/50).

➡ Applications are normally processed in 48 hours.

➡ You need three passport photos.

➡ In Morocco's neighbouring countries, there is a Moroccan embassy in Madrid (Spain) and consulates-general in locations including Algeciras; an embassy in Nouakchott (Mauritania) and a consulate-general in Nouâdhibou; and diplomatic missions in Algeria including an embassy in Algiers.

➡ Further information, including a list of Morocco's diplomatic missions, is available from the **Moroccan Ministry of Foreign Affairs and Cooperation** (www. diplomatie.ma/en).

➡ As visa requirements change, it's a good idea to check with the Moroccan mission in your country or a reputable travel agency before travelling.

Visa Extensions

➡ Most travellers requiring a visa extension find it easiest

VISAS FOR NEIGHBOURING COUNTRIES

Embassies for the following countries are in Rabat.

Algeria

➡ Diplomatic disputes have kept the Morocco–Algeria border closed since 1994. Periodic bouts of rapprochement raise hopes that it may one day reopen. In the unlikely event this happens during the lifetime of this guidebook, the main border crossing would be between Oujda and Tlemcen in Algeria.

➡ Visas are required by everyone except nationals of Arab League countries.

➡ Algeria prefers applicants to apply in their country of residence.

➡ For more information, check out www.sahara-overland.com and Lonely Planet's *Africa*, which covers Algeria.

Mauritania

➡ Everyone, except nationals of Arab League countries, needs a visa to enter Mauritania.

➡ At the time of writing, Mauritanian visas were not being issued at the border.

➡ The Mauritanian embassy in Rabat issues 30-day and 90-day visas (Dh380/720). Multiple-entry visas are sometimes available, but purely at the discretion of the consular officer on the day.

➡ From Monday to Thursday, apply early in the morning and pick up the following day. Get there well before the embassy opens at 9am and be prepared for queues. In the crowd of applicants, there's often someone organised enough to operate a list of those queuing – if so make sure your name is added, to keep your place in the queue.

➡ You need two passport photos and a photocopy of your passport. Local touts may approach you offering forms and help filling them in (and pointers to the nearest copy shop), for a small fee.

➡ For more info see www.sahara-overland.com and Lonely Planet's *West Africa*, which covers Mauritania.

Spain

➡ Spain is in the European Union and the Schengen Area.

➡ The Schengen Area covers 30 European countries, including Spain and all other EU-member countries apart from the UK and the Republic of Ireland.

➡ Ceuta and Melilla, the two Spanish enclaves in Morocco, have the same visa requirements as mainland Spain.

➡ Nationals of EU-member countries do not need a visa to enter Spain.

➡ Nationals of countries including Australia, Canada, Israel, Japan, New Zealand and the USA do not need a Schengen visa to cross a Schengen border.

➡ Your passport will be stamped upon arrival in the zone, and you can then stay for up to 90 days (straight or cumulative) within 180 days. This means, for example, that when you leave the zone at the end of a three-month stay, you are not permitted to re-enter for three months.

➡ For more information, see Spain's **Ministry of Foreign Affairs and Cooperation** (www.exteriores.gob.es) and Lonely Planet guides, including *Mediterranean Europe*, which has chapters on Spain and Morocco.

to head to mainland Spain, or one of the Spanish enclaves in Morocco, and re-enter after a few days.

➡ Although doing a visa run generally presents few problems other than travel costs, it leaves you at the mercy of individual immigration officers on re-entry. Travellers have occasionally come unstuck this way.

➜ A harder alternative is to apply for a visa extension, issued by the Directorate General of National Security.

➜ Residence (a Carte de Sejour) is also available, but it is difficult to get and usually requires proof of employment.

➜ Go to the nearest police headquarters (Préfecture de Police) to check what documents they require.

➜ If possible, take a Moroccan friend to help you deal with the bureaucrats.

➜ In addition to your passport and three passport photos, the police will likely require a letter from your embassy requesting a visa extension on your behalf.

➜ Applications can take days or weeks, and the different procedures employed by different police headquarters may hold up proceedings.

International Health Certificate

If you're coming to Morocco from certain parts of Africa and South America where yellow fever is endemic, you'll need to show you've been vaccinated by producing a yellow-fever certificate or international certificate of vaccination.

In practice this is usually only required if you've travelled overland up through Mauritania, where yellow fever is endemic (although anecdotal evidence disputes how rigorously the order is enforced at the land border), or arrived from an African country on, say, a Royal Air Maroc flight.

We would recommend, however, that travellers carry a certificate if they have been in an infected country during the previous month to avoid any possible difficulties with immigration.

There is always the possibility that a traveller without a legally required, up-to-date certificate will be vaccinated and detained in isolation at the port of arrival for up to 10 days, or possibly repatriated.

You may need to prove you've been vaccinated against cholera if you are arriving from an afflicted zone.

Volunteering

There are many international and local organisations that arrange voluntary work on regional development projects in Morocco.

They generally pay nothing, sometimes not even providing lodging, and are aimed at young people looking for something different to do for a few weeks over summer.

Some of these organisations are really summer camps and international exchange programs.

A good starting point is Lonely Planet's The Big Trip, a guide to gap years and overseas adventures that includes a chapter on volunteering and working overseas, as well as a directory of resources.

Organisations

International or local organisations that sometimes have Morocco placements or camps:

Baraka Community Partnerships (www.barakacommunity.com) At the Tijhza Village Project in the High Atlas, this organisation needs help with schemes such as a reforestation program, repairing and renovating poorer homes, supporting the two schools, establishing a preschool and mothers' group, and developing compost toilets and bee-keeping programs.

Chantiers Sociaux Marocains (CSM; ☎0537 26 24 00; www.csmmorocco.org) Rabat-based NGO engaged in nationwide health, education and development projects, with international volunteers aged 18 to 35.

Jeunesse des Chantiers Marocains (http://perso.menara.ma/youthcamps) A nonprofit, youth-focused travel and cultural exchange organisation.

Programs in Marrakesh include volunteering at a nursery school or orphanage, with accommodation in a homestay organised.

Morocco Exchange (www.moroccoexchange.org) Offers short-term student exchange and travel programs with a focus on cross-cultural education through visiting cities and rural villages. Previous custom-made programs have explored Morocco's medical system, the use of the French language, and women's rights.

Peace Corps (www.peacecorps.gov) Long-established US volunteer scheme with deep roots in Morocco; volunteer programs lasting two years.

Projects Abroad (www.projects-abroad.co.uk) The UK-based organisation offers Moroccan volunteering holidays from healthcare to working with nomads.

Idealist.org (www.idealist.org) Has volunteering and job opportunities in Morocco.

Volunteer Abroad (www.volunteerabroad.com/Morocco.cfm) A good place to start looking for volunteer places, as it provides links to organisations with Moroccan programs.

International Cultural Youth Exchange (ICYE; www.icye.org) Allows you to search for upcoming Moroccan volunteer opportunities.

Women Travellers

➜ Prior to marriage, many Moroccan men have little opportunity to meet and get to know women, which is a major reason why Western women receive so much attention.

➜ Not bound by Moroccan society and Islamic law, foreign women are seen as excitingly independent and generally available.

➜ Increased tourism to Morocco has also brought female visitors who are unprepared – or simply unaware that cultural mores in Muslim countries are different from the West.

➔ Around 70% of Morocco's population is under the age of 30, and by the end of their trip most Western women may think they've met every male in this group.

➔ The constant attention is impossible to shake off, no matter what tactic is employed, and soon becomes wearing.

➔ If it's your first time in Morocco, the first few days may be something of a shock, but you'll quickly develop a thick skin to deal with the unwanted looks and comments.

➔ The key to not spending your trip feeling hassled is to be wary but not paranoid – the low-level harassment rarely goes any further.

➔ Moroccans are eager to help any traveller and there are times when being a woman is a distinct advantage, especially when lost or in some form of distress. Moroccans tend to be genuinely concerned for the 'weaker sex' and will offer protection and support if you feel you're in a potentially bad situation.

➔ Another benefit is that unlike male travellers, you'll have opportunities to meet local women.

Attitudes & Relationships

➔ The common attitude that a Westerner is a walking visa out of a country where unemployment is rife can affect women travellers.

➔ This perception is partly fuelled by Western women having holiday romances with local guys.

➔ Bored young men may have little to lose by wooing someone who can offer them an opportunity in another country, or a sexual liaison unavailable from Moroccan women.

➔ Some locals could be juggling several relationships at once.

➔ More positively, there are many success stories about relationships of mixed nationality.

Dress

➔ Dress modestly. Despite some tourists' attire, hot pants and cleavage in the Marrakesh medina are never appropriate. It's best to cover your shoulders and knees, and avoid low-cut tops altogether.

➔ Bikinis attract attention and sunbathing topless on the beach is totally inappropriate.

➔ At the other end of the scale, sporting a headscarf or even a jellaba (Moroccan-style flowing cloak) will earn you respect, particularly in the countryside, as well as questions about why you're wearing it: Are you Muslim? Are you Moroccan? Are you married to a Moroccan?

Havens & Pitfalls

➔ If the hassle gets too much, look for the ever-increasing number of places accustomed to having the business of single Moroccan women.

➔ The upper floor of a *salon de thé* (teahouse), a restaurant or a hotel terrace are also good bets.

➔ Hammams are good male-free zones for a relaxing reprieve.

➔ Hotel and public swimming pools usually attract groups of men, whether they be swimming or drinking at a poolside bar.

➔ Be aware that some budget hotels double as brothels; any cheap hotel above a popular locals' bar is a likely contender.

➔ If you want an alcoholic drink, head to a large hotel rather than braving a bar, as these are generally rough, male-dominated establishments. Local women who frequent watering holes, even the

posher ones, are generally prostitutes.

Male Travelling Companions

➔ Women travelling with male companions are less likely to experience much of the hassle that solo women inevitably encounter.

➔ It may be better to claim to be a married couple rather than just friends (the latter concept is usually greeted with disbelief).

➔ If you are a Moroccan woman (or Moroccan in appearance) travelling with your non-Moroccan spouse, it is advisable to carry a copy of your marriage certificate. Premarital sex for Muslims is forbidden and Morocco has a stern attitude to prostitution.

➔ For the same reason, if your partner is thought to be Muslim you may meet with some uncomfortable situations at hotel reception desks. This is less of an issue in larger cities.

Transport

➔ Try to sit next to a woman on public transport, especially in grands taxis where you're squeezed in closely, and on trains, where you could potentially be trapped inside a compartment.

➔ Many women travel in grands taxis without problems, regardless of where they sit, but you could pay for two seats to get a ride by yourself in the front. It would be considerably more comfortable.

➔ Don't hitchhike.

Safety Precautions

Crimes against women remain extremely rare. More common is verbal abuse from both men and women. In places that have seen a large influx of tourists in recent years, problems can occur. For example, we've received reports of physical harassment at music festivals in Essaouira.

Women travellers should take a few sensible precautions:

➡ Never compromise your safety for the sake of economy.

➡ Don't wander about alone at night, as there's an attitude that all 'good women' should be at home after dark; take a taxi.

➡ Don't walk alone in remote areas like isolated beaches, forests and sand dunes.

➡ Wearing dark glasses is good for avoiding eye contact, but don't spend your entire Moroccan journey hiding behind them.

➡ Don't react with aggression – it could be returned in kind. A good-humoured *non merci* or *la shukran* ('no thank you') is much more effective than abuse.

➡ The key word to use is 'respect', a concept that most Moroccans hold dear. *Hashouma!* ('shame!') can also be used to embarass would-be harassers.

➡ A wedding ring may help you avoid unwanted attention – along with a photo of your 'husband' and 'child'. The fact that you're travelling without them will arouse suspicion, but you could counter this by saying you'll be meeting them at your next destination.

➡ Many Moroccan men aren't too concerned whether you're married or not. They may insist they're just being friendly, and might even invite you home to meet their mother.

Work

➡ With huge unemployment and a largely out-of-work youthful population, Morocco isn't fertile ground for job opportunities.

➡ A good command of French is a prerequisite and some Arabic would help.

➡ If you secure a position, your employer will have to help you get a work permit and arrange residency, which can be a long process.

➡ There are more volunteering opportunities.

Teaching English

There are a few possibilities for teaching English as a foreign language in Morocco, although they are not terribly well paid. Rabat is one of the best places to start looking.

The best times to try are around September and October (the beginning of the academic year) and, to a lesser extent, early January. Having a TEFL (Teaching English as a Foreign Language) qualification will be useful.

American Language Centers (www.aca.org.ma) Ten schools around the country.

TEFL.com (www.tefl.com) Has a database of vacancies.

Transport

GETTING THERE & AWAY

Entering Morocco

The Moroccan government's 'open skies' policy has allowed the European budget airlines into the country, while there are numerous ferry services from Europe. Morocco also serves as the gateway country for African overlanders.

Border formalities are fairly quick and straightforward. Regardless of where you enter, your passport must be valid for at least six months from your date of entry.

Flights, tours and rail tickets can all be booked online at lonelyplanet.com/bookings.

Air

Airports & Airlines

Direct flights are available from cities across Europe, the Middle East, West Africa and North America. **Royal Air Maroc** (RAM; ☑0890 00 08 00; www.royalairmaroc.com) is Morocco's national carrier. For information about Moroccan airports, visit the website of **Office National des Aéroports** (www.onda.ma). Casablanca's Mohammed V International Airport is the country's main gateway, followed by Menara airport (Marrakesh). Other important airports include Fes–Saïss (Fez), Ibn Batouta International (Tangier), as well as Ouazazarte, Agadir and Nador.

Land

Border Crossings

Algeria This border remains closed and Algeria is reluctant to reopen it until the status of the Western Sahara is resolved.

Mauritania The only crossing is in the Western Sahara between Dakhla (Morocco) and Nouâdhibou (Mauritania).

Spain You can cross to mainland Spain via the Spanish enclaves of Ceuta and Melilla in northern Morocco.

Continental Europe

BUS

Buses mostly enter Morocco on the ferries from Spain, with connections from across Europe. Routes are busiest during major Spanish or French holidays, as buses fill up with Moroccans working abroad.

CTM (☑in Casablanca 0522 45 80 80; www.ctm.ma) Compagnie de Transports au Maroc, Morocco's national line, operates buses from Casablanca and other Moroccan cities to Spain, France, Belgium, Germany and Italy.

Eurolines (www.eurolines.com) A consortium of European coach companies operating across Europe and into Morocco (partnering with CTM).

Supratours (www.oncf.ma) Run by train company ONCF, has weekly departures from the

---

CLIMATE CHANGE & TRAVEL

Every form of transport that relies on carbon-based fuel generates CO_2, the main cause of human-induced climate change. Modern travel is dependent on aeroplanes, which might use less fuel per kilometre per person than most cars but travel much greater distances. The altitude at which aircraft emit gases (including CO_2) and particles also contributes to their climate change impact. Many websites offer 'carbon calculators' that allow people to estimate the carbon emissions generated by their journey and, for those who wish to do so, to offset the impact of the greenhouse gases emitted with contributions to portfolios of climate-friendly initiatives throughout the world. Lonely Planet offsets the carbon footprint of all staff and author travel.

major northern Moroccan cities to destinations across Spain, France and Italy.

CAR & MOTORCYCLE

⇒ European hire companies do not usually permit their vehicles to be driven to Morocco.

⇒ If you intend to take a Moroccan hire car to the Spanish enclaves of Ceuta or Melilla, you must have a letter from the hire company authorising you to take the car out of Morocco.

⇒ Some hire companies will not allow you to take their car out of the country.

⇒ If you're entering Morocco via Ceuta or Melilla, take the opportunity to fill up on duty-free fuel.

TRAIN

You can travel from London to Tangier via Paris and Madrid in less than 48 hours, with a night in Algeciras (Spain).

Morocco is not part of the InterRail/Eurail systems, so you will have to buy tickets locally to add the country onto a European trip.

In Algeciras, the train station is about 10 minutes' walk from the ferry terminals for Morocco. If you arrive during the day you should be able to quickly transfer to the ferries.

Useful resource:

Man in Seat 61 (www.seat61. com) Comprehensive, regularly updated information on getting to Morocco by train.

Mauritania

The trans-Saharan route via Mauritania is the main route from North Africa into sub-Saharan Africa.

From Dakhla follow the N1 south along the coast for 328km to the border, past Nouâdhibou and south to the Mauritanian capital, Nouakchott.

While this route is generally regarded as safe, check Mauritania safety advice before travelling. Take plenty of water and food, and set off early in the morning.

This route is entirely paved (apart from a 5km stretch in the no-man's land between the two border posts). Moroccan border formalities are processed at Guergarat. The border is mined, so stay on the road. From the border, it's a 41km drive along the peninsula to Nouâdhibou.

Mauritanian currency (ouguiya, UM) is available at the border, and on the black market in no-man's land.

Vehicle searches and requests for a *petit cadeau* (little present) are not uncommon, particularly if the Mauritanian officials find alcohol on you (illegal in Mauritania).

Prepare a *fiche* (form) or *ordre de mission* (itinerary) for Mauritanian checkpoints. List all your passport and visa details, occupation, destination and your vehicle's make, colour and registration number. Make plenty of photocopies.

Useful resources include Horizons Unlimited's **Sahara Travel Forum** (www.horizonsunlimited.com) and **Sahara Overland** (http://saharaoverland.wordpress.com).

CAR & MOTORCYCLE

⇒ Some stations south of Dakhla may be out of fuel,

in particular the last station 50km before the border.

⇒ As well as getting stamped in by the police, you need to buy a 30-day temporary-vehicle-import form (€10).

MINIBUS & JEEP

There are ad hoc transport links from Dakhla to the Mauritanian border and beyond. Minibuses and 4WDs leave from the military checkpoint on the road out of Dakhla. Grands taxis occasionally run to the border from the main station (Dh220). You'll then need to hitch to get to the Mauritanian checkpoint, as walking across the border is forbidden. A lift all the way to Nouâdhibou is preferable, or you will likely have to pay extortionate fees to travel on from the border.

In Dakhla, hotels Erraha and Sahara and the Sahara Regency are good places to pick up information and arrange transport.

From Nouâdhibou, bush taxis to the border/Dakhla cost around UM2000/11,500, leaving in the early morning.

Sea

There are extensive ferry links between northern Morocco

FERRY COMPANIES & ROUTES

Direct Ferries (www.directferries.com) sells tickets for most of the below. The Europe-wide service has sites in most European languages.

Acciona Trasmediterranea (www.trasmediterranea. es) Almería–Melilla, Almería–Nador, Algeciras–Ceuta, Algeciras–Tangier, Barcelona–Tangier, Málaga–Melilla.

Baleària (www.balearia.com) Algeciras–Ceuta, Algeciras–Tangier.

Comarit (www.comarit.es) Algeciras–Tangier, Sète–Tangier, Tarifa–Tangier.

FRS (www.frs.es) Algeciras–Ceuta, Algeciras–Tangier, Gibraltar–Tangier, Tarifa–Tangier.

Grandi Navi Veloci (GNV; www.gnv.it) Barcelona–Tangier, Genoa–Tangier.

Grimaldi Lines (www.grimaldi-lines.com) Livorno–Tangier, Valencia–Tangier.

Ferry Routes

and southern Europe, the most popular of which is Algeciras (Spain) to Tangier.

➡ From southern Spain and northern Morocco, you can just turn up at the dock and buy a ticket for the next ferry, but book in advance during high season (mid-June to mid-September, Christmas, New Year and Easter). Tickets can also be purchased online.

➡ In Tangier and Algeciras, avoid the touts who try to guide you towards their favourite travel agency for their bit of commission.

➡ Discounts for students and young people with an ISIC card or similar, and InterRail or Eurail pass-holders are common. Children aged between two and 12 often travel for half the fare, those aged under two travel free, and over-60s can often get reductions.

➡ Vehicles can be taken on most ferries for an extra fee; bicycles are normally free.

➡ Cabins are available on longer crossings.

➡ Ferries to Tangier now dock at the new Tanger Med terminal, except for those from Tarifa (Spain).

France

➡ The journey from Sète (two hours by train from Marseilles) to Tangier takes 36 hours; to Nador takes 28 hours.

➡ There are about five sailings weekly to Tangier, and one to Nador.

➡ Advance booking is recommended.

Gibraltar

➡ There's one fast ferry a day to/from Tangier.

➡ The trip takes a similar length of time to sailings to/from Algeciras, and tickets cost the same.

➡ Algeciras is a better option as it's a busier port with more choice.

Spain

➡ Ferries from Spain to Morocco are plentiful. Tickets start at about €30.

➡ Hydrofoils and catamarans (also referred to as fast ferries) are used extensively, but are more expensive.

➡ Spanish passport control is uncomplicated, but non-EU citizens and Schengen visa-holders should make sure they get an exit stamp before boarding the ferry.

➡ You need to fill in an embarkation form on board, and get your passport stamped before disembarking.

➡ Customs can be slow on the Spanish side if you're coming from Morocco.

ALGECIRAS TO TANGIER

➡ The most popular and frequent crossing between Europe and Morocco. Ferries run at least every 90 minutes, and hourly in the summer. The crossing typically takes an hour.

➡ Services typically run from 7am (or 6am in summer) until 10pm, but during peak demand in August 24-hour services aren't unknown.

ALGECIRAS TO CEUTA

➡ Several daily high-speed ferries (30 minutes to one hour) leave in both directions between about 7am and 10pm.

ALMERÍA TO MELILLA

➡ Ferries depart daily from Almería, and on Monday morning and Sunday afternoon from Melilla, taking up to eight hours.

ALMERÍA TO NADOR

➡ There are five crossings a week in either direction, taking five/eight hours to Nador/Almería.

BARCELONA TO TANGIER

➡ Two companies offer this route to Tangier, one

stopping in Barcelona en route from Genoa (Italy).

➡ Three weekly sailings; takes about 29 hours.

MÁLAGA TO MELILLA

➡ The daily (apart from Sunday) service is normally an afternoon/night ferry to/from Melilla.

➡ It takes up to eight hours.

TARIFA TO TANGIER

➡ Catamarans leave every hour or so and cross the strait in 35 minutes, making this the fastest and most practical route.

➡ The fare includes a free bus transfer to Algeciras on presentation of your ferry ticket.

➡ The transfer takes 50 minutes, making the trip via Tarifa a faster way to get to Algeciras than the slower direct ferries.

VALENCIA TO TANGIER

➡ This service is part of the Tangier–Livorno (Italy) sailing.

➡ This leg of the journey takes 20 hours, leaving around midday and arriving at 8am in both directions.

Italy

➡ Three companies sail the Mediterranean from Italy to Tangier, from Livorno via Valencia and Genoa via Barcelona.

➡ The Livorno service takes 56 hours.

➡ The three weekly Genoa sailings take about 50 hours.

GETTING AROUND

Getting around Morocco is pretty straightforward – transport networks between towns are good, and even off the beaten track there's often something going your way. RAM offers internal flights, the rail network is excellent in linking the major cities, and large bus compa-

nies like CTM are comfortable and efficient. Local networks are cheaper and more cheerful and do the job.

Car hire is relatively expensive but gives you the most freedom, although navigating the big cities can be stressful. Good sealed roads are generally the order of the day, with much investment being poured into areas like the Rif to improve their connectivity. Roads in remote mountain and desert areas are often just *piste* (unsealed track or road).

Bicycle

Mountain biking can be a great way of travelling in Morocco. There are plenty of opportunities for getting off the beaten track, with thousands of kilometres of remote *pistes* to be explored.

Hazards Surfaced roads are generally well maintained once completed, but they tend to be narrow and, in less-frequented areas, may have jagged edges, which can be hairy given the kamikaze drivers. Beware of gangs of stone-throwing children in remote areas.

Hire You'll find bicycles for hire in places like Essaouira and Taroudannt, but don't expect to find the latest models of mountain bike.

Transport Bus companies will generally carry bicycles as luggage for an extra fee. Likewise on trains, although it's generally only possible to transport bikes in the goods wagon.

Bus

The cheapest and most efficient way to travel around the country, buses are generally safe, although their drivers sometimes leave a little to be desired.

Bus stations Some Moroccan bus stations are like madhouses, with touts running around calling any number of destinations of buses about to depart. Most cities and towns have

a single central bus station (*gare routière*), but Supratours and CTM sometimes maintain separate terminals, and often have offices outside the station. Occasionally, there are secondary stations for a limited number of local destinations.

Touts Touts will happily guide you to a ticket booth (and take a small commission from the company). Always double-check that their recommended service really is the most comfortable, direct and convenient option.

Luggage Bus stations in the main cities have left-luggage depots (*consigne*), sometimes open 24 hours. Padlock your bags. More often than not you'll be charged for baggage handling, especially if your gear is going on top of the bus – Dh5 is common.

Costs Bus travel is cheap considering the distances covered. CTM fares from Casablanca to Agadir, Marrakesh, Fez and Tangier are Dh220, Dh130, Dh70 and Dh100 respectively. Companies including Supratours offer 1st- and 2nd-class tickets, although the difference in fare and comfort is rarely great.

Reservations Where possible, and especially if services are infrequent or do not originate in the place you want to leave, book ahead for CTM and Supratours buses. Particularly busy routes are Marrakesh–Essaouira and Casablanca–Marrakesh, where you may need to reserve seats two days in advance in high season.

Daytime journeys Many buses have rather meagre curtains, so to avoid melting in the sun, pay attention to where you sit. Heading from north to south, sit on the right in the morning and the left in the afternoon; east to west, sit on the right, or on the left if travelling from west to east. You will often be assigned a seat when you purchase your ticket, but you can ask to choose a place.

Night-time journeys Operating on many intercity routes, night buses can be both quicker and cooler, although not necessarily more sleep-inducing.

Supratours & Train Network

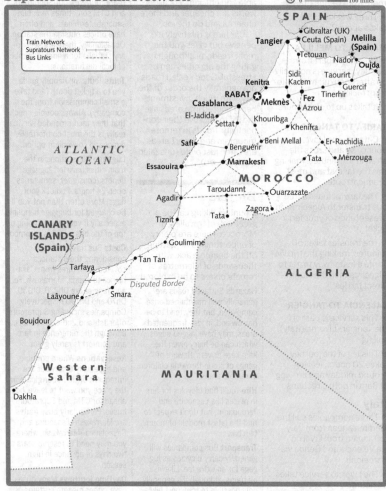

Stops Most bus trips longer than three hours incorporate a scheduled stop to stretch your legs and grab a snack. Buses are often delayed at police check-points for about 10 minutes – longer than grands taxis, whose local drivers usually know the police.

Bus Operators

CTM

With the most comprehensive nationwide service, **CTM** (www.ctm.ma) serves most destinations of interest to travellers. Established in 1919, it's Morocco's oldest bus company.

➡ On CTM buses, children aged four years and over pay full fares, which tend to be 15% to 30% more expensive than most other lines – comparable to 2nd-class fares on normal trains.

➡ Tickets can normally be purchased in advance; check departures with the online timetable.

➡ Most CTM buses are modern and comfortable, and some 1st-class buses have videos (a mixed blessing), air-conditioning and heating (they sometimes overdo both).

➡ There is an official Dh5-per-pack baggage charge on CTM buses.

➡ Once you have bought your ticket, you get a baggage tag, which you hand over when you've reached your destination.

SUPRATOURS

The ONCF train company runs **Supratours** (www.oncf.ma) to complement its rail network. For example, train passengers continuing south from Marrakesh link up at the station with buses to destinations including Agadir and Ouarzazate.

➡ It's possible, at train ticket offices, to buy a ticket covering a complete trip with both rail and bus components.

➡ On trains, travellers with tickets for connecting buses have priority.

➡ Supratours is similar to CTM in terms of both its fares and the comfort of its buses. Check departures with the online timetable.

OTHER COMPANIES

In the south of the country, Satas and SAT are good second-tier choices, as is Trans Ghazala in the north.

At the bottom end of the price range, and on shorter routes, there are a fair number of two-bit operations with one or two well-worn buses. These services depart sufficiently full, and frequently stop to recruit more passengers.

Car & Motorcycle

Morocco is a country made for touring, and offers freedom to explore the more unusual routes in your own time.

Daylight driving is generally no problem and not too stressful, though Moroccan drivers need to be treated with more caution than their counterparts in the West.

The roads connecting Morocco's main centres are generally good, and there's an expanding motorway network. A new motorway along the Mediterranean coast is set to join the three already in place:

➡ From Tangier down the Atlantic Coast to El-Jadida.

➡ From Rabat inland to Fez via Meknès.

➡ From Casablanca south to Agadir via Marrakesh.

Bringing Your Own Vehicle

➡ Every vehicle should display the nationality plate of its country of registration, and you must always carry proof of ownership of a private vehicle. Moroccan law requires a Green Card (carte verte, or International Motor Insurance Card), as proof of insurance. A warning triangle (to be used in case of breakdown) is compulsory.

➡ Obtain insurance and a Green Card before leaving home. Otherwise local insurance (assurance frontiere), costing about Dh650 for 10 days, must be purchased at the ferry port or a nearby broker (bureau d'assurance).

➡ Ask for the optional constat amiable form, which both parties fill out in the event of a minor road accident. They can also be purchased at tabacs in cities.

➡ At the port, or on the ferry on longer crossings, you must also fill in the TVIP form (temporary vehicle importation declaration – declaration d'admission temporaire de moyens de transport), valid for six months. Present this form when you (and your vehicle) leave the country. You can also download the form from the website of **Morocco Customs** (www.douane.gov.ma), where it's referred to as D16TER.

➡ There is no need for a carnet de passage en douane for temporarily importing your vehicle to Morocco.

Driving Licence

➡ International driving permits are recommended for Morocco by most automobile bodies, but many foreign, including EU, licences are accepted provided they bear your photograph.

➡ You must carry your licence or permit and passport when driving.

Fuel & Spare Parts

➡ The country is well served with petrol stations, although they become fewer and further between south of Goulimime. If you're travelling off the beaten track, refuel at every opportunity. Keep a close eye on the gauge in the southern desert and fill up wherever you get a chance, as stations don't always have supplies of fuel.

➡ Leaded and less-common unleaded (sans plomb) petrol cost around Dh12.50 per litre and diesel (gasoil) is around Dh8.50. In the Western Sahara, tax-free petrol is about 30% cheaper. Fuel in the Spanish enclaves of Ceuta and Melilla is comparably priced to Morocco.

➡ Moroccan mechanics are generally good and decent-sized towns should have at least one garage, most with a range of spare parts for Renaults and other French cars. If you can fit replacement parts yourself, ask a Moroccan friend to help you buy the parts, as this may help to keep the price closer to local levels.

Hire

➡ Most Moroccan car-rental companies require drivers to be at least 21 (or 23 in a few cases).

➡ Renting a car costs about Dh300 per day for a week or so with unlimited mileage. For longer rentals, lower daily rates are sometimes available. Pre-booking gives the cheapest deals. Most companies demand a (returnable) cash deposit (Dh3000 to Dh5000) or take an impression of your credit card.

➡ With international firms such as **Hertz** (www.hertz.com), **Budget** (www.budget.ma), **Europcar** (www.europcar.com), **National** (www.nationalcar.com) and **Avis** (www.avis.ma), you can pre-book online. There are also numerous local agencies.

➡ Make sure you understand what is included in the price and what your liabilities are. Always check the car's condition before signing up, and make sure it comes with a spare tyre, tool kit and full documentation – including insurance cover. Keep the car's documents and your licence with you, rather than in the car, as you'll need them if the car is stolen or damaged. Keep receipts for oil changes or mechanical repairs; these costs should be reimbursed.

➡ Insurance must, by law, be sold along with all rental agreements. Make sure that prices include collision damage, insurance and tax (20%). You should also take out Collision Damage Waiver insurance, typically about Dh35 to Dh60 a day (often with an excess of up to Dh5000). Super Collision Damage Waiver, which eliminates or minimises the excess, may be available for an extra Dh60 or so a day.

➡ Unless you hire a 4WD, your rental agreement will probably not allow off-road (*piste*) driving, making you liable for potential damages.

Motorcycle

➡ Motorcycle touring is popular, but many bikes are unfamiliar in Morocco, particularly those with larger capacity engines, so repairs can be tricky.

➡ Carry a good tool kit and all necessary spares, including cables and levers, inner tubes, puncture repair kit, tyre levers, pump, fuses, chain, washable air filter and cable ties.

➡ Some insurance policies do not allow foreign motorcycle licences to be used in Morocco.

➡ Some companies offer motorcycle (Dh300 per day for a DT 125cc Yamaha) and scooter (from Dh150 per day) hire.

➡ See **Horizons Unlimited** (www.horizonsunlimited.com) for detailed advice on biking in the region.

Parking

➡ Parking zones are often watched by *gardiens de voitures* (car-park attendants). Payment of a few dirhams gives a trouble-free parking experience.

➡ In the big city centres, parking tickets are issued from kerbside machines (Dh2 to Dh3 per hour for a maximum stay of two hours). Parking is free on Sundays.

➡ Parking is not allowed at kerbsides painted in red and white stripes. Stopping is not allowed on green and white stripes.

➡ Fines for illegally parked cars can reach Dh1500.

Roadblocks

➡ Police control points are common on main roads in and out of most sizeable towns.

➡ Foreigners are unlikely to be stopped, but it's still a good idea to slow down and put on your best smile.

➡ Roadblocks are also common in sensitive areas like the Western Sahara, the Rif Mountains around the cannabis-producing region of Ketama, and the road to Figuig near the Algerian border.

➡ Police are more vigilant in these areas, but at most, you'll be asked to show your passport, driving licence and the vehicle's papers, and asked the purpose of your visit and destination.

Road Hazards

Morocco ranks 6th worldwide in road accidents. Treat all vehicles as ready to veer out and cut you off at inopportune moments.

Cyclists and pedestrians often have poor traffic awareness. Roads are often busy with people (including groups of schoolchildren), bicycles, horse and carts, donkeys and so on.

Desert In the *hammada* (stony desert), tar roads sometimes disappear without warning, replaced by stretches of sand, gravel and potholes. If a strong *chergui* (dry, easterly desert wind) is blowing and carrying a lot of dust, you'll have to wait until it eases off if you don't want to do your car considerable damage.

Mountains High and Middle Atlas passes are often closed due to snow in winter. Seek local advice before travelling, or check the road signs along the routes.

Medinas Entering cities and towns, park outside the medina or find out if the route to your accommodation is easily driveable – narrow medina streets weren't designed for cars.

Night Driving at night is particularly hazardous: it's legal (and very common) for vehicles travelling under 20km/h to drive without lights.

Road Rules

➡ Drive on the right-hand side of the road.

➡ Give way to traffic entering a roundabout from the right when you're already on one.

➡ The fine for missing a red stop sign is Dh700.

➡ The speed limit in built-up areas is 40km/h, and 100km/h outside the towns (120km/h on motorways). Police with radar guns are common, so watch your speed.

➡ It's the law to wear a seatbelt.

➡ Tolls apply on the motorways – for example, Rabat–Tangier is about Dh60 and Rabat–Casablanca is Dh20. You take a ticket upon entering the motorway and pay at the end.

➡ In the event of an accident, especially involving injuries, drivers are officially required to remain at the scene. Vehicles cannot be moved until the police have arrived – this may take hours.

➡ Pick up a *constat amiable* form in case you have an accident; they can be purchased at *tabacs* in cities.

Local Transport

Bus

➡ The bigger cities have public bus services.

➡ Tickets are typically Dh4.

➡ Buses can be ludicrously overcrowded and routes often hard to discern.

➡ Petits taxis are often an easier and faster option.

Grand Taxi

The elderly Mercedes vehicles you'll see on Moroccan roads and gathered near bus stations are shared taxis (*grands taxis* in French or *taxiat kebira* in Arabic).

The Ziz and Drâa Valleys, the Tizi n'Test and the Rif Mountains, all scenic areas not well-served by buses, are good to visit in a taxi.

➡ Grands taxis link towns to their neighbours, often in a relay system that may necessitate changing a few times on longer journeys. Taxis sometimes ply longer routes but these services are rarer and usually leave first thing in the morning.

➡ Grands taxis take six cramped passengers (two in the front, four in the back) and leave when full. It can often be advantageous to pay for two seats to get the taxi going earlier, and give yourself more space. This is particularly useful for lone women, as you should get the front seat to yourself.

➡ The fixed-rate fares are a little higher than bus fares, but still very reasonable. Make it clear you want to pay for *une place* (one spot)

in a *taxi collectif* (shared taxi). Another expression that helps explain that you don't want the taxi to yourself is *ma'a an-nas* (with other people). If you've got particularly heavy/bulky luggage, there might be a surcharge.

➡ Hiring an entire taxi is sometimes a good option – especially if you're travelling with a small group, or you want to travel along an unpopular route without waiting hours for other passengers. The fare should be six times the cost for one place. If you'll be travelling through a scenic area, make sure plans for stopping en route are clear.

➡ Grand-taxi drivers often have a boy-racer mentality. Overtaking on blind corners can be a badge of honour, and speed limits are only adhered to when there's a police roadblock in sight. Night-time journeys are best avoided. Seatbelts are a rarity – and questioning this may be taken as a slur on your driver's skills.

Petit Taxi

➡ Cities and bigger towns have local petits taxis, which are a different colour in every city.

➡ Petits taxis are licensed to carry up to three passengers, but are not permitted to go beyond the city limits.

➡ They are usually, but not always, metered. To ask in French for the meter to be switched on, say '*tourne le conteur, si'l vous plaît*'. Where taxis are not metered, agree on a price beforehand.

➡ If the driver refuses to use the meter and won't give you a price, ask to stop and get out. Most petit-taxi drivers are perfectly honest, but those in Marrakesh and Casablanca are notoriously greedy with tourists.

➡ Multiple hire is common. The price should be the same whether you hail an empty taxi and pick up other passengers en route, or there are already others in a taxi you wave down, or you travel alone.

➡ From 8pm (often 9pm in summer) there is normally a 50% surcharge – or just Dh1 or so where a fixed-fare system is in place.

Pick-Up Truck & 4WD

➡ In more remote areas, especially the Atlas Mountains, locals travel between villages in Berber *camionettes* (pick-up trucks), old vans or the back of trucks.

→ When travelling between remote towns and villages, the best time to find a lift is early on market days (generally once or twice a week). Waits for departures can be considerable.

→ 4WD taxis operate on remote *pistes* that would destroy normal taxis.

Tours

Atlas Sahara Trek (Map p52; ☏0524 30 39 01; www. atlas-sahara-trek.com; Marrakesh) Winter camel treks to Erg Chigaga and summer hikes into the M'Goun valley.

Authentic Morocco (www. authentic-morocco.com; Marrakesh & UK) This reliable company supports local communities and practises low-impact tourism, offering itineraries from camel treks to tours of Roman ruins.

Desert Majesty (Map p114; ☏0524 89 07 65; www.desert majesty.com; 18 Pl al-Moua-hidine) A highly recommended local agency offering trips to the High Atlas and the desert. Airport pick-ups, multilingual guides originating in Erfoud, Merzouga, M'Hamid and Taouz, and reassuringly safe drivers are offered at competitive prices. Booking queries are handled by Felicity who is fluent in English, German, French and Darija.

Equatorial Travel (www. equatorialtravel.co.uk; UK) Tailor-made trips and set itineraries, focused on areas including music, photography and walking, run by a small agency based on the fair-trade concept.

Journeys Elite (www. journeyselite.com; UK) Offers tailor-made trips such as Anti Atlas by 4WD, and High Atlas gorges to Erg Chebbi.

Nature Trekking Maroc (www.maroctrekking.com; Marrakesh) Off-the-beaten-track trekking, horse riding,

mountain biking, skiing and 4WD trips.

Wildcat Adventures (www. wildcat-bike-tours.co.uk; UK) Offers road- and mountain-bike tours in the High Atlas and Anti Atlas, plus a bike-trek-camel itinerary.

Wilderness Travel (www. wildernesstravel.com; USA) Much-applauded culture, wildlife and hiking specialist, with itineraries from High Atlas treks to cruising the coastline.

Yallah (www.yallahmorocco. com; Marrakesh & UK) The decade-old company offers tailor-made tours plus two itineraries covering the Imperial cities and southern Morocco, both ending in luxury in Marrakesh.

Train

Morocco's excellent train network is one of Africa's best, linking most of the main centres. Trains are reasonably priced, and preferable to buses where available. Trains are comfortable, fast and run closely to their timetables. The **Office National des Chemins de Fer** (ONCF; www.oncf.ma) runs the network.

→ There are two main lines: Tangier down to Marrakesh via Rabat and Casablanca; and Oujda or Nador in the northeast down to Marrakesh, passing Fez and Meknès before joining the line from Tangier at Sidi Kacem.

→ A high-speed (TGV) line to link Tangier, Rabat and Casablanca is under construction and due to open in December 2015.

→ Also operated by ONCF, Supratours buses link many destinations to the train network.

→ Trains are particularly convenient around Casablanca and Rabat, with services leaving every 30 minutes between the two cities.

→ The overnight Tangier–Marrakesh and Oujda–Casablanca trains have sleeping cars.

Classes

There are two types of train, and the main difference between the two is comfort, rather than speed:

→ *Rapide* (Train Rapide Climatisé, TCR) – standard for intercity services.

→ *Ordinaire* (Train Navette Rapide, TNR) – less comfortable, without air-conditioning, apart from the double-decker TNR Rabat–Casablanca shuttle. Mostly late-night and local services.

Additional information:

→ Prices given here are for *rapide* trains (*ordinaire* trains are around 30% cheaper).

→ First- and 2nd-class fares are available, with six seats in 1st-class compartments and eight in 2nd class.

→ First-class tickets include a reserved seat, while in 2nd class you just sit in an empty seat.

→ Second class is more than adequate on short journeys.

→ Shuttle services operate regularly between Kenitra, Rabat, Casablanca and Mohammed V International Airport, and they supplement the *rapide* services on this line.

Costs

Sample 2nd-class fares:

→ Casablanca to Marrakesh (Dh90, three hours)

→ Rabat to Fez (Dh80, three hours)

→ Tangier to Marrakesh (Dh205, 8½ hours)

Additional information:

→ All journeys in sleeping cars cost Dh350 in a four-bed couchette, and Dh450/600 for a single/double compartment.

→ Children aged under four travel free.

→ Children between four and 12 years get a discount (normally 50%, less in a few cases including sleeping cars).

→ At weekends travellers get a 25% discount on return trips, or one-way trips longer than 180km, on major-line trains.

Stations & Timetables

→ Stations aren't usually well signposted, and announcements (in both French and Arabic) are frequently inaudible, so keep an eye out for your stop.

→ Most stations are located in the ville nouvelle. In cities such as Tangier, Marrakesh, Fez and Rabat, the main stations are sleek affairs with free wi-fi and decent restaurants.

→ Stations usually have left-luggage depots, which only accept luggage that can be locked.

→ Timetables for the whole system are posted in French at stations, or check on the ONCF website for times and prices.

Tickets

→ Buy tickets at the station, as a supplement is charged for buying tickets on the train. Automatic ticket machines are becoming more widespread at stations.

→ Buy your ticket the day before you want to travel if possible, particularly if you want to travel 1st-class. Second-class seats cannot be reserved. First-class tickets can be bought up to a month before travel – advisable if travelling during major holidays, and for sleeper services.

→ Inspectors check tickets on the trains.

Train Passes

Rail Pass This is available for seven/15/30 days (Dh600/1170/2100 to travel in 2nd class, Dh900/1600/3150 for 1st class). Pass prices drop for travellers aged under 26, and again for those under 12 years.

Carte Chahab (six months Dh249) If you're under 26, this offers 25% to 50% discounts.

Carte Hikma (six months Dh99) For those aged over 60, this offers 25% to 50% discounts.

Carte Ousraty (one year, Dh50 per person) For families, this offers 10% to 25% on group tickets.

Tram

Casablanca and Rabat both have new and modern tram networks, which are excellent for exploring those cities. See p173 for more details.

Health

Prevention is the key to staying healthy in Morocco, and a little planning before departure will save you trouble later. With luck, your worst complaint on your trip will be a bad stomach; infections are usually associated with poor living conditions and poverty, and can be avoided with a few precautions. Car accidents are a common reason for travellers to need medical help. Medical facilities can be excellent in large cities, but in more remote areas may be basic.

BEFORE YOU GO

Vaccinations Don't leave health matters to the last minute: some vaccines don't ensure immunity for two weeks, so visit a doctor four to eight weeks before departure. Before leaving home, ensure that all your routine vaccination cover is complete. Ask your doctor for an international certificate of vaccination, listing all the vaccinations you've received.

First-aid courses Those heading to very remote areas may like to do a first-aid course, such as those offered by the American Red Cross and St John's Ambulance. Particularly if you're going trekking, you could take a wilderness medical training course, such as that offered by the **Royal Geographical Society** (www.rgs.org).

Medications Bring them in their original, clearly labelled containers. A signed and dated letter from your physician describing your medical conditions and medications, including generic names, is also helpful. If carrying syringes or needles, ensure you have a physician's letter documenting their medical necessity. See your dentist before a long trip; carry a spare pair of contact lenses and glasses (and take your optical prescription with you).

Insurance

➡ Adequate health insurance is vital when travelling to Morocco. The national health service isn't always great and the few good private hospitals are expensive.

➡ You may prefer a policy that pays the medical facility directly rather than you having to pay on the spot and claim later, although in practice most Moroccan doctors and hospitals insist on payment up front.

➡ If you have to claim later, make sure you keep all documentation.

➡ Carry proof of your insurance with you; this can be vital in avoiding any delays to treatment in emergency situations.

➡ Some policies ask you to call (reverse charge) a centre in your home country, which makes an immediate assessment of your problem; keep your insurer's emergency telephone number on you.

➡ Find out which private medical service your insurer uses in Morocco so that you can call them direct in the event of an emergency.

➡ Your policy should ideally cover emergency air evacuation home, or transport by plane or ambulance to a hospital in a major city, which may

RECOMMENDED VACCINATIONS

Although no specific vaccinations are required for Morocco, America's Centers for Disease Control and Prevention (CDC) suggests the following as routine:

➡ Diphtheria

➡ Tetanus

➡ Measles

➡ Mumps

➡ Rubella

➡ Polio

The CDC also suggests the following for Morocco:

➡ Hepatitis A and B

➡ Typhoid

➡ Rabies

be essential for serious problems.

→ Some policies offer lower and higher medical-expense options; the higher ones are chiefly for countries such as the USA, which have extremely high medical costs.

Medical Checklist

Consider packing the following items in your medical kit:

→ antibiotics (if travelling off the beaten track)

→ antibacterial hand gel

→ antidiarrhoeal drugs (eg loperamide)

→ paracetamol or aspirin

→ anti-inflammatory drugs (eg ibuprofen)

→ antihistamines (for hay fever and allergic reactions)

→ antibacterial ointment (eg Bactroban) for cuts and abrasions

→ steroid cream or cortisone (for allergic rashes)

→ bandages, gauze and gauze rolls

→ adhesive or paper tape

→ scissors, safety pins and tweezers

→ thermometer

→ pocket knife

→ DEET-containing insect repellent

→ insect spray for clothing, tents and bed nets

→ sunblock

→ oral rehydration salts (eg Dioralyte)

→ iodine or other water-purification tablets

→ syringes and sterile needles (if travelling to remote areas)

Websites

Useful to consult prior to departure:

CDC (www.cdc.gov/travel) US website.

Health Canada (http://tinyurl.com/4tj653u)

International Association for Medical Advice to Travellers (IAMAT; www.iamat.org) Gives access to its online database of doctors with recognised training.

Lonely Planet (www.lonelyplanet.com)

MD Travel Health (www.mdtravelhealth.com) US website.

NHS (www.fitfortravel.nhs.uk) UK website.

Smarttraveller (www.smarttraveller.gov.au) Australian website.

WHO (www.who.int/ith)

IN MOROCCO

Availability & Cost of Health Care

Primary medical care is not always readily available outside major cities and towns. Your hotel may be able to recommend the nearest source of medical help, and embassy websites sometimes list doctors and clinics. In an emergency, contact your embassy or consulate.

Pharmacies These are generally well stocked, and pharmacists can provide advice (usually in French) covering common travellers' complaints. They can sell over-the-counter medication, often including drugs only available on prescription at home, and advise when more specialised help is needed. Double-check any unfamiliar purchases; readers have reported receiving incorrect and potentially dangerous medication for their conditions.

Doctors and clinics If you are being treated by a doctor or at a clinic, particularly outside the major cities, you will often be expected to purchase medical supplies on the spot – even including sterile dressings or intravenous fluids.

Dental care Standards are variable – Marrakshi street dentists around the Djemaa el-Fna aren't recommended! Travel insurance doesn't usually cover dental work other than emergency treatment.

Infectious Diseases

Hepatitis A

Spreads Through contaminated food (particularly shellfish) and water.

Symptoms and effects Jaundice, dark urine, a yellow colour to the whites of the eyes, fever and abdominal pain. Although rarely fatal, it can cause prolonged lethargy and delayed recovery.

Prevention Vaccine (Avaxim, VAQTA, Havrix) is given as an injection, with a booster extending the protection offered. Hepatitis A and typhoid vaccines can also be given as a combined single-dose vaccine (hepatyrix or viatim).

Hepatitis B

Spreads Through infected blood, contaminated needles and sexual intercourse.

Symptoms and effects Jaundice and liver problems (occasionally failure).

Prevention Travellers should make this a routine vaccination, although Morocco gives hepatitis B vaccination as part of routine childhood vaccination. It is given singly, or at the same time as hepatitis A.

HIV

Morocco has an HIV infection rate of 0.15%, primarily found in cities such as Agadir and Marrakesh, and rising to around 5% among men who have sex with men, sex workers and intravenous drug users.

Spreads Through infected blood and blood products; sexual intercourse with an infected partner; 'blood to blood' contacts, such as through contaminated instruments during medical, dental, acupuncture and other body-piercing procedures, or sharing used intravenous needles.

Leishmaniasis

Spreads Through the bite of an infected sandfly or dog. It may be found in rural areas in the Atlas Mountains, where sandflies are more prevalent between June and October.

Symptoms and effects Slowly growing skin lumps or sores. It may develop into a serious, life-threatening fever, usually accompanied by anaemia and weight loss.

Prevention and treatment Avoid sandfly bites. There is no vaccine, but treatment with an antimonial drug such as Glucantime or Pentostam is straightforward, usually involving an injection.

Rabies

Spreads Through bites or licks on broken skin from an infected animal. Rabies is endemic to Morocco.

Symptoms and effects Initial symptoms are pain or tingling at the site of the bite with fever, loss of appetite and headache. If untreated, both 'furious' and less-common 'dumb' rabies are fatal.

Prevention and treatment People travelling to remote areas, where a reliable source of post-bite vaccine is not available within 24 hours, should be vaccinated. Any bite, scratch or lick from a warm-blooded, furry animal should immediately be thoroughly cleaned. If you have not been vaccinated and you get bitten, you will need a course of injections starting as soon as possible after the injury. Vaccination does not provide immunity; it merely buys you more time to seek medical help.

Tuberculosis

Spreads Through close respiratory contact and, occasionally, infected milk or milk products.

Symptoms and effects Can be asymptomatic, although symptoms can include a cough, weight loss or fever months or even years after exposure. An X-ray is the best way to confirm if you have tuberculosis.

Prevention BCG vaccine is recommended for those mixing closely with the local population, whether visiting family, planning a long stay, or working as a teacher or health-care worker. As it's a live vaccine it should not be given to pregnant women or immuno-compromised individuals.

Typhoid

Spreads Through food or water that has been contaminated by infected human faeces.

Symptoms and effects Initially, usually fever or a pink rash on the abdomen. Septicaemia (blood poisoning) may also occur.

Prevention Typhim Vi or typherix vaccine. In some countries, the oral vaccine Vivotif is also available.

Yellow Fever

Travellers arriving in Morocco from a yellow-fever-endemic area need to show proof of vaccination before entry.

Spreads There is a small risk of yellow fever, borne by mosquitoes, in rural Chefchaouen province between May and October.

Symptoms and effects Muscle aches, fever, headache, nausea and vomiting subside after a few days, followed in up to a quarter of cases by anaemia, liver inflammation, hepatitis, jaundice and kidney damage. Most patients who also experience bleeding from the nose, mouth and stomach (leading to blood in vomit and faeces) die in a short space of time.

Prevention The risk is so small that the World Health Organization does not recommend vaccination. It must be given at a designated clinic, and is a live vaccine so must not be given to immuno-compromised or pregnant travellers.

Traveller's Diarrhoea

Causes Strains of travel – unfamiliar food, heat, long days and erratic sleeping patterns – can all make your body more susceptible to an upset stomach.

Prevention Water is generally safe to drink in cities, but elsewhere you should only drink treated water. Eat fresh fruits or vegetables only if they are cooked or if you have washed or peeled them yourself. Buffet meals, which may have been kept sitting warm for some time, can be risky; food should be piping hot. Meals freshly cooked in front of you (like much street food) or served in a busy restaurant are more likely to be safe. Be sensible, but not paranoid: food is one of the treats of visiting Morocco, so don't miss out.

Hygiene Pay close attention to personal hygiene. Many Moroccan meals are eaten with the hand, so always wash before eating and after using the toilet. Even the smallest restaurant will have a sink, but soap is less common, especially at cheap hotels. Antibacterial hand gel, which cleans without needing water, is useful.

Treatment Drink plenty of fluids, and preferably an oral rehydration solution; pharmacies stock these inexpensive *sels de réhydration orale*. Avoid fatty food and dairy products. A few loose stools don't require treatment, but if you start having more than four or five a day, take an antibiotic (usually a quinolone drug) and an antidiarrhoeal agent (such as loperamide). If diarrhoea is bloody, persists for more than 72 hours, and is accompanied by fever, shaking, chills or severe abdominal pain, seek medical attention.

Environmental Hazards

Altitude Sickness

Causes Lack of oxygen at high altitudes (over 2500m) affects most people to some extent. The effect may be mild or severe, and occurs because less oxygen reaches the muscles and the brain at high altitudes, requiring the heart and lungs to compensate by working harder. There is no hard-and-fast rule as to what is too high: Acute Mountain Sickness (AMS) has been fatal at 3000m, although 3500m to 4500m is the usual range.

Symptoms and effects Symptoms of AMS usually (but not always) develop during the first 24 hours at altitude. Mild symptoms include headache, lethargy, dizziness, difficulty sleeping and loss of appetite. Potentially fatal, AMS may become more severe without warning. Severe symptoms include breathlessness, a dry, irritative cough (which may progress to the production of pink, frothy sputum), severe headache, lack of coordination, confusion, irrational behaviour, vomiting, drowsiness and unconsciousness.

Prevention If trekking, build time into your schedule to acclimatise, and ensure your guide knows how to recognise and deal with altitude sickness. Morocco's most popular trek, to Jebel Toubkal, reaches the 4167m summit relatively quickly, so many people may suffer even mildly. The longer treks in the M'Goun Massif also reach heights of around 4000m. Treks in the Rif Mountains and Jebel Sarhro are considerably lower, so don't carry the same risks. You can download free booklets, including *Travel at Altitude* and *Children at Altitude,* from the website of the **British Mountaineering Council** (BMC; www.thebmc.co.uk).

Treatment Treat mild symptoms by resting at the same altitude until recovery, or preferably descend – even 500m can help. Take paracetamol or aspirin for headaches. If symptoms persist or become worse, immediate descent is necessary. Drug treatments should never be used to avoid descent or to enable further ascent. Diamox (acetazolamide) reduces the headache of AMS and helps the body acclimatise to the lack of oxygen. It is only available on prescription, and those who are allergic to sulfonamide antibiotics may also be allergic to Diamox.

Heat Illness

Causes Occurs following heavy sweating and excessive fluid loss with inadequate replacement of fluids and salt. This is particularly common in hot climates when taking unaccustomed exercise before full acclimatisation.

Symptoms and effects Headache, dizziness and tiredness.

Prevention Dehydration is already happening by the time you feel thirsty – drink sufficient water such that you produce pale, diluted urine. Morocco's sun can be fierce, so bring a hat.

Treatment Consists of fluid replacement with water, fruit juice, or both, and cooling by cold water and fans. Treating salt loss consists of consuming salty fluids such as soup or broth, and adding a little more table salt to foods than usual.

Heatstroke

Causes Extreme heat, high humidity, physical exertion or use of drugs or alcohol in the sun, and dehydration. Occurs when the body's heat-regulating mechanism breaks down.

Symptoms and effects An excessive rise in body temperature leads to sweating ceasing, irrational and hyperactive behaviour, and eventually loss of consciousness, and death.

Treatment Rapid cooling by spraying the body with water and fanning is ideal. Emergency fluid and electrolyte replacement by intravenous drip is usually also required.

Insect Bites & Stings

Causes Mosquitoes, sandflies (found around the Mediterranean beaches), scorpions (common in southern Morocco), bees and wasps, bedbugs and scabies (both found in cheaper accommodation).

Symptoms and effects More likely to be an irritant than a health risk. Sandflies have a nasty, itchy bite, and can carry the rare skin disorder leishmaniasis. Scorpions have a painful sting that is rarely life-threatening. Bedbugs lead to very

itchy, lumpy bites. Tiny scabies mites live in the skin, particularly between the fingers, and cause an intensely itchy rash.

Prevention and treatment DEET-based insect repellents. Spraying a mattress with an appropriate insect killer will do a good job of getting rid of bedbugs. Scabies is easily treated with lotion available from pharmacies; people you come into contact with also need treatment to avoid spreading scabies between asymptomatic carriers.

Snake Bites

Causes The chances of seeing a snake in Morocco, let alone being bitten by one, are slim. Nevertheless, there are a few venomous species, such as the horned viper, found in the southern desert areas. Snakes like to bask on rocks and sand, retreating during the heat of the day.

Prevention Do not walk barefoot or stick your hand into holes or cracks.

Treatment If bitten, do not panic. Half of those bitten by venomous snakes are not actually injected with poison (envenomed). Immobilise the bitten limb with a splint (eg a stick) and apply a bandage over the site, with firm pressure, similar to applying a bandage over a sprain. Do not apply a tourniquet, or cut or suck the bite. Get the victim to medical help as soon as possible so that antivenin can be given if necessary.

Water

Tap water is chlorinated in Morocco's cities and generally safe to drink – certainly safe to clean your teeth with. Elsewhere, stick to treated water – filter or purify it.

Bottled water is available everywhere, although there is an environmental cost through the mountains of discarded (and unrecycled) plastic bottles.

Off the beaten track, water drawn from wells or pumped from boreholes should be safe, but never drink water from rivers or lakes, as this may contain bacteria or viruses that can cause diarrhoea or vomiting.

Women's Health

Condoms, tampons and sanitary pads are widely available in Morocco.

Contraception If using oral contraceptives, remember that some antibiotics, as well as diarrhoea and vomiting, can stop the pill from working, so take condoms just in case. Condoms should be kept in a cool, dry place or they may crack and perish.

Pregnancy Take written records of the pregnancy and your blood group, which will be helpful if you need medical attention. Antenatal facilities vary greatly in North Africa, so think carefully before travelling to out-of-the-way places, bearing in mind the cultural and linguistic difficulties, not to mention the poor medical standards, you could face.

Language

The official language in Morocco is Arabic, which is used throughout the country. Berber is spoken in the Rif and Atlas Mountains. Most Berbers also speak at least some Arabic. French is still regularly used in the cities, but much less so among rural Berbers.

MOROCCAN ARABIC

Moroccan Arabic (Darija) is a variety of Modern Standard Arabic (MSA), but is so different from it in many respects as to be virtually like another language. This is the everyday spoken language you'll hear when in Morocco.

All publications and signs, however, are written in Modern Standard Arabic (MSA), which is the common written form in all Arabic-speaking countries. Note though that in Morocco, standard Western numeric symbols are used rather than those normally used in Arabic.

In this language guide we've represented the Arabic phrases with the Roman alphabet using a simplified pronunciation system. The vowels are:

a	as in 'had'
aa	like the 'a' in 'father'
ai	as in 'aisle'
ay	as in 'day'
e	as in 'bet'
ee	as in 'beer', only softer
i	as in 'hit'
o	as in 'note'

WANT MORE?

For in-depth language information and handy phrases, check out Lonely Planet's *Moroccan Arabic Phrasebook*. You'll find it at **shop.lonelyplanet. com**, or you can buy Lonely Planet's iPhone phrasebooks at the Apple App Store.

oo	as in 'food'
ow	as in 'how'
u	as in 'put'

Note that when double consonants occur in the pronunciation guides, each consonant is pronounced. For example, hammam (bath) is pronounced 'ham-mam'. The apostrophe (') represents the glottal stop (like the closing of the throat before saying 'Oh-oh!'). Other consonant sounds to keep in mind are:

dh	like the 'th' in 'this'
gh	a throaty sound like the French 'r'
h	a strongly whispered 'h'
kh	as the 'ch' in the Scottish loch
q	a strong, throaty 'k' sound

Basics

When addressing a man, the polite term more or less equivalent to 'Mr' is aseedee (shortened to see before a name); for women it's lalla, followed by the first name. To attract the attention of someone in the street or a waiter in a cafe, the word shreef is used.

The abbreviations 'm/f/pl' (male/female/plural) are used where applicable.

Hi.	la bes (informal)
	bekheer (response)
Hello.	es salaam alaykum (polite)
	wa alaykum salaam (response)
Goodbye.	bessalama/m'a ssalama
Please.	'afak/'afik/'afakum (said to m/f/pl)
Thank you.	shukran
You're welcome.	la shukran 'la wejb
Excuse me.	smeh leeya
Yes./No.	eeyeh/la
How are you?	keef halek?
Fine, thank you.	bekheer, lhamdoo llaah

What's your name?	asmeetek?
My name is ...	esmee ...
Do you speak English?	wash kat'ref negleezeeya?
I don't understand.	mafhemtsh

Accommodation

Where is a ...?	feen kayn ...?
campsite	shee mukheyyem
hotel	shee ootayl
youth hostel	daar shshabab

Is there a room available?
wash kayn shee beet khaweeya?

Can I see the room?
wash yemkenlee nshoof lbeet?

How much is a room for one day?
bash hal kayn gbayt l wahed nhar?

I'd like a room ...	bgheet shee beet ...
for one person	dyal wahed
for two people	dyal jooj
with a bathroom	belhammam

air-conditioning	kleemateezaseeyun
bed	namooseeya
blanket	bttaaneeya
hot water	lma skhoon
key	saroot
sheet	eezar
shower	doosh
toilet	beet lma

Directions

Where is the ...?
feen kayn ...?

What is the address?
ashnoo hoowa l'unwan?

Please write down the address.
kteb l'unwan 'afek

Please show me on the map.
werri liya men l kharita 'afak

How far?
bshhal b'ayd?

Go straight ahead.
seer neeshan

Turn ...	dor ...
at the corner	felqent
at the traffic lights	fedo elhmer
left/right	'al leeser/leemen

Question Words – Arabic

How?	keefash?
What?	ash?
When?	eemta?
Where?	feen?
Which?	ashmen?
Who?	shkoon?
Why?	'lash?

behind	men luy
here	hna
next to	hedda
opposite	'eks
there	hunak

north	shamel
south	janoob
east	sherq
west	gherb

Eating & Drinking

A table for..., please.
tabla dyal ... 'afak

Can I see the menu, please?
nazar na'raf lmaakla lli 'andkum?

What do you recommend?
shnoo tansaani nakul?

I'll try what she/he is having.
gha nzharrab shnoo kaatakul hiyya/huwwa

I'm a vegetarian.
makanakoolsh llehem

I'd like something to drink.
bgheet shi haazha nashrubha

Please bring me ...	llaa ykhalleek zheeb li ...
a beer	birra
a glass/bottle of red/white/ rose wine	kaas/qar'a dyal hmar/byad/ roozi shshrab
a napkin	mandeel
some bread	shwiyya dyaal lkhoobz
some pepper	shwiyya dyaal lebzaar
some salt	shwiyya dyaal lmelha
some water	shwiyya dyaal lmaa

I didn't order this.	tlabtsh had shshi
Without ...., please.	bla ... 'afak
This is excellent!	had shshi ldeed bezzef!
Cheers!	bsaha!
The bill, please.	lahsaab, 'afak

Meat & Fish

anchovies	shton
beef	baqree
camel	lehem jemil
chicken	farooj/dujaj
cod	lamoori
fish	hut
kidneys	kelawwi
lamb	lehem ghenmee
liver	kebda
lobster	laangos
meat	lehem
sardines	serdeen
shrimp	qaimroon
sole	sol
tuna	ton
whiting	merla

Fruit & Vegetables

apple	teffah
apricot	meshmash
artichoke	qooq
aubergine	lbdanzhaal
banana	banan/moz
cucumber	khiyaar
dates	tmer
figs	kermoos
fruit	fakiya
garlic	tooma
grapes	'eineb
green beans	loobeeya
lentils	'aads
lettuce	khess
mushroom	fegg'a
olives	zeetoun
onion	besla
orange	limoon
peas	zelbana bisila
pomegranate	reman
potatoes	batatas
tomato	mataisha tamatim
vegetables	khoodar
watermelon	dellah
white beans	fasooliya

Other

bread	khoobz
butter	zebda
cheese	fromaj/jiben
chips	ships
eggs	bayd
oil	zit
pepper	filfil/lebzaar
salt	melha
soup	shorba
sugar	sukur
yoghurt	zabadee/laban/danoon

Emergencies

Help!	'teqnee!
Help me, please!	'awennee 'afak!
Go away!	seer fhalek!
I'm lost.	tweddert
Thief!	sheffar!
I've been robbed.	tsreqt
Call the police!	'ayyet 'la lbùlees!
Call a doctor!	'ayyet 'la shee tbeeb!
There's been an accident!	uq'at kseeda!
Where's the toilet?	feen kayn lbeet lma?

Numbers – Arabic

1	wahed
2	jooj
3	tlata
4	reb'a
5	khamsa
6	setta
7	seb'a
8	tmenya
9	tes'ood
10	'ashra
20	'ashreen
30	tlateen
40	reb'een
50	khamseen
60	setteen
70	seb'een
80	tmaneen
90	tes'een
100	mya
200	myatayn
1000	alf
2000	alfayn

I'm sick.	ana mreed
It hurts here.	kaydernee henna
I'm allergic to (penicillin).	'andee lhsaseeya m'a (lbeenseleen)

Shopping & Services

Where is the ...?	feen kayn ...?
bank	shee baanka
barber	shee hellaq
chemist/pharmacy	farmasyan
... embassy	ssifaara dyal ...
market	souk
police station	lkoomeesareeya
post office	lboostaa
restaurant	ristura/mat'am
souvenir shop	baazaar
travel agency	wekaalet el aasfaar

I want to change ...	bgheet nserref ...
some money	shee floos
travellers cheques	shek seeyahee

I'd like to buy ...	bgheet nshree ...
I'm only looking.	gheer kanshoof
Can I look at it?	wakhkha nshoofha?
I don't like it.	ma'jebatneesh
How much is it?	bshhal?
That's very expensive.	ghalee bezzaf
Can I pay by credit card?	wash nkder nkhelles bel kart kredee?

big	kabeer
small	sagheer
open	mehlool
closed	masdood

Time & Dates

What time is it?	shal fessa'a?

yesterday	lbareh
today	lyoom
tomorrow	ghedda

morning	fessbah
afternoon	fel'sheeya
evening	'sheeya

day	nhar
week	l'usbu'
month	shshhar
year	l'am

early/late	bekree/m'ettel
quickly/slowly	dgheeya/beshweeya

Monday	nhar letneen
Tuesday	nhar ttlat
Wednesday	nhar larb'
Thursday	nhar lekhmees
Friday	nhar jjem'a
Saturday	nhar ssebt
Sunday	nhar lhedd

January	yanaayir
February	fibraayir
March	maaris
April	abreel
May	maayu
June	yunyu
July	yulyu
August	aghustus/ghusht
September	sibtimbir/shebtenber
October	uktoobir
November	nufimbir/nu'enbir
December	disimbir/dijenbir

Transport

Public Transport

When does the ... leave/arrive?	wufuqash kaykhrej/ kaywsul ...?
boat	lbaboor
city/intercity bus	ttubees/lkar
train	tran
plane	ttayyyaara

I'd like a ... ticket.	'afak bgheet wahed lwarka l ddar lbayda ...
return	bash nemshee oo njee
1st/2nd class	ddaraja lloola/ttaneeya

Where is the ...?	feen kayn ...?
airport	mataar
bus station	mhetta dyal ttobeesat
bus stop	blasa dyal ttobeesat
ticket office	maktab lwerqa
train station	lagaar

What's the fare?
shhal taman lwarka?

Please tell me when we get to ...
'afak eela wselna l ... goolhaleeya

I want to pay for one place only.
bgheet nkhelles blaasaawaheda

Stop here, please.
wqef henna 'afak

Please wait for me.
tsennanee 'afak

Driving & Cycling

Where can I hire a ...?	feen yimkin li nkri ...?
bicycle	bshklit
camel	jmel
car	tumubeel
donkey	hmar
horse	'awd

Can I park here?
wash nqder nwakef hna?

How long can I park here?
sh-hal men waket neqder nstatiun hna?

How do I get to ...?
keefesh ghaadee nuwsul l ...?

Where's the next petrol station?
fin kayna shi bumba dyal lisans griba?

I'd like ... litres.
bgheet ... itru 'afak

Please check the oil/water.
'afak shuf zzit/lma

We need a mechanic.
khesna wahed lmikanisyan

The car has broken down at ...
tumubeel khasra f ...

I have a flat tyre.
'ndi pyasa fruida

BERBER

There are three main dialects among Berber speakers, which in a certain sense also serve as loose lines of ethnic demarcation.

In the north, in the area centred on the Rif, the locals speak a dialect that has been called Riffian and is spoken as far south as Figuig on the Algerian border. The dialect that predominates in the Middle and High Atlas and the valleys leading into the Sahara goes by various names, including Braber or Amazigh.

More settled tribes of the High Atlas, Anti Atlas, Souss Valley and southwestern oases generally speak Tashelhit or Chleuh. The following phrases are a selection from the Tashelhit dialect, the one visitors are likely to find most useful.

Basics

Hello.	la bes darik/darim (m/f)
Hello. (response)	la bes
Goodbye.	akayaoon arbee
See you later.	akranwes daghr
Please.	barakalaufik
Thank you.	barakalaufik
Yes.	yah
No.	oho
Excuse me.	samhiy
How are you?	meneek antgeet?
Fine, thank you.	la bes, lhamdulah
Good.	eefulkee/eeshwa
Bad.	(khaib) eeghshne

Practicalities

food	teeremt
mule	aserdon
somewhere to sleep	kra lblast mahengane
water	arman

Is there ...?	ees eela ...?
Do you have ...?	ees daroon ...?
How much is it?	minshk aysker?
Give me ...	fky ...
I want ...	reegh ...
a little/lot	eemeek/bzef
no good	oor eefulkee
too expensive	eeghla

I want to go to ...	addowghs ...
Where is (the) ...?	mani gheela ...?
Is it near/far?	ees eeqareb/yagoog?
straight	neeshan
to the left	fozelmad
to the right	fofasee

mountain	adrar
river	aseef
the pass	tizee
village	doorwar

yesterday	eedgam
today	(zig sbah) rass
tomorrow	(ghasad) aska

GLOSSARY

This glossary is a list of Arabic (A), Berber (B), French (F) and Spanish (S) terms that are used throughout this guide. For a list of trekking terms, see p38.

agadir (B) – fortified communal granary

'ain (A) – water source, spring

aït (B) – family (of), often precedes tribal and town names

Alawite – hereditary dynasty that has ruled Morocco since the late 17th century

Allah (A) – God

Almohads – puritanical Muslim group (1147–1269), originally Berber, that arose in response to the corrupt Almoravid dynasty

Almoravids – Muslim group (1054–1147) that ruled Spain and the Maghreb

bab (A) – gate

babouches (F) – traditional leather slippers

banu (A) – see *beni*

baraka (A) – divine blessing or favour

Barbary – European term used to describe the North African coast from the 16th to the 19th centuries

ben (A) – (or *ibn*) son of

beni (A) – 'sons of', often precedes tribal name (also *banu*)

Berbers – indigenous inhabitants of North Africa

borj (A) – fort (literally 'tower')

brigade touristique (F) – tourist police

bureau des guides (F) – guides' office

caid/caliph – town official

calèche – horse-drawn carriage

calle (S) – street

camionette (F) – minivan or pick-up truck

capitol – main temple of Roman town, usually situated in the forum

caravanserai – large merchants' inn enclosing a courtyard, providing accommodation and a marketplace (see also *funduq*)

chergui (A) – dry, easterly desert wind

Compagnie de Transports Marocaine – CTM; national bus company

corniche (F) – coastal road

corsair – 18th-century pirate based at Salé

dar (A) – traditional town house with internal courtyard

Délégation Régionale du Tourisme – tourist office; see also ONMT

derb (A) – lane or narrow street

djemaa (A) – Friday mosque (also *jami'*, *jemaa* and *jamaa*)

douar (A) – generally used for 'village' in the High Atlas

Eaux et Forêts – government ministry responsible for national parks

eid (A) – religious festival

Ensemble Artisanal – government handicraft shop

erg (A) – sand dunes

fantasia (S) – military exercise featuring a cavalry charge

faux guides (F) – unofficial or informal guides

foum (A) – usually the mouth of a river or valley (from Arabic for 'mouth')

funduq (A) – *caravanserai* (often used to mean 'hotel')

gardiens de voitures (F) – car-park attendants

gare routière (F) – bus station

gîte, gîte d'étape (F) – trekkers' hostel, sometimes a homestay

Gnaoua – bluesy Moroccan musical form that began with freed slaves in Marrakesh and Essaouira

grand taxi (F) – (long-distance) shared taxi

haj (A) – pilgrimage to Mecca, hence *haji* or *hajia*, a male or female who has made the pilgrimage

halqa (A) – street theatre

hammada (A) – stony desert

hammam (A) – Turkish-style bathhouse with sauna and massage

hanbel (A) – see *kilim*

haram (A) – literally 'forbidden', the word is sometimes used to denote a sacred or forbidden area, such as the prayer room of a mosque

Hejira – flight of the Prophet from Mecca to Medina in AD 622; the first year of the Islamic calendar

ibn (A) – son of (see also *ben*)

Idrissids – Moroccan dynasty that established a stable state in northern Morocco in the 9th century

iftar (A) – breaking of the fast at sundown during Ramadan; breakfast (also *ftur*)

imam (A) – Muslim cleric

Interzone – name coined by author William Burroughs for the period 1923–56, when Tangier was controlled by nine countries

jebel (A) – hill, mountain (sometimes *djebel* in former French possessions)

jedid (A) – new (sometimes spelled *jdid*)

jellaba (A) – popular flowing garment; men's *jellabas* are usually made from cotton or wool, while women's come in light synthetic fabrics

kasbah (A) – fort, citadel; often also the administrative centre (also *qasba*)

kif (A) – marijuana

kilim (A) – flat-woven blankets or floor coverings (also *hanbel*)

koubba (A) – sanctuary or shrine (see also *marabout*)

ksar (A) – fort or fortified stronghold (plural *ksour*)

mâalem – master artisan

Maghreb (A) – (literally 'west') area covered by Morocco, Algeria, Tunisia and Libya

maison d'hôte (F) – guesthouse, often a restored traditional Moroccan house

majoun (A) – sticky paste made of crushed seeds of the marijuana plant

marabout – holy man or saint; also often used to describe the mausoleums of these men

mechouar (A) – royal assembly place

medersa (A) – college for teaching theology, law, Arabic literature and grammar (also called *madrassa*)

medina (A) – old city; used to describe the old Arab parts of modern towns and cities

mellah (A) – Jewish quarter of the medina

Merenids (A) – Moroccan dynasty (1269–1465), responsible for the construction of many of Morocco's *medersas*

mihrab (A) – prayer niche in the wall of a mosque indicating the direction of Mecca (the *qibla*)

minbar (A) – pulpit in mosque; the *imam* delivers the sermon from one of the lower steps because the Prophet preached from the top step

moulay (A) – ruler

Mouloud – Islamic festival celebrating the birth of the Prophet

moussem (A) – pilgrimage to *marabout* tomb; festival in honour of a *marabout*

muezzin (A) – mosque official who sings the call to prayer from the minaret

muqarna (A) – decorative plasterwork

musée (F) – museum

ONMT – Office National Marocain du Tourisme, national tourist body, sometimes called Délégation Régionale du Tourisme

ordinaire (F) – less comfortable train, slightly slower than a *rapide*

oued (A) – river or stream, including dry riverbeds (sometimes *wad* or *wadi*)

oulad (A) – sons (of), often precedes tribal or town name

palmeraie (F) – palm grove

pastilla (A) – a rich, savoury-sweet chicken or pigeon pie made with fine pastry; a dish of layered pastry with cinnamon and almonds served as dessert at banquets

pasha – high official in Ottoman Empire (also *pacha*)

pensióne (S) – guesthouse

petit taxi (F) – local taxi

pisé (F) – building material made of sundried clay or mud

piste (F) – unsealed tracks, often requiring 4WD vehicles

place (F) – square, plaza

plage (F) – beach

plazas de soberanía (S) – 'Places of sovereignty', the name given to the Spanish possessions in North Africa

Prophet (Mohammed), the – founder of Islam, who lived between AD 570 and AD 632

qissaria (A) – covered market sometimes forming the commercial centre of a medina

Quran – sacred book of Islam

Ramadan (A) – ninth month of the Muslim year, a period of fasting

rapide (F) – type of train more comfortable and slightly faster than an *ordinaire*

refuge (F) – mountain hut, basic hikers' shelter

riad (A) – traditional town house set around an internal garden

ribat (A) – combined monastery and fort

Saadians – Moroccan dynasty that ruled in the 16th century

sharia (A) – street

sherif (A) – descendant of the Prophet

Shiites – one of two main Islamic sects, formed by those who believed the true *imams* were descended from the Prophet's son-in-law Ali (see also *Sunnis*)

sidi (A) – honorific (equivalent to 'Mr'; also *si*)

souq (A) – market

Sufism – mystical strand of Islam that emphasises communion with Allah through inner attitude

Sunnis – one of two main Islamic sects, derived from followers of the Umayyad-caliphate (see also *Shiites*)

Syndicat d'Initiative (F) – government-run tourist office

tabac (F) – tobacconist and newsagency

tadelakt (A) – waterproof lime plaster mixed with pigments and polished with a stone to give it a smooth, lustrous finish, originally used for the walls of *hammams* but now a favourite of interior designers

tariq (A) – road, avenue

téléboutique (F) – privately operated telephone service

tizi (B) – mountain pass

Tuareg – nomadic Berbers of the Sahara, also known as the Blue Men because of their indigo-dyed robes

ville nouvelle (F) – new city; town built by the French alongside existing towns

vizier – another term for a provincial governor in the Ottoman Empire, or adviser to the sultan in Morocco

zawiya (A) – religious fraternity based around a *marabout*; location of the fraternity (also *zaouia*)

zellij (A) – ceramic

Behind the Scenes

SEND US YOUR FEEDBACK

We love to hear from travellers – your comments keep us on our toes and help make our books better. Our well-travelled team reads every word on what you loved or loathed about this book. Although we cannot reply individually to postal submissions, we always guarantee that your feedback goes straight to the appropriate authors, in time for the next edition. Each person who sends us information is thanked in the next edition – the most useful submissions are rewarded with a selection of digital PDF chapters.

Visit **lonelyplanet.com/contact** to submit your updates and suggestions or to ask for help. Our award-winning website also features inspirational travel stories, news and discussions.

Note: We may edit, reproduce and incorporate your comments in Lonely Planet products such as guidebooks, websites and digital products, so let us know if you don't want your comments reproduced or your name acknowledged. For a copy of our privacy policy visit lonelyplanet.com/privacy.

OUR READERS

Many thanks to the travellers who used the last edition and wrote to us with helpful hints, useful advice and interesting anecdotes:

A Mikko Ahvenainen **B** Gary Badham, Austin Beasley, Udo Berg, Monique Bergeron, Hassan Boulamjouj, Nicholas Brown **C** Tim Carpentier, Adrian Clement, Tony Collins, Jeremy Coyd, Dorothy Crookshank, Alex Curry **D** Carine De Groodt, James Deng, Michele Di Nunzio, Tessa Ditner, Iain Dolan, Jakub Dominowski, Kevin Dugmore **E** Els van den Eertwegh, Ron Eijlander **F** Marios Forsos, Thomas Fox, Lucille Frauenstein **G** Patrick Gallagher, Andra Ghent, Lucinda Gibson, Alina Gruppe **H** Valerie Hackl, Tracy Hall, Mulle Harbort, Reineke Hollander, Natalie Howell, Angela Hubinger, Laura Schollert Hvalsum **J** Benjamin Jahn, Anders Jeppsson, Emily Jones, Robert Jones, Sue Jones **K** Sharon Keld, Sertac Keles, Ineke Kamphuisen, Gregory Kipling, Fritz Gerd Koring, Nicole Korpell, Dimos Kyritsis **L** Jakub Lasek, Houda Lazrak, Jeremy Lemarchand, Dominik Linder, Ruth W Lo, Matthew Lombardi, Ailsa Lord, Vince Lungley, Brian Lynch **M** Andy McLandrich, Takis Markopoulos, Fabrizio Marras, Richard Maurer, Sunil S Mehta, Bas Meijerink, Patricia Miró, Sarah Mitchell, Silvia Moens, Anouska Moynagh **N** Julie Nicaisse

O William O'Neill, Guy Oram **P** Colin Payne, Jorge Peregrin, Robbert Petterson, Anna Preston, Andrea Previtali, Louise Pybus **R** Tamsin Ranger, Andy Rees, Matty Renshaw, Jon Rothwell, Ester Rubio **S** Noel Sanborn, Jonathan Shapiro, Chris Silver, Mica Silver, Lene Smith, Ann Steadman, Sarah Sutcliffe **T** Jiameng Teah, Sally Thelen, Assen Totin **V** Rich Venezia **W** Kirstie Wielandt, Tom Wilkinson, Christine Williams, Chi-Ki Katie Wong, Debra Wood **Z** Bettina Zurek, Luis E Zuzunaga, Jessica Anne van der Zweth

AUTHOR THANKS

Paul Clammer

As always, friends in Marrakesh and Fez provided great company to bookend the research trip. You all know who you are – shukran. In Casablanca, thanks to Tahir Shah for his fine hospitality. In Assilah, particular thanks to Carin Cowell. Thanks to my co-authors Paula, James and Helen for all their hard work. Finally, thanks and love to Robyn, who put up with me during the write-up.

James Bainbridge

A muezzin-worthy song of appreciation goes to everyone who aided my progress through the southern medinas and mountains, including Christophe in Aglou Plage; Sally in Mirleft; Jawad and Driss in Tarfaya; Isam in Tata; Said and Latifa in Taroudannt; Rachid in Oumesnate; Houssine and Brahim in Tafraoute; Mahfoud in Tazekka; Yassine and Ben in Taghazout; Aneflous in Immouzer; Mohammed and Hassan at Jardin de Olhão; Sissi in Taliouine; and Valerie in Dakhla. Thanks also to the camel who towed my car out of Banana Beach; to my brother Andy for coming along for the ride; and to my South African family for all the cups of tea during my write-up.

Paula Hardy

Doors opened in Marrakesh and beyond thanks to the generous insights of Mohammed Nour, Peter and Hassan at Dar Zaman, Peter Mana'ch, Emily Burrows, Bachir El'Ammari, Mike Richardson, Melissa Topacio, Cloe Erickson, Youssef Oulcadi, Nora Fitzgerald, Hamza Weinman, Norya Nemiche, Elsa Bauza, Eveline Donnez and the staff at Dar Housnia. Thanks also to co-authors Paul, Helen and James and Alison Bing, and, at Lonely Planet, Glenn van der Knijff. Last, but never least, thank you to Rob for seeing Morocco through new eyes and sharing the adventure.

Helen Ranger

Thanks to Paul for his guidance and for taking on Fez medina guesthouses. In Morocco, I thank Jess Stephens for being artistic in Sefrou, Ricky Martin for blooming in Oujda, John Wilkinson and Abdeslam Mouden for knowing so much about Chefchaouen, and Si Mohamed Baghdadi for his impressive expertise in Arabic and Tarafit. Robert Johnstone and Mike Richardson provided scintillating company when reviewing smart restaurants, and driver Lofti M'hamid got me there and back safely.

ACKNOWLEDGMENTS

Climate Map Data Climate map data adapted from Peel MC, Finlayson BL & McMahon TA (2007) 'Updated World Map of the Köppen-Geiger Climate Classification', Hydrology and Earth System Sciences, 11, 1633¬44.

Cover photograph: Streetside pottery seller, Keren Su/Getty.

BEHIND THE SCENES

THIS BOOK

This 11th edition of Lonely Planet's *Morocco* guidebook was researched and written by Paul Clammer, James Bainbridge, Paula Hardy and Helen Ranger. This guidebook was commissioned in Lonely Planet's Melbourne office, and produced by the following:
Commissioning Editor Glenn van der Knijff

Coordinating Editors Kate James, Simon Williamson
Senior Cartographer Corey Hutchison
Book Designer Katherine Marsh
Managing Editor Angela Tinson
Senior Editors Catherine Naghten, Karyn Noble
Assisting Editors Michelle Bennett, Nigel Chin, Gabrielle Stefanos

Assisting Cartographers Anita Banh, Mark Griffiths, Valentina Kremenchutskaya, Alison Lyall
Cover Research Naomi Parker
Language Content Branislava Vladisavljevic
Thanks to Shahara Ahmed, Ryan Evans, Larissa Frost, Genesys India, Jouve India, Trent Paton

Index

NOTES

NOTES